UNDERSTANDING BANGLADESH

S. MAHMUD ALI

Understanding Bangladesh

HURST & COMPANY, LONDON

First published in the United Kingdom in 2010 by
C. Hurst & Co. (Publishers) Ltd.,
41 Great Russell Street, London, WC1B 3PL
© S. Mahmud Ali, 2010
All rights reserved.
Printed in India

The right of S. Mahmud Ali to be identified as the author of this
publication is asserted by him in accordance with
the Copyright, Designs and Patents Act, 1988.

A Cataloguing-in-Publication data record for this book
is available from the British Library.

ISBN: 978-1-85065-997-6 *clothbound*
      978-1-85065-998-3 *paperback*

This book is printed using paper from registered sustainable
and managed sources.

www.hurstpub.co.uk

CONTENTS

LIST OF TABLES

LIST OF TABLES

PREFACE

Late in the afternoon on 16 December 1971, Lt. General A.A.K. Niazi, commander of Pakistan's armed forces and civilian state institutions in the country's eastern wing, East Pakistan, surrendered his command to Lt. General Jagjit Singh Aurora, Commander-in-Chief of the Indian Eastern Command, and of Bangladesh's *Mukti Fauj*, or 'liberation army', in Dhaka. Bangladesh, the eastern two-thirds of traditional Bengal, was now a separate, putatively independent, state. The surrender ceremony, however, illustrated the circumscribed nature of that transition. The two Bangladeshi military officers present hovered at the margins and played no visible role in the proceedings. The sovereignty of Eastern Bengal, its map redrawn several times since 1905, passed from Pakistani masters to Indian allies. Shattered by a nine-month long civil war ended by a *coup de grace* delivered by Indian forces in the last month of the conflict, with over nine million of its citizens driven to Indian refugee camps and destitution, and its pre-eminent leader locked up in Pakistani prison facing an uncertain future, Bangladesh was born utterly debilitated.

The debility was not just physical and economic; there were issues of political philosophy, moral probity and legal precedents that further darkened its prospects. Bangladesh was the first state to be created since 1945 by a combination of third party intervention in support of an autonomist-turned-secessionist campaign forcing the dismemberment of a member-state of the United Nations, and Great Power polarization deepening regional fissures. The *sui generis* nature of its independence, the scale of destruction, dislocation and disruption, and a virtual absence of institutional bases of statehood made it a unique experiment in political change. In the days and months after the Pakistani surrender, there were many more questions about its future than there were answers. Nearly four decades on, many of those questions have been answered, but new ones have arisen. Some questions are no closer to resolution now than they were then.

Since its emergence, this extremely densely-populated delta country has been blighted by natural and man-made turbulence. The depredations of nature and of rulers, who have ranged from charismatic autocrats through military dictators to venal coalitions of incompetent 'democrats,' have compounded its congenital challenges. An apparent focus on victimhood as a *raison d'être*, limited recourse to rational-empirical approaches to challenges, and a failure to forge a national consensus on fundamental principles have compounded complexities. A tiny middle class of sorts, a proto-bourgeoisie, has evolved in the urban centres but neither representative institutions nor a service-oriented political philosophy have dug deep roots in Bangladesh's benighted soil. But the people live in hope.

While many Bangladeshis saw the independence of their country as the most epochal event of their times, their focus has been on the proximate, local and national aspects of what was a variegated conflict operating at three different levels of the security milieu. The three levels were closely interconnected, with action in one resonating within the others. The acute immediacy and narrow specificity of the Bangladeshis' concerns robbed their painfully violent experience of any appreciation of the complex nature of their struggle and its consequences once the guns had fallen silent. Externally, the most visible conflict, given the restrictions imposed on media coverage of East Pakistan's civil war by Islamabad, was between the regional rivals, Pakistan and India. These, after all, were the internationally recognized actors pursuing conflicting interests which, because of their mutually incompatible founding principles and cross-cutting linkages straddling arbitrarily-drawn artificial borders, generated a battle unto the death. Seeking to establish their own legitimacy by demolishing the other's validity, the former Empire's twin post-colonial successor states exploited every opportunity to undermine each other.[1] Weakening, indeed dismembering, Pakistan by dividing its physically and culturally disparate wings would forever marginalize Pakistan and limit its irritating ability to challenge India's regional supremacy. The moral superiority of supporting the East Pakistani electorate's clearly expressed democratic will against Islamabad's violent repression of the Bengalis made the Indian case far more amenable to domestic and external approval than it otherwise would have been. But above the 'national' Bangladeshi and sub-systemic South Asian layers lay an equally imposing set of external inter-actions. This was the region's variable relationship to the formative—as yet fluid—tri–polar peak of the systemic hierarchy represented by the dynamic US-China-USSR strategic triangle.[2]

Although Pakistan and India were the key actors defining the con-tested future of Bangladesh, their 'softness'[3] ensured sub-systemic intru-sion by the systemic core. Both regional players were dependent in their different ways on superpower patrons. Since independence, both had been allied to US security interests, India covertly and Pakistan, more explic-itly.[4] However, Washington's loss of interest in the region since the 1965 India-Pakistan war and a focus on Indochina had encouraged Soviet efforts to play the role of honest broker in mediating the 1966 'Tashkent accord,' and establish a partial balance in Moscow's treatment of India and Pakistan. Although this balanced approach eventually proved short-lived, it restored the *status quo ante-bellum* in Indo-Pakistani relations, partly mitigated Pakistan's military-security weaknesses with modest Soviet support, and secured peace, but did not address the core Indo-Pakistani disputes.

Richard Nixon's quest to liberate America from its Indochinese bur-dens, to help the nation recover from that traumatic haemorrhage and restore its strategic vigour, transformed superpower relations. The Guam Doctrine enunciated US encouragement of Asian clients to play a leading role in their own defence against presumably communist subversion and aggression.[5] Washington pursued a tacit alliance with Beijing against the Kremlin's growing global assertiveness. With China the potential partner in this dramatic strategic endeavour, India was increasingly viewed as an irritant. As Pakistan's military leader Yahya Khan provided an effective, and secret, conduit between Washington and Beijing after other initia-tives had failed, the two diarchies—Nixon and his National Security Adviser Henry Kissinger in the White House, and Chairman Mao Zedong and Premier Zhou Enlai in *Zhongnanhai*—saw Indian pressure on Pakistan over East Bengal as a manifestation of the formative Soviet-Indian alliance collaborating against shared Sino-US interests in South Asia, and the wider world more generally.

On 3 December 1971, after open warfare broke out between India and Pakistan on both eastern and western fronts, Washington accused Delhi of being responsible, although action on the western front had been trig-gered by poorly-executed Pakistani air attacks on Indian bases. On 6

December, as Indian forces pressed their multi–pronged offensive into East Pakistan, Indian Prime Minister Indira Gandhi noted Moscow's warning that Beijing might 'rattle the sword' in Ladakh and Chumbi Valley but the Soviet Union would 'counter-balance any such action'.[6] On the same day, Nixon cautioned Brezhnev that America had major interests in Pakistan's survival and would act to protect these if Moscow or Delhi seriously threatened Pakistan's viability. The Soviet Union urged restraint on all sides but its pro-Bangladesh sympathies were evident.

The convergence of concentric circles of interest, perceptions and policies of these disparate actors rendered the Bangladeshi 'freedom fighter' guerrillas and civilians subordinate players in a sanguinary convulsion tearing apart their lives and rearranging the South Asian regional subsystem. As each party adjusted its rhetoric to the rapidly changing reality, national mythologies and history were rewritten in particular versions that had limited consonance with each other and carried varied reflections of 'the truth'. The emotive nature of clashing perspectives has meant that within Bangladesh, there has only been modest consensus on what happened. A failure to unify the narrative has led to a polarization of the polity along divergences that have deepened over time despite the absence of major policy differences among the leaderships of most mainstream political groupings. The divisive discourse has prevented Bangladesh from overcoming its basic challenges and realizing the often-expressed aspirations of its elite and masses since those heady days of struggle against repressive 'colonial exploitation' by Pakistan's rulers.

This book aims to examine Bangladesh as an unusual case of stateformation, offering a detached but empathetic account of some of the watersheds marking its political experience, an attempt to reveal the tendencies and forces that generated the sequence of key events, and an effort to examine their likely consequences. The rational-empirical model, often foreign to the national discourse and tradition, is founded on establishing causal linkages—or demonstrating a lack of these—on the bases of evidence rather than instinct or preference. The enterprise is premised on the belief that evidentiary narratives can make a positive contribution to advancing a logical framework crucial to the grasp and management of Bangladesh's myriad and profound challenges.

The book is organised in six chapters. The first sheds light on elements of the country's political legacy, its fragmentary inheritance, the confounding etymology of its national identity-formation process and internally inconsistent crystallisation of founding principles. The contradictions between its stated original purpose and the enforced incongruity of the reality are fundamental to comprehending the incomplete and contrived nature of the Bangladeshi ideational construct. In temporal terms, it charts the evolution of the Bengali–Muslim (some would later claim Muslim-Bengali) identity of Eastern Bengal's polity from the first modern partition of Bengal in 1905 by the Viceroy, Lord Curzon, to Operation Searchlight, Pakistan's military crackdown on East Pakistan's nationalist autonomist movement in March 1971.

The second chapter shows up the struggles of the country's charismatic father-figure as he fought the contradictions between his almost magical vision and the more sordid reality of post-war Bangladesh, contradictions which eventually consumed him and set the context for the growing influence of the soldiery in the evolution of the revolutionary state. Soldiers abandoning the first principle of sworn loyalty to the state and rebelling against their suspicious Pakistani commanders played a crucial role in establishing the new republic. The military-political dynamics of a civil war triggered by the Pakistani ruling elite's fear of losing control to the hitherto subordinate Bengali compatriots who had won a legislative majority in free and fair elections were rendered more complex by the unavoidable involvement of Pakistan's perennial rival India. This was overlain by even greater complexity of the systemic fluidity engendered by Nixon's secret enterprise to build security bridges to Beijing and reduce perceived threats from the Soviet Union by building up a strategic counterweight in the form of a secret ally, China. Sino-Indian tensions, Sino-Soviet hostility, Sino-Pakistani fraternity and US efforts to utilise Pakistani links as the conduit for this clandestine endeavour built the context in which an Indo-Soviet alliance rendered Pakistan's dismemberment inevitable given Sino-US inability to physically intervene in Pakistan's behalf. Despite a US 'tilt' toward Pakistan, Washington remained a key player in this dramatic state-creation by secession aided by third-party intervention. Once Bangladesh became a reality, the USA moved to aid the war-ravaged republic although its strategic interest was focused on securing residual Pakistan's survival and the reduction of Indo-Soviet influence. The first years of independent Bangladesh were marked by efforts to avoid a famine and restore calm. Famine eventually hit in 1974 and the veneer of normalcy dissolved in a coup taking the lives of the national leader, Sheikh Mujibur Rahman, and his extended family. This violent transition deepened cleavages and established lasting patterns of bitterness.

The third chapter examines the role of the military in the evolution of the Bangladeshi state. The army's initial marginalisation by its new political masters, its violent rejection of this leadership and its bloody ouster, and subsequent bouts of military rule in various guises defined Bangladesh's early history. The inability of the party-political elite, fragmented by the war and its aftermath and persuaded to accept a one-party system, to respond to the basic needs of the penurious populace, the failure of the country's first rulers to establish representative institutions and pluralist practices, and the legitimization of violence as a political instrument brought sections of the poorly-led military to the fore as an instrument of change. The bloody disruption their action caused allowed the rise of the radical left as a militant and popular force. The combined efforts of the left and rebellious soldiers brought General Ziaur Rahman to power. Despite his debt to another war hero, the radical leader, Colonel Abu Taher, Zia identified with the centre-right, restored state control and neutralised the left. But his efforts to build a pan-Bangladeshi superstructure bringing together mutually incompatible elements from across the political spectrum alienated his former nationalist allies within the military. They killed him.

Now arose the centre-right forces—first Zia's own political party but, soon, his successor as army commander, General H.M. Ershad. A man of many gifts, Ershad nonetheless stood out as a colourful but uncharismatic pragmatist in a land enamoured of magnetic predecessors. For nine years he engaged in state-building in the face of increasingly vituperative and obstreperous opposition, but his inability to establish legitimacy in the urban centres eventually cost him the devoted loyalty of the military and thus ended that second bout of military rule. But the tradition died hard, attracting even Western interest as the first decade of the twenty-first century approached its end, and will likely colour the country's continuing political evolution.

The fourth chapter examines the party-political dynamic dominating Bangladesh's civilian polity, its development into a centrist, moderate mainstream that formally espouses liberal, representative pluralism and market economic principles but has, in fact, demonstrated no ability to rise beyond acquisition by graft and accumulation by abuse of office by a handful of families and their party-political and bureaucratic-commercial acolytes. The main parties have remained tied to personalities rather than principles or even policies. The subjugation of the state and exploitation of its institutions for individual- and group benefit have robbed party-politics of their lustre. Enforced reforms might change things, but the quality of the long-term outcome remains uncertain at best. The two Rahman dynasties—Sheikh Mujibur Rahman's daughters, and General Ziaur Rahman's widow and sons—retained control over the two largest political parties and the devotion of the masses, their members, and supporters. Despite depredations during fifteen years of cyclical election to office, first by Khaleda Zia's BNP in 1991–96, then by Sheikh Hasina's Awami League in 1996–2001, and then by the BNP again in 2001–06, the leaders remained popular, and their parties, unchallenged, except by each other. Authoritative accounts by Bangladeshi and foreign observers repeatedly pointed to the gross abuses and myriad failings they visited on their compatriots, and yet, they exercised a rationally inexplicable magnetism on the voting public which troubled their critics.

Chapter five looks at several subsidiary but influential phenomena—political extremism, student activism, and the philosophical need of 'the other' to define Bangladesh. Extremism grew in the late 1960s, culminating in a curious set of circumstances in 1971 when the religious right joined hands with Pakistani forces and *Muhajir* communities, fighting nationalist activists and guerrillas, and etching their abhorrent credentials permanently on many minds. The radical left, in contrast, viewed both Pakistani and Indian bourgeoisie as the enemy, and the nationalist Bengali leadership as a *lumpen* agency shifting allegiance from one to the other. Its cadres fought both Pakistani forces and nationalist guerrillas. Secular nationalists, centrists and extremists from the left and the right have vied for control, creating conflicting imageries of 'the other' against which they have tried to take the rest the country with them. The result has been mixed in more senses than one, with incoherence one outcome. The conflict among proponents of very different visions of Bangladesh's national goals and power configurations continues.

The future, of course, is another country, and the country's future lies in its students. Historically active and idealistically driven, Bangladesh's students, especially those from state-funded universities, have led political activism. Starting from the campaign to establish Bengali as a state language in Pakistan in 1948 leading to police action in 1952 in which several were killed, forcing the Pakistani authorities to concede, Bangladeshi students have combined ideals and street muscle to shape the country's political culture. Many have risen to the top via terms spent in jail. They could play a crucial role in defining Bangladesh's future. In terms of ideas, the war of independence was fought as a survivalist campaign more against everything Pakistan stood for, than for what the imagined Bangladeshi nation-state might specifically represent. This crystallisation of national identity as a revisionist challenge to the status quo did not resolve the elemental discordance between the assumed primacy of primordial Bengali cultural definition of the polity, and the permanence of Bengal's confessionally-defined partition which injected religiosity into the new-fangled state's *raison d'être*. A struggle for the nation's soul contributed to the transformation, in Bangladeshi eyes, of India from ally-in-chief to the ever looming shadow of 'the other' against which to define the self.

The epilogue sums up the contradictions of the Bangladeshi experience. Despite an abysmally poor record of governance, Bangladesh's macro-economic performance has, at approximately 5.5 per cent of annual GDP growth over the past two decades, not been totally dire. In some years, the economy has, in fact, grown much more robustly, demonstrating the potential for significant acceleration given the right policy framework and international circumstances. In fact, in 2006–07, some studies underscored Bangladesh's ability to join the ranks of second-tier economies within the next two decades. This would be a surprising, but not entirely unrealistic, prospect. However, the systemic weaknesses of Bangladeshi politics and the challenges they created for around 150 million excruciatingly poverty-stricken people demanded, in the eyes of the friendly donor community, radical surgery. The instrument of this drastic enterprise was the military which was encouraged to take charge, establish a civilian administration, implement major political and economic reforms and transfer power to a newly-elected government. This the military did, with parliamentary elections being held in December 2008, and establishing an administration massively reflecting the popular will in governing the land.

As this work goes to press, the success of this enterprise remains moot, but over the longer term, fundamental challenges—demographic burdens of Malthusian proportions, resource-deficits, an unsympathetic regional and international milieu and, crucially, adverse impact of climate change—add up to a level of threat that not even the most effective administration could cope with any degree of confidence. The book sums up this mixed picture and attempts to draw out possible lessons for the multitudes and those brave souls who seek to lead them over the coming decades. An appreciation of the challenges and choices facing Bangladesh—potentially a grim microcosm of the planetary future—resulting from a work of this genre is perhaps the most apparent benefit to flow from it. If Bangladesh succeeds and survives its myriad demons, there is hope for humanity on this increasingly fragile earth. The alternative does not bear contemplation.

1

THE PAST AS PROLOGUE
1757–1971

Abstract: In December 1971, Bangladesh emerged as the world's newest republic. Formed from the eastern two-thirds of Bengal, it had been known as East Pakistan since the Partition of Britain's Indian Empire in 1947. A nine-month civil war between Pakistan's western elite and eastern majority, which transmuted into Bangladesh's war of independence, separated Pakistan's two wings. But there had been an even earlier partition in 1905. That short-lived separation of Bengal's Muslim-majority east from its Hindu-majority west, the latter centred around the colonial capital, Calcutta, fashioned the template on which first East Pakistan and then, in 1971, Bangladesh came into being.

Bengali–Muslim separatism was rooted in the cycles of imperial expansion, consolidation and fragmentation which shaped South Asia. As northern Indian Hindu kingdoms gave way to Afghan, Turkic and Central Asian Muslim successors, power changed hands, as did wealth, status and elite composition. By the eighteenth century, non-Bengali Muslim rulers from the *Ashraf* aristocracy, having co-opted some pre-existing Hindu noble houses, had taken charge of Bengal. Internecine squabbles among the elites weakened the rulers. With key sections of this elite siding with the British East India Company against other sections, Bengal was, by the end of the eighteenth century, a Company governorate, a nucleus around which the Company built and expanded a colonial satrapy in northern India. In the bloody aftermath of the 'Sepoy Mutiny' of 1857 the Crown assumed imperial control over India. Significant reforms had, in the meanwhile, generated a renaissance among India's non-Muslim majority. As the rational discourse and scientific inquiry at the heart of

1

Britain's industrial revolution and liberal-democratic reforms touched the native intermediary classes, largely Hindu nationalist movements began to crystallise. Partly to counter this growing challenge, Viceregal authority aided the emergence of a new Muslim elite.

Bengal's first Partition in 1905, the establishment in Dhaka of the Muslim League the following year, and the reunification of Bengal in 1911 in the face of massive 'Hindu nationalist' protests deepened the divide and sowed the seeds of future discord. Bengal's second Partition, effected in 1947 on the basis of confessional differences, resolved none of the philosophical or political-economic conundrums inherent in the Indo-Pakistani post-colonial design. Pakistani state consolidation processes, the rise of a Punjabi–Muhajir-bureaucratic-feudal elite in West Pakistan which marginalised the East, and the latter's rejection of this marginalisation created the context in the 1950s and 1960s for growing unhappiness with the status of Pakistan's Bengali majority. With political power concentrated in the hands of the Pakistani military, East Pakistan's Bengali population increasingly supported Bengali nationalist autonomist aspirations espoused and promoted by the centrist Awami League and its leftist political allies.

Not all East Bengalis challenged the Pakistani edifice. Centre-right forces did not seek structural changes—just policy modifications. Conservative Islamists on the fringes, however, saw the nationalists as Indian agents seeking the destruction of Muslim autonomy on a subcontinental canvas. They supported Pakistani forces' attempts to crush the nationalist movement. Indian aid to the nationalists secured victory for Bangladesh but by leaving too many questions unresolved, generated the potential for future discord.

First blood

On 16 October 1905, Lord George Curzon, Britain's Viceroy in India, partitioned Bengal, thereby initiating, perhaps inadvertently, a process that would be repeated in August 1947, when eastern Bengal became the eastern province of Pakistan. This, in turn, would trigger a sequence of events culminating in the secession of East Pakistan and the establishment of Bangladesh in 1971. Those events were watersheds in a continuum shaped by the convergence, divergence, and occasional reconfiguring, of diverse tendencies to refashion the region's socio-economic features and political landscape in a dynamic dialectic. Bengal's first partition brought to the surface the many currents which had evolved since the arrival of Muslim rulers several centuries earlier and which had taken on a sharper profile after their British successors began reengineering its economic, legal and political structures and practices. For the region's future, the most critical of these currents would be the sharpening juxtaposition of confessionally-defined emerging political forces.

The British had taken Bengal and parts of Bihar and Orissa from *Nawab* Siraj-ud Dowlah, scion of a Muslim ruling family, in the battle of Plassey near his capital, Murshidabad, in 1757. Given the East India Company's success in secretly purchasing the loyalty of the *Nawab's* army commander, Mir Zafar Ali Khan, before the battle, its outcome was a foregone conclusion. The intrigues and stratagems employed by the British and their Muslim rivals[1] obscured the fact that power passed over the heads of Bengal's pauperized peasants from one 'foreign' master to another. Both Muslim and British rulers engaged intermediaries to manage their fiefs, for example. The Company's suspicion of the occasionally rebellious Muslim aristocracy led to policies that subverted its wealth and authority by superimposing a new class of loyal intermediaries whose interests lay in sustaining the British dispensation, by force, if necessary. They were the *Zamindars*, newly-ennobled revenue collectors 'permanently settled' on the land whose revenue they collected on the Company's behalf from their tenant-farmers. While the peasants' status changed little, more efficacious revenue collection sharpened the divide between those whose labours grew the fruit and those who enjoyed it. In eastern Bengal, the former were mostly *atraf* Muslims, converted from the lower rungs of the Hindu hierarchy by *Sufi* mystics; the new landed aristocracy was overwhelmingly caste Hindu. Some *ashraf* Muslim noble families survived the changes but with their ties to aristocrats elsewhere in India, they were as foreign to the peasantry as were their freshly-minted Hindu fellows.

In the nineteenth century, British authority steadily expanded in all directions from the empire's Bengal nucleus, which also included what would eventually become the separate provinces of Bihar and Orissa. Administrative boundaries were repeatedly adapted to this expansion. In 1836, the upper districts of the Presidency were partitioned off under a Lt. Governor; in 1854, the Governor General-in-Council transferred Bengal's administrative responsibilities to a Lt. Governor; in 1874, Assam and Sylhet were placed under a Chief Commissioner; and in 1898, the Lushai Hills region was added to it. By 1903, when partition plans were broached, the writ of Bengal's Lt. Governor had spread to over 189,000 sq. miles with a population of 78.5 million. A concentration of political, economic and judicial authority and resources in and around the imperial and provincial capitals in Calcutta meant the administration of eastern districts, totally agricultural and with poor communication links, suffered. If nothing else, efficient revenue generation required an improvement. Not surprisingly, Curzon's plans stated three prosaic objectives:

- Ensure more effective administration of Bengal's outlying districts and reduce the burdens borne by the province's government.
- Promote the development of the landlocked and—compared to the Bengal plains—relatively backward hilly districts of Assam by providing these with an access to the sea via the Chittagong port in southeastern Bengal.
- To these ends, unite disparate Oriya-speaking districts under a single administration, transfer Chhota Ngapur from Bengal to the Central Provinces, and detach Dhaka, Chittagong and Mymensingh areas from Bengal and attach them to Assam.

The proposals were formally published in January 1904. The following month, Curzon toured the eastern districts, consulting and addressing local luminaries in Dhaka, Chittagong and Mymensingh. The visit by the Viceroy-and-Governor General, accompanied by his wife and their large retinue, created a stir in the usually somnolent agricultural east. Curzon was escorted by an honour-guard of fifteen cavalrymen riding finely caparisoned steeds; but for the locals, his fleet of 1902–model Dechamp-Tonneau cars proved more fascinating as the group slowly processed along paths snaking across Bengal's rice paddies.[3] The Viceroy's exchanges with local leaders helped to refine the proposals: a self-contained new province would be created in eastern Bengal under a Lt. Governor. It would have a legislative assembly and enjoy revenue authority. It would be sufficiently large to require and justify semi–autonomous administrative functions and capabilities. The new province would comprise the administrative Divisions of Dhaka, Chittagong and Rajshahi—the last excluding Darjeeling but including Malda, as well as the Tripura state and Assam. In addition, Bengal would exchange several Hindi–speaking districts with the Central Provinces for Oriya-speaking ones. The residual, somewhat circumscribed, province of Bengal would have a population of 54 million and occupy an area of 141,580 sq. miles.

Eastern Bengal and Assam, the proposed new province, would be administered from the former *Mughal* provincial capital Dhaka, with subsidiary headquarters in Chittagong. Its 106,540 sq. miles would be home to some 31 million people. Its Lt. Governor would be assisted by a Legislative Assembly and a two-member Board of Revenue, but in judicial matters, the Calcutta High Court would retain jurisdiction. In administrative terms, the province would unite the region's jute- and tea-growing areas (except in Darjeeling) under a single authority, attenuate the influence of the largely Calcutta-based Hindu *zamindars* over their mainly Muslim *ryots* (tenants) in the eastern districts and, given the confessional distinctions articulated by the separation,[4] effectively shape a communally-defined future for the region. While Curzon did not overtly express support for this particular aspect of the outcome, many among Bengal's *bhadrolok* (literally, civil folk) middle classes focused on it early on. As it happened, this class was exclusively Hindu.

The partition threatened diverse elite interests. British-India's most articulate and potentially problematic progeny, lawyers, were well-represented among Bengali *bhadrolok*. They feared a possible decline of the Calcutta-based judicial system's pre-eminence across the province and the consequent clouding of their prospects. Bengal's growing and increasingly influential press, too, worried about likely competition from Dhaka and other eastern towns. Traders and their many beneficiaries suddenly saw threats emerging from Chittagong, the port that would serve Eastern Bengal and Assam, and rival Calcutta's regional clout. Feudal interests also converged. Absentee *zamindars* would need to set up duplicate establishments in Eastern Bengal and manage relations with its new revenue authorities. The consequent costs and avoidable hassle brought them into play on the side of the middle classes. Although many of the plan's critics saw it as a manifestation of Britain's *divide et impera* stratagem against the Indian National Congress's growing nationalist campaign, some of Bengal's Muslim leaders also protested against the planned partition. However, their concerns were over a possible weakening of the recent advances made by Muslims in education and professional employment, and were expressed in much more moderate language than the rhetoric used by Congress activists. These protests notwithstanding, the Government of India promulgated Bengal's new administrative arrangements on 19 July 1905, and these took effect on 16 October.

Bengal's Muslim middle classes and remaining aristocrats welcomed the partition, viewing it as British recognition of their community as deserving of separate and equal treatment after a century-and-a-half of animosity and neglect. Even the conservative *Wahabi* and reformist *Faraizi* groups supported the partition. Liberal Muslims who opposed it and endorsed the *Swadesi* movement, did not support the latter's violent 'Boycott' campaign. In 1906, Salim ul-lah, the *Nawab* of Dhaka, convened a gathering of co-religionists who went on to form the All India Muslim League, a confessionally defined political grouping designed to protect and promote the interests of the empire's Mohammedan community. The Muslim League welcomed the partition. The British appeared to be reversing their stance. Having fought and overthrown India's Muslim rulers and nursed the rise of mainly Hindu feudal and professional inter-mediaries, they now sponsored the crystallisation of a countervailing Muslim polity. As the Muslim elite took advantage of an apparent endorsement by the British of the emergence of a counterpoint to the Congress's anti–colonial nationalist campaign, Hindu anger and secular reaction spread from Calcutta to India's northern, western, central and southern cities and provinces.

Two strands emerged—a political-economic campaign to boycott British goods in favour of domestic products, especially in textiles, and violent attacks on the institutions and personae of imperial control, termed 'terrorism' by the authorities. Militant Bengali activists—almost wholly from the Hindu community—carried out a large number of attacks on colonial officials and premises in the first three decades of the twentieth century. In 1906–17, over a thousand 'terrorists' reportedly carried out 210 'revolutionary outrages' and 101 unsuccessful attempts in Bengal. After a relatively quiet decade, Bengal officials recorded 189 such incidents in 1930–34.[5] Support for the popular *swadesi* (indigenous) campaign increased demand for local manufactures and handicrafts. While numerically marginal, the 'terrorists' posed a more immediate threat, although the effect of bombings and shootings targeting govern-ment offices and officials was more psychological than physical. The retribution was severe, but their campaign continued and set a precedent for the future. The parallel strands—peaceful and legally organized oppo-sition to unacceptable decisions, and violent challenges to the authorities imposing such decisions—divided the Congress. This split became evi-dent at its 1907 annual session in Surat. On one side, Bal Gangadhar

Tilak endorsed violence against all manifestations of the partition, symbolising an unstated challenge to the imperial order. Surendranath Banerjea, a vocal critic of the partition, nonetheless warned against unpredictable consequences of a violent campaign. Moderate leaders like Gopal Krishna Gokhale and Banerjea won the day, but the two strands never reconciled, co-existing uneasily until a more profound partition divided the empire itself in 1947.

The years following the 1905 partition saw parallel developments. In East Bengal, Muslim leaders and organisations consolidated their support among their co-religionists, especially among Bengali middle-farmers—*jotedars*—who had assumed intermediary roles in rural Bengal, sharpening the Bengali–Muslims' collective identity. In the rest of Bengal, the Boycott campaign and the 'terrorist' movement grew more violent and threatening. Curzon's successor, Lord Minto, generally supportive of the rise of a Muslim polity, cracked down on its violent critics. But the strength of feeling and organisation brought to bear on the authorities on this issue began to tell and, in August 1911, the new Viceroy, Lord Hardinge, recommended restoration of a united Bengal. King George V, at his Durbar in Delhi in December, revoked the partition. At the same time, the decision to move the imperial capital to Delhi, seat of the Mughals ousted by the British, was announced. The reorganised Bengal, administered by a Governor-in-Council, comprised the Bengali–speaking Presidency, and the Divisions of Burdwan, Chittagong, Dhaka and Rajshahi, bringing together a population of 42 million over 70,000 sq. miles. The Muslims were in a slight majority. On 1 April 1912, Bihar, Chhoto Nagpur and Orissa became a separate province, while Assam reverted to Chief Commissioner's rule. The aftershocks of these changes would be felt for decades.

Hindu leaders and their supporters were pleased with Bengal's reunification, even if Calcutta's relegation to the status of a provincial capital took some of the shine off their victory. The Muslims, on the other hand, saw this as a restoration of the *status quo ante* in which their interests had been subservient to those of all the other actors. The perception that this reversal had been effected by violent means and that the Congress had supported that campaign created the context in which Hindu-Muslim differentiation took on sharply political contours. By then, the confessionally defined electorates produced by the Morley-Minto reforms of 1909 had formalised and institutionalised this polarization. One apparent lesson from the episode was that agitational capability rather than loyalty or moderation was the more effective path for pursuing political objectives, especially from a position of weakness. Another suggested that irrespective of its avowedly secular nationalist rhetoric, Congress defended Hindu elite interests and would pursue these at the cost of Muslim ones. The scene was set for India's communally charged future.

The Pakistan experience

East Bengal's transition to East Pakistan passed many way stations but only three leaders of note stood out along that journey. Two of them—AK Fazlul Huq and Maulana Abdul Hamid Khan Bhashani—were rooted in the soil and represented the interests of the penurious peasantry of the northern and western districts of eastern Bengal and southern districts of Assam. The third, Huseyn Shaheed Suhrawardy, belonged to a prominent Calcutta Muslim family and played an important, if eventually tragic, role in Bengal's second partition. In the 1930s, all three were members of the Muslim League which provided a superstructure for Muslim political activism without limiting pursuit of specific and local interests. Huq and fellow lawyers formed the *Krishak Proja* (peasants, tenants) party, later renamed *Krishak Sramik* (peasant, worker). They mobilised farmers and labourers irrespective of their religious creed. In the 1937 elections, the party secured the largest share of the vote in eastern Bengal and Huq formed a coalition government with the Hindu *Mahasabha*, a communal body that nonetheless agreed to cohabit with a Muslim dominated party. Huq's eminence earned him the honour of being chosen to put forward the 'Pakistan resolution' at the Muslim League's 1940 conference in Lahore. His willingness to work with all Bengalis, including Hindus, meant he soon lost the League's love and felt constrained to focus on the Bengali aspect of his politics. This schizoid tension was a defining feature of East Bengal's search for political identity.

While war raged in the Middle-East and across South-East Asia, India generally and Bengal in particular saw other forms of conflict that proved equally deadly. The 'Quit India' movement led India's British authorities to imprison most leaders of the Congress and thousands of its activists. One renegade Congress leader, Bengal's Subhas Chandra Bose, rejected his colleagues' formalistic resistance and sought more direct action against imperial control. Fleeing India in dramatic fashion, he first sought German assistance to establish an Indian army of liberation to be manned by Indian soldiers taken prisoner by Axis forces in Europe and Africa. This attempt, given Hitler's reluctance to provide substantive help, proved abortive. Bose then travelled east and secured Japanese support in setting up the Indian National Army (INA) with British-Indian prisoners of war (POW) in Japanese custody. The INA played a secondary role in Japan's advance across Burma into the empire's north-eastern ramparts. This led, inadvertently, to a catastrophic famine in Bengal. As the Japanese-INA advance appeared close to entering India from the east, British forces implemented contingency plans to impede enemy progress across eastern Bengal's estuarine delta-land. Their strategy included the destruction of local transport systems and grain-stocks that, if captured, would boost enemy logistics. In the event, British-Indian defenders held the Japanese-INA forces in Manipur and Nagaland before turning them back, but their scorched-earth policy led to a cataclysmic famine in eastern Bengal in 1943. More than a million penurious peasants starved to death.[6]

Bhashani made his name as an activist fighting for the rights of peasants in northern Bengal and landless Bengali settlers in Assam. The latter had started colonising largely uninhabited tracts of the Brahmaputra Valley and surrounding sub-montane regions in Assam when Bengal and Assam were conjoined administratively. Local resentment of the settlers led the British authorities to impose increasingly rigorous restrictions on the Bengalis, many of them Muslim. Bhashani found his calling in helping the illiterate and pauperised settlers organise themselves to demand their rights. Although a religious scholar by training, he would be best known for his work with peasants who had settled on the Bhashan islet on the Brahmaputra River; hence the name Bhashani, given to him by grateful beneficiaries. The Assam Government had laid down geographical limits to where Bengali peasants could settle, causing much hardship among communities that had already moved beyond the 'line'. Encouraging settlers to resist restrictions, Bhashani was repeatedly jailed. He was in prison in Assam when Partition was implemented.

Suhrawardy, a member of the regional Muslim elite, led the Bengal Muslim League to victory in the 1946 elections. His was the only Muslim League administration in the empire at the time. The League's electoral success reflected the crystallisation among Bengal's Muslims of a distinct confessional identity driven by and strengthening the Pakistan movement. As the last Chief Minister of united Bengal in that crucial period in the subcontinent's history, Suhrawardy initially opposed Partition, demanding instead an independent united Bengal in post-colonial South Asia. This would cost him the affections of Jinnah and Liaquat Ali Khan, the League's central leaders. His role in the Muslim League's Direct Action Day on 16 August 1946, when party activists attacked Hindu critics of the Pakistan movement and communal violence burst forth like a volcanic eruption, sweeping away hopes of maintaining Bengali, or Indian, unity, was equally controversial. Suhrawardy was accused by Hindu commentators of doing nothing to prevent the carnage. As violence spread first across Bengal between Hindus and Muslims, and then engulfed the Sikhs as well across the Gangetic plains, Punjab and the North-West Frontiers in orgiastic bloodletting, the need to separate the communities in newly-defined successor states assumed great urgency. Later, Suhrawardy joined Mahatma Gandhi in calling for peace but by then many lives had been lost and Partition had become inevitable. This was the backdrop against which East Pakistan was born.

Once Britain's final attempt to avoid breaking up the empire in the form of the May 1946 Cabinet Mission Plan had been swept aside in the wake of widespread bloodshed, the inevitability of partition was acknowledged by almost all the parties. Lord Mountbatten presented his plans to the leaders of the major groupings—Jawaharlal Nehru, Vallabhbhai Patel and Acharya Kripalini for Congress, Mohammad Ali Jinnah, Liaquat Ali Khan and Abdur Rab Nishtar for the Muslim League, and Baldev Singh for the Sikhs—on 2 June 1947. Although the single largest concentration of Indian Muslims lay in Bengal, they were not directly represented at the talks. After agreement was obtained, details were published the following day. Elaborate procedures included voting by members of the Hindu-majority and Muslim-majority areas of the Bengal Legislative Assembly sitting separately to determine their preferences, a referendum in Assam's Sylhet district on its choice of its future affiliation, and a Boundary Commission to demarcate borders that would 'partition' Bengal. Punjab legislators would similarly vote for dividing up their province, and a referendum would also be held in the North West Frontier Province. On 20 June members of the Bengal Legislative Assembly voted for the Partition of their province. Hindu-majority western Bengal opted to stay in India; Muslim-majority eastern Bengal elected to join Pakistan. A referendum held on 7 July determined Sylhet's future within East Bengal. Sir Cyril Radcliffe's Boundary Commission demarcated the borders defining the newly-created successor states but their details were not published until after India and Pakistan had violently come into being in mid-August, 1947.

The scale of the trauma around the Partition can only be gauged from estimates of the number of people killed or forced to leave their ancestral homes to seek refuge across suddenly proclaimed, and often evidently contrived, international borders. Estimates of Partition's death toll range from 200,000 to over a million; the number of people forced to migrate in 1947–1951 has been estimated at between 10 million and 17 million.[7] These figures provide some indication of the turbulence that rocked the subcontinent as it emerged from nearly two centuries of British rule. Most of the displacement and forced-migration occurred in the empire's north-western quadrant, but Bengal did not escape. Around 2.5 million Hindus fled East Bengal, 2.06 million heading for West Bengal, and 173,000 moving to Assam, mostly from Sylhet. Similarly, 671,000 Muslims left West Bengal, Bihar and Assam and sought refuge in East Pakistan. West Bengal's net gain was 1.4 million.[8] The flight of Hindus out of East Bengal and a reciprocal migration of Muslims from India into East Pakistan would continue, subtly changing the demographic, confessional and social makeup of the two parts of Bengal over the years. 'Communal' rioting occasionally boosted this traffic, but the bitterness engendered by the Partition, the motif of a wholly new genre of art, literature and cinematography, would remain unmatched.

East Bengal inherited a Muslim League government led by the local *ashraf* elite, many of its members bilingual in Urdu and Bengali. They seized the property of the Hindu *zamindars* and others who had fled to India, redistributing it mainly among the incoming *muhajirs* from India. Many of the latter were technically skilled or commercially experienced Urdu-speaking entrepreneurs. Generically (and somewhat pejoratively) termed *Biharis* by the host community, they brought with them both a staunch belief in Pakistan and a devout faith in Islam, burnished by the horrors of Partition, that stood in contrast with the more relaxed approach taken by those East Bengalis whose lives had not been directly touched by these events.[9] *Biharis* tended to live in their own communities in something of a splendid isolation, maintaining their more austere and orthodox practices and rarely if ever communing with the Bengalis except at the workplace and religious functions. They were far more at home with the West Pakistani soldiers, civil-servants, traders and entrepreneurs who increasingly assumed important positions in the province than they were with members of the host community. Disdain was often mutual. Even in the early days of Pakistan, East Bengal already bore the seeds of disquiet and dissention.

The divergent experiences and expectations shaping the perceptions and worldviews of the Bengali majority and the *Bihari* immigrants built fissures that neither party was able to bridge. The refugees spoke in Urdu, the reviled language of the West Pakistani elite; for the Bengalis, the language of literary giants such as Rabindranath Tagore, Nazrul Islam, Jibananda Das, Sarat Chandra Chattapadhyay and Mir Mosharraf Hossain, among others, was the hallowed core of their cultural identity and the fountainhead of their ideational essence.[10] The immigrants shared values and interests with Pakistan's western rulers; the Bengalis resented the privileges granted to the newcomers in the form of assets left by fleeing Hindus, and employment generated by their skilled labour and assisted enterprise. Many *Biharis* owed allegiance to the orthodox *Deobandi* school of Sunni Islam, or shi'ism; most Bengali Muslims were descended from low-caste Hindus converted by *Sufi* saints whose belief in the universality of *noor-i-khuda* (divine light) gave them a tolerant, even syncretic, perspective considered heretical by the orthodox. The discriminatory treatment of the Bengalis by their West Pakistani rulers ensured these cleavages deepened over time as *Biharis* and Bengalis lived parallel yet distant lives.

The language of schizophrenia

Pakistan was born challenged and no challenge was more profound than the philosophical one. It was conceived as the homeland of the empire's Muslim community, but the movement for its creation was led by Jinnah and his acolytes who came from India's northern and south-western provinces where Muslims were in a minority and which stood no chance of becoming part of the new Muslim homeland. The leaders had to uproot themselves physically and emotionally, and migrate to the empire's Muslim-majority north-western provinces where the Muslim's League's campaign call—'Islam is in danger'—stirred few native souls. Here, Pakistan's *muhajir* founders teamed up with feudal barons and upcoming industrialists to establish *de novo* the superstructure of a brand new polity. Many of their native compatriots among *Punjabi*, *Pashtun*, *Sindhi* and *Baloch* national groups did not share the leadership's view of the ideational bases and physical boundaries of the new dispensation. The Hindu-ruled Muslim-majority princely state of Jammu & Kashmir, represented by the letter 'K' in the formulation 'Pakistan', did not join Pakistan and, despite desultory warfare lasting fifteen months, remained in India. The Khan of Kalat, the largest feudal estate in Balochistan province, refused to join Pakistan and was forced to do so by military pressure. As regards Pakistan's largest component, East Bengal, few of Pakistan's leaders had much time for its concerns, leaving it as they did in the hands of Dhaka's *ashraf* elite running the provincial Muslim League administration. Despite its size, East Bengal languished on the margins of Pakistan's rulers' consciousness. But this was, in relative terms, a secondary problem.

The 'two-nation theory' espoused by the Muslim League posited that South Asia's Hindus and Muslims were two distinct nations that merited separate national-states for the healthy development of their post-colonial future. Britain's partition plans tacitly acknowledged the validity of this claim without any fanfare. The empire's last Viceroy, Lord Mountbatten, stayed on as the first Governor-General of the Dominion of India without, apparently, noting the irony of his position. The India he formally presided over strongly rejected the two-nation formulation on the basis of which he had created two successor states from the empire and its associated princely states and frontier agencies. The India ruled by the Gandhian-Nehruvian Congress was founded on the premise that India was an ideational, historical, cultural, economic and political association in which religious faith played no role in determining policy, and Pakistan's two-nation theoretical basis was a violation of the secular principles on which the Indian Union was founded.[11] So, August 1947 saw two new states created from the division of a single, largely unified, political-economic entity on the bases of two mutually exclusive founding principles struggling with the consequences of their sanguinary separation.

If the theoretical bases of the Indian Union were accepted as legitimate, then the philosophical notions on which the Pakistani state was founded could not be—and vice versa. The strength of logic and the ethnic, societal and cultural overlaps straddling the contrived boundaries between the contiguous successor states created an environment in which their rival leaderships felt driven to demonstrate the validity of the foundational myths of their own state by subverting and de-legitimising the organising principles underpinning the other. Since their birth, then,

India and Pakistan were engaged in a philosophical duel unto the death. Disputes over the princely states of Jammu & Kashmir, Hyderabad, and Junagadh & Manvadar, the division of armed forces, national assets and foreign reserves, distribution of shared waters, and myriad differences that clouded diplomatic prospects and led to war weeks after independence, were symptomatic of the elemental discord that characterised post-colonial South Asia. Each state thrived on the negation of 'the other'. Indian energy and imagination were focused on demonstrating Pakistan's 'illegitimacy', while the latter was engaged in a survivalist programme that could not countenance even the slightest challenge to its centralising and 'nationalising' endeavours. Perceived challenges from Baloch, Pashtun, Sindhi and Bengali nationalist tendencies would be painted in colours of treason and 'Hindu conspiracy' before being crushed. This was the highly charged backdrop against which East Pakistan evolved.

Consolidating a diverse and disparate collection of communities and cultures into a brand new political-economic entity separated by a thousand miles of hostile Indian territory posed a monumental challenge to Pakistan's émigré leaders. South Asia offered the post-colonial world a template for building successor states, but the metropolitan Westphalian nation-state paradigm left it little choice in charting an independent course.[12] An elite mind-set shaped in British campuses and Inns of Court took to creating reflections of the British polity in post-colonial South Asia. The Congress managed the task much better than the Muslim League did. Jinnah's assertion during his first visit to East Bengal as Governor-General in 1948 that Urdu, and Urdu alone, would be Pakistan's national language caused the first breach. Bengali middle-classes, with university students at their leading edge, vociferously rejected the 'father of the nation's' statement. Advised by the province's often Urdu-speaking *ashraf* elite, Jinnah must have been surprised by the strength of vernacular feeling among East Pakistanis. He could not let this challenge to the nation-building mission jeopardize his life's work. He would allow no compromise to weaken what he thought were fundamental tasks of giving Pakistan political coherence.

This insistence on a unitary vision of Pakistan, which left no room to accommodate local specificities, caused a schism within the East Pakistan Muslim League. One of Bengal's more illustrious sons, Suhrawardy, had been hounded out of East Bengal by the Muslim League administration under Khawaja Nazim-ud-din, himself a scion of the *Nawabs* of Dhaka.

After the bloodshed of Partition, Suhrawardy, still a resident of Calcutta, began a campaign aimed at restoring communal harmony, focusing on the residual but substantial Hindu minority in East Bengal. Here, he met leaders of both majority and minority communities, urging mutual respect and tolerance. Provincial officials soon reported he was conspiring with likeminded locals to restore a united Bengal, possibly within India but certainly not a part of Pakistan. Thrown out of the province, Suhrawardy denied the allegations, pleading for justice to Pakistan's Prime Minister Liaquat Ali Khan. Although Khan refused to intervene[13] and Suhrawardy was forced out of the League, he was allowed to move to the national capital, Karachi. Here he set up a party called the *Awami* (people's) Muslim League. Restrictions imposed by the Pakistani authorities meant that this organisation was limited to having an office and printed stationery but few members and little activity. However, in June 1949, the League's other discontented leaders—Bhashani and Fazlul Huq—called a party-workers' convention in Dhaka. Nearly three hundred delegates from across East Pakistan attended. Supported by second-tier figures like Huq's aide Ataur Rahman Khan, and Suhrawardy's student acolyte from his Calcutta days, Sheikh Mujibur Rahman, Bhashani proclaimed the formation of a new party, the East Bengal *Awami* Muslim League, with himself as President. Fazlul Huq decided not to join the new party, electing to concentrate on the activities of his *Krishak Sramik* organisation instead, but his tacit support was helpful. Thus, less than two years from the Muslim League's achievement of Pakistan, a faction challenging its status as the symbol of East Bengali aspirations took root in the city where the League itself had been born in 1906.

East Bengal's turbulent traditions began early. In October 1949, *Awami* Muslim League leaders began a hunger strike in protest against the Muslim League administration's 'failure' to address famine-like conditions in the province. As they marched towards the provincial secretariat in Dhaka, the leaders were arrested in a move that would establish the pattern of provincial politics. The administration would be seen to have failed to provide essential services; the opposition would mount strikes and protest marches; faced with threatened violence the authorities would crack down on the protesters, arresting and jailing them; eventually, detained politicians would be released and emerge stronger than when they went in. This would be the template of political activism in East Bengal and, later on, in Bangladesh. In 1950, when Suhrawardy was in Dhaka to represent a politician whose victory in a May 1949 by-election over his Muslim League rival had been quashed by the government, the authorities imposed strict restrictions on the former Chief Minister who was jailed for violating some of these. Protests against these restrictions led in July 1950 to a meeting among Suhrawardy, Bhashani, and Sheikh Mujibur Rahman at the central jail in Dhaka. The following month, after he was allowed to return to Karachi, Suhrawardy announced the merger between his Awami League and Bhashani's. Now there was a political vehicle to represent East Bengal's distinct aspirations and sophisticated leadership to drive it.

Structural differences, too, divided the Wings. With most Hindu *zamindars* having left for India, East Bengal legislated for an end to feudal practices in 1950, abolishing absentee-landlordism, imposing ceilings on land-holdings in this very densely populated delta country, and handing much recovered land to the tillers in tiny plots that merely provided for subsistence farming for the majority of the rural popultion. This transformation in land-ownership reduced the threat of penury to peasant farmers whose earlier need to borrow money from usurious lenders often landed them in bondage. Fleeing Hindu *zamindars* had often been unpopular among their tenants. The assets they left behind, officially called 'enemy property', were distributed among their grateful former subjects or acquired by the state. East Bengal's new political elite, principally middle-class professionals in origin, actively worked to reduce the extremes of feudal imposition. While rural poverty would remain a major feature of eastern Bengal's socio-political experience, the structural bases of inequity—in contrast to the continuing practice in West Pakistan—were removed. This created the space for the emergence of a new class of middle-peasants—*jotedars*–who would acquire the surplus necessary for assuming local leadership in socio-economic and eventually, political, activities in rural East Pakistan. The rise of this newly influential group would transform the province's political landscape.[14] When representative electoral practices reached the region, parties that attracted these men would reap numerical advantages that others could only dream of.

As a result, in terms of elite-formation, East Bengal became even more distinct, and distant, from West Pakistan. There, feudal barons continued to exercise influence in concert with the Muslim League's *muhajir* leaders, Pakistan's emergent *bourgeoisie*, and members of the British-trained civil-military bureaucracies whose ranks boasted few Bengalis. State-building from scratch, consolidation of control over troublesome princely states and tribal agencies, the many disputes with India—including the first war over Kashmir—Jinnah's declining health and eventual death, the assassination of his successor Liaquat Ali Khan by army officers in 1951, and a series of turbulent political changes at Pakistan's political centre meant governmental focus was rarely on East Pakistan. The majority province appeared to be treated like a troublesome appendage. Not surprisingly, Bengali resentment steadily grew. It was against this backdrop that the East Bengali movement which demanded that Bengali be given the status of a national language reached a climax. The imposition of Urdu, a largely alien language spoken by some among Bengal's exploitative *ashraf* aristocracy but foreign to the masses, aroused a resentful reaction among the vernacular middle classes whose cultural identity had been sharpened since Jinnah's 1948 assertion. As professional and political groups became better organised and the student community grew in size and influence, the campaign for securing for Bengali the status of a national language in the Pakistani state acquired the character of an ethno-cultural nationalist movement. Bereft of visible or material assets, Bengali middle- and political classes saw their linguistic heritage and literary traditions as the essence of who and what they were.[15] Pakistani attempts to demean this one source of collective pride proved so thoroughly unacceptable that protests turned violent.

On 21 February 1952, provincial policemen opened fire on demonstrators in Dhaka, killing four youths, including students. Although Bengali blood had been shed by Bengali constables, this became a watershed in the coalescence of East Bengal's nationalist aspirations, generating a protracted and painful campaign for autonomy and eventually, independence. The youths were seen to have become martyrs to the Bengali cause struggling to secure national honour within a repressive Pakistani state structure. In a way, this violent encounter marked a parting of ways, although it also underscored the violence inherent in the regional patterns of political discourse which often was as absolutist as it had been during the British *Raj*. So, while for East Bengal 21 February 1952 was a fork in the road in its role within Pakistan, bloody encounters between instruments of state and those who questioned policy were part of the region's political traditions which post-colonial elites refused to discard. Although South Asia's new *sahibs* were brown, they were *sahibs* nonetheless, and state behaviour often proved it.

A fragmented polity

This new version of East Bengali nationalism found effective expression in the formation of a five-party coalition called the United Front, led by Bhashani, Suhrawardy, Huq, Haji Mohammad Danesh and Sheikh Mujibur Rahman (Mujib). The Front demolished the Muslim League in provincial elections held in March 1954, capturing 223 seats; the League managed to take seven. From this point on, the Muslim League, the party of Jinnah and Pakistan's most significant political organisation, would never again exert any visible influence in Pakistan's eastern 'wing'. The loss of affection between Pakistan's central elite and East Bengal's emergent political leadership posed a challenge parallel to the development of a schism between Pakistan's feudal politicians on the one hand and its civil-military bureaucrats on the other. Fazlul Huq, as the pre-eminent leader of the United Front, was the putative chief minister of East Bengal. But his openly expressed support for a benign relationship between Pakistan and India was seen in Karachi to threaten national integrity. Although Huq was never formally charged, he was accused of treason and prevented from forming the provincial administration. Instead, a civil-military bureaucrat named Iskander Mirza was appointed the province's martial law administrator and authorised to govern the province as an extension of Pakistan's federal government.[16]

The loss of an opportunity to exercise power earned through electoral processes placed the United Front under strain. The Awami League under Suhrawardy now sought to exploit the fluidity in Karachi to secure power for itself. In October, Governor-General Ghulam Mohammad abolished the Muslim League-dominated constituent Assembly at the centre. Suhrawardy was among the few Pakistani politicians who endorsed this move, earning the Governor-General's gratitude. Following secret discussions between the two men later in the year, Suhrawardy joined Muhammad's technocratic 'cabinet of talents' as Pakistan's law minister. In January 1955, the Awami League formally left the United Front. Negotiations between the Governor-General and Suhrawardy led, in the run up to the drafting of Pakistan's constitution, to proposals of the formation of a coalition government at the centre with Suhrawardy as the prime minister and Ataur Rahman Khan as East Bengal's chief minister. In formal terms, the Awami League had replaced the Muslim League as Pakistan's dominant political party at both national and provincial levels. However, with Fazlul Huq already marginalised, major differences now emerged between Suhrawardy and Bhashani on key principles being enshrined in Pakistan's draft constitution. Bhashani rejected the separation of the electorate on religious grounds while Suhrawardy supported it. This would become a major bone of contention between Pakistan's central authorities and East Bengali politicians, but for now, it threatened the Awami League's cohesion. The two men also differed on Pakistan's foreign policy.

Suhrawardy backed the civil-military bureaucracy's decision to incorporate Pakistan into America's military alliance network designed to thwart 'communist threats'; Bhashani questioned the wisdom of such alliances and urged the development of close ties to China instead. As the Cold War heated up, the debate superimposed the global on the local, increasingly reflecting and reinforcing regional fissures and national cleavages. But both men may have shared disquiet over the Pakistani elite's transparently disingenuous efforts to reduce the relative weight of East Pakistan's demographic preponderance. By administrative fiat, the four provinces of West Pakistan were brought together in 'One Unit' giving this western 'Wing' the same importance as the eastern 'Wing.' But this did not generate sufficient pressure for unifying political forces in either wing and eventually, the 'One Unit' faded as a contentious political issue for the next fifteen years.

Suhrawardy's demands—that Bengali be made a national language, that Pakistan be constituted as a federal republic with its provinces enjoying substantial autonomy, and that joint geographical constituencies replace the confessionally determined and divisive separate electorates—proved unacceptable to Pakistani leaders. They anointed a senior bureaucrat, Chaudhri Mohammad Ali, as the next prime minister. Ali took up the Muslim League banner, throwing out Suhrawardy from the cabinet and replacing his Awami League in the central coalition with Huq's *Krishak Sramik* Party. Huq became Pakistan's Home Minister and his KSP formed the provincial government in Dhaka under Abu Hussain Sarkar as chief minister. Pakistan's 'revolving door politics' thus churned the parties and their leaders—raising some momentarily, and then discarding them while lifting others—fragmenting the polity and rendering the formation of coherent ideological policy platforms virtually impossible. Politicians appeared to be driven by the need to establish their domain, secure the power of patronage, and exercise what could charitably be described as extreme pragmatism.

This process ensured that Huq and his party, by joining an administration that lacked popular legitimacy, lost influence in the province where their roots lay, despite the formal trappings of power. This created fresh opportunities for the Awami League. It abandoned the term 'Muslim' from its name, announced plans to recruit members from among all Pakistani nationals irrespective of their religious beliefs, began a campaign for equal civic rights for all citizens and demanded the replacement of separate electorates with joint ones. Not surprisingly, many West Pakistani officials at the centre accused the Awami League of conspiring to break Pakistan up. Awami League activists led by Mujib frequently and vigorously protested against the provincial government's many failings, with strikes and demonstrations making civic life almost unbearable in Dhaka and other towns and cities.

The adoption of Pakistan's constitution in 1956 addressed few of the country's problems. While it adopted the structures of a republic, tensions between its bureaucracies and politicians on the one hand, and between politicians from the two wings on the other, further complicated by differences among East Pakistani politicians themselves, meant the country never fulfilled the obligations its leaders had imposed on themselves. Nowhere was the challenge more severe than in famished East Pakistan.

Meanwhile, Iskander Mirza had, with army commander-in-chief General Ayub Khan's connivance, replaced Ghulam Mohammad as Pakistan's head of state. Mirza was moved by a letter from Suhrawardy which narrated the latter's experiences during his tour of the province's starving hinterlands. Mirza flew to East Bengal, saw the appalling conditions in rural districts, and ordered the army to feed the destitute. The Awami League and the Muslim League, despite previous hostility, now joined hands in calling for the ousting of the Sarkar government in Dhaka. Mirza invited Sarkar, Fazlul Huq and Suhrawardy to Karachi for talks, following which the Sarkar government resigned. After fifteen months in opposition, the Awami League was ready to take power, which it did in September 1956. Ataur Rahman Khan became the chief minister of East Pakistan—as East Bengal had been renamed in the constitution; ten days later, Suhrawardy was invited to form a coalition government at the centre. He teamed up with the Punjabi feudal-dominated Republican Party and assumed the office of the prime minister of Pakistan.

Although the Awami League now controlled both the central government of Pakistan and the provincial government in East Pakistan, it appeared to be more focused on ideological demands than administrative needs. Both chief minister Ataur Rahman Khan and Mujib—party Joint Secretary and provincial minister—demanded the establishment of joint electorates for all citizens as a priority. Politicians in the two wings of Pakistan had different perspectives on the issue. East Pakistan had a substantial Hindu community while most Hindus had left West Pakistan. East Pakistani politicians were much more sensitive to the needs of their Hindu compatriots than West Pakistani colleagues could be. Also, anti-Hindu and anti–Indian emotions ran much higher in West Pakistan than they did in the East. East Pakistanis tended to be emollient and pragmatic on India-Pakistan relations; West Pakistanis viewed this as symptomatic of a 'Hindu Indian conspiracy' to 'subvert' Pakistan and accused East Pakistanis of 'treason'. Despite much furore in the National Assembly, the ruling coalition eventually struck a compromise—separate electorates to be continued in West Pakistan and joint electorates to be established in the East—that won a substantial majority. The legislative defeat of the Muslim League's argument that Muslims and Hindus were different nationalities whose differences must be reflected electorally convinced many Pakistanis of the Awami League's 'perfidy.'

Suhrawardy, however, had to fight on many fronts. Within the Awami League, Bhashani demanded that Pakistan renounce its military alliances with the USA and chart a more non-aligned course, with friendship with China a key objective. Suhrawardy defended Karachi's military-dictated strategic priorities while also noting Pakistan's growing ties to Beijing. However, Anglo-French collusion with Israel in their attack on Egypt in October 1956 weakened his arguments as Bhashani and his left-wing faction attacked Karachi's weak-kneed response to the assault. Suhrawardy's point that abandoning the alliances would leave Pakistan prey to Indian machinations found little favour among those who urged 'normal' relations with Delhi. In December, Chinese premier Zhou Enlai visited Pakistan amid much fanfare. His trip to Dhaka was notable for the enthusiasm with which he was received. In an address at Dhaka's *Paltan Maidan* grounds, Zhou blasted the USA and the West generally, condemning their global policies and embarrassing Suhrawardy's central government in Karachi. At the end of the speech, Zhou embraced his host, Bhashani, leaving no doubts about where his sympathies lay.

1957 proved to be a crucial year. In January, India provided inadvertent succour to the beleaguered Suhrawardy by proclaiming that the state of

Jammu & Kashmir would come under the control of its army. Even Sheikh Mujibur Rahman, who had endorsed Bhashani's views over those of his mentor on Pakistan's national security priorities, decided Delhi had demonstrated its unreliability. He now made statements supportive of Suhrawardy who, visiting Dhaka, took the opportunity to explain his position to the influential student community and secured their endorsement. He then went to see Bhashani. Having been utterly disillusioned with Suhrawardy and his handling of the Awami League-led government, Bhashani had called a party conference at Kagmari, which proved to be a critical moment in the evolution of East Pakistani politics.

Here, Bhashani made a bitter attack on Suhrawardy's foreign policy preferences, making it clear that it would no longer be possible for the two men and their supporters to work as one. Next, he resigned from the Awami League and invited leftist politicians from across Pakistan to Dhaka. There, Bhashani launched the National Awami Party (NAP), with himself as president. A West Pakistani socialist, Mahmudul Huq Osmani, became the leftist party's first secretary general. Suhrawardy told Mujib he had decided to retire from politics when his prime ministerial term ended and that he wanted Mujib to succeed him as the leader of the Awami League and lead it in a moderate, centrist, direction as opposed to the clearly leftist stance Bhashani and his faction had taken. Mujib took charge of the residual Awami League. Fragmentation could now only accelerate.

Mujib's Awami League and Bhashani's NAP followed parallel tracks on several scores. Both believed in a secular state with all citizens guaranteed equal rights irrespective of their religious affiliations, and both sought a measure of regional autonomy. In April 1957, before NAP was formally launched, East Pakistan's provincial assembly passed a resolution demanding full autonomy although Mujib hastened to clarify that economic autonomy was what his party demanded. And the NAP, soon after it was formed, urged the dissolution of West Pakistan's 'One Unit' formulation, decreed in 1955. Bengalis saw the merger of Punjab, NWFP, Sindh and Balochistan into the 'One Unit' as a ploy to permanently deny East Pakistan's majority status in a federal Pakistan and to marginalise it in national political and economic decision-making processes. Suhrawardy, attacked by West Pakistani leaders for his party's 'separatist' tendencies, downplayed the resolution and openly denounced it. This led to Ataur Rahman Khan, East Pakistan's Chief Minister and

Suhrawardy's Awami League colleague, to point out that the party took provincial autonomy with utmost seriousness, placing Suhrawardy in an impossible situation.

Events underscored the artifice and contrivance that shaped Pakistan's parliamentary politics. Suhrawardy's coalition colleague, the leader of the Republican Party and West Pakistan's chief minister, Dr. Khan Sahib, facing difficulties in the provincial legislature where the Awami League could not offer any assistance, teamed up with Bhashani's NAP. Despite serious ideological differences, they forged a coalition to continue the Republican control over West Pakistan. Despite this alliance with West Pakistan's feudal interests, however, the NAP persisted in its demand that the One Unit be dissolved; ironic, since the One Unit had been initiated by the Republicans. When the matter was brought before Pakistan's National Assembly, Suhrawardy was forced to defend a formulation initiated by the Republicans and now challenged by their coalition-partners. President Iskander Mirza supported the Prime Minister and announced he would not allow any 'tampering' with the constitution. Behind the scenes, Pakistan's Army Commander-in-Chief, General Ayub Khan, having hurriedly returned from a conference abroad, urged Mirza to take whatever steps he considered necessary to prevent the One Unit's dissolution and consolidation of the leftist, anti–American, NAP's influence. In the end, West Pakistani feudal interests won the day. Dr. Khan Sahib urged Mirza to sack Suhrawardy. This Mirza did in October 1957. Suhrawardy, refusing to budge, summoned a special session of the National Assembly to test his legislative strength first. Mirza, using presidential prerogative, barred such a session and Suhrawardy stepped down. This unconstitutional and unedifying display of Pakistan's feudal, military-bureaucratic power jarred with the Awami League's efforts to chart a moderate course, seeking to neutralise the growing popularity of the NAP's leftward march across East Pakistan.

Meanwhile, Pakistan's revolving-door politics gave rise to a succession of governments, as first the Muslim League and then the Republicans formed short-lived coalitions which failed to deliver on their pledges and barely survived in office while the country's needs went unaddressed. The situation was little better in East Pakistan. Staunch in opposition, the Awami League under Ataur Rahman Khan and Sheikh Mujibur Rahman found it difficult to manage the poverty-stricken province's myriad administrative needs. Corruption among the party's leaders and activists was rife[17] as Western—mostly American—aid kept the province going. With the clamour for improved governance growing in the provincial assembly, the League tabled a motion to curb the Speaker's authority in March 1958. This was to secure for the Awami League untrammeled powers, since Speaker Abul Hakim was seen to lack the power to be useful. While opposition leader Abu Hussain Sarkar and chief minister Ataur Rahman Khan argued about the niceties of parliamentary democracy, the province's governor, the founder of the KSP, Fazlul Huq, decided that the Awami League had lost the confidence of the legislature. Ignoring Karachi's instructions to avoid giving any impression of partisanship, Huq swore in Sarkar as the new chief minister and prorogued the assembly.

Sarkar would need time to organise a legislative majority, but he was given none. The Awami League now manoeuvred in Karachi for Huq's dismissal. The following morning, the province's Chief Secretary, East Pakistan's senior-most civil servant, operating on the orders of Pakistan's central government, proclaimed 'president's rule,' assumed the Governorship, fired Huq, sacked Sarkar and reinstated Ataur Rahman Khan. Huq returned to the leadership of the KSP and promised a comeback after Pakistan's first general elections, scheduled for 1959. When Bhashani and Huq appeared to unite against the Awami League government, Mujib invited a West Pakistani Muslim League leader, Abdul Qayyum Khan, to come to Dhaka, lend support, and demonstrate the Awami League's pan-Pakistani appeal. Meanwhile, Dr. Khan Sahib's assassination had complicated matters for the federal government. Mujib and Khan held president Mirza responsible for Pakistan's many ills. It was against this backdrop that a NAP-KSP legislative front deprived the Awami League of a majority in the provincial assembly, forcing the Ataur Rahman Khan ministry to resign. When Sarkar formed another KSP-NAP administration, Mujib linked up with Mahmud Ali, the leader of NAP's *Ganatantri Dal* (democratic party) faction, promising to accept NAP's political programme and repudiating Suhrawardy's leadership of the League. The outcome of this new legislative alliance caused the Sarkar government to fall within three days of taking office.

Mujib, now the driving force within the Awami League, demanded that president's rule be lifted from the province and a sum of $30 million be transferred as a share of the US aid given to Pakistan in recent years. Neither Mirza nor any of West Pakistan's political leaders responded to these demands but they were concerned about the Awami League-NAP coalition, especially since Bhashani had indicated that if West Pakistan did not pay heed to East Pakistani demands for redressing their many grievances, he would bid them farewell.[18] A trip to Karachi by the former chief minister Ataur Rahman Khan failed to elicit any positive results on either of these scores. While disappointed NAP and Awami League leaders fulminated against 'West Pakistani negligence', tensions mounted as 20 September 1958, the date scheduled for reopening the East Pakistan Legislative Assembly, approached. Against this backdrop, a sequence of events followed which would melodramatically raise questions about the ability of East Pakistani politicians to appreciate the essence of pluralist politics and conduct themselves accordingly.

On the day, in keeping with the Awami League's demands, Pakistan's central government decreed by ordinance that the powers of the Speaker be reduced. It was widely assumed that Pakistan's Prime Minister Feroz Khan Noon, a former governor of East Pakistan, was sympathetic towards the Awami League and the ordinance was his gift to his provincial allies. Speaker Abul Hakim complained to President Mirza that he had been threatened with physical violence by Awami League leaders including Mujib if he entered the legislative building. Despite the threats he did assume the speaker's chair when the assembly convened. But legislators began physically assaulting each other, liberally using as weapons whatever they could find to hand, including microphones and the staff bearing the national standard. The Speaker shouted out an adjournment order and fled the chambers. As the Awami League members refused to obey that order, Deputy Speaker Shahid Ali took over. The treasury bench tabled a motion to set up a board to establish if the Speaker was fit to continue in his post. Unable to conduct a proper debate and voting, the Deputy Speaker ruled the motion had been carried.

The assembly remained calm for the following two days, perhaps helped by the fact that neither the Speaker nor the Deputy Speaker attended either session. The Awami League then advised the Deputy Speaker to chair the session on 23 September. Despite illness and a reluctance to get embroiled in the Awami League's disputes with its critics, Shahid Ali conceded and arrived at the chamber, where Awami League guards escorted him to the Speaker's chair. Opposition legislators, surprised by the unannounced arrival of the indisposed Deputy Speaker, immediately began a fracas. Their Awami League colleagues reciprocated. Missiles including parts of the chamber's furniture were thrown and a chair hit the Deputy Speaker in the head. At this point, Dhaka's District Magistrate, East Pakistan's Inspector General of Police and several constables entered the chamber, routing opposition legislators, and injuring some of them. These men and the Deputy Speaker were taken to hospital where, two days later, Shahid Ali expired. Sarkar and several senior party colleagues were arrested on charges of 'attempted murder' and rioting. The General Officer Commanding of Pakistani land forces in East Pakistan, Major General Umrao Khan, filed a detailed report to General Ayub Khan who discussed the situation, and political problems in West Pakistan, with President Iskander Mirza.

Mirza and Ayub Khan agreed Pakistan needed drastic action to arrest the slide to what looked like potential anarchy in the hands of politicians who were apparently unable to either constitutionally rule the country or manage their partisan differences in a civil fashion. They decided to assume executive authority, abrogate the constitution, dissolve all legislative bodies and prohibit all political organisations and activities. On 7 October, Mirza proclaimed martial law throughout the country and appointed Ayub Khan the Chief Martial Law Administrator, handing him the state's executive powers. Three weeks later when differences arose between the two men, Ayub Khan deposed Mirza, sent him into exile and assumed the presidency as well. Pakistan's early experimentation with pluralist representative politics had come to an end. The army announced plans to 'clean up' the civil administration, arresting officials and politicians on charges of corrupt or inefficient conduct in office, and trying hundreds under military provisions. Pakistan's administrative system gained in efficacy, but there was little else over the next four years.

The military and Pakistan's 'basic' democracy

After months of planning, Ayub Khan presented Pakistan with a new constitution which changed the structure of legislative and executive authority from parliamentary to presidential. The presidency sat at the peak of a hierarchy of 'basic democrats' whose lowest rungs were directly elected and served as the electoral college for the next tier up, until this indirectly elected pyramid reached the National Assembly, the new legislative body. Basic Democrats, or 'BDs', as they came somewhat disdainfully to be called, were elected on a non-party basis, and established political parties could not campaign for any of their candidates, who were to be elected solely on the merit of past performance, or faith in their future potential, by local electors. Each wing elected an equal number of BDs—60,000—and these eventually elected the MPs who legislated at the president's pleasure. Having established a framework that marginalised political parties and their irksome leaders, Ayub Khan promoted himself to Field Marshal, retired from the military, established a faction of the Muslim League with his civilian and retired military backers and set himself up as its candidate in presidential elections in 1964. Most of Pakistan's other parties teamed up as the 'combined opposition' and nominated Fatema Jinnah, sister of the 'father of the nation', to run against Ayub Khan. Despite active country-wide campaigning with the help of her many supporters, she lost.

Now began a transformative episode. Ayub Khan centralised control, laying the foundations of a national-security state.[19] Judging the changes his regime made against the characteristics of other national security states, he appeared to make rapid progress.

The military's status as the highest authority: Pakistan's post Jinnah-Liaquat order derived its authority from three distinct groups operating in a fluid combination—the *Muhajir*-Punjabi party political elite, Pakistan's civil bureaucracy, and the military. Following Liaquat Ali Khan's assassination, a civil-military bureaucratic coalition with the army as the junior partner overshadowed party political elites. US assistance promoted the military's relative power and influence while other institutions remained stunted and Ayub Khan's domineering personality soon made the army the senior partner in the bureaucratic coalition. The imposition of martial law secured for the military supremacy within the domestic structure.

Suspicions of democratic institutions and practices: Rigorous implementation of military regulations, prohibition of political parties and activities, and vigorous prosecution of cases against many notable political figures reflected the state's abhorrence of the often clumsy routine of democratic pluralism. Ayub Khan's 'basic democratic' constitution with its multi-tiered electoral college reflected his lack of faith in the messy rough-and-tumble of 'usual' democracy.

Political-economic clout of the military-security organs and their associates: Ayub's economic policy, especially his distributive and surplus-accumulation formulations, assisted the flowering of new elites by focusing resources in the hands of a select group of capitalists—the so-called twenty-two families—and levers of political and economic management in the military-civil bureaucracy. While these steps consolidated the coherence of the Pakistani state, West Pakistani control deepened East Bengal's sense of marginalisation and hardened its resentment.

Obsession with 'enemies': Although India had remained the looming adversary since Partition, Pakistan's politicians had been concerned with the many domestic challenges facing the new republic. Ayub Khan's administration, like other military regimes, stressed the 'Indian threat' to Pakistan's continuing existence and wellbeing. Those who questioned the legitimacy of the martial authorities were equated with enemies of Pakistan.[20] Ayub Khan, who promoted himself to Field Martial, did not restrict himself to anti–Indian rhetoric but also mounted military operations—first in the south, in 1964, and then, in the north, in the following year, with mixed results. The Bengalis in East Pakistan did not share either the military regime's obsession with India or the former's determination to avoid all contacts with it. Not surprisingly, their loyalty was seen as questionable.

Acceptance of any means to destroy 'enemies': In a national security state, an ideological focus on the enemy means state institutions are geared to identifying, containing, defeating and destroying the 'cunning and ruthless' enemy—including those consorting with the adversary from within. Pakistani security organs saw in East Pakistan's Bengali majority, especially the large Hindu minority, a dangerous pocket of potentially disloyal people, possibly with many fifth-columnists.[21] Manoeuvring legal and political processes to eliminate such dangerous 'threats to Pakistan's national security' and employing massive violence to destroy these were aspects of the same mindset.

Restrictions on debate and limits on popular participation: National security states concentrate power in the hands of security-obsessed, highly regimented and defensive elites who view challenges to their authority as existential threats. The Ayub regime was no exception. Its centralisation of Pakistani state power led to the marginalisation and near-elimination of domestic countervailing forces by the rigorous enforcement of restrictions on representative groups and activities. Its 1962 'basic democracy' constitution institutionalised these restrictions, bottling up resentment and anger until an eruption would sweep Ayub Khan himself away.

Having played a key role in forging strong military links with the West generally and the USA in particular, he enjoyed the support of Western governments anxious to build a bulwark against the expansion of Soviet influence across Asia. Much American military and economic aid was directed towards helping his government meet Pakistan's many challenges. Boosted by election results and keen to take advantage of apparent Indian weakness, Ayub Khan mounted a border incursion along the vaguely defined, disputed, border in the salt marshes called the Rann of Kutch, between Pakistan's southern Sindh province and Gujarat in western India. Although the eventual resolution of the dispute would require international arbitration lasting many years, the immediate outcome suggested Pakistan could try to resolve more substantive territorial disputes in similar fashion.

The sudden death of Prime Minister Jawaharlal Nehru and the apparent vacuum it created at the apex of India's political leadership may have encouraged Ayub Khan and his aides to make a move on Jammu & Kashmir. Sending a cadre of Special Forces to infiltrate across the 1949 Ceasefire Line in the summer of 1965, Pakistani authorities sought to trigger an uprising by Kashmiris angry at Delhi's forcible annexation of their disputed land. In the event, an uprising failed to materialise. Early in September, Indian forces mounted an operation to gain control of a Pakistani salient that overlooked and threatened the only motorable road linking India's mainland to Kashmir. Pakistan then launched a counter-attack, triggering major armoured and infantry battles. Both sides made full use of their modest air and naval forces but most of the action was limited to the Kashmir and Punjab sectors with secondary operations in the Sindh-Rajasthan area. Both forces suffered heavy casualties, but by the time they accepted a ceasefire, they had made only limited gains on the ground. This stalemated war had ramifications a thousand miles to the east.

Operations spread from the Ceasefire Line dividing Jammu & Kashmir into Pakistani– and Indian occupied provinces, most heavily across the line partitioning Punjab, and to a lesser extent, in the southern desert. There was no action in East Pakistan. Pakistani forces, almost exclusively non-Bengali in composition, only had a modest presence in East Pakistan. Four depleted infantry brigades, commanded from divisional headquarters in Dhaka and supported by very small air and naval detachments based in Dhaka and Chittagong respectively, offered no more than symbolic support. Stretched to the limit in trying to match Indian force-levels, Pakistani military doctrine claimed the defence of the East lay in the West. The view was that with only limited resources available to meet the Indian threat, Pakistani forces must secure the defence of the 'national core' before any other mission. Only when West Pakistan was safe and flourishing would it be able to protect East Pakistan. India, on the other hand, needed to maintain its defensive strength along its long and disputed Himalayan frontiers with China where only three years earlier Delhi had received a drubbing in the hands of the People's Liberation Army.

In September 1965, India saw no mileage in attacking the weakly defended East Pakistan; there was, in fact, some danger that such an attack could attract unwelcome Chinese attention to the North. East Pakistan was thus saved, but only by default. East Pakistani politicians—Mujib among them—were worried about the level of importance Pakistan's military leaders attached to defending their province from possible Indian threats. East Pakistani politicians and their supporters began to seriously consider the need to develop a military or paramilitary option for the province outside federal control. For Pakistan's India-obsessed, centralising and deeply insecure military ruling elite rooted and based in West Pakistan, a proposal to establish an armed force beyond the control of the central military command structure would be tantamount to treacherous heresy. But in 1966, that was a key element of the charter of demands that Sheikh Mujibur Rahman, now the President of the Awami League, presented before West Pakistani politicians.

However, long before the Awami League formalised its demand for provincial autonomy Bengali academics at home and abroad had pointed to what they considered deliberate discrimination against East Pakistan in all spheres of national endeavours. A particularly contentious issue was the manner in which state sector employment was skewed against East Pakistanis. Bengalis noted that while East Pakistanis totaled 57.69 per cent of all Pakistanis, all the prize appointments among the civilian and military posts in the public sector had gone to West Pakistanis. Even in terms of the provision of basic services since independence, West Pakistan enjoyed an overwhelming preponderance:

Table 1.1: Inter-Wing 'disparity' in Pakistan's state sector[22]

Category	Pakistan	West Pakistan	East Pakistan
Population	130m	55m	75m
Total number of doctors	20,000	12,400	7,600
Total number of hospital beds	32,000	26,000	6,000
Rural Health Centres	413	325	88
Urban Community Development Centres	133	81	52
Primary schools in 1968–69	67,726	39,418	28,308
Secondary schools in the same period	7,953	4,472	3,964
Colleges of various types	433	271	162
Engineering/Medical/Agricultural colleges	26	17	9
Universities	10	6	4
Number of post-graduate scholars	27,539	18,708	8,831
Prized State Sector Employment			
Central Civil Service—percentage	100	84	16
Pakistan Foreign Service—percentage	100	85	15
Head of Mission Abroad—number	69	60	9
Armed forces personnel—number	520,000	500,000	20,000
Army personnel—percentage	100	95	5
General Officers—number	17	16	1
Navy technical services—percentage	100	81	19
Navy non-technical services—percentage	100	91	9
Air Force General Duty Pilots—percentage	100	89	11
Pakistan International Airlines (PIA)—number	7,280	7,000	280
PIA Board Directors	10	9	1
PIA Area Managers	5	5	0
Pakistan Railway Board Directors	8	7	1

Statistical data such as the table above, while damning, did not tell the whole story. Investment in key sectors of state activities such as education gave West Pakistan a significant advantage. At the time of independence, for instance, West Pakistan had 8,413 primary schools, East Pakistan had 29,663; two decades later, West Pakistan had 39,418 primary schools while the number in East Pakistan—despite the province's bigger population—had actually fallen to 28,308. The number of secondary schools in West Pakistan had risen by 176 per cent while growth in East Pakistan was 114 per cent. West Pakistan saw a 675 per cent rise in the number of colleges, the corresponding figure in East Pakistan was 320 per cent. The number of specialist technical colleges grew by 425 per cent in West Pakistan, and 300 per cent in East Pakistan. In those two decades, the number of post-graduate scholars grew thirty-fold in West Pakistan, and five-fold in the East. This growing gap in human resource development had ramifications across the spectrum of Pakistan's national life. Nowhere was this difference more apparent than in economic exchanges. Per capita income—in Pakistani Rupees (Rs.)—had grown from 355 in 1960 to 492 in 1970 in West Pakistan; this compared to 269 and 308 over the same period in East Pakistan. The GDP per capita figures were differentiated equally sharply.

Between 1959 and 1960 and 1964 and 1965 the West Pakistani figure rose from 312 to 391, that in the East from 242 to 297. On both counts, then, the gap between the two provinces rose as time passed. The most graphic illustration of the marginalisation of East Pakistanis in the 'basic democratic' dispensation came in the juxtaposition of the widening income gap between the provinces and the difference in the price of staple food grains, which impacted on calorific intake and nutritional levels. Wheat, the primary cereal grown in West Pakistan, sold at Rs. 10 per 82lbs in that province and at Rs. 35 in the East. Inexplicably, rice, East Pakistan's primary cereal, sold at Rs. 50 per 82lbs in that province while selling at Rs.18 in the West.[23] In cash crops, East Pakistan's jute fibre and goods earned 43 per cent of Pakistan's total export revenues[24] although price and subsidy differentials gave little benefit to the farmers. The picture in the manufacturing sector was more telling. Whatever modern industrialisation had taken place in the province was either state-controlled or owned by non-Bengali entrepreneurs. Among the latter, six houses—Adamjee, Dawood, Bawani, Ispahani, Amin and Karim—owned more than 40 per cent of the province's total manufacturing assets, 32 per cent of industrial production, and 81.5 per cent of the national jute indus-try.[25] Many East Pakistanis demanded change.

The Awami League's 'Six Points,' as the demands came to be known, summarised East Pakistan's many grievances. The essence of these was a quest to end perceived political and economic discrimination against the country's majority province, in favour of 'parity'. Mujib's accusations dis-tilled long–held and widely believed suspicions among politically active Bengalis that the Pakistani state, centred as it was in the Western wing's ruling elite, which had few representatives of the East in its ranks, con-centrated its energies on the needs of the West, ignoring those of the East. His allegations, resonating well beyond the Awami League's mem-bership, both reflected and reinforced a more general Bengali antipathy toward their West Pakistani compatriots, especially Pakistan's military-bureaucratic-feudal elite. The most visible result of this perceived struc-tural inter-wing discrimination was in the differences in economic development. East Pakistani leaders from non-Muslim League parties often made general complaints about Karachi's 'step-motherly' treatment of the East. In early 1966, Mujib would specify the province's economic complaints:[26]

(a) 'East Pakistan has earned bulk of the annual foreign exchange of Pakistan.

(b) East Pakistan's earnings have been spent in West Pakistan in indus-trialising that wing and earnings from those industries have been reinvested in West Pakistan as the earnings of that wing.

(c) East Pakistan's earnings are not being spent in East Pakistan on the basis that it is unable to absorb them due to absence of capital formation.

(d) Imports to East Pakistan are less than her exports, whereas the reverse is true in West Pakistan.

(e) Two third's of Pakistan's foreign exchange is earned by jute; but that earning is utilised neither for the benefit of the jute-growers nor for East Pakistan.

(f) Almost all foreign aid and loans are secured against foreign exchange earned by East Pakistan; but they are spent in West Paki-stan on the same premise that East Pakistan cannot absorb it. The irony is that interest on these loans and their instalments (sic) is being borne by East Pakistan.'

These discriminatory practices by Pakistan's central authorities were said to have had a highly negative cumulative impact on East Pakistan:[27]

(i) 'East Pakistan has not been industrialised sufficiently,

(ii) The little industrialisation that has been done has been done by West Pakistanis or by people other than East Pakistanis, with all the characteristics of foreign investments both in the matter of employment and profit earning,

(iii) There is chronic inflation causing soaring high prices of commodities with all its concomitants like black-marketing and profiteering bringing untold miseries to the life of the people,

(iv) Not only are Jute-growers not getting a fair price for their produce but they are not even getting the cost of production, resulting in their perpetual indebtedness and progressive impoverishment.'

The road to Bangladesh

In February 1966, after the dust of the previous year's India-Pakistan war had settled, West Pakistan's opposition politicians stirred. They set up what they hoped would be a 'democratic action committee' that would challenge Ayub Khan's military-backed government and initiate steps towards replacing 'basic democracy' with a more familiar version. Given that this would require the abrogation of the 1962 constitution sponsored by the army, they needed all the help they could get. Invitations were sent out to all opposition parties in both provinces but from the East, only Sheikh Mujibur Rahman and his Awami League colleagues showed up, bringing with them a stunning message for their hosts. Mujib revealed a six–point charter of demands that would, if implemented, transform Pakistan from an army-controlled unitary state to a loosely-held confederation. Much of what happened thereafter flowed from these 'Six Points,' a milestone in East Bengal's progression from East Pakistan to Bangladesh. These were as follows:[28]

- The constitution should provide for 'a Federation of Pakistan in its true sense on the basis of the Lahore Resolution, and Parliamentary form of Government with supremacy of Legislature directly elected on the basis of universal adult franchise.' Mujib elaborated the seven 'ingredients' of the proposed arrangement:

    a. 'Pakistan shall be a federation,

    b. It shall be based on the Lahore Resolution,

    c. Its Government shall be of Parliamentary form,

    d. It must be responsible to the Legislature,

    e. The Legislature must be supreme,

    f. It must be directly elected, and

    g. Elections must be on the basis of universal adult franchise.'

- The 'Federal Government shall deal with only two subjects, viz: Defence and Foreign Affairs, and control over all other remaining subjects shall lie with the Federating States…what makes a Federation strong is not heaps of subjects under it. A Federation becomes strong by the loyalty and affection of its citizens in times of peace, and the allegiance they owe and obedience they show it in war.'

- With regard to Pakistan's national currency, either of the following two options:

    a. 'Two separate but freely convertible currencies for the two wings may be introduced, or

    b. One currency for the whole country may be maintained. In this case, effective constitutional provisions are to be made to stop flights of capital from East to West Pakistan. Separate Banking Reserve is to be made and separate fiscal and monetary policy to be adopted for East Pakistan.'

- 'The power over taxation and revenue collection shall lie with the federating units and…the Federal Centre will have no such power. The Federation will have a share in the state taxes for meeting their required expenditure. The Consolidated Federal Fund shall come out of a levy of a certain percentage of all state taxes.'

- '(1) There shall be two separate accounts for foreign exchange earnings of the two wings,

  (2) Earnings of East Pakistan shall be under the control of the East Pakistani Government and that of West Pakistan under the control of the West Pakistani Government,

  (3) The foreign exchange requirement of the Federal Government shall be met by the two wings either equally or in a ratio to be fixed,

  (4) Indigenous products shall move free of duty between two wings,

  (5) The Constitution shall empower the unit Governments to establish trade and commercial relations with, set up trade missions in and enter into agreements with foreign countries.'

- 'Set up a militia or a para-military force for East Pakistan...East Pakistan is the home of the majority of Pakistanis. To defend it is the political obligation as well as moral duty of the Government of Pakistan.'

Not surprisingly, despite their democratic opposition to Field Marshal Ayub Khan's 'basic democratic' regime, Mujib's West Pakistani hosts in Lahore were aghast at the scale, ambition and implications of the Six Point charter he urged them to consider. They rejected it out of hand. This may only have reinforced the Awami League's, and Bengali, suspicions that pluralistic or representative inclinations notwithstanding, West Pakistani elites of all political hues were united in their determination to maintain their colonial over-lordship over East Pakistan.[29] Mujib and his party colleagues returned to Dhaka deeply disillusioned but also determined to pursue what they saw as the only way forward—provincial autonomy. To this end, they had sought the co-operation of West Pakistani politicians, who then rebuffed them. Frustrated by the failure of this licit approach to redressing East Pakistani grievances, the Awami League now sought a radical alternative.

In May 1966, Mujib, along with a large number of other activists, was arrested on suspicion of pursuing seditious objectives, although no specific charges were brought against him at this time. It was only on 6 January 1968 that Pakistan's Home Ministry issued a press release in which the Government claimed that in December 1967 federal security services had detected a conspiracy 'detrimental to the national interests of Pakistan.' The note revealed that eight men, including two members of the Civil Service of Pakistan (CSP), had been arrested for their involvement 'in attempting to separate East Pakistan through an armed revolt.' On 18 January, Pakistan's Home Ministry issued another statement in which Mujib was directly implicated in the 'conspiracy'. He and several other detainees were released from police custody to be immediately detained by military personnel under martial law regulations and taken to the Dhaka Cantonment in preparation for trial by court martial. The prosecution claimed that Mujib and a number of other Bengalis, many of them junior military officers and 'other ranks', had conspired with Indian intelligence officials to organise the armed secession of East Pakistan. Since the alleged discussions between the two parties had taken place in Agartala, capital of the Indian state of Tripura, the *cause célèbre* became the 'Agartala conspiracy case.'

Later in the spring, the Government decided against conducting a court martial, instead, framing charges under Pakistan's criminal procedure code. A special, three-member, tribunal was formed with two Bengali judges working to a West Pakistani chairman. The trial began at a high-security building inside the army garrison in Dhaka. Pakistan's former foreign minister Manzur Quader led the prosecution; the defence was headed by a British parliamentarian, Thomas William QC. Charges were framed against Mujib and thirty-four other men—among them three CSP officials, and a large number of junior armed forces officers and enlisted personnel. The case was titled 'State vs. Sheikh Mujibur Rahman and others.' During the hearings, 227 witnesses including eleven approvers were summoned to give evidence. The prosecution sought to demonstrate that Mujib had attempted to secure Indian assistance in mounting a violent secessionist campaign to break Pakistan with the aid of the accused service personnel and civil officials. The charges, if proven, could lead the accused to the gallows. But several of the approvers changed their testimony during the hearings, alleging that security service personnel had forced them under duress to file false accusations against Mujib and his 'co-conspirators.'

While national attention was riveted on the proceedings, the evidence against Mujib and the others increasingly appeared contrived. William's appeal to the High Court calling into question the legality of the special tribunal did not help the prosecution. As popular anger rose in East Pakistan against what many saw as a transparent attempt to eliminate the province's most vocal champion on trumped-up charges, Bhashani, the veteran politician, launched a popular campaign to free him. His leadership and the street muscle provided by the newly-formed *Sarbadaliya Chhatra Sangram Parishad* (all-party student campaign council) proved to be a formidable combination confronting the state's efforts to destroy Mujib's political career and remove him as a troublesome autonomist. Violent confrontations between the police and the protesters caused much damage and many casualties. Civic life was badly disrupted in Dhaka and the troubles began spreading to East Pakistan's other towns. As more and more people—students, workers and peasants—joined the campaign in a surging protest against the trial, the movement appeared in danger of becoming a confrontation between Ayub Khan's provincial administration and almost the entire politically active segment of East Pakistan's population.

Against that backdrop, Sergeant Zahurul Haq, one of the accused men in the Army's custody, was shot dead. Although officials claimed he was shot while trying to escape, violence exploded in the streets of Dhaka. Mobs set fire to state guesthouses where the prosecution team was staying and other government property. Although Manzur Quadir and his team managed to escape, much documentary evidence was destroyed. With pressure mounting and little incontrovertible evidence in the hands of the prosecution, the government withdrew the case on 22 February 1969 and freed the accused. The case had given a shot in the arm to East Pakistan's political crystallisation as an autonomy-seeking polity. A collective sense of victimhood, the apparent chicanery of Pakistan's leadership against the most vocal proponent of the East's interests, and the 'success' of the violent campaign to free him transformed the protests into a mass nationalist movement. At a rally in Dhaka's *Paltan Maidan* grounds the day after his release, Mujib accepted the name given to him by student leaders. He was now *Bangabandhu*, the friend of Bengal, East Pakistan's undisputed popular leader. His word would be gospel in East Bengal.

By this time, though, trouble was seething not just in East Pakistan, but throughout the country. In October 1968, when the government marked the tenth anniversary of Ayub Khan's assumption of power as 'the decade of development,' students in both wings began agitating against his dictatorial regime and for the restoration of representative governance. The timing was propitious for the campaigners. Similar movements in the USA, France, Germany and several others countries had rocked governments there and a handful of Pakistani student-activists now returned home to assist their colleagues there. Although feelings were less strong in West Pakistan than in the East, Ayub Khan's failure to 'make progress on Kashmir', widespread perceptions of corruption, and a sense of *Punjabi* and *Pashtun* domination contributed to alienation in the West. However, the opposition was divided by rivalries between East and West Pakistani politicians, and among regional groups within West Pakistan. Besides, Ayub Khan's key opponent in the West, Zulfiqar Ali Bhutto, 'the leftist ex–foreign minister Ayub jailed—is a drunkard.'[30]

By late August 1968, Ayub Khan had confidentially written to the US Ambassador, Benjamin Oehlert, that he dreaded the prospect of campaigning for the presidency again.[31] His health had suffered later that year and this may have encouraged his detractors. His recovery seemed to spur his critics to more vigorous protests. In January 1969, as curfews were imposed to disrupt demonstrations and troops were deployed to restore normalcy in most Pakistani cities, leaders of eight centre-right parties announced the formation of Democratic Action Committee (DAC) to coordinate their campaign. The DAC issued an eight-point charter of demands including the release of Mujib, Bhutto and NAP leader Wali Khan, and holding of elections on the basis of adult franchise. The NAP, staying outside the DAC, endorsed its programme; the Pakistan People's Party (PPP), formed the previous year as Bhutto's political platform, also staying outside the DAC, criticized its opposition to holding elections. Coordinated by the DAC and an 'all-party student campaign council,' protesters rioted in Dhaka in late January, facing the police and para-military East Pakistan Rifles. In the scuffles that followed on 20 January, a student was shot dead. Rioting now spread from Dhaka to other cities across Pakistan.

By the end of January, the violence had led to over thirty deaths; scores had been injured and hundreds arrested.[32] Ayub Khan's prospects looked bleak. On 1 February, he invited all 'responsible' politicians to an all-party conference to calm passions. It was not clear, though, if the imprisoned Mujib and Bhutto, and the former chief of the Air Force, retired Air Marshal Asghar Khan, an increasingly influential critic of the regime, would be asked to attend the talks. The depth of Ayub's plight was underscored by his decision to replace the very unpopular Governor of East Pakistan, the Muslim League's Monem Khan, with another provincial party stalwart, Sabur Khan. But these changes made little difference.[33] On 5 February, the invitation was modified to include virtually all opposition figures to attend the proposed talks. Five days later, DAC leader Nawabzada Nasrullah Khan asked Ayub Khan to free Mujib, Bhutto and Wali Khan—a difficult demand for the President to accept. But clearly he did not have much of a bargaining position. Thomas L. Hughes, Director of Intelligence and Research to the US Secretary of State, wrote: 'The situation in Pakistan is one of chaos, in places approaching anarchy…In East Pakistan, opposition to Ayub has taken on strong overtones of anti–West Pakistani sentiment to the point that secession can no longer be ruled out.'[34]

Political turbulence and economic challenges worked in a symbiotic spiral. East Pakistan, already in deficit in terms of food supply, had suffered severe flooding in the winter of 1968–69. This damaged the rice crop and reduced stocks, raising prices. West Pakistan had a surplus of both rice and wheat, but the East Pakistani government had moved slowly to arrest rising prices; limited port- and shipping/transportation capacity served to heighten popular anger as severe shortages loomed.[35] Ayub Khan conceded, releasing all the prominent detainees and accepting many of the preliminary demands made by his critics. A 'Round Table Conference' was convened on 13 March and Sheikh Mujibur Rahman's detailed presentation left little doubt that he was determined to push his Six–Point agenda.[36] Yet the Government's failure to accept the more substantive demands meant that the conference failed and rioting resumed with full vigour. After more troops were deployed to East Pakistan on 25 March 1969, Ayub Khan proclaimed martial law, with the words 'I cannot preside over the destruction of my country,' appointed the army commander, General Agha Mohammad Yahya Khan, as Pakistan's Chief Martial Law Administrator, and then resigned.[37] Calm was largely restored after Yahya Khan told the nation his only aim was to establish normalcy, consult politicians to create an agreed framework for holding elections, and then transfer power to the elected representatives.[38]

In several other radio and television addresses that followed, and in encounters with the press during visits to Dhaka and other Pakistani cities outside the capital, Yahya Khan fleshed out his pledges, furnishing more details of his thinking on Pakistan's future political and economic structures and how he planned to hold elections to secure those changes. In November, he said wide consultations had convinced him that on key issues 'such as the parliamentary federal form of government, direct adult franchise, fundamental rights of citizens and their enforcement by the law courts, independence of judiciary and its role as the custodian of the constitution, and the Islamic character of the constitution which should preserve the ideology on which Pakistan was created, there is no disagreement.'[39] As regards the future of West Pakistan's 'One Unit' configuration, he said the unit would be dissolved and the four separate provinces restored. Future elections would be held on universal adult franchise. He admitted that 'the people of East Pakistan did not have their full share in the decision-making process on vital national issues…they were fully justified in being dissatisfied with this state of affairs. We shall, therefore, have to put an end to this position. The requirement would appear to be maximum autonomy to the two Wings of Pakistan as long as it does not impair national integrity and solidarity of the country.'[40] To begin the process of democratic restoration, non-violent political activities would be allowed from 1 January 1970.

Despite some violence stemming from party-political campaigning beginning on that date, Yahya Khan assured his compatriots that his promised process of transferring power to the people's elected representative was on course. At the end of March, he presented the Legal Framework Order (LFO), which both set out the procedural details of elections to a constituent assembly which would draft a new constitution within 120 days from its first session, and established the principles underpinning Pakistan's democratic future. The LFO incorporated many of the opposition's demands, including most of the Six–Points. It stressed the need to remove inter-wing administrative and economic disparities within an agreed period and reflect East Pakistan's majority status in state institutions. Federal polls would be held on 5 October 1970 and provincial ones by 22 October, and the allocation of seats reinforced the institutionalisation of East Pakistan's stature in the new Pakistan.[41] In addition the LFO also specified a number of seats to be reserved for women in each elected assembly without barring women from contesting any of the elected seats.

Table 1.2: The framework for the restoration of democracy
in Pakistani Schedule I-Art. 4 (2)

National Assembly of Pakistan

Province/region	Directly elected seats	Women's reserved seats
East Pakistan	162	7
The Punjab	82	3
Sindh	27	1
Balochistan	4	1
North-West Frontier Province (NWFP)	18	1
Centrally Administered Tribal Areas (CATA)	7	0
Total	300	13

Schedule II-Art. 5 (I), Provincial Assemblies

Province	Directly elected seats	Women's reserved seats
East Pakistan	300	10
The Punjab	180	6

Sindh	60	2
Balochistan	20	1
NWFP	40	2

The LFO also made clear that all legislative and constitutional proceedings would be conducted and recorded in the two national languages—Urdu and Bengali—and in English. Shortly after its publication, political parties issued election manifestoes setting out the philosophical bases of their vision for Pakistan and more prosaic policy positions. The Awami League's restated the Six Points and explained how these would be implemented:

- Minorities would enjoy complete equality before the law and equal protection of the law: 'They shall enjoy the full rights of citizenship.'
- The constitution would acknowledge the state's 'fundamental responsibility' to ensure every citizen has access to 'food, clothing, shelter, education and the opportunity of employment at reasonable wages.'
- Citizens' fundamental rights and freedoms would be ensured and the constitution would guarantee these could not be 'curtailed except during a period of actual hostilities during a war. No such curtailment would be permitted on the pretext of "national emergency".'
- The constitution would ensure that citizens represented their region in all federal services 'on the basis of population.' Existing under-representation, especially of East Pakistan, would be promptly remedied with accelerated recruitment: 'An initial corrective measure would be to shift the Naval Headquarters and training establishments... from Karachi to Chittagong.'
- All-Pakistan and Central Superior Services would be abolished. New federal services would be established to administer the federal subjects—defence and diplomacy—with personnel recruited from provinces 'on the basis of population.'
- A 'socialist economic order' would ensure 'the just distribution of the fruits of... growth among all sections...and the different regions... Our task is to bring about a social and economic revolution...within a democratic framework.' To this end, key sectors of the economy would be nationalised:
  1. Banking
  2. Insurance

3. Heavy industry—iron and steel, mining, machine-tools, heavy engineering, petrochemicals, fertiliser, cement, fuel and power.
4. Foreign trade—export and import of jute, cotton, iron and steel products, coal, food grain, cement and fertiliser.
5. Arterial, inter-wing and international transport including shipping.
6. Other key industries to be determined by the national planning agency

Demonstrating its pan-Pakistani concerns for establishing an equitable state structure, the Awami League also pledged to abolish *zamindari, jaigirdari*, and *sardari* (various forms of feudal and tribal over-lordship) systems in West Pakistani provinces, prohibit *jirga* (tribal councils that dispensed traditional justice and took local administrative decisions in parts of the NWFP) and repeal 'all discriminatory tribal laws.' It promised to replace the use of English 'in all walks of life' with Bengali and Urdu. The League committed itself to an 'independent, non–aligned foreign policy,' non-dependence on foreign aid, 'struggle against imperialism, colonialism and apartheid', and the withdrawal from 'SEATO (South East Asian Treaty Organisation), CENTO (Central Treaty Organisation) and other military pacts.'[42] As masses of Bengalis demonstrated their wildly enthusiastic support for this manifesto at rally after rally in which Mujib aroused populist passions across East Pakistan, the programme proved extremely popular, even among many who did not otherwise support Mujib or the League. It was not popular in West Pakistan.

Other problems also loomed. As the One Unit in West Pakistan stood dissolved on 1 July 1970, and the four provinces were revived, electioneering rhetoric took on a new regionalist edge. Partisanship was already bitter and divisive—now ethnic, linguistic and geographic factors further deepened cleavages. Retaining national cohesion would be a major challenge. Yahya Khan warned politicians that the One Unit's dissolution was meant to improve governance and deliver services to people, not to widen parochial gaps. He stressed that since preparations for the polls were well in hand, there would be no occasion to treat violent or criminal conduct with leniency. His government would maintain order to ensure the elections and transfer of power took place in a peaceful environment, noting that the country was still under martial law. He also cautioned the electorate against taking the unrealistically optimistic promises of rapid economic development being made by many leaders at face value, pointing out limits on what the new government could realistically deliver, given national and global circumstances, and how soon after the elections.[43] The elections themselves faced delays. Extensive floods had severely damaged East Pakistani property and infrastructure, and National Assembly polls were postponed to 7 December; provincial ones would be held by 19 December.

As the floods receded, campaigning resumed in East Pakistan. Then, on the night of 12–13 November, a cyclonic storm and a tidal bore tore through its coastal districts, killing several hundred thousand people, and devastating the meagre lives of many more across a large swathe of territory.[44] It was the region's worst ever natural disaster. Many East Pakistanis saw Islamabad's response to this cataclysm as unconscionably tardy and inadequate. Mujib, having toured the area, estimated that a million people had been killed and attacked the government's failure to provide warnings before, and relief afterwards. From this point on, Islamabad's 'criminal negligence' toward the plight of East Pakistan, which he now called 'Bangla Desh,' was the focus of his campaign speeches.[45] It touched a chord among a populace increasingly aware of the repeatedly alleged 'disparity' it had been subjected to since 1947. A substantial relief and rehabilitation operation led by the United Nations (UN) and funded by the Organisation of Economic Cooperation and Development (OECD) and other donors—the USA prominent among them—eventually began. Yahya Khan, having just returned from Beijing where he conveyed Nixon's confidential message of his interest in making covert contacts to Zhou Enlai, defended Islamabad's response to the devastation during a visit to Dhaka in late November—'I did not bring the cyclone; it was not my fault. My fault begins taking shape only when I do not do anything for the surviving people.' When journalists reminded him of Mujib's allegations of neglect, Yahya said, 'Let them come to power as quickly as possible. I hope they come to power and do better. I have tried to do my maximum.'[46]

Against this backdrop, the elections' outcome in East Pakistan was not surprising, but the scale of the Awami League's victory was. In the National Assembly polls, League candidates won 160 of the province's 162 seats. With the seats reserved for women and allocated in proportion to its electoral success, the League had 167 of the National Assembly's 313 seats—a majority enough to secure for the party the right to form

Pakistan's first government elected on the basis of universal adult franchise. Its success in the provincial elections was more sweeping. Awami League candidates won 288 of the 300 general seats in the provincial assembly. With all ten of the seats reserved for women, the League controlled 298 seats in the 310–seat assembly. The opposition—with the Pakistan Democratic Party's two seats, and the NAP, the Jamaat-i–Islami and the Nizam-e-Islami with a seat each, and seven seats going to independents, was negligible. East Pakistan's voters had given the Awami League, Sheikh Mujibur Rahman and their Six–Point manifesto a mandate that could not now be discounted. As soon as the results were published, Mujib assured Pakistanis that the Six–Point programme would definitely be realised. The League's confederal designs for Pakistan's democratic future, at both the central and provincial levels, were now an essential part of the country's political landscape. This, though, proved to be the nub of the problem that Pakistan was faced with.

The elections reflected East Pakistan's demographic, hence democratic, preponderance and the Awami League's success in mobilising provincial opinion in support of its confederal agenda. But they also reinforced the inter-wing and regional polarisation that Yahya Khan had warned against a year earlier. Bhutto's PPP won eighty-three elected seats in Punjab, Sindh and NWFP; with the five seats reserved for women that fell to it, the PPP controlled eighty-eight National Assembly seats—all of them in West Pakistan, giving it a massive majority as far as the federal legislators elected from that wing were concerned. But it had not contested nor won a single seat in East Pakistan, just as the Awami League had neither contested nor won a single seat in West Pakistan. The polarisation between the two provinces represented by this dichotomous dominance of Mujib's Awami League in the East and Bhutto's PPP in the West, in the context of the marginalisation—if not elimination—of other parties in both wings placed Pakistan's future in the hands of two men who could not have had more divergent perspectives.

In order to draft a constitution with the newly-elected National Assembly that would prove acceptable to the majority of Pakistanis in both wings of the country, Mujib and Bhutto would have to make significant compromises and sell these compromises to their parties and support bases. Given the expectations raised by the ouster of Ayub Khan and the highly charged pre-election campaigns mounted by the key actors, there were few signs that either was willing or able to risk the consequences of making such compromises. Bhutto did not openly criticize Mujib or his manifesto but his statements made clear his preference for a strong centre with, ideally, himself in charge. With Mujib repeatedly vowing to realise the League's confederal charter, neither had much room for manoeuvre. The man in the middle, Yahya Khan, was believed to 'have accepted the need to work with Sheikh Mujib, but this decision was doubtless predicated on a belief that the present West Pakistani elite would be well-represented by centrists who could work with and control the Awami League leader and thus protect West Pakistani interests.'[47] Bhutto's sweeping success in the West destroyed those hopes.

To make sure there were no doubts about his position, Bhutto refused to sit in opposition for the next five years, asking how the PPP would realise the pledges it had made to the people if it did not take office. Pointing out that his party had won majorities in the assemblies of Punjab and Sindh, and that 'real power of the Centre lay in those two provinces,' he insisted that no central government could therefore be run without the PPP's cooperation. He acknowledged Sheikh Mujibur Rahman's success in leading the Awami League to the National Assembly with a majority, but argued that 'majority alone doesn't count in national politics.'[48] The Awami League promptly challenged this contention, saying that Punjab and Sindh could no longer aspire to be 'bastions of power.' A democratic course charted on the basis of 'one man one vote' could not countenance such 'bastions'. In this new system, 'a party enjoying a comfortable, indeed an absolute, majority as the Awami League does, with a clear electoral mandate, is quite competent to frame the Constitution and form the Central Government. This can be done with or without any other party. Such cooperation as may be obtained will be for the Awami League to choose.'[49]

To break the stalemate, Yahya Khan visited East Pakistan in January 1971. After three days of talks with Mujib, other Awami League leaders and officials in Dhaka, Yahya indicated that Sheikh Mujibur Rahman would soon be assuming the leadership of the Government of Pakistan and that Yahya himself would retire from the presidency—'When he comes and takes over I won't be there. It is going to be his Government soon…I inherited a bad economy and I am going to pass it over to Sheikh Sahib.'[50] He also hinted that the National Assembly session would be convening in Dhaka. However, he could not yet say exactly when that all-important session would begin. Pushed by Yahya Khan to reach a compromise, Bhutto arrived towards the end of January and consulted Sheikh Mujib and his colleagues for three days. He admitted that 'genuine difficulties' born of serious differences separated the two sides. Although he had accepted several of the Awami League's demands, he could not agree to the institutionalisation of provincial autonomy on the basis of the 1940 Lahore Resolution and the framing of a constitution based on the Six Points.[51] The two sides agreed on other points, especially on nationalising key sectors of the economy, and Bhutto wanted negotiations to continue, but he could not bend further. Behind the scenes, things took a turn for the worse. In private talks with Mujib, Bhutto threatened dire consequences if the Sheikh did not agree on an accommodation.[52] Mujib, angered by this, also refused to bend. The deadlock deepened.

Both men demanded an early transfer of power to the elected representatives. Mujib insisted on the Awami League's majoritarian right to frame the constitution and form the government; Bhutto insisted neither could be done without an agreement with the PPP. In mid-February, Bhutto announced his party would not attend the National Assembly simply to ratify a constitution drafted on the basis of the Six Points which 'could not provide a viable future for the country.'[53] The Members of the National Assembly (MNA) were expected to gather in Dhaka by 2 March 1971 when the elections for the women's seats would be held. The full session of the Assembly would formally begin on the following day. Bhutto said he would not go just for the formalities. If other West Pakistani leaders wished to attend the Assembly, 'Let them go, but they will have to come back also!'[54] Unperturbed by that implicit warning, several West Pakistani politicians criticised Bhutto's attempts to 'seek solutions to constitutional problems outside the National Assembly.' The Awami League, however, prepared to assume office. Its parliamentary party elected Sheikh Mujibur Rahman the leader, effectively nominating him as Pakistan's next prime minister. Party vice president Syed Nazrul Islam was elected Deputy Leader. Party general secretary AHM Kamruzzaman was elected the secretary of the parliamentary party. The party elected a Chief Whip and two whips, and hinted that veteran leader Khondkar Mushtaq Ahmed would be nominated for the post of Speaker. The members of the planned Awami League cabinet in the central government, too, were listed. In short, by 16 February, Mujib was ready for Pakistan.

Bhutto, presuming to represent West Pakistan, was not, however, ready for him. In late February he said there was no room for further negotiations with the Awami League. Mujib noted that he had no wish to impose the Six Points on West Pakistan. If the western provinces wished to exercise autonomy under that framework, the Awami League would help them to do so; if they wished not to, that too would be fine. Bhutto said if one province was to enjoy autonomy, then all provinces must, in equal measures—Pakistan's two wings must not have two distinct constitutional arrangements. He also said it would be impossible for him to stay in Dhaka to attend the Assembly session for 120 days 'when Indian troops were massed on the West Pakistan borders.' His duty was to be with his people 'when their security was threatened.' He offered two options to Yahya Khan—either waive the 120–day limit on drafting the new constitution or postpone the National Assembly session. He warned that if elections to the women's seats were held on 2 March as scheduled and if the National Assembly was convened on 3 March without the PPP's participation—which he had foreclosed—he would launch a popular movement starting with a 'complete general strike over the length and breadth of this wing of the country.'[55] In other words, Bhutto lit a fuse underneath Yahya Khan's plans to transfer power.

Yahya Khan himself, by this time, was very worried about the deadlock between the two leaders. But he was more anxious about a constitution based on the Six Points. He had no intention of sanctioning a constitution 'which had inherent within it factors which could bring about the dissolution of Pakistan.' Like Ayub Khan, he too did not intend to preside over his country's dissolution.[56] Meanwhile, on 30 January, in an apparently unrelated incident, two Kashmiri men had hijacked an Indian airliner to Lahore where, after being welcomed by Bhutto and other politicians—but not Pakistani officials—they released the passengers and crew and then blew up the aircraft. Delhi, condemning Islamabad's 'complicity,' tightened security along the borders and banned all over-flights of Pakistani aircraft. Conspiracy theories abounded across South Asia[57], but the effect was an end to Pakistan's ability to maintain direct interwing air-links and a significant rise in logistical costs to its military deployments and operations in the East. These domestic and regional complexities confounded Yahya Khan's plans for ending martial law and transferring power to the elected politicians. He wrote to President Nixon and briefed the US ambassador on these matters while using the 'backchannel' via Kissinger on the China initiative. He also sought help on economic aid for East Pakistan and military hardware for the armed forces, and Nixon's good offices in restoring normalcy with India.[58]

Nixon had struck up a rapport with Yahya Khan during their meetings in the USA and Pakistan. Having decided to utilise the General's services in establishing covert contact with Chinese leaders, Nixon ordered the administration to be helpful in meeting Pakistani requests for assistance. The most controversial of these exercises was making a one-off exception to existing restrictions on the delivery of military hardware to the Pakistani armed forces, dependent as the latter were on US arms and equipment. Progress was slow and the US bureaucracy extremely reluctant to go along with the White House on this. Economic assistance, especially relief provision to East Pakistan, proved much easier. Both men clearly shared a degree of empathy and convergent strategic perspectives. But Nixon was unable to help Yahya Khan in resolving Pakistan's domestic political crisis.[59] Yahya confided his worries in the US ambassador, Joseph Farland—he had invited Mujib to talks in Islamabad twice in recent weeks; Mujib had declined on both occasions. Yahya then flew to Karachi to see Bhutto. If the impasse were not broken by 3 March, he would have to defer the National Assembly session 'for a week or two.' Despite unfounded rumours that Washington was encouraging Mujib to pursue secession, Yahya urged Farland to fly to Dhaka and see the East Pakistani leader 'as soon as possible.' Yahya's sense of desperation was obvious.[60]

Meanwhile, in February, the Pakistan army's General Staff updated 'Operation Blitz,' the military contingency plan to suspend political activities and wrest control over East Pakistan if so ordered. Later that month, a trebling of troops and weapons in East Pakistan flown from the West began.[61] Around the same time, Yahya Khan dismissed his civilian cabinet, concentrating military control over Pakistan's administrative machinery. Justice A.R. Cornelius, a former chief justice, was one of two remaining civilian advisers to the President. General-officers considered hardliners even by Pakistani observers now took over decision-making. Against that backdrop, as the military prepared for a possible eastern showdown, two parallel developments shook Pakistan. On 1 March, Yahya Khan announced the postponement *sine die* of the opening of the National Assembly session scheduled for two days later. Vice Admiral S.M. Ahsan, until recently Commander-in-Chief of the Navy and Deputy CMLA, and currently Governor of East Pakistan, warned Yahya Khan about the dangerous consequences of this step; he was relieved of his duties. The Commander, Eastern Command, Lt. General Sahibzada Yaqub Khan, took over the additional responsibilities of provincial governor but East Pakistan was seething.

As street protests and clashes with security forces spilled more blood in East Pakistan, hardening positions on both sides, Yaqub Khan, fearing further military action would be disastrous, urged negotiations with the Awami League.[62] On 3 March, when Bengali activists marked the postponed opening of the National Assembly with even more bloody clashes, Yaqub Khan appealed to Yahya for 'political direction'. There was little sympathy for his 'pro-Bengali' inclinations in Rawalpindi at this time. Unable to prevent the spiral to a bloody *denouement*, Yaqub Khan, who had learn Bengali and read *Rabindranath Tagore's* literary works, key components of the Bengali cultural core, with affection, resigned. The two senior Pakistani military officers most sensitive to Bengali grievances and aspirations thus passed from the scene, to be rapidly replaced. Visiting Karachi, where he contacted Bhutto, Yahya Khan appointed Lt. General Tikka Khan as Governor and Martial Law Administrator of East Pakistan, and later, Lt. General A.A.K. Niazi as Commander, Eastern Command. They were markedly different to their predecessors. Yahya Khan also announced that the National Assembly would convene on 25 March and that he would consult both Mujib and Bhutto to ensure both leaders and their parties attended this important event so that power could be transferred to the elected politicians.

The US Consul-General in Dhaka, Archer Blood, saw Mujib three days after Farland's encounter with Yahya Khan. Mujib had little positive to say about Bhutto whom he considered a representative of Pakistan's military elite. Mujib criticised Bhutto's 'love for Communist China and his intransigent position vis-à-vis India.' In terms of domestic politics, Mujib refused to budge on the Six Points. He also noted clashes between Awami League activists and East Pakistani communists in which three of his men were reportedly killed. Mujib promised that for each of his men killed, 'he would kill three of theirs and 'this we have done.'[63] There was little sign that Mujib would make any compromises with his West Pakistani fellows. Against that backdrop, on 1 March, Yahya Khan announced the postponement of the opening of the National Assembly without giving out a fresh date. He cited the PPP's decision to boycott the planned session as the trigger behind this decision. Protests in Dhaka turned violent and when the police opened fire, several demonstrators were killed or wounded. The rhetoric emanating from the two camps now turned more vitriolic.

On 3 March, at a rally organised by the leaders of the League's student wing, Mujib made an emotional address, demanding that martial law should be ended and power transferred to the elected representatives immediately. He ordered a province-wide general strike from six in the morning to two in the afternoon every day until 7 March, when he would issue further instructions. Mujib told his West Pakistani colleagues, 'If you do not want to frame one constitution, let us frame our own constitution and you frame your own. Then let us see if we can live together as brothers.' Urging the citizens of Bangla Desh to begin 'peaceful non-cooperation,' he ordered League volunteers to maintain strict discipline.[64] The volunteers, however, may have paid limited attention to Mujib's pledge that the immigrant *Bihari* community (and non-Muslims) 'are our sacred trust.' As they spread out across the province, effectively taking over from the local administration and police forces, their anger focused on the Urdu-speaking and other pro-Pakistani 'traitors' in their midst.[65] As the autonomists and conservatives clashed, 'the miscreants indulged in large-scale massacres and rape against pro-Pakistan elements. Attacks were recorded in Dhaka, Narayanganj, Chittagong, Chandraghona, Rangamati, Khulna, Dinajpur, Thakurgaon, Kushtia, Iswardi, Noakhali, Sylhet, Maulvi Bazar, Rangpur, Saidpur, Jessore, Barisal, Mymensingh, Rajshahi, Pabna, Sirajganj, Comilla, Brahman Baria, Bogra, Naogaon, Santahar and several smaller towns.[66]

Clashes between Awami League activists and soldiers deployed in and around urban centres on 'martial law duty' became frequent, with the number of victims growing on both sides. Islamabad started sending additional troops and equipment to the East. The former traveled by air along a circuitous route via Sri Lanka but the hardware came on ships. One of these, the *M.V. Swat*, faced difficulties when stevedores at the Chittagong port refused to unload the military gear from it. The 8th battalion of the East Bengal Regiment, an infantry outfit manned almost entirely by Bengali soldiers but with a mixed body of officers from both wings, was given the responsibility of ensuring the kit was unloaded without further delay or damage. The commanding officer, a West Pakistani, assigned his second-in-command, Major Ziaur Rahman, a Bengali, to oversee this mission. Zia, as he was known, set to with his usual professional capability. Many other Bengali soldiers and policemen stationed in the province were, however, by this time, reluctant to carry out orders that entailed violence against their compatriots. This posed a challenge for the federal and provincial security forces. It became difficult. Mujib rejected another invitation to talks from Yahya Khan and issued directives to banks, government offices and private organisations to ensure staff were paid salaries, cash transactions were conducted within the province, and essential services like medical and emergency services and utilities continued to function during the extended general strike. Effective authority had shifted away from Islamabad's men.

The following day, 5 March, after several incidents in which troops shot dead protesters across East Pakistan, the Martial Law authorities withdrew the soldiers from city streets. Casualty estimates varied widely but by the last day of the five-day strike, 6 March, hundreds had been admitted to hospitals with gunshot- and other wounds. Yahya Khan told the nation he had briefly postponed the National Assembly session to provide the leaders with a little time to work out a compromise formula. To this end he had invited the two principal leaders to a conference but Mujib had turned down the offer. Yahya Khan said the postponement had been 'completely misunderstood.' Having failed to secure agreement between the Awami League and the PPP, he could wait no longer. The Assembly would meet on 25 March.[67] Mujib agreed to attend if four conditions were met:

- Martial law be withdrawn.
- The troops be sent back to the barracks.
- Inquiries be held into the 'killings of people' during the strikes.
- Power be transferred to the people's elected representatives.

The following day, Mujib issued a series of directives to all civilian government, semi–government and private organisations, educational institutions and essential services. He also addressed a massive rally in Dhaka. His office announced a ten point programme, virtually assuming control of the province, and published an expanded set of demands:

- Immediate withdrawal of martial law.
- Transfer of power to the elected representatives of the people.
- Immediate withdrawal of all military personnel to the barracks.
- Immediate cessation of the military build-up and the heavy inflow of military personnel from West Pakistan.
- Non-interference by military authorities in 'the different branches of the Government functioning in Bangla Desh' and an end to 'victimisation' of staff.
- Maintenance of law order 'to be left exclusively to the police and Bengali East Pakistan Rifles (para-military force), assisted, whenever necessary, by Awami League volunteers.'[68]

There was excited speculation in Dhaka and other East Pakistani cities that Mujib would formally declare independence on 7 March—he did not. He ceremonially accepted a newly-designed flag of Bangladesh—with a golden map of East Bengal superimposed on a red circle at the centre representing the rising Sun set against a green background reflecting the verdant delta—from student leaders at the rally, but did not unfurl or fly it. However, he did proclaim, 'the struggle this time is for liberation, the struggle this time is for independence.' Mujib also ordered the establishment of *sangram parishads* (campaign councils) from the union—the lowest tier of local government—to the district level, under Awami League leadership. Most civil servants and public and private organisations obeyed these instructions. As a result, administrative authority in the province effectively transferred to the Awami League. Clashes between protesters and soldiers continued.

In mid-March, while military reinforcements flowed in from West Pakistan, and clashes were reported across East Pakistan between central forces and Awami League activists, students, workers and sundry Bengali youths, Yahya Khan sent an emissary to Mujib, asking him not to take any precipitate steps and await his arrival for talks. On 14 March, on his way to Dhaka, the President met Bhutto in Karachi; at a rally later that day, Bhutto urged the transfer of power to the PPP in West Pakistan and to the Awami League in East Pakistan. This was a new formulation and suggested that Bhutto had accepted, and now demanded, the effective partitioning of Pakistan into two separate administrative and legislative units so long as he could take power. The following day Yahya Khan arrived in Dhaka. Talks produced an agreed framework and both sides issued optimistic statements, although neither provided any details.[69]

Bhutto then joined them, promising to 'make every effort to reach an understanding' and end this 'most unfortunate and tragic' crisis.[70] While the talks were continuing, military preparations for a sudden offensive against 'anti–Pakistan elements' were completed. As events progressed towards what may have been an inevitable *denouement*, General Tikka Khan, who had, in the meanwhile, assumed the offices of provincial Governor and Martial Law Administrator, and Commander Eastern Command, told other senior Pakistani army officers in the East 'to be ready.'[71] Pakistan marked the anniversary of the Lahore Resolution on 23 March, but there was no celebration in East Pakistan. Most buildings, instead of flying Pakistan's national standard, hoisted black flags in protest against the denial of the Awami League's right to govern. On 24 March, stern military action against Bengali activists was reported in Chittagong, Rangpur, Saidpur and other areas. The crunch came that day when the Awami League delegation brought a new draft proclamation to be issued by the President, stating, 'After the Constitutions of the State of Bangladesh and States of West Pakistan have been framed...the President shall summon a meeting of the National Assembly, at which all the members shall sit together as a sovereign body for the purpose of framing a Constitution for the Confederation of Pakistan.'[72]

The presidential delegation would not consider this a negotiable draft. Kamal Hossain, a leading member of the Awami League team, insisted that this was a summary of all the points that had been agreed on by the two parties—except for the term 'confederation' which could be negotiated between Mujib and Yahya. The talks were over. When it became clear that there was no possibility of the National Assembly convening or power being transferred to the elected politicians, Mujib called a 'general strike throughout Bangladesh' on 27 March in protest. He declared that the only way to resolve the crisis was to 'accept Awami League demands *in toto*.' In the evening, Yahya Khan and the West Pakistani entourage flew out. Hours later, Mujib and several senior aides were taken into custody as the military fanned out across Dhaka and other major East Pakistani cities. 'Operation Searchlight' was underway. The Pakistan established in 1947 was coming to an end and Bangladesh's bloody genesis had begun.

2

WAR, INDEPENDENCE AND BLOOD-FEUDS

1971–1975

Abstract: The failure of the leaders of Pakistan's two Wings to reach a compromise after parliamentary polls held in late 1970 pushed Pakistan to the brink of civil war. Negotiations punctuated with demands from Mujib's Awami League, especially its student wing, for confederal autonomy, left little room for manoeuvre. Once a zero-sum stalemate had been reached, Yahya Khan and the army, against the backdrop of growing violence in East Pakistan, decided to 'crush' the Bengali autonomist movement.

A military operation in late March 1971, employing massive force against ill-equipped students, party-activists, policemen and paramilitary troops, swiftly took control of the capital and other cities. Many Bengalis were killed or wounded. Attacks against Bengali–manned army units were less successful. Rebellious soldiers gave battle and some managed to flee to the border with their equipment. Their commanders established a nucleus of resistance, preparing for protracted war against Pakistani 'occupation forces' while inviting surviving politicians to assume leadership. With Mujibur Rahman in army custody, an Awami League official, Tajuddin Ahmed, became the acting Prime Minister, and Colonel M.A.G. Osmany, a retired officer, assumed command of the resistance.

Yahya Khan's intermediary role in President Nixon's covert initiative to establish links with China, Sino-Soviet hostility, and Indo-Soviet alliance ensured that Pakistan's civil war and Bangladesh's war of independence would assume a global strategic significance. By September 1971, 80,000 Pakistani personnel, supported by around '1–2 million' *Biharis* and 'some ardently anti–Hindu Bengalis' faced 50,000 guerrillas of the resistance. A combination of impossible logistical constraints, a hostile populace, a scorched earth policy driving millions to India, and Delhi's willing aid to the guerrillas sealed Pakistan's fate. Pakistan's inept offensive in early December elicited India's 'lightning campaign' in the East, with Pakistani forces being forced to surrender in mid-December. While Islamabad and Delhi grappled with the subcontinent's transformed strategic circumstances, donors kept Bangladesh alive as millions of destitute people returned home. Mujibur Rahman, freed by Pakistan's new President, Bhutto, assumed Bangladesh's presidency to wild acclaim.

However, his new republic faced so many challenges that even with substantial assistance, he was unable to meet the expectations raised during the campaign for autonomy and the ensuing war of independence. A new constitution and electoral victory did not reduce the threat from a reinvigorated left. To counteract this challenge, he set up a paramilitary force, and pardoned thousands of men accused of collaborating with Pakistan. A famine in late 1974 revealed the frailty of power and fragility of the state. Mujib decided to turn Bangladesh into a one-party state, and assume absolute authority. As rumours of conspiracies against *Bangabandhu* spread, US officials advised him to take precautions—advice he dismissed out of hand. By mid-1975, when preparations for launching the one-party state—which left no constitutional alternatives available to challenge the new dispensation—nearly in place, a small band of renegade army officers took it upon themselves to rid the land of its charismatic father-figure and his close circle of advisers. On 15 August, they struck, decapitating Bangladesh's first elected leadership. The bloody aftermath stamped itself indelibly on Bangladesh's future.

The darkness of 'Operation Searchlight'

Late in the evening on 25 March 1971, as Yahya Khan's aircraft entered West Pakistani airspace, Pakistan army's 14th Infantry Division, headquartered in Dhaka, launched 'Operation Searchlight', deploying combat troops armed with automatic weapons and mortars—some in M-24 Chaffee tanks—to the city's central districts. They focused on areas seen as hotbeds of the Awami League's autonomist activism—the university campus, halls of residence, including one used by female students, and a district of narrow alleyways in the old part of the city largely inhabited by the Hindu community. In simultaneous moves, troops also entered *Peelkhana*, the Moghul stables for elephants, where the mainly Bengali–manned East Pakistan Rifles (EPR) paramilitary force was headquartered. According to foreign observers, among the riflemen present at the time '700 (were) killed, 200 overpowered, and 100 escaped.' Pakistani troops also attacked the police headquarters and lines at *Rajarbagh*, and Reserve (armed) Police barracks in central Dhaka. An estimated 1,800 policemen were killed.[1] Pakistani army units mounted similar assaults on EPR and police barracks elsewhere across the province. Attacks on Bengali soldiers of the army's East Bengal Regiment (EBR), six of whose battalions were stationed in penny-packets across the country, followed.

The surprising nature and scale of the Pakistani assaults on men until recently seen as loyal members of the state's armed bureaucracies led to the decimation of many police and paramilitary units, most personnel being either killed, wounded or captured. Some managed to obtain light arms during the confrontation and gave battle. Resistance was patchy and imbalanced with the few survivors fleeing to disappear among an angry but fearful populace. Most of them joined the nucleus of the national resistance being forged by the remnants of the EBR's 1st, 2nd, 3rd, 4th, 8th and 10th (National Service) battalions. The main engagements that night were fought by the paramilitary EPR and Reserve Policemen. In Peelkhana, the EPR had around 2,500 mostly Bengali troops, including 250 recruits undergoing basic training. Many were killed in the first bursts of unexpected fire. Bengali junior commissioned officers (JCOs) took command of the survivors, and battle raged through the night. Hundreds were killed.[2] Eventually, the remnants ended their hopeless defiance, crossed the *Buriganga* River and prepared to fight another day. The experience of the 2000–odd reserve policemen in Rajarbagh,[3] and hundreds of their colleagues in Dhaka's police stations, and the staff of its Fire Brigade, was similar.

Pakistani forces paid equally violent attention to the university campus, a centre of nationalist activism. Three halls of residence—Iqbal Hall, Jagannath Hall, traditionally open to Hindu students, and Rokeya Hall, housing women students—were attacked, as were faculty residences. Dozens of students were killed[4] and many others arrested. At least ten faculty members, and possibly eleven, were reportedly killed[5] while a number of others disappeared. Troops reportedly 'acted with no provocation on part of Bengalis except barricade erection.' Supported by the soldiers, 'non-Bengali Muslims [were] systematically attacking poor people's quarters and murdering Bengalis and Hindus.'[6] This was in addition to targeted killing of Awami League politicians, student activists, faculty members and Bengali former service personnel. Areas believed to house such 'enemies,' especially Hindus and other Awami League supporters, were set ablaze. Flames lit up the night sky while shot and shell carved their fiery trajectories across it. The violence unleashed on East Pakistan in Operation Searchlight was so severe that Ambassador Farland, who described Mujib's control over the province since early March 1971 as the Awami League's 'act of insurrection', nonetheless noted the USA could not 'hold the brief for what seems to have been the brutal, ruthless and excessive use of force by Pak military not only in putting down limited resistance but in seeking out and destroying presumed opponents in East Pakistan.'[7] Even the Pakistani General A.A.K. Niazi, himself accused of ordering many atrocities after taking charge of Eastern Command forces from General Tikka Khan on 11 April 1971, later said:

Military action was based on the use of force primarily, and in many places indiscriminate use of force was resorted to which alienated the public from the army. Damage done during those early days of the military action could never be repaired, and earned for the military leaders names such as 'Changez Khan' and 'Butcher of East Pakistan.'[8]

Awami League leaders were with Sheikh Mujibur Rahman at his Dhanmandi residence in Dhaka when the fireworks began. Mujib decided to stand fast while his colleagues disappeared into the night, eventually to cross the border and seek refuge in India.[9] A Pakistani commando platoon arrested Mujib very early on 26 March.[10] His closest confidante, Kamal Hossain, surrendered the following day. They were subsequently flown to West Pakistan to stand trial. On 26 March, Yahya Khan addressed the nation, explaining how the Awami League had brought the country to the brink of catastrophe by engaging in 'an act of treason' and how the soldiers, whom he complimented 'on the tremendous restraint that they have shown in the face of grave provocation,' had saved the day.[11] The application of massive force against a largely civilian population in Dhaka and the province's other cities wrested bloody control of urban centres by the end of March 1971. This brief, pyrrhic, victory proved to be the death-knell of united Pakistan.

The rise of the resistance

The six battalions of the EBR stationed in East Pakistan—the 5th, 6th and 7th being deployed in West Pakistan—were largely Bengali–manned but led by a mixed crew of Bengali and non-Bengali officers. Following 'Operation Searchlight', commanders were ordered to disarm these, and the troops and recruits stationed at the EBR Regimental Centre (EBRC) located in Chittagong. Major Ziaur Rahman, second-in-command of 8 EBR, also based at Chittagong, was sent to the port by his commanding officer (CO) on the night of 25 March, ostensibly to help unload the *M.V. Swat*, a ship carrying military hardware that Bengali stevedores had refused to touch. Discovering that this maritime assignment was a trap set to eliminate him and his men, Zia returned to the battalion's base camp, announced his plans to defect, disposed of his 'treacherous' CO, and moved his troops out of the city to a suburb called Kalurghat. Here, on 26 March, using a local radio transmitter, he announced a war of independence against Pakistani forces, proclaiming himself president of Bangladesh. The next day, he made a more reasoned announcement, describing himself as the 'provisional commander-in-chief of the Bangladesh liberation army,' and proclaimed, 'on behalf of Sheikh Mujibur Rahman, the independence of Bangladesh.'[12] Almost simultaneously, EPR troops in Chittagong under Major Rafiqul Islam mounted pre-emptive attacks on key points across the city, thwarting Pakistani efforts to take control of East Bengal's main port. But their success was mixed and brief. Soon, battle ensued as Pakistani forces began hunting for Zia and his men. Eight EBR and EPR units would fight several engagements, losing men and *materiel*, and be forced steadily to move towards the Indian border, setting a pattern.

A similar fate awaited two other battalions—2 EBR stationed at Joydebpur outside Dhaka and 4 EBR, scattered across north-eastern districts. After much local action, the remnants of the two units were taken over by their seconds-in-command, Majors K.M. Safiullah and Khaled Mosharraf respectively. With surviving EPR and police personnel, and angry students from the cities joining their depleted ranks, these battalions fought a series of battles with Pakistani regulars who employed artillery and the Pakistan Air Force's (PAF) F-86 Sabre Jets against these rag-tag bands. Bengali personnel serving in other EBR battalions were less fortunate. 1 EBR, 3 EBR and 10 EBR were taken to pieces. Although subunits of the 1st and 3rd battalions extricated themselves to the border, eventually joining up with the remainder of what became known as the *Mukti Fouj* (liberation army), 10 EBR virtually disappeared from the scene. 9 EBR, which was being raised at the time, would not surface for many months. EBRC recruits too died in their hundreds. Bengali personnel serving in other units were either killed or captured, with a handful managing to escape and join the rebels. Intense Pakistani pressure meant that initially, rebel units operated with little co-ordination.[13] On 30 March, Major Safiullah, unaware of Major Zia's proclamations broadcast a few days earlier, issued another call to arms using the EPR's wireless net. The response from remnant EPR subunits was most encouraging.[14]

However, the Pakistani forces' superior organisation, combat proficiency, firepower, mobility and logistics meant the rebels suffered reverses, being steadily pushed towards the border. It was only on 4 April that physical coordination proved possible. On this day, M.A.G. Osmany, a recently retired Colonel who had served in the Pakistani General Headquarters (GHQ) and as Colonel Commandant of the EBR, became known as 'Papa Tiger,' chaired a gathering of rebel commanders at 2 EBR's operational headquarters at Teliapara on East Pakistan's eastern borders. The group decided to conduct 'the war of liberation' under a central command headed by a senior army officer. Osmany himself would be the commander-in-chief once approval had been obtained from the future 'government of Bangladesh'. The *Mukti Bahini* (liberation force), to be built around the nucleus provided by 2nd, 4th and 8th EBR, was given geographical areas of responsibility: Safiullah was made commander of the Brahmanbaria-Sylhet area; Khaled Mosharraf, the Comilla-Noakhali belt, and Ziaur Rahman, Chittagong and Chittagong Hill Tracts (CHT).[15] This was a preliminary step; the demarcation of areas of responsibility across the province would follow, and combatants from the other surviving EBR, EPR, police and other paramilitary elements too would be brought together in new infantry battalions. The commanders decided to urge East Bengal's political leaders to immediately form a government. They sent out emissaries to bring as many elected members of the National Assembly (MNA) and provincial assembly (MPA) to Agartala, capital of India's Tripura state, as possible.

Agartala was where, after all the controversy over the trial of Mujib and his acolytes in the late 1960s, Bangladesh's putative administration took shape. On 10 April, a number of East Bengal's elected representatives gathered there under Tajuddin Ahmed, until now the Awami League's provincial Party Secretary, and issued Bangladesh's Proclamation of Independence Order. Backdating the proclamation to 26 March, the order confirmed the earlier declaration broadcast in Mujib's name. It appointed Mujib Bangladesh's president and supreme commander of its armed forces, and Syed Nazrul Islam the vice president. During the period of Mujib's inability to exercise his powers, the vice president would act as president.[16] Next, Tajuddin Ahmed, the consensus leader of the residual Awami League, went on air to broadcast the declaration of independence, announcing the formation of a national military built around an EBR-EPR nucleus under the command of Colonel Osmany as Commander-in-Chief. Tajuddin authorised the establishment of six operational commands covering contested districts—Sylhet-Comilla, Chittagong-Noakhali, Mymensingh-Tangail, Faridpur-Barisal, Khulna-Patuakhali and North Bengal, nominating commanders for the sectors which were later reorganised.[17]

Beyond those large towns that were defended by army garrisons, rebel regulars and guerrillas of various spontaneously raised militias continued to harass Pakistani forces and their supporters in these areas. The *Mukti Bahini* commanders, all former officers from the Pakistani army, had already been fighting in these areas on their own; now they became part of a national army-in-the-making. A unified command structure theoretically consolidated the diverse rebel units and guerrilla bands. A few days later, a cabinet under Tajuddin as premier was formed with Awami League legislators taking all the portfolios. This was a provisional government with no writ in East Bengal outside rebel-controlled enclaves. On 17 April, the cabinet was sworn in at 'Mujib Nagar' just inside western Bangladesh in the presence of a number of foreign journalists. Immediately afterwards, the government-in-exile, with the tacit but evidently warm endorsement of the Government of India (GOI), established its headquarters in Calcutta.

Sanctuary, support and the regional dynamic

The 'Mujib Nagar' ceremony symbolised the formal birth of the 'democratic republic of Bangladesh'. Publicity in the Indian and other media meant that, at least in the minds of millions of Bengalis in East and West Bengal and elsewhere, Bangladesh had come into being. The reality was more complex, but a basis for developing both political and military elements of Bangladesh's national leadership had now been laid. Although war was being waged by the Bengali 'liberation forces' and their Pakistani adversaries, the location of the Government-in-exile and its modest paraphernalia, including its *Swadhin Bangla Betar Kendra* (Free Bengali radio station) in Indian territory, and *materiel* being supplied to the guerrillas by Indian state organs,[18] particularly the Border Security Force (BSF), elevated the conflict to a higher level—that between India and Pakistan. Pakistani forces controlled Dhaka and Chittagong, Bangladesh's two main cities, but the resistance, by destroying several key bridges, rail-tracks and river ferries, made military movement across the delta difficult. 'The prospects are poor that the 30,000–odd West Pakistani troops can substantially improve their position, much less reassert control over seventy-five million rebellious Bengalis. This is likely to be the case even if the expeditionary force is augmented.'[19] The key to the Bangladesh enterprise's success lay in the nature and scale of Indian support and this transformed the East Bengal civil war into a regional confrontation. The potential for conflict between the rival successor states, as has been noted, was driven by an elemental need to subvert each other. Bangladesh's 'liberation war' thus became a core around which Pakistan faced an existential conflict with India.

Pakistan, especially a military-led Pakistan, had been considered the principal immediate threat to the multitudinous, diverse and democratic Indian polity by India's leaders. Bengali success in separating the two wings would weaken and discredit West Pakistan's militantly anti–Indian elite. East Bengal posed no direct security threats to Delhi. In fact, Mujib had advocated cordial relations with India—another reason behind West Pakistani loathing of East Bengal's pre-eminent politician. India also worried that an extended insurgency in East Bengal could throw up 'a new, extremist leadership as opposed to the relatively moderate Awami League one—which would eventually take over the new country.'[20] A radical regime in East Bengal would create 'very severe problems for India,' especially in West Bengal, where radical leftists challenging state authority had been contained with great difficulty. Delhi would, therefore, not only help the Bengalis secede from Pakistan, but also seek to establish an acceptable administration in Dhaka. To this end, Delhi would provide clandestine military assistance to the *Mukti Bahini*, in the form of sanctuary, arms and ammunition, training, and possibly advisers, and help the rebels to 'develop at a minimum the kind of insurgency capability which the army cannot entirely suppress.' Indian involvement could lead to progressively wider clashes between the two armies; 'even open military intervention by India could not be ruled out.'[21] Given the difficulties facing Islamabad's forces in confronting East Bengali resistance, which enjoyed even covert Indian support, the prospects for united Pakistan looked bleak.

Having only recently won an overwhelming majority in parliamentary elections and taken control of the Indian National Congress, Prime Minister Indira Gandhi initially responded cautiously to the Pakistani crackdown in the East. Her statements and that of her Foreign Minister in the Indian parliament on 27 March indicated Delhi's deep concern over the violence unleashed by Pakistani forces in East Bengal. Four days later, after intense discussions at the highest levels of India's political elite and security bureaucracies, Mrs Gandhi moved a resolution in the *Lok Sabha* (lower house) expressing 'deep anguish and grave concern' and setting out the perspective guiding Delhi's actions:

A massive attack by armed forces, dispatched from West Pakistan, has been unleashed against the entire people of East Bengal with a view to suppressing their urges and aspirations. Instead of respecting the will of the people so unmistakably expressed through the election in Pakistan in December 1970, the Government of Pakistan has chosen to flout the mandate of the people…Situated as India is and bound as the people of the subcontinent are by centuries old ties of history, culture and tradition, this House cannot remain indifferent to the macabre tragedy being enacted so close to our border…This House expresses its profound sympathy for and solidarity with the people of East Bengal in their struggle for a democratic way of life…This House calls upon all peoples and Governments of the world to take urgent and constructive steps to prevail upon the Government of Pakistan to put an end immediately to the systematic decimation of people which amounts to genocide. This House records its profound conviction that the historic upsurge of the seventy-five million people of East Bengal will triumph. The House wishes to assure them that their struggle and sacrifices will receive the whole-hearted sympathy and support of the people of India.[22]

Operationally, Pakistani forces took control of all of East Bengal's urban centres by the end of April 1971 and, on 6 May, Pakistani authorities felt confident enough to allow foreign journalists—expelled from East Pakistan after 25 March—to return to the province. Only the CHT and the narrow Cox's Bazaar coastal strip in the south-east remained in rebel hands for some time. Other rebel units managed to retain tiny salients elsewhere for a length of time, but their value was more senti-mental than tactical. Despite the immense obstacles facing the *Mukti Bahini*, apparent only after three weeks of combat, it was clear that 'the vast majority of Bengalis now reject the concept of a united Pakistan… Psychologically the concept of a united Pakistan is dead in Bengal.'[23] The violence of Pakistani action, mainly directed at Awami League activists and supporters, and Hindus, triggered an exodus of refugees from East Bengal to the neighbouring Indian states of West Bengal, Meghalaya, Assam and Tripura. Their numbers would remain controversial—with India claiming very large groups were crossing over to its territory while Pakistan insisted the figures were no more than a third or even a quarter of Delhi's claims. By 25 May, 3.4 million mostly Hindu East Bengalis had sought refuge in India and more than 100,000 were crossing the bor-der daily.[24] This 'flood' of Bangladeshis, unless arrested and reversed, could inundate eastern India with 'as many as 8 million refugees. In Indian eyes this would pose an intolerable burden on the social and economic struc-ture of the area.'[25]

The humanitarian crisis in Bangladesh and the neighbouring Indian states, Pakistani failure to restore normalcy, continuing violence and dis-ruptions, and looming fears of a famine concentrated minds in world capitals. But Islamabad's refusal to consider political changes, essentially signifying a compromise with the Awami League, whose leader had been described by Yahya Khan as 'a traitor,' limited the options open to all actors in this unhappy drama. Meanwhile, the *Mukti Bahini* reorganised itself. A *Niyomita Bahini* (regular army) would raise a number of infantry battalions and later, brigades, to prepare for conventional warfare when the Pakistani forces had been sufficiently worn down by guerrilla warfare; other Bangladeshi youths willing to fight for the independence of their country would be organised as guerrillas of the larger *Gonobahini* (people's forces) to wage non-conventional warfare in the meanwhile.[26] The refugee camps established by the Indian authorities close to Bangladesh's borders provided a large pool of willing volunteers for both forces. The BSF set up special camps where, by the end of May, 10,000 Bengalis were receiv-ing training in 'guerrilla and sabotage tactics'. Indian forces were provid-ing arms, ammunition and training, and some advisers had crossed the border to train fighters in Bangladeshi territory.[27] Indian and Pakistani border units had clashed several times and Pakistani aircraft had violated Indian airspace at least once.

Given the charged atmosphere and the emotional rhetoric on all sides, an escalation of the conflict seemed distinctly possible. Delhi, 'faced with something approaching genocide of the Hindus in East Pakistan and inundated with an unmanageable Hindu refugee inflow', might act to stop both and establish a friendly government in Dhaka. Pakistani forces might cross the border in 'hot pursuit' of the guerrillas and their Indian advisers and protectors, or attack Indian-staffed guerrilla training camps and bases.[28] Either move would trigger an India-Pakistan war which could engulf the subcontinent. As desultory action continued across Bangladesh, the threat of famine driving even more refugees into India and forcing tensions up a notch, hampered diplomatic efforts, especially at the UN and aid agencies.

In late May, after a visit to some of the 335 camps Delhi had established for the refugees, Mrs Gandhi chaired a war-cabinet meeting on the crisis. The Home Minister noted that by mid-May, more than 2.5 million refugees had sought shelter and the situation along the border had become 'desperate'; the refugees would place 'an impossible burden' on the Indian economy; the GOI ought to take 'every step to force' the Government of Pakistan (GOP) to 'stop pressuring East Pakistanis to flee', and repatriate the refugees. The External Affairs Minister said formal recognition of Bangladesh was contingent on 'the specific material help that India was prepared to make available' to the Bangladeshi separatist movement; recognition should only be formalised 'when India made the decision to risk military action against Pakistan'; while other powers had reacted extremely negatively to the East Bengal situation, the superpowers had adopted a 'wait and see attitude'. The Defence Minister noted Indian military preparedness and Pakistani operational weaknesses but still recommended against unilateral military action because of the indeterminate nature of possible Chinese involvement, the willingness of Turkey, Iran and other Muslim states to help Pakistan, and uncertainty over assured military supplies from the Soviet Union for 'what could be a long war.' Additionally, an Indian invasion of East Pakistan would impose a two-front war on India requiring 'the military occupation of all of Pakistan.'[29]

Mrs Gandhi issued the following instructions: defer recognition of Bangladesh for the immediate future, maintain constant military readiness, take every diplomatic step to force the GOP to stop the refugee flow and repatriate those who have crossed into India, 'including hints that India might take unilateral military action' to this end; seek financial aid from all possible sources to temporarily support the refugees.[30] Faced with pressure from the opposition, especially from the Left and Right, to initiate strong actions against Pakistan, Mrs Gandhi stressed her plans to continue urging the major powers to press GOP to change its policy. Given the seriousness of the situation, she also pleaded for support for her policies. She sounded more restrained than her interlocutors, but noted that about 3.5 million Bengalis had entered India and basic care for them could cost over Rs.1,800 million over six months. She said, 'What was claimed to be an internal problem for Pakistan, has also become an internal problem of India. We are, therefore, entitled to ask Pakistan to desist immediately from all actions which it is taking in the name of domestic jurisdiction, and which vitally affect the peace and well-being of millions of our own citizens. Pakistan cannot be allowed to seek a solution of its political or other problems at the expense of India and on Indian soil.'[31] The scene was set for inevitable confrontation.

Meanwhile, in East Bengal, the monsoons made large-scale operations difficult and both sides needed to recoup their losses, reorganise their forces and prepare for stronger action when the rains eased. Col. Osmany restructured the resistance. He divided Bangladesh into eleven sectors, appointing new commanders, incorporating some officers who had arrived after escaping from West Pakistan, and taking advantage of the arrival of thousands of regular- and guerrilla fighters trained by Indian and Bangladeshi instructors. A typical sector would have a commander and, when available, a deputy commander. A local legislator would serve as the civil affairs adviser. Accountants and logistics officers, usually civilians, helped the commander to maintain control over the flow of money, rations and equipment. Each sector had thousands of fighters, with manpower often exceeding firearms. Ill-equipped youthful combatants, armed with little more than the 'freedom fighters' fiery zeal, went into battle against professional Pakistani soldiers and paramilitary troops month after month, wearing the enemy down. Despite the cost in Bengali blood and Indian treasure, mostly the former, this was perhaps inevitable.

The orders given by the GOP to its army were: 'To defend the territorial integrity of Pakistan, in the process destroying the maximum number of enemy and capturing as much enemy territory as possible. The main battles would be fought in the West (the Punjab). It was envisaged that the fate of East Pakistan would hinge upon whatever operations were undertaken in the West.[32] Eastern Command's mission was to 'defend Dhaka at all costs, and within permissible limits delay the enemy invading East Pakistan.'[33] However, Yahya Khan had determined that the rebels could, possibly with Indian support, occupy a chunk of East Pakistani territory, declare Bangladeshi control over it, establish a government there and seek international recognition. To preclude this unacceptable eventuality, he ordered that every single inch of East Pakistani territory be defended 'to the last man last round'[34] chasing the *Muktis* across the border and defending the frontiers from strong-points built around border outposts (BOP). This dispersion along a 2,500–mile border with few defensible geographical features dissipated Pakistan's military strength in 'penny-packets'. Pakistan's General Headquarters (GHQ) repeatedly urged Eastern Command to defend nodal points and Dhaka, but Yahya Khan's determination to deny the Bangladeshi forces a recognisable bridgehead and Eastern Command's focus on that mission allowed the freedom fighters to operate successfully in the hinterland and, despite losses in pitched battles, inflict severe pain on the Pakistanis.[35]

The global palimpsest

It was during this interregnum that global influence began to be felt in relation to the local and regional situation. Even before assuming the presidency, Richard Nixon had concluded that the Indo-China war had become an unacceptable drain on America's resources and a threat to its moral authority. The USA needed to honourably withdraw and recuperate before it could once again effectively defend its global interests. To this end, the supposed Sino-Soviet alliance behind Hanoi's war effort had to be severed; Washington had to build bridges to Beijing before 'peace with honour' could be secured in Vietnam.[36] Despite some resistance from the US executive branch bureaucracies, Nixon, with the help of his Assistant for National Security Affairs, Henry Kissinger, pursued a confidential 'opening to China'. President Yahya Khan, advised by Foreign Secretary Sultan Khan, acted as the bridge-builder.[37] This had an impact on Nixon's views of US interests in Pakistan's welfare and shaped the White House's decisions regarding the Bangladesh crisis. What is more, Nixon and Kissinger liked Pakistani leaders and wished to help them while they disliked Indian leaders equally strongly. This combination of rational choices and subjective ones would influence events.[38]

The US establishment view had been that Washington had 'no vital interest in the South Asian subcontinent.' However, as a global power, America was 'inevitably concerned for the stability and well-being of an area in which one-fifth of mankind resides and which holds geopolitically significant position between China and the Soviet Union.' Accordingly, US interest lay in Indian and Pakistani success in economic development, in building 'politically open societies,' and avoiding 'the dominance of an external power in the region.'[39] As far as the regional protagonists were concerned, this typical interagency study noted, 'Within South Asia itself both India and Pakistan are important to US interests. Our interests in India, however, are of greater significance.'[40] This rationalistic, pragmatic and self-interested perspective shaped the views of the State Department, Department of Defence (DOD), and the Central Intelligence Agency (CIA). What these bureaucracies did not know was that Nixon's strategic initiative toward China demanded the continued survival, indeed good health, of the Yahya regime in Islamabad[41] and that the White House was determined to pursue these objectives irrespective of the obstacles.

The dynamics of Cold War great power relations were making an impression on both of the underlying processes shaping the conflict—the civil war pitting Bangladeshis against Pakistanis, and the India-Pakistan confrontation over it. The fact that the USA was the biggest economic benefactor to both India and Pakistan, making both dependent on American economic largesse—military aid had been cut off during the 1965 India-Pakistan War—gave America leverage, making it the most influential external actor. However, 'non-aligned' India maintained close ties to the Soviet Union and Moscow was the biggest supplier of military hardware to Indian armed forces. While India's domestic military-industrial capability was substantial and its more sophisticated economy was very much larger and better able to withstand shocks, Pakistan lagged on both counts and the civil war severely strained its modest economy.[42] Nixon wished to ensure there was no breach of the peace between India and Pakistan, at least until his China mission had reached fruition. China, Pakistan's 'all-weather friend,' had serious territorial and other differences with both India and the Soviet Union, and would stand by Islamabad. Beijing had already written to Delhi accusing India of 'interfering in Pakistani affairs.'[43]

In contrast, Moscow was expected to support Delhi. Since 1966, the USSR had acted as an honest broker, mediating negotiated resolution of Indo-Pakistani disputes, and providing Pakistan with some economic and even military assistance, but Indian outrage had ended Soviet military aid to Islamabad. Moscow seemed keen to retain some influence in Pakistan but its pro-Delhi preferences now became clear. President Nikolai Podgorny had written to Yahya Khan that 'the complex problems that have arisen in Pakistan of late can and must be solved politically without the use of force.'[44] This admonition left little doubt that on Bangladesh, Moscow sided with the Bengalis and their sympathisers in India. This set of linkages erected two contrasting coalescent alignments—with the USA and China supporting Pakistan while urging behind the scenes moderation in dealing with the Bangladeshis, and the Soviet Union supporting India in its aid to Bangladesh's campaign for independence and seeking to prevent any US-Chinese initiative in support of Pakistan. Still, as early as 26 March, Soviet Ambassador Anatoly Dobrynin had asked Secretary of State William Rogers how Washington planned to respond to Pakistani army action with hints that Moscow was willing to engage in a dialogue with America on this subject.

Against that backdrop, Nixon wished to suggest neutrality between India and Pakistan in their confrontation over Bangladesh while being privately supportive of Pakistan's Yahya regime. He also focused on providing economic aid to both countries, especially for people in East Bengal, and Bengali refugees sheltering in India. This was the line he took in mid-June when the Indian Foreign Minister, Swaran Singh, called on him. Offering an additional $70 million to help India manage the refugee problem, Nixon said America was keen to avoid bloodshed and further danger to the region's people. Singh insisted Delhi had 'no fixed position' on the preferred outcome of the Pakistani crisis between a united Pakistan and an independent Bangladesh but sought an end to the flow of refugees—with six million already in India and one arriving every second.[45] Responding to Singh's request for pressure on Islamabad, Nixon said overt pressure would not help and that he would act tactfully while offering practical aid and encouraging allies to do so.

This was the line pursued by Kissinger in discussions with Indian leaders during a trip to Delhi in July. However, he also focused on India's relations with China and the situation along their disputed borders, a sensitive issue. The Indian Defence Minister Jagjivan Ram and his aides briefed him on Chinese troop numbers and dispositions, Indian concerns, and the capability of either side to sustain operations without reinforcements. This exchange on tactical matters was followed by a warning from Kissinger to Ram that, although he thought Beijing would be unlikely to act against India without provocation, 'the Chinese would intervene if there was a war with Pakistan.'[46] Kissinger noted that he had been 'scolded by everyone' he met in Delhi for not pressing Yahya Khan to stop the violence in East Bengal, explaining that US policy was 'to try to avoid a confrontation with Pakistan and have some influence on developments.' However, while America was 'in favour of a political solution' that would permit the return of the refugees, it did not favour secession. Ram and his aides raised the question of the supply of US arms and spare parts to Pakistan. They feared this supply, while small, could affect the regional balance of power. Kissinger replied, 'the only balance of power the US is concerned with is the global balance—and the problem of preventing an outside power from dominating South Asia. The local balance within South Asia is not an American concern.'[47]

Having explained Nixon's global strategic preoccupations, Kissinger flew to Islamabad for a meeting with Yahya Khan and a rendezvous with history. As choreographed by Yahya Khan via secret correspondence, Kissinger, pretending to fall ill during a banquet hosted in his honour by the Pakistani President, excused himself. Early next morning, an NSC colleague, wearing his sunglasses and hat drove to a northern hill station ostensibly to recuperate; Kissinger himself, in the company of two NSC aides and several PLA security staff, flew in a PIA airliner to Beijing. There, in secret sessions lasting seventeen hours with Zhou Enlai, Kissinger conveyed Nixon's wish to overcome past hostility, build trust, and erect a tacit alignment against Soviet 'hegemonism'. Zhou, representing Mao Zedong and challenging conservative Chinese factions led by Mao's anointed successor, Marshal Lin Biao, responded favourably, extending a formal invitation to Nixon to visit Beijing and conduct face-to-face discussions on normalising relations.[48] The peak of the global strategic hierarchy was thus shaken to its roots, injecting a degree of fluidity in a system frozen in place by the apparent immutability of superpower nuclear deterrence.

Bangladesh's rice paddies were a world away from these systemic realignments. The Pakistani forces were pursuing their enemies somewhat less vigorously than before, and the flow of refugees had fallen from a high-point of 100,000 per day in May-June to a little over 30,000 daily in late June and early July, but the fundamentals had not changed. 'Although military action against Hindus has declined, it has not ceased and communal tensions have not been checked', a report read.[49] Mrs. Gandhi had urged Congress leaders to counter political pressures for immediate military action against Pakistan, but Delhi was still making contingency plans for such intervention.[50] Nixon faced many pressures, but few stronger than those at home. Congress and the media sympathised vocally with the Bangladeshis and demanded that Administration policy reflect that stance. Nixon was angered by the apparent lack of appreciation of his efforts to prevent India from dismembering Pakistan which could, by spreading Hindu-Muslim and Bengali–non-Bengali tensions from East Bengal to across the region, trigger widespread violence. There were fears that if faced with insurmountable challenges, Yahya Khan would 'commit suicide.'[51]

Nixon harboured resentment against antagonists at home and abroad. He worried that India, aiming to undermine East Pakistan so that forces capable of unraveling West Pakistan would be unleashed, was training Bengali guerrillas at twenty-nine camps identified by Islamabad, that Bengali fighters were killing eighteen Pakistani soldiers and blowing up two bridges daily, that the US ambassador to India, Kenneth Keating, had joined a propaganda 'campaign...against Pakistan,' that the State Department was 'basically pro-Indian,' and that the State Department and AID officials stationed in Dhaka had blown 'the whistle on the whole thing.'[52] Meanwhile, US officials in Islamabad and Dhaka warned of a looming famine in East Pakistan which could approach the 1943 catastrophe in which millions were killed.[53] Washington asked Yahya Khan to appoint a 'food czar' for East Pakistan and replace General Tikka Khan with a civilian governor in East Pakistan. Yahya appointed an eminent Bengali, Dr. A.M. Malik, as Special Assistant for Displaced Persons and Relief and Rehabilitation Operations in East Pakistan.[54] Yahya said Malik outranked Tikka Khan and this would effectively ensure civilian control of the province without forcing him to transfer power to Bhutto, who was 'standing in the Wings' in the West.[55] Nixon ordered as much food- and economic aid to Pakistan as possible.

Secretary of State William Rogers told Nixon that India was 'doing everything it can to prevent the refugees from returning.' Director of Central Intelligence (DCI) Richard Helms advised Nixon that Pakistan was 'going broke' and pressure was building in India to go to war. Kissinger, fresh from his trip to Beijing, warned that 70,000 Pakistani troops could not 'hold down East Pakistan' and that Delhi was thinking of 'using the war as a way of destroying Pakistan.' He reported that the Indian Army Chief of Staff, General Sam Manekshaw, had said Indian forces could take on East Pakistan, West Pakistan and China 'all at once.' Nixon asked what China would do—Kissinger thought the Chinese would 'come in' to fight the 'insufferably arrogant' Indians. Nixon, admitting to a 'bias' in the dispute, said that Delhi would not 'get a dime of aid, if they mess around in East Pakistan.' He said especially in view of the Chinese invitation to him, he 'could not allow—over the next three or four months until we take this journey to Peking—a war in South Asia if we can possibly avoid it.'[56] This, then, was to be the American policy for the time.

The focus on emergency food aid for Bengalis on both sides of the border forced Yahya Khan to offer some concessions. He declared an amnesty and invited the refugees to return, agreed to establish reception centres for returnees, and to station UN personnel to monitor their treatment at the border. However, he did not recall the army to the barracks, nor let the UN supervise food transportation and distribution. For its part, India received additional US funds for helping the refugees but refused to station UN or other foreign officials along its side of the border. When Delhi did not respond to Pakistani steps, Kissinger asked Dobrynin if reports of Soviet encouragement to India to initiate 'military adventures' were accurate. Dobrynin admitted Moscow extended political support to Delhi but discouraged 'military adventures'. Kissinger warned that a war between India and Pakistan could not be limited to East Pakistan and might extend beyond South Asia.[57]

Kissinger's inter-departmental Senior Review Group (SRG) focused on a famine expected to hit East Bengal by October and ways of preventing it. Yahya Khan's refusal to accept a political solution in the East, India's refusal to accept anything but, continuing rebel operations from across the border and a steady flow of Bengali refugees to India meant US hands were tied. Efforts to prevent a war, maintaining aid flow to Pakistan despite Congressional bars and administrative blockages, and sustaining the newly promising Beijing initiative presented Nixon and his aides with contradictory demands. Reassuring India also became important, especially as Kissinger had given no indication of his secret assignment during his sessions with Indian leaders just before flying to China. Rogers briefed Ambassador L.K. Jha that Kissinger's mission was aimed at establishing high-level contact, arranging a visit by Nixon, trying to 'normalise' relations and strengthen stability. Jha worried that, given Pakistan's role in the drama, America might not remain sensitive to Indo-Pakistani tensions or the 'troubled Sino-Indian relationship and Chinese support of Pakistan.'[58] Rogers assured him that America's China initiative would not be at the cost of its other relations. Jha did not indicate how reassured he felt.

Rogers also had to respond to Pakistani requests for additional wheat and funds with which to lease river craft to distribute the cereals in riverine East Bengal's remote hinterland. Rogers decided he would inform the Pakistani Ambassador, Agha Hilaly, as soon as US decisions in this regard had been taken. At the end of July, the SRG decided to set out a comprehensive relief programme for East Bengal, draft a telegram for Nixon to be sent to Yahya Khan telling him what needed to be done regarding refugees, food relief etc, consult the British on a joint or parallel approach, consult the Soviets on an assessment of the South Asian situation, and 'develop a contingency plan for a possible Indian-Pakistani war.'[59] The discussions made it clear that despite Nixon's instructions to maintain the pipeline of economic, technical and non-lethal military aid to Pakistan, these had been shut down. An exasperated Kissinger complained, 'The President has said repeatedly that we should lean toward Pakistan, but every proposal that is made, goes directly counter to these instructions.'[60] When officials explained Pakistani obstacles to effective aid distribution, Kissinger asked AID Deputy Director, Maurice Williams, to 'go there and tell Yahya what is needed to break the bureaucratic log-jam.'

But a bigger challenge came from another direction. After several years of desultory talks on security collaboration, in August 1971, a year after China and Pakistan had opened the Karakorum Highway linking China's Xinjiang province to Pakistan's Arabian Sea coast, the Soviet Union and India signed a Treaty of Friendship with mutual security clauses. Three days later, Foreign Ministers Andrei Gromyko and Swaran Singh issued a joint statement stressing that Moscow and Delhi grasped the US-PRC initiative's strategic significance to their shared interests in South Asia, and would trump it with formalised collaboration. Coincidentally, on 9 August, the day the treaty was signed, Islamabad announced plans to try

Sheikh Mujibur Rahman for 'waging war against Pakistan' and other crimes. A week later, the Soviet ambassador in Islamabad delivered a message from Kosygin to Yahya Khan: the Indo-Soviet treaty was not aimed against any country; however, if Mujib was given a 'severe sentence' following his trial, 'serious consequences would follow.'[61]

The plot thickens

Bangladeshi forces started receiving more and better arms, ammunition and explosives from their Indian supporters. Guerrilla activities by the *Mukti Bahini's* sector troops intensified and expanded, and became more effective. Most road, rail and river transportation systems came to a stand-still.[62] Agricultural production and manufacturing pretty much came to an end. Pakistani troops, divided into small sub-units deployed along the border in 'strong-points', lost much of their mobility and effectiveness. Against that backdrop, Maurice Williams visited Pakistan, meeting Yahya Khan and his senior aides in Islamabad and traveling across East Bengal to assess the refugee- and relief situation. Yahya Khan accepted much of his advice, allocating $20m for emergency relief in the East and promising to welcome returning refugees back. However, on the ground, things were unpromising. *Mukti Bahini* fighters were 'gradually stepping up the intensity and sophistication of their operations'. The security situation continued 'to deteriorate and the Hindu population is still leaving the province...India is "fighting" Pakistan by proxy through its support to the *Mukti Bahini* insurgents and Pakistan, indirectly, is fighting back by pursuing policies which will encourage the entire eleven million Hindu population of East Pakistan to go to India and not return.'[63] Yahya Khan, anticipating US pleas, appointed Dr. A.M. Malik as East Bengal's civilian—and Bengali—Governor, succeeding General Tikka Khan. However, administrative control was vested in General Niazi who, as the Martial Law Administrator and Commander, Eastern Command, exercised final authority.

The outcome reflected the superficiality of the changes. Since June, when Pakistan set up reception centres for returnees, only 34,000 refugees had come back from India. And despite Pakistani efforts, 20,000–30,000 Bengalis were fleeing to India daily with the total running to eight million.[64] More worryingly, the Pakistani military, by employing the most orthodox Muslims they could find in the province, established 'peace committees' which replaced the local councils led by traditional local leaders, thereby threatening social stability. One result of this radical social engineering would be an intensification of Hindu-Muslim tensions and growing threats to communal harmony. More fundamentally, this disruption 'would force traditional village leadership into opposition, extend the conflict' and radicalise rural areas. 'Normally, it would be difficult to imagine a way to completely disrupt a traditional subsistence society and economy like that of East Pakistan. But Pakistani officers are capable of doing it, as they seek to solve an immediate and increasingly urgent military problem.'[65] Williams urged his bosses to collaborate with other donors and dramatically expand relief operations and aid to Pakistan and India. He requested Yahya Khan to lift the ban on the Awami League and make a political approach to it; Yahya said he had gone 'as far as West Pakistani opinion would tolerate.'[66] The failure of US State Department's secret attempts to bring Islamabad and Bangladesh's government-in-exile to the negotiating table outside the reach of the latter's Indian hosts[67] may have made compromise even harder.

By September 1971, 80,000 Pakistani military and paramilitary personnel, supported by around '1–2 million' *Biharis* and 'some ardently anti–Hindu Bengalis' faced 50,000 guerrillas of the resistance.[68] Perhaps 15,000 operated inside East Bengal at any one time, but the bulk of the resistance forces appeared to be waiting. Every six weeks, 1,000–1,500 guerrillas trained at the Indian camps joined the *Mukti Bahini*.[69] Pro-Awami League nationalists may have comprised the largest element, but extreme left-leaning activists similar to West Bengal's urban guerrillas were also there.[70] By attacking transport, communications, power and other essential elements of East Bengal's already paltry infrastructure, as well as logistics including essential supplies, the guerrillas had weakened Islamabad's hold on the province and drained Pakistani military capacity. The proxy engagement of India's traditional rival explained India's substantial assistance to the Bengali resistance. However, the cost to East Bengal had been enormous. Economic activity had fallen to 30–35 per cent of the pre-March 1971 level; some 200,000 people had been killed and over eight million of the region's seventy-six million people had been forced to flee. Probably 80–90 per cent of them were East Bengali Hindus running in fear of their lives.[71] Yahya Khan had installed a civilian provincial government but his insistence on Mujib's trial and the highly contrived exercise meant to replace those Awami League legislators who had been killed, fled or gone missing since March 1971 left little room for those who might pursue negotiations.

The resistance was now sufficiently large, strong, and combat-savvy for the Bangladeshi commanders to start thinking of conventional engagements with Pakistani forces. The first step had been taken in July when Ziaur Rahman was asked to raise the 'Z Force', the first infantry brigade. In September, Safiullah and Khaled Mosharraf raised the 'S Force' and the 'K Force' respectively. The rebels now had both the nucleus of a three-brigade-strong conventional army and thousands of sector troops who had acquired skills and experience of guerrilla fighting. In October these combined forces began attacking salients along the 2,500 mile-long border, putting Pakistani BOPs, strong points and 'fortresses' under added pressure, and pinning the latter down along the frontiers while guerrillas operated in the countryside with relative impunity. They also attacked ocean-going shipping at the ports of Chittagong and Chalna, killed members of the pro–Pakistan 'Peace Committees' that had replaced local government at the lowest levels, and attacked administration figures and their relatives. As well as challenging Pakistani control in a wide swathe across the Dhaka, Noakhali, Comilla, Faridpur, Sylhet and Mymensingh districts, Bangladeshi fighters also occupied parts of Khulna and Rangpur by early October. Pakistani soldiers still mounted indiscriminate reprisal attacks on villages and markets.[72] Along the borders, Indian artillery often backed Bengali rebel forces in their assaults on Pakistani positions. A large-scale *Mukti Bahini* offensive was expected in October-November after the monsoon rains had ended and trainees from Indian camps had been 'unleashed.' While Islamabad tried to forge a united Muslim League party that could, with new seats gained in East Pakistani 'by-elections', forge a coalition government, the guerrillas were changing the ground reality. When the US Ambassador saw Yahya Khan in late September to advise him that Mujib could be the 'trump card' for a political settlement, Yahya 'did not react adversely'[73] but nor did he act.

With signs of a Bangladeshi–Indian military offensive building against a Pakistan frozen in political and tactical paralysis, Indira Gandhi began a trip to major capitals to advance India's case. She saw Nixon on 4 November. Nixon received her warmly, mainly to avoid giving offence and to prevent Delhi from using that as an excuse to initiate overt hostilities against Pakistan.[74] Mrs. Gandhi focused on the military situation along India's border with West- rather than East Pakistan. Nixon told

her that Pakistan would disengage its forces in the West if India reciprocated. The following day, they discussed global security issues including
Vietnam and the Middle East. Gandhi endorsed Nixon's China initiative
and the meeting ended pleasantly. South Asia was not discussed.[75] While
the leaders chatted amiably, aides discussed possible approaches to the
Bangladesh crisis. Assistant Secretary of State Joseph Sisco told Mrs
Gandhi's aide T.N. Kaul that Yahya Khan would be willing to open talks
with Awami League leaders who could represent Mujib. Kaul said this
would be a non-starter 'since the Bengalis are bent on independence and
only Mujib would have a chance of settling for less.' Sisco broached
Yahya's offer of a unilateral Pakistani military withdrawal; Kaul assured
him India had no territorial designs, was not trying to impose a settlement on East- and West Pakistan, but could not 'afford to take security
risks until the political problem in East Pakistan was resolved.' Insisting
that 'all the refugees, irrespective of their religion, must return,' Kaul noted
that, if attacked, 'India was determined that it would be a decisive war
with decisive results.'[76]

Despite Nixon's efforts to maintain the modest military pipeline to
Pakistan, only economic aid was getting through, most of it for the victims of natural and man-made disasters afflicting East Bengal's destitute
millions. In late October, Maurice Williams returned to Pakistan, receiving high-level briefings in both wings. The army in the East had achieved
'nearly autonomous control of the province' and Niazi's reports were mis-
leading Yahya Khan.[77] Yahya told Williams that 'civilianisation' of the
provincial administration was stabilising the situation and that after by-
elections filled legislative seats vacated by renegade Awami League members, 'political accommodation' for a loyal provincial government would
have been completed. This would deny Delhi its objectives of supporting
the insurgency. Williams was struck by the 'wide gap between the myth
of growing stability as seen by Yahya Khan, and the reality of political
deterioration.'[78] General Rao Farman Ali Khan, military adviser to Governor Malik, told Williams that at least eighty per cent of East Pakistan's
Hindus had left and the remaining 1.5 million 'refugees would probably
go to India before the situation settles down.'[79] Khan said the army was
getting the 60,000 badly-trained and poorly led *Razakar* militia to fight
the *Mukti Bahini*. Williams thought the conflict between these two armed
bands was squeezing the middle peasantry, the basis of rural stability, to
either flee to the cities or to India.[80] Nixon's aides knew that Pakistan and

India were staggering towards war. An inter-agency contingency paper on US options in case of war breaking out noted that 'US interests would be best served by an early end to the conflict and by negotiations among all parties leading to a withdrawal of Indian troops and an overall political settlement.'[81]

Although General Gul Hassan Khan, Pakistan's CGS, had alerted the Chief of Staff (COS), General Abdul Hamid Khan, in early September that 'an Indian invasion was a foregone conclusion,' urging that General Niazi reorder Eastern Command's deployments to defend Dhaka, neither Hamid nor Yahya appeared to have taken note.[82] It was only in mid-November that Yahya Khan sent Foreign Secretary Sultan Khan, privy to the US-China initiative, to see Nixon and seek help. After months of vigorous support for Yahya Khan's policies, Nixon told his emissary that the Pakistani political crisis 'is one of those terrible problems that, frankly, must be solved by a political solution; it must not be solved by force.'[83] Nixon and Kissinger assured Sultan Khan that America would do everything diplomatically possible to prevent a war from breaking out—they were talking to India, Russia and China and would continue to do so. No intervention was promised. The reason may have been that while Nixon believed Yahya Khan was 'a thoroughly decent and reasonable man; not always smart politically, but he's a decent man,' and India was 'more at fault' for deepening the crisis, he knew that Yahya Khan would 'be demolished' in East Bengal.[84] He seemed to pin his hopes on Yahya Khan's promise to present a new constitution to Pakistan by the end of the year and transfer power to elected representatives soon afterwards. If only Yahya Khan's Pakistan could hang on that long.

Denouement

The *Mukti Bahini* had established bases in salients all along the border, posing serious threats to Pakistani BOPs and 'strong-points'. One of these, close to the Indian village of Boyra on the Jessore-Calcutta road, was a particularly painful thorn. On 20 November, Pakistani troops, with artillery and air cover, attacked the guerrillas while shells fell on Boyra itself. That night, an Indian infantry brigade with armour, artillery and air support, mounted a counter-attack in the Jessore sector while smaller battle-groups pushed into Rangpur, Sylhet and the CHT sectors.[85] Three Pakistani aircraft were shot down and their pilots taken prisoner. This was the first major assault by Indian forces. On 22 November, General Gul Hassan Khan briefed Yahya Khan on the attacks, urging an immediate counter-offensive from West Pakistan. Yahya told him, 'serious negotiations are in progress at this time and if we opened a front in the West, these would be jeopardised.'[86] However, he declared a state of emergency the following day. On 24 November, Mrs Gandhi told parliament that Indian forces had been ordered to enter East Bengal in 'self-defence.' The *Mukti Bahini*, with Indian support, mounted a series of attacks in home territory. Chaugachha, Meherpur and Kaliganj in the west, Hilli and Bhurungamari in the north-west, Kamalpur, Shamshernagar and Chhatak in the North, and Belonia and Akhaura in the East saw major assaults with the Bangladesh forces making significant gains,[87] although casualties were heavy on both sides.

On 18 November, Gandhi had written to Nixon repeating her requests to push Yahya Khan towards a political solution to the crisis, to end the flow of Bengalis into India and to take all the refugees back. She also urged Nixon not to involve the UN Security Council (UNSC).[88] After Boyra, Nixon and Kissinger worried that a traumatic resolution of the East Pakistan crisis, as seemed likely now, would unravel West Pakistan, too. Their hope was to draw in Soviet and Chinese influence in exercising restraint, and offering Pakistan third-party military help in the West to counter-balance Indian superiority in the East. But they also saw this as a dress rehearsal for Soviet and proxy action against allies of the West, including China.[89] Discussions among US, Indian and Pakistani officials in the three capitals underscored US interest in preventing escalation, Yahya Khan enthusiastically endorsing US proposals to deploy UN observers along the eastern borders and unilaterally withdraw Pakistani troops from the western ones, and India reluctant to reciprocate. On 27 November, Nixon wrote to Gandhi, acting as the sole intermediary between the two antagonists.[90] He also wrote to Yahya Khan and Alexei Kosygin. His assurances of friendship to Yahya noted America's emphasis on diplomatic efforts. His missive to Kosygin was more prosaic:

The recent border incidents which have involved engagements between Indian and Pakistani aircraft, tanks, and artillery in the Jessore sector of East Pakistan have been of particular concern to me, as I am sure they have been to you. The situation has reached a point at which there appears to be an imminent danger of full-scale hostilities between India and Pakistan.[91]

Nixon described the proposals for de-escalation that he had communicated between Yahya Khan and Indira Gandhi in the hope that these would lower tensions, making a political solution possible. He sought Soviet support for these measures. By then, Delhi had admitted to having crossed the border but insisted it was only in self-defence. Pakistani forces hoped to limit Indian penetration to ten to fifteen miles and hold the province for a month. Ambassadors Keating and Farland met Gandhi and Yahya Khan respectively urging restraint, but nothing changed. At this point, the *Mukti Bahini* was doing most of the fighting, with the occasional support of Indian artillery, armour and infantry.[92] Delhi had trained and armed the guerrillas to defeat the Pakistani forces and would have preferred if it were 'done internally, strictly by the *Mukti Bahini*.' But the latter were 'only effective when stiffened by the Indians.'[93] With foreign relief experts being withdrawn to Dhaka and grain-stocks and transports being captured or destroyed by the combatants, the food situation was again deteriorating. Nixon ordered that all military supplies to India be cut off and economic aid be squeezed. The exercise was made difficult by the complexities of the military aid system and the fact that America funded repairs to US-built C-119 aircraft in the Indian Air Force (IAF), built roads linking Indian military facilities in Nepal and paid for an Indian radar there which monitored the Chinese air force, the information being shared by India and the USA.[94]

Mrs Gandhi's response to Nixon's letter was polite but firm: her 'duty was to see what was in the interests of her country.' Pakistan had moved the troops to the border first and only after India responded did Yahya Khan offer disengagement. He had created his own problems and 'we are not in a position to make this easier for him.' India would not 'allow' Yahya Khan's 'misdeeds to stand.' She 'wouldn't like to take this country to war' but 'this war and this situation are not of our making.' Many countries had promised to press Yahya Khan but did nothing. Now, Yahya Khan, with 'his back to the wall, wants to be bailed out. We have to take steps which will make us stronger to deal with this situation.' The 'farcical' by-elections Yahya had held in East Bengal were 'not going to make any differences whatsoever.' As for US pleas for restraint following the Boyra battle, Mrs. Gandhi noted, 'We can't afford to listen to advice that weakens us.'[95] Keating was instructed to inform Delhi that except for items covered by existing licenses worth $11.5 million, all military supplies to India stood cancelled. Other aid, too, would be limited.

On 29 November, Yahya Khan, in consultation with the Army Chief of Staff, and the Commander-in-Chief, PAF, decided to open the Western front. The naval Commander-in-Chief was briefed later. The D-Day, initially 2 December, was postponed to 3 December. According to plans approved in August, a corps comprising an armoured- and two infantry divisions would mount an offensive, to be reinforced after the first battles. The aim was to 'seize maximum territory of political and strategic significance.'[96] However, given India's four-to-one superiority, Pakistani operations could not last longer than thirty days—Pakistani artillery in the East was already restricted to firing ten shells per day per gun—and India's eventual victory even in the West was assured.[97] By 2 December the Indian and *Mukti Bahini* offensive had gained momentum. 'Relentless pressure' was forcing the abandonment of provincial towns to the guerrillas and some localities only seventeen miles from Dhaka had been lost.[98] Yahya Khan wrote to Nixon invoking Article 1 of the US-Pakistan Bilateral Agreement of 5 March 1959, seeking direct military assistance against Indian aggression.[99]

Early in the afternoon on 3 December, Pakistan's Army COS advised General Niazi, 'Total war imminent (.) Redeploy forces in accordance operational tasks (.) Consider areas of tactical strategic and political importance (.),[100] Yahya Khan saw the US and Chinese ambassadors for separate briefings regarding Pakistani air attacks 'in response to Indian incursions.' He also recorded an address to the nation to be broadcast by Radio Pakistan at 5.40 pm, just after PAF aircraft mounted attacks on several Indian air bases in Kashmir and Punjab. Mrs. Gandhi told her compatriots that Pakistani aircraft had bombed six Indian bases; Pakistani artillery was shelling Indian territory in the West and India 'had no option but to adopt war footing.'[101] Pakistan alleged that Indian fighters had conducted 'aggressive reconnaissance' over West Pakistan for three or four days 'as a prelude to attacks' launched by Indian forces at 3.30—4.00 pm. on 3 December at several points stretching between Kashmir in the North and Rahim Yar Khan in the south. Pakistani air raids were 'necessary countermeasures.'[102] Pakistani formations in the West mounted a limited offensive on the night of 3–4 December, making modest gains at some points. But in the East, India no longer needed to maintain the cover of the *Mukti Bahini*.

India's aircraft severely damaged the air base in Dhaka, virtually grounding the fourteen F-86 Sabre Jets which had no night-fighting capability. The Indian Eastern Command under Lt. General Jagjit Singh Aurora, with its three army corps and substantial air and naval support, launched what came to be called the 'lightning campaign'.[103] *Mukti Bahini* guerrillas, exploiting local intelligence contacts and overwhelming popular support, led the way. The Indo-Bangladeshi 'Joint Command', eliminating or bypassing Pakistani resistance, using paratroopers and heliborne forces to overcome river obstacles and outflank enemy defences, and enjoying almost total air- and naval supremacy, rapidly advanced along a broad front. General Niazi's Eastern Command, Yahya Khan's military leadership in Islamabad and their allies in Washington found it difficult to keep pace. Nixon was angered by the very slow cutting off the aid pipeline to India, recipient of $8.3bn in US aid since 1947,[104] while diplomats argued over the language of UNSC draft resolutions. The Americans, perplexed by the inconsequential nature of the Pakistani air raids,[105] failed to determine who had attacked first. When Kissinger called the Soviet *Charge d'Affaires*, Yulie Vorontsov, to protest against the Indian offensive, he was told it would be over in a week or so. Nixon asked Kissinger to advise the Kremlin that this was 'a watershed in our relationship if it continues to go on this way.'[106] Nixon had pursued *détente* with the Soviet Union to restore strategic calm, pledging to share with Moscow the diplomatic onus of addressing the Middle East problem and other global issues. He was scheduled to visit Moscow in May for a summit with the Soviet leadership. A new era of superpower peace, still being painstakingly built, looked fragile. Washington faced difficulties in that it had secret agreements with both India and Pakistan aimed at helping them in case they were attacked.[107] Nixon's China initiative and his very different views of Yahya Khan and Indira Gandhi pushed him towards 'tilting' in favour of Pakistan and he was infuriated by his Administration's inability to abandon 'balance' between the two. US efforts to secure third-party support for Pakistan were only slightly more effective.

At Pakistani request, Nixon and Kissinger urged the Shah of Iran and Jordan's King Hussein to send combat aircraft and other munitions to restock Pakistan's rapidly dwindling inventory, promising that America would replace the items they sent.[108] They also worked with China, Britain, France, Italy and other allies and friends to get the UNSC to press the belligerents to stop hostilities and withdraw forces from captured territories. In all, over a dozen draft resolutions were discussed, tabled, voted on or vetoed on the subject without affecting the dynamics on the ground.

The Soviet Union, India and their allies demanded an immediate end to Pakistani military action in the East, return of all Bengali refugees from India and a political settlement of East Bengal's political-military crisis; the USA, China, Pakistan and their allies sought an urgent end to hostilities, withdrawal of forces from each other's territory and then, negotiations. So many vetoes were applied that the UNSC was frozen in polarised futility. US officials closely consulted Pakistani and Chinese diplomats but the momentum of the Indian-*Mukti Bahini* offensive in the East,[109] and the stalemate in the West, offered them little leverage.

By 4 December, Kissinger privately acknowledged, 'Everyone knows we will end up with Indian occupation of East Pakistan.'[110] India's destruction of Pakistan's POL depots in Karachi threatened Islamabad's capacity to defend the West itself. Nixon agonised over whether he should have been tougher during Gandhi's visit just weeks before Boyra in warning her against launching a war. As far as the great powers were concerned, Nixon and Kissinger worried about losing Soviet respect by appearing ineffectual. This would have consequences for global power balances and management of strategic security affairs.[111] While Washington cut off its modest arms supply to both belligerents, Moscow supplied Delhi. On 6 December, Nixon wrote to Leonid Brezhnev, cautioning him that unless Indian military action was restrained, US-Soviet relations would gravely suffer: 'It is clear that the interests of all concerned states will be served if the territorial integrity of Pakistan were restored and military action were brought to an end. Urgent action is required and I believe your great influence in New Delhi should serve these ends.'[112]

On that day, the Indian government extended diplomatic recognition to Bangladesh, ending any subterfuge in waging war in Bangladesh's favour or on its behalf. Pakistan broke relations with India. With 'Joint Command' victory in the East now certain, the White House feared India would soon move some of its forces from there to the West to threaten Pakistan's existence. As this would be happening at a time of America's global retrenchment in consonance with Nixon's 'Guam doctrine', a Soviet-aided Indian success in securing Bangladesh's secession from US-ally Pakistan would 'prove that countries can get away with brutality.'[113] Nixon noted that 'The US cannot be responsible for maintaining peace (in) every place in the world. We can use our influence, may not always be successful.'[114] Sharing strategic responsibility, he wanted to get the Chinese to act by telling them that 'some movement on their part toward the

Indian border could be very significant.' He asked Kissinger to tell Beijing's UN envoy Huang Hua, Kissinger's secret 'backchannel', that if China considered 'it necessary to take certain actions we want you to know that you should not be deterred by the fear of standing alone against the powers that may intervene.'[115] This is the message Kissinger would give Huang.

There were now worries about the fate of 'about a million and a half Urdu-speaking people' in Bangladesh and the 300,000 Bengalis in residual Pakistan. Washington now began to consider whether these people could be saved from possible violence with organised mass evacuation efforts.[116] America was also anxious 'not to let India extinguish the Pakistan Government'.[117] On 7 December, Yahya Khan wrote to Nixon:

If India should succeed in its objective, the loss of East Pakistan with a population of seventy million people dominated by Russia will also be a threat to the security of South Asia. It will bring under Soviet domination the region of Assam, Burma, Thailand and Malaysia. The far-reaching consequences of such a development to the future of Asia need no comment. In this critical hour for Pakistan I request your Excellency to do whatever you can to relieve the pressure from our borders.[118]

Nixon replied just hours later, recounting the steps he had taken to help Pakistan and discourage India and the Soviet Union, at the UN and other fora. He promised to continue in the same vein, while 'keeping the People's Republic of China fully informed about the various measures we are taking in your support and have made it clear that we welcome the strong efforts it is making in your behalf.'[119] Nixon's domestic dilemma was underscored when he told his aides how to get the message across to the media about what Washington had done and what it could do to end the crisis: 'You should also get across (that) we have no influence, we have no responsibility for either. It's not our job. The Russians have an interest in India. The Chinese have a hell of an interest in Pakistan. We only have an interest in peace. We're not anti–Indian, we're not anti–Pakistan. We're anti–aggression.'[120] In Bangladesh, in the meanwhile, events had overtaken diplomacy.

The drama in Dhaka

Niazi had sought help, particularly Chinese aid, pledged by his superiors in Rawalpindi. He received encouragement and reassurances, but no material support. At 11am on 7 December, he was summoned by Governor Malik for a briefing. After Niazi briefed the Governor, his Military Adviser General Farman Ali and Chief Secretary Muzaffar Husain, Malik ordered the drafting of a message to Yahya Khan:

From Governor East Pakistan For President of Pakistan (.) It is imperative that correct situation in East Pakistan is brought to your notice (.) I discussed with Gen. Niazi who tells me that troops are fighting heroically but against heavy odds without adequate artillery and air support (.) Rebels continue cutting their rear and losses in equipment and men are heavy and cannot be replaced (.) The front in Eastern and Western sectors has collapsed (.) Loss of whole corridor East of Meghna river cannot be avoided (.) Jessore has already fallen which will be a terrible blow to the morale of pro-Pakistan elements (.) Civil administration ineffective as they cannot do much without communications (.) Food and other supplies running short as cannot move from Chittagong or within the Province (.) Even Dacca city will be without food after 7 days (.) Without fuel and oil there will be complete paralysis of life (.) Law and order situation in areas vacated by army pathetic as thousands of pro-Pakistan elements being butchered by rebels (.) Millions of non-Bengalis and loyal elements are awaiting death (.) No amount of lip sympathy or even material help from world powers except direct physical intervention will help (.) If any of our friends is expected to help that should have an impact within the next 48 rpt 48 hours (.) If no help is expected I beseech you to negotiate so that a civilised and peaceful transfer takes place and millions of lives are saved and untold misery avoided (.) Is it worth sacrificing so much when the end seems inevitable (.) If help is coming we will fight on whatever the consequences there may be (.) Request be kept informed.[121]

Yahya Khan's response assured 'All possible steps are in hand.' Diplomacy at the UN, 'full scale and bitter war' in the West and advice on fresh military strategy were listed. The need for 'strongest measures' in food rationing and essential supplies was stressed. Yahya Khan's closing words, 'God be with you. We are all praying'[122] exposed Pakistan's frailty before the rapidly approaching climax. By 8 December, Brahmanbaria, a nodal point in the east, had fallen; another important town, Comilla, was encircled, and an Indian column was rushing south to Chittagong. Meanwhile, Dhaka remained under intermittent but heavy aerial attacks. In Washington, Nixon accepted Kissinger's suggestion to order an aircraft carrier from Vietnamese waters to the Bay of Bengal, ostensibly to evacuate American nationals from Bangladesh.[123] Nixon also ordered all aid to India be cut off and except for already approved goods worth $124 million, all aid was stopped. Kissinger noted that America was 'in a position where a Soviet stooge, supported with Soviet arms, is overrunning a country that is an American ally.' The USA now had to 'prevent an Indian attack on West Pakistan.'[124] When China came up, Kissinger pointed out that Beijing not only faced a million Soviet troops along its border, 'they've just had semi–revolt in the military.' With Lin Biao's abortive coup against Mao Zedong and Zhou Enlai, Beijing was incapacitated. Next, Brezhnev wrote to Nixon proposing a ceasefire between India and Pakistan provided Pakistan agreed to negotiate with the Awami League. Nixon noted that 'the partition of Pakistan is a fact.'[125]

This recognition dawned in Dhaka, too. Indian forces had advanced from Akahura to Ashuganj on the Meghna River where retreating Pakistanis had blown up a major bridge. The local populace came forward with boats and ferries to transport the allied troops across the river. Indian forces used helicopters and paratroopers to carry out 'vertical envelopment' of Pakistani positions that rapidly became untenable. Malik telegraphed:

From Governor East Pakistan for the President (.) Military situation desperate (.) Enemy is approaching Faridpur in the West and has closed up the river Meghna in the East bypassing our troops in Comilla and Laksham (.) Chandpur has fallen to the enemy thereby closing all river routes (.) Enemy likely to be at the outskirts any day if no outside help forthcoming (.) Secretary General UN's representative in Dacca has proposed that Dacca City may be declared as an open city to save lives of civilians especially non-Bengalis (.) Am favourably inclined to accept the offer (.) Strongly recommend this be approved (.) Gen. Niazi does not agree as he considers that his orders are to fight to the last and it would amount to giving up Dacca (.) This action may result in massacre of the whole army cmm WP police and all non-locals and loyal locals (.) There are no regular troops in reserve and once the enemy has crossed the Ganges or the Meghna further resistance will be futile unless China or USA intervenes today with massive air and ground support (.) Once again urge you to consider immediate ceasefire and political settlement otherwise once Indian troops are free from East Wing in a few days even West Wing will be in jeopardy (.) Understand local population has welcomed Indian army in captured areas and are providing maximum help to them (.) Our troops are finding it impossible to withdraw and manoeuvre due to rebel activity (.) With this clear alignment sacrifice of West Pakistan is meaningless.[126]

Yahya Khan gave Malik 'my permission to take decisions on your proposals to me (.) I have and am continuing to take all measures internationally but in view of our complete isolation from each other decision about East Pakistan I leave entirely to your good sense and judgement (.) I will approve of any decision you take and I am instructing Gen. Niazi simultaneously to accept your decision and arrange things accordingly.'[127] The following day, General Farman Ali handed Malik's message to the UN envoy, Paul Mark Henry, suggesting an immediate cease-fire, 'repatriation with honour' of Pakistani armed forces and West Pakistani personnel to West Pakistan, and guaranteed safety of all personnel settled in the East since 1947—all in preparation for power being transferred to the people's elected representatives.[128] The signal was communicated via UN channels to US and Indian leaders but soon, Yahya Khan heavily revised the message, deleting any mention of repatriation of Pakistani troops and West Pakistani personnel. He wanted to 'make it clear that this is a definite proposal of ending all hostilities and the question of surrender of armed forces would not be considered and does not arise…The question of transfer of power and political solution will be tackled at National level which is being done.'[129] Meanwhile, Yahya Khan was considering establishing a civilian government with the Bengali politician Nurul Amin as prime minister and Bhutto as his deputy.

To launch a diplomatic initiative at the UN, he dispatched Bhutto to New York. Bhutto got there just as the crossed wires over Malik's message and Yahya's revision of it were being untangled by Pakistani diplomats in New York and Washington. On 11 December, Yahya Khan asked Malik not to take any further action on the messages recently exchanged between Dhaka and Islamabad on a UN-mediated ceasefire. In Washington, Kissinger told Nixon that 'somewhat at our pressure,'[130] Yahya Khan had accepted Brezhnev's 9 December formulation for an end to hostilities: an immediate cease-fire in place without withdrawal of forces, and resumption of negotiations with the Awami League where they had been broken off in March. This meant to secure the defence of West Pakistan, Yahya was accepting the loss of the East. Later, though, he changed his mind—possibly under pressure from Pakistan's other Generals—and rejected the Brezhnev proposal. The US Navy's Task Group 74, led by a nuclear-powered aircraft carrier, steamed west-ward, pausing east of the Malacca Strait while Kissinger secretly consulted Huang Hua in New York. Before that, he saw Yulie Vorontsov and mentioned President Kennedy's 1962 commitment to Ayub Khan. Kissinger told Vorontsov, 'we're moving some military forces, but it will not be visible' for a couple of days yet, 'in effect it was giving him a sort of veiled ultimatum.'[131] This was important in view of the White House's calculation of the urgency of the military time-frame: India would 'wrap up' its operations in the East after which it would need ten days to ship all the major formations from there to the West. Once these additional Indian forces joined battle, West Pakistan could last just two weeks; a cease-fire had to be imposed before that deadline.[132]

While the fate of Pakistan, especially that of residual or West Pakistan, was important, it was part of a much bigger calculus—'if the outcome of this is that Pakistan is swallowed by India, China is destroyed, defeated, humiliated by the Soviet Union, it will be a change in the world balance of power of such magnitude' which had to be prevented.[133] Although India's Defence Minister Jagjivan Ram and military leaders wished to 'liberate' parts of southern 'Azad (Pakistan-administered) Kashmir' before accepting a cease-fire resolution passed by the UN, Mrs. Gandhi herself would accept such a resolution after an Awami League administration had been installed in Dhaka. Soviet and Indian officials had been in close consultation in Delhi and Moscow and the Soviet Union was concerned that China might intervene in Pakistan's behalf. However, Mrs. Gandhi believed Beijing knew Moscow would itself press China in Xinjiang and provide air support to India and this made Chinese intervention unlikely. She sent senior envoys including the head of her Policy Planning Commission to Moscow to assure Soviet leaders that Delhi had no plans to annex any West Pakistani territory. Mrs. Gandhi believed India would emerge from the war as the region's dominant power. 'China will respect India and may even decide to improve relations with India.'[134] She thought Pakistan, on the other hand, would become a weak power suffering from so many domestic challenges that America and China would lose interest in it.

On the morning of 12 December, with TG-74 edging into the Malacca Strait *en route* to the Bay of Bengal, Moscow assured Washington that Mrs. Gandhi had pledged to the Soviet leadership that 'the Government of India has no intention to take any military action against West Pakistan.'[135] There was an opportunity now for the great powers to work out a formulation for the imminent emergence of Bangladesh without causing systemic disruption. Although fighting would continue for a few more days and none of the parties involved yet spoke about a final outcome, the apex of the international security system was assured that the Pakistani state would not be extirpated and a superpower conflagration would not follow. The scale of immediate human problems was big enough—up to 10 million Bengali refugees in India, over 600,000 non-Bengali Muslims in East Bengal (out of a total of 1.5 million) anxious to go to West Pakistan, some 50–100,000 Bengalis living in West Pakistan, almost all of whom would wish to return to Bangladesh, an undetermined number of people displaced by fighting within Bangladesh, and around 70,000 Pakistani soldiers,[136] and another 20,000 paramilitary personnel, civilian staff and their dependents stranded in Bangladesh. Solving their problems was challenge enough.

By now, Indian and Bangladeshi 'allied forces' had surrounded most Pakistani brigades and battalions, and cut off access to Dhaka. Indian paratroopers were moving towards the city from Tangail in the north and Narsingdi in the east. Some Indian units were already accepting the surrender of locally-deployed Pakistani units. General Sam Manekshaw, Chief of Staff, Indian Army, broadcast his first message to Pakistani commanders and troops in the East to surrender. All India Radio broadcast his message three times, with considerable effect on the defenders' morale. Intense diplomacy at the UNSC continued to draw great power efforts to bring the hostilities to an end. The USA and China came round to accepting a cease-fire in place while the Soviet Union seemed to support discussions as Indian and Bangladeshi forces rushed toward Dhaka. On 13 December, leading units of the Indian column advancing toward Dhaka from the north crossed Joydebpur and pushed toward Tongi, an industrial suburb north of the city.

Early in the afternoon on 14 December, Yahya Khan finally gave Malik and Niazi the authorisation they had sought four days earlier: 'I have done all that is humanly possible to find an acceptable solution to the problem (.) You have now reached a stage when further resistance is no longer humanly possible nor will it serve any useful purpose (.) It will only lead to further loss of life and destruction (.) You should now take all necessary measures to stop the fighting and preserve the lives of all armed forces personnel all those from West Pakistan and all loyal elements.'[137] Niazi sought the US Consul-General's help in contacting General Manekshaw. Malik, having determined that he could no longer serve a useful purpose, resigned and moved from the Governor's House to the sanctuary established by the Red Cross at Hotel Intercontinental in Dhaka.

On 15 December, Manekshaw replied to Niazi, guaranteeing the safety of Pakistani forces provided they surrendered to Indian commanders.

Permission for surrendering to the Indian commander was secured from the Pakistani COS, General Abdul Hamid Khan, and on the night of 15–16 December, classified military and government documents, code books, treasury cheques and Pakistani currency were burnt by Pakistani officers and officials. On 16 December, the Chief of Staff, Eastern Command, Indian Army, Major General J.F.R Jacob, arrived in Dhaka to discuss the details of the surrender. The team was briefed at the headquarters of the Pakistani Eastern Command at Dhaka Cantonment. Later, as TG74 led by the *USS Enterprise* sailed from the Indian Ocean into the Bay of Bengal,[138] a fleet of Indian military aircraft brought Lt. General Jagjit Singh Aurora, Commander, Eastern Command of the Indian army, and his entourage, to Dhaka. Early in the evening, as *Mukti Bahini* fighters began fiery and noisy victory celebrations, a teary-eyed General Niazi signed the instrument of surrender and handed East Bengal over to his Indian counterpart. East Pakistan was transformed, by third party military intervention supporting a secessionist campaign, into the People's Republic of Bangladesh. Few senior Bangladeshi officials were on hand to witness, far less to participate in, this event.

Return of the Bangabandhu

Early in the afternoon of 16 December, Indian officials announced a unilateral ceasefire in the West, to be effective the following day. Delhi demanded an immediate response from Islamabad accepting this offer. After intense American pressure, Yahya Khan eventually reciprocated hours before the Indian offer was to expire. In Pakistan there now began a period of cathartic soul-searching. The tensions were reflected in the army itself. Several brigade commanders in the 6th Armoured Division, apparently in consultation with their fellows elsewhere, demanded the military leadership's resignation. The following day, a gathering of army officers in the Rawalpindi garrison close to the capital resulted in an unprecedented challenge to the command of Yahya Khan and his closest aides.[139] Yahya Khan asked the Deputy Prime Minister-designate, Z.A. Bhutto, to return to Pakistan immediately and, having taken the decision on 19 December to resign, handed the presidency and the office of the Chief Martial Law Administrator to Bhutto the following day.[140] Bhutto stopped the promulgation of Pakistan's third, Yahya-drafted, constitution, promising to embark on writing a new one 'soonest.'[141] He appointed Lt.

General Gul Hassan Khan the new army commander-in-chief, and retired several Yahya aides to replace them with younger men. He told his angry and despondent compatriots that 'East Pakistan is an insepa-rable and indissolvable (sic) part of Pakistan,' but he was willing to engage East Pakistani leaders in negotiations over a 'loose arrangement' on the condition that Indian forces must first 'vacate my motherland…and East Pakistan.'[142] Some Pakistanis, outraged by the turn of events, rioted, while others assaulted soldiers outside barracks.

In Dhaka, meanwhile, incipient factional differences within Tajuddin's cabinet, and across the wider polity, threatened to burst forth and desta-bilise the new country. Things became so 'desperate' that on 2 January 1972, Foreign Minister Abdus Samad Azad, who had replaced Khanda-kar Moshtaque Ahmed, saw the US *Chargé d'Affaires* and sought Ameri-can help in pressing Bhutto to release Mujib.[143] Just days later, Bhutto moved Mujib from death row in a Pakistani prison, placed him under house arrest, then held a secret meeting with him, suggesting that he, Bhutto, as President of Pakistan, was granting East Pakistan the auton-omy Mujib had struggled for. In custody, Mujib had been kept *incom-municado*, had had no access to the news media and probably was unaware of the dramatic and bloody changes that had swept his country. The two men appeared to have agreed to maintain some 'links' before Bhutto sent Mujib and his constitutional adviser, Kamal Hossain, on a PIA jet to London, where he arrived in the morning on 8 January 1972.[144] Follow-ing rounds of deferential briefing by Bangladeshi, Indian and British officials, Mujib left for Dhaka via Delhi. He was accorded a hero's wel-come in both. His reception broke protocol boundaries, underscoring the admiration in which he was held. The president and prime minister of India led the reception line at Delhi's Palam airport on 10 January. With them stood the members of the Indian cabinet, service chiefs, the diplo-matic corps and assorted other VIPs. Thousands of other Indians thronged patiently beyond the security perimeter for a glimpse of the Bengali leader.

The reception in Dhaka, where he arrived a few hours later, was even more tumultuously worshipful. Hundreds of thousands of Bangladeshis, in a demonstration of love, affection and admiration, and perhaps curios-ity, crowded the airport, the streets of the city and the *Suhrawardy Udyan* grounds where Mujib had stirred the nation's spirits into rebellious frenzy on 7 March 1971 and where he spoke again on his return. The response from a crowd grateful that their leader, *Bangabandhu*, had returned, suggested Mujib could have asked his emotional compatriots for virtually anything, and got it. And he would have a lot to ask. Seventy-five million Bangladeshis lived in '53,000 sq. miles (of)... waterlogged lowland of floodplains and delta formations' and faced 'difficulties of staggering dimensions—a huge population, widespread poverty, inadequate food production, serious war damage, uncertain trade prospects, internal dissension, and a none too competent bureaucracy saddled with major new responsibilities.' Observers could be forgiven for suggesting that Bangladesh's 'prospects are hopeless.'[145] The civil war had left deep scars across society—very large numbers of people had been killed, injured, dispossessed, evicted, brutalised and forced into subhuman subsistence.[146] The survivors expected things to fast improve.

At the heart of the Mujib administration's power-centre stood Mujib himself. Two days after returning to Dhaka, relying on a close circle of trusted aides, he handed over the presidency to Justice Abu Sayeed Chowdhury, a loyal ally, appointed Tajuddin Ahmed the finance minister and himself took over as prime minister. He was thus not only the father of the nation and president of the ruling party, he was also the country's chief executive. Taking virtually total charge of the devastated land, with few assets other than a charismatic command over the populace, he left himself open to criticism whenever his administration failed to deliver. As a backstop, Mujib cultivated relations with the two countries that had extended most support to the Bangladeshi enterprise—India and the Soviet Union. Mujib traveled to India on 6 February on his first state visit. His discussions with Mrs. Gandhi laid the foundations of bilateral relations encompassing diplomatic, economic and security parameters. Bangladesh faced many challenges and needed urgent assistance. India would provide much of this aid as the proximate patron, just as it had to the country's independence campaign. The two neighbours would soon formalise their allied status in a Treaty of Peace, Friendship and Cooperation on the template of the August 1971 Indo-Soviet Treaty.

To ensure this was not seen as a satellite's submission to the regional hegemon, Mujib first asked Gandhi to withdraw Indian forces. This was done on 17 March.[147] Two days later, Mrs. Gandhi, on the first state visit by a foreign leader to Bangladesh, signed a twenty-five-year treaty binding the security of the two states. The Treaty would strengthen the hands of those demanding close Indo-Bangladeshi relations and outraged those who saw this as a symbol of the Awami League's servility to India, and a hegemonic tool with which Delhi would defend its protectorate from legitimate democratic opposition.[148] The assurance of Indian strategic support boosted Mujib's domestic independence, reducing the national military's potential role, a source of much concern. With security assured and friendship secured, Mujib traveled to Moscow on 1 March to thank Bangladesh's superpower patrons and underscore Dhaka's position within the Indo-Soviet orbit. Nonetheless, in early April, having consulted Islamabad and London, Nixon wrote to Mujib extending recognition to the People's Republic of Bangladesh.[149] Having lost the tactical round to Moscow and Delhi, Washington now sought to repair the damage:

In our relations with Bangladesh and with other countries of South Asia we seek no special advantage or position of influence in political, economic or military sense. At the same time we will pursue policy of encouraging restraint among outside powers in the subcontinent, with no great power seeking dominant influence. We believe this policy is in the interest of all countries of South Asia. In this context we fully respect Bangladesh's desire to play a neutral and non-aligned role in international affairs. For our part we will take no action that would abridge BD neutrality and non-alignment.[150]

Given the consequences of Washington's pro-Pakistan 'tilt' during the war, and the support Delhi and Moscow had given the Bangladesh movement, US emphasis on Dhaka's 'neutrality and non-alignment' acknowledged the limits of US options. However, it also reflected a determination to ensure Dhaka's policy formulation was not just rhetoric and that Bangladesh would be held to its pledge. Although on the fringes of the Cold War's bipolar confrontation, Bangladesh would continue to receive the attention of patrons whose interests widely diverged. Given the state's severe weaknesses, as the external overlaid itself on the domestic, local and regional cleavages could only deepen.

With the Pakistani infrastructure violently overturned, the writ of the new state was modest. Indian civil servants, administrators and soldiers established a framework which was gradually supplanted with a patchy Bangladeshi successor. The destruction of the constabulary, magistracy and judiciary during the civil war left Bangladesh in turmoil. In addition to the regular forces of the *Mukti Bahini*, 'some 30,000 well-armed guerrillas' had infiltrated from India.[151] The war left an estimated 350,000 weapons of various calibres and massive quantities of ammunition and explosives—some Indian supplied, some captured from Pakistani forces—in private hands.[152] Despite the government's efforts including televised ceremonies showing former guerrillas surrendering token arsenals to Mujib, large illegal stockpiles remained outside official control. By the end of 1972, officials estimated around 100,000 such arms were still unaccounted for.[153] No wonder that armed violence and banditry flourished across Bangladesh. There was some progress: a new police force was established with about 30,000 personnel—to eventually number 75,000. However, the training and equipment of the force left much to be desired. The regular army numbered 20,000 men. Another 20,000 men were inducted into paramilitary units. The authorities initially permitted several semi-official militias to operate, with mixed outcomes.[154] The government awaited the eventual repatriation of some 24–28,000 service personnel locked up in Pakistani 'concentration camps,' expected to be integrated into the national military on their return.

If law and order posed daily challenges, economic prospects were even bleaker. The UN Relief Operation Dhaka (UNROD), initially handling most food relief and related activities, had prevented what many believed was an inevitable famine. The war cost the country a quarter of its truck fleet; and nearly a year after independence, the railway system was working at 40 per cent of its pre-war capacity. Much of the tracks, rolling- and coaching stocks, bridges and signaling equipment remained unserviceable.[155] The sector was especially disrupted by the death, imprisonment and flight of *Bihari* railway personnel during and after the war. In the wider economy, smuggling across the now open Indian-Bangladeshi borders, hoarding, black-marketing and profiteering in a crisis economy heightened the plight of most citizens who were left without a steady income. Non-Bengali owners and managers had fled Bangladesh and the country's few industrial, commercial, banking, shipping, and processing units had either been shut down damaged, or destroyed. The new government took over all these organisations, nationalised others and handed them over to inexperienced civil servants or individuals whose qualification was loyalty. A bureaucratic-political elite was created by transferring assets rather than by generating wealth. Before independence, manufacturing contributed six per cent of the GDP; modern sectors including industry made up 15 per cent. Agriculture, largely subsistence in nature, contributed more than two-thirds of GDP.[156] There was, therefore, little reinvestable surplus. In 1970, the GDP stood at $4.5 billion; in 1972, it was 'somewhat smaller'.[157] Bangladesh's jute, timber products, tea, leather and a few other exports had given it a trade surplus until the mid-1960s; then, rising imports, mainly foodgrains, made it an aid-dependent economy. Since independence and by August 1972, Dhaka received aid commitments of over $900 million—for immediate relief and rehabilitation and medium-term reconstruction.[158] It was a challenge to ensure the funds were utilised for the intended purpose and at the speed necessary to arrest the spiral of deprivation, popular frustration turning to anger and violence, and deepening criminal and subversive threats.

The destruction of agricultural stocks, poor harvests and increasing demand—with refugees returning from India and the internally displaced to their homes—together rendered the fragile situation even more delicate. A comparative study[159] looked thus:

Table 2.1: Bangladesh's food shortages (all in 'thousands of metric tons)

Crop year (ending 30 June)	Rice harvest	Food grain import		
		Wheat	Rice	Total
1970	12,010	1,045	502	1,547
1971	11,140	898	381	1,279
1972 (preliminary)	9,970	1,350	500	1,850

The government was trying to procure rice domestically and from international markets. A fall in global cereal stocks, drought in some districts, and 'considerable smuggling of food from certain areas of Bangladesh into India in the summer of 1972' encouraged by price differentials and an open border meant that a UN study released in late 1972 predicted that in 1973, Bangladesh would need to import 2.5 million tons of grains to meet its basic demands—the same volume as in 1972.[160] There was no assurance that this demand would be met. Although top officials appeared to be 'generally well-trained and competent,' those from the middle- and lower-ranks were not. 'Considerable meddling by Awami League notables in administrative matters,' and the control over some areas by guerrilla commanders meant the administration 'suffered from widespread incompetence, inefficiency, and corruption.' Emergency relief distribution, post-war reconstruction and large-scale project management showed some results 'due to the direct activity of foreign governments and personnel.'[161] Similar challenges afflicted other aspects of freedom.

The delicacy of civil-military relations partly arose from the fact that while Tajuddin Ahmed's 'government-in-exile' had provided a veneer of political leadership to the resistance, the *Mukti Bahini* and its allied militias—with all enrolled personnel adding up to between 125,000 and 175,000 fighters[162]—fought under the commander of their own *Bahini* (Force) or Sector, with little visible influence of the Calcutta-based Awami League leaders. The latter's Indian patrons also established a separate force with selected recruits from among ardent Awami League cadres under leaders such as Mujib's trusted nephew, Sheikh Fazlul Haq Moni. This force was called the Bangladesh Liberation Force (BLF) or *Mujib Bahini*. Although set up as an Awami League militia, *Mujib Bahini* trained directly under Indian officers; *Mukti Bahini* commanders exercised no control over its personnel or activities. The two *Bahinis* occasionally clashed.[163]

After Tajuddin's cabinet returned to Dhaka in late December 1971 and took over from Indian commanders and civil servants, he set up Central Board of National Militia with the Prime Minister as chairman. The Board would have overseen a national militia which would absorb all Freedom Fighters. Mujib, while sharing Tajuddin's concerns, changed the direction of Bangladesh's civil-military relations. Early in April 1972, General Osmany, the wartime Commander-in-Chief, resigned and the post was abolished. Instead, Mujib authorised the establishment of an army, navy and air force, each with its own chief of staff. Col. Safiullah of K-Force fame became the first Chief of Army Staff (CAS). The army was authorised a strength of 50,000, about twice the current figures. Col. Ziaur Rahman was appointed Safiullah's deputy (DCAS) and Col. Khaled Mosharraf, CGS. Commodore Nurul Huq was appointed the Chief of Naval Staff (CNS) and, Group Capt. A.K. Khondker, the Chief of Air Staff (COAS). A foundation was laid for the growth of regular armed forces, but there was already trouble in the ranks.

The presence of many armed men roaming freely, and recent experience of the depredations of a civil war, fragmented the locus of authority. The BLF had around 15–20,000 fighters;[164] the left-wing NAP had around 10,000; Kader Siddiky claimed he had 16,000 armed men and 75,000 unarmed supporters.[165] Many other militias did not share their records with the authorities. The government estimated that in addition to arming BDF regulars, Delhi had issued over 140,000 arms to irregular formations.[166] Later estimates rose above 200,000.[167] Despite the presence of 150,000 Indian soldiers,[168] lawlessness was rampant. Without recovering the bulk of unauthorised weapons from the populace, the government could not hope to establish itself as the sole fount of collective violence, and did not do so. Partisan politics, with Awami League cadres being issued with automatic arms and ammunition from government stocks 'to defend themselves,' made the effort to recover illegal arms desultory and ineffective. The army was one of those organisations which noted these failings with grave disquiet.

Rumbles in the jungle

Mujib, Bangladesh's unquestioned leader, faced several simultaneous crises. At the heart of his difficulties lay the Awami League's lack of administrative skills and experience, a failure to grasp the enormity of the challenges, and the absence of an overarching vision of the kind of polity Bangladesh should be—a vision around which national consensus could coalesce. The war that dismantled Pakistan delegitimised the beliefs underpinning it, releasing new and dormant forces, but established no single, dominant idea offering an alternative framework to hold society together. Contending philosophies crystallised in the crucible of war and vied for supremacy, preventing a monocultural polity from taking form. As long as the Pakistani threat had existed, nationalist forces acquiesced in the Awami League's leadership. Once the enemy fell, divergences surfaced.[169] In the absence of mediatory institutions, traditions and practice, differences were settled violently. For the new state, this would be a framework of individual and collective behaviour. Force, the motor of the war of independence, remained a key component of state power in independent Bangladesh. However, the army was not to be its instrument.[170]

A defence budget of $34 million in 1972 gave the nascent armed forces little room for growth, but with the GNP at $3,750 million and total public expenditure of $1,029 million, even this was a burden.[171] In 1973, defence outlays would be slashed to $18 million, angering many officers. It was not so much budgetary allocations that outraged some commanders, however. Some Indian troops had taken whatever they could from the relatively well-appointed Pakistani garrisons in Bangladesh while others collected the arms and ammunition left behind by the four surrendering army divisions.[172] Major M.A. Jalil, the Sector Commander in the Khulna area, challenged Indian military's right to ship captured ordnance.

Under Indian pressure, he was detained and tried. Exonerated by the court, Jalil left the military and became the President of the formative National Socialist Party—JSD—*Jatiya Samajtantrik Dal*, a radical leftist group which, breaking off from the Awami League's student wing, challenged the Awami League's authority and sought to build a truly 'people's republic' using 'scientific socialism,' on the ruins of the petit-bourgeois state of Bangladesh.[173] Other, more respected, military commanders, too, challenged the new order. Two of them, close friends who had defected from Pakistan in 1971, stood out.

Colonels Abu Taher and M. Ziauddin, war heroes who shared a vision very different to that of the Bangladesh that emerged from East Pakistan's ashes, rose to be commanders of the army brigades in Comilla and Dhaka respectively. Having spent much of the war in the mud and blood of the frontline—Taher had lost a leg in the November 1971 battle of Kamalpur in northern Bangladesh—they rejected the class-ridden order they discerned in the military in particular and the elite-mass divide generally. Taher said the military could not afford to be a burden to this land of penurious peasants and must become a productive force. He ordered his units to grow their own victuals, organise the farmers in the villages near the garrison in cooperatives and banish the barriers dividing the troops from the populace they were to defend. Ziauddin, critical of the conduct of some officers and men after the war, ordered them to collect looted 'white goods' at a central location in the Dhaka cantonment and then lit a bonfire as a lesson in incorruptibility. This was not enough. Driven to despair at the government's failure to mitigate the poverty haunting millions of Bangladeshis, he wrote a signed article in the weekly *Holiday* in which he chastised Mujib by name. Challenging the government's dealings with Delhi, he demanded disclosure of the 'secret clauses' of the treaty with India, warning, 'We fought without him and won. And now if need be we will fight again.'[174]

Summoned by Mujib and ordered to retract his commentary or apologise, Ziauddin refused and was dismissed later in the year. Taher and other comrades who supported Ziauddin were eased out of service. Taher was given the responsibility of running a dredger unit based in Narayanganj, an industrial river-port outside Dhaka. Both men would begin a secret new career in the politics of the radical left in Bangladesh. Taher would become the clandestine commander of the JSD's armed cadre active in colleges and universities, and with sleeper cells within the army;

Ziauddin would embark on a journey of 'declassification' before becoming the senior military figure in the *Purbo Banglar Sarbohara Party* (PBSP—East Bengal Proletarian Party) led by Siraj Sikder. His armed men would operate from bases in the Madhupur forests and, when chased from there, from the CHT's sylvan uplands. Some factions would seek refuge in the *Sundarban* mangrove forests in the south-west. The JSD and the PBSP posed the most radical threats to Mujib's administration in the early 1970s.

The downturn in Mujib's popularity became apparent four months after his return when Dhaka University students, the traditional vanguard of national politics and now counting many Freedom Fighters (FF) in their ranks, rejected Mujib's student wing, the *Chhatra League* (BCL) in campus elections. These were won by the Students Union, a wing of the leftist NAP, which had split into pro-Moscow and pro-Beijing factions. Fragmentation rocked the ruling elite, too. The BCL had split into warring factions representing left-radical and centrist activists. The Awami League itself appeared close to splitting into similar factions. The Administration seemed frozen by internal disputes. Outside Dhaka, former provincial civil servants stayed at their posts but exercised little authority; district-level Awami League leaders vied with FF commanders for control. Nothing got done without approval from Dhaka. In the capital, 'even cabinet ministers are unsure of their position and are unable to give directives to their subordinates.' In both administrative and policy matters, 'all questions must be decided by Sheikh Mujib himself.'[175] The Constituent Assembly, a gathering of surviving representatives elected in 1970, simply appointed a constitution drafting committee and then adjourned its first session. Student- and labour leaders from non-Awami League groups urged Mujib to replace his administration with a 'revolutionary' regime, without offering detailed proposals.

Partly to see things for himself and partly to re-establish his authority, Mujib toured many districts in early 1972, assuring everyone he was dedicated to solving the country's myriad problems but also announcing he would not be able to 'deliver anything for three years.' He complained of 'conspirators' creating a 'crisis of confidence' and pledged to punish party cadres or government officials found to be corrupt. He then dismissed several and jailed a few. His frequent pleadings with donors also brought in, between 1 January and 30 June 1972, relief assistance worth $796.91 million. With $263.27 million, the USA was the top donor;

twenty other countries, the European Economic Community (EEC), and private donors made up the remaining \$533.64 million.[176] With UNROD's help, this aid alleviated the distress of millions of returnees and the internally displaced. This did not silence the JSD or the PBSP and other radical leftist critics of the Awami League's 'bourgeois' government, but calmed things down somewhat. While Bangladesh struggled with ideological and practical problems, Nixon sent his friend, Treasury Secretary John Connally, to South Asia. Connally saw Foreign Minister Azad in Dhaka in early July, just after Mrs. Gandhi and Bhutto had concluded their summit meeting with the 'Simla Declaration' resolving key post-Bangladesh war questions. While GOB was not represented, Delhi had closely consulted Dhaka before the summit and Azad was satisfied that Bangladeshi interests had been addressed. However, advising Connally the war had cost three million Bangladeshi lives and ten million returnees had had to be rehabilitated,[177] Azad urged him to use American 'influence with GOP to expedite the return' of the about 500,000 Bengalis detained in Pakistan, and repatriation of the *Biharis* to Pakistan. Stressing Dhaka's non-aligned stance, Azad sought US support for Bangladesh's UN entry bid.

Connally then met Mujib alone and conveyed Nixon's congratulations on swiftly restoring order to a war-torn country, 'a great tribute to the qualities of leadership.' Mujib thanked 'President Nixon and the US for his life, saying "I know that you interceded to save me and I am very grateful."'[178] Assuring Connally of his neutral and non-aligned stance, Mujib described his country's bankruptcy and dire administrative condition. Reiterating that there were 'three million people killed and ten million returnees from India', Mujib sought the urgent return of 'some 20,000 Bengali soldiers' and 500,000 Bengalis, 'many civil servants, and many business people' from Pakistan. Replying to Connally's question about Dhaka's plans to try 1,500 Pakistani POWs on war crimes charges, Mujib said, 'We must try them. They must pay for these crimes. Not all 1,500, but maybe 300, maybe 200, or maybe 100. But we must have some trials.'[179] Connally noted:

His discussions reflected an acute awareness of his problems of administration. The thrust of much of what he said, including his adamant stand on having the Bengalis in Pakistan returned to Bangladesh, was interpreted by me to mean he was desperate for the 20,000 soldiers to come back to help him form the nucleus of his army and police force in the country. His desperate need for the knowledge and the abilities of the civil servants, the professionals and business people (was evident)...The clear implication was that he needed the soldiers to build his army and the business and professional people to help him build an economy.[180]

Pakistan would not begin returning the Bengalis Mujib wanted for over a year and their ability to fulfill his hopes remained uncertain at best. Meanwhile, he led an inept and corrupt administration failing millions of victims of deprivation, criminal injustice and hopelessness.[181] Many who questioned his ability to meet the country's challenges did so violently. The pre-independence brutality of the religious right was replaced by the terror of the radical left and armed criminals. Despite the nearly insuperable difficulties, his government—with foreign help— reorganised the bureaucracy, rehabilitated nearly ten million returnees, restored much of the transport and communication system, banned 'un-Islamic activities' such as gambling, horse-racing and consumption of alcohol, nationalised 40,000 primary schools, all the banks and insurance firms abandoned by Pakistanis, and 580 industrial units left behind by non-Bengali owners, and secured recognition from a large number of countries.[182] On 16 December 1972, Mujib's parliament adopted a constitution which proclaimed Bangladesh a parliamentary republic with the following key features:

- Authority was vested in the parliament and would be exercised by a cabinet led by the prime minister; the president would act on the prime minister's advice.
- The unicameral parliament comprised three hundred members directly elected from single territorial constituencies for five-year terms; fifteen seats were reserved for women.
- Bangladesh's principal ideology was socialism, which was said to embody nationalism, secularism, and democracy.
- The judiciary was independent but lacked the power of judicial review.
- An ombudsman would investigate complaints against the executive; the aim was to expose corruption or conduct considered detrimental to the national interest.[183]

The constitution provided the basis for parliamentary polls in March 1973. Almost as important, in November, Mujib established a Joint Rivers Commission with India, giving his country—built on the world's largest delta drained by hundreds of rivers, fifty-four of which crossed into Bangladesh from India—a forum in which the lower riparian state's riverine interests would theoretically carry the same weight as the upper riparian state's.

In the New Year, Dhaka issued a very critical statement in response to renewed US bombing of North Vietnam. Leftist students attacked several US facilities across Bangladesh. After two students were killed in police firing at the US Information Service (USIS) library in Dhaka, the police withdrew on 2 January and the students occupied the building. Renaming the library in the memory of the two 'martyrs,' the students replaced the Stars and Stripes with the flags of North Vietnam and the Viet Cong. Troubled by the government's apparent reluctance to restore 'normalcy' before polls due on 7 March, Secretary of State Rogers wrote to Mujib seeking restoration of 'this property to us.'[184] This proved effective; the police forced the students off the library and Dhaka repaired the damage done to it. Mujib sent a 'warm congratulatory message' to Nixon when a US-North Vietnam ceasefire agreement was signed. White House staff recommended the immediate grant of $30 million from existing budgetary allocations for procuring fertiliser and cotton to help revive Bangladeshi agriculture and industry. This would raise bilateral US grant aid to Bangladesh to $145 million. Kissinger held up authorisation for a fortnight.[185]

In South Asia, India and Pakistan had implemented most clauses of the Simla Agreement.[186] However, the fate of the Pakistani POWs in India, Bengalis detained in Pakistan and *Biharis* ('stranded Pakistanis') in Bangladesh remained uncertain as Dhaka insisted on trying 195 POWs for 'war-crimes' and Pakistan refused to countenance any such trial. While India and Pakistan had agreed to exchange POWs who were sick and other detainees with humanitarian concerns, Pakistan's refusal to recognise Bangladesh and continuing disagreements between the two, left the war's aftermath unresolved. Other than the state of limbo in which several hundred thousand people found themselves, strains over repayment of Pakistan's pre-Bangladesh debts, and Dhaka's demand that Pakistan's assets and liabilities be shared out between Bangladesh and the residual Pakistan caused much stress as officials from the three countries tried to thrash out a consensus from their conflicting impulses and imperatives. The lack of direct Pakistani–Bangladeshi contacts further complicated efforts to draw a line under the war.[187]

More immediately, Bangladesh's first parliamentary polls concentrated urban minds on the diverse visions vying to define the polity's nature and future direction. The pro-Moscow NAP (Muzaffar) and Communist Party of Bangladesh (CPB)—often described as the Awami League's 'B-team,' did not challenge the League's fundamental goals but stressed corruption, political repression and the law and order situation. Earlier, their criticism of Mujib following the police shooting of NAP students at the USIS had lost them popular support. Later, when they apologised to Mujib for criticising him personally, they lost credibility.[188] NAP's pro-Peking (Bhashani) faction and the similarly oriented Jatiya League focused on Indo-Bangladeshi relations, trying to exploit growing anti–Indian sentiments. The JSD, driven by both idealism and ideology, and reflecting the frustrations felt by the many FFs in its ranks, stressed 'scientific socialism', challenging the petit-bourgeois order. Apart from the JSD, no radical-leftist group contested the elections, but all the opposition parties fared badly. NAP (M) received 8 per cent of the vote, NAP (B), 5 per cent, and the JSD, 6 per cent. The Awami League received 73 per cent.[189]

Mujib's victory—the Awami League won 293 of the 300 seats—both legitimised his rule and focused popular aspirations on him. He remained immensely popular but his inability to ensure stable and affordable supply of foodgrains, especially rice, across Bangladesh, and to control law and order in Dhaka and Chittagong, confronted the country with 'unpredictable consequences'. In 1973, Dhaka needed to import 2.5 million tons of grains to maintain subsistence-level supplies for its population. By late June, Bangladesh had purchased 1.1 million tons from the world market, obtained pledges of 700,000 tons from Washington, and won assurance of another 700,000 tons from other donors. If the pledges were honoured, and effective distribution ensured, Bangladesh could meet its basic cereal needs. But to meet the biggest seasonal demand in November-December, US supplies must leave port by September 1973. However, given America's 'unusually tight' grain position, this schedule would be missed unless the White House issued exceptional instructions to the Department of Agriculture.[190] The lives of millions of Bangladeshis thus came to be tied to the efficacy of Washington's bureaucratic mechanisms.

While America was seeking ways of honouring its pledges on supplying wheat, edible oil and other victuals to Bangladesh, two army Majors visited the embassy in Dhaka with a shopping list of arms, ammunition and spare parts, especially for the ex–PAF F-86 Sabre Jets grounded since the war. It was not clear if the officers represented GOB, or military commanders or, indeed just themselves. Since there had been no 'official' approaches from a minister or a departmental Secretary, the US *Chargé d'Affaires* felt Washington should make no formal response. The embassy noted US interest in Bangladesh was purely humanitarian and that this was challenge enough. Should Washington respond positively to the inquiry, Indo-Soviet reaction would likely be adverse. GOB's own response might be volatile—it seems to have been forced to accept a squadron of Soviet MiG-21 fighters with no means of paying for these. Besides this, one might ask 'where is the threat?'[191] Who would Bangladeshi jet fighters—of Soviet or US provenance—combat? The Majors thus raised more questions than they answered. One question the US *Charge* did not mention was whether the Majors' visit indicated a breach between the military and the civilian administration, or if the Majors were being used as a cat's paw for making contact for purposes other than military procurement. After all, a longstanding US ban on military supplies to South Asia was well-known and no government would make a serious effort to lift it simply by dispatching two Majors to the local American mission.

Intrigue aside, diplomacy made some headway. In Late August, with Washington serving as a conduit between Islamabad and Dhaka,[192] India and Pakistan agreed on a triangular swap. Most Pakistani POWs and civilian detainees in India would be repatriated; terms for the release of the 195 soldiers wanted by Dhaka for war-crimes would be decided later. Bengalis living in Pakistan, including detained service personnel, and 80,000 of the approximately 300,000 Pakistanis 'stranded in Bangladesh' would be exchanged.[193] The International Committee of the Red Cross (ICRC), which had maintained some links with the detainees and provided for the 'stranded Pakistanis' at 'Geneva camps' established across Bangladesh for these communities, now arranged the exchange by land, sea and air. By September, the first POWs had returned to Pakistan; by March 1974, most of the agreed exchanges had been completed. However, more than 200,000 *Biharis* still awaited an uncertain future in Bangladesh's 'Geneva camps.'

For Mujib, that was another problem. In the face of growing opposition, especially from the radical left, he again followed the students of Dhaka University. There, the NAP (M)'s student-affiliate, the Bangladesh Students Union, allied itself to the Awami League's student front, the BCL, before the student body elections in September. Once the student wings had joined hands, Mujib established a 'United Front' combining the Awami League, the CPB, and NAP (M). Given his party's overwhelming parliamentary majority, this joining of forces suggested the legislature was not enough to legitimise Awami League rule. Radical leftists were accused of attacking AL cadres and killing many of them. The Front's leaders pledged joint action against those 'anti–socials.'[194] The second half of 1973 saw increasing challenges to the state's control, especially in the countryside. Fifty-two police stations were attacked, many of these in the Dhaka, Barisal, Kushtia and Rajshahi districts, in June-November.[195] In response, Mujib mounted a series of 'combing operations', with police and paramilitary units searching the rural strongholds of the radicals and detaining suspects who were given limited access to the judicial process. A constitutional amendment enacted in September empowered the president to declare a state of emergency if he felt 'a grave emergency exists,' and that Bangladesh was threatened by 'war or external aggression or internal disturbance.'[196] Although a state of emergency was not yet declared, officials began harassing editors and journalists critical of the government, a few being briefly jailed and one weekly temporarily shut down.

With growing anti–AL violence and charismatic war-heroes in the army having shown leftist tendencies, Mujib needed a more reliable alternative with which to counter the radical left. Members of the war-time *Mujib Bahini* and loyal party cadres were formed into the *Jatiya Rakkhi Bahini* (national defence force-JRB), dressed in olive-green fatigues similar to the Indian military's and distinct from the Bangladesh army's Khaki drill, and ensconced in secluded, well-appointed modern barracks across the country. Majors Vohra and Reddy of the Indian army recruited, trained, armed and initially directed the men. The JRB's secretiveness, the presence of Indian officers in its midst, the similarity of its uniform to the Indian military's, its relatively opulent bases, and a flaunting of new arms and equipment created suspicions in some military minds that the JRB was an instrument of Delhi's control and a threat to national sovereignty and the army's position.[197] While the military coped with these anxieties, the arrival of the 28,000 servicemen from Pakistan virtually doubled its ranks overnight. The returnees added to the army's skills-set but also, with institutional divisions put in place by the government on the advice of the military's FF commanders, ensured the force was divided right down the middle and focused on internal competition.[198]

Mujib, fighting many fires almost single-handedly, balanced the needs of diplomacy with domestic crisis-management. He went on state visits to Yugoslavia and Japan, attended a Commonwealth summit in Ottawa and a NAM conference in Algiers. During the Arab-Israeli War, he supported the Arabs, sending a medical mission to help, and secured the recognition of a number of Muslim states. He attracted substantial aid from both the East and West, preventing a long-predicted famine. Although more than a hundred countries recognised Bangladesh, the refusal of Pakistan and China to do so kept Dhaka out of the UN. At home, disadvantaged groups, especially wage-labourers, led by radical students and activists, mounted a series of attacks on party and state apparatus, but not enough to force drastic changes. However, Mujib did seek to widen his support base and build consensus against the radical left. On 29 November, he released nearly 33,000 men, mostly activists of the religious right, held as 'detained collaborators' since the Pakistani surrender.[199] A general amnesty applied to all pro-Pakistani elements except for those facing specific criminal charges. By the end of 1973, threats from the left had forced Mujib to move to the centre, seeking national reconciliation, and bringing the right in from the political wilderness. He initiated a trend that would shape Bangladesh.

Horsemen of the Apocalypse

The centrist drift gained momentum in early 1974 when the Organisation of the Islamic Conference (OIC), led by Egypt, initiated reconciliation between Dhaka and Islamabad prior to the OIC's summit in Lahore, Pakistan. With quiet US backing,[200] OIC ministerial teams shuttling back and forth between the two capitals managed to work out a consensus by persuading Mujib not to try 195 Pakistani soldiers on war-crimes charges. This ended Pakistani objections to recognising Bangladesh. On 9 April, the Indian and Bangladeshi foreign ministers, Swaran Singh and Kamal Hossain, were joined by Aziz Ahmed, Pakistan's Minister of State for Defence and Foreign Affairs, in Delhi. They signed a tripartite agreement that finally ended the post-war imbroglio, with all parties acknowledging the outcome of Bangladesh's independence. Mujib flew to Lahore to attend the OIC summit. Later, Bhutto paid a visit to Dhaka. The crowds gathered to see him grew so large and unruly that the JRB forcefully dispersed them. Two flamboyant, charismatic and mercurial leaders, central to the South Asian drama, thus came together as the dust settled over the fall-out from their determined pursuit of particular and contrary interests. Both stressed 'democracy' and 'socialism' as key political values but pursued policies that appeared violently to contradict these stated objectives.

The challenges facing Bangladesh appeared starker. Smuggling, hoarding, profiteering, and black-marketing apparently contributed to rising food prices in March. This presented such a threat to social peace that in early April, a coalition against Mujib formed. Disillusioned with the level of corruption, declining production, price rises and the emergence of an Awami League-based *nouveau riche* class, six left-of-centre parties established a United Front with Bhashani as the president.[201] It demanded repeal of the Special Powers Act—which allowed the state to detain citizens indefinitely without preferring charges—and the Rakkhi Bahini Act, the introduction of a country-wide rationing system, and the eradication of corruption, smuggling and profiteering.[202] The Front threatened to mount a national campaign in June 1974 unless its demands were met. This threat was easily countered; the government detained several leaders and placed Bhashani under house arrest. However, the complaints could not be brushed aside.

Later in April, Mujib deployed the military in 'Operation Silver Lining' along the border to both curb smuggling and retrieve illegally held firearms. Smuggling, a function of supply-demand dynamics and price differentials across contrived borders, was difficult to control at the best of times. After the war, the two governments had opened the Indo-Bangladesh border to free trade in 'essential items' for those living within 16 kilometres on either side to ease their plight.[203] This effectively legitimised smuggling—defined as trans-border transfer of goods without revenue accrual to either government. The army, given local control over some police and BDR units but not the JRB, established camps across the country, built intelligence networks, set up border patrols, started detaining suspects, and recovering goods being smuggled and ordnance held illegally. Many local Awami League leaders and activists were rounded up, questioned—sometimes harshly—and then handed over to the police for legal processes. In many cases, despite apparently unimpeachable evidence of culpability, those detained were released by the police on instructions from senior party officials.[204] This outcome of the exercise deepened the gulf between the Awami League and the soldiery. Several officers, accused of breaking the law in their treatment of detainees including Awami League members—were either dismissed from service or prematurely retired. In many areas, the army was ordered back to the barracks before what soldiers considered the completion of their mission.

Things were not helped by a rapid deterioration of economic circumstances across rural Bangladesh, from which the majority of soldiers had been recruited. By early 1974, food grain stocks had fallen to 150,000 tons, forcing a drastic reduction in the public food distribution system which, in turn, 'led to a collapse of confidence in the government's ability to stabilise the price situation.'[205] Wholesalers refused to release their stocks and the market offers shrank even further. As prices of rice, wheat, salt and chilli—essential elements of the subsistence diet—spiked and continued to rise,[206] the press started reporting food scarcity. Smuggling across the 'open' border was popularly blamed for causing much of this.[207] Although officials denied the 'open border' was a problem, in May Mujib visited Delhi where Mrs. Gandhi and he signed a border agreement which allowed the two governments to delineate and demarcate the international boundary between their two countries, establish BOPs and check-points along it, and deploy border security forces—the BSF and the BDR—to guard it against unauthorised crossing.

In July, the monsoons brought very heavy rains and with all three major river systems—the *Ganges/Padma, Brahmaputra/Jamuna*, and the *Meghna/Kushiara*—in spate, much of the delta was flooded. With the summer crop destroyed in the field, transportation made more difficult, and stocks low, prices shot up again. The government made it compulsory for all farmers to sell their rice to 'procurement' agencies 'according to a graduated scale' and the movement of rice from surplus areas was prohibited in order to ease procurement; but total yield in 1974 was barely 130,000 tons.[208] Committees set up to help the process proved ineffective. Expectations of a shortfall in the next harvest and compulsory official purchases aggravated fears 'of future shortages,' and encouraged hoarding. In the absence of 'a high degree of public confidence in the government,'[209] Mujib failed to persuade traders and hoarders to release their stocks. Flood damage, low stocks, hoarding perhaps compounded by some smuggling, weak administrative and distributive mechanisms, and party-political corruption brought millions of Bangladeshis, especially wage-labourers dependent on daily wages, to the brink of starvation. The global environment imposed additional burdens which proved insurmountable. Both the Soviet Union and China had bought large quantities of grains and the USA had had a 'disappointing corn crop,' which strained its stocks.[210]

Starting in mid-1973, Dhaka had gradually reduced its request for US food aid from 300,000 tons to 220,000 tons.[211] But in late May 1974, with rice prices steadily rising, Washington informed Dhaka that Bangladesh's export of four million jute bags to Cuba for $5 million legally barred it from receiving any American food assistance. Only the president could waive the ban with a certificate that such aid was in US national interest. In July, GOB provided written assurances that the deal with Cuba, made in ignorance of US law, would not be repeated. However, until the last bags had been shipped out of Bangladesh in October, Washington could not release fresh food aid.[212] In late September, Mujib visited the USA. By the time Kissinger called on him in Washington on 30 September, America had committed 150,000 tons of grains to Dhaka for October-December 1974, and Kissinger promised to add another 100,000 tons before Mujib saw President Ford the next day.[213] In this meeting, Mujib laid out Bangladesh's difficulties flowing from the 'oil shock' and the famine ravaging his country. Ford confirmed America would provide 250,000 tons of grain in the last quarter of 1974.

However, by the time this bounty arrived in Bangladesh, the famine had peaked. In October, 3.3 million Bangladeshis received daily meals of cooked food from 5,283 government-run 'gruel kitchens.' As of 2 November, 4.2 million people were receiving such meals from 5,757 kitchens. At the famine's height, nearly 6,000 kitchens served daily meals to 4.35 million people.[214] With the winter crop harvested and foreign aid arriving, the pressure eased and by the end of November 1974, most 'gruel kitchens' had been closed. However, food prices went up again in early 1975 as did the number of unclaimed bodies in the streets of Dhaka.[215] Estimates of famine deaths varied widely. The Minister for Food, Relief and Rehabilitation told parliament that as of 22 November, 27,500 people had starved to death. A UN estimate suggested that in one of the three worst-affected districts, '80,000 to 100,000 persons died of starvation and malnutrition in 2–3 months.'[216] Most observers agreed that in 1974, 30,000–100,000 rural landless poor adults starved to death; if the number of children and the elderly who succumbed to the same causes in this period were added, the toll would be much higher.[217] Although there would be no consensus on how many people had starved to death, the famine shook Bangladesh up almost as profoundly as had the war. The loss of innocence was now complete.

While open opposition to Mujib was rare, covert violence against his party grew. In 1973–74, 3,000–4,000 Awami Leaguers, including several MPs, were killed.[218] Many more had been attacked. His aides demanded protective measures. In late December, Mujib proclaimed a 'state of emergency,' suspending fundamental rights, subordinating the judiciary to the executive, i.e. himself, and tabled a constitutional amendment which was quickly passed with little debate. This Fourth Amendment laid the foundation of a one-party state, giving Mujib, as the Chairman of the future 'National Party' and President of the Republic, absolute power, leaving no scope for any legal opposition.[219] Parliamentary democracy gave way to presidential authoritarianism as the legislature became an advisory body. On 26 January 1975, Mujib assumed executive presidency in what he called the 'second revolution.' He shuffled his cabinet of acolytes, promoting Home Minister Muhammad Mansur Ali to prime minister, but nobody had any doubts about where the authority lay. As power was further concentrated in Mujib's hands, he deployed the army to the CHT where the radical left-wing PBSP had sought refuge after being chased out of northern forests. The army's *Operation Dragon Drive* was designed to comb the forested hills in a 'hammer and anvil' exercise, forcing party leader Siraj Sikder and military commander Col. Ziauddin into a dragnet. Sikder, having escaped the soldiers in the hills, was caught by intelligence agents in Chittagong town. Ziauddin and other PBSP leaders escaped.[220] Sikder, brought before Mujib and ordered to recant, refused. He died in custody, allegedly 'shot while trying to escape' although few found this explanation credible.[221] The PBSP was marginalised as a threat to the regime, but new threats had emerged.

By late 1974, the administration's failings had become so apparent and the consequences so dire that rumours of conspiracies and coups ran rife in Dhaka. Evidence exists of at least two sets of plots running in parallel, and possibly converging in mid-1975. In November 1974, a group of Bangladeshis contacted the US embassy to broach the need for bringing about changes to the country's leadership. A series of informal meetings with US diplomats continued until January 1975 when the embassy decided to break off all contact with these men. While there was no evidence of US complicity in the plot, there clearly was foreknowledge.[222] The parallel plot was by disgruntled military officers, whose discovery of

Awami League malfeasance during the various operations 'in aid of civil power,' compounded by post-famine disgust, the JRB's ill-concealed brutality toward all dissidence, and a steady concentration of power in Mujib's hands created a context in which the plotters, all Majors, found sympathy but no support among senior commanders. The chief plotter, Major Syed Farook Rahman, second-in-Command of the Bengal Lancers, the Bangladesh army's solitary armoured regiment, sought the leadership of Major General Ziaur Rahman, Deputy CAS, on 20 March 1975. Zia declined but did not urge the Major to desist, nor did he bring the force of his command to bear on the conspirators. He, too, had foreknowledge.[223] By then, Washington had informed Mujib about the plots against him without naming names, but 'he brushed it off, scoffed at it, said nobody would do a thing like that to him.'[224]

The imminent transformation of the 'People's Republic' into a single-party monolith may have given Mujib the confidence he expressed to his American friends. The constitution authorised a 'National Party', and Mujib planned to merge the Awami League, its youth, labour and farmers wings with sympathetic groups and call it the Bangladesh Krishak Sramik Awami League (Bangladesh peasants', workers', Awami League, BKSAL). This would be the only legal political party in the new dispensation. Although no formal order was issued, it became clear that civil servants, professionals including journalists, and even soldiers would be expected to sign up if they wanted their careers to progress.[225] Radical leftists were prominent hold-outs. Ignoring the 'emergency,' the JSD, formally underground, held a massive anti–government rally in the capital on 17 March and then, in accordance with a secret understanding with Mujib,[226] marched to Home Minister Mansur Ali's residence and attacked it. The fact that an anti–Mujib rally in the capital attracted large crowds suggested Mujib's magnetism was on the wane. Nine days later, on the anniversary of the country's declaration of independence, Mujib outlined the four elements of the 'second revolution' to be realised through BKSAL's establishment—first, 'elimination of corrupt people'; second, increased agricultural and industrial production; third, population control through family planning; and finally, 'our national unity.'[227] At the time of the passage of the Fourth Amendment, he had told parliament BKSAL was aimed at realising the four state principles—nationalism, democracy, socialism and secularism.

In early June, Mujib formally launched BKSAL, taking charge of the country's destiny with no recourse to redress or alternatives open to his

compatriots. The new system was built on parallel political and administrative strands with Mujib heading both as Party Chairman and President. On the political side, he chaired a fifteen-member Executive
Committee filled with old party allies. The tier below was a 115–member
Central Committee. Under this were five committees with 21–32 members each leading BKSAL's labour, students, youth, peasants and women's
wings. Mujib's powerful nephew Sheikh Fazlul Huq Moni was a member
of the Executive Committee. His eldest son, Kamal, was a key leader of
the youth committee. Administratively, Mujib divided Bangladesh into
sixty-one districts and appointed a governor to administer each under his
direct command. They would control the activities of all security, paramilitary and military units stationed in their districts and collaborate with
respective BKSAL District Secretaries. As a result, the country's political
and executive edifice would be fused into a BKSAL framework loyal and
accountable to Mujib alone. The new dispensation would take effect on
1 September 1975.

Mujib was to deliver an important speech at the Dhaka University
convocation, setting out his vision of Bangladesh's future, on the morning
of 15 August. All national figures including the sixty-one Governors-
designate had been invited to attend. Apart from the historical-political
import of the address, there was a sentimental element to it, too. After
the Partition, Mujib had left Calcutta and taken admission in the Dhaka
University, but continued political activism consumed his energies. After
organising protests on behalf of a junior employee who had aired grievances against the University management, he was thrown out of the institution without completing his formal higher education. Now, almost
three decades on, as the *ex–officio* Chancellor, he would be presiding over
the graduation of students who had. Just hours before making that historic speech, very early in the morning, Mujib was killed in a coup executed by a number of junior and recently retired army officers led by
Major Syed Farook Rahman. With him was his friend and brother-in-
law, Major Khandaker Abdur Rashid, Commanding Officer, 2nd Field
Regiment, Artillery. Several hundred soldiers from their two units, joined
by a rag-tag band of other soldiers loyal to their retired colleagues,
attacked Mujib who was killed at home along with his family except his
two daughters, then travelling abroad. The 'Killer Majors' also attacked
Mujib's nephew, Sheikh Moni, and Mujib's powerful brother-in-law and
party colleague, Abdur Rab Serniabat. The latter and many members of

their families too died that dawn. By the time the sun rose over Dhaka, *Bangabandhu* Sheikh Mujibur Rahman and his closest allies had either been killed or rendered inoperative. Mujib's Second Revolution had led to an unheralded, sanguinary, third.[228]

3

IN THE VALKYRIES' SHADOW

1975–1990

Abstract: A period of violent uncertainty overtook Bangladesh after Sheikh Mujibur Rahman's assassination. The army Majors leading the putsch put up an Awami League leader, Khandakar Mushtaq Ahmed, as the new president. He detained several of his senior colleagues but the remaining Awami League legislators fell in line, endorsing the new dispensation. Mushtaq replaced the Chief of the Army Staff with a war-hero, General Ziaur Rahman, who focused on absorbing Mujib's loyal militia, the JRB, into the army, and expanding the armed forces for an era of martial eminence. The 'Killer Majors,' however, stayed beyond the chain of command, keeping their tanks and guns deployed across the capital. Disputes between Zia, who did not force their return to the garrison, and Chief of the General Staff, Khaled Musharraf, who insisted they come back, triggered a counter-coup. Musharraf deposed the president, arrested the CAS and assumed command. Zia's radical left-wing friend, Colonel Abu Taher, activated secret cells within the army, and freed Zia. In the violence that followed, several officers, including Musharraf, were killed. A wave of rebellions and mutinies shook the military.

Zia assumed command of the martial law administration and then, the presidency. Using force against Awami League supporters who attacked Bangladeshi border towns from sanctuaries in India, and montagnard autonomists in the Chittagong Hill Tracts also aided by Delhi, Zia built a conservative coalition of entrepreneurs, professionals, and moderate leftist and right-wing politicians. This eventually emerged as the Bangladesh Nationalist Party, the vehicle for his political ambitions. Using religious iconography and creating a 'Bangladeshi' nationalist framework distinct from the 'Bengali' symbolism used by the Awami League, Zia erected a new ideational superstructure. Directing Bangladesh away from a statist economy and pro-Indo-Soviet diplomacy to business-friendly policies and an orientation towards the West, China and Muslim states, he alienated sections of nationalists within the military. A group of army officers killed him in May 1981.

A brief interregnum dominated by the BNP's civilian leaders demonstrated the fragility of Bangladesh's polity. Factional feuds, alleged corruption and apparent inefficiency led to Zia's military successor, General H.M. Ershad, taking over in 1982. Despite a nuanced approach to politics and an enforced stability bringing some economic benefits, Ershad never gained popular legitimacy, but not for a lack of effort. He used the template Zia had left behind—promoting himself from Chief Martial Law Administrator to President, then negotiating with politicians from across the spectrum, fashioning a party-political platform and being elected as head of state. But his Jatiya Party failed to establish the organisational weight of either the Awami League, now led by Mujib's daughter Hasina, or the BNP, under the leadership of Khaleda, Zia's widow.

Ershad secured sympathy from the OECD and Arab donor community during periods of natural calamity—cyclonic storms and devastating floods wreaking particular havoc. But at home, his rule united Hasina and Zia with sundry critics and a sustained campaign dogged his administration right to the end. Manipulation of differences kept his rivals at bay for nine years. Then, the army withdrew its support. Ershad promptly resigned. An ingenious constitutional innovation then restored a democratically elected government.

The cavalry in a turkey shoot

Sheikh Mujibur Rahman was killed in a coup executed by two Majors commanding the 1st Bengal Lancers, Bangladesh Army's only armoured unit, and 2nd Field Artillery Regiment, their men and machines, and another dozen or so officers, several of them friends cashiered by Mujib in recent years. The latter brought along troops loyal to them joining in from battalions whose commanding officers (COs) had no idea where their defecting troops, or the arms, ammunition and vehicles they commandeered, were. Majors Farook and Rashid, as the two men came to be called, had failed to secure the support of the Generals at the Army

Headquarters (AHQ) but, aware of their own political vulnerability, had linked up, on 2 August, 1975, with Khandakar Mushtaq Ahmed, Mujib's foreign trade minister and leader of the Awami League's conservative faction.[1] A convergence of factional interests of the League's right-wing, army officers outraged by Mujib's failings, and conservative global forces anxious to prevent the success of what many saw as an Indo-Soviet client-state was widely noted,[2] but factual errors[3] in some accounts raise questions about the validity of analyses offered by these authors.

Most, however, agree that the root of the anti–Mujib coup lay in the particular history of the formation of the Bangladesh Forces (BDF). The war of independence, variegated in intensity and structure, shaped the national military that emerged in 1972. The irrational events of the civil war had forced Bengali soldiers to look at their land and themselves in a new light. The imperative of self-preservation transferred loyalty from the fratricidal Pakistani state to the imagined Bangladeshi one. Revolt required not just the rejection of all earlier beliefs but their replacement with opposite ones. Cathartic trauma, compressed within the last week of March 1971, catalysed the transformation of loyal Pakistanis into rebellious Bengali nationalists. The events of 1969–70 and Islamabad's post-election intransigence had created grounds for disaffection but most Bengali soldiers did not challenge Pakistani authority until the attacks on 25 March underscored an existential threat facing them.

Apolitical professionalism had persuaded some personnel to see the Pakistani crackdown as tragic but understandable security overkill, given Pakistan's praetorian urge of self-preservation. The military mind is geared to restoring certitude in an environment in flux. Rigid structures, hierarchical authority and a strict reward-and-punishment regime create a disciplined mindset that values conformity and abhors nonconformity. Soldiers are trained into team-workers loyal to authority; revolt and mutiny are not just crimes, but are irredeemably sinful.[4] So, the rejection of the Pakistani status quo demanded an enormous leap of the imagination into the realm of uncertainty. Order lost respectability as rebellious rejection of authority gained high value; violence, the trigger behind this change, became the core of a new worldview. Rebellious Bengali troops were transmogrified into personae so different that they could never again identify with their original selves or the beliefs and practices that had hitherto shaped their behaviour. Neither the fighters themselves nor their political masters grasped the import of this change.

The civil war, which blurred distinctions between combatants and non-combatants, also broke the traditional barriers between soldiers and civil society. The haphazard nature of the early resistance, and the guerrillas' reliance on the populace for goodwill in the form of food, shelter, information and recruits eroded these distinctions and those separating officers and men. Amorphous homogeneity replaced the conventional army's rigorously maintained hierarchy. The fraternity in arms was real for the students, party activists, trade unionists and peasants who joined the resistance. Guerrillas addressed officers as 'brother.' Informal camaraderie tied the freedom fighters (FFs) in powerful bonds not experienced by those who did not share the excitement and dangers of betrayal, mutilation and death peculiar to civil wars. The bonds, forged in war, outlasted it and bound FFs into an exclusive fraternity challenging the peacetime chain of command.

With barriers collapsing, FFs were exposed to diverse ideas, often very different to those nurtured in a conventional army. Political activists playing leading roles in guerrilla bands introduced theories and socio-economic concepts novel to the professional soldier. In the tumultuous exuberance and youthful innocence of nationalist rebellion, egalitarian socialist ideals impressed many guerrillas although few undertook serious study of Marxist theory and practice. A handful of commanders saw the war as a struggle of the oppressed Bengali peasantry against capitalist exploitation[5] and sought social transformation as the war's objective. The civil war also brought revolutionaries into the army. Trained to fight the status quo they had been born into and had then rejected, these men carried seeds of rebellion in the Bangladeshi armed services.[6] Two groups stood out. Several junior officers serving in the Pakistani forces in West Pakistan or elsewhere outside East Pakistan abandoned their relatively comfortable lives, most of them escaping to India in the summer of 1971 and then joining the *Mukti Bahini* as commanders or staff officers. Members of the top quartile of their classes at the Pakistan Military Academy, they apparently enjoyed substantial career prospects when they defected. Driven by a sense of being 'special,' the 'escapees' fought well. In independent Bangladesh, former Majors M.A. Manzoor, Abu Taher, and M. Ziauddin, Captains Syed Farook Rahman, Sharful Haq Dalim, Motiur Rehman and S.J. Noor, and Lieutenant Bazlul Huda, among others, would seek to reshape both the army and the country, to devastating effect.

Another significant group was a band of young, hitherto apolitical, college students from the upper strata of East Bengal's minuscule middle classes. Most joined the war motivated by a passionate nationalist ardour triggered by the searing brutality Pakistani troops unleashed on their campuses. Men of intelligence and tenacity, they too fought well and, in the summer of 1971, were selected for officers' training. Commissioned in October, many earned gallantry awards in the war's closing stages. A second batch of cadets was selected, but the Pakistanis surrendered before their training was completed. These cadets had to wait a while before being commissioned. Officers from these two batches, but especially the first, more influenced by the experience of combat than by the regimental traditions of peacetime conventional soldiering, brought to the Bangladesh army a degree of politicisation unheard of in either the Indian or the Pakistani services.[7]

The treatment the FFs received from the Awami League and its Indian patrons did not help. The gulf between the politicians leading a comfortable life in exile and guerrillas in the frontline has been noted.[8] Indian generosity toward the fighters notwithstanding, Delhi also built up alternatives like the BLF or the *Mujib Bahini* with special treatment in terms of armament, training and facilities. Their command structure left them beyond the authority of the government-in-exile and their purpose remained unclear. Indian forces, spearheading the final offensive in December 1971, exploiting the *Mukti Bahini's* preparatory success, marginalised the latter and denied the FFs the role of victors in national liberation. Indian forces occupied Pakistani garrisons, stripping them bare of *materiel* and furnishings. Forced to the margins of the victorious *finale* in their life-and-death struggle, disappointed FFs challenged the Indians on several occasions.[9] Indian troops removed all arms, ammunition, explosives, vehicles, communication gear, radars and other Pakistani military items, material that would have equipped the nascent Bangladeshi forces well. Neither the Awami League nor its Indian patrons responded to the fighters' bitter complaints.[10] Against this backdrop, the usually nationalist military mindset was confounded by the national leader Sheikh Mujibur Rahman's assertion to his own CAS, Major General K.M. Safiullah, that he needed no army and that whenever he needed military support, Indira Gandhi would provide it.[11] Rumours of secret clauses in the Indo-Bangladesh treaty providing for such 'aid' stirred military angst.[12] Delhi's direct involvement in building up the JRB, seen by many soldiers as a rival force loyal to Mujib personally, deepened anger. Unable to shake off its dependence on an ally of dubious fidelity and denied any material reward or moral prize of victory, the military developed a defensive insecurity vis-à-vis India which would pit it against its political masters.[13] This, and the shocking surprise of the act, explain why a small group of renegade officers, breaking the chain of command to kill the President, faced no immediate reprisal from the military.

A sanguinary interregnum

Just hours after Mujib's death, Khandakar Mushtaq Ahmed (Mushtaq) invited the Chiefs of Staff of the three services, along with the DCAS, Major General Ziaur Rahman, and CGS, Brigadier Khaled Mosharraf, to the radio station in Dhaka where, after some discussion, all swore allegiance to Mushatq's presidency. This was broadcast. The Director General of BDR, the Inspector General of Police and other senior officials made similar pledges of fidelity. The sequence of these broadcasts underscored the significance of the military in the new dispensation. However, tensions also surfaced. Some military leaders, the CGS most prominent among them, demanded immediate restoration of the chain of command. This proved to be a forlorn hope. With tanks and artillery guns under their command deployed across Dhaka, Majors Farook and Rashid repaired with Mushtaq to *Bangabhaban*, the presidential palace, from where they passed the president's orders—essentially their own advice to Mushtaq—to the Generals. This rankled with the latter.

Mushtaq soon promoted the Majors to Lt. Colonel, appointing them as his advisers. He formed a new cabinet with nineteen ministers and nine ministers of state—all civilians—of which eleven of the ministers and eight of the ministers of state had held positions in Mujib's administration.[14] So, an impression of continuity, or Awami League leadership bereft of Mujib, was apparent. Although Bangladesh would honour all its international obligations and commitments, including its friendship treaty and various agreements with India, a shift away from the broadly Indo-centric foreign and security policy framework in place since 1972 became evident. The signs were random and superficial—Bangladesh *Betar* was renamed Radio Bangladesh; speeches were ended with declamations of 'Bangladesh *zindabad*' rather than '*Joy Bangla*' from the war;[15] Radio Bangladesh started playing both Pakistani and Indian popular music in its entertainment programmes. Several countries which had held up diplomatic recognition—China and Saudi Arabia prominent among them—swiftly announced plans to exchange ambassadorial missions with Bangladesh. Mushtaq confirmed the Majors' announcement of the imposition of martial law, ordered a countrywide curfew with a three-hour break for Muslims to attend Friday congregations, and had several of Mujib's confidantes arrested. Identifying the army as the potential source of the gravest threats to his authority, Mushtaq moved to box its leadership in. First, on the Majors' advice, he retired Major General Safiullah, appointing Major General Ziaur Rahman as the CAS, and inducted Group Captain M.G. Tawab from Germany as the new COAS, promoting him to Air Vice Marshal. Then, to institutionalise his own authority, Mushtaq created the post of Chief of Defence Staff above the three service chiefs, appointing Major General Khalilur Rahman, DG of BDR, to that post. Finally, he appointed General M.A.G. Osmany, the wartime commander, as presidential military adviser. As a corollary, Colonel H.M. Ershad, then attending the National Defence College in Delhi, was promoted in his absence and made Zia's DCAS. These changes failed, however, to secure Mushtaq control over the army.

His efforts to reduce threats from the Awami League were more effective. Weeks after Mujib's death, the four men potentially capable of mounting a political challenge to Mushtaq—the political leader of the resistance in 1971, Tajuddin Ahmed, former Vice President Syed Nazrul Islam, former Prime Minister Mansur Ali, and former Commerce Minister A.Q.M. Kamruzzaman—were arrested and detained at the Central Jail. In late September, Mushtaq issued 'The Indemnity Ordinance, 1975,' a decree which protected the 'Majors' and their men from any legal proceedings flowing from the planning and execution of the plot against President Mujib and twenty-one members of his extended family. He sought to balance the need to legitimise his own authority and the demands of the Majors on whose proverbial back he rode. The contradiction inherent in trying to boost institutional frameworks and stabilise the functions of the state, and maintaining the Majors' (now Lt. Colonels Farook and Rashid) extra-institutional status within the presidency strained Bangladesh to breaking point. CGS Mosharraf repeatedly urged CAS Zia to bring the two officers and their tanks and guns back to the cantonment and restore the chain of command. As the public mood had swung behind the changes wrought by the plotters,[16] and they enjoyed Mushtaq's confidence, attempts to rein them in would be fraught. Zia tried but failed to bring the tanks back in October, and did not persevere.

Mosharraf did not forgive Zia for this failure. Meanwhile, Mushtaq made other changes. He repealed sections of the constitution which had replaced multi–party democracy with the solitary 'national party'— BKSAL; he scrapped Mujib's plans to divide the country into sixty-one districts to be administered by sixty-one BKSAL governors; he repealed Presidential Order no. 9 of 1972 which had given Mujib the power to dismiss civil servants without assigning reasons; and he disbanded the JRB, ordering its merger with the army. He released 1,000 of around 5,000 political prisoners detained by the Mujib government.[17] Early in October, Mushtaq announced that multi–party parliamentary democracy would be restored, political activities be permitted from 15 August 1976, and general elections held on 28 February 1977. Until then, though, the government used provisions of Mujib's Special Powers Act (SPA) and the state of emergency he declared in 1974, and the martial law regulations promulgated by Mushtaq, to exercise unlimited authority:

a. The SPA let most criticism of the government be interpreted as 'prejudicial acts' against the state and gave the latter extensive powers of arrest and detention.

b. Emergency Power Rules (EPR) suspended citizens' fundamental rights and removed checks on the state's power to arrest and detain.

c. Martial Law Regulations (MLR) reinforced the powers of the state and curtailed the rights of the citizen to seek redress against those.[18]

While the legal superstructure was being refined to legitimise the state's 'emergency' powers, the fragility and marginalisation of the civilian elite structure became clear early on 3 November 1975 when the military embarked on an internecine enterprise. Brigadier Khaled Mosharraf, with troops from Colonel Shafat Jamil's Dhaka-based 46 Brigade, mounted a partial coup aimed at returning the 'Killer Majors' and their units to the garrison and restoring the chain of command with himself at the top. The political intent and alleged partisan affiliations of this coup are contested.[19] The facts are known, though. Troops surrounded Zia's official residence forcing him to sign a letter of resignation and accept house arrest. The sudden withdrawal of two infantry companies guarding *Bangabhaban* was the sign of an impending assault on the tanks and those they protected. But a frontal assault was averted as Mosharraf sent a delegation of officers to Mushtaq with his demands:

- The tanks of 1ˢᵗ Bengal Lancers must be disarmed and then returned to the cantonment; a corollary—Colonels Farook and Rashid must surrender.
- A new CAS must be appointed to succeed Major General Ziaur Rahman.
- Mushtaq could stay on as president but national policy must change to reflect the alliances with countries which had supported Bangladesh's war of independence.[20]

Mushtaq rejected the demands but announced his own resignation effective at 6.00am that morning. The nonplussed Mosharraf now reduced his demands to just the return of the tanks and the appointment of a new CAS. Farook had left *Bangabhaban* to take personal command of his tanks deployed in the vicinity; Rashid, negotiating along with Mushtaq, insisted only a showdown could decide which side prevailed. Then, at around 10.00am, the Inspector General of Police rang to say that unidentified soldiers had forced open the cells at the Central Jail the previous night—as Mosharraf's coup had got under way—and killed the four Awami League leaders detained there. It was then that the 'Killer Majors' agreed to concede. Mushtaq persuaded Khaled Mosharraf to let the 'Majors' go into exile, to be arranged by Air Vice Marshal Tawab, the COAS, and the Foreign Ministry. Eventually, seventeen members of the team flew to Bangkok. Mosharraf, with the apparent support of Tawab and CNS M.H. Khan, insisted that Mushtaq appoint him CAS.

During the period 3–5 November 1975, Bangladesh had no effective government. The presidency was in a state of limbo with Mushtaq's verbal resignation and nobody willing to take his place. The cabinet did not function although Mushtaq convened a meeting to decide how to deal with the consequences of the dramatic military factional conflict playing out in the garrisons. Administrative functions in the capital only continued by bureaucratic inertia as the threat of civil war resuming hung heavily over the country.

What became clear was that if the military chose to intervene, however sophisticated or popular the civilian political elite, it would be both helpless and marginal to events. And in November 1975, the political elite did not appear to carry either endowment. The danger of intra-mural military conflict wrecking an already weak state structure would have been apparent but the actors in the grim drama seemed to have taken little notice. With order crumbling on the inside, the players sought to maintain a semblance of formal normality. While negotiations between Mushtaq's advisers and Khaled Mosharraf's aides continued, Colonel Shafat Jamil, entering the cabinet room with armed officers, demanded Mushtaq's resignation. By then, the murder of the four imprisoned Awami League leaders had become common knowledge, and the 'ouster' of the 'Killer Majors' had led to widespread demonstrations by Awami League members and their allies from other political parties. Jamil insisted that Chief Justice Abusadat Mohammad Sayem be appointed the next president, and after much persuasion, Sayem agreed to take the oath of that troubled office on 6 November. By then, Mosharraf had promoted himself to Major General—with Tawab and M.H. Khan pinning the badges of rank on his dress-uniform epaulettes—and taken the office of Chief of the Army Staff.

While Mosharraf appeared finally to have got his wish, he was troubled by reports of his mother and brother, both Awami League members, leading a party procession through the city celebrating the apparent restoration of the Mujibist order. As activists of the Awami League, NAP (M) and pro-Moscow CPB observed 'Mujib Day' on 4 November and planned to hold mass memorial prayers in Mujib's honour on 7 November, the Indian press and state media mounted a hagiographic campaign reminding everyone of the late, great leader, Mujib.[21] Press reports of joyous Awami League gatherings, Mosharraf's family links to some of these, and the 'defeat' of the 'anti–Awami League' campaign soured that segment of Bangladeshi opinion which had welcomed the post-Mujib changes. Politically conscious citizenry appeared polarised between those who cheered the Majors'ouster' and the return of the Indo-Soviet alignment, and those who questioned that line of thinking. Anxiety born of uncertainty and fear, and evidence of divisiveness within the military created an environment in which a third group would emerge from the shadows, confounding an already complex web of inter-factional power-play. This would come to be called the *Sepoy biplob* (mutiny)' that unfolded early on 7 November 1975.

Shortly after being placed under house arrest, Ziaur Rahman called up Abu Taher,[22] his wartime comrade,[23] and now leader of a radical leftist party, ten thousand of whose members were in prison at the time.[24] After retiring from service and taking up responsibility for the government's dredger operations based in Narayanganj, a port and industrial centre outside Dhaka, Taher secretly assumed the JSD's vice presidency,[25] took command of JSD's clandestine armed wing, the *Biplobi Gono Bahini* (revolutionary people's army—BGB), and set up secret cells of the *Biplobi Shainik Sangstha* (revolutionary soldiers' organisation—BSS) in several military units. Comprising mostly junior- and non-commissioned officers (JCOs and NCOs) drawn to the egalitarian ethos of socialist ideals, these cells attracted soldiers unhappy with the stern justice of peacetime regimental discipline and the often-poor leadership provided by commissioned officers, seen as the most retrograde section of this class-ridden conservative institution.[26]

Taher's JSD cells were preparing for a revolutionary campaign aimed at overthrowing the petit bourgeois Bangladeshi state before Mujib's sudden assassination forced a change of plans. The JSD welcomed the changes made on 15 August but denounced Mujib's assassination since it did not alter the state's class structure. With turbulence in the armed services hinting at a power struggle within that conservative state organ, Taher decided to strike as soon as Zia sought help. Radicalised soldiers, moved by a JSD pamphleteering campaign launched on 5 November describing Mosharraf's coup as an Indian conspiracy to subvert national sovereignty and restore Indo-Soviet primacy in Bangladeshi affairs,[27] prepared a twelve-point charter of demands. If met, these would transform the Bangladesh army and, indeed, Bangladesh itself. The Charter (Appendix I) demanded the end of the colonial military structure and the establishment of 'a revolutionary army.'[28]

With many soldiers, armed JSD cadres and civilian FFs agitated by recent events and ready to accept JSD leadership, Taher chaired a meeting of the BSS on the evening of 6 November with cell leaders from units based in Dhaka in attendance. He issued orders for two prongs of the 'revolution'. The first prong would free Zia and detain Mosharraf and his aides; the second would, with BSS and BGB cells in Dhaka and other garrisons working with activist FFs, mount a revolutionary surge to capture organs of state authority and to establish a hierarchy of revolutionary councils with Zia as its formal leader. Every military unit would form its own BSS which would link up with a 'central revolutionary army organisation' in Dhaka which Zia would command but not control:

This central organisation will decide all policies. General Zia will not take any decision without consulting the general committee. Only after consultation will

General Zia be able to take any final decisions. This central body will keep contact with the other cantonments, the bodies of revolutionary students, peasants, workers, and the common masses of the country. We must remember that with this revolutionary army all the progressive revolutionary students, peasants, and workers are linked up.[29]

Both prongs would be launched early on 7 November. The insurrection's goals were to:

- shatter the unity of the most active, organised and oppressive armed group of the bourgeois state machinery;
- minimise the organising capacities of the bourgeoisie;
- weaken the imperialist, revisionist and hegemonist forces which are the patrons of the national bourgeoisie;
- force the new rulers to bring back a democratic situation as far as possible with a view to ultimately eliminating the elements of bourgeois democracy;
- prepare the ground for the introduction and growth of proletarian state power and political forces parallel to the bourgeois system of state power.[30]

The operation began early on 7 November. The first prong was an immediate success. Troops from 2nd Field Regiment Artillery and 1st Bengal Lancers overpowered infantry-men guarding Major General Ziaur Rahman's residence and took him to the Field Artillery lines. Other BSS soldiers in Dhaka and elsewhere broke into regimental armouries, helped themselves to arms and ammunition, and ordered officers to doff their badges of rank and take orders from JCOs and NCOs commanding respective cells. Some officers refused to obey and were killed. As the chain of command melted away and those officers who had not joined the revolutionaries fled—many abandoning their families to their fate—anarchy overwhelmed several garrisons, Dhaka and Rangpur prominent among them. Soldiers, who had revolted without fully grasping the political implications of their action, went to the nearest town centre and engaged in sporadic looting. The streets of Dhaka, unlike on 15 August and 3 November, filled with crowds as civilians joined JSD cadres and radical soldiers in chanting *Sepoy janata bhai bhai, officer-er rakta chai* (soldiers and civilians are brothers, we want the blood of officers).

The number of officers killed was relatively small, but that was mainly because not many physically challenged the radicals. Once the failure of his coup became clear to Mosharraf, he and two allied officers, Colonel K.S. Huda, the brigade commander from Rangpur, and Lt. Colonel Haider, a battalion commander from Chittagong, fled in a car. The car broke down near the billets of an infantry unit near Dhaka's new parliament complex at Sher-e-Bangla Nagar. They sought shelter there but were later shot, not by revolutionary soldiers or JSD activists, but by two captains from the battalion.[31]

At the 2nd Field Regiment Artillery, Taher and Zia had an emotional meeting. They were comrades who had worked closely together during the war. As the DCAS, Zia quietly supported the approach taken by Colonels Ziauddin and Taher, then commanders of the Dhaka- and Comilla brigades. Besides, Zia took no action when Taher began establishing his secret BSS cells in military units. Most of all, when he called Taher for help, he must have known the retired war hero would utilise his radical resources to free him. This may explain why Taher launched his revolutionary insurrection with plans to free Zia and make him the revolution's nominal leader integral to the uprising.[32] Zia asked to see several senior officers he believed he could trust, and his rescuers brought them in. They pledged their fealty to the man proclaimed by the revolutionaries as their leader and restored in his office of CAS. Zia then made a broadcast from Dhaka's radio station, now under radical control. Announcing that he had temporarily taken over as the Chief Martial Law Administrator (CMLA), he pledged to restore order. He ordered all offices, factories, public services and educational institutions—closed since Mosharraf's coup—to reopen. Urging national unity, hard work and dedication to address the country's monumental challenges, Zia promised to build a prosperous land with divine blessings and popular support. Under the circumstances, and rekindling memories of his declaration of the war of independence in March 1971, his speech resonated widely.

This time round, though, soldiers and citizens, many of them armed, had mingled and were riding tanks and other military vehicles on city streets. The capital's crowds cheered them as they charged along in impromptu victory marches. Against that backdrop, at a gathering of BSS soldiers, BGB cadres and sympathetic onlookers, Taher presented the twelve-point charter of demands to Zia, seeking his commitment to implementing it, and to transforming Bangladesh and its army into leftist entities. BSS soldiers loyal to Taher surrounded Zia and urged him to pledge his loyalty to the 'sepoy revolution.' Zia signed the document. A professional soldier of the traditional mould, he nonetheless agreed to some of the demands and, after consolidating his authority, implemented several of them. The most high-profile of these were the immediate release, on 8 November, of JSD leaders Major Jalil, A.S.M. Abdur Rab and several others, and the abolition of the 'batmen' system which employed soldiers as officers' men-servants; but Zia could not countenance a radical transformation. Besides, the JSD had not won control over the state. During a party rally at the national mosque complex on 9 November, the policemen trying to disperse the gathering injured A.F.M. Mahbubul Huq, leader of the JSD-affiliated student wing. The party later acknowledged its failure to utilise Zia as an instrument with which to revolutionise the Bangladesh army and, using it, the country: 'shortly after having been put in such a powerful position, Zia understood that his personal class-based hopes and ambitions would not be realised if he remained under the influence of progressive forces…By 10–11 November 1975, he assumed a fully reactionary role. Notwithstanding his various correct initial statements, Zia moved towards the reactionary camp early on.'[33]

While blood—mostly military—was being shed, Zia and his army colleagues moved to establish a leadership which would recognise his own elevation but keep it within a formal, semi–constitutional, framework. After some debate, the Generals and Colonels decided Justice Sayem would remain president and assume the role of CMLA; Zia, with the two other service chiefs, would become one of three DCMLAs. However, he would be pre-eminent among martial law administrators[34] by force of events, personality and personal popularity in the military and among the general populace. This proved crucial as JSD-inspired mutinies rocked army units and garrisons across the country. Military commanders, unprepared for this drastic challenge to their authority by rank-and-file soldiers, often failed to grasp the structural nature of change being sought by radical troops and their civilian allies. Trying to address the mutinies as a disciplinary problem, they often aggravated the situation, with more officers being shot and, in some cases, killed, by their soldiers. Often, it was Zia's personal intervention and the combination of his charm, blackmail—on several occasions he threatened to resign if rebellious troops did not directly return to barracks and surrender stolen arms and ammunition—and authority gained during the war and since, that ended mutinous acts.[35] This consolidated his command, bolstering his reputation to near-mythical heights.

This mixture of cajolery and threatened application of the law had different facets. Zia saw the military as the key instrument with which to pursue the construction of the national edifice. For a professional soldier, this was natural. The army was, after all, his only power base. As the CAS, 'fixing' the army was his first challenge and this could not be accomplished without eliminating the radical threat and restoring discipline. The JSD and the BSS were at the root of the problem as he saw it. Mutinous soldiers appeared to come in two distinct strands—a radicalised group linked to the JSD via the BSS seeking revolutionary transformation, and a strongly nationalist group whose anti–Indian fervour had been aroused by JSD activists to rebellious levels for radical purposes.[36] The latter did not pose a fundamental threat to the traditional order and could be recast in helpful ways; indeed, its role in freeing Zia on 7 November 1975 and reinstating him as the CAS was celebrated annually by successive governments. The former, however, did, and had to be neutralised. Zia ordered the arrest of JSD leaders on 23 November. Colonel Taher, held the next day, was sent to prison in Rajshahi in the north-west. Security forces, searching for illegal arms, detained many JSD activists and sympathisers, forcing others into hiding. An attempt by JSD cadres including Taher's brothers to abduct the Indian High Commissioner in Dhaka, and seek an exchange with Taher, ended in bloody failure.

In late May 1976, Taher was brought to Dhaka and placed in solitary confinement at the Central Jail. There, beginning in June, a special military tribunal chaired by Colonel Yusuf Haider, tried him, twenty-two soldiers and eleven JSD leaders and champions—some in absentia. Taher's JSD colleagues on trial included Major M.A. Jalil, A.S.M.A. Rab, Serajul Alam Khan, Mohammad Shahjahan, Mahbubur Rahman Manna, Hasanul Haq Inu, Akhlaqur Rahman and K.B.M. Mahmood. Hearings began *in camera* on 21 June under strict security and media control. On 17 July, Colonel Haider announced the verdict. Colonel Taher was convicted of serious anti–state activities including 'propagating political opinion' among service personnel, and sentenced to death.[37] President Sayem rejected the clemency petition Taher's lawyers filed and early on 21 July 1976 Colonel Taher was hanged. Although his execution removed immediate threats to the administration, it tarnished Zia's nationalist credentials.[38]

A cavalcade of Generals

With open challenges to his authority in the military—and the country more generally—ended, Major General Ziaur Rahman embarked on consolidating both his own power, and the solidity of the Bangladeshi state. Although a foundation had been laid under Mujib, recent turbulence had shown up its frailties and underscored the need to rebuild state institutions, sometimes from scratch. In key aspects of the Bangladeshi experience—political and economic—Zia initiated policies which shifted the focus of domestic organisation and external alignments. As the CAS and principal DCMLA, Zia's primary interest was in restoring military discipline and building a professional, relatively modern, force capable of performing its fundamental tasks of defending the state's independence and sovereignty from external threats and internal challenges. He pursued this course zealously. But he was also responsible, over varying periods, for the ministries of Finance, Home Affairs, Commerce & Foreign Trade, and Information and Broadcasting. With both the military and security forces taking orders from him, and the state's financial and planning organisations working to his vision, Zia transformed both.

The ineffectiveness of non-military institutions apparent at a time of military turbulence and the vulnerability of the military's institutional carapace to radical intrusions gave Zia the purpose with which he drove changes. In the process, he built up the military and its intelligence organs as key institutions of state, subordinated other organs, liberalised economic activities to generate wealth and revenue, and transferred much of the latter to the armed forces. The enlarged and improved forces were then better able to maintain the order he established, reinforcing the 'peripheral-capitalism' Bangladesh pursued, and establishing a symbiotic relationship linking the international money- and arms- markets dominated by the OECD donor countries which proved to be more generous to the new order in Dhaka.[39] The expansion of the military's strength and capacity enlarged its space in domestic politics, allowing its leaders to shape the contours of policies that reinforced the tendencies congruous to their conservative and orthodox perspectives and weaken those that challenged these.[40] Non-radical leftist analyses of Zia's objectives focused on the rise of militarist elites in Bangladesh, starting with Zia. He was seen to be seeking:

- the unity and survival of military institutions
- the autonomy of military institutions over any other sector, group or organisations
- attributes of an exclusivist, authentic but non-responsible national representative
- millenarian and revolutionary approaches ending turmoil and decadence and starting a new, more hopeful and beneficent, era
- the conception of a 'missionary role' in protecting the state and defining national values and goals
- economic policies that could generate the surpluses needed to ensure security needs
- building up the international personality and presence of the state, and
- a permanent supervisory role in governmental processes to ensure the aforementioned aims[41]

The military was expanded with new battalions, regiments and training establishments being launched frequently. Zia visualised an army comprising several infantry divisions with the existing brigades stationed in Dhaka, Chittagong, Comilla, Jessore, and Rangpur forming the nucleus. With the JRB being merged with the army, trained manpower needs for two divisions were easily met. The first to be launched was the 9th Infantry Division in Dhaka. This was a politically crucial formation, designed to secure the capital from renegade elements. Next came the 24th Light Infantry Division in Chittagong. Inheriting a counterinsurgency operation in the Chittagong Hill Tracts from the previous government, Zia devoted considerable resources to this formation. Engaged in combat with the tribal insurgents of the Chakma *Shanti Bahini* (peace force) guerrillas from the start, 24th Infantry Division would grow to comprise four infantry brigades, discard the appellation 'light,' and as the army's only 'active' formation, become a training school for most units and personnel who were routinely rotated among its operational sectors and brigades.

Zia changed the top level of the military hierarchy, bringing in officers he had worked with or had confidence in. Major General Kazi Golam Dastgir, commander of Operation Dragon Drive in the CHT, was brought over to Dhaka as the new Director-General BDR, replacing Major General Khalilur Rahman, who was retired. Brigadier Abul Manzoor, an escapee from Pakistan and a wartime sector commander, was brought back from Delhi where he had been the Defence Attaché, and made the CGS. Brigadier Mir Shaukat Ali became the first GOC of the 9th Infantry Division. Brigadier Atiqur Rahman raised the 24th Light Infantry Division in Chittagong. Brigadier Mohabbat Jan Chowdhury, Zia's friend from his Pakistan Military Academy days, was appointed Director General, Forces Intelligence. Colonel, later Brigadier, Nurul Islam, Principal Staff Officer to Zia, served as his key political adviser. All of them were soon promoted to Major General. As the army expanded, other senior officers, too, were promoted. Since there were more repatriated officers than FF ones, arithmetical progression increased the number of repatriated officers in senior ranks and many FF officers felt marginalised. The nature of military service, with the inherent authority and privilege of seniority, made the senior-junior disparity a sensitive issue. This group differentiation became a divisive factor as some commanders from each group solicited the support of junior officers, building fiefdoms that challenged the chain of command.[42]

Eventually, the three other brigades, too, grew into infantry divisions. New, independent brigades were to be raised. JRB resources including arms, communications gear, vehicles and barracks would be redistributed. New equipment was procured from a wide variety of sources and this multiplicity of *materiel* imposed training, maintenance and servicing challenges. Military expenditure increased dramatically. In 1975, the year Zia took office, military expenditure was $42 million out of total public expenditure of $567 million; in 1980, the last complete year of the Zia regime, the comparable figures were $138 million and $2.15 billion respectively.[43] Table 3.1 shows the progression:

Table 3.1: Military and other expenditure growth in the
Ziaur Rahman regime[44]

Year	GDP $m	Central budget $m	Defence spending $m	arms imports $m
1975	7,458	567	42	12
1976	8,404	1,192	86	12
1977	8,533	1,493	136	34
1978	9,199	1,600	140	5
1979	9,612	1,823	135	0
1980	9,955	2,156	138	27

Zia traveled widely, building up defence and security relationships with Western countries, oil-rich Arab and Muslim states, and with China. OECD donors and aid agencies increased their economic contributions, as did the Arab states with oil revenues. He expected much of America, asking the US ambassador if Washington could help with building recreational facilities e.g., swimming pools and gymnasiums for university students, offering them 'some useful channel for their energies,' and helping to train and equip the Bangladeshi police force. He also sought budgetary support.[45] Once Zia appeared solidly ensconced in office, the USA allocated food aid, loans to pay for fertiliser, funding for rural electrification, and a waiver allowing Bangladesh to export jute goods to Cuba without triggering aid cancellation.[46] China and Saudi Arabia, swift to accord recognition to Dhaka after Mujib's death, gave much needed economic and diplomatic support. China also began providing substantial military assistance at 'friendship rates.' All three services expanded and this gave Zia the capacity to resist recalcitrants on two fronts.

First, Kader Siddiky, a former guerrilla commander from the northern Tangail region who had earned both fame and notoriety during the war of independence, crossed the frontier into India's Meghalaya state where the BSF provided sanctuary, arms and ammunition to his *Kader Bahini* fighters. These men started attacking Bangladeshi BOPs and police stations close to the northern borders. There were also frequent firefights between the BSF and the BDR along several disputed stretches of the border. The BDR was expanded on the light-infantry model with equal stress on combat capability and its traditional anti–smuggling role. Officered by army personnel, the BDR became an effective counter to the *Kader Bahini* offensive in the north, although in the eighteen-month confrontation many soldiers were killed, and many more wounded, in these operations. It would take political change in Delhi to end this warfare.

India was also involved in providing sanctuary and clandestine support to another group of angry Bangladeshis—the Chakma tribal *Shanti Bahini* militia operating in the CHT, a 5,000 square mile territory of low, forested hills in Bangladesh's south-eastern corner.[47] In the 1970s, this approximately 10 per cent of national territory was home to around 600,000 people or 0.7 per cent of the total.[48] With a population density elsewhere in land-hungry Bangladesh one of the highest in the world, and Bengali immigration into the hills barred, first by colonial and then, by Pakistani law, demographic and political tensions between plainlander Bengali–speaking Bangladeshis and the CHT's non-Bengali tribal groups were high. Chakmas, the largest, most articulate and best organised of the CHT's fourteen tribes,[49] were troubled by the rise of Bengali separatism in 1970–71. Young Chakmas, with the acquiescence of their King, Tridiv Roy, developed a mutually supportive relationship with the Pakistani military's Inter-Services Intelligence Directorate (ISI) whose officers had built secret camps in the CHT for Mizo separatists from the neighbouring Indian state of Mizoram. The ISI armed some Chakma youths to guard these bases. When Pakistani forces fled in late 1971 ahead of advancing Indian and Bangladeshi units, many of these young Chakmas resisted and faced an unpleasant initiation into the new Bangladeshi dispensation. Tridiv Roy fled to Pakistan to join the Bhutto cabinet. After the 1973 polls, the Chakma MP and tribal leader M.N. Larma asked Sheikh Mujibur Rahman to constitutionally guarantee the separate status of the CHT within Bangladesh. Mujib advised the tribals to 'become Bengalis' instead. This led to Larma, his brother J.B. Larma and their aides establishing the *Parbattya Chattagram Jana Sanghati Samity* (Chittagong Hills People's Solidarity Association—JSS) and its armed wing, the *Shanti Bahini* (SB) militia, to challenge the Bangladeshi state's authority in the CHT.

In the early years, the SB was small, weak and nebulous. It lacked the capacity to challenge Dhaka's writ. Besides, in 1974, the PBSP, a radical leftist organisation led by Siraj Sikder and Colonel Mohammad Ziauddin, forced out of the forests of north-central Bangladesh by security forces, occupied western CHT. Its Marxist struggle against the petit bourgeois Bangladeshi state was stifled but the presence of its armed cadres in the CHT's eastern half constrained the SB's autonomist exertions. The absence of substantial security presence in the area meant the PBSP and SB deterred each other. The Bangladesh army's Operation Dragon Drive against the PBSP in December 1974–February 1975 eliminated the PBSP as a counterpoise as Sikder was caught and killed and Ziauddin was forced to flee with the group's remnants. The removal of the PBSP and the subsequent withdrawal of the military, leaving behind small, isolated camps, expanded the SB's room for manoeuvre. In addition, the tribal populace's encounter with the Bangladeshi military had been unpleasant—with soldiers suddenly appearing in large numbers at tiny hamlets of fearful tribals and harassing—occasionally torturing—them for information. Troops cordoned off and searched most scanty and flimsy highlander hutments along their axes of advance. They showed no respect for the locals' rights, customs, or privacy. They humiliated the *Karbaris* and Headmen, key figures in the traditional tribal system, weakening the hierarchy holding montagnard society together.[50] Demoralisation, anger and fear among the locals may have served the military's immediate purpose, but the longer-term outcome could not. Resentment against the troops, and the state they represented, could only build a recruitment pool for the SB. This combination of circumstances led to an explosion of SB activism from 1976 onward.

Given their military intelligence background, Ziaur Rahman and his 'kitchen cabinet' pursued a complex and multi–faceted response to the insurrection. They saw it as another Indian plot to subvert Bangladesh's sovereignty by assisting malcontents, and turning a domestic political issue into a regional military-security challenge to their state.[51] One prong of their effort was military—to locate, identify and engage the insurgents in battle, destroying their combat capacity. Another was socio-political and economic—to restore the authority of the three traditional kings recognised by the British but weakened by the wartime turbulence in 1971 and post-independence policy thereafter, and to grant the region developmental assistance to generate employment opportunities and alternatives to militancy. A third prong was a strategic device designed to integrate the region to the rest of the country ethnically and demographically. Zia rescinded key elements of the CHT Regulation of 1900, organising mass resettlement of landless Bengali peasants and rural workers to villages established on *khas* (public) land, offering material aid and land titles to these Bengalis, with the protection of the security forces. The idea was to ensure the CHT's population eventually reached a Bengali majority which would, in this view, legally and politically secure the area's integration into Bangladesh.

Tribal, mainly Chakma, reaction was violent. SB attacks on army, BDR and police patrols and encampments mounted. The insurgents also attacked Bengali settlements. Battle was joined. The 24th Infantry Division was expanded to include four—rather than the usual three—infantry brigades with battalions from the rest of the army regularly rotating. It was the army's only operational formation and drew personnel, arms and equipment to its full authorisation. The BDR Sector responsible for the CHT too was reinforced with fresh battalions brought in from elsewhere. Additionally, the constabulary deployed some of its new Armed Police Battalions to the CHT, all operating under the command of the General Officer Commanding (GOC) 24th Infantry Division. With its combat capacity, and high priority in resource allocation and operational status, this Division soon assumed a political role within the military. As the GOC was granted civil and military power to both lead operations and supervise regional developmental efforts, he effectively became a 'prince among men.' This would later have unforeseen effects on national politics.

Meanwhile, as the scale of counter-insurgency operations grew, so did mutual bitterness. Both soldiers and insurgents were accused of committing atrocities but, with far greater resources to draw on, the army would have defeated its adversaries on that count. Simultaneous hunting of the guerrillas, investing large sums in development projects, and expanding Bengali settlements proved to be only a partly effective stratagem. As soldiers and settlers violently responded to alleged SB atrocities, many tribals were killed or wounded in encounters and counterattacks. Thousands fled into the neighbouring Indian state of Tripura in a modest re-enactment of the flight of Bengalis in 1971. As Indian intelligence and security forces aided SB operations, the CHT issue grew from a local or national challenge to a regional-interstate confrontation. As with the *Kader Bahini*, the SB too took on the contours of an instrument of proxy war. Dhaka-Delhi relations plunged to their nadir. It would change only when Mrs Gandhi lost power.

The SB had its own problems. Ideologically leftist, it was unable to work with the even more left-wing PBSP and, in fact, often clashed with it. Theoretically inclusive, the SB attracted only a handful of other tribes into its ranks and few Marma or Murong, for instance, shared its combative approach. Its charismatic leadership posed challenges too. M.N. Larma and his brother J.B. Larma were its dominant leaders. As co-founders and the most articulate proponents of tribal autonomy, the elder Larma was the political leader, while the younger Larma commanded the armed wing. After the BDR apprehended J.B. Larma and he was jailed for four years, central Committee member Priti Kumar Chakma took over the command of the SB. Help from the BSF and India's foreign intelligence body, the Research and Analysis Wing (RAW), turned the SB into a more active militia as it mounted more vigorous attacks on Bangladeshi forces. Priti Chakma and his aides, J.L. Tripura and Bhabatosh Dewan sought independence while M.N. Larma sought a more modest goal—autonomy within Bangladesh.[52] Differences led to factional fighting. This became critical after J.B. Larma was released and sought immediate reinstatement.

Priti Chakma and his aides demanded that M.N. Larma treat his brother as he would any other 'returnee' and keep him under observation before reinstatement. Unsuccessful attempts at reconciliation followed. In June 1983, Larma loyalists attacked the Priti camp and killed several key commanders. Despite a subsequent agreement to restore peace, in November, Priti faction fighters attacked the JSS headquarters and killed nine leaders including M.N. Larma. After more skirmishing, J.B. Larma—popularly known as Shantu—emerged as the leader with most support. Indian sponsors saw Priti Chakma's influence within the movement decline and abandoned him. Grasping an opportunity to weaken the resistance, the government announced an amnesty to those SB members who surrendered. In April 1985, 223 fighters of the Priti faction did so. By extending the amnesty, Dhaka was able to increase this number to 2,500.[53] Now, Shantu emerged as the unchallenged political and military leader of the tribal resistance with whom negotiations could be initiated. However, in 1976, this was still a decade away. As Zia saw it, the SB threat to Bangladesh's sovereignty and territorial integrity, with the tribals acting as Delhi's agents, had to be beaten into submission. A campaign of mutual virulence that would consume much national substance for two decades began. As a result, with the civil bureaucracy subordinated to the military, and the CAS heading the ruling elite, the pre-eminence of the military in national affairs became systemic.

Nationalist politics and the clash of ideas

Although Zia was the pre-eminent DCMLA and President Sayem was CMLA in name—all CMLA instructions and decrees were first approved at meetings of the President with the DCMLAs—Zia sought the CMLA's formal trappings of power. After a series of meetings on the subject, the longest being on the evening of 29 November 1976, Sayem gave in. Zia was promoted to CMLA and Sayem was reduced to the titular presidency. Zia could now appoint and fire his deputies, enact martial law regulations, and take any action 'in the national interest.'[54] With the force of MLR, EPR and SPA combined in his office, Zia, theoretically at least, enjoyed absolute authority. In April 1977, he persuaded Sayem to resign and nominate him as the successor. Now, Zia controlled both the levers of power and the formal trappings of it. With rumbles continuing in the garrisons and the CHT, Zia wished to expand his power base beyond the military, and build an ideological basis of popular support. He created the post of Vice President, appointing a retired judge and former head of Pakistan's election commission, Abdus Sattar, to it. He also expanded his Council of Advisers—his cabinet—with senior bureaucrats, military commanders, academics, professionals and businessmen. Later, he invited a few sympathetic politicians to join him; many did. Frequent reshuffles ensured cabinet members did not grow any political moss and remained loyal to Zia. While retaining absolute control, Zia sought to legitimise his rule while he embarked on reshaping Bangladesh. A series of electoral and legislative steps would create both new political players, and a new type of politics.

Soon after taking over as president, Zia announced a nineteen-point programme, seen as the instrument of his will to transform Bangladesh. It combined elements of ideational change with socio-economic objectives, effectively a wish-list that would appeal to the broadest spectrum of popular opinion. It was difficult to question the programme. For instance, it began with, 'To preserve the country's independence, integrity and sovereignty at all costs;' included 'to make the nation self-reliant in every possible way;' 'to encourage the spirit of public service and nation-building among government employees and to improve their financial situation;' 'to check the population explosion;' and ended with 'to safeguard the rights of all citizens irrespective of religion, colour and sect and to consolidate national unity and solidarity.'[55] (See Appendix II). A month later, on 30 May 1977, Zia held a referendum on the question, 'Do you have confidence in President Major General Ziaur Rahman and the policies and programmes enunciated by him?'[56] The government announced that 88.5 per cent of the voters had cast their ballots and 76.63 per cent, or 15.73 million people had voted 'yes.'[57]

Critics questioned the claimed turnout and the accuracy of the announced outcome.[58] Zia saw the result as a ringing endorsement of his nineteen-point programme and proceeded accordingly. He inducted former members of the Civil Service of Pakistan (CSP)—some accused of collaborating with Islamabad in 1971—into senior positions and, with their help, changed the 'socialist' or state-centric economic management

system. What he adopted was described as the 'Ayub Khan model'—
'encouragement of private enterprise, in emphasis on export-oriented
industries within the private sector, and in boosting of exports through
private foreign trade.'[59] Additionally, Zia stressed agricultural production
with public subsidies and his rural-focused 'self-help development policy'
targeting population growth.[60] He mobilised villagers with a countrywide scheme of manual excavation of canals, built family planning centres
with staff providing birth-control information, advice and material, and
ensured high grain prices to encourage food production. By subsidising
seeds, irrigation costs and fertilisers, and avoiding redistributive land
reforms, he secured the support of middle-peasants and *jotedars*.

In the urban sector, Zia emphasised private enterprise, raising the
investment ceiling from Tk 30 million to Tk 100 million, initiating partial disinvestment of nationalised enterprises, and offering incentives to
both domestic and foreign investors. Policy shifts increased aid flows
from $553.50 million in 1973–74 to $1,282.40 million in 1974–75 and
$930.4 million in 1975–76, with most funds being provided by OECD
donors.[61] High rates of money supply and bank credit and other incentives turned some traders into manufacturing entrepreneurs—establishing
a proto-national bourgeoisie that would be built on by his successors. In
1977–81, narrow money supply grew at 21 per cent and bank credit, at
25 per cent, annually; between 1975 and 1976–81, the revenue: GDP
ratio rose from 5 per cent to 9 per cent while the expenditure: GDP ratio
grew from 8 per cent to 17 per cent.[62] In 1976–81, the annual budget
deficit averaged at 8 per cent. However, the combination of a high rate
of monetary growth and large budget deficits did not generate high inflation because Zia was able to sustain low inflationary expectations in a
stable politico-economic environment while delivering annual GDP
growth of about 6 per cent.[63] Good harvests and a benign donor-com-
munity helped.

But perhaps the key substrate holding this improved economic picture
up was domestic political shifts. Pummelled by repeated radical leftist
violence in the armed forces—1977 turned out to be a particularly vicious
year—and challenges from the Awami League and its allies, Zia sought
to build a rainbow confederation uniting the right, left and the centre on
a nationalist, anti–India platform.[64] Several strands emerged to redefine
Bangladesh's dominant political character. Delhi's opposition to the post-
Mujib order, its unilateral withdrawal of Ganges water at the much-re-

viled Farakka Barrage just west of Bangladesh's north-western Rajshahi district during the January-May 'lean period' in 1976, its aid to armed dissidents in northern and south-eastern Bangladesh, and its refusal to honour the spirit of the twenty-five-year Treaty of Peace, Friendship and Cooperation built a groundswell of anti–Indian opinion across Bangladesh which the religious right, discredited in 1971 and barred from politics by Mujib, exploited to the full. The pro-Beijing left, driven underground by the past Awami League administration, too, loudly criticised what many saw as 'Indo-Soviet hegemonism.' As Zia's government leaned away from a Delhi–Moscow alignment towards the West, the Arab bloc and China, it found popular support but also faced violent reaction. Taking advantage of a changed popular mood, Zia urged the pro-Beijing Left to participate in open politics and legendary figures like Moahammad Toaha, Abdul Haq and Abdul Matin emerged from the shadows, followed by Tipu Biswas, Shanti Sen and Wahidur Rahman and others.

Zia allowed the religious right to do the same. Engaging in discussions with key figures from both camps, he sought to forge a national consensus on the ideational basis of an independent Bangladesh. This discourse was crystallised in a presidential proclamation issued on 23 April 1977, announcing that citizens of Bangladesh would be known as 'Bangladeshi' as opposed to Bengali, and the state ideology would be 'Bangladeshi nationalism' as opposed to 'Bengali nationalism.' The rationale offered was that not all the country's citizens were ethnic Bengalis, that many different tribal and linguistic groups called Bangladesh home and that to describe Bangladesh as the Bengali homeland would be to deny the respect and rights of national equality to the country's non-Bengali minority communities. The problem was that Bangladesh's struggle for autonomy and war of independence had been waged on the basis of Bengali nationalism as the defining framework. Cultural identity and political-economic repression had been the drivers of the autonomist movement. Now, by replacing 'Bengali' with 'Bangladeshi' in the constitution, Zia was seen to be moving away from Bangladesh's secular foundations to a more religiously defined future.

Zia wished to broaden the concept of nationalist idealism to incorporate the cultural, linguistic, religious and environmental values of all the communities making up the nation but also define its spatial and geopolitical separation.[65] What remained unstated was that irrespective of the Bangladeshi concept's historical evolution, Bangladesh was constrained to rationalise two irreconcilable facts: it was founded on the Muslim three-fifths of the original Bengal partitioned on the basis of confessional politics and had to acknowledge that aspect of its history; nor could it deny the fact that it sought and won independence on grounds that rejected the confessional *raison d'être* of Partition without overcoming the consequences of Partition. Was it, then, Bengali first and Muslim second—as the essence of its autonomist struggle suggested, or Muslim first and Bengali second, as its continued separation from the rest of Bengal in secular India indicated? This rather esoteric question, troubling only the political cognoscenti, nonetheless challenged efforts to establish a meaningful and rationally sustainable nationalist idea. Zia's Bangladeshi formulation rationalised an inherently and internally inconsistent political reality. The contradictions this generated would tear the Zia regime apart and violently end his life.

Arguably the defining and controversial step Zia took was to 'Islamise' the constitution. He inserted *Bismillah-ar-Rahman-ar Rahim* (in the name of Allah, the Beneficent, the Merciful) above the preamble; in the chapter on the Fundamental Principles of State Policy, he substituted 'Secularism' with 'the principle of absolute trust and faith in the Almighty Allah,' a phrase that was repeated several times, for instance, 'pledging that the high ideals of absolute trust and faith in the Almighty Allah… shall be the fundamental principles of the Constitution.' Article 12, which incorporated secularism and freedom of religion as a state principle, was deleted. This outlined the shift from a culturally-defined secular polity to a more confessionally orientated one with the place of Islam marked out as pre-eminent in state policy, perceptions and prescriptions. In the first paragraph of the Preamble to the constitution, 'the historic struggle for national liberation' was substituted with 'a historic war for national independence,' a phrase considered less revolutionary and more declarative of nationalist aspirations than the former. Semantics also changed. Zia began all official pronouncements, proclamations and addresses with an expression of faith in Allah and he ended these with the declamation 'Bangladesh Zindabad' (long live Bangladesh—in Persian). *Joy Bangla*,' the 1971 Bengali war cry (approximating 'victory to Bengal') fell into disuse and this was seen by many as the abandonment of the 1971 campaign's areligious aspects. This became the pattern of official pronouncements. In short, Zia's use of language was as radical a break with the past as were his politics.

Another bloody mutiny!

While Zia tried to stabilise national politics and reform state structures, his powerbase in the garrisons was convulsed by mutinies and rebellions. The fragility of his power was demonstrated by the ease with which Lt Colonels Rashid and Farook, the leaders of the 'Killer Majors' from 1975, returned to Dhaka from their Libyan exile in late April 1976 and attempted to mount another putsch, this time against Zia. Despite intelligence foreknowledge of Farook's plans, he was able to travel from Singapore to Dhaka and then, to Savar garrison, north of the capital, where the troops of an armoured regiment welcomed him with rare warmth. Shortly afterwards, DCMLA Air Vice Marshal M.G. Tawab and Lt Col. Sharful Haq Dalim, another of the August 1975 'Majors,' flew in to Dhaka on the same flight from Dubai. Although Tawab claimed this was purely coincidental, Zia would later use this incident as an excuse to oust Tawab, retire him and deport him to Germany whence he had been brought in by Mushtaq in 1975. Meanwhile, soldiers of Farook's original unit, the 1st Bengal Lancers, now stationed in the north-western garrison, and coincidentally Zia's hometown, of Bogra, wrote to Zia asking him to allow Farook to visit them. With signs of unease in many cantonments, Zia let Farook visit the Lancers in Bogra. Instead of calming things down, Farook's arrival stoked the fires of mutiny. Zia now had Rashid and Dalim packed off to Bangkok.

As the Bengal Cavalry in Savar and the Bengal Lancers in Bogra, along with other dissident elements, raised the standard of mutiny, infantry units from the 9th and 11th Infantry Divisions respectively surrounded the tank regiments with anti–tank weapons and challenged them to make a move. After a stand-off lasting several days, Farook again agreed to abandon his mutinous regiment and fly abroad. Worryingly, Farook's departure did not restore calm. Further disturbances continued in which infantry and other units too were involved. Zia took drastic steps against mutinous soldiers, disbanding an armoured regiment, putting over two hundred transgressors on trial by courts martial[66] and jailing or dismissing a large number of them. Sporadic outbreaks of mutiny continued throughout 1976 but nothing matched the violence of what happened in 1977. Early in June that year, Farook returned to Dhaka using a fake passport and passing himself off as someone else. However, he was arrested at the Dhaka airport and tried by court martial for carrying 'unauthorised arms, objectionable literature and a false identity.'[67] He was sentenced to five years in prison. His presence in Bangladesh may have triggered another mutiny.

During a visit to Egypt in late September, Zia was warned by President Anwar el-Sadat that Egyptian intelligence had uncovered a plot by radical left-wing Bangladeshi soldiers and airmen to kill Zia and his senior military aides, take over the state and proclaim a revolutionary republic akin to the one outlined in the twelve-point charter on 7 November 1975.[68] Forewarned, Zia dropped plans to inaugurate a new Air Force Officers' Mess in Dhaka soon after returning home, the alleged event at which the plot would unfold. This aborted the planned mutiny on 28 September but on the night of 29–30 September, troops from a Bogra-based infantry unit—22nd EBR—broke open the battalion armoury, helping themselves to arms and ammunition, shouted revolutionary slogans similar to those heard on 7 November 1975, killed a couple of young officers trying to stop them, detained the commander of 93rd Armoured Brigade—the local formation—and his officers, and tried to instigate the 4th Horse Regiment, a new armoured unit built on the ashes of the disbanded Lancers. Having failed to win the latter over, the infantrymen went to the town and looted several banks and shops. They also broke open the local prison and freed a number of soldiers imprisoned after the rebellion in 1976.[69] Zia alerted his senior aides to the possibility of an attempted coup in Dhaka and ordered preparations to counter it.

While the authorities were coping with military indiscipline, the Japanese Red Army Faction, a radical left-wing group, hijacked a Japan Airlines (JAL) airliner with 156 passengers as it took off from Bombay for Bangkok. The five hijackers, demanding a ransom of $6 million and the release of nine comrades from Japanese prisons—and threatening to kill the passengers if their deadline was not met—forced the pilot to land in Dhaka, where preparations for handling an emergency of this nature were entirely absent. Zia ordered Air Vice Marshal A.G. Mahmud, Tawab's successor as COAS, to resolve the crisis peacefully. Mahmud stationed himself at the airport terminal building with several aides and began negotiating with the hijackers. Bangladeshis were glued to their radios and TV sets as the national networks broadcast the exchanges live. Early on the morning of 2 October, soldiers from the Army Field Signals Battalion and collaborators from the Bangladesh Air Force (BAF) Provost Unit in Dhaka began a mutiny akin to the *Sepoy Biplob* of 7 November

1975. The slogans and the demands were the same but instead of describing Zia as their hero, they called him a traitor. The rebels were joined by disparate groups of soldiers from non-infantry units in Dhaka. They looted armouries and, boarding convoys of trucks equipped with loudspeakers, began shouting revolutionary slogans and firing into the air. One group raided the Central Ordnance Depot, stealing a large quantity of arms and ammunition. Another occupied the radio station where a BAF Sergeant proclaimed himself president, announcing that a revolution had taken place and a revolutionary council formed by soldiers, students and workers would from now on administer Bangladesh. Before he could go into details, the transmitter was switched off, abruptly ending his address. There was little spontaneous public support for this putsch.

Meanwhile, a third rebel column moved to the airport where the COAS was still negotiating with the hijackers. The mutineers shot dead a number of air force officers, decimating the BAF's operational capacity at a stroke. The COAS survived only by hiding in a cupboard. Once the rebels had overrun the airport and heavy firing began, the hijackers of the JAL airliner hurriedly released a number of the hostages and forced the pilot to take off. It was then that troops from 29 EBR, the Divisional Support Unit of 9th Infantry Division, were deployed to engage the mutineers. One Company rushed to the airport and cleared it, neutralising most of those who had killed the BAF officers. Another took control of the radio station. Yet another traversed the capital's streets, fighting mutineers who had taken their convoys to the city. The revolt had cost the lives of about two hundred people including eleven BAF officers and seventeen civilians.[70] By breakfast time on 2 October, the mutiny was effectively over, but its reverberations would ring for a while.

Zia addressed the nation, assuring it that 'patriotic forces' had put down a revolt staged by 'disgruntled elements' and 'undisciplined soldiers.'[71] He urged unity against forces out to destroy Bangladesh's independence and sovereignty. In the days that followed, Zia said nothing to disabuse compatriots of the line taken by right- and left-wing politicians and the press that 'pro-Indian forces' with the connivance of the Awami League and the JSD, had mounted the attempted coup. He moved rapidly to devise a political response to the serious challenge the mutiny represented. Nine days after the attempt, he invited leaders of all the main political parties to discuss the rebellion, indirectly blaming India for instigating the violence.[72] A few days later, Zia addressed the nation again, accusing 'anti-

Bangladesh forces' of conspiracy, and warning political parties against
infiltrating military and security services. He banned the JSD, the pro-
Moscow Communist Party and Mushtaq's Democratic League, implying
their involvement in the revolt. He ordered the arrest of the CPB's leaders. Mushtaq was already in jail on corruption charges. Parallel to a political initiative, he set up a number of military courts with benches
comprising JCOs and NCOs as well as commissioned officers. These
reportedly 'processed' around 1,500 'cases' of mutinous soldiers. Over a
thousand were summarily dismissed and around 488 executed; about 500
had deserted out of fear.[73]

However, the scale of the violence and the deliberation with which the
local military formation responded highlighted major security lapses.
These provided the pretext for a reshuffle among senior military officers.
Major General Mir Shawkat Ali, GOC, 9th Infantry Division, was sent
out from Dhaka to Jessore as the GOC there. Major General Abul Manzoor, the CGS, was posted to Chittagong as the GOC of 24th Infantry
Division, and ordered to bring the *Shanti Bahini's* insurrection in the
CHT to an end. Air Vice Marshal K.M.A. Islam, DG of Forces Intelligence (DGFI), considered the President's closest intelligence confidante,
was pensioned off. They were relieved by senior repatriate officers whose
loyalty to Zia, or greater effectiveness in command—which the reshuffle
apparently implied—widened the nationalist-conservative cleavage
already dividing the officers' corps.[74] Other senior officers eased out were
Major General Kazi Golam Dastgir, DG of BDR, who was retired and
sent abroad on an ambassadorial assignment, and Air Vice Marshal A.G.
Mahmood, COAS, who was retired but retained as a minister. Stern
action may have dealt a severe blow to rebellious tendencies in the rank
and file, but polarisation among officers deepened as Zia moved to supplement his military support base by cultivating new constituencies
among the civilian polity.

On 16 December 1977, 'Victory Day,' Zia announced plans to establish
a political front with like-minded groups, uniting the political spectrum
under a 'nationalist patriotic' umbrella. This loose group would combine
FFs and other pro-independence elements, revolutionary and pro-Peking
leftists, and rightists who had supported Yahya Khan's government in
1971. Zia held interminable meetings with leaders of these parties but
did not engage with the *Jamaat-e-Islami* (JI) or mainstream Muslim
League chiefs. His effort was to bring together professionals, entrepre-

neurs, former civil-and-military bureaucrats, academics and politicians sharing his anti–Indian nationalist beliefs.[75] Only 'pro-Indian' parties such as the Awami League, its offshoot the JSD, the CPB, and NAP (Muzaffar)—the latter two pro-Moscow—were not welcome, but some members of these parties too defected to Zia's *Jatiotabadi Ganatantrik Dal* (nationalist democratic party—JAGODAL) which was formed in February 1978. To deepen the support base, Zia boosted the personal networks he had established across rural Bangladesh.

Soon after taking over as the CMLA, Zia had begun visiting remote ramparts so far removed from the urban power centres and national consciousness that some of the villages he suddenly appeared in had never seen a national leader. He traveled by jeep or helicopter and on foot, dragging along reluctant bureaucrats and later, sycophantic politicians, with him. His disarming approach to the rural poor gave him insights into the reality in which the majority of Bangladeshis found themselves and established bonds that would create a network of supporters in the hinterland. While his policies aided accumulation and acquisition by the *jotedars* in the villages and the proto bourgeoisie in the cities, his personal relations with the common rural folk laid the foundations of popular mobilisation which would stand him in good stead when he moved to establish a party-political platform not entirely dependent on the urban-based left- and right-wing support he also cultivated. An archetypal centrist, Zia established contact with leaders of extremist movements from both ends of the spectrum, and with some Awami Leaguers. By late 1976, he had decided that given the India-aided insurgencies in the north and southeast of the country, polls scheduled for February 1977 could not be held on time.[76] President Sayem was persuaded to postpone general elections but schedule first-tier local elections in January 1977. Zia also had Mushtaq—now a severe critic—arrested on charges of 'prejudicial activities' and tried by a military court. His imprisonment for five years pleased many right- and left-wing leaders who had nursed grievances against Mushtaq. With key rivals neutered, Zia forged ahead.

JAGODAL united established political factions—the left-wing NAP (Bhashani) led by Mashiur Rahman, and the United People's Party led by Kazi Zafar Ahmed, and a Muslim League offshoot led by Shah Azizur Rahman. Senior figures, such as former provincial chief minister Ataur Rahman Khan, negotiated long and hard, but eventually rejected Zia's vision of a strong presidency operating with a multi–party but subsidiary parliament, taking Bangladesh in a right-of-centre direction domestically and diplomatically. While they supported the latter aspect of Zia's goals, they could not countenance a centralising executive. Three smaller parties made up the remainder of JAGODAL. Once the party had gelled, Zia moved to further legitimise his position. His victory in the May 1977 referendum was not considered enough for the democratic political system that he now sought to build. Constitutional amendments were decreed in April 1978 and the following month, a large number of political prisoners were released. Simultaneously, with JAGODAL at the core, Zia formed the Bangladesh *Jatiayatbadi* (nationalist) Front which nominated him as its candidate in the planned presidential elections. At the end of April, he retired as the CAS but had himself promulgated as the Supreme Commander of the Armed Services in his capacity as the CMLA. He left day-to-day affairs of the army to his DCAS, General H.M. Ershad, but did not immediately promote him to CAS.

With emissaries making the rounds, Zia persuaded the Awami League to participate in the presidential elections. Revived from its BKSAL straitjacket and working with its CPB and NAP (M) allies, the Awami League forged a nineteen-party group—*Ganatantrik Oikkya Jote* (democratic unity front—GOJ) which nominated General M.A.G. Osmany— Zia's wartime commander-in-chief. Demonstrating Zia's popularity across the spectrum, right- and left-wing parties like the JI, Muslim League, Islamic Democratic League, *Shamyabadi Dal* (socialist party), and the East Bengal Communist Party supported Zia. Even the JSD, embittered by Colonel Taher's execution, urged voters not to return the Awami League to power. Osmany campaigned against 'Mujib's killers,' vowing to bring them to justice and restore parliamentary democracy. Zia stressed the relative peace, prosperity and security his regime had established and compared this state to the period under the Awami League. In the polls held in early June, 53.59 per cent of registered voters took part; Zia secured 67 per cent of the votes; Osmany received 21.70 per cent; other candidates polled 1.63 per cent.[77] The opposition criticised the results, accusing Zia's supporters and officials of massive rigging. But the polls changed the political landscape. Zia emerged as the unchallenged national leader, and his victory confirmed the popularity of a strong executive. More significantly, his rainbow coalition was seen as the new nationalist and dominant force in national politics. Zia was now able to stress his popular credentials to the military, while retaining his military credentials for handling civilian politicians. He had taken a major step towards democratisation, but the concentration of power in his own hands meant there was little real change. On the other hand, the legitimisation of the religious right, anathema to the pro-independence nationalists, generated tensions within Zia's key support base early on.

This, however, was not enough. Zia needed to establish a system that would enable him to pursue his programmes, now expanded to thirty-one-points, to conclusion. A strong executive had to be backed up with a credible legislature which would give him the two-thirds majority needed, firstly, to ratify his actions and, secondly, to preserve presidential power in his hands. He could not be certain of victory in parliamentary elections using the front as his vehicle. The front's member parties could nominate their own candidates and then, having used Zia's popularity to win seats, go their own legislative ways if they wished to. Zia needed a unified party with countrywide organisation and support that could compete with the Awami League. Painful negotiations led, in September 1978, to the dissolution of JAGODAL, NAP (Bhashani) and the front's smaller parties and the emergence of the Bangladesh *Jatiyatabadi Dal* (Bangladesh Nationalist Party- BNP). Zia became its founder-chairman. With him sat men of diverse inclinations and antecedents: Mashiur Rahman and Kazi Zafar Ahmed—leftist politicians; Obaidur Rahman—a liberal democrat; Shah Azizur Rahman—an allegedly anti–independence former Muslim Leaguer; Badruddoza Chowdhury—medical specialist and TV personality; A. Momen Talukder—a former bureaucrat; Majedul Haq and Mustafizur Rahman—retired soldiers; and L.K. Siddiqui and Jamaluddin Ahmed—wealthy businessmen. Several Awami Leaguers e.g., Nurul Islam, Sujat Ali and former president Mohammad Ullah, too, joined this variegated party.[78] With such diversity prominent at the highest levels, the BNP was faction-ridden from the start. However, an anti–Indian, staunchly nationalist, pro-Western capitalist, progressive Islamist framework united the many camps under the same umbrella.

The BNP's constitution gave nearly absolute power to the chairman. Zia nominated all the ten other members of the National Standing Committee, the most powerful party organ. He also would convene its meetings, set agendas and preside over sessions. The chairman was the party's chief executive and could amend the party's constitution and have these amendments ratified by the appropriate council. He could dissolve any of the committees and councils that made up the party hierarchy.

At the early stages, the chairman exercised the cumulative powers of these councils and committees. The BNP was, therefore, both a vehicle for and a reflection of Zia's plans for Bangladesh. And a key plan was to establish a pliable parliament. In November, he announced plans to hold general elections in late January 1979. While established parties like the Awami League wanted to resume political activities, they questioned Zia's motives behind holding elections under martial law and demanded the restoration of parliamentary democracy. Zia's aides convinced them that the withdrawal of martial law before an elected parliament could sit in session would create a legislative vacuum. A compromise was finally reached.

Elections to the second parliament were held on 18 February 1979. 1,709 candidates from thirty-one parties including the BNP, two factions of the Awami League, the JSD, and the Bangladesh Muslim League-Islamic Democratic League alliance, and around 300 independent candidates, contested the 300 seats. The BNP won 207 seats on the strength of 7.93 million votes, or 41.17 per cent of the total. The Awami League's main faction, led by Abdul Malek Ukil, won the second highest number of seats—thirty-nine, with 4.73 million or 24.56 per cent of votes.[79] In the presidential system, the parliament was a secondary player, but the participation of all the major parties and groups in the polls, and a reasonably free and fair voting performance, legitimised the political process, 'normalised' the proto bourgeois state, and permitted a stable political–economic system to evolve. The parliament was convened on 1 April; five days later, it ratified all the martial law orders, regulations and proclamations promulgated between 15 August 1975 and 9 April 1979. This Fifth Amendment to the constitution was condemned by the opposition. There was, however, relief that as promised, martial was lifted and constitutional rule began.

Zia formed a new council of ministers in mid-April. Justice Abdus Sattar, Zia's deputy, became vice president; Shah Azizur Rahman was appointed prime minister. Badruddoza Chowdhury and Moudud Ahmed became deputy prime ministers. Politicians from the BNP's many factions were allocated various portfolios. But key ministries and divisions like Finance, Planning, Home Affairs, Foreign Affairs, and Establishment were given to reliable former civil- and military bureaucrats. Zia himself retained Defence, Cabinet Affairs, and Science & Technology. He then issued a gazette notification in which he had himself promoted to Lt. General backdated to 28 April 1978, and retired on the following day.[80]

Lt. General Ershad was promoted to CAS after a year of effectively doing the same job while serving as Zia's DCAS. Ziaur Rahman was now a civilian politician, almost entirely focused on his political programme for rebuilding Bangladesh. What he had begun with his nineteen-point programme was now driven with party-political panache.

A death foretold

Once the urban political elite had been co-opted, Zia cast his net wider, building new networks deep in rural Bangladesh. An experimental semi–official campaign to build 'swanirbhar (self-sufficient) Bangladesh' led by Mahbubul Alam Chashi was now adapted to building 'self-reliant and self-sufficient villages.' Zia sought to recast local government and direct resources to rural elites sympathetic with his vision. He persuaded BNP colleagues to erect a rural base by taking over the existing swanirbhar infrastructure and extending it across the country. Combining administrative fiat and party organisation, Zia sponsored local government institutions in every village and called these *gram sarkar* (village government). Each *sarkar* had ten members representing different sections of local community working under a Village Chief. The landless had two representatives, as had the land-owning section; there were two women, and two businessmen. Fishermen and artisan communities had two representatives. These ten members elected the chief. The *sarkar* was given modest magisterial and administrative authority with a view to encouraging grassroots leadership and engagement for political mobilisation. By the end of 1980, nearly 70 per cent of the country's 65,000 villages had its own *sarkar*. All the villages had their own *sarkar* by February 1981.[81] As a corollary, Zia established Village Defence Parties (VDP), unarmed rural auxiliaries with modest training and equipment who supplemented the local constabulary and helped to maintain law and order. By 1981, their numbers had grown to ten million across the country; Zia planned to double the number.[82] This was a remarkably cost-effective organisation that successive administrations would sustain. The other pro-BNP grouping that spread the party's tentacles were *Juba* (youth) Complexes which united local youths, gave them access to funds via auctions of village markets and organised them into partisan musclemen. The originally urban BNP now had a network of national organisations able to compete with the Awami League. Lt. General Ziaur Rahman was no longer a captive of his military colleagues. He had broken free.

Zia's domestic and foreign policies were intricately intertwined. With a centrist, middle class-based, party and political vision shaping domestic politics, he openly courted the West, Muslim countries and China. His stance angered India[83] and the USSR and their allies at home, but the results were generally positive. With development policies reliant on large infusions of aid, Zia needed both money and diplomatic support to establish the country as an independent, nationalist actor. The recognition of the post-Mujib regime by Saudi Arabia and China went a long way to that end. He secured a total of $808.63 million in aid from Muslim states; of this, $541.84 million came from Saudi Arabia.[84] China offered both financial and technical assistance. Significantly, Zia established a security relationship with Beijing. Chinese diplomatic support at the UNSC, and the transfer of military hardware at 'friendship prices,' aided Bangladesh's quest for autonomy and the wherewithal to deter threats to it. Bangladeshi forces acquired infantry and artillery hardware, anti–tank and anti–aircraft weaponry, patrol craft for the navy and, training facilities for service personnel. This would lay the basis for even stronger relations.

But most assistance came from the USA, its Western allies, and Japan, which would eventually become the single largest bilateral contributor to Bangladesh's development. Under US auspices, the World Bank (WB), the International Monetary Fund (IMF) and the Asian Development Bank (ADB) would become key advisers and providers of funds to fuel semi–capitalist economic growth and a restructuring away from statist policy and planning. America's leading position in helping Bangladesh was crucial to the efficacy of the 'Paris Club' of OECD donors whose annual meetings would increasingly shape Dhaka's fiscal and monetary policies. Over the duration of the Zia regime, US aid to Bangladesh added up to $1,177.15 million disbursed as follows:

Table 3.2: US aid disbursement to Bangladesh during Ziaur Rahman's rule[85]

Financial Year	Amount of Aid in $m
1975–76	185.51
1976–77	85.59
1977–78	142.27
1978–79	242.64
1979–80	88.47
1980–81	261.91
1981–82	170.76

With the economy growing at a reasonably steady clip, Zia raised Bangladesh's profile with high-energy diplomacy. It was elected to the UN Security Council. Dhaka raised the Farakka Barrage-Ganges water dispute with India at the Council to Delhi's utter dismay, and then withdrew the complaint after India offered to negotiate an agreement. Zia was appointed to the OIC's three-member *al-Quds* committee charged with evolving 'a new strategy to liberate *al-Quds al-Sharif* (also known as the Dome on the Rock) and to restore to the Palestinians their inalienable rights.'[86] He was invited to address the 11th Special Session of the UNGA in August 1980. He initiated regional co-operation within a formal framework which, in 1985, was launched as the South Asian association for Regional Cooperation (SAARC). He was on the OIC team appointed to mediate a truce between Iran and Iraq as the two neighbours waged a bitter war in 1980. In short, Zia managed, despite enormous difficulties, to put Bangladesh on the map.

At home, economic circumstances had changed. Although agricultural real wages did not move substantially, with manufacturing capacity expanding, urban real wages rose; the rates of domestic savings and investment grew. As both revenue and spending increased, the budget deficit remained static; current account and trade deficits grew significantly as limits on imports were lifted but exports did not grow comparably. Deterioration in the external terms of trade was partially balanced by improvements in the internal terms of agricultural transactions. Real deposits and loan rates of interest increased without deepening of the national finances; debt liabilities and debt servicing obligations grew significantly although as a percentage of total foreign exchange earnings, debt service obligations did not impose a larger burden. As a result, despite an increase in income inequality, overall, there was an improvement in the standard of living.[87] In economic terms, therefore, Bangladesh had become a different country.

In military-political terms, though, some things did not change. In 1979, some of the 'Killer Majors' got together abroad to discuss changing the government. Two of them, Anwar Aziz Pasha and Sharful Haq Dalim, flew to Dhaka to contact serving officers and left-wing activists and develop a network that would be willing and able to act against the government when they, the 'Majors,' gave the signal. An artillery officer, Lt. Colonel Didarul Alam, and an Electrical & Mechanical Engineering (EME) Corps officer, Lt. Colonel Nurunnabi Khan, responded to their call. Several left-wing activists, too, joined the group. Pasha and Dalim gave some money to the leftists and promised some to Didarul Alam to buy printing machines to 'educate the people', and to buy a bus for a commercial operation that would generate income and advance the cause.[88] The 'Majors' met in Ankara in December 1979 when the Bangladeshi ambassador there, a retired Major General, chanced upon them. They dispersed, but not before the ambassador had filed a report. They would return to Ankara five months later for their final session.

In the meanwhile, Didar and Nurunnabi Khan had gathered some troops and NCOs, contacted local JSD leaders and maintained links to the 'Majors' abroad. With signs of military security personnel getting close to them, the two Colonels planned to move on 17 June 1980. As Zia was scheduled to be traveling abroad, artillery and infantry troops working under the two colonels would kill CAS Ershad, arrest all the other officers in Dhaka in their quarters, and proclaim a revolutionary council that would implement the unmet demands from 7 November 1975.[89] When it became clear that intelligence staff had cottoned on to their plans, Didarul Alam decided to postpone the 'D-Day', but the soldiers he had commandeered for the purpose refused to delay things. So, with the mutinous officers and men working at cross purposes, the '17 June revolt' was a short-lived but nonetheless frightening affair. Didarul Alam fled to India and was arrested on return in November. Pasha was summoned from Ankara by the Foreign Office and was detained on arrival. Nurunnabi Khan, probationary bank official Mosharraf Hossain, and a JSD student Leader, Kazi Munir Hossain, were the other three men charged by a military court with conspiring to overthrow the government and subverting the loyalty of service personnel. The trial began on 10 March 1981. Pasha and Munir Hossain pleaded guilty and turned state's evidence. On the basis of their evidence, the other three were convicted and on 20 May, Didarul Alam was sentenced to ten years imprisonment, Nurunnabi Khan to a year, and Mosharraf Hossain, to two years. Munir Hossain was pardoned. Zia not only pardoned Pasha, but reinstated him as First Secretary at the embassy in Ankara. Ten days later, another group of mutinous officers would kill President Ziaur Rahman.

This last attempted coup which took Zia's life on 30 May 1981, led to much debate in its aftermath, characterised by a lack of consensus as to its causes. One theory popularised by an Indian journalist accused repatriated officers and some politicians of conspiring to eliminate FF officers by encouraging the charismatic FF officer, Major General Abul Manzoor, to kill the senior FF, President Ziaur Rahman, implicating FF officers as a group and thereby bringing to the fore repatriated officers at the national level.[90] Another theory claimed Zia's efforts to effect 'too critical changes in the traditional power relationships' and 'shift his power base from a military-bureaucratic-industrial combine to a mass-oriented institutional framework' aroused the passions of sections of the military who felt their position was being threatened and decided to strike.[91] Another Bangladeshi analyst saw Zia's assassination as the outcome of the violence through which the Bengali soldiery of the Pakistani forces had first been converted into rebellious guerrillas, then thoroughly politicised and radicalised by the traumas of the civil war in 1971, and then, further stressed by the convulsions of the rebellions and mutinies that had rocked the forces in 1975–1980, and Zia's eventually rigorous attempts to enforce discipline in the forces.[92] Other academics noted causal links between the 'democratising' president's death and his efforts to reduce the military's role in governance, and the consequent outrage among commanders anxious to prevent the erosion of the military's corporate interests.[93]

Given the erudition behind these theories, the possibility that each has some merit has to be taken into consideration. The facts, as they are known, can be interpreted to support any of these formulations. And the key fact is that a group of army officers, working under Major General Abul Manzoor, the GOC 24th Infantry Division, killed the president very early on 30 May 1981. Zia was not unaware of the divisions within the country and the army. He had personally resolved some of these. In fact, he was traveling to Chittagong on 29 May to intervene in an unpleasant dispute between two BNP leaders that had fragmented the party there. As for the army, he may inadvertently have widened the FF-repatriate breach by promoting many of the latter and marginalising the former. Once a confidant, Manzoor had become a critic. Charged with resolving the *Shanti Bahini's* insurrection in the CHT, Manzoor came round to the view that the engagement of more than four infantry brigades and ancillary forces against several thousand guerrillas could not end the insurgency and that a political solution was needed. Zia insisted that coercive tools alone would persuade the 'India-sponsored' guerrillas that their cause was hopeless and they must accommodate themselves within the unitary Bangladeshi state.[94] This difference was embittered by Zia's appointment of Ershad, a repatriated officer, as CAS.[95] Manzoor treated Ershad with disdain during official visits; this, in turn, raised questions about military discipline and respect for the chain of command.[96] Some intelligence briefings portrayed Manzoor as a political threat; Zia offered first to post Manzoor to Bogra and then, to send him abroad as ambassador.[97] Manzoor's swift rejection of the offers did not go down well.

On 20 May, the two men met at the regular Formation Commanders' Conference at the AHQ in Dhaka. These conferences had been initiated by Zia as CAS and were now continued by him, as the Supreme Commander, to discuss national security and military issues with the commanders of the army. While proceedings of these conferences remain classified, it is known that an argument broke out between Zia and Manzoor. Manzoor accused Zia of 'betraying the army' and threatening the nationalist cause by his increasingly 'civilian political stance.'[98] Manzoor was thought to be complaining about Zia, having attained power riding on the back of his military power-base, now abandoning it, the only national and nationalist institution, for party-political interests. But the import of his position was that he was 'challenging the very rationale of the national consensus on which Zia's programme was based.'[99] Manzoor also accused Zia of tolerating corrupt practices among BNP leaders and several army commanders, appearing to hold the president responsible for many of the nation's ills. Zia vigorously defended himself but found no open support from the other Generals present. This may have given Manzoor the impression, or illusion, that his fellow Generals were with him on these points.

Around 25 May, a written order transferring General Manzoor to Dhaka as Commandant of the Defence Services Command and Staff College (DSCSC) was issued. Manzoor had built a reputation as a cerebral soldier, equally at home in the field and the classroom, and the DSCSC was then the seat of highest professional military learning in the country. But the posting also meant a loss of command—especially of the only operational formation—and since the Commandant DSCSC had to take orders from the CGS, a post Manzoor had held several years earlier, this posting was seen as humiliating. Zia's instruction that Manzoor not receive him on the presentation line at the Chittagong airport, and insistence that Manzoor report to the DSCSC by 1 June, Manzoor's request that the posting be put off notwithstanding, provoked an angry reaction. Since his 'ouster' from the AHQ in the wake of the October

1977 mutiny, Manzoor's leadership qualities had impressed a number of FF officers who idolised him and had made a couple of abortive attempts to assassinate the president.[100] They now prepared to defend their General by bringing down the source of his humiliation. Two officers played a leading role in planning and executing the successful attempt on the night of 29–30 May: Lt. Colonel Mehboob-ur Rahman, CO, 21 EBR, Manzoor's nephew, and a rising star in the FF constellation thrown out of the AHQ on vague suspicions of an earlier anti–repatriate plot; and Lt. Colonel Matiur Rehman, the senior counter-insurgency staff officer at Manzoor's Divisional Headquarters, an 'escapee' FF, and like Manzoor and Mehboob, a decorated war hero. Working closely together, they had recruited several other FF officers to their cause. Among them, the Assistant Director of Ordnance Services (ADOS) at the Divisional Headquarters, Lt. Colonel Dilawar Hussain, and Brigade Major, 69th Infantry Brigade, Major S.M. Khaled, would play important roles in the assassination.

Early on the rainy morning of 30 May, sixteen officers who had met up at Kalurghat, the Chittagong suburb where Zia made his historic declaration of independence in March 1971, drove to the Chittagong Circuit House[101] where Zia was staying, and mounted a commando-style attack. They first demolished local defences with anti–tank rockets and automatic weapons. There was no resistance by the policemen in a cordon around the president's residence. Soldiers from the President's Guard Regiment (PGR) detachment guarding the president did try to fire back but were either killed or seriously injured in the first minutes of the raid. Lt. Colonel Moinul Ahsan, the president's Chief Security Officer, and Captain Ashraful Khan of the PGR, awakened by the explosions, rushed towards the attackers but were swiftly cut down. Zia himself, awakened by the noise, came out of his room to inquire what the attackers wanted. Moti fired bursts of automatic fire at Zia and he fell, mortally wounded. The attack was over in about twenty minutes.[102]

When the assailants reported success to Manzoor, he ordered measures to defend Chittagong from possible attacks by loyal forces.[103] All telephone lines linking the city to the rest of the country were cut; one infantry brigade was deployed to defend the city and another was tasked to protect the port, the airport and the radio transmitter at Kalurghat; a third was sent north to prevent landings at Kumira beach and block possible entry of forces from Comilla in the north at the Shuvapur Bridge choke point on the Feni River. The GOC chaired a conference of subordinate commanders early on 30 May at which he said the government was riddled with corruption which was now polluting the army, too; despite repeated warnings Zia had taken no corrective steps. Now, a group of young officers had killed Zia and he supported them. The officers present at the meeting were asked to swear their allegiance to the new order on the Koran, and they did. Later, senior civilian officials did the same. Manzoor then addressed 'the nation' in a radio broadcast laying out the reasons behind the 'takeover' and outlining his plans for Bangladesh.

Next, he announced the appointment of a seven-member revolutionary council chaired by him to head the administration. He abrogated the constitution, dissolved the parliament, dismissed the cabinet, suspended party-political activities and imposed martial law across the country. In the military, he dismissed General Ershad from the post of CAS and appointed Major General Mir Shawkat Ali, Principal Staff Officer at the Supreme Commander's Secretariat, to relieve Ershad, and dismissed Major General M.J. Chowdhury, DG of Forces Intelligence. He also abolished the institutions of *Gram Sarkar* and Youth Complexes, prohibited drinking and gambling, and cancelled the twenty-five-year Indo-Bangladesh Treaty of Friendship, Co-operation and Peace. He then announced the formation of revolutionary councils in other garrisons and urged officers and men in those stations to join hands with his revolutionary order. This appeal did not change the minds of most officers and men even in Chittagong, many of whom were shocked by the manner in which Zia had been killed.[104] Beyond Chittagong, the military chain of command remained unimpaired as Ershad and his aides began counter-measures.

Later in the morning of 30 March, the plotters sent several officers to the Chittagong Circuit House to lift the bodies of Zia, Lt Colonel Ahsan and Captain Khan, take them some distance away from Chittagong, and secretly bury them in an unmarked grave.

The Sattar interregnum

The news of Zia's death electrified Dhaka. Demonstrating the army's crucial role not only in marginalising the BNP's civilian administration, but also in restoring it, CAS General Ershad visited Vice President Abdus Sattar, then under treatment at the Combined Military Hospital in the cantonment. Ershad assured Sattar of the army's loyalty to the legally constituted authority, persuading him to take over temporarily. Sattar went to the *Bangabhaban* and at 6.00am, took the oath of office in Ershad's presence. The government broadcast condemnations of the attempted coup but perhaps because of ongoing negotiations with Manzoor, desisted from naming him. The latter sent messages to Major Generals Shawkat Ali and Moinul Hussain, the former having just been named the new CAS and the latter the Adjutant General, saying he would contact them as soon as telephone links had been restored. Uninvolved in the coup, the two Generals were embarrassed. Manzoor did not command any loyalty outside his own formation and even in Chittagong, many units refused to support him. His orders proved to be just a bluff which the AHQ and even some officers under his own command called.

By mid-day on 30 May, the AHQ had rejected Manzoor's pleas to support the new dispensation and radio broadcasts from Dhaka began naming him in attributing the 'illegal acts' that had begun with Zia's assassination. Troops from the formation in Comilla, north of Chittagong, were ordered to proceed to the renegade region. Commanders from other formations and garrisons swore allegiance to the centre and by 31 May, the government's warnings to all military units in Chittagong to cross the Shubhapur Bridge and surrender by a fixed deadline or face the consequences began taking effect. Dhaka rejected all the demands made by Manzoor, insisting on the restoration of the chain of command. After failing to secure support from the officers and men of the local units whose COs had not been in on the plot, Manzoor spoke to Ershad early on 1 June in a final attempt at a negotiated resolution. Faced with the demand for unconditional surrender, Manzoor decided to abandon Chittagong with his key aides and their families for destinations unknown. Lt. Colonels Mehboob and Motiur Rehman sped off on their own. Intercepted by troops of an Engineers unit, they got involved in an argument and were killed. Manzoor and his companions abandoned their vehicles at the foothills near Fatikchhari, walked for a while and then stopped at a tea-garden worker's hut for a meagre meal. Here, the police arrested Manzoor and the accompanying officers.

Manzoor asked to record a statement, which he was allowed to do. Noting that he had been dismissed from service and was, therefore, a civilian, he asked to be taken to the civil prison in Chittagong. Deputy Inspector General of police A.S.M. Shahjahan, the senior police officer in the region, would have complied, but soon, an army detachment led by a Captain arrived and demanded the General be handed over. In the charged atmosphere which roiled the country following Zia's death, the police officer could only take a written receipt of the individuals being transferred to army custody.[105] Shortly after arriving in the cantonment that he had only recently left, Manzoor was shot dead. A single bullet left a 'big gaping hole' in the right occipital region of his head, forcing brain matter out. He died of 'shock and haemorrhage from bullet injury' to his head.[106] By this time, loyal units from Comilla had taken over Chittagong cantonment while most local troops had crossed the Shubhapur Bridge and surrendered. Manzoor's abortive coup was over but Zia and he were dead, as were several other officers. The Zia era had ended but what would follow remained unclear. Bangladesh's vulnerability to violent intra-military convulsions was now as apparent, as was the marginal capacity of the political elite to maintain civilian rule—which now survived simply at the sufferance of Lt. General H.M. Ershad, CAS. What followed was the consequence of the tensions generated by the two elite groups with often contrary interests seeking to establish supremacy in a 'soft state'.

On 1 June, soldiers recovered Zia's shattered and decomposing body from the secret grave. The following day, it was flown to Dhaka. Hundreds of thousands of mourners joined the funeral procession, underscoring Zia's popularity and the pall his death had cast over the country. Zia was buried with full military honours near the new parliament complex. Now began the task of rebuilding his shattered edifice. Justice Sattar and General Ershad sought to maintain the continuity of government while taking severe punitive measures against the plotters of the abortive coup. All three strands to this effort—the army, the BNP and the administration—had pivoted round the personality of Zia, who had largely fashioned them around his own leadership. The army and the administration with their own structures could retain cohesion independently of Zia, but the BNP's disparate segments had not gelled sufficiently. Now, with his violent death, all three institutions were convulsed. Sattar ordered a judicial commission of inquiry into the president's assassination. Ershad instituted a military court of inquiry headed by a Major- General, and later, a General Court Martial chaired by another, to try the officers alleged by the former to have been involved in the plot. Twenty-four officers were charged with causing a mutiny leading to the death of the president and others, and with inciting mutiny by spreading rumours of a plot by repatriated officers to kill their FF colleagues. Seven other officers were charged with joining the mutiny and failing to inform their superiors or appropriate authorities of the existence of this mutiny. The accused were either FF officers or junior officers commissioned after Bangladesh's independence; no repatriated officers were charged or tried.[107]

The court martial began the trial on 10 July 1981 and ended it on 26 July. The court martial sentenced twelve officers to death and awarded varying prison sentences to ten others. The remaining defendants were acquitted but were dismissed from service. The convictions and sentences were appealed against at the Supreme Court, but both the High Court and the Appellate Division noted they had no jurisdiction over the proceedings of courts martial. Following the trial and executions, the army conducted a 'screening' operation among its officers, which led to the retirement or dismissal of about a hundred officers—all of them FF.[108] The army was now largely commanded by General Officers repatriated from Pakistan and officered by other repatriates, and officers either trained at the Bangladesh Military Academy, or commissioned from among JRB leaders. There was much scepticism over the nature and probity of the legal processes but Ershad and his aides were able to establish order within the military, if at a lower level of intellectual attainment and professional rigour. The most volatile element in the state structure was thus stabilised, promising to maintain stability within the state and polity generally. But the situation within the BNP, and the wider administration, was less secure.

A few days after taking office, Sattar announced he would stand as the BNP's candidate for the presidency and that he would make no changes to the presidential system installed by Zia. This immediately revived the BNP's factions. A right-of-centre team representing anti–Indian and conservative Islamist elements led by the Prime Minister, Shah Azizur Rahman, coalesced around Sattar. The other group, describing themselves as nationalist and pro-independence, formed around Zia's former Deputy Prime Minister, Moudud Ahmed. The factional dispute had grown so bitter in late 1979 that Zia decided in January 1980 to retain the right-wing faction in office and relieved Moudud Ahmed of his ministerial duties. Moudud did, however, remain an MP and a key aide to the President. Now, he demanded that the party- and national constitutions be edited to reflect changes occasioned by Zia's death; essentially to loosen the presidency's grip on the government and the Chairman's absolute control over the BNP. Moudud's faction demanded an elected Vice President to lend representative weight to the presidency. They also sought consideration of the opposition's demand to amend the constitution to restore parliamentary supremacy. Sattar and Moudud met several times but failed to agree. The BNP's parliamentary party, too, split along factional lines on these issues and on Sattar's candidacy. The government appeared on the brink of collapse. The BNP's ruling faction tabled the sixth constitutional amendment enabling Sattar to run for the presidency while still the substantive Vice President and acting President, but the rebel faction's MPs, and the opposition, boycotted the session. This is when Ershad took an openly political step.

The CAS met Moudud Ahmed on 6 July 1981, and told him, 'although we are not yet prepared to take over,' if the amendment was not passed 'the army would have no alternative but to do so.'[109] That evening, Ershad arranged a meeting between Sattar and Moudud with their aides at the *Bangabhaban*, where they worked out a compromise. Under pressure from Ershad, Moudud Ahmed's dissident faction agreed to support the passage of the 6th Amendment and then prepare for a 7th Amendment converting the Vice Presidency to an elected office.[110] But before that could happen, three weeks after Zia's assassination, Sattar fired two members of the cabinet—retired Major General Nurul Islam and Lt. Colonel Akbar Hossain—both Zia's confidants and his fellow FF officers. Now, the cabinet was almost entirely dominated by men who had either opposed independence or had played no active role in the war. This shift to the right angered both dissident BNP leaders and the opposition, especially the Awami League, reinvigorated by the return from India of Mujib's older daughter, Hasina, and from Britain of his adviser, Kamal Hossain. The AL led a campaign supported by most opposition parties demanding the lifting of the state of emergency imposed after Zia's death, the formation of a national government and the replacement of the presidential system with a parliamentary one. So, when the government announced that presidential polls would be held on 21 September, there was much anger outside the ruling faction of the BNP.

Different opposition parties and fronts wanted different changes before they would take part in the elections. Their lack of unity gave the BNP's ruling faction the space it needed to make its case. While the government negotiated with key opposition parties and twice postponed the polls, first to 15 October and, then, to 15 November, the opposition put up dozens of candidates representing the diversity of political platforms and personalities. Of the eighty-three individuals who signed themselves up as presidential candidates, only seventy-two were declared valid by the Election Commission. In the end, after initial campaigning using public funds and facilities by thirty-one men, only a handful made a mark. Apart from acting-president Sattar, General M.A.G. Osmani, the wartime commander, ran as the nominee of a citizens' group, while Dr Kamal Hossain was the Awami League's candidate. Differences in organisational strength and campaign-financial muscle reduced the contest to a duel between Justice Sattar and Kamal Hossain. 21,873 polling stations were set up for the 38.95 million registered voters. Turn out was reported to have been 55.47 per cent. Sattar was credited with receiving 21.60 million votes; Kamal Hossain got 5.69 million.[111] The other twenty-nine candidates, having failed to attract the threshold number of votes, lost their deposit. This landslide victory established Sattar as Bangladesh's new popularly elected leader, underscoring a public anxiety to maintain stability. The BNP was given a fresh mandate to rule and the validity of demands from the dissident faction and opposition groups for change was weakened, but not silenced. The Awami League launched a new campaign.

Opposition parties alleged the BNP's vote rigging and its muscle men's coercive tactics had prevented their supporters from casting their ballots. Given the tradition of coercive politics throughout the country's post-1947 history, this was not new and, following an official announcement of results, Sattar took the oath of office on 20 November. While the BNP was thus restored to formal authority, the hollowness of its own organisation now returned to the fore. As Prime Minister Rahman pushed for Sattar's elevation to the post of party chairman, the dissidents persuaded Zia's widow, Khaleda, that the BNP was being taken over by the 'opponents of independence' and her late husband's legacy faced ruin. Khaleda Zia agreed to run for the office of the party chairman on behalf of the rebels who also wanted her to become the country's vice president and balance the right-wing's pre-eminence. This fresh round of debilitating internal feud in the BNP ranks drew the army back into the fray. General Ershad and his aides persuaded Khaleda Zia to withdraw her nomination, weaken the rebel faction, and allow Sattar to become party chairman unopposed. He now had the authority to shape the party and the government to reflect his priorities and preferences. However, the existence within the BNP's leadership of apparently irreconcilable differences raised questions about Sattar's ability to pursue coherent policies that could be sustained over the term of his office. It also created room for intervention by an organisation that seemed able and willing to supplant politicians.

Consistent in his public support for the constitutionally established government since Ziaur Rahman's assassination, General Ershad had repeatedly acted to secure Sattar's succession. He also had brought the leaders of the BNP's feuding factions together to try to resolve their differences without disrupting administrative continuity. Exposure to the BNP leaders' incoherence impressed on army commanders the politicians' inability to organise themselves sufficiently for effective discharge of their official duties.[112] Against this backdrop, Ershad repeated his long-standing view that without an institutional role for the army in national governance, the pattern of violent insurrections by sections of the army could not be ruled out. Ershad had set out this formulation in writing in late 1980, while Zia was at the apparent peak of his authority: 'The role of the military, especially in the context of a national army, should very much be that of a participant in the collective effort of the nation.'[113] Writing in the inaugural edition of the Bangladesh Army Journal, Ershad could be certain that his comments would be noted by virtually every military officer, including those retired officers working in the higher echelons of the ruling elite. This view chimed with some of the remarks made by war-hero-turned renegades like Colonels M. Ziauddin and Abu Taher, and Major General Abul Manzoor, but it also challenged Zia's active attempts to professionalise the military and keep it outside the political-administrative leadership structure. As a loyal professional, Ershad's objectives may have been uncertain, but that the military could not be ignored by the rulers was clear. Whether Zia and his aides took note was less so.

Now, just before and after Sattar's electoral victory, Ershad issued statements and gave interviews to local and foreign journalists in which he explained what he wanted.[114] He noted that the separation of society's civilian and military segments was a colonial legacy that had no relevance to an independent country which needed to muster all its human and material resources, including those in the military to 'build democracy' and pursue development, establish law and order, maintain state security and alleviate mass poverty.[115] He insisted he sought no power for himself, nor a leadership role for the military in this 'collective national enterprise,' but declared that unless the armed forces were given a role in the policy making processes 'within the constitutional framework,' future turbulence could not be ruled out.[116] In other words, Ershad warned the politicians to accept the reality of their own vulnerabilities. Given the 'softness' of the polity's key components in contrast to the military's relative 'hardness,' now that he had revamped and united the force under his own leadership, Ershad may have felt he could not be disciplined by an internally divided ruling elite which he had helped, as the CAS, to maintain its authority. The government had to seriously consider his demands.

Institutionalising a role for the military in national administration proved controversial. Leaders of the Awami League, the JSD, the Nizam-e-Islami and the *Mukti Joddha Sangsad* (Freedom Fighters' council), and General Osmany condemned Ershad's comments. The formerly underground Leftist parties advocated closing the gap between citizens and soldiers but sought clarity on and detailed consideration of the practicalities. BNP leaders did not directly question Ershad's statements, but coming as these did so soon after Sattar's election, they and other politicians were demoralised.[117] Sattar and his aides agreed to the establishment of a National Security Council (NSC) at the highest level of the administration. A council bearing this name had been in operation since the mid-1970s. Chaired by the Home Secretary—the senior bureaucrat in the ministry—it comprised senior civil and military officials who regularly reviewed security issues, recommending action to the cabinet. The armed forces had demanded that the council be upgraded to comprise six members—the president, vice-president, prime minister and the three chiefs of staff from the services.[118] The NSC would vet all major ministerial decisions with the three service chiefs exercising the same voting rights as the civilian leaders. In short, the service chiefs sought implicitly to control the cabinet.[119]

On 1 January 1982, the government announced the formation of the NSC chaired by the president and with the vice president, prime minister, and ministers of industries, finance and home affairs, as well as the service chiefs, as members. The latter's voting powers were thus diluted. The NSC would advise the government on national defence, coordinate the activities of the armed forces, paramilitary organisations and civil armed forces, and examine if the armed forces could be utilised in non-military state activities; it was not, however, a 'super cabinet.'[120] While one of the military's demands had apparently been met, however partially, other problems dogged Sattar's administration. Reports of ministerial impropriety and administrative failings made the headlines in an increasingly vocal press. With the BNP's factions trying to undermine each other, credible reports against senior figures undermined the administration's authority. In early February, a dramatic event pointed to the government's vulnerability. Imdadul Huq, a young BNP member sought by the police on serious criminal charges, was found sheltering at the official residence of the Youth Minister, Abul Kashem, who was away at the time. The police surrounded the house on orders of the Home Minister who advised Kashem to return home. Kashem persuaded Huq, armed with a firearm, to surrender. The sensational incident triggered demands that Sattar take drastic steps to reform his administration.

Three days later, following a cabinet meeting at which Sattar pleaded for party unity, six uniformed army officers led by Major General Abdur Rahman, GOC, 9th Infantry Division based in Dhaka, entered the *Bangabhaban*. Criticising the government's inability to get rid of corrupt members from within its ranks, they demanded that Sattar hand over power to them.[121] After hours of discussion, Sattar agreed to dissolve the cabinet and announced this on radio, accusing ministers of graft and incompetence. However, the following day he reshuffled the cabinet, dropping only a few ministers. The newly established NSC sat for the first time and took charge of major national issues. Sattar ordered that charges be brought against several senior former ministers, reconstituted the BNP's Standing Committee, and appointed Mohammad-ullah, a former president during Mujib's reign, as the Vice President. His was a short-lived vice-presidency. Hours later, early on 24 March 1982, General Ershad proclaimed martial law and assumed 'all and full powers of the Government of the People's Republic of Bangladesh.'[122] Sattar announced he was resigning and was handing over to General Ershad in 'the national interest.' Ershad persuaded Chief Justice Ahsanuddin Chowdhury to assume the presidency while he, Ershad, became the country's chief executive officer. The BNP's rule was over.

In Zia's footsteps

Nominating himself as the Chief Martial Law Administrator (CMLA) and appointing a number of Deputy- and Zonal Martial Law Administrators (DCMLAs and ZMLAs) from among senior armed forces officers, Ershad assumed executive, legislative and judicial authority. He proclaimed his right to appoint, dismiss, or cancel the nomination of the president, the formal head of state. Martial Law Regulation no. 1 of 1982 established an array of military tribunals, special- and summary military courts whose jurisdiction placed them beyond the reach of the civil judiciary's appellate benches. A series of Martial Law Regulations and Orders brought the spectrum of group activity and personal conduct within the military's purview. For instance, Martial Law Order no. 1 forbade holding seminars and workshops without permission from martial law authorities; Order no. 2 prohibited foreign travel by government employees without clearance; Order no. 3 instructed citizens on the maintenance and cleanliness of property and equipment in their care; Order no. 4 dissolved the Youth Complexes set up by Zia and forbade the collection of tolls which had sustained the groups as the BNP's strong-arm bands; *Gram Sarkars* (village governing councils), too, were abolished;[123] Order no. 5 laid down the president's oath of office.[124] The detailed nature of the regulatory framework proclaimed within hours of Ershad's putsch suggested the military had been preparing for sometime to take power. Ershad and his aides may have been making contingency plans since 1980.[125]

Fragmentation among political parties, and the decline of cleavages within the armed forces, allowed Ershad to present the military as a body united under his command, ready at a moment's notice to implement his orders, using massive violence if necessary. This possibility, and a general disillusionment over the well-publicised malaise afflicting the ousted BNP administration, may have deterred overt opposition.[126] Ershad's was the first bloodless coup in the country's brief, turbulent, history. By discrediting and marginalising party-political organs and personalities, it weakened the polity's ability to build the capacity to organise the population, lead groups in meaningful pursuits and institute pluralist self-rule. It also negated the trend set by Zia to erect civil political structures and practices that could, over time, evolve into a more confident polity under effective civilian leadership. Other than that, though, Ershad's military administration essentially followed the course charted by Zia in the mid-1970s. In addition to his offices of the CAS and CMLA, Ershad appointed himself Supreme Commander of the Armed Forces, and Defence Minister. Like Zia in his early years, Ershad took the Cabinet, Establishment and Science & Technology portfolios, securing personal control over the civil and military bureaucracies. His Council of Advisers, made up of senior military commanders and bureaucrats, replaced Sattar's cabinet. Initially, Ershad called himself 'President of the Council of Advisers.' In December 1983, he assumed the presidency.

The CMLA conducted affairs of state from the CMLA's Secretariat, effectively the office of the chief executive. He commanded the army in his capacity as the CAS. He controlled the Navy and the Air Force from the Supreme Commander's Secretariat where he was aided by a Principal Staff Officer (PSO) and a tri–service staff coordinating national defence and security management on his behalf. As Defence Minister, he oversaw the civil-military interface at the bureaucratic-administrative level. And he kept an eye on potential sources of trouble—civilian and military— with the help of trusted aides running the Directorate General of Forces Intelligence (DGFI) and National Security Intelligence (NSI). Placing men he believed were loyal to him in charge of these key organs, Ershad, like Mujib, established personal loyalty as a key criterion of policymaking, weakening the institutionalisation of authority. Concentration of power held in place with a network built on personal loyalty remained his regime's weakness that lasted until the very end of his period in office.[127] But in the spring of 1982, that was years in the future.

There were differences, however. Unlike Zia, Ershad had not fought in the war of independence, having commanded a battalion of the EBR in Pakistan until being taken prisoner in early 1972 along with other Bengali service personnel.[128] And yet, as the *ex–officio* patron of the official association of the Freedom Fighters, he frequently spoke on behalf of FFs, which some other FF leaders found difficult to stomach. Outraged by his demand that the armed forces be involved in non-military affairs of state, they had freely vented their anger claiming this was an expression of Ershad's ambition.[129] Not even Ershad's friends would describe him as a charismatic figure[130] as Zia and Mujib had been. Zia evoked strong feelings among soldiers and civilians alike—the many attempts on his life and office underscored the hostility felt by some while the large gatherings he commanded in life, and after death, demonstrated the affection millions felt for him.

Ershad, on the other hand, was less well known outside the forces, and evoked a modest emotional response. Zia had been a soldier and war-hero who grew into a political leader with a pluralist vision of his country and paid the price of his efforts to realise it. Ershad was seen in a more pragmatic light, willing and able to manage the more practical aspects of state-building but carrying pretensions of literary excellence, an aspect of his image much reviled in urban intellectual circles. Zia was seen as personally incorruptible although he allowed his aides to engage in graft;

Ershad and his team were accused of massive corruption. Following his ouster Ershad would become the first former president to be convicted and jailed on corruption charges. Zia's stature as a war-hero did not prevent the bloodletting which afflicted the military until his assassination; violent militancy ended in the relatively more professional military Ershad's team built. Unlike Zia, Ershad did offer prime ministership to the veteran politician, and former Chief Minister of East Bengal, Ataur Rahman Khan, and honour that offer, if temporarily. Both Zia and Ershad fashioned political vehicles with disparate elements that nearly collapsed in fratricidal bickering after they left the scene, but Ershad did effect a measure of troubled stability.

Like many other military putsch leaders, Ershad initially announced a set of objectives[131] which arguably resonated with a large section of Bangladesh's cognoscenti:

- Restoration of a democratic system reflecting the needs and hopes of the people.
- Checking inflation, increasing food supply, reducing aid-dependency and turning state-owned enterprises into profitable, commercially-run private businesses.
- Reducing public expenditure, expanding agricultural and industrial investment, and implementing land reforms to encourage food production.
- Eradicating corruption by using the powers of martial law regulations and orders.
- Implementing administrative reforms ensuring that 'bribery, corruption, nepotism, misuse of power, negligence in duty and waste of national wealth would end.'
- Reforming the national judiciary and educational systems, and
- Addressing the problems of population explosion and mass unemployment.

Soon after Ershad proclaimed martial law, security forces arrested a number of former ministers, other politicians, senior officials and prominent businessmen on graft charges. Many were charged under martial law regulations and tried by military courts; some officials lost their jobs without being charged or tried. To increase efficiency and reduce costs, Ershad reduced the number of ministries from forty-two to seventeen, slashing Directorates from 256 to 180.[132] Apart from these high profile measures, Ershad pursued longer-term changes. He set up commissions to examine areas of perceived weaknesses. Civil and Foreign services were reorganised, formalising the induction of military officers on a quota system; banks, financial institutions and public-sector enterprises, too, received soldiers on their boards. But educational reforms, stressing technical training, were set aside when political parties grasped this issue as the focus of an agitational campaign mounted by Dhaka University students and taken up by fellow scholars elsewhere. The recommendations of a commission tasked to review the country's ancient land tenure system were only partly implemented in recognition that substantive land reforms would be impossible without making fundamental changes to elite structures and social norms. However, a certain amount of change was implemented. In short, Ershad tried to alter key aspects of collective activities without forcing revolutionary change. Success was partial. His attempts at revamping the macro-economic framework, liberalising private enterprise and investment in manufacturing and agriculture, enhancing local governance, healthcare, and the judiciary evoked mixed responses. But his primary challenge was political.

For nearly nine years, Ershad would seek to establish the legitimacy of his rule which, given that he had repeatedly pledged loyalty to constitutional processes before and after Sattar's landslide victory in presidential polls, and then ousted him, would prove elusive. His 'civilianising' framework built on Zia's template: local elections and a referendum; forming supportive groups by co-opting defectors from existing parties and allied fronts; using executive authority, especially intelligence and security assets, to weaken parties and leaders opposed to him while buying off those willing to be bought; building up rural support and urban organisation by melding disparate if sycophantic factions into a new front and, then, a new party; then, holding presidential and parliamentary elections; finally, to secure *ex–post facto* parliamentary endorsement of all action by amending the constitution with the help of a supportive legislature.

To this end, Ershad allowed indoor political activities from 1 April 1983 and lifted bans from all political activities in mid-November, relaxing martial law regulations. He announced plans to hold presidential polls on 24 May 1984, and parliamentary elections on 25 November 1984. Building electoral momentum, on 27 December 1983, shortly after assuming the presidency, Ershad held Union Council elections—at the lowest tier of local government. In February 1984, he held elections to municipal councils except for those in Dhaka and Chittagong. These polls, held on a non-party basis, created new groups of elected officials with a stake in Ershad's rule. Having established a new tier of local administration at the *Upazila* (sub-district) level, he announced plans to hold elections to those councils on 24 March 1984. The main political parties rose in unison against this plan. Ershad invited all the major parties and their leaders to discuss ways of civilianising the administration and restoring democratic rule. Some 360 leading members of seventy-five political parties met Ershad in the first two months of 1984. Long overnight sessions failed to bridge the gap between the two sides—the politicians questioned the validity of polls held under martial law; Ershad pointed out that the withdrawal of martial law before the election of a new parliament would create a legislative vacuum which could lead to anarchy which must be avoided—essentially the argument General Zia had made.

At the end of March 1984, Ershad struck political gold, appointing veteran political leader and former provincial chief minister, Ataur Rahman Khan, as his Prime Minister. This allowed him to establish a veneer of civilian authority over the administration while he pursued his party-political game of chess. Throughout 1984, Ershad and his rivals played a game of chicken, with each raising the stake and calling the other's bluff. The quality of Ershad's challenges changed with the BNP's ruling council electing Khaleda Zia its leader. Now, both the main parties, the Awami League and the BNP, diametrically opposed on power and legitimacy issues, shared an enduring feature of Bangladeshi politics—the mass appeal of charismatic, semi–feudal and dynastic leadership which the rationally-organised military and civil bureaucratic state structure could neither countenance nor countermand. This structural dichotomy between the empirical-rational model pursued by state functionaries and their OECD donors on the one hand, and the emotional, almost mystical, subjectivity binding the populace to its 'leaders' on the other would remain a major challenge for General Ershad's administration and its successors.

On 28 November, opposition activists surrounded the central secretariat, broke the police cordon, and breached the boundary wall, threatening to enter the offices of the ministers and their bureaucrats. Much violence ensued. Ershad reimposed the full rigour of martial law, banning outdoor political activities and warning against violations. The Zonal, Sub-zonal and District martial law administrators were reinstated and special- and summary military courts revived to try recalcitrant opponents. He then proceeded to hold the *Upazila* elections in February 1985, and scheduled a referendum on his presidency on 21 March 1985.[133] The referendum, which addressed the voting public directly, bypassed and weakened the party political elite. The ballot asked if the citizens endorsed his 'policies and programmes and have confidence in him to continue as the President of the country till national elections are held in accordance with the provisions of the suspended constitution.'[134] With his critics boycotting the polls, Ershad won 86 per cent of the vote and claimed the right to stay in office with massive popular support.[135] His political rivals begged to differ; the Awami League's fifteen-party alliance and the BNP's seven-party front, with occasional and indirect coordination, mounted a campaign of general strikes, marches and a national demolition derby in which activists attacked vehicles and premises that violated their strike calls, and the police counter-attacked the picketing public. Considerable damage was done to the economy and civic life, but once blood had been shed and the martial law authorities had failed to stamp out 'resistance,' short of unacceptable coercion being applied, calm could not be restored.

Ershad now embarked on another political enterprise, inviting defectors from the major parties and widening his support base. The BNP and the Awami League were further fragmented as several of their leaders joined the General. Ershad set up student, youth and labour fronts which could, over time, attract support, neutralise their Awami League and BNP counterparts, and erect a platform for a political coalition akin to Zia's *Jagodal*.[136] By the spring of 1985, Ershad had drawn several senior politicians into working arrangements, amongst them Korban Ali, Shah Moazzam Hossain and Mizan Chowdhury from the Awami League; Abdul Halim Chowdhury, M.A. Matin, Shah Azizur Rahman, Shamsul Huda Chowdhury and Anisul Islam Mahmood from the BNP; Kazi Zafar Ahmed of the UPP; Serajul Hossain Khan of the *Ganotantri Dal* (democratic party); Salahuddin Kader Choudhury of the Muslim League; and Anwar Hossain Monju, Editor of the influential daily, *Ittefaq*, and son of an eminent Awami League leader. Zia's former deputy prime minister, Moudud Ahmed, too, would soon join him. On 16 August 1985, Ershad launched his National Front with his own *Janadal* party and faction leaders who had defected to him. The *Janadal's* eighteen-point programme, similar to Zia's nineteen-point one, became the front's platform. Persuading the members of the front to dissolve their own organisation into a new political party that would eventually be chaired by Ershad, on New Year's Day 1986 the General floated his own political platform, the *Jatiya* (national) Party.

Ershad targeted the BNP, especially Khaleda Zia's leadership, and was able to denude it of key leaders. His attacks on the party and efforts to marginalise it turned Khaleda Zia into an implacable adversary. In contrast, Ershad cultivated Sheikh Hasina, the Awami League's leader, secretly meeting her at least twice and pledging to restore Mujib to the position of the national father-figure. He devoted much skill and resources to widening the breach between the Awami League and the BNP, and their two leaders.[137] In the first five years of his rule he attained notable success in this enterprise. In March 1986, keen to legitimise his office, Ershad agreed to hold parliamentary polls before presidential ones. If the opposition parties took part in the polls, nobody associated with the administration would run while in office, and he would dissolve all military courts and withdraw martial law administrations at the Zonal level and below.[138] Nearly three weeks later, he made further concessions— nobody associated with the government, including local bodies chairmen, would support the campaign of any candidate for the legislative polls, and he personally guaranteed that these would be free and fair. If the opposition still boycotted the polls, however, he would have no alternative to re-imposing the full force of martial law.[139] After several nights of secret negotiations, just before the deadline imposed by the Election Commission, Hasina announced that the Awami League would take part in the parliamentary elections. The BNP and other opposition groups were put on the back foot by this move. By taking part, Hasina partly legitimised the elections held on 7 May 1986. Apart from the Awami League and the JP, twenty-six other parties contested the polls. Much violence and alleged vote-rigging accompanied the voting.

The results, when they were eventually announced, outraged the Awami League. Of the 300 seats contested, it only won 76 to the JP's 153.[140] While Hasina and her aides rejected the results and Khaleda Zia accused both Hasina and Ershad of betraying the nation's trust, many of the independents and members elected from the smaller parties would gravitate to the JP, giving the party a significant majority in the new legislature. This allowed the JP to take all thirty of the additional nominated seats reserved for women. This was crucial to Ershad being able to secure the minimum of 220 votes out of the total of 330 needed to win *ex–post facto* endorsement of his martial law regulations and actions via yet another, the seventh, constitutional amendment. With the ratification of his coup and post-coup actions accomplished, Ershad announced plans to hold presidential elections. In July 1986, he replaced Ataur Rahman Khan with Mizanur Rahman Chowdhury as the prime minister. He resigned as CAS, appointed Lt. General M. Atiqur Rahman as his successor, and retired from service. He also assumed the formal leadership of *Jatiya Party* (JP). Hasina and her eight-party alliance opposed the presidential form of government and did not wish to endorse its continuation by taking part in presidential polls; Khaleda Zia preferred the presidential system to the parliamentary one but vehemently objected to elections being conducted by 'the illegitimate, autocratic, Ershad regime.'[141] So, when the polls took place in mid-October 1986 in the midst of boycotts and general strikes called by the opposition, Ershad won handsomely in a contest without any challenger worth the name.

Although the government claimed Ershad had taken 84 per cent of votes cast from a 50 plus per cent turnout, opposition leaders and much of the foreign media 'estimated a far lower percentage and alleged voting irregularities.'[142] Undaunted, Ershad took the oath of office as an elected head of state and proceeded to garner the parliamentary support needed to amend the constitution legalising his coup and all subsequent action. This was accomplished in November 1986. Ershad then lifted martial law, and the Awami League and other opposition parties which had won parliamentary seats, joined the legislature. The 'civilianisation' of Ershad's rule was now complete but without the legitimacy he sought. Khaleda Zia's adamant opposition to Ershad's rule had won her high praise in circles critical of Ershad's 'autocratic rule.' In July 1987, Hasina had occasion to join her. Ershad ordered the enactment of a law authorising the presence of military officers in local administrative councils. Politicians of most non-JP shades saw this as an intolerable institutionalisation of military intrusion into civilian affairs and the 'loyal' opposition walked out of the parliament to organise protests. By October 1987, mainly under Zia's leadership, BNP's student- and youth wings made civic life in the capital uncomfortable. The BNP-led seven-party alliance and the Awami League-led eight-party alliance found common cause and began coordinating their agitation, demanding Ershad's resignation and the holding of free and fair elections. The two groups issued a joint declaration adopting a common programme and scheduled a 'million-strong' rally in Dhaka on 10 November.

This combined effort, hitherto unseen in independent Bangladesh, aroused much enthusiasm and led to considerable violence. Unwilling to allow such a massive show of force, Ershad declared a state of emergency, arrested and interned opposition leaders, restricted public gatherings and tightened security arrangements. The big rally, in the end, did not produce the results the organisers were hoping for, but dissent did not end. As some opposition MPs prepared to resign their office in early December, Ershad dissolved the parliament and scheduled elections in March 1988. In late January, as Hasina was campaigning in Chittagong for a boycott of the elections, two local groups clashed around her. The police opened fire and a number of activists were killed close to where Hasina was speaking. The authorities promptly ordered an inquiry into the incident which nonetheless triggered countrywide protests, further inflaming the situation. All the major opposition parties stayed away and only A.S.M.A. Rab of JSD brought in other factions to take part in these polls. Foreign observers reported the turnout at 10–15 per cent. The result was predictable. Rab's combined opposition bagged thirty-five seats; Colonel Farook's Freedom Party won four; JSD (Shahjahan) took three and independents, six. JP won the other 252.[143] With a newly elected government ready to implement his vision, Ershad replaced Mizanur Rahman Chowdhury with Moudud Ahmed as prime minister. But his troubles were not over.

The key opposition parties' absence had rendered this an unrepresentative parliament and it lasted barely three years. And yet, with Ershad using his party as a legislative battering ram with which to enact laws and amend the constitution, it achieved more than more 'legitimate' National Assemblies. It passed the national budgets for FY1988–89, FY1989–90, and FY1990–91; it enacted the Eighth Amendment to the constitution proclaiming Islam as the state religion and creating six permanent benches of the High Court outside Dhaka; the Ninth Amendment to the Constitution limited the president's tenure to two terms and provided for an elected vice president; the Tenth Amendment created thirty parliamentary seats reserved for women on a permanent basis. Ershad's refusal to acknowledge the weight of the opposition's efforts against his rule loosened the tentative links between the two alliances and their leaders who began a vituperative campaign as much directed against each other as against Ershad. With this fresh lease of political life, Ershad focused on addressing the consequences of floods which visited devastating losses on the country, destroying much property and crops in 1987–88. This period of relative calm also allowed Ershad to focus on several reform programmes he had begun early on.

An unlikely reformer

Despite the almost continual, often violent, agitation by urban political activists, Ershad's nine years did bring about a measure of stability, allowing him to pursue substantial changes to Bangladesh's economics and social circumstances by reforming aspects of the underlying relationships.

Industry and investment

Ershad lifted limits on domestic and foreign investment in most sectors of the economy, retaining control over only a few areas. Trade, too, was liberalised, with market forces allowed to shape economic dynamics. Over six years, he privatised hundreds of industrial units nationalised in the early 1970s. One nationalised bank was returned to its owners; minority shares in another were handed to local owners; six scheduled banks and nineteen insurance companies were licensed to operate in the private sector.[144] Industrial units still in the public sector were to be gradually privatised. The operations of the Export Processing Zone, initially limited to Chittagong, were expanded; a Board of Investment was set up to attract and ease direct foreign investment. Entrepreneurs were encouraged to invest untaxed 'black' income into manufacturing after 'whitening' it by paying a 15 per cent tax. Ershad aided the consolidation of a national *bourgeoisie*, actively promoting a new and expanding class of trading-and-manufacturing entrepreneurs into the national elite.[145] Some of the beneficiaries of his policies would join his political platform when he civilianised his administration. If he secured political gains from these policies, the country gained too. His term in office saw the construction of over 6,000 miles of motorable roads and 500 bridges; installed power generating capacity rose from 650 MWe to 2,250 MWe;[146] he committed the country, and the donor club, to the construction of the Jamuna multi-purpose road-rail bridge which would connect the often-neglected western third of the country to the remainder.

Agriculture and land tenure

With 120 million people sharing a country just 144,000 square kilometres in area, or about 728 persons per sq. km,[147] Bangladesh was the most densely-populated state on earth outside of city-states. As an agrarian society, it had traditionally relied on land to provide subsistence, employment, income, surplus-based wealth, social standing and security. Ownership had historically been iniquitous, reflecting the stratification of a tiny landed aristocracy and mass tenancy by penurious peasant-farmers.[148] Successive administrations had, in the 1950s and 1970s, imposed some ceilings and carried out modest redistribution, but the vast majority of Bangladeshis either owned no land, or possessed just the homestead and a plot providing bare subsistence. The need for loans to buy inputs and service previous loans, and the lack of banking facilities, forced many small farmers to mortgage their land to *jotedars* or moneylenders at usurious rates of interest. Unmet loans led to the loss of ownership. The Land Reforms Ordinance of January 1984 granted important rights to tenants for the first time.[149]

The ceiling on individual holdings was reduced from 33.33 acres to 20; the right of individuals to acquire property in someone else's name and bypass the ceiling was cancelled; the right of landholders to evict tenants was revoked; tenants would have contractual rights which the state would protect; in case a tenant died, his next of kin would execute the contract for the remainder of the contract's term; tenants and owners would share the fruits of their efforts, each claiming a third of harvests—the remaining third being shared in proportion to investment made in providing inputs; if the owner wished to sell the land, the tenant would have first option to buy it. In addition, government-owned *khas* land would be given to landless farmers to build homesteads on a preferential basis. In February 1984, Ershad proclaimed another rule fixing minimum wages for agricultural labourers. While his reforms did not transform land-ownership or power relations, they did make the first serious attempt at alleviating the plight of the rural poor.

Healthcare and pharmaceuticals

In theory, Bangladesh's public health service provided basic healthcare to the urban poor and the rural majority. But the reality was grim. For most people, medical care was often distant, very expensive, and difficult to sustain to the end of a course of medication. Widespread poverty meant many patients could not afford to travel to the nearest town with public health facilities. Many of these were just buildings with few therapeutic assets.[150] Surgery and other complex services were almost beyond reach. State resource allocation had been meagre and private or charitable institutions only filled some of the void. A part of the problem was the concentration of facilities and doctors at the urban centres, especially Dhaka. Another was the price of medicaments which were available. Ershad wished to address these issues soon after taking over. Appointing several eminent physicians to a 'National Drugs Committee,' he sternly implemented their recommendations as the new national policy.[151]

The policy stipulated what were 'essential' drugs and what were not, what drugs could be locally manufactured and what was allowed to be imported, and prohibited the rest. Within the first three months from the enactment of this ordinance, stocks of 265 medicinal items were destroyed; the manufacture and sale of 134 items were restricted within six months; 742 items were banned. Official control was imposed on the import of active ingredients and sale of imported products. Restrictions were imposed on multinational firms selling or manufacturing items other than essential ones. Despite resistance from some traders and multinational firms, improvements were soon apparent. Before the reforms, eight multinationals controlled 65 per cent of production and 75 per cent of the market by value; a decade later, local producers controlled 60 per cent of both production and market. The latter now supplied nearly 70 per cent of the drugs used by the state system. While prices generally rose by 173 per cent over this decade, those of the twenty-five essential drugs went up by just 20 per cent.[152] The efforts to spread the benefits of medical training and facilities across Bangladesh, on the other hand, failed. Ershad's administrative decentralisation plans included posting out doctors on state employment from Dhaka and other cities to rural health centres for fixed terms. This compulsion triggered a campaign by doctors spearheaded by the Bangladesh Medical Association which eventually merged into the 'dump Ershad' campaign mounted by the opposition parties and other groups in the late 1980s.

Local government and devolution

Having disbanded Zia's *Gram Sarkars*, Ershad proceeded to erect a more substantial edifice of devolved authority and local governance. The jurisdiction of each of the around 460 police stations or *Thana*[153] was to be organised as the lowest tier of administrative hierarchy, in theory bringing the benefits of governance closer to the citizenry. Each *Upazila* (sub-district) would overlay several Unions, each of which, in turn, brought together a number of villages. The *Upazila* would be managed by elected representatives, and focus on poverty alleviation and development. The *Upazila* Chairman, elected under adult franchise, would chair a council comprising the elected chairmen of the union councils within that *Upazila*, and representatives of various sections of the local populace. The Chairman would have a broad brief:

- be responsible for all administrative and developmental work in the area
- implement all government policies and programmes in the area
- supervise all relief work in a post-disaster situation
- administer all educational institutions
- implement the national family planning programme
- supervise the work of all civil servants in the area; write their annual reports assessing performance
- initiate, identify, prepare and implement development projects
- realise taxes and other revenues and receive funds on the council's behalf
- maintain and operate the *Upazila's* accounts and funds in correct order
- implement the decisions of the *Upazila* Council

To assist the Chairman, the government created three dozen civil servant posts from different cadres representing most of the central ministries focused on domestic affairs. They included a chief executive officer,[154] a magistrate, a financial officer, a project implementation officer, a medical team with eight graduate doctors to staff the local health and family welfare centre, and other officials and staff to represent line ministries and functions. Infrastructural development and the establishment of small urban centres brought an infusion of resources, pumping around Tk 14 billion in 1984–90 into semi–rural Bangladesh,[155] generating both employment and inflation, and reducing the gap between the state's colonial-era administrative structure and the people it was intended to serve. The reverse flow of resources energised a significant share of the population and built the basis for urbanisation outside the metropolitan cities. Consolidating this devolutionary process, Ershad raised administrative sub-divisions to districts, forcing the focus and capabilities of the government from the cities to over five dozen medium-sized towns, decentralising developmental and state-building functions from Dhaka outward. For a ruler whose quest for legitimacy never ended, this was radical reform that outlasted his presidency.

Justice and the judiciary

A corollary to more proximate administration was the dispensation of justice. The judicial system had been operating at the district level with higher courts and courts of appeal established in the capital. Both of the Supreme Court's two divisions, the High Court, and the Appellate Division, were located in Dhaka, forcing many to travel to and find accommodation in that crowded city for indefinite periods of time in the hope that their cases would finally be resolved. At lower levels, a limited establishment of courts, judges and judicial staff and facilities meant thousands of people waited for years—many in jail as 'under trial prisoners'—before getting any verdict. Sometimes, plaintiffs died without having their cases resolved; in other instances, children, held with parents as 'under trial prisoners,' grew into adulthood in jail.[156] With caseloads piling up all the time, justice for many was seen to be denied. At the lower end of the spectrum, the establishment of an Upazila-level magistracy immediately expanded the judiciary by a thousand judges and ancillary staff. Ershad took equally drastic measures to devolve the upper end of the spectrum, establishing seven permanent benches of the High Court in towns outside the capital.[157]

After Ershad withdrew martial law and revived the constitution, those benches were dissolved, but the Chief Justice, on the President's advice, established sessions benches in Barisal, Chittagong, Comilla, Jessore, Rangpur and Sylhet. In 1988, Ershad enacted the Eighth Amendment to the Constitution, providing for the establishment of High Court benches in these towns. This triggered an uprising by the Supreme Court Bar Association whose members, perhaps driven more by concerns for personal prospects in a devolved judicial structure, nonetheless dressed their complaints as outrage at the executive's unacceptable interference with the judiciary.[158] Lawyers not only boycotted the courts for months and accused the Chief Justice of siding with 'the autocrat Ershad', they also began a campaign which boosted the anti–Ershad agitation mounted by the parties and other organised groups. Eventually, at a time when Ershad was abroad, the Supreme Court's Appellate Division struck down the section of the Eighth Amendment endorsing the establishment of High Court benches outside Dhaka, thereby dissolving those benches. However, the sessions courts established by the Chief Justice could continue to operate. That was the visible fruit of Ershad's battle with the lawyers and the judiciary.

A regime challenged

Ershad, like Zia, ultimately relied on his command of the military to maintain authority. Although he, too, established a political party and retired from service, he paid much more attention to his former colleagues, many of whom remained close aides, during his presidency than Zia had done as a 'civilian' ruler. During the first two years when he ran his military administration as the CMLA, Ershad heavily relied on the army to serve as the instrument of his will and defender of his vision. He had inherited a modest GDP of $13.22 billion growing very slowly, while a population of 96 million rose rapidly and high inflation neutralised much of the gains.[159] And yet, defence allocations rose from $153 million in 1981 to $240 million in 1982.[160] That growth reflected Ershad's support for improved pay and conditions for personnel, modest procurement plans and a limited expansion in numbers.

As Table 3.3 shows, sustained financial support and steady growth meant Ershad's rule consolidated military professionalism, with new schools and facilities for specialist training and some new hardware, mostly Chinese, coming on stream.[161] This concentration of resources and the positioning of army officers in many key administrative, diplomatic and financial or corporate positions built a military carapace around the state[162] which civilians found irksome. Direct military involvement in civilian affairs would wax and wane with Ershad's enthusiasm for civilianising his government and the resistance put up by politicians, students, trades union and assorted critics, but a core of uniformed personnel in state organs was a reality which could not ignored. The 'rise' of the military within the state and the relative weakening of other institutions and groups in the polity generated a lasting power imbalance in favour of the armed services.

Table 3.3: Military expenditure by the Ershad Administration in 1984–1990[163]

Year	GNP $bn	Mil Pers	Milex $m	Milex/GNP	Arms Imports $m
1984	12.38	81,000	234	1.9%	30.00
1985	13.31	91,000	231	1.7%	60.00
1986	14.23	91,000	242	1.7%	70.00
1987	15.32	102,000	281	1.8%	50.00
1988	16.36	102,000	274	1.7%	50.00
1989	17.56	103,000	279	1.6%	120.00
1990	19.54	103,000	301	1.5%	30.00

The growth of the military in numbers of formations and units, in its ability to carry out orders—operational and domestic—and in professionalism, made the forces a different category to what they were when Ershad had become CAS. In many ways, his continuing close association with the services—like Zia, he lived in his military residence even as president—stood him in good stead when the civilian polity was up in arms. But as the forces grew more professional and Ershad assumed a more party-political persona after retiring from service, a certain distancing became inevitable.

One aspect of these changes became apparent in the CHT where the *Shanti Bahini's* montagnard insurrection and the army's counter-insurgency operations had reached a bloody stalemate. In the mid-1980s, while fighting raged, the government contacted Shantu Larma, using a former Marxist MP, Upendra Lal Chakma, to mediate. Six meetings followed, the first on 21 October 1985 at Panchhari, near the Larmas' home village in northern CHT. Led by field commanders from the two sides, the delegates established a negotiating framework. Rupayan Dewan ('Major Rip'), the insurgent chief delegate, reiterated demands for regional autonomy with a tribal legislature, an end to military and security forces' operations in the CHT, removal of Bengali settlers from the area, and positive discrimination for tribal students and workers in educational institutions and employment. The Bangladeshi Brigadier leading the army team rejected these demands but pledged not to encourage further Bengali settlement.[164]

While the army conducted talks, tribal attacks on Bengali settlers peaked. In early 1986, in a series of raids at Assalong, Sentilla, Taindong and Tanokkopara, the guerrillas killed thirty-eight and wounded twenty-four Bengalis. Violent reprisals by outraged settlers and their uniformed defenders on montagnards led to the exodus of thousands of tribals, mostly Chakmas, to the neighbouring Indian state of Tripura, where the authorities set up camps for the refugees. The latter boosted the *Shani Bahini's* morale, gave it a measure of legitimacy as the champions of an oppressed minority, provided it with a recruitment pool and afforded Delhi some leverage in a low-intensity confrontation with Dhaka. India claimed it was sheltering some 50,000 tribal refugees; Dhaka insisted only 29,000 had fled and of them, 8,000 had already returned.[165]

With talks ineffective, Dhaka adopted a two-pronged approach—keep military pressure on the insurgents, and develop a politico-economic arrangement which would alleviate the montagnard population's pain and bypass the guerrillas. In August 1987, planning minister Air Vice Marshal A.K. Khandkar (retd) was appointed head of a high-powered council with a brief to identify the CHT's problems and recommend solutions. Working with Major General M. A. Salam, GOC of the 24th Infantry Division deployed in the area, Khandkar negotiated with local non-militant luminaries a plan for regional autonomy while launching a special five-year plan for the CHT parallel to the national economic plans. The regional plan allocated $15.55 million annually on seventeen projects redressing some of the imbalance in public services and facilities. Nine hospitals, 938 primary schools, thirty-three junior high schools, sixty-two secondary schools, eight colleges, two residential schools and a second vocational training centre were built. 30,000 acres of land was rehabilitated and most of it restored to montagnard owners.[166] In parallel, talks lasting around eighteen months led to a consensus on reorganising the region's administrative structure, giving autonomy to regional councils and restoring the authority of the traditional 'kings,' the Chakma Raja of Rangamati, the Mong Raja of Manikchhari and the Bohmong Raja of Bandarban.

The CHT was trifurcated into three districts founded on these three 'circles.'[167] Ershad set up a thirty-one-member elected council for each in such a fashion that montagnards and settlers would elect their own representatives in proportion to their population but the chairman and a majority of the councillors would be from the tribal community. The council would ensure that the montagnard community controlled the area's land and maintained law and order as well as managing education, health, agriculture, livestock and other areas of local governance. The council would authorise any transfer of land within the district and command the police force, appointing all personnel up to Sub-Inspectors. These sensitive issues at the core of the insurrection were thus legally addressed in the hope that the guerrillas would now have no reason to fight and peace would descend on the sylvan hills. In addition to receiving central funds, each council could levy certain taxes and decide how to spend it. The centrally appointed Deputy Commissioner of each district would be the *ex–officio* Council Secretary, assisting the elected chairman.[168] The three traditional kings could attend sessions of their respective councils if they wished to.

The restoration of the pre-independence feudal system challenged a key goal of the semi–Marxist JSS and *Shanti Bahini*, but by changing the legal and administrative frameworks under which the CHT was ruled, Ershad addressed some of the montagnard demands and created alternative power-centres with a stake in the Bangladeshi state. This stole much of the insurrection's thunder and, coupled with repeated amnesties, reduced the attraction of combat with the military. The most important outcome of this process was persuading Bangladesh's plainlander majority, and especially the military whose role was crucial here, that the montagnards had some genuine grievances which their own country, Bangladesh, must address, and that while secession must not be tolerated, demands for significant regional autonomy guaranteeing the ethnic minorities' material, legal and cultural rights were legitimate. Although some guerrillas would continue battling the army for several more years, the foundation for an eventual peace accord had been laid.

Ershad's many successes were, however, tinged with frailty. His quest for legitimacy never succeeded. This uncharismatic leader aroused much passion among his critics but little love among his acolytes, yet the opposition's almost continuous and fairly concerted campaigns since 1986 had failed to dislodge the General. And by frequently moving members of his cabinet about, he retained virtually absolute control over the politicians. In August 1989, Moudud Ahmed was promoted to vice president while Kazi Zafar Ahmed took over as prime minister. In early 1990, the main alliances seemed demoralised, ineffective and unable to affect the country's political milieu. Against this backdrop, Ershad's bold assertion that he would stand in the forthcoming presidential elections not only aborted whatever prospects there may have been of negotiations, but in fact, galvanised the many parties and politicians arrayed against him into action. Given the certainty that no major party would take part in polls with Ershad in office, his determination to go ahead regardless shook into life myriad civic and professional groupings such as the Bangladesh Medical Association, the Supreme Court Bar Association, the University Teachers' Association, a 'Citizens' Committee,' an 'Open Forum,' a Combined Cultural Front, the *Sramik Karmachari Oikkya Parishad* (workers and employee' unity council—SKOP), and several other *ad hoc* organisations. These began protesting against Ershad's plans, joining hands in a final push against his government. While the political parties did not openly associate themselves with these groups, they collaborated behind the scenes via their own factions and wings with links to the professional bodies and trades union.

Despite, or perhaps because of, pressures from the student wing of the *Jatiya Party*, elections to the Dhaka University Central Students Union (DUCSU), the most crucial student body in the country in terns of political activism, was swept by the BNP's student wing. Its members performed well on other major campuses, too. Khaleda Zia's repeated incarcerations and refusal to compromise with Ershad had won her and her party strong degree of credibility. Now, with her student wing dominant on the campuses and professional affiliates active on the street, she made a move. Ershad, apparently confident he could overcome this episode as he had others in the past, traveled abroad on a series of official visits. In early October, five protesters were killed in police firing in front of the ruling party's offices in Dhaka's central business district. This triggered a series of joint strikes and demonstrations which usually turned violent and caused even more anger than there was at the beginning. Throughout October, demonstrators battled the police, attacked government offices, private businesses and vehicles and destroyed much property. The appearance of the government losing control was unacceptable and the authorities cracked down even harder. A spiral of violent confrontation and bloodshed led to the emergence of the All Party Student Unity (APSU), led by Zia's student acolytes and forged with the support of other political parties. With the APSU spearheading the movement and lending muscle to it, its leaders persuaded Zia and Hasina to unite under the banner of a countrywide anti–Ershad campaign, mobilising support among urban and semi–urban populaces. With left-of-centre parties and the *Jamaat-e-Islami* too pursuing the same objectives without physically joining the major alliances and the APSU, Ershad was left with only the bureaucracy, the *Jatiya Party*, and the army on his side.

While his party remained loyal, the army had changed. Ershad's drive for the increasing professionalisation of the officer's corps proved ironic. Over time, many officers commanding battalions and brigades—now that FF-repatriate tensions had evaporated—came to see themselves as soldiers of a non-partisan national military, not obliged to defend the interests of any particular party or politician over those of another. This view resonated with the hopes of the main opposition parties—certainly as long as they were in the opposition.[169] It was a question of timing—when the consensus on the army's corporate interests tipped against those of its principal benefactor-cum-beneficiary, and the more neutralist and careerist officers asserted greater influence on shaping collective views than that of the interventionists. The two tendencies had roughly balanced each other into the late 1980s when two senior appointments turned things around.

Ershad had appointed Lt. General Nooruddin Khan as the CAS when General Atiqur Rahman retired. Major General Abdus Salam was appointed as the CGS. Neither man had demonstrated any political inclinations and this evident disinterest may have been a key consideration behind their promotion. With them in command, the neutralist, apolitical tendency among the officers came to the fore. When a joint campaign coalesced against the president and took on the character of a national—if urban—movement with growing popularity, a large section of the officers' corps, keen to promote a nationalist image of the military and prevent an impression of being the dictator's tool taking root, grew anxious.[170] As police and paramilitary assaults on protesters shed more blood, thereby encouraging the activists to even more passionate outbursts, Ershad formed a cabinet committee under Vice President Moudud Ahmed to work out measures to restore calm while he traveled abroad. Efforts by his cabinet colleagues to establish a framework for politically addressing the opposition's demands failed. A coincidental event in Ayodhya, an ancient town in northern India, where Hindu extremists pulled down an ancient mosque to force their demand for the construction of a 'Ram temple' on the spot, created a temporary distraction. As riots led Muslim blood to be shed in India, some Muslims attacked Hindu temples in Bangladesh. Ershad tried to calm passions but eventually, in late November, he imposed a state of emergency. Curfews were openly violated and the death of Dr Milon, a BMA office-holder, and Jehad, a student activist, triggered more agitation. The state's authority appeared to have been severely eroded.

The combined opposition now demanded that Ershad hand over power to a caretaker government under the leadership of a person of their choice. Constitutional difficulties would be overcome by Ershad asking his Vice President to resign, then appointing the nominee of the opposition to the vice presidency, and finally himself resigning, handing over the presidency to this acting vice president. The new president would form a non-partisan interim government whose sole objective would be to restore calm, hold free and fair elections to the parliament, and then, transfer power to the party that commanded a majority in the newly-elected legislature. The audacity of the demand and the scale of the violence backstopping it may have convinced Ershad that it might be best to leave office with some honour in tact. On 2 December, he decided to do this and revealed this to only a few key aides. However, to ensure continuity of government and a constitutionally acceptable transfer of power, he announced detailed plans for holding elections in which he would play no role and that he would resign fifteen days before the deadline for filing nominations. This announcement on 3 December could have restored a measure of normalcy if the public had had an opportunity to hear it first hand. As it happened, with most newspapers out of action, the press was unavailable and a foreign radio station, perhaps inadvertently, misinformed audiences in Bangladesh that Ershad would resign fifteen days before the planned elections, rather than fifteen days before the deadline for filing nominations as he himself had announced.[171]

To opposition leaders, this may have appeared to be another attempt by the General to ignore their demands and maintain control by marginalising them. Politicians and student leaders immediately rejected Ershad's 'plans' and agitation intensified. It was at this time that the army's senior commanders called a meeting of field-grade officers and above in Dhaka where they sought their views on the army's role in domestic political disturbances. Breaking convention, an infantry Colonel stood up and made very clear his view that President Ershad was a civilian party-political leader like others in that profession and that the army was a national institution designed to defend the nation, not to protect individual political leaders or their governments.[172] Once this statement had been made, other officers vocally endorsed this view. The CAS then conferred with other senior commanders and PSOs, and all agreed that the national military could not back the president and fight the popular campaign mounted by much of the urban citizenry. When the CAS informed the president that this was the collective view of the officers' corps and senior commanders, Ershad decided immediately to resign, as soon as procedural details had been worked out.

He had been elevated to office at the beginning of his nine-year term by the strength of his military command, and now, the loss of military confidence swiftly brought about his fall. 'People power' had won, but only because the military had elected to become its indirect instrument. The army now made the emergence of a new democratic era possible. This was General Ershad's ironic legacy.

4

THE PLIGHT OF PARLIAMENTARY POLITICS
1990–2007

Abstract: Once the army decided to withdraw support from its chief patron and General Ershad resigned, the military maintained scrupulous neutrality while politicians worked out the mechanics of a transition to representative governance. Parliamentary polls saw the electorate broadly divided between supporters of two coalitions, led by the BNP and the Awami League. The former won with a modest margin in popular vote. Shortly after taking office, Khaleda Zia's government was faced with the devastation visited by a tropical storm which killed many on the coast. Domestic and foreign relief efforts, with US support preponderant, helped the survivors to cope. But success was short–lived as the Awami League-led opposition challenged the government's authority and, boycotting the parliament, took its dispute to the capital's streets. Strikes and attendant violence cost Bangladesh nearly a tenth of its GDP in the last two years of Zia's rule.

Overcoming an abortive mutiny, Zia held two elections in 1996, the first boycotted by the opposition and producing a parliament giving her party almost total control. She then amended the constitution in keeping with the opposition's demands and held a second set of polls which the Awami League won. Despite questioning most of her rival's policies, Shekh Hasina built on her predecessor's socio-economic legacy. Investment in health and education sectors rose, but so did public sector corruption and political violence. Zia followed Hasina's footsteps in leading her party out of the parliament and challenging her rival's authority in street battles between musclemen of the two parties. As in the early 1990s, domestic and external efforts to mediate between the two sides proved abortive, but Hasina pressed ahead and only left office after completing her five-year term. As in 1996, an unelected caretaker administration took charge and held parliamentary polls.

This time round, the BNP-led coalition won a massive majority. The polls confirmed the establishment of a two-party system, but Hasina and her supporters rejected the results, accusing the army and the BNP of 'subtle rigging.' She and her coalition partners again boycotted the parliament, reducing the legislature to a toothless executive sidekick. The executive's own authority was eroded by divisions appearing within the BNP, with corruption allegedly rampant among the ruling elite, and reports that the real power lay with Zia's elder son and his team of enforcers. While macro-economic performance improved somewhat, mainly on the strength of the growing success of private entrepreneurs and beneficence of donors, political violence and an air of vicious discomfiture robbed Bangladeshis of any sense of satisfaction. The rulers' inability to establish a framework of shared values intensified competition to a zero-sum category.

Both the BNP and the Awami League claimed credit for devising the non-party interim administration which would hold elections and ensure the state remained neutral during the transition. However, neither acknowledged that this reflected and reinforced the utter mistrust dividing key actors, rendering the give-and-take of parliamentary politics impractical. Against such a charged backdrop, the BNP's decision to move regulatory goalposts was seen as subverting the system to secure the incumbents unfair advantages the 'caretaker government' was designed to preclude. As violence challenged the caretaker system in late 2006, the army, now encouraged by the donor community, intervened.

A legacy of ghosts

As soon as the CAS, Lt. General Nooruddin Khan, and the CGS, Major General M. A. Salam, advised President Ershad the army would not support his struggle with his party-political rivals, he offered to resign. Negotiations soon delivered an agreement. The Awami League and the BNP asked that the Chief Justice of the Supreme Court, Shahabuddin Ahmed, take over as interim president, head a caretaker government (CTG) and hold parliamentary elections within ninety days from taking office, and then hand power over to an elected government which enjoyed a majority in the newly elected legislature. Once agreement was reached, this sequence swiftly followed. The three main alliances—the Awami League's eight-party, the BNP's seven-party, and the five-party socialist bloc—and the Jamaat-e-Islami, overcoming mutual suspicions and differences, issued a joint declaration that soon after the polls, the new legislature would restore parliamentary pre-eminence irrespective of the election's outcome. The military pledged to support constitutional and electoral reforms and, distancing itself from its former CAS and Supreme Commander, kept out of the fray as Ershad was jailed on charges of corruption and abuse of office.

This was the outcome of a rational appreciation of the situation. The strength and scale of the anti–Ershad campaign persuaded Nooruddin Khan and Salam that a move to defend Ershad would lead to a blood-bath, not an option they would countenance. Ershad had failed to develop a credible support base and his reputation was dragging the army down.[1] The service's corporate interests demanded that the army cut its losses, let politics take its own course, and restore its own image and stature in the national milieu. A few officers considered this a cynical betrayal of their leader but in a minority, they were outmanoeuvred by Nooruddin and Salam. After Ershad's fall, the latter charted a scrupulously neutral course, maintaining contact with both Khaleda Zia and Sheikh Hasina while strongly supporting Justice Shahabuddin Ahmed's interim administration.[2]

In this period of transition the army presented a united front, serving as an instrument of the state's authority. Its deterrent role helped maintain stability but could not hold the various alliances together. Once the focus of the opposition's agitation disappeared from the scene, the glue cementing their collaboration evaporated; the Awami League and the BNP drifted apart. During the election campaign which followed, the Awami League complained that the BNP had been a product of 'garrison politics' and its victory would return Bangladesh to indirect martial law. There was, however, no evidence that the Generals evinced preference for one party or the other. Zia's aides included several retired officers,[3] but there was no suggestion that their former military ranks rather than their loyal service first to the late General Zia and now to his widow brought them the rewards of office,[4] or that they exercised any influence with the army. Such linkages would have challenged the army's chain of command and would be seen as unwelcome interference.

Elections to the Fifth Parliament were held on 27 February 1991. Seventy-five parties fielded candidates. They and 424 independent candidates contested the 300 elected seats. The BNP won 140 with 30.81 per cent of the votes cast; the Awami League took eighty-eight seats with 30.08 per cent of the votes; Ershad's Jatiya Party won thirty-five seats—including the five Ershad himself won from his prison cell—polling 11.92 per cent of the votes cast; Jamaat-e-Islami, under its controversial leader, Golam Azam, recently allowed back from Pakistan, took eighteen seats with 12.13 per cent of the votes.[5] The Awami League's BKSAL faction and the Communist Party of Bangladesh (CPB) won five seats each; independents took three; six other parties secured a seat each. Bangladesh's first-past-the-post system and the thirty nominated seats reserved for women[6] ensured that despite the similar shares of the popular vote polled by BNP and Awami League candidates, the BNP enjoyed a significant advantage. Its temporary alliance with the Jamaat secured twenty-eight of the thirty reserved seats while Jamaat took the remaining two. With their combined strength at 288 seats out of 330, the BNP-Jamaat coalition was able to demonstrate a majority and President Shahabuddin Ahmed asked Zia to form a government, which she did. The Awami League accepted its position as the main opposition party with some reluctance but became a vigorous critic and appraiser of the Treasury Bench's legislative activities.

Democracy had been restored with Bangladesh's 'first fairly held poll'[7] which revived the Awami League and the BNP as the country's two main political parties, each supported by approximately a third of the voting public. All the other parties were shown to be minnows when compared with these two giants. The fact that despite the dominance of these two parties, there were another seventy-odd groups willing to fight for a slice of power and its rewards showed up the fragmentation of the polity around the AL–BNP core. The differences between the two parties in ideology, background of the leadership groups, support base, and policy preferences underscored a polarisation of the polity which, while not unusual in resource-hungry, zero-sum political systems, made the fashioning of consensus on key issues difficult. The parties did share similarities in the nature of their leadership. The Awami League had elected Sheikh Hasina—daughter of Sheikh Mujibur Rahman, a charismatic leader killed in a 'partial coup' mounted by disgruntled junior officers—as its President. The BNP had chosen Khaleda Zia, widow of the late General Ziaur Rahman, another charismatic leader killed in an abortive coup executed by another group of junior officers, as its Chairperson. The two parties, little more than political vehicles for their larger-than-life leaders until their violent death, had fought to establish democracy without permitting internal democracy. Now, their dynastic and populist successors, controlling these largely unaccountable organisations, would manage Bangladesh's democratic dispensation.[8] The euphoria was short-lived.

On the night of 29–30 April, a tropical storm dubbed Cyclone Marian hit Bangladesh's southern coasts stretching from the island of Bhola in the west to the tip of the Teknaf peninsula in the east. Winds in excess of 235 kilometres per hour whipped up 15–20 foot waves as Marian made landfall. The islands of Bhola, Manpura, South Hatia and Sandwip were inundated while the coastal belt from Chittagong to Cox's Bazar was severely lashed. About 139,000 people were killed overnight and millions left homeless as the cyclone destroyed over a million homes. More than a million cattle and 74,000 acres of crops were destroyed; another 300,000 acres of cropland was flooded as sea water covered rice paddies and contaminated drinking water.[9] The port of Chittagong was severely damaged and blocked with sunken ships, some from the Navy. Many bridges, including several key ones, and miles of road and embankment, were washed away, affecting the airport, and disrupting the city's water supply.[10] Bangladesh's cyclone warning system worked well and many local residents were evacuated before the storm struck, but with only 6 per cent of the required shelters available, many people had nowhere to go when the warning was sounded. Besides having a young, inexperienced government, 'Bangladesh had to deal with the legacies of the military's rule and the limits placed upon one of the poorest countries in the less-developed world.'[11]

Notwithstanding the BNP's long struggle against military rule, in office it had few tools other than the military with which to address the cyclone's devastating fallout. The Navy and the Air Force were badly mauled. A large number of naval vessels, berthed at the main base in Chittagong, were torn from their moorings and sunk, or lay battered. As for the Air Force, around two squadrons of F-6 fighter aircraft donated by Pakistan, and located at the Chittagong airport, were either destroyed or badly damaged.[12] The army, emerging from the catastrophe relatively unscathed, was able to respond to the government's efforts to organise relief and reconstruction. The disaster's scale soon made it clear that national resources were inadequate and help was sought. Government stores did hold relief supplies, and the country benefitted from foreign assistance, with local charity soon supplementing these. However, moving the material from the stores in Dhaka and other cities to Chittagong, and then on to the affected areas required vessels, aircraft and helicopters, and trained manpower to operate these, which Bangladesh lacked. Foreign relief teams with military vessels and helicopters came from many countries including the UK, India, Pakistan, China, Japan and Saudi Arabia, but the biggest contribution arrived from the USA.

On 10 May, President George Bush ordered the Department of Defence (DOD) to provide practical assistance to Bangladesh. The US Pacific Command (PACOM) established a Contingency Joint Task Force (CJTF) using troops from Amphibious Group 3 and the 5th Marine Expeditionary Brigade, then *en route* home from the Persian Gulf, and supplemented with US army and air force elements. They brought in equipment, material and skills and, coordinating with local and foreign military units, aid agencies and NGOs, mounted operations to locate survivors and extend immediate succour to them.[13] In much of the coastal belt and many of the islands, troops from the 24th Infantry Division headquartered in Chittagong played the key role alongside US counterparts. In most cases, they were well received by the local populace. However, in a few instances when it became apparent that the local Bangladeshi military commander was 'hoarding food for his personnel,' the survivors turned hostile. The problem was solved when 'civil authorities were notified and took charge of the relief effort.' These rare cases of unpleasantness 'had one positive aspect: when the civilian government fixed the problem, they enhanced their own credibility with the local populace.'[14]

Operation Sea Angel, the US relief effort, began with the arrival of Major General H.C. Stackpole, CJTF Commander, in Dhaka on 12 May, and the distribution of relief stores started four days later. The US operation ended on 13 June. While significantly boosting relief efforts,[15] Operation Sea Angel also underscored the softness of the Bangladeshi state. The American mission followed a Bangladeshi request but the opposition began a disinformation campaign early on, insisting that the primary purpose behind the US deployment was to 'establish a permanent base.'[16] Keen to prevent such rumours taking hold, honour Bangladesh's sovereignty, and maintain a minimal military 'footprint,' Stackpole kept the bulk of his forces afloat rather than ashore. No more than five hundred US service personnel spent a night on Bangladeshi soil on any day.[17] A member of Zia's cabinet confided in him that the government was uncertain about the popular perception of several thousand US troops arriving;

however, their sea-basing turned them into a clear 'asset.'[18] The presence of Indian and Pakistani military personnel, in much smaller numbers, too, proved sensitive,[19] hinting at the delicate nature of Bangladesh's national confidence and the fluidity of purpose to which its party-political leaders worked.

Another early challenge facing the government was the festering insurgency in the CHT and the thousands of tribal refugees it had forced to flee to the neighbouring Indian state of Tripura. Bangladesh's relationship with India, fraught since Mujib's assassination, had been made more complicated by the sanctuary the *Shanti Bahini* enjoyed in Tripura. Zia took the initiative of raising the issue during a visit to Delhi in May 1992. At the end of her visit, the two governments pledged in a joint declaration their commitment to the speedy repatriation of the refugees to the CHT. Two months later, Zia established a nine-member committee headed by a trusted member of the cabinet to study the CHT problem and recommend measures to resolve it. Just weeks after the formation of the committee, the PCJSS, the *Shanti Bahini's* political wing, declared a unilateral cease-fire making negotiations feasible. Although discussions would continue behind the scenes and no final accord would be reached, the situation calmed down and the blood-letting eased.

Warfare by another name

Elemental fragility became apparent as Zia and Hasina established their authority as the national leader and leader of opposition respectively. Hasina would later claim that ninety of ninety-four bills passed by the fifth parliament originated as ordinances earlier issued by the executive and later ratified by a pliant legislature.[20] She complained that the committee system did not work and democracy had become a 'dictatorship of the Prime Minister.' The two benches clashed so often that legislative debates became combative and even vituperative. The BNP passed the 11th constitutional amendment, legalising the *sui generis* CTG under Justice Shahabuddin Ahmed, and then, the twelfth amendment in July 1991, formalising the restoration of parliamentary democracy, despite the Awami League's abortive demands to link it to repealing the 1975 Indemnity Ordinance Bill. The BNP thus gave up its preferred form of governance, formally adopting the parliamentary principle as demanded by the Awami League and its allies. On 19 September, Zia took the oath of office as prime minister under the new system, but this did not secure peace. The BNP's election of Abdur Rahman Biswas as president in October 1991, when Shahabuddin Ahmed returned to the Supreme Court as chief justice, triggered another dispute as the opposition alleged Biswas had opposed the Bangladeshi cause in 1971.

The confrontation between the two benches intensified. Between April 1991 and March 1994, opposition parties individually or jointly walked out of parliament or boycotted its sessions on fifty-seven occasions.[21] When a minister made derogatory comments about the opposition,[22] refusing to retract, the latter began a longer boycott. Then, in March 1994, came the Magura by-election. A mid-sized town in south-western Bangladesh, Magura had little to distinguish it apart from the fact that the Awami League MP who represented it in parliament had won successive elections with a substantial majority. On his death, a by-election was arranged. Both the major parties conducted robust campaigns typical of the local practice. In the event, the BNP candidate, a senior party leader, won 'through mechanisms that brought the fairness of the electoral system into question.'[23] The by-election had taken on national significance because it followed the BNP's unexpected defeat at the Awami League's hands in the key mayoral elections in Dhaka and Chittagong. These results apparently confirmed to the Awami League the validity of its claims that it would win all free and fair elections; for the BNP, the stunning loss in the capital and the second city reflected an unacceptable degree of unpopularity and inefficacy which simply must be reversed if its authority was to be maintained.

That zero-sum drive explained the violence and alleged vote-rigging which marked the Magura polls. The Awami League, outraged by the result and already seeking to institutionalise the holding of elections under a non-partisan CTG rather than by the incumbent administration, mounted fiery protests. The debate evolved into a substantive dispute in which the BNP saw the Awami League's demands as a challenge to its constitutional and electorally sanctioned mandate; the latter could not countenance the prospect of being defeated in another election conducted by the BNP administration. The Awami League's parliamentary boycott escalated into a multi–party agitational campaign aimed at forcing the BNP to institutionalise the holding of elections under a neutral, unelected, CTG. General strikes, violent clashes between pickets, processions and the police, vandalism and arson, destruction of property, loss of lives and livelihoods and economic decline tore urban Bangladesh asunder. With neither the BNP nor its opponents ready to concede, concern about the country's future grew both at home and abroad.

Following a visit by the Secretary General of the Commonwealth in mid-1994, both sides agreed to receive his personal envoy, Sir Ninian Stephen, in an effort to resolve the increasingly bitter dispute. Sir Ninian's mediation failed to break the impasse between the BNP's stance that no solution which violated the current constitution was acceptable, and the Awami League's demand that elections must be held under a neutral CTG. His disappointed departure inflamed anger, confrontation escalating to intermittent conflict. There was another round of exchanges in December when Zia reportedly agreed to step down thirty days before the next election, scheduled in early 1996 and allow the installation of a neutral interim administration. In exchange, she sought the opposition's pledge that they would not 'orchestrate street protests and political strife' ahead of the polls. This the opposition would not pledge. When talks were stalemated again, Zia accused the opposition's violent campaign of derailing her efforts to reform the economy and attract overseas investment. In response, the opposition MPs resigned *en masse* on 28 December 1994. Their campaign turned into running battles with the police and other security forces on city streets as vehicles and factories disobeying strike calls were frequently set ablaze.

There was no respite for the citizenry from the unending cycle of violence, the virtually legitimised violation of the law, and the state's failure to restore order. Troubled by the rioting in October 1995, by which time Bangladeshi cities and the modern economic sectors had been in a state of crisis for eighteen months, a citizens' group formed a team of five eminent men, the G5, to mediate between Khaleda Zia and Sheikh Hasina.[24] The G5's experience revealed the depth of elite polarisation. Between 9 October and 8 November, the G5 shuttled between the two women who often met the mediators alone. As the opposition continued its campaign of general strikes including one lasting seventy-two hours, and frequently-armed processions while the police robustly challenged violent acts, mediation took on a measure of unreality. The only visible movement was Zia's conceptual acceptance of an interim government to conduct elections once the parliament had completed its five-year term. However, Hasina demanded an interim administration be headed by an apolitical person while Zia insisted the head must be an MP from the ruling party.

There were some occasional rays of hope. On one such occasion, Zia offered to discuss the concept of a neutral CTG with Hasina,[25] asking the G5 to convey this to her rival. She then wrote to Hasina inviting her to discuss 'all issues with an open mind.'

The absence of a specific mention of Zia's willingness to consider establishing a neutral interim government was seen by the Awami League, and by the G5, as the reason behind the initiative's 'infructuous conclusion' and the reinvigoration of street battles. The G5's initiator conceded that negotiations were 'constrained by the deep suspicions about the mutual good faith of either side which divides both parties. These suspicions are no doubt further aggravated by the mutual antipathies of the two principal protagonists who command enormous authority as the respective leaders of their parties.'[26] The government asked the Election Commission to arrange parliamentary by-elections to fill the 140–plus seats vacated by the opposition. Polls were scheduled for 15 December 1995. By the third week of November, however, it became clear that the Awami League and its allies would boycott the by-elections. On 25 November, President Biswas dissolved the parliament on Zia's advice. The Election Commission now scheduled general elections for 15 February, within the constitutionally mandated ninety-day time-limit.

The opposition repeated demands that Zia step down before the polls; all the major parties, represented by their student, youth, and labour wings, engaged in vigorous demonstrations which frequently led to clashes, death and destruction. While the police and the BDR dealt with the violence, the Election Commission deployed military units to retrieve illegally held arms before the elections. So, political activists and state security personnel often found themselves in clashes which made the run up to the election to the sixth parliament especially bloody. At a rally at the National Press Club in Dhaka, the Awami League warned voters, 'anyone who goes to vote will come back dead.'[27] Just before and even on polling day, the opposition set ablaze several hundred polling stations across the country. Around sixteen persons were killed and five hundred injured in political violence in the fortnight before the elections, forcing polling to be deferred in several areas.[28]

The Awami League and its allies set the precedent for rejecting the parliament's *locus* at the heart of government. In 1991–96, the parliament sat on a total of four hundred working days; the Awami League, working alone or in concert with its allies, boycotted its sessions on three hundred.[29] The transfer of political debates from the legislature to the capital's streets hurt the parliament's standing and lowered the value of parliamentary politics. Political violence had by then caused serious economic dislocation. Leaving aside the costs of local or regional strikes called by opposition factions, general strikes affecting the entire urban sector and key rural sectors across Bangladesh escalated during Zia's term of office. Data compiled by the United Nations and local institutions highlighted the haemorrhaging of the national substance while politicians battled for power. By the time Zia left office, the number of countrywide general strikes had multiplied, and the loss of national wealth approached a tenth of the GDP, far higher than the losses sustained in the tumultuous last six months of General Ershad's rule, as Table 4.1 shows.[30]

Table 4.1: Economic costs of *Hartals*, 1990–96, in million Taka, constant market prices

FY	GDP	GDP/day	General Strike days	GDP loss	GDP loss %
1990–91	1,325,226	4,477	1	4,477	0.3
1991–92	1,392,005	4,703	5	23,514	1.6
1992–93	1,455,680	4,918	7	34,425	0.2
1993–94	1,515,139	5,119	13	66,543	4.4
1994–95	1,589,762	5,371	27	145,012	9.1
1995–96	1,663,241	5,619	28	157,334	9.5

The impact on mass poverty of this level of losses to the formal economy[31] is not clear, but the outcome of the government's pledges and efforts to alleviate poverty remained patchy. However, there was some improvement over the Ershad regime's performance. One measure of declining poverty was the rate of growth in per capita GDP. In 1972–82, the decade between independence and Ershad's coup, per capita GDP grew at 2.2 per cent annually; it fell to 1.5 per cent in 1982–90. In 1990–95, covering the bulk of the Khaleda Zia administration, the annual average stood at 4.6 per cent, higher than anything seen before.[32] That general improvement did not, however, translate into a substantial fall in headcount poverty, this index falling from 53 per cent in 1991–92 to just 51 per cent in 1995–96.[33] The government thus failed to leave any major mark on the national economy.

Despite that weakness, Zia remained adamant on the political front. Insisting that the constitution, as it existed, be fully honoured, she refused to countenance calls for handing power over to an unelected CTG when her term of office ended. The constitution stipulated that unless the president, acting on prime ministerial advice, or during an emergency, prorogued or dissolved the parliament before its five-year life came to an end, the parliament would stand dissolved on the fifth anniversary of its first session. The Election Commission then had to hold fresh legislative elections. The opposition, led by the Awami League, sought to prevent the ruling BNP from holding elections before April 1996 by creating 'enough political pressure through a concerted mass movement of lockouts and general strikes' which often turned violent.[34] This would have led to the parliament's automatic dissolution after its five-year term. If this were the case Zia would have had to transfer power to a non-BNP interim government. But form took precedence over substance; Zia refused to concede in the face of mounting pressure. Voting for the sixth parliament was held on 15 February 1996, marred by 'attacks on polling centres by opposition activists and credible allegations against the ruling party of vote rigging.'[35]

The BNP won 205 of the 207 seats for which results were declared. Fresh polling was ordered for the remaining ninety-three where alleged violence or irregularities had forced the suspension of voting. Turnout, estimated at 5–10 per cent,[36] robbed the results of any legitimacy. With opposition 'non-cooperation' continuing, Hasina declared the polls 'illegal,' ordering an indefinite campaign starting on 9 March. Violence in the first three months of 1996 resulted in an estimated 120 deaths, injury to thousands, and widespread damage to property and economic activity. With ports, railway stations and road transport severely disrupted, Bangladesh's recently-built readymade garment (RMG) export sector faced near-collapse. On 19 March, Khaleda Zia took the oath of office and appointed a new cabinet. As the country apparently teetered on the brink of civil war, in an unprecedented revolt, civil servants joined professional bodies in echoing the opposition's demand for fresh polls to be held by a neutral interim government. The short-lived sixth parliament, an exclusively BNP-staffed affair, now enacted the thirteenth constitutional amendment which met most of the demands the opposition had made.

It provided for an eleven-member CTG to be appointed by the President and headed by a Chief Adviser—who should, in the first instance, be the most recently retired Chief Justice—whose primary responsibility would be to hold elections within ninety days of the parliament's dissolution. The amendment stipulated that this would be the practice before all future parliamentary polls. The CTG would conduct only routine administrative functions and transfer power to the leader of the newly-elected parliament. Advisers would have no party affiliations and would not contest elections. During the CTG's tenure, the President would exercise executive supreme command of the armed forces. President Biswas signed the bill into law on 28 March; two days later, as agitating civil servants and opposition activists prepared to besiege *Bangabhaban*, he dissolved the parliament. As Zia stepped down, Biswas appointed former Chief Justice Habibur Rahman as Chief Adviser to head an interim government. Rahman appointed ten advisers and ordered the Election Commission to prepare to hold legislative polls within the ninety-day limit. The Commission scheduled these for 12 June 1996.

If these developments suggested a pragmatic resolution of the country's political plight, the citizenry was swiftly disabused of that illusion. A new threat emerged from the military in May. As the formal head of the CTG and the Supreme Commander of the armed forces, the President ordered the army to deploy some troops on election duty. While preparing for such deployments, two senior officers—one the General Officer Commanding (GOC) an infantry division stationed in north-western Bangladesh—were found to have engaged in discussions with a retired army officer who was currently a prominent member of the Awami League. Although their telephonic exchanges did not suggest partisan collusion, the President, advised by the Director-General of Forces Intelligence (DGFI), saw these contacts as detracting from the military's supposedly explicit and implicit apolitical stance, especially given the seniority of the two officers.[37] The President terminated the service of the two officers and notified the AHQ of his decision. Lt. General A.S.M. Nasim, the CAS, outraged by this decision having been taken without he being consulted first, refused to retire the two officers.

When President Biswas insisted that his order be immediately executed, General Nasim challenged the President's authority and ordered some troop movements to bolster his hands. Biswas then announced his decision to fire the CAS, but ensconced in his offices at the AHQ, Nasim refused to budge. Soldiers and armoured vehicles from the 9th Infantry Division stationed at Savar just outside the capital were sent roaring along Dhaka's thoroughfares, but it was not clear if they were demonstrating General Nasim's authority or the President's. Only a small troop of tanks from an armoured brigade in Bogra moved towards Dhaka on Nasim's order but was halted on the Jamuna River's western bank as the ferries needed to ship the tanks were not available. The bulk of the army refused to obey the sacked CAS's orders. The stalemate between the rather modest forces loyal to Nasim and the rest of the army soon ended as Nasim was led out of the AHQ without offering resistance. No blood had been shed, but the fragility of civil-military relations and the army's cohesion, and the inability of the civilian polity to order military conduct were again evident. Only the DGFI's steadfast backing of the president and the other GOCs' decision to desert their CAS defeated Nasim's abortive coup.

Blood Brothers and Sisters

Nasim's surrender and the ouster of officers who had obeyed him after his dismissal by President Biswas were interpreted in polarised Bangladesh as the Awami League's loss and the BNP's gain.[38] However, Nasim had been promoted to Lt. General and appointed CAS by Khaleda Zia on the assumption that he was most likely among senior Generals to handle military affairs in a manner favourable to her leadership. This suggested that the professional dynamics shaping military decision-making were more complex than was apparent. Nasim would not countenance partisan bias among his commanders; nor would he let a party-political president such as Biswas cashier senior officers on flimsy grounds presented by the DGFI in the form of secret recordings of telephone conversations whose legal status was unclear. Nasim was also determined to protect his office's command prerogatives, especially at a time of delicate transition between elected governments. Allowing the temporary supreme commander to remove senior officers at will could set precedents and erode the authority of service chiefs; this would have to be prevented.[39]

The DGFI and the GOCs other than the one sacked by Biswas too saw things clearly, but differently. The army was the one national institution that backstopped the CTG's neutral authority. It had to be, and had to be seen to be, scrupulously neutral itself to remain credible and effective in this crucial role. If senior commanders engaged in discussions with party-political figures, in the febrile electoral atmosphere they would be seen as partisan. This potentially posed a challenge to the army's ability, as the state's ultimate law-and-order instrument, to guarantee a free and fair election. Equally important was the principle of civilian primacy and the Supreme Commander's authority spelt out in the 13th constitutional amendment. If the CAS violated this sensitive provision, the army could be seen as a threat to the constitutional order. That eventuality had to be obviated in the interest of national stability and of the army's benign role in a democratic dispensation.[40] In late May 1996, this latter view prevailed. Biswas promoted Major General Mahbubur Rahman, the CGS, to Lt. General and CAS. Once Nasim left the AHQ and Rahman assumed command, calm was restored.

The army had both gained and lost under Zia. Identifying the military as a potent player in national politics, she had adopted a hands-on role in its management. As Defence Minister, she appropriated the Supreme Commander's office, until now the president's prerogative, and renamed it the Armed Forces Division (AFD) of the Prime Minister's Secretariat. The three services were to be managed from her chambers in this revamped and renamed body. The autonomy enjoyed by the Service Headquarters was curbed as the AFD assumed control over movement of units and formations, and postings and promotions of officers. Despite other preoccupations, Zia found time to personally issue orders affecting the armed forces, with most of her attention devoted to the army. The navy and air force, while technologically more sophisticated than their pedestrian brothers-at-arms, had little political influence. The army, larger and more lethally armed than other state organs, was more visible. To ensure it did not pose even potential challenges to her authority, Zia acted against those her aides considered unreliable. In the democratic order, the direction of flow of influence in civil-military relations stood reversed. Breaking taboos and setting precedents, Zia appeared in operational areas, inspecting troops during exercises. She visited barracks, cultivated officers and presided over military ceremonies. Increased familiarity eased some of the tensions.[41] The direction of Zia's policy towards the military was set by a group of former officers who had provided physical protection to her from General Ershad's musclemen in the 1980s.

Several of them, who saw themselves as 'nationalists' and had succeeded in business, extended covert support to the BNP leader. When Khaleda Zia became Prime Minister, they became influential aides. Their knowledge of the military and her trust in them resulted in these men becoming her most significant advisers on military matters. Among them was her young brother who had left the army as a Captain but retained close links to his course-mates and contemporaries still in service. With advice from these stalwarts, she followed the example set by Generals Ershad and Zia, appointing trustworthy men to sensitive posts, replacing heads of the main intelligence organs, the DGFI and NSI and later, of the army itself. Within two years, nearly two dozen officers of flag rank were thrown out; several were arrested and put on trial while others were sent abroad on diplomatic assignments.[42] Officers down to battalion commanders received prime ministerial attention. The majority of the sacked officers belonged to the 'repatriate' camp, triggering speculations that a purge of 'repatriates' on the scale of Ershad's 1981–82 ouster of Freedom Fighters was in the offing. By early 1993, insecurity born of uncertainty and suspicions had brought back earlier tensions.

Inheriting Ershad's defence budget, which appears below for comparison, Zia initially made a significant reduction in military allocations as other demands took precedence. However, as her efforts to reshape the forces took effect, she increased defence expenditures, ordering a modest expansion, as Table 4.2 shows.

Table 4.2: Defence allocations and expansion in the Khaleda Zia administration[43]

Year	Defence Budget/Exp.$m		ArmsImport $m	GDP $bn	Defence Strength
1990	321.68	326.90	40	21.71	103,000
1991	303.31	—	90	21.92	106,500
1992	327.00	355.00	40	23.30	107,000
1993	375.00	461.00	30	23.96	107,000
1994	467.00	467.00	30	25.60	115,500
1995	500.00	500.00	70	29.00	115,500
1996	503.00	542.00	20	31.00	117,500

While these figures were small in absolute terms, they suggested growing investment in military capacity and sophistication. Procurement of foreign military hardware rose to $130 million in 1994–6 as firepower and communications were improved.[44] If the expansionary allocations were intended to 'buy' the military's loyalty, however, Zia and her advisers were proved mistaken. Lt. General Nasim's appointment as CAS should have, in this set of calculations, assured Zia and the BNP of the military's collective support even after her administration had handed power to a CTG. But as General Nasim's difficulties with President Biswas in May

1996 demonstrated, such assurances could not be taken for granted. Given the history of close interaction between Bangladesh's civil society and its armed forces, civil-military relations could be described as having attained a symbiotic balance of sorts. As long as neither partner disturbed, nor was seen to disturb, the balance, the status quo would likely persist. In 1991–96, the emergence of new centres of influence, the revival of factionalism and an atmosphere of anxiety among some officers in the new dispensation presaged turbulence in civil-military relations. Zia's failure to manage this critical relationship was symptomatic of her government's many failings.

However, there were successes, too. The government faced increasingly rigourous conditions for the distribution of funds from the IMF and the World Bank (lead OECD donor agencies); domestic and external pressures for reducing widening fiscal and other deficits mounted; foreign aid availability also declined.[45] That combination of difficulties reduced the room for fiscal manoeuvre, forcing the government to introduce a value-added tax (VAT), for instance, and gradually withdraw direct public investment from productive sectors. The macroeconomic picture slowly improved. The GDP grew at an annual average of 4.4 per cent compared to 3.9 per cent achieved in General Ershad's last five years; its components too changed—with agriculture falling from 37.6 to 31.4 per cent, industry rising from14.3 to 17.4 per cent, and services growing from 48.1 to 51.2 per cent. Gross domestic savings rose from 3.3 to 7.7 per cent of GDP; current balance of payment deficit shrank from 6.2 to 2.9 per cent; and foreign reserves grew from the equivalent of three months of imports to 5.8 months.[46] Several areas saw progress.

Zia pursued a number of developmental objectives with vigour and imagination. Primary education, especially for girls, was one. Identifying early education as key to the national future, her government introduced free and compulsory primary education, tuition-free education for girls up to class ten, and stipends for girl students. Later, a 'Food for Education' (FFE) programme, by offering basic food-items to parents of poor students, increased incentives for sending children to school, reducing pressures for putting them to work. As Table 4.3 (overleaf) shows, funding for primary and mass education steadily increased in both the Revenue Budget and the Annual Development Programme (ADP).[47] The figures for 1990–91 show the allocations in General Ershad's final year in power for comparison. Later administrations built on the trend Zia established.

Table 4.3: Funding of the Education sector and primary-mass sub-sector
in 1990–96[48]

Year	Education sector funding			primary-mass education funding		
	Rev Budget	ADP Budget	Total	Rev Budget	ADP Budget	Total
1990–91	11,820.10	3,124.10	14,944.20	5,385.00	1,986.60	7,371.60
1991–92	13,815.80	5,272.70	19,088.50	6,704.10	3,615.40	10,319.50
1992–93	16,743.90	5,930.40	22,674.30	7,621.60	4,028.40	11,650.00
1993–94	18,057.50	9,550.90	27,608.45	8,478.80	6,485.20	14,964.00
1994–95	20,077.30	15,185.30	35,262.60	8,659.60	8,928.00	17,587.60
1995–96	21,514.50	13,711.70	35,226.20	9,504.40	8,213.50	17,717.90

Zia impressed donors with her determination to expand public education services. As a result, donor contribution to the sector, especially the
primary-mass education sub-sector, increased by about 224 per cent in
the first year of her rule and stayed around the same level until she left
office. State funding of the sub-sector increased significantly in 1993–94
although aid allocations fell slightly. Table 4.4 shows the distribution of
domestic funding of and foreign aid for the sub-sector. Once again,
1990–91 data allows comparison with the last year of Ershad's rule.[49]

Table 4.4: Domestic and Foreign Funding of Primary-Mass Education
in 1990–96

Year	State funding	Foreign aid	Total for sub-sector
1990–91	5,974.30	1,397.30	7,371.60
1991–92	7,185.80	3,133.70	10,319.50
1992–93	8,249.40	3,400.60	11,650.00
1993–94	11,588.70	3,375.30	14,964.00
1994–95	14,306.60	3,281.00	17,587.60
1995–96	14,562.10	3,155.80	17,717.90

While increased resources made an expansion of facilities and services
possible, the quality of teaching, textbooks and methods remained poor.
In the 1990s, an average of 3.12 million four-year olds became five-year

olds each year, joining the primary schooling stream, while 3.53 million five-year olds became six–year old, moving up to the second grade. In 1991, there was a teacher for every sixty-one pupils and increased resources did not improve that ratio.[50]

The government began providing free text-books to poor children, reduced tuition fees and abolished them for girls, developed some infrastructure and, perhaps most helpfully, launched the FFE programme. The idea was to encourage poor parents to send their children to school instead of engaging them in earning a living. Families headed by widows or single-mothers, day-labourers, low-income artisans e.g., fishermen, potters, blacksmiths, weavers and cobblers, and landless or poor parents owning no more than half an acre were included in the programme. The food given under FFE served as an income entitlement enabling families to release their children for education and keep them in school. One child from each eligible family received 12kg of rice or 15kg of wheat every month. Eligible families with two or more school-going children would receive 16kg of rice or 20kg of wheat per month. Although the pilot programme was small, steady expansion would soon make countrywide coverage possible. In 1993 405,797 children, including 191,370 girls, benefited from the programme; in 1995, the figures rose to 481,204 and 235,027 respectively with attendance rates rising from 71.10 per cent to 77.70 per cent in this period.[51] Few areas of success shone so brightly in the five years of the first Zia administration. It was a legacy on which her successor would build.

A New Helmswoman

Justice Habibur Rahman, the Chief Adviser to the CTG, appointed a new Chief Election Commissioner, and reshuffled a number of civil and police officials to end any residual influence of the previous administration. He was nonetheless accused of favouritism by both the Awami League and the BNP.[52] However, neither party took any steps to hold its activists to account for widespread violation of the law, death and injury inflicted on rivals and destruction of public and private property caused during the months of turmoil. Nor did the CTG or the criminal justice system take action against people responsible for disregard of the law. Violent activism born of the pre-1972 political culture was in effect legitimised by the democratic order.[53] As an extension of this process, the two main parties intensified their 'enemy discourse' stressing the elemental divergences in their national narratives.[54] The Awami League built its historiography on a 'foundational discourse' based on Bengali nationalism, its leadership in the 'Liberation War,' the *Bangabandhu's* central role in the formations of the nation-state, the party's secular and populist values, and the Bengali cultural essence of national identity. The BNP, in contrast, narrated a 'saviour discourse' claiming it had saved Bangladesh from an autocratic regime descending into a dynastic mode, that it was the only nationalist force capable of defending sovereign independence from an overbearing India, and that it reflected the centrality of Islamic values in social life. It distinguished 'Bangladeshi nationalism' as the driving force behind the 'War of Independence' and Bangladesh's autonomous existence, distinct from the Awami League's 'Bengali nationalism' which, in its view, subverted national freedom by insisting on ideals that invited Indian hegemony.

While the BNP described the Awami League as the 'authoritarian other' which treated Bangladesh as its chattel, the Awami League saw the BNP as a destroyer of the spirit of the 'War of Liberation' and its secular values—in short, the 'malevolent other,'[55] Given this level of mutual alienation, campaign violence was not surprising. The CTG's brief tenure saw 102 instances of party-political violence. The comparable figure for the whole of 1996 was 453, the highest since the democratic restoration.[56] Such dislocations notwithstanding, the polls held on 12 June, much more effective as an instrument of the popular will than the earlier election, consolidated the evolution of a two-party system. Of the 56,670,022 voters registered by the Election Commission, 42,418,262 or 74 per cent exercised their franchise.[57] Of the dozens of parties which fielded thousands of candidates, only five won seats, as did one independent MP. As Table 4.5 shows, the polls weeded out numerous parties from the electoral-elite, strengthening the centrist trend.

The elections marginalised a number of small parties and their high-profile leaders, noted for vocal protests against incumbent administrations and a capacity to organise disruptive strikes and agitation. Electoral failures of factions of the CPB, NAP, Workers Party and the ten-party Left United Front reinforced the centralising trend. The Islamist parties and the Left barely maintained a presence. In contrast, General Ershad's Jatiya Party made notable gains. The General repeated his 1991 feat of winning the five seats he was allowed personally to contest, again from prison, re-

Table 4.5: Results of the elections to the sixth National Assembly[58]

Party affiliation	No. of candidates	Votes polled	Percentage of votes	Seats won
Awami League	300	15,882,790	37.40	146
BNP	300	14,255,882	33.60	116
Jatiya Party	293	6,954,981	16.40	32
Jamaat-e-Islami	300	3,653,013	8.60	3
Islami Oikkya Jote (IOJ)	165	460,997	0.10	1
JSD—Rab	67			1
Independents	350	450,132	0.10	1

establishing his democratic credentials. Sheikh Hasina and Khaleda Zia too won multiple seats, but the first-past-the-post system shifted the balance of support from the BNP to the Awami League. The latter, with the bulk of the nominated seats reserved for women, secured absolute majority in the House. Hasina invited the Jatiya Party and the JSD to join a 'government of national consensus,' forming a cabinet with Ershad's aide, Anwar Hossain, and JSD's faction leader A.S.M.A. Rab, as non-Awami League ministers in the new administration.

One of her first steps in office was to try to bring to justice the killers of her father and the rest of her family. In fact, much of the administration's legislative, executive and diplomatic efforts and resources were devoted to this end. The parliament which enacted the Indemnity Bill after Mujib's assassination had been dominated by the Awami League; Hasina now got the new Awami League-dominated parliament to repeal that Act, in November 1996. In the months that followed, actors from that coup, Colonel Farook Rahman, Majors Shahriyar Rashid Khan, and Bazlul Huda, former minister Taheruddin Thakur and several junior personnel would be arrested and put on trial while the government launched diplomatic initiatives to bring back the others from various countries where they had sought refuge. This quest for justice would take years and the appeals process would defeat Hasina's efforts to see those responsible convicted and sentenced; Bangladesh's judicial system appeared unable to move fast enough.

Despite an overwhelming desire to seek justice taking precedence over almost everything else, Hasina reformed the parliamentary committee system. She set up a joint committee with opposition MPs to explore ways of improving the legislative process. As a first step, the practice of cabinet members chairing particular standing committees was discarded for a system in which chairmen of all such committees were to be elected. This changed the rubber-stamp quality of committee discussions, injecting a degree of vigour in the examination of drafts and bills, as well as official records, improving legislative oversight and the executive's accountability, even if modestly. The ruling party also enacted laws making voter registration with individual photographic identity documents mandatory, and freeing up the Election Commission from executive control, by making the Commission accountable to the legislature.[59] However, implementation did not quite match the verve seen in tabling bills and passing laws. Voters' registration with photo-ID would remain an aspiration for a decade, and the Election Commission remained beholden to the executive. Initially reluctant to concede defeat, the BNP eventually accepted its position as the opposition in the new parliament. Soon, however, it accused the police and Awami League activists of targeting, harassing and jailing large numbers of BNP members. Its leaders began showing the same impatience with legislative processes, now utterly dominated by their rival party, which the Awami League had displayed while it was in opposition.

Despite that unpromising backdrop, Hasina took the initiative to address two major national challenges that had been festering for decades. Her close ties to the establishment in Delhi, whose protection she had enjoyed in 1975–81, stood her in excellent stead on both counts. The first related to the availability of water in the Ganges River which flowed from India into north-western Bangladesh. The Ganges was the core of one of three river systems—the others being the Brahmaputra and the Meghna—whose silt accretions had built the delta on which Bangladesh stood, and sustained its critically important water cycle. All three flowed into Bangladesh from India, and debouched into the Bay of Bengal south of its coastal lowlands. Born of a combination of glacier melt-water and monsoon rains hitting the Himalayas and the Tibetan plateau, these three rivers were central to networks formed by hundreds of tributaries and distributaries, many of which also originated in India and passed into Bangladesh. Together, these networks, rising and falling seasonally, made up the lifeblood of the delta's ecosystem—recharging its aquifers, irrigating its rice paddies, sustaining its flora, fauna and fisheries, providing protein to the populace, preventing saline intrusions from the sea, serving as the main mode of transportation, and employing millions in myriad professions linked to the water's ebb and flow.

The rivers, the Ganges most prominent among these, made the Bengal delta a human habitat. In the 'critical period' from 1 March to 10 May, part of the January-May 'lean season' when the flow from the headwaters declined, the delta's eco-system faced a major natural challenge. The advent of the Monsoons in June reversed the situation and by August-September, much of the delta was flooded. The cyclical nature of water-flow lent the delta's ecology a periodicity which, over time, had fine-tuned its biomass cycle. The occasional failure of the river to deliver the minimal water-flow in the 'critical period' confronted the region with grim diffi-culties. Poor Bangladeshis suffered grievous losses as crops and fisheries failed, aquifers dropped and many economic activities were made impossible.

This danger was made more severe by a barrage India built at Farakka, 17km upstream from where the Ganges entered Bangladesh, to divert its water to the Hooghly, a distributary, which turned south near Farakka to flow past Calcutta into the Bay of Bengal. The barrage and its 42km feeder canal began operating in April 1975 without consultations with the lower riparian Bangladesh, at the time an Indian ally. Immediately, the January-May flow at the Hardinge Bridge, several miles downstream in Bangladesh, fell from the 1934–1975 average of 2,340 cubic metres per second (cmps) to 1,236 cmps in 1975–1995.[60] The barrage had been built with two objectives—to flush out silt deposits blocking navigability in the Calcutta port, and to prevent saline intrusions into Calcutta's water supply.[61] Throughout the 1960s when the barrage was under construction, the then-Pakistani government repeatedly complained that the with-drawal of water at the barrage during the 'lean season' would seriously affect East Pakistan's economy.[62] Bangladesh's protests, initially mild but increasingly anxious and shrill, contributed to the cooling of relations. Within years of being commissioned, the Farakka Barrage, seen from Bangladesh, had become the most serious threat to 'normal' ties between the neighbours.

In 1976, in the context of worsening relations between post-Mujib Dhaka and an angry Delhi, Bangladesh registered a protest against the withdrawal of dry season water with the UN General Assembly (UNGA). The UN advised the two countries to negotiate a mutually acceptable resolution. Mrs Gandhi's government was unable to effect any improvement before being swept away in elections. In recognition of the seriousness with which Bangladeshis viewed the impact of the withdrawals, and as part of efforts to improve relations with neighbours, the Morarji Desai administration signed an agreement in November 1977 which assured Bangladesh of roughly 60 per cent of the water-flow from 1 January to 31 May.[63] Precise quantum of the share of the two neighbours was spelt out for every ten-day period over the five dry months. The agreement established a joint-committee to observe and record daily flows at the barrage, in the feeder canal and at the Hardinge Bridge in Bangladesh. It established a mechanism for resolving disputes which the joint-committee failed to. It also provided for negotiating a long-term solution to the challenge of meeting rising demand upstream with static dry season flow, empowering the Joint Rivers Commission to find an agreed augmentation plan which would increase the flow of water into Bangladesh. The agreement worked very well with few complaints from either side. A month before it expired in November 1982, the two governments signed a memorandum of understanding (MOU) on sharing the Ganges' dry season flow, largely on the expiring agreement's framework, covering 1983 and 1984. In November 1985, another MOU was signed; it expired in May 1988. No accord replaced it to ensure water was shared out on the basis of agreed principles. The Khaleda Zia administration failed to secure agreements with India on any major issue, and apart from complaining about the loss of crucial water-flow in the dry season,[64] achieved little.

Relations improved as soon as Sheikh Hasina took office. Both governments sent out signals indicating interest in addressing disputes. Bangladesh invited the Indian Foreign Minister, I.K. Gujral, to visit Dhaka in September 1996. His counterpart, A.S. Azad, went to Delhi in November. These visits established the framework for jointly tackling the biggest issues dividing the neighbours, and to remove obstacles to the revival of earlier warmth. On 10 December, Sheikh Hasina arrived in Delhi and was treated with the friendship only someone who had sheltered there as a self-exiled state guest for years could elicit.[65] On 12 December, she presided over the signing of a 'historic Treaty' between the two governments on sharing of Ganges water during the 1 January to 31 May dry season. The general outline of the Treaty was similar to that underpinning the 1977 Agreement and the MOUs which followed it. However, the new Treaty was valid for thirty years—guaranteeing predictability for a long time, and tying the two neighbours down to respective shares of water agreed on. Whereas the 1977 Agreement assured Bangladesh the provision of approximately 60 per cent of the dry season water flow at Farakka, the 1996 Treaty offered Bangladesh approximately 52 per cent of the flow.[66] The Treaty also specified the two neighbours' share in case the flow at Farakka fell below given minimums.[67] The price of long-term friendship appeared to be reduced guaranteed flows.

The other success of the Hasina administration also relied on friendship with India. Keen to end the bloodletting in the Chittagong Hill Tracts between security forces and Bengali settlers on the one hand, and *Shanti Bahini* guerrillas and the montagnard tribal people on the other, Hasina solicited Delhi's help. This was crucial since many thousands of tribal, mostly Chakma refugees, had fled the violence to the Indian state of Tripura where they provided a ready manpower pool to the guerrillas and a handy instrument of leverage to Delhi. Without Indian sanctuary and covert support, the guerrillas stood little chance of maintaining their autonomist struggle, although the Bangladeshi forces' counter-insurgency operations too did not show many signs of success.[68] In October 1996, Hasina set up a twelve-member National Committee on CHT chaired by her party's Chief Whip to negotiate a peace accord. It included MPs from the Awami League, the BNP and the Jatiya Party and retired officials. The committee met PCJSS leaders in December, and several later sessions followed. The first sign of success came in March 1997 when, with Indian mediation, the National Committee traveled to Agartala, capital of Tripura, where it negotiated an agreement with tribal activists on 9 March. The government offered an amnesty to refugees facing criminal charges in Bangladesh, gave assurances of safety, guaranteed jobs and financial help to build houses and regain land. The tribal refugees agreed to return home, the first batch of 5,000 arriving in Rangamati on 28 March 1997. Over the next three years, all 64,000 came back to the CHT.[69] Greater success followed.

On 2 December 1997, the National Committee on CHT, representing the government of Bangladesh, signed a 'peace accord' with the PCJSS at a ceremony attended by the Prime Minister. The accord required changes to Bangladeshi law in transferring local administrative authority to a newly-established CHT Regional Council comprising the previously set up three Hill District Councils (HDCs). The twenty-two-member

Regional Council would have a five-year term. Its chairman, who would invariably be a member of the tribal community, would have the status of a minister of state. The chairman and the other members were to be elected by the members of the three HDCs. The Regional Council would have twelve tribal members and two tribal female members, six non-tribal members and a non-tribal female member. In addition, the chairmen of the three HDCs would be *ex officio* members. Of the tribal members, five would be from the Chakma tribe, three from the Marma tribe, two from the Tripura tribe, one from the Mro and Tanchangya tribes and the other from among the Lushai, Bom, Pankho, Khumi, Chak and Khiang tribes. Of the two tribal female members, one would be Chakma; the other would represent the other tribes. Two non-tribal members would be elected from each of the three Hill Districts; the non-tribal female member would be from any of these districts.[70]

The chairman would exercise the Regional Council's executive authority in supervising the three HDCs, intermediating between them and the government. A senior bureaucrat appointed to the Council as its Chief Executive Officer would assist the Chairman. The government would consult the Regional Council before enacting any new law concerning the CHT. Pending the election of a Regional Council, the government appointed an interim one. The Act extended a general amnesty to former members of the *Shanti Bahini* who surrendered their arms, and to unarmed members of the PCJSS; it ordered the withdrawal of warrants of arrest issued, cases filed, and sentences passed against them, and the release of any such member already in prison on such grounds.[71] The accord provided for the rehabilitation of those tribals who had fled to India or had been internally displaced. It pledged to hold a land survey to 'finally determine land ownership of the tribal people through settling the land-disputes on proper verification and shall record their lands and ensure their rights thereto.'[72] It authorised the constitution of a Land Commission which would settle 'disputes regarding lands and premises' including those between returning refugees and illegal settlement of Bengalis.[73]

The accord obliged both parties to uphold the 'characteristics of tribal creed and culture,' and committed the government to a phased withdrawal of all military and Village Defence Party (VDP) camps after the PCJSS/ *Shanti Bahini* members had returned to a 'normal life.' The two sides would fill all job vacancies in the CHT with the region's permanent residents, with priority given to tribal candidates. The accord established a Ministry for the CHT with a minister appointed from among the tribal populace. It also set up an Advisory Committee comprising the Chairman/representative of the Regional Council, Chairman/representative of each of the three HDCs, the three MPs from the CHT, the three tribal chiefs, and three non-tribal members from among the CHT's permanent residents 'to lend support' to the new Ministry. The accord appeared to address the key political and economic grievances of the CHT's montagnard population, concerns of the settler community, and issues of national territorial integrity. However, it did not receive universal accolades within the country. The BNP, which had reinvigorated the peace process begun by General Ershad, rejected the accord turning it, like many other national endeavours, into another pawn in Bangladesh's party-political divide. The BNP boycotted the parliamentary debate on the accord, and did not vote on the legislation which granted it legal status.

The government's slow and partial implementation of the agreement was compounded by the rising assertiveness of several dissident tribal groups which saw it as symbolic of their failure to achieve autonomy. Three disaffected organisations came to the fore—*Pahari Gano Parishad* (PGP—Hill People's Council), *Pahari Chhattra Parishad* (PCP—Hill Students Council), and Hill Women Federation (HWF). Rejecting the accord as an unacceptable compromise by the PCJSS, they claimed the deal had failed to 'reflect the genuine hopes and aspirations of the peoples of the CHT and has failed to fulfill the main demands of the *Jumma*[74] people namely, constitutional recognition of the national ethnic minorities of the CHT with guarantees for Full Autonomy (sic), restoration of traditional land rights, demilitarisation of the area, and withdrawal and resettlement of the Bengali settlers in the plain land.'[75] The PCJSS, keen to be seen as responsible representatives of the montagnard populace, sought to curb the extremism espoused by these groups which challenged its authority. An Implementation Committee responsible for enforcing the accord's clauses met four times between March and November of 1998 but its proceedings were not minuted and its decisions were not implemented.[76] The authority for collecting the Land Development Tax was not transferred by the Deputy Commissioners to the Regional Council; internally displaced persons were not fully rehabilitated; scholarship stipends to tribal students were not increased; and many of the security forces' 'temporary camps' had become permanent.

The accord's critics, the BNP foremost among them, complained that by giving the CHT's montagnards special privileges, by denying Bengali plainlanders unrestrained right of abode, of movement and of property in a part of the national territory, and by treating a small group of armed insurgents as a legitimate political organisation, the government had violated the constitution's precepts and compromised the state's unitary character.[77] Nonetheless, the accord did restore a measure of peace and normalcy to the CHT. By 5 March 1998, about two thousand *Shanti Bahini* guerrillas had surrendered their arms and the group was considered to have disbanded.[78] Most criminal cases against former guerrillas, including those for 'waging war against Bangladesh,' were dropped, although a few cases remained pending. Uncertainties plagued the accord's full implementation, but a basis for ending decades of futile squandering of blood and treasure had been laid.

'The flood of the century'

The Bengal delta, as noted, relies on seasonal flooding of the Ganges, Brahmaputra and Meghna river systems to maintain the health of its water cycle. During the 'flood season' (July-September), with the peak water levels in the three river systems varying over time, water descending from upstream typically covers about a third of the country at any one time, depositing fertile silt. More than 90 per cent of the catchment area of these systems lies in India, Nepal, Bhutan and Tibet, and the Himalayan uplands that link them.[79] Rainfall in these lands determines the volume, velocity and timing of the flow passing through Bangladesh. When water levels peak in all three systems simultaneously, the result is severe flooding in Bangladesh.[80] In early July 1998, the government's Flood Forecasting and Warning Centre reported water-levels rising in all the major rivers with large areas going under water in all the basins. Over the next three months, 100,250 sq. km, or 68 per cent of the country, would be flooded and remain under water for weeks.

Although in 1988 flooding had been almost as severe, it had affected a smaller part of the country and the major rivers had stayed above the 'danger level' for a shorter period of time. In 1998, the average water-level across the three systems stayed above the danger level for fifty-nine days, with many areas remaining swamped for longer than two months.[81] The floods affected nearly 31m people, causing 918 deaths. Economic losses were substantial, as the comparative data from 1988 and 1998 presented in Table 4.6 shows:

Table 4.6: Damage and losses caused by floods in 1988 and 1998[82]

Affected category	1988 Floods	1998 Floods
Flooded area—in sq.km	89,970	100,250
Average duration of flood—in days	34	59
Number of people affected	45,000,000	30,916,351
Number of deaths	2,379	918
Rice production lost—in million tons	2.00	2.04
Number of cattle lost	172,000	26,564
Roads damaged—in km	13,000	15,927
Embankments damaged—in km	1,990	4,528
Number of bridges and culverts damaged	1,160	6,890
Number of houses/homesteads affected	7,200,000	980,571
Number of schools damaged	19,000	1,718
Number of displaced people	n.a.	1,049,525

Rural life was particularly badly affected. In low-lying districts, floodwaters were at almost double their usual level—137cm compared to 73cm; on medium-high land, they were on average 88cm higher than normal; even high fields not usually flooded were under an average of 22cm of water. As a result, 69 per cent of the *aus* rice, 82 per cent of the deep-water (broadcast) *aman*, and 91 per cent of the transplanted *aman* rice was lost. This added up to 24 per cent of the total agricultural production anticipated that year.[83] But that was just the rice crop lost. Some 47 per cent of families suffered damage or loss to housing averaging 59 per cent of the pre-flood value. Average monthly days of paid work fell during the flood. Day labourers suffered the most: their employment declined from nineteen days per month in 1997 to eleven days in July-October 1998. Such loss of earning in those households which subsisted on a single income posed grim nutritional challenges. The average flood-affected person consumed 272kcal less per day than his non-affected compatriot; 15.60 per cent of flood-affected households became 'food insecure.'[84]

On 24 July, Prime Minister Hasina chaired the first meeting of the National Disaster Council (NDC). Over the next three weeks, some relief aid reached the most vulnerable as military units began deploying to rescue marooned people. In mid-August, the government decided to cope with the floods using internal resources, but as the damage spread and the scale of the disaster became clearer on 26 August, it sought international help. Combining its own resources and donor assistance, the government expanded the Gratuitous Relief and Vulnerable Group Feeding (VGF) programmes. By 25 September all major rivers had receded below the danger level, but with the fear of famine looming, the government, by 1 October, expanded the VGF programme to cover four million people.[85] The combination of family coping mechanisms, official coordination, NGO activism and donor assistance generated sufficient vigour in the relief operations to avert a famine. The government's efficacy in handling the consequences of 'the flood of the century' did not, however, arouse universal support for its policies. In fact, critics became more vocal.

Comparisons with the performance of the previous administration were inevitable. In 1991–96, the GDP had grown at an average rate of 4.5 per cent, slashing poverty levels from 43 per cent of the population to 36 per cent when Khaleda Zia left office.[86] Could the Awami League government do better? Its economic management came under scrutiny directly after Hasina took office. In July-November 1996, share prices in the Dhaka- and Chittagong Stock Exchanges multiplied nearly four times; market capitalisation jumped from insignificant to nearly 20 per cent of the GDP; and the price to earning ratio climbed to eighty.[87] The two cities faced a law-and-order situation when, in that febrile environment, more than twenty thousand unemployed locals, students, and musclemen gathered outside the two bourses to join bands of overenthusiastic traders inside, jostling to skim off the top of an apparently endlessly expanding pie. Some traders and agents did well in the boom, but in mid-November, the index began to move down, within months falling below the July 1996 starting point. For most of the approximately 500,000 retail investors who had joined the rush to take a position in the market with money taken out of 'savings and fixed deposits, real asset sales and borrowings,' their dreams 'turned into a nightmare.'[88]

Having taken credit for the confidence necessary for vigorous popular investment activities, the government moved slowly to address the 'glaring weaknesses in the way securities markets have been managed and regulated.'[89] It set up an Inquiry Committee to investigate what had happened, apportion responsibility and recommend corrective measures. The committee, and the government, then argued that several senior member-dealers of the two bourses and a few listed companies had manipulated the market, but the cases it filed against them went nowhere. The government then strengthened the legal framework within which private capital markets must operate. The dangers of such manipulation recurring were thus significantly reduced but the economy suffered a net outflow abroad of $120 million in direct portfolio investment,[90] a large sum relative to the size of the equity market. Some rich Bangladeshis got richer but the retail investors were not helped by the government's corrective action or Bangladesh's criminal justice system.

There were other difficulties. While the Awami League and the BNP were engaged in a frequently violent struggle for power in early 1996, the OECD donor community, led by the World Bank, in consultation with officials and public actors, established an agenda for action that needed urgently to be implemented by whichever party eventually took office.[91] The country's economy had moved along since its lacklustre performance under General Ershad, but reforms considered necessary to unleash the vigour of domestic investment and consumption, essential to widen and deepen the market, raise income and reduce poverty had stalled. A commitment from the elected administration was sought to revive economic reforms and reinvigorate the production-distribution-consumption dynamic. The Awami League, as the leading opposition party, treating this is as a critique of the BNP administration, enthusiastically endorsed, and indeed contributed to, this discourse. And yet, eighteen months after taking office, the Hasina administration's performance in implementing the recommendations was at best very mixed.[92]

Macroeconomic stability for growth: The government had maintained fiscal deficit within 5 per cent of GDP, with current account deficits within 3 per cent, but no restraint on current expenditures or strict prioritisation of the ADP allocations was apparent. 'Unrestrained domestic financing of the deficit' threatened Bangladesh's 'tenuous' macroeconomic stability.

Promoting private sector development: Trade liberalisation had slowed; import controls remained in place; some back-sliding was noticed in scaling down tariffs. Banking reforms had made some progress, as had strengthening the Securities and Exchange Commission (SEC). However, the stock exchanges needed much greater transparency and efficiency before investors' confidence was restored.

More efficient and productive agriculture: Bangladesh Agricultural Research Council, the premier institution in the field, had been given greater autonomy but there had been little movement toward 'market-friendly' policies guiding fertiliser and seed distribution, food grain procurement and storage, agricultural research and extension, and streamlining rural finance. NGOs partly filled the gap between demand for agricultural credit and its supply, but institutional help was missing.

Human development: The Ministry of Education's new Primary Education Development Policy laid the basis for radically reforming the sector. The government's health and nutritional programmes, too, marked watersheds. The establishment of a ministerial committee to review progress in both areas showed considerable improvement. A government-NGO consultative council to expand the NGOs' role in education, health and poverty alleviation would further help.

Energy and Infrastructure: Harnessing gas reserves to provide the energy for growth required private sector participation, and a 'rational gas pricing structure.' Lack of competition in telecommunications and the poor transport system hampered commerce, stifling growth. A 'Road Master Plan' was expanding the road network, but privatisation of the energy sector and improving the efficacy of the ports remained problematic. The government had not established the 'Apex Task Force' recommended in the Agenda to swiftly resolve such challenges.

Governance and Institution building: Urgent public sector reforms, the announcement of a 'policy vision' for improving performance, and the establishment of lead institutions for driving change did not materialise. The government appointed a new chairman of the privatisation board and approved the divestment of nearly thirty public enterprises, but did not transfer the enterprises to private owners. Hopes generated by the formation of a Public Administration Reforms Commission were dashed by the resignation of two successive chairmen.

Despite these failings, the economy apparently developed a self-sustaining momentum which provided some 'autonomous' growth on which policies could build. Before the 1998 floods swamped the country, the GDP was expected to grow by 5.5 per cent in 1997–98, driven by rising exports and a 'minimal' impact of East Asia's economic turbulence.[93] However, currency devaluations by ASEAN countries generated greater competition in the export sector and unresolved structural issues continued to threaten volatility. There now was an additional worry—deepening corruption.

The spreading rot

Although graft had been spreading ever since Bangladesh became independent,[94] the scale of corruption now broke new ground. Most administrative sectors were seen to have become venal and grasping with rent-seeking most widespread among the police, local government, the magistracy, education and health services. In 1997, more than two-thirds of surveyed families reported they had had to bribe the police while filing complaints; almost half reported having to negotiate bribes before the police would process their cases; nearly two-thirds of those involved in court cases reported they had to bribe court officials; more than half bribed court officials directly while more than a quarter bribed them through their lawyers; nearly three-fourths felt the police deliberately delayed filing court cases. With education becoming more competitive, three quarters said they had to employ 'extra-regular methods' to get their children into school; half said it was not possible for children to get good results or promotion without hiring teachers as private tutors. State medical services, designed to provide basic healthcare to the urban poor and the rural majority, were found to be equally grasping. 40 per cent of surveyed families reported having to make extra payments to get admitted to hospitals; 41 per cent reported they did not get prescribed medication without paying extra; and 58 per cent of those surveyed considered the police to be the most corrupt government institution.[95]

While no empirical study has been conducted of the reasons behind this explosive growth of graft, perceptions indicated where citizens thought the problem was rooted. The same survey showed that three-fourths believed greed to be the driving force; 58 per cent saw 'moral degradation' as another cause; 51 per cent thought 'lack of accountability' was a key contributor; 32 per cent also considered 'inadequate salary' as an explanation.[96] These subjective assessments were made by citizens directly affected by the conduct of those in the Republic's pay. An equally damaging aspect of rent-seeking involved large public sector corporations whose trade unions and managers abused their bargaining rights and offices to enrich themselves at the cost of the customers and the state.

The Power Development Board (PDB) provided an example of both levels of corruption: the payment of a small percentage of bills by contractors to the accounts department before bills were paid was now 'standard practice' and 'taken for granted.' Similar gratification was required by junior officers 'for certifying measurements, recommending quoted rates for unscheduled works, and for higher level officers approving bills.' Engaging 'ghost labour' particularly during emergencies was 'fairly common.' These types of corrupt transactions were 'fairly common in most government agencies and departments.'[97]

In addition, PDB had several specialist areas where rent-seeking was rampant. The most notorious was 'system loss,' a term used to describe power which was generated, distributed and consumed but was not paid for. Although the distribution system's inefficiencies led to certain losses in transit, 'system loss' in Bangladesh came to indicate theft. Under the Hasina administration, such theft was substantial. In 1998–99, for instance, PDB generated 14,150 MkWh of electricity, purchased another 450 MkWh from private producers, but billed customers for only 11,462 MkWh, showing a system loss of 22 per cent. Bangladesh's other two electricity corporations, the Dhaka Electric Supply Authority (DESA) and the Rural Electrification Board (REB), too, recorded system losses in that financial year,[98] at 40 per cent and 17 per cent respectively.[99] The weighted average system loss across the power sector was 35 per cent of which 21 per cent was 'technical loss' due to systemic inefficiencies; the balance, i.e. 14 per cent, was due to theft and unauthorised use. In 1999–2000, total power generation by the energy sector was projected at 17,535 MkWh. At 14 per cent theft of this generated power would amount to 2,434 MkWh. At an average tariff of Tk 2.10 per kWh, the value of the theft would be Tk 5 billion, or approximately $90 million.[100] Public knowledge of such illegal usage and media reports notwithstanding, system losses occurred every year and nobody was held accountable.

Another major public service utility which was riddled with corruption, the Dhaka Water and Sewerage Authority (DWASA), provided evidence of institutionalised graft. Its revenue covered only 29 per cent of its expenditure; it only billed for 44 per cent of the water it supplied. Of the remainder, 31 per cent was shown as 'administrative losses'; 25 per cent was attributed to 'technical losses.'[101] 'Administrative losses' included incomplete customer database, un-metered service connections, illegal-and illegally reconnected connections, tampered-with connections, incorrect metre-reading, inaccurate invoicing, and 'rent-seeking behaviour by revenue inspectors.''Technical losses' included leaking pipes and connections, inoperative fittings, and overflow. Such corruption existed 'in all the state-run corporations and agencies.'[102] Graft continued to grow as an administrative, legal and developmental issue throughout Hasina's term in office. Bangladesh was repeatedly described as the most corrupt country in the world, or amongst the top few, in Transparency International's global ranking year after year. Even in 2000, close to the administration's term coming to an end, the situation remained grim. Of the 1,345 cases of corrupt behaviour by public servants and others linked to the administration in January-June 2000, for instance, 927 could be traced to specific strands of the executive branch while the remaining 418 cases related to other branches of government. Together, they cost the exchequer Tk 115 billion ($2.1 billion) in lost revenue.[103] Compared to similar cases reported in January-March 1997, in the third quarter of the first twelve months of the Hasina administration, there was an increase in most areas, as Table 4.7 shows:

Table 4.7: Comparative distribution of cases of corruption in 1997 and 2000[104]

Govt. departments	Jan–March 1997 %	Jan–June 2000 %
Police, BDR, Ansar etc.	46.00	30.00
Local government	13.00	17.00
Education	10.00	16.00
Health	5.00	11.00
Taxation—income, customs, VAT etc.	6.00	6.00
Banks, micro-credit lenders etc.	7.00	6.00
Forestry	4.00	6.00
Water including Water Board	4.00	5.00
Transport including water transport	4.00	2.00
Sub-total	(390 cases) 100.00	(927 cases) 100.00
Other complaints recorded	cases: 188	cases: 418
Total reported cases	(over three months) 578	(over six months) 1,345

Analyses of the reported cases of corruption exposed widespread bribery among law enforcement agencies, taxation and land administration officials, and telecommunications personnel. Analyses also showed that embezzlement, extortion and abuse of discretionary power and misuse of resources because of weak monitoring were just as prevalent[105] in the higher rungs of administration. Offices with the most corrupt staff were police stations, lower judicial courts, public hospitals, Sub-registrar's offices, land records offices, 'Tehsil' office and scheduled banks.[106] Despite the frequency and prominence with which private media reported such incidents, there were few attempts by the administration to address this malaise. No wonder that while over 90 per cent of respondents surveyed in 1999 supported elected governments over other forms, more than half had no confidence in Bangladesh's political system or its political parties.[107]

The Awami League had a particular approach to addressing corruption. General Ershad, jailed in December 1990 and then convicted of corruption under the BNP administration, was released on bail in 1997 after he agreed to support Hasina's 'government by consensus,' allowing a senior Jatiya Party official, Anwar Hossain, to join the cabinet. Three years later, disillusioned with Hasina's policies and offered a more attractive deal by Khaleda Zia, Ershad pulled his party out of the government and joined the BNP-led opposition instead. In keeping with local political traditions, Anwar Hossain broke away from Ershad and remained in the cabinet as the leader of his one-man faction of Jatiya Party. Days later, in August 2000, Ershad was again convicted of corruption and abuse of office during his presidency, barred from contesting elections for five years, fined Tk 50 million ($1 million) and jailed by the Hasina government. Ershad's decision to abandon the ruling coalition in favour of Zia's opposition front was seen as a betrayal meriting punishment.

In April 2000, Zia had claimed that the Hasina administration had misappropriated Tk 4 billion ($75 million) while buying eight MiG-29 combat aircraft for the Bangladesh Air Force.[108] Shortly thereafter, prompted by similar complaints regarding the purchase of a frigate for the Bangladesh Navy from South Korea, the Parliamentary Standing Committee on Defence began investigating allegations that senior leaders had receiving kickbacks worth Tk 5 billion ($90 million).[109] In September, Khaleda Zia, two former ministers, and seven officials were convicted of taking bribes worth $32 million, allegedly paid during the purchase of two Airbus airliners for the national airlines while she was prime minister. In February 2001, the Supreme Court ruled that Ershad could be released on bail after he had paid a fine. Before his lawyers could move on this award, Ershad was detained by the government under the Special Powers Act. He was, however, released on bail in April when he announced that he was leaving the BNP-led four-party opposition alliance, 'lending credence to allegations that he had struck a deal with the Awami League government.'[110]

Domestic observers and donor agencies repeatedly pointed to the excesses committed by politicians and officials in their rent-seeking activities, 'imposing a considerable burden on the economy' during Hasina's premiership. One report estimated that because of corruption, Bangladesh received 50 per cent less foreign direct investment (FDI) in 1999 than it should have.[111] Corruption at the Chittagong Port was said to cost the economy $1.1 billion annually.[112] Power supply across Bangladesh suffered 'system loss' which, in turn, caused the country lost industrial production worth $1 billion every year.[113] Telephone lines could not be installed without paying bribes; citizens trusted neither the law enforcement agencies nor the judiciary; the public health and education sectors failed to deliver necessary services paid for by the state. In a country with extreme levels of mass poverty, petty corruption imposed high costs on grassroots consumers who could least afford to suffer additional afflictions. From the ground up, graft spread its tentacles to the higher reaches of the administration. The context for this persistent abusive impunity in the administration was no secret:

The absence of transparency and accountability in public life can in large part be attributed to a lack of political will, a result in turn of the confrontational nature of politics in Bangladesh. Since its resurrection in 1991, parliament has not functioned to its full potential. Sessions are often abandoned because of opposition boycotts. *Mastaans* (thugs) are commonly deployed by politicians to realise their goals. Meanwhile, political party funding procedures are far from scrupulous, and corrupt networks between politics and local businesses are entrenched.[114]

Confrontational politics resumed within months of the Awami League taking office. In late March 1997, describing the government's agreements with India on sharing Ganges water, importing electricity, and the formation of an economic bloc as tantamount to surrendering sovereignty, Zia called general strikes. These led to violence between her supporters and the police, leading to several deaths and many injuries. At the end of July, dissatisfied with the government's stance over public-sector wages and privatisation of SOEs, workers belonging to a federation of seventeen trades union known as SKOP called a general strike, their second since Hasina had assumed office. BNP-affiliated workers led demonstrations which resulted in some violence. At a donor conference in November 1997 in Dhaka, the 'Aid Bangladesh Consortium' expressed hope in Hasina's ability to free Bangladesh from 'administrative inefficiency, rampant corruption, political aberrations and economic stagnation with bouts of natural calamity. By the end of the year, this optimism had largely evaporated.'[115] In November 1998, Khaleda Zia led an anti–government demonstration protesting against alleged repression of the opposition, and called for a series of general strikes. The ruling party accused her of 'conspiring to destabilise the political situation by creating artificial crises.'[116] The BNP did not desist.

Throughout the summer and autumn of 1999, a BNP-led coalition of opposition parties which included General Ershad's Jatiya Party faction and the Jamaat-e-Islami, carried out street protests against what they insisted were the government's repressive policies and criminal abuse of power. The Awami League's willingness to grant Delhi transit rights to move goods and personnel between the Indian mainland and India's remote north-eastern states provided a popular stick with which to beat the administration.[117] The opposition also boycotted the parliament and, in an ironic reversal of roles, the BNP now demanded that the Awami League's 'failed government' step down and allow fresh elections. Showing the same resilience that Zia had displayed in the mid-1990s, Hasina refused to comply, insisting polls would be held only when her five-year term was over. The BNP soon found another excuse to mount yet another series of strikes which turned violent. Trying to enforce municipal laws and land rights and reduce mounting pressures of rapid urbanisation— shorthand for landless villagers rushing to Dhaka in search of jobs, and establishing or expanding slums lacking basic facilities—the government launched a campaign of relocating unemployed slum-dwellers. With nowhere to go and little to lose, many objects of this municipal attention resisted attempts to evict them from their shacks.

After around 50,000 slum-dwellers had become homeless, a Supreme Court injunction stopped further eviction. By then, the opposition had exploited this opportunity to the full. In September, the BNP and its allies called a three-day strike during which opposition activists engaged the police in cities across Bangladesh. In clashes which followed, at least one person was killed and hundreds were injured.[118] These confrontations created grounds for others. In early 2000, the BNP's coalition comprising Ershad's Jatiya Party, Jamaat-e-Islami and the Islami Oikkya Jote (IOJ—Islamic United Front), mounted a fresh campaign to unseat Hasina. The exercise comprised a continuing boycott of the parliament, street protests and processions which usually turned violent, and general strikes which almost invariably led to bloodshed as state agencies and Awami League supporters engaged opposition activists in an apparently zero-sum contest for the control of city streets and the nation's soul. Violence intensified after the Chief Election Commissioner—recipient of much BNP vitriol—resigned and Hasina appointed a new one without consulting the opposition. In June, just before the deadline for the boycotting opposition MPs losing their parliamentary seats, perks and privileges expired, Zia led her colleagues to the National Assembly, registered their presence, attended a session thereby ensuring they retained their seats, and then, triumphantly walked out again. In July, what became the first in a series of similar action that would follow over the next few years, two bombs were discovered and defused at a venue visited by the prime minister. Hasina accused the opposition of plotting to kill her, and criticised the judiciary for having become a 'sanctuary for criminals and terrorists.'[119]

Violent political polarisation was now the established reality of democratic Bangladesh. Just as Hasina and her supporters had held Bangladesh hostage demanding Zia's resignation during the BNP's rule, Zia and her acolytes in opposition now returned the favour. The sixth parliament met on 382 working days; the BNP boycotted its sessions on 156 of those.[120] On most occasions when opposition MPs boycotted the National Assembly, they were either holding fiery rallies and processions, or enforcing general strikes. As in 1991–96, these activities imposed a substantial cost on the national economy in lost production, earnings, consumption, distribution and trade, and death, injury, and damage to private and public property. The lawlessness generated by the state's inability to resolve internal disputes increased the sense of insecurity, especially in urban areas.[121] Donors appeared to be far more anxious than national politicians were about the impact of the violence on Bangladesh generally and its economy in particular. The cost of countrywide strikes was substantial, with the GDP actually falling slightly even with fewer strikes between 1999 and 2000, as Table 4.8 shows:

Table 4.8: Economic costs of countrywide general strikes in 1996–2000[122]

FY	GDP Tk.m	GDP/ dayTk.m	Strike days	GDP loss Tk.m	GDP% lost
1996–1997	1,762,847	5,956	7	41,689	2.40
1997–1998	1,844,436	6,231	8	49,850	2.70
1998–1999	1,934,370	6,535	28	182,981	9.50
1999–2000	1,934,291	6,535	15	98,022	5.10

In the decade of the democratic restoration, equally divided between BNP and Awami League administrations, fourteen days on average were lost to productive processes annually because of countrywide strikes called by the opposition. The annual average cost of these strikes to the economy worked out to 4.5 per cent of GDP.[123] Clearly, even ignoring loss of lives and livelihoods, injuries and damage to property, the strikes imposed on Bangladesh a massive cumulative direct cost and a comparable cost in terms of lost opportunities. But this did not appear to concern either the two major parties or their leaders, or the thousands of supporters and activists, *mastaans* (local toughs) and rent-collectors who made up the rank and file of the largest 'political' organisations. By the end of this 'democratic decade' the combination of money and muscle had emerged as the key denominator in Bangladeshi politics—as evidenced by editorials in the better-circulated dailies and the many seminars and 'round-tables' organised by newspaper editors, NGO leaders and donor bodies. The outlook in 2000 was particularly grim.[124]

Although the Awami League and the BNP differed on many issues, on one point they seemed to agree—that the military was a source of grave insecurity and needed to be handled with care, and by the prime minister herself. As with Khaleda Zia, Sheikh Hasina too sought to exercise command over the army. Just as Zia had appointed officers she considered loyal and reliable to senior positions, so did Hasina. In her case, though, the move proved to have been more effective. As Defence Minister, she too presided over military ceremonies, celebrations, briefings and exercises. She too commanded the services of the AFD and appointed apparently dependable officers to head the DGFI and NSI, the two main intelligence services. She appointed as Military Secretary to the Prime Minister (MSPM) the son of one of the four Awami League leaders killed in the Dhaka Central Jail on 3 November 1975, a brigadier with modest professional accomplishments but unimpeachable party pedigree. Just as Zia had relied on the advice of her brother, Hasina sought the advice of this officer and his friends in the service, as well as a handful of other aides, to 'manage' the army. The latter included two former CAS, Generals K.M. Safiullah and Nooruddin Khan, both MPs and the latter a minister.

But this was not considered enough. As the tenure of General Mahbubur Rahman, made CAS after General Nasim's abortive putsch in 1996, approached its end in late 1997, Hasina looked for a reliable General to succeed him. It said a lot about Bangladesh's civil-military relations and the views of the country's elected leader regarding the military force that she could not find one serving General who met her expectations. Instead, she recalled from leave pending retirement Major General Mustafizur Rahman, a former Engineer–in–Chief, promoted him to Lt. General, and appointed him CAS. The fact that the two shared family links provided a credible explanation of that unusual, albeit legal, decision. Hasina also promoted a number of FF and ex–JRB officers whose careers were not advancing especially well. One of them rose to Major General and commanded 24 Infantry Division in the Chittagong-CHT area where pacifying a former insurgency-wracked region demanded considerable political skill and actuarial integrity in disbursing substantial resources. The fate of two senior subordinates working under this General reflected some of the army's command problems. Both Brigadier-Generals had trained in Pakistan and later, abroad; both commanded brigades although not at the same time; the professional careers of both had traced respectable trajectories before they were posted to this, their last appointments. One was found shot dead in his billet during an exercise in which he was acting as the GOC; the other, some months later, resigned and fled abroad after refusing to sign documents showing that his troops had distributed a large amount of foodgrains among penurious local residents when, in fact, they had not.[125]

Another challenge facing the military was the continuing efforts by the political leaders to establish groups of officers who would potentially support particular party-political lines. This deepened factionalism among the senior- and mid-level commissioned ranks. Hasina, by building up a retinue of favoured colonels and brigadier-generals, and promoting a number of officers without the endorsement of their professional superiors, consolidated this process of fragmentation initiated by Ershad and later, Khaleda Zia. Towards the end of her term, Hasina authorised a new infantry regiment—the Bangladesh Regiment—to supplement the long-established East Bengal Regiment (EBR) of 1971 fame. This led to a modest expansion of the corps of infantry. She also changed the command structure of the Bangladesh Rifles so that BDR battalions would be commanded by Lt. Colonels rather than Majors seconded from the army. This opened up many new posts allowing the promotion of a back-log of army majors without having to expand the army. An expectation that the beneficiaries of these policies would develop a measure of empathy with the benefactor was not irrational. The cohesion of the chain of command was thus further eroded, straining the army's institutional efficacy.[126] If politicians wished to subvert the military, they could not have been more effective.

Hasina also continued the trend established by Zia to steadily increase defence allocations, including those for procuring new hardware. The most substantial gains were made by the Navy and the Air Force. She ordered an air-defence frigate for the navy from the South Korean firm Daewoo, and purchased eight MiG-29 combat aircraft from Russia for the air force. Given the obsolescence of most of Bangladesh's defence hardware, these measures were a major advance. However, both procurement initiatives later became controversial as allegations of receiving massive kickbacks were made against the prime minister and senior aides, and investigated.[127] Hasina also agreed to the establishment of engineering and medical colleges for the armed forces, and authorised the National Defence College, the highest seat of professional military learning. Budgetary allocations and personnel strength modestly grew during her term. In FY 1997–98, she allocated $563 million to the armed forces, marking a small rise from Zia's last budget. Allocations rose to $602 million in FY 1998–99, and registered smaller increases over the remainder of her term, rising to $692 million in FY 2000–01.[128] Actual expenditure was allowed to exceed allocations, although not alarmingly, absorbing costs of naval and air force procurement, expanding uniformed manpower from 121,000 to 125,500, and building new institutions.[129] Whether national security was boosted remained moot.

Saving grace

There were clearer gains elsewhere. The most substantial was perhaps in the education sector, most prominently in primary and mass education strands where Hasina built on Zia's initiatives and expanded existing programmes. Allocations were increased and aid was sought to turn pilot projects into expanded mainstream programmes covering much larger catchment areas. Budgetary support, including figures from the last financial year of the Zia administration for comparison, is summarised in Table 4.9:

Table 4.9: Education sector and primary sub-sector funding in 1995–2000 in TkMln[130]

Fin. Year	EduRev	EduADP	EduTotal	PriRev	PriADP	PriTotal
1995–1996	21,514.50	13,711.70	35,226.20	9,504.40	7,895.10	17,399.50
1996–1997	22,955.40	15,517.80	38,473.20	9,982.00	8,059.10	18,041.10
1997–1998	26,957.40	14,830.40	41,787.80	11,475.10	6,821.20	18,296.30
1998–1999	29,680.00	17,510.00	47,190.00	11,990.00	8,171.20	20,161.20
1999–2000	32,200.00	19,250.00	51,450.00	13,340.00	8,835.00	22,175.00

The expansion of primary education and the Food for Education (FFE) programmes showed the potential effect of consistent application. In 1995–96, the last year of the Zia government, allocations for primary and mass education totaled Tk 17,717.90m. Of this, the state paid Tk 14,562.10m while donors contributed Tk 3,155.80m. In 1998–99, donor assistance fell to Tk 2,762.50m, but by increasing state contribution to Tk 19,007.50m, the government was able to raise total allocations to Tk 21,770m.[131] By the end of 1998, state-funded primary schools had grown to 37,710 out of a total of 63,534. Teachers' training efforts too were paying some dividends. Overall, 68 per cent of all primary school teachers now had the necessary qualifications. Although only 53 per cent of male teachers could claim such qualifications, almost 100 per cent of female teachers, whose numbers grew fast during this period, did. Despite this improvement, however, demand had also risen. As a result, the number of pupils per teacher had only fallen from sixty-one in 1991 to fifty-nine in 1999. In state-funded schools, though, the ratio stood at 76: 1.[132] Initiatives begun by Zia were now integral part of the system: poor students received free textbooks, many of them paid reduced tuition fees, female students had tuition-free access to education, and school buildings and other infrastructure were gradually improved. The FFE programme now covered 1,243 Unions in the country's 460 Thanas with the number of beneficiaries expanding from 481,204—235,027 of them girls—in 1995 to 533,469 and 268,632 respectively in 1998. Enrollment and attendance rates too had improved.[133]

Healthcare showed similar promise, especially in reducing child and maternal mortality. There had been steady but slow progress in both areas since the 1980s and early 1990s. In 1996–2001, the term of the Hasina administration, these trends continued. Child mortality rates (under-five years old) include infant mortality (to the age of one year). In 1996, infant mortality stood at 67 per thousand live births, and child mortality, at 117. In 2001, the figures fell to 56 and 82 respectively.[134] Expanding immunisation against childhood diseases such as measles explained some of the success. From a high-point of 71 per cent coverage in 1994 during the first Zia administration, immunisation had fallen to zero in 1996 because of the widespread disruptions caused by the violent clashes between BNP and Awami League activists. Immunisation was resumed by the administration in 1997, with coverage reaching 59 per cent that year, improving slightly over the next few years, and reaching 64 per cent in 2001.[135] Maternal mortality, another of the most basic healthcare issues, also exposed the contrast between opportunity costs and the potential. During the Zia administration, maternal mortality per 100,000 live births had slightly declined from 472 in 1991 to 444 in 1996. The Hasina administration brought this down to 315 by 2001 when she left office.[136]

Some areas of administrative darkness persisted, though. The widening and deepening of graft as an aspect of public life have already been noted. Torture, part of Bangladesh's extra-judicial culture, was another. A few cases which at the time aroused popular passions, stood out. The rape of women held in police custody exemplified the utter helplessness of some of society's most vulnerable sections and their victimisation by those supposed to protect them. Occasionally, media exposure caused public outrage forcing the authorities to take palliative if not corrective action.[137] But the cases only highlighted the depth of desperation into which many members of the citizenry found themselves. One such victim was the eighteen year-old Shima Chowdhury. In February 1997, she died while being held in what the magistracy and constabulary said was 'safe custody' in Chittagong Jail while an investigation into her alleged rape in police custody in October 1996 proceeded. In July 1997, four police officers accused of raping Chowdhury while she was in their custody were acquitted by a trial court in Chittagong. The judge criticised the prosecution for presenting a weak case. An outcry of human rights and women's rights groups forced the government to appeal against the court's verdict. In another such case in August 1997, three police officers were found guilty of the rape and murder of fourteen year-old Yasmin Akhter in 1995, and sentenced to death. Then, in July 1998, Shamim Reza Rubel, a student, was picked up from his parents' home in Dhaka and allegedly beaten to death within five hours of being arrested. The Criminal Investigation Department conducted an inquiry into his death and thirteen policemen as well as an Awami League leader were charged in connection with it. A judicial inquiry which followed confirmed Rubel's death had not been accidental but the government refused to release its full report. These were not isolated incidents.[138]

Nonetheless, when in 2001 Hasina claimed victory in not giving in to the BNP's campaign demanding her resignation, celebrated her government's completion of its 'five-year mandate' and handed power to a non-partisan CTG, she could take credit for certain socio-economic gains. While her party negatively compared the former BNP administration's performance, international observers, especially the donor community, acknowledged successes. In the 2001 Human Development Report,[139] Bangladesh's ranking in the global human development index rose from 146 in 2000 to 132 in 2001, reflecting advances in life expectancy, population growth, child and maternal mortality, access to sanitation, safe water and essential drugs.[140] Macroeconomic stability had expanded the GDP from $26 billion in 1995 to $46 billion in 2001 with only moderate inflation. Successive policy shifts had reduced debt-servicing liabilities from 2.6 per cent of the GDP in 1990 to 1.7 per cent in 2001. Most significantly, the greater allocation of resources to social sectors, especially health and education, had achieved 'a positive, qualitative shift.'[141] This was a rare success indeed, but its high costs would soon be revealed.

The political economy of democratic governance

Hasina had invited retired Chief Justice of the Supreme Court and Bangladesh's first head of interim government, Shahabuddin Ahmed, to become president. His handling of the post-Ershad democratic transition in 1990–91 had won him respect across the political spectrum. As president, Ahmed hewed to a non-partisan, rationalist line. As the Awami League's term approached its end and party–political activism began dominating ruling party discourse, differences between him and Hasina emerged. These became public in January 2001 when Hasina told journalists that if the president resigned, the parliament would elect a successor. Ahmed's silence did not quash rumours of difficulties between the centres of executive and moral authority. Against a backdrop of tensions at the top levels of government, and violent opposition protests, a series of bomb-explosions which killed a number of people and injured many more heightened a sense of insecurity.

On 11 July, Hasina stepped down and four days later, Shahabuddin Ahmed swore in former Chief Justice Latifur Rahman as Chief Adviser to his CTG. Almost immediately, Rahman transferred a large number of civil servants and police officers, and suspended several high-profile commercial contracts signed by the Hasina administration in its final weeks. Hasina now publicly identified the CTG as an adversary and much bitterness ensued. Meanwhile, despite an official drive to recover thousands of illegal firearms, political and criminal violence surged. Police records noted that since the CTG took office, nearly 230 people were killed and more than 1,500 injured in the run up to the polls in October.[142] Not surprisingly, this caused much anxiety. The CTG's mandate to hold elections within ninety days of taking office appeared threatened by disagreements on details between the major parties, and because of general insecurity.

At the closing stages of a violent campaign, the CTG deployed 500,000 security personnel across Bangladesh, ensuring calm.[143] The polls held on 1 October 2001 were generally peaceful, free and fair. The BNP and its allies took two-thirds of the 300 contested seats; the Awami League was reduced to about a fifth. By-elections made necessary by those candidates who had won multiple seats and had to give up all the secondary ones consolidated the BNP-Jamaat-IOJ-JP (N) coalition's massive majority, as Table 4.10 shows. The polls further strengthened the polity's two-party features with the BNP and the Awami League increasing their electoral base at the cost of other parties. In voting strength, the BNP had a slight edge over the Awami League, taking 41.4 per cent of votes cast, with 40.02 per cent going to the latter. However, the first-past-the-post system, and the BNP's alliance with Jamaat-e-Islami, translated into a massive victory for the alliance over the outgoing coalition.[144] Of the fifty-three parties which put up 1,451 candidates, only eight won seats; of the 486 independent candidates, only six did.[145] Once again, a large number of prominent political personalities leading small groups of supporters failed to make any impression.

Table 4.10: Results of the October 2001 parliamentary polls[146]

Party affiliation	Seats contested	Seats won	Votes obtained	% of valid votes
BNP	259	193	23,074,714	41.40
Awami League	300	62	22,310,276	40.02
Jamaat-e-Islami	31	17	2,385,361	4.28
Islami Jatiya Oikya Front	280	14	4,023,962	7.22
Jatiya Party (Naziur)	7	4	521,472	0.94
Islami Oikya Jote	6	2	312,868	0.56
Krishak Sramik Janata League	39	1	261,344	0.47
Jatiya Party (Monju)	140	1	243,617	0.44
Independents	486	6	2,262,045	4.06

Once the dust had settled, the victors shared the thirty additional seats reserved for women, and independent MPs too moved towards the BNP. As a result, Khaleda Zia's team had the mandate to amend the constitution if they chose to without having to worry about the opposition's legislative challenges. The BNP-Jamaat tactical coalition resulted in a strategic rightward shift in Bangladesh's political dynamics. Alleging massive and 'subtle rigging' by the BNP and its military allies,[147] Hasina announced a boycott of the parliament. There were more rational explanations behind the Awami League's defeat: there was a general shift across the country away from the Awami League towards the BNP. The change was notable in Dhaka and pronounced in fifty-eight 'swing constituencies.' In the capital, a combination of mounting violence, 'high profile terrorist activities with which the names of some Awami League leaders and MPs appeared in the newspapers,' and the government's inability or unwillingness to 'expose the real criminals' stirred up a potent brew of anger and anxiety which was reflected in the results.[148] Hasina also appeared to be in denial over the scale of 'corruption, mismanagement in the Dhaka City Corporation and its mayor, load shedding, increase in hijacking, kidnapping and extortions etc.'[149] Local and foreign election monitors refuted her accusations but it would be a while before the Awami League's disappointment subsided sufficiently for its MPs to end the boycott and take their parliamentary seats.

Khaleda Zia took the oath of office on 10 October and swore in a cabinet that, for the first time in Bangladesh's history, included two members of the Jamaat-e-Islami. The political revolution marked by the award of ministerial office to men who had, in 1971, opposed national independence, was much remarked upon; the dire state of the economy drew less attention. In January 2000, donors had expressed concern that the Hasina administration's 'ongoing loosening of policies and signs of weakening investor confidence and donor support in the face of governance and political problems' threatened the post-1998 recovery.[150] 'Persistent pursuit of expansionary fiscal and monetary policies along with slow progress on needed structural reforms' especially in the banking and SOE sectors had driven up the government's deficit to 5–6 per cent of GDP in 1999–2001. Credit from the banking system to the government had grown at an annual rate of nearly 35 per cent in 1999–2001.[151] In that period, public external debt grew by 4 per cent of the GDP to $16.5 billion, or 36 per cent of the GDP, adding to the pressures on the economy.[152]

This, added to sharply declining exports and imports, and international reserves falling from $1,751 million in 1997–98 to $1,302 million in 2000–01, meant the economy was showing 'growing fragility.'[153] There were fears that real GDP growth would fall from 5.25 per cent in 2000–01 to 3.75 per cent in 2001–02.[154] With most indicators following a similarly negative trend, Bangladesh faced a serious challenge. Donors made these points in talks with the Hasina government in February, Justice Latifur Rahman's CTG in July, and the new BNP-led administration in November 2001. The near-crisis situation forced the administration to focus on the primacy of the economy. It also led to further negotiations in January and February 2002 when the Zia government told its aid partners it would 'adopt a comprehensive set of measures to be supported' by the IMF starting from July 2002. From then on, the government engaged in regular, periodic consultations with the World Bank, the IMF and the ADB on macroeconomic, monetary and fiscal policies, in addition to the annual meeting of the Aid Bangladesh Consortium. The key socio-economic challenge was that although Bangladesh had reduced extreme poverty by 20 per cent over the 1990s, a third of its citizens were still subsisting in that category. Donors agreed with the government that 'the main task will be to lift the rate of economic growth sufficiently to achieve a significant reduction in the prevailing high levels of poverty.'[155]

To that end, the government and the donors agreed on supporting more flexible interest and exchange rate regimes. The former was less sure about the timing of the shift and Bangladesh Bank's ability to handle the complications such flexibility would impose. The complexity of the situation forced Bangladesh to accept tough reformatory measures in exchange of concessionary loans. One condition was the flotation of the Taka which was done in May 2003. By then, some of the government's action had borne fruit. Macroeconomic stability had been restored, structural reforms initiated, industrial production and exports rebounded by 5 per cent, and international reserves had been rebuilt from $1 billion in November 2001 to $1.8 billion in May 2003.[156] The Taka had been devalued; the world's largest jute mill, Adamjee, a loss-making SOE employing 26,000 people, was closed in July 2002 at a cost to Tk 4 billion in redundancy payments; another twenty-four SOEs had been closed while eleven were launched on closure or privatisation at a cost of Tk 7.6 billion in retrenchment packages. In January–September 2002, energy subsidies were slashed—petrol by 22 per cent, natural gas, diesel and kerosene by 10 per cent, and electricity by 7–8 per cent. In January 2003, petrol and diesel prices were again raised by 17 per cent.[157] The government also pledged to expand Bangladesh Bank's independence in managing exchange- and interest rates, and oversee commercial banks. An IMF-aided study concluded that structural changes were needed. To increase 'pro-poor' allocations and investment in health and education, the state needed to withdraw from productive and commercial financial activities which imposed massive burdens on its meagre resources.

Plans had been made to shut down or privatise another 105 SOEs employing 75,500 workers at a cost of Tk 64 billion. Money owed to the state was another challenge. Arrears worth Tk 4 billion owed to utility companies were one example. Total SOE arrears at the end of 2002 amounted to Tk 145 billion or 4.8 per cent of GDP.[158] Reforming SOEs and nationalised commercial banks (NCBs) could cost 8–12 per cent of GDP,[159] an unbearable burden. Reforms initiated in June 2003 were supported by an IMF-aided three-year package worth SDR 347 million aimed at reducing poverty by increasing growth. Despite difficulties, the export of ready-made garments (RMG) and frozen food picked up, pushing exports up by 15.5 per cent in July 2003–April 2004. After the Taka was floated, foreign exchange reserves grew, reaching $2.7 billion on 30 June 2004. The currency's depreciation by 3 per cent in this period also boosted Bangladesh's competitive edge.[160] Responding to rising world energy prices and working to a formula agreed on with the World Bank, the government cut subsidies on kerosene by 17 per cent in May. However, energy SOEs remained a burden on the economy. The government's efforts to modernise the four NCB's—Sonali, Rupali, Janata and Agrani—towards efficient management so that they could recover much of their very large outstanding loans, the last three could be privatised, and minority shares in Sonali Bank could be sold, proved painfully slow.[161]

Against that backdrop, and in the context of growing reliance on the RMG sector's revenues, the imminent termination of the Multifibre Arrangement (MFA) regime at the end of 2004 deeply concerned the government. It feared that the loss of duty-free access to European Union and North American markets and the expected rise in competition from exporters with comprehensive textiles industries would slash earnings by $1.4 billion in 2005–06, or an annual loss of 1 per cent of GDP.[162] To complicate matters, floods swamped nearly half the districts in July 2004, affecting a quarter of the population. The World Bank and the ADB estimated losses to assets and output at $2.2 billion, or 3.75 per cent of GDP.[163] Most losses stemmed from damage to crops, housing and infrastructure. The IMF released SDR 53 million as part of its poverty reduction aid. Smaller scale floods hit the country in September and food prices rose steeply during the fasting month of Ramadan in October-November. Funds were reallocated for urgent agricultural relief, housing and infrastructure reconstruction, and restoration of power and water supplies and other basic services in affected areas. Besides mustering domestic resources, the government secured aid worth $200 million from the World Bank, $185 million from the ADB, and $35 million from the UK Department of International Development (DFID), to be disbursed in 2005–07.[164] However, crop production suffered a decline. There was some good news from the export sector—monthly exports in July-October 2004 averaged $720 million compared to $600 million in July-October 2003, with gross foreign reserves rising to $3 billion on 30 September. But exports fell back to a monthly average of $644 million in November 2004–February 2005.[165]

Post-flood reallocation of resources for relief and reconstruction, slow reforms in the SOE and NCB sectors, rising costs of improving civil service compensation packages, an oil price surge in late 2004 and its impact on food grain prices combined in a difficult milieu forcing the government to seek donor assistance for reforming energy SOEs. IMF aid was needed to strengthen Bangladesh Bank and monitor the floating exchange rate. ADB support helped with examining the Chittagong port's bottle-necks. The World Bank, ADB and USAID provided 'technical assistance' towards developing 'an anti–corruption strategy' and improving 'the law and order situation.'[166] To encourage Bangladesh's poverty reduction efforts, in June 2005, the IMF extended the three-year programme begun in June 2003 to the end of 2006. So, critical areas of economic manage-ment and governance were being addressed with substantial donor involvement. Despite a 'difficult political environment,' Bangladesh achieved per capita GDP growth of 4.8 per cent in 1996–2003, helped by a 'sharp decline in the population growth rate' beginning in the early 1990s. With strong NGO involvement in social sectors, the population below the poverty line fell from 59 per cent in 1991 to under 50 per cent in 2000. Still, compared to other low-income countries (LIC), Bangla-desh's performance remained below par:[167]

- Financial markets were relatively inefficient, undermining growth performance.
- Physical and human capital development, e.g. percentages of paved roads and number of mobile- and fixed-line telephone subscribers per thousand people, pupil-teacher ratios and adult literacy rates were well below the South Asian average.
- Large amounts of foreign assistance received over thirty years generated mixed results, with disbursements declining since the mid-1990s; the slack was taken up by rising remittances which topped 6 per cent of GDP in 2004.
- Trade, reflecting a 'closed' framework, accounted for 20–30 per cent of GDP, well below the LIC average; FDI receipts were low, with some in the RMG sector.
- The 'strong positive relationship between better governance and good institutions, and high per capita incomes and better growth' explained some of the failings.[168]

Acknowledging these challenges, the government launched the National Strategy for Accelerated Poverty Reduction (NSAPR) in Octo-ber 2005, setting 'pro-poor growth, human development, and good gov-ernance as the pillars' of the development agenda. But failures to meet structural reform deadlines were blamed on 'delays in the disbursement' of aid money.[169] The government claimed some progress: despite the floods and energy price rises, the GDP had grown by 5.5 per cent in 2004–2005 and the deficit contained at 3.5 per cent; a 'rebound in food production' and tighter monetary policies countered inflationary consequences of rising fuel prices; to meet pressures in the foreign exchange market, Bangladesh Bank sold $600 million in March-November 2005, helping the depreciation of the taka/dollar exchange rate by 9 per cent in 2005; tax reforms increased the number of tax–payers by 26,000, raising income tax receipts by 16 per cent in the first four months of FY05.[170] However, Bangladesh Petroleum Corporation (BPC) and DESA continued to haemorrhage. The government had passed on 60–75 per cent of rising fuel costs to consumers over the past two years, with retail price for kerosene and diesel rising by 76 and 50 per cent respectively, and those of petrol, by 27–29 per cent.[171]

But this was not enough. The one bright spot lay in the RMG sector—despite the end of the MFA quotas, Bangladesh's RMG exports and RMG-linked imports, and investments in the sector, grew. The government admitted that port operations remained 'a major problem and governance problems will also need to be addressed.'[172] The irony of the Finance Minister's admission just a few months before his government's five-year term ended may have been lost on him and his cabinet colleagues. After a review in February 2006, donors concluded that Bangladesh had met most of the poverty reduction programme's objectives—growth had been sustained, inflation contained and international reserves increased; poverty had been reduced and progress made toward meeting Bangladesh's Millennium Development Goals (MDGs). Except for revenue collection, the 'quantitative performance criteria' for judging performance had been met.[173] In fact, despite political and governance difficulties, the GDP grew by more than 6 per cent annually between July 2003 and June 2006, a better performance than in any comparable period since independence.[174] Donors still believed the country's potential for progress had remained unrealised as the Zia administration approached its end.[175]

The politics of power

Nothing proved the point better than the record of the opposition's legislative activities. As with the two previous parliaments, the National Assembly was often a stage for high drama of shouted imprecations, shrill exchanges of mutual vituperation and opposition walkouts and boycotts. There was little serious effort to present bills and argue their pros and cons with measured consideration. In 1996–2001, the BNP-led opposition had boycotted the parliament on 156 days out of the 382 days when the National Assembly met in session; in 2001–2006, the Awami League-led opposition boycotted the parliament on 223 days out of 373.[176] In 1991–1996 and 2001–2006, the Awami League had boycotted the BNP-led parliament on 523 days out of 773 days when the legislature had met. Between them, the two parties, when in opposition, had boycotted the National Assembly on 679 days out of a total of 1,155 days when the legislature met. This meant the parliament was boycotted by the opposition 57.78 per cent of the time it was in session.[177] No institution could maintain its credibility, or justification, on that scale of brazen power-politics. The theatre, occasionally entertaining, may have filled a void in the lives of Bangladeshis, but it marginalised the legislature in policy-making and confirmed the institution's peripheral role. This was a gift of the three terms served by the BNP and Awami League governments elected since the 1991 democratic restoration.

Even when MPs from all the main parties attended sessions, parliamentary discussions descended into troubling displays of inanity, banality or even profanity. MPs used the opportunity to speak to build their own positions within the party hierarchy by praising 'the leader' in terms that were often irrelevant to the subject under discussion or unacceptable in polite company. On other occasions, they would engage in ill-tempered exchanges with colleagues from rival benches. Some utilised their slots to raise issues not relevant to the bill or subject under discussion. On many of these occasions, the Speaker would warn particular MPs and, *in extremis*, switch off their microphones. Data collected by Transparency International's Bangladesh chapter is instructive. In 2003–6, for instance, MPs switched discussions to irrelevant issues on 962 occasions—BNP MPs were responsible 70.79 per cent of the time while the opposition accounted for 29.21 per cent. MPs exchanged impolite accusations and counter-accusations on 990 occasions; BNP parliamentarians were guilty 71.01 per cent of the time while opposition MPs reciprocated with 29.09 per cent. MPs praised Khaleda Zia or Sheikh Hasina respectively a total of 1,058 times—Treasury Bench MPs were responsible for 74 per cent of these unnecessarily hagiographic interventions while opposition MPs accounted for 26 per cent. The Speaker, a BNP nominee and presumably sympathiser, cautioned MPs 547 times for engaging in irrelevant discussions—BNP legislators received 67 per cent of these warnings while opposition MPs received 33 per cent. Things got so unacceptable on 66 occasions that the Speaker was constrained to switch off the microphone while an MP was in full flow. Treasury Bench and opposition MPs shared these occasions equally.[178]

The two rival parties shared one other common proclivity: by the time the Awami League left office in 2001, Bangladesh was ranked the most corrupt country in the world, in the Corruption Perception Index compiled by Transparency International. By the time the BNP stepped down in 2006, Bangladesh had once again descended to the bottom of that index.[179] In opposition, both parties blamed the incumbent for bringing the country to such a pass; in office, they defended their own performance while playing down the 'substance of perceptions.' Pecuniary abuses were just an aspect of the 'corruption' in which leaders and their acolytes engaged. Allegations filled the air but no action followed. Ever since General Ershad's ouster, successive administrations had accused their predecessors of massive corruption and had filed cases against leading personalities although Ershad was the only national figure to be convicted and forced to serve his sentence. Only in 2007 would a new CTG take drastic action against the 'two Begums,' their aides, and other prominent figures in an anti–corruption campaign which would partially reveal the scale of high-level graft lubricating Bangladesh's elite system. In BNP-ruled Bangladesh, abuse apparently was as much about power as money.

The Awami League's 'repression' of the BNP in 1996–2001 and the latter's inability to mount an effective response while in opposition—apart from parliamentary walk-outs and boycotts, and violent strikes and street-protests—appear to have forced changes. One was the growing clout of Zia's sister, brothers and sons in the decision-making process. The party's constitution gave the Chairperson near-absolute authority and this translated into her power to select or discard advisers at will. In opposition and under pressure, Zia came increasingly to rely on her family for advice and, in turn, empowered relatives within the party hierarchy. The most prominent sign of this shift occurred when she appointed her elder son, Tareque Zia, a senior BNP official. Tareque, as he was widely known, had initially concentrated on building up a commercial empire in collaboration with his mother's brother, the former army officer, Syed Eskander. Now, with money and political clout, he began erecting an edifice of proxy power based at a commercial building called 'Hawa Bhaban' in one of Dhaka's better districts. Here, with a collection of close aides and business partners, he built a network of influence and money which eventually became a source of parallel authority within the BNP whose youth wing fed from and into this dynamic and, occasionally, threatening establishment.

Tareque's success in leveraging political and commercial enterprise mutually reinforced both strands of his operations. As would be revealed from investigations in 2007–08, his men would persuade other commercial organisations into sharing some of their largesse for influence, protection and further gains. Those who disagreed with this formulation fell foul. One of the most prominent of these victims was Mahi Chowdhury, son of another prominent BNP leader, Badruddoza Chowdhury, a co-founder of the BNP with General Ziaur Rahman. Mahi Chowdhury, a young entrepreneur who went into politics and was elected an MP, had been Tareque's associate for years when they fell out. In the late 1990s, when Prime Minister Sheikh Hasina visited Mahi Chowdhury's constituency, the latter, breaking with Bangladesh's zero-sum traditions, organised a colourful reception for her. This marked him out as a 'traitor' among the BNP's youthful ranks. Commercial links between 'the two sons' soon were eroded by growing political differences.

Still, after Zia assumed prime ministerial office in 2001, she had B. Chowdhury—as he was known—elected as Bangladesh's president. In this formal capacity, B. Chowdhury remained punctiliously non-partisan. In BNP leaders' view, he took this neutrality too far when he politely declined to attend memorial services at Ziaur Rahman's mausoleum on the anniversary of Zia's death on 30 May 2002. He was swiftly replaced by Speaker Jamiruddin Sircar and on 6 September 2002, by Prof. Iajuddin Ahmed, a BNP-affiliated academic.[180] Father and son, B. Chowdhury and Mahi, broke away from mainstream BNP, and teamed up with several centrist political and civic figures, forming *Bikalpa Dhara* (alternative stream), challenging Bangladesh's violently polarised politics with a measure of reasoned civility. Although in numerical terms this new body could not challenge the BNP behemoth, its rising prominence was seen as an unacceptable threat, particularly bitter because of its intramural origins. The group was attacked and its leaders physically threatened. Eventually, Mahi Chowdhury's house was set ablaze by people he thought were acting on the orders of his political rivals.[181] He escaped from the burning house with his young family but the law provided neither protection nor redress. This malevolence marking Khaleda Zia's second term did not, however, do justice to her team's successes. Zia handed over a relatively robust economy to the new CTG when she stepped down in October 2006. The data in Table 4.11 indicate the economic development attained over the second term of the BNP's coalition administration in 2001–06.

Table 4.11: Economic progress attained during the BNP administration in 2001–06[182]

Fin. Year	GDP Tk.trn	GDP $bn	GDP per capita $	GDP growth %
2001	2.50	45.40	320.00	4.50
2002	2.73	47.30	348.00	4.90
2003	3.00	51.70	373.00	6.50
2004	3.30	55.50	392.00	7.00
2005	3.60	57.30	392.00	5.80
2006	4.10	58.80	399.00	6.50

Despite significant growth, expanding population in a finite landmass reduced per capita resource availability and for a majority of Bangladeshis, life remained brutish and short. With healthcare, education, sanitation and life expectancy rising, and mortality in general and child mortality in particular falling, population growth continued to put pressure on quality of life indicators. The population grew from 128 million on 1 July 2000 to at least 138.80 million on 1 July 2006.[183] Although annual growth stabilised at 1.3 per cent in 2002–2006, in that latter year Bangladesh's population density stood at 940 per sq.km,[184] the densest among countries other than city-states. Nonetheless, there was progress in many areas: under-five mortality fell from 149 per thousand live births in 1990 to 69 in 2006; infant (under one-year) mortality, from 100 to 52.[185] Life expectancy at birth rose from 54 years in 1990 to 63 in 2006.[186] Adult literacy reached 48 per cent in 2005; primary school attendance hit 81 per cent in 2006 while enrolment exceeded 100 per cent.

Secondary school enrolment reached 44 per cent for boys and 45 per cent for girls; attendance stood at 36 and 41 per cent respectively.[187] By increasing social sector budgetary allocations, the government achieved 'most of the objectives' of the IMF-aided June-2003 poverty reduction programme.[188] In 1995–2005, spending on the health sector reached 7 per cent of the total, and education 17 per cent; defence spending stood at 10 per cent.[189] Once again, the potential for change was tantalising if unrealised. Defence remained a sensitive area. Like her predecessors, Khaleda Zia also sought to control the armed forces, particularly the army, for her own purposes, using resources as an instrument of leverage. The chief executive's reliance on budgetary tools reduced the efficacy of leverage since the room for manoeuvre was small to start with. Zia began by slightly reducing defence expenditure after taking office. However, she soon had to raise allocations. Actual defence expenditure exceeded yearly allocations throughout her administration. This could have indicated either lax accounting procedures or an inability or unwillingness on her part to control what the Generals, Admirals and Air Vice Marshals were doing. Table 4.12 compares the defence budgetary allocations and manpower in the Hasina administration's last FY with those during Zia's term:

Table 4.12: Defence allocations and military manpower in FY 2001–2007[190]

Fin. Year	Def.Exp.$m	GDP Percentage	Service personnel	Paramilitary strength
2001	608.00	1.30	125,500	54,000
2002	607.00	1.30	125,500	63,200
2003	644.00	1.20	125,500	63,200
2004	777.00	1.38	125,500	126,200
2005	840.00	1.46	125,500	126,200
2006	938.00	1.58	126,500	63,200
2007	999.00	1.47	150,000	63,910

Some of the data can be a little confusing. For instance, the sudden increase in the strength of paramilitary forces recorded in FY 2004 and then reverted to the original in FY 2006 is explained by the inclusion of all *Ansar* militia personnel in FY 2004 and then, in FY 2006, the exclusion of the 'unembodied' volunteers who would not be available for service at all times. The sudden increase of regular service personnel by 24,000 in FY 2007 did not record a dramatic expansion of the armed forces; instead, it acknowledged the discovery by overseas observers that the Bangladesh Army's Corps of Infantry actually comprised fifty battalions rather than around twenty-six as registered in earlier accounts. The changes in the command structure were, however, more compelling.

When Lt. General Mustafizur Rahman retired as CAS in December 2000, Hasina appointed Lt. General Harun-ar-Rashid, the senior FF officer in the army at the time, to succeed him. General Rashid had won an award for bravery in combat in 1971, had risen through the command-and-General Staff chain of career progression, performed well at military schools of instruction at home and abroad, and commanded a UN peace-keeping force in the Caucasus. By all accounts, he was an apolitical, pro-fessional commander, an impression widely shared.[191] As it happened, his appointment coincided with the closing months of the Hasina adminis-tration when party-political rhetoric grew shrill as the Awami League vied with its rivals for the moral high ground, especially over its role in the war of independence. Anniversaries from recent history were exploited by all sides, but especially the ruling party, to reinforce their national cre-dentials in a milieu steeped in an emotional search for identity in which differences were seen as elemental and beyond compromise. In one such event, the CAS was inveighed into addressing a gathering that could be construed as partisan and in the febrile political atmosphere his speech was interpreted as such. There was no rational basis for such an appraisal, but as President B. Chowdhury's dismissal demonstrated, reason was not of the essence. In fact, General Rashid was retired a week before Chow-dhury was, and sent abroad as an envoy.

Khaleda Zia, operating on the advice of her military aides, recalled Gen-eral Hasan Mashhud Chowdhury, a repatriate officer who had been sent abroad on diplomatic assignment by a previous government, and appointed him CAS. Chowdhury was reputedly a devout Muslim, an incorruptible disciplinarian and a soldier bereft of ambition, in short, a safe pair of hands.[192] He built on Rashid's legacy, concentrating on training and consoli-dation of the army's operational capability. This came in handy because Zia, having inherited a worrying erosion of law-and-order and surging criminal violence, wanted to utilise the army in cracking down on crime. Public lynching of suspected criminals in the capital's streets in broad daylight may have forced Zia's hands.[193] In October 2002, Chowdhury mounted 'Operation Clean Heart,' with about 40,000 troops deployed alongside police and paramilitary units across Bangladesh. In the eighty-five days of 'Operation Clean Heart,' troops detained more than 10,000 suspects of whom around fifty died in custody.[194] Officials usually attributed these deaths to 'heart attacks.'[195] 'Clean Heart' wound down in early 2003 with-out any permanent impact on criminal violence. Zia now established a special team of policemen called the Rapid Action Team, RAT, to be trained by army special services. But the RAT made little impression.

In June 2003, the Zia cabinet decided to establish Rapid Action Battalions—RAB—to counter serious criminal violence on a permanent basis. Once necessary legislation was passed, RAB units were formed in March 2004 and began operating in June that year. They brought together elite personnel from the armed forces, the BDR, and the police, who were seconded to this organisation with its distinctive black-dress uniforms, sunglasses and bandanas and with apparent sanction to operate with little fear or favour. Trained by army special services in operational tactics, RAB would provide internal security, conduct intelligence into criminal activities, recover illegal arms, arrest criminals, assist other law enforcement authorities and investigate offenses as ordered by the government.[196] Commanded mostly by army officers, RAB soon evoked complaints of enforcing 'martial law in disguise.'[197] Although the army was only partially involved in RAB operations, the fact that between March 2004 and December 2006, RAB was implicated in 'the unlawful killings of at least 350 people in custody'[198] cast a shadow on the image of the military and on the Zia government more generally.

General Chowdhury served as CAS for exactly three years, stepping down on 15 June 2005. On the advice of her closest aides, Zia appointed Lt. General Moeen Ahmed, a contemporary and friend of her brother Sayeed Eskander, as the new CAS. Ahmed was the first officer to have been trained and commissioned in independent Bangladesh to take charge of what arguably was the country's key institution. Not having shone particularly brilliantly as an ambitious officer until now, he may have been given the job as another safe pair of hands. Looking ahead, Zia similarly prepared yet another safe pair of hands for when she left office. In 2005, she enacted a constitutional amendment to extend the retirement age of chief justices from sixty-five years to sixty-seven. This would ensure her appointee Chief Justice K.M. Hasan would retire just before she herself stepped down. He would then in accordance with constitutional provisions assume the role of Chief Adviser to the CTG assigned the task of holding general elections.

Anxious over potential subversion of the CTG's neutrality, the Awami League's fourteen-party alliance placed a twenty-three-point charter of demands seeking electoral reforms. When the two main parties failed to agree on the formation of a new election commission and CTG, violence erupted. After more than twenty-five people were killed and scores injured in street battles, Justice Hasan stepped aside.[199] Instead of appointing the former chief justice who had preceded Hasan, Iajuddin Ahmed appointed himself his Chief Adviser, concentrating all executive authority in his person. He appointed ten advisers who took on cabinet portfolios but faced with growing scepticism over the neutrality of a CTG led by a BNP-appointed president who also was the Chief Adviser and Supreme Commander of the armed forces, and the bloody protests this scepticism generated, four advisers resigned on 11 December.[200] Foreign observers, troubled by the political impasse threatening the polls, conducted their own analyses, with one group complaining the voters' list drawn up by the BNP-led administration contained 'over 12 million false names.'[201] With party activists and the police clashing regularly, the death toll topped fifty by 31 December.[202]

When things went beyond the capacity of the police to manage, Iajuddin Ahmed deployed the army to the capital's streets. However, General Ahmed and his commanders remained scrupulously non-partisan in the robustness shown by the soldiers in dispersing mobs. It was then that rumours started floating that the President, urged by BNP leaders, was considering relieving the CAS with a General more amenable to working along lines favourable to the BNP.[203] Envoys of donor countries and organisations informally called the 'Tuesday Club'[204] because of their weekly meetings, met the General Secretary of the Awami League and the Secretary General of the BNP, urging them to negotiate a compromise deal. In the backdrop of street violence in which an activist was beaten to death near the national mosque before TV crews filming live, and the zero-sum nature of the Awami League-BNP rivalry, the talks failed. Immediately, the European Union suspended its election monitoring mission on the grounds that polls would not meet international standards.[205] The UN suspended all assistance to the electoral process, shutting down its International Coordination Office for Election Observers in Dhaka.[206]

The UN's Resident Coordinator, Renata Dessallien, now made public what she and her diplomatic colleagues had been warning General Ahmed for some time: an election held under the current dispensation would not be free and fair, would be boycotted by the Awami League and its allies, and could not produce internationally acceptable results; if the army allowed this to happen, it would lose its lucrative role in UN peace-keeping operations.[207] This was a price the army would not pay. The Generals visited the president at the *Bangabhaban* where, after several hours of unpleasant exchanges, Iajuddin Ahmed stepped down as Chief Adviser, although he remained president. The Advisers to his CTG resigned, general elections were postponed and a state of emergency came into effect from 11 January. Bangladesh's democratic future was to be defended and defined by the military at the donor community's behest. Besides the armed forces and their foreign allies, few Bangladeshis had had any direct role in shaping these events. Once again, Bangladesh had become an anxious onlooker at its own banquet. That was the legacy of Khaleda Zia's second democratic administration.

5

A 'REFORMIST' INTERREGNUM

2007–2009

Abstract: Growing concerns over the consequences of an apparently zero-sum conflict between Khaleda Zia's BNP-led administration and the Awami League-led opposition headed by Sheikh Hasina, and the absence of a constitutional solution to a crisis which threatened to become a chronic malaise, reached a peak in late 2006. The combination of their unquestioned authority over their respective party organisations, their countrywide support-base, and their inability or unwillingness to compromise, or even extend a measure of civility to each other, built a downward spiral which threatened to take Bangladesh down with them. The army was encouraged by OECD donors and India, but warned that if the BNP-designed interim administration was allowed to conduct polls which were boycotted by the Awami League, as Hasina had threatened to do, the United Nations and the donors would not recognise the newly-elected government as legitimate. This would end the lucrative peacekeeping assignments the army had come to depend on. This threat proved effective.

The donors and the army agreed they had a two-year window in which to address Bangladesh's many ills, especially gross corruption and incompetence afflicting the political-bureaucratic elite about which the donors had regularly been warning the government in their annual report to the 'Aid Consortium Conference.' Operating from behind the scenes, although not entirely invisible, the army forced President Iajuddin Ahmed to relinquish executive authority, imposed a state of rigorously enforced emergency, arrested a large number of politicians, businessmen and other 'untouchables' on charges which occasionally appeared flimsy, set up a technocratic Caretaker Government, and set about reforming the political

251

system. However, popular relief and appreciation proved fickle. Eminent national figures, identified as alternative messiahs, themselves beneficiaries of the discredited system, failed to elicit the passionate popularity enjoyed by the 'two Begums,' Zia and Hasina, held in comfortable proximity in the parliament complex on allegations of abuses of power and corruption. The army's efforts to get rid of the two women, whose history of personal antipathy was viewed as central to the country's ills, proved abortive. Although other influential figures, including Zia's sons, suffered the indignity of painful incarceration and unthinkable interrogation, the two women remained impregnable. Hasina agreed to go abroad for 'medical treatment' but Zia refused to leave.

Consumer price inflation, especially affecting food items and energy, allegations of abuse and corruption against those exercising absolute power, modest improvement in the quality of civic life, and occasional outbursts of popular anger challenged the regime's reformist zeal. Nonetheless, electoral mechanisms were revamped, earlier follies shown up and corrected, and a relatively even playing field created for the restoration of elective governance. A foundation was thus laid for an improved system for addressing the needs of Bangladesh's severely neglected majority. However, the regime's failure to rid the land of the two charismatic inheritors whose popularity defeated efforts to reform their parties, showed up the polity's passionate irrationality. Once failure was acknowledged, the regime endeavoured to restore the two leaders to their original glory so that a credible election could be engineered. Whether the result would be equally credible, or accepted by the defeated, and what the legacy of the reformist drive would be, remained uncertain.

A restoration of sorts

Towards the very end of 2008, Bangladesh abandoned indirect military rule for the third time and held elections to the parliament, its ninth. Emergency regulations, substantially relaxed since early December, were finally lifted twelve days before the polls, and an elected government led by the Awami League's Sheikh Hasina was sworn in to office on 6 January 2009.[1] This electoral outcome appeared to restore the dynastic cycle in which Hasina and her BNP rival, Khaleda Zia, alternated in office while the other was consigned to political wilderness in marginalised opposition, and their parties confronted each other in city streets. However, the political game had partly changed in the two years between the street violence in October-November 2006 and the December 2008 polls. The army, in the guise of 'joint forces'—operating in concert with the other armed services, the BDR, the RAB, the Police, the security and intelligence organs and the magistracy—had detained several hundred thousand men in this period. Most were released after interrogation and, in some cases, trial; but a large number remained in custody. They included many senior politicians from the BNP, the Awami League and the Jamaat-e-Islami, creating a vacuum in the party hierarchies, most visibly, the BNP's.

This was designed to ensure that even if the military's early efforts to rid the land of the 'two Begums'—Hasina and Zia, in the 'minus two' formulation—failed[2], fresh blood would rise to fill the gaps. Also, the conviction and detention of senior party figures served to remind the political classes that they needed to observe certain restraints while in office. The fact that Zia and Hasina themselves had suffered imprisonment—albeit in comfortable circumstances—and continued to face allegations of corruption and abuse of power acted as a deterrent to a return of profligate indiscretion. Or at least, that was the hope.[3] However, many uncertainties remained. The Awami League, confident of victory, had early on demanded the polls be held on schedule on 18 December; the BNP, severely weakened by factional feuding and the military's anti–corruption drive, insisted that polls be deferred by two months. Then, in November, it diluted its demands and following fresh rounds of talks among CTG leaders, the Election Commission (EC) and the two main parties, agreed to participate if the polls were held on 28 December and local elections were further delayed. For about a week, uncertainties over whether the BNP would take part in polls if these were held without the party's demands being met and, if elections went ahead without the BNP, what the consequences might be, exercised many.

The CAS, General Moin Uddin Ahmed, then reportedly advised the CTG that polls should take place on 18 December,[4] but the EC finally announced that parliamentary elections would be held on 29 December 2008 and local elections, on 22 January 2009. Faces having been saved, these dates satisfied all the parties registered by the EC. With assurances from the CAS and Chief Adviser Fakhruddin Ahmed that emergency rules would be lifted at an 'early date,' party leaders began campaigning. Whether they would accept the results—with BNP figures complaining the army had struck a deal with the Awami League[5]—remained unclear. However, the rules of the game had changed. The CTG had issued several electoral regulations changing the legal framework for holding elections. Of these, the Representation of the People Order 2008 (RPO) was the key innovation. Others were the Code of Conduct for Parliament Elections (2008), the Political Party Registration Rules (2008), the *Upazila* Ordinance (2008), and the *Upazila* Election Rules (2008). The last two would define the parameters for the local government polls in January 2009; the remainder would shape the conduct of the general elections. Political parties had to register themselves with the EC, undertaking to organise and conduct themselves in conformity with a set of norms which challenged past practice. These included regular internal elections, reserving a third of leading positions for women to be achieved by 2020, severing ties with affiliated student, youth and labour wings, and nominating candidates named by local committees rather than by central fiat. Party constitutions could no longer contradict the state's constitution and nor could membership be exclusively based on gender, language, faith, race or caste. The maximum number of parliamentary seats a candidate could contest was reduced from five to three.[6]

Although both the Awami League and the BNP had protested against the ban on student wings, compromises were found by formally delinking these affiliates from the main body of the parties while retaining an 'unofficial' association—thereby defeating the reform's purpose. The Jamaat-e-Islami was forced to change its constitution, acknowledging Bangladesh's 1971 war of independence as such—as opposed to its past insistence that this had been a civil war between factions within Pakistan—and changing its name from Jamaat-e-Islami Bangladesh to Bangladesh Jamaat-e-Islami. The party also claimed it had already attracted around five thousand non-Muslim members to its rolls.[7] These histrionics suggested the CTG's political reforms, designed to transform the ground rules, had been subverted by its inability to secure fundamental changes in the major parties.

Although the EC agreed to amend its proposed electoral laws as requested by the Awami League and the BNP, both violated provisions of the RPO and the Electoral Code of Conduct. The latter required candidates to seek permission from local officials before holding campaign rallies and similar events, prohibited campaigning at places of worship, and imposed punishments of six months in prison and/or a fine of up to the equivalent of $725 for breaches.[8] The EC issued warnings but took no punitive action against violators. The BNP was warned that by holding a pre-election rally in Chittagong before the campaign period had begun, Khaleda Zia had violated the electoral code of conduct.[9] The Awami League's massive rally summoned to receive Sheikh Hasina when she returned from abroad in November 2008 was similarly criticised as unauthorised electioneering.[10] The Awami League also violated the RPO's Article 90(B) by rejecting six candidates selected by their respective local party organisation and, nominating candidates picked by the party's central body instead.[11] The BNP followed suit.[12] Although the RPO stipulated that for this infraction parties could lose their registration, the EC imposed no sanctions.

The CTG gradually lifted restrictions imposed under Emergency regulations. Electoral campaign activities including processions and rallies, public criticism of the government, and media coverage of these were partly allowed from 3 November. Many troops working under 'joint forces' supervisory commands erected across the country were withdrawn. Most of the remaining Emergency restrictions were lifted on 12 December when candidates including party leaders were already out campaigning. All EPR-related constraints were removed five days later,[13] but police investigations and court cases begun under EPR would continue 'as if the rules had not been repealed.'[14] The ordinance repealing the Emergency regulations also dissolved the National Coordination Committee on Corruption and Serious Crime (NCC) established on 8 March 2007, but its 'administrative functions' would continue until 1 January 2009. Importantly, for the army and the CTG, the repeal ordinance also pointed out that the indemnity granted to these entities under Section 6 of the EPO would continue in force as though the EPO 2007 had not been repealed. Section 6 asserted that no legal proceedings could be instituted against any individual for taking action 'in good faith' and on orders given by superior authorities under the EPO 2007 and the EPR 2007.[15] These caveats notwithstanding, the repeal ordinance drew a line under the army's efforts, aided by OECD donors, to redesign Bangladesh's political landscape. Its anti–corruption drive, mounted partly as an instrument with which to refashion the polity, had led to the incarceration of more than two hundred leading politicians and high-profile entrepreneurs. The detained included many 'untouchables', most prominently Sheikh Hasina, Khaleda Zia, and her sons Tareque Rahman and Arafat Rahman. Many other politicians and businessmen, either on the list of 'absconders,' or fearing imminent arrest, fled abroad. To lead the drive, the army had reconstituted the Anti–Corruption Commission (ACC) under former Chief of Army Staff, Lt. General Hasan Mashhud Chowdhury, and established the NCC, initially under Lt. General Masud Chowdhury, Principal Staff Officer at the Armed Forces Division and, later, under the Adviser in-charge of Home Ministry, Major General M.A. Matin.[16]

The CTG had promulgated 144 ordinances[17] and established ten special judge's courts in the National Assembly complex, which also housed a special sub-jail in which Sheikh Hasina and Khaleda Zia spent their period of confinement. These courts tried corruption cases under emergency rules. More than two thousand such cases were filed, mostly on charges of bribery, extortion, tax evasion and abuse of office. The ACC had filed 472 anti–corruption cases while police and other organs had processed 710.[18] More than three hundred men and women, including about sixty politicians and their close relatives, were convicted in trials held under emergency rules. They included former ministers and MPs. Several university teachers and students, too, had been jailed under emergency rules following disturbances in August 2007, but they were later released on presidential clemency. Once it became clear that the CTG and the army had exhausted alternatives to restoring Sheikh Hasina and Khaleda Zia to the leadership of their parties and polls were the only practical exit strategy, courts began challenging the CTG's authority, questioning key ordinances.

A High Court bench, responding to a public interest litigation (PIL) writ petition in July 2008, asked the government to explain the legality of the state of emergency. Another High Court bench, responding to another PIL writ petition, ruled in December 2008 that four provisions of the EPO were illegal. These had barred individuals being tried under emergency regulations from seeking bail or appealing against orders issued by lower courts, and higher courts from staying sentences awarded by lower ones. The High Court also quashed the EC's decision to reject nominations filed by a number of candidates from the major political parties on the ground that they had defaulted on loans taken from banks and other public financing organisations and had failed to reschedule these within the stipulated time-frame. Nearly eighty candidates—thirty named by the EC as defaulters and the remainder, by Bangladesh Bank, the country's central bank—whose nominations had initially been questioned under the new electoral rules, obtained stay orders from the High

Court and proceeded to contest the elections.[19] The EC insisted it would challenge the High Court's decision at the Supreme Court's Appellate Division after the elections, but to avoid disrupting the polls, would, for now, carry out the High Court's orders.

A tattered legacy

As the national mood swung towards restoration of the familiar party-political system headed by charismatic dynasts, cases against key figures began to unravel. A businessman who had accused Sheikh Hasina of 'extorting' a large sum of money over the contract for building a power project via her cousin who was then a minister in her cabinet, thereby triggering a series of such allegations against the Awami League leader, applied to the CTG in mid-December 2008 to have his original allegation 'withdrawn.' He claimed his action had been the result of 'a misunderstanding in an adverse environment,' and that 'it was an unexpected incident...I did not directly file any case. Neither did I name anyone. There was a misunderstanding, which will be over when the case is withdrawn...I was compelled to file the case on 13 June 2007 due to changed circumstances.'[20] Almost immediately afterwards, another businessman who had filed a similar complaint of extortion—of Tk 10 million—against Khaleda Zia's eldest son and heir apparent, Tareque Rahman and his close aide, Mian Nuruddin Apu, announced plans to withdraw his complaint. Inviting reporters to his Dhaka office, this construction magnate told his guests he had been 'forced to file the case' against Tareque Rahman 'amidst an adverse situation against his will.' The police had later submitted a charge-sheet against Tareque and Apu to the court of the capital's Chief Metropolitan Magistrate who passed it on to Dhaka's 'Speedy Trial Court no. 2' whose Magistrate fast-tracked proceedings, ensuring investigations were completed within seven days as stipulated in the Speedy Trial Act.[21] Now there was a possibility that those exertions might have been futile.

The NCC and the ACC, which had spearheaded the regime's anti-corruption drive, were thwarted when the High Court ruled that the Truth and Accountability Commission (TAC), set up by the CTG to address mass graft in an imaginative and non-judicial manner, was illegal. By the time of this ruling, 389 individuals had applied to the TAC to make voluntary disclosures of illegal acquisitions. They included more than 270 officials and thirty businessmen. More than 200 had applied to the TAC via the ACC, 167 had done so via the NCC, ten had approached via trial courts while another twenty arrived at the TAC on their own. Two-hundred-and-fifty-nine applicants had admitted to possessing illegally acquired assets worth Tk 277.90 million; of this, Tk 144.60 million had already been deposited with the state treasury.[22] By the time Bangladesh went to polls, the High Court had stayed 134 anti–corruption cases and was considering another 328 while the ACC was still processing 194 cases whose future now looked uncertain.[23] Perhaps the most telling comment on the drive was made by Sheikh Hasina who told business leaders that while politicians were being accused of extortion, and many businessmen had been detained and interrogated on 'who had paid how much to us, there was no account of how much changed hands between the detained and their interrogators.'[24] These moves raised serious questions about the *raison d'être* cited by the military for its assumption of control, the CTG's actions over its two-year tenure, and the prospects of the anti–corruption drive continuing beyond the polls.

The delicate and febrile nature of national politics had led to much toing and fro-ing. Government mediators and ambassadors from major donor states visited Hasina and Zia, urging them to work together to ensure polls were peaceful, that the victors did not wreak vengeance on their rivals after results were announced, that both the rulers and the opposition collaborated in restoring representative governance, and that MPs carried out their proper legislative and other duties once the newly elected National Assembly sat in session. But most of all, they urged the 'two Begums' to work together. Having refused to speak to each other in a civil fashion for almost two decades, Hasina and Zia agreed to meet in November 2008.[25] This caused quite a stir, underscoring the persistence of an abnormal, hitherto dysfunctional, political culture. To ensure traditional electoral violence did not vitiate the 29 December polls, the CTG prohibited carrying firearms in public, ordered that all licensed weapons in the possession of civilians be deposited with the police before the elections, and stopped issuing fresh arms licenses. It also ordered the pre-election deployment of substantial bodies of 'joint forces' personnel across the country to ensure there was no recurrence of the habitual displays of partisan 'muscle.' On 20 December, tens of thousands of troops, paramilitary and police personnel freshly deployed by the CTG on 'election duty' to ensure voting was 'free and fair,' went into action. Unusually, there was little adverse reaction to these deployments.

However, the EC's decision to redraw the boundaries of 133 of the country's 300 electoral constituencies had proved controversial with senior political figures questioning the move. The boundaries, drawn up before the 1973 polls, had been partially modified in 1979, 1984 and 1995, but did not reflect demographic changes which had transformed Bangladesh since the country gained independence. Objections reflected fears that modifications could seriously affect the electoral prospects of parties, especially given the electorate's polarisation and a preponderance of 'swing seats' in constituencies where a modest switch in party-support among voters could change the winning side. This required previously defeated candidates contesting in these constituencies to increase their support by just 10 per cent to secure victory. At the root of these anxieties lay Bangladesh's 'first past the post' winner-take-all electoral system. The most recent previous elections, in 2001, had demonstrated the volatility which resulted from the combination of these factors. Then, the BNP raised its share of votes by just 8 per cent from its 1996 performance, enough to increase its parliamentary seats by 44 per cent. The reverse was true for the Awami League whose share of the vote declined by 3 per cent, costing it 57 per cent of the seats it had won in 1996.[26] Not surprisingly, challenges were filed against proposed changes to the constituency demarcations but on 12 November, as the end of emergency regulations approached, the Supreme Court ruled in favour of the EC.

A new system of registering political organisations with the EC reduced the number of parties from over a hundred to thirty-eight,[27] forced these to amend their constitutions, diluted the party leader's dictatorial powers by introducing collegial practices, and extracted pledges of transparency, accountability and regular internal elections. The EC revised the electoral rolls, reducing duplications and other anomalies and cut the number of registered voters by twelve million.[28] The Commission announced that on 14 October 2008, the electoral roll carried the names of 81,130,973 registered voters.[29] The army issued national photo-identity cards intended in part to reduce electoral fraud and other popular criminal activities. Transparent ballot boxes were introduced to boost voting transparency—literally. Protracted negotiations between the CTG and the major parties appeared to have included agreements that parties would not nominate convicted criminals as electoral candidates, victors would not use legal instruments to victimise their critics, incumbents would not abuse their offices for private gain, and the actions of the CTG and its military backers taken in 2006–08 would be indemnified. The ACC and the NCC elected not to pursue allegations of criminal abuse they and the police had earlier made against Hasina and Zia although not all the cases were immediately withdrawn. The Awami League appeared willing to honour such tacit accords,[30] but the BNP insisted it had made no secret deals with anyone. The opacity of the army's thinking about its post-election 'exit strategy' kept the nation in suspense until the very end.

Despite efforts by state organs, some politicians in particular and the country more generally continued to face threats from the radical extremes of the political spectrum. The *jihadi* challenge proved to be particularly troublesome, especially as indirect Indian intervention raised its profile at a difficult time. Just days before the polls, a Delhi–based TV channel quoted unnamed Indian intelligence officers as saying that 'a six-member suicide squad of the banned Harkat-ul-Jihad-al-Islami Bangladesh (HuJI-B), had been assigned to kill' Sheikh Hasina and that she had been warned accordingly 'by Indian intelligence agencies.'[31] Hasina limited her campaign visits to major towns and cities, announcing, 'I'm the daughter of *Bangabandhu* Sheikh Mujibur Rahman and I'm not scared of any threats.' She then accused the previous BNP-Jamaat alliance government of 'patronising terrorists' who had attacked her in the past.[32] The BNP, for its part, claimed that the arrest of militants and the recovery of grenades after Khaleda Zia's rally near Comilla on 23 December demonstrated that there was a plot to kill her.[33] The authorities swiftly deployed additional security personnel to protect both Sheikh Hasina and Khaleda Zia, but these developments begged several questions: why did Bangladeshi security services fail to discover specific threats to the leaders of the country's two main parties when foreign intelligence services were able to do so in one case? How accurate and reliable were Indian intelligence activities in Bangladesh? Did Indian intelligence services directly warn a Bangladeshi politician of national stature before advising the government of Bangladesh? In short, more questions were raised than were answered.

These did not, however, detract from the continuing Islamist challenge to Bangladesh. In mid-November 2008, RAB personnel, hunting for the alleged new 'Amir' of Jamaat-ul Mujahideen Bangladesh (JMB), Moulana Syed, raided a house in the capital's Mirpur district. Although the Moulana eluded them, they recovered 150 'improvised grenades' and 70kg of explosives, bomb-making equipment and 'jihadi literature'. They also arrested a man named Hanif a.k.a. Kamal who they believed was JMB's new military commander. Hanif told the media, when RAB presented him at a press conference, that he had been 'told to manufacture powder. The definition of jihad is the armed struggle in Allah's way against the apostates who change Allah's laws and establish man-made laws.'[34] In the following weeks, security personnel arrested a number of other suspected radical Islamists along with arms, ammunition, explosives and equipment reportedly used to fabricate grenades. This unapologetic pursuit of 'divinely sanctioned' regime-change using terrorist violence underscored the persistence of Islamist extremism as a potent threat to the secular-liberal state which the CTG and the military, their OECD patrons, and the wider political establishment generally, sought to fashion in Bangladesh.[35]

Such grim portents notwithstanding, on 29 December 2008, elections to Bangladesh's ninth parliament passed off fairly peacefully; it was the results which caused trouble. The Chief Election Commissioner claimed around 86 per cent of the electorate had cast their votes[36] at over 35,000 polling centres across the country to elect MPs from among 1,538 candidates including 141 independents.[37] More than half a million security personnel deployed across the country maintained calm.[38] Of the 299 seats being contested—voting for the 300th was deferred because of the death of a candidate during the campaign period—results for 295 were published on 30 December when an Awami League landslide victory became evident.[39] The scale of the BNP's defeat became clear even before the final tally was published. This showed the Awami League and its partners in the 'grand alliance' had won 262 seats; the BNP-led four-party front took thirty-two. Among the former, the Awami League itself won 230 seats, General Ershad's Jatiya Party took twenty-seven, the left-wing JSD won three and the Workers Party, two. The BNP itself won twenty-nine, Jamaat-e-Islami took two, and the Bangladesh Jatiaya Party, one. Outside of the two alliances, a breakaway BNP faction, the Liberal Democratic Party, won one seat; independents secured four.[40]

The results transformed Bangladesh's political landscape, giving the Awami League an unusually sweeping mandate and casting the BNP to the margins.[41] On polling day, BNP spokesmen repeatedly complained of intimidation, rigging by officials and Awami League activists, and other abuses. When the Awami League's massive victory became clear, Khaleda Zia rejected the results of the 'stage-managed polls.'[42] While voting had taken place relatively peacefully, there was some violence afterwards—mostly against BNP-Jamaat supporters.[43] As fears grew of agitation by the losers, Sheikh Hasina offered the post of Deputy Speaker and the chairmanship of several parliamentary committees to the BNP; it responded with pledges of co-operation.[44] On 6 January 2009, Sheikh Hasina took the oath of office as prime minister. Her cabinet of twenty-three ministers and eight state ministers, mostly novice politicians, surprised even some of her party activists.[45] Two weeks later, in an officially non-party-based election to local government positions, the Awami League and its supporters defeated those of the BNP and its allies, further consolidating their hold on party-political Bangladesh. This overwhelming dominance did not automatically translate into a resolution of all of the country's myriad problems.

Indeed, by raising expectations, it may have built up the potential for disillusionment, frustration and future difficulties. The conduct of the local elections with the Awami League back in office underscored the potential for trouble. Polls were held to elect the Chairmen and other local government officials in 481 *Upazilas* across the land, but violence by ruling party activists forced the EC to postpone polling in six. The results from 295 showed the trend early on—Awami League-backed candidates took nearly two-thirds of the posts of chairmen.[46] These polls, unlike the parliamentary ones, were marked by low turnout, much violence and relatively lax security arrangements while the Chief Election Commissioner himself accused newly-appointed ministers and Awami League legislators of trying to affect the outcome of the elections.[47] To an extent then, by early 2009, Bangladeshi politics had reasserted its time-honoured patterns which the army and its CTG had worked hard to eradicate. As the Awami League and the BNP bickered over how legislative practices would reflect the plural nature of the electorate, the Awami League's massive majority notwithstanding, some urban Bangladeshis were concerned that the reforms initiated in 2007–8 would soon be turned into footnotes of Bangladesh's tortured history.[48]

A smorgasbord of troubles

As if politics were not enough, Dhaka faced yet other challenges. Violent agitation by students had been damped down with considerable difficulty. Efforts to exile the 'two Begums' and encourage the germination of new political parties having collapsed, other tacit exercises aimed at developing more 'democratic' factions within the existing parties were launched, but these too failed. Much of 2008 was spent in repairing the damage wrought by these abortive exertions. Before that process could begin, in November 2007, a tropical storm, 'Cyclone Sidr,' tore in from the Bay of Bengal, devastating much of the country's south-western quadrant. Mercifully, with early warning systems and storm shelters playing a life-saving role, Sidr only took just over 3,000 lives. However, large stretches of rice paddies, prawn and other fisheries, mangrove forests, and cattle and wildlife in those habitats were destroyed. Millions were left homeless. Saline surges from the Bay ensured that agricultural recovery would be painfully slow. More urgently, providing food, water, medicine, shelter and clothing to the survivors challenged the CTG's capacities. Foreign assistance, including from the US military, alleviated the acute nature of the aftermath, but even a year after the cyclone, only a quarter of the 78,000 new, sturdy family-homes pledged by donors and charities had been built. Another 276,000 families had received no reconstruction aid and subsisted in unsafe temporary shelters as a new cyclone season approached.[49] The CTG had not had time to address their plight.

In fact, its first financial year in office, which ended in June 2007, did not see much change from the performance of the elected governments which preceded it. Partisan and graft-driven elements of decision-making and resource allocation processes were replaced but by taking action which discouraged domestic lending and investment, the CTG effectively reduced liquidity, putting a brake on economic activities. Meanwhile, 'low revenue collection, poor infrastructure, low skill levels, and corruption' remained 'the main impediments to sustained growth and poverty reduction.'[50] The CTG was prompted to act against these tendencies but the worldwide economic crisis of 2008 stretched Bangladesh's ability to feed its citizens, provide basic services and maintain socio-economic equilibrium. As international prices of cereals and other food products and petroleum shot up in early 2008, and Dhaka balanced efforts to stabilise food prices with cutting energy subsidies, politicians used rising prices and power shortages as evidence of the CTG's incompetence. Bangladesh increased imports and sought help from friendly countries, using the paramilitary BDR to distribute basic victuals at 'fair prices.' Food prices were an issue during the 2008 election campaign.

Despite the rising prices of food grains and fuel, and complaints of inefficiency and corruption,[51] supplies remained adequate, averting large-scale hunger. Macroeconomic performance in FY 2007–08 appeared 'remarkably resilient in a year of multiple natural disasters and elevated international food and fuel prices.'[52] Agriculture and RMG exports led the rejuvenation. Growing remittances and increased aid helped ease balance of payments difficulties. Private sector credit rebounded quickly, and improved revenue collection also helped. Nonetheless, Bangladesh remained a very poor country with average per capita income stuck at $550.[53] Vulnerability to cyclonic storms and flooding, and the impact of external economic shocks combined to push some groups back under the poverty line. Large harvests of rice in April-June 2008 partly mitigated the shortages seen over the previous year, but prices remained much higher than in neighbouring India, for instance, limiting access for many Bangladeshis. However, at least one donor agency calculated that given the strong growth in income in 2006–08, poverty rates had fallen lower than the 2005 estimates. This was made possible by the GDP growing, despite major challenges, at an estimated 6.2 per cent in 2008.[54]

The picture darkened considerably as the CTG prepared to hold parliamentary elections at the end of 2008 and transfer power to elected successors. In late November, the donors assessed the country's economic prospects with much pessimism. They calculated dramatic declines in key areas—export growth, remittances by workers employed abroad, the balance of payments, revenue and expenditure, and GDP growth. The impact of the global economic downturn would force both export orders and remittances downward in FY 2008–09 to the extent that exports could decline by 4.3 per cent and remittances by 20 per cent compared to the previous financial year. The current account balance could suffer a deficit of $303 million compared to a surplus of $672 million in the preceding financial year. Similarly, revenue collection in FY 2008–09 could drop from an estimated Tk 693.80bn to Tk 684.60bn, forcing a reduction in budgeted expenditure from Tk 999.60bn to Tk 963.20bn.[55] For an economy overwhelmingly dependent on public sector expenditure, this portended much collective pain. There was a silver lining, however. If the trend towards lower food- and fuel costs continued, the budget deficit could fall from an estimated Tk 305.80bn to Tk 278.70bn.[56] However, this was unlikely to cheer up the millions of RMG workers dependent on export orders, and members of the families of expatriate workers who relied on the regular arrival of foreign remittances.

Still, Hasina inherited a lively economy. Domestic activity picked up in July-December 2008 and the country recorded a 'robust growth in exports and remittances. Continued growth in RMG production, together with improvements in business confidence and recovery in housing and construction, stimulated industrial activity in the first quarter of FY 2009. Falling prices of construction materials and a rise in demand for real estate because of the growth in bank credit and higher remittances helped to revive the construction sub sector. Services, especially wholesale and retail trade and transport and communications, also performed well in the first quarter of FY 2009.'[57] Donors noted the changing global economic and commercial context in which Bangladesh's performance would slow a little but managed well, the fall in international commodity prices and costs of importing energy should stand the country in good stead.[58] The key medium-to-long term economic tasks before the government were 'to raise infrastructure investment and government revenue mobilization, accelerate ADP implementation, address deficiencies in institutional capacities in key line agencies, and create more jobs.' Addressing power and gas shortages would be critical to encouraging private investment to enhance long-term growth prospects. But 'Confrontational politics, if it reappears with the restoration of democracy, will also slow down economic activity.'[59] The new government's decision to transfer a large number of government officials[60] suggested that not much had changed politically and that in economic terms things could still go wrong.

Politics, never fully extirpated, returned to the fore as polls approached. Both Hasina and Zia lambasted the CTG's apparent inability to meet 'the people's demands.' Campaign rhetoric suggested that political Bangladesh, having sleepwalked through two years of indirect military rule, had stirred awake. Post-election, Hasina's cabinet line-up surprised even many of her supporters. Only a handful of the new ministers had had any experience of high office[61]; most were first-time MPs. There was much comment on neophytes effecting a generational change and the role of experience in public life. The most heavily analysed appointments were those of Sahara Khatun as Home Minister, and Dipu Moni as Foreign Minister. The former, a lawyer and an activist with experience of street-agitation, promised to reform the constabulary and other instruments of domestic tranquility. The latter, a doctor-cum-lawyer by training, was the head of the Awami League's women's wing before her appointment to the cabinet. Once there, she worked to rearrange the diplomatic corps. But perhaps the biggest changes were signaled by the new Law, Justice and Parliamentary Affairs Minister, Shafique Ahmed, who announced the government's plans to 'restore the constitution of 1972.'[62] This pledge, if honoured, would revoke the fourteen amendments enacted since 1972, thereby challenging the shift to the right effected by various administrations since the constitution's promulgation.

Whether the schism polarising Bangladesh would be healed remained unclear but that change was in the air was not. Some things, however, stayed the same. Soon after the outcome of the parliamentary elections had become clear, Awami League members began attacking their counterparts from the BNP and, occasionally, supporters of parties allied to the BNP. Several people were killed and many injured. In the cities, activists from the Awami League's student wing took control of major campuses, throwing out anyone considered hostile or not sufficiently supportive. Although senior figures from the ruling party insisted they were opposed to such violence and would act to stop it, little was actually done to stop it for several days. Asked what action she was taking to stop her party men from attacking BNP members since the election, the Home Minister said, 'Do you not remember what they did to us in the past?'[63]

Neighbourhood delights

Meanwhile, as Bangladeshis were absorbed in following every nuanced twist and turn of the unfolding domestic drama, Burma's military junta picked the moment to test the CTG's resolve. In early November, two Burmese warships escorted South Korean hydro-carbon survey vessels including a drilling rig into an area of the Bay of Bengal disputed between Dhaka and Naypyitaw. Myanmar had licensed the Daewoo Corporation, working with Myanmar Oil and Gas Enterprise, the Korea Gas Corporation, and two Indian state-owned firms—ONGC and GAIL—to explore for hydrocarbons in the area. For its part, Bangladesh based its claims on its Territorial Waters and Maritime Zones Act 1974 which resulted in the two neighbours claiming overlapping zones south of their land borders. After its diplomatic protests elicited Burmese rebuffs, Dhaka deployed three naval combat platforms to the area.[64] While a naval stand-off ensued, Bangladesh sent its Foreign Secretary at the head of a team to explain its claims and dissuade continued Burmese activities in the disputed waters. Burma's leaders insisted they were fully within their rights and would continue working where they were. Dhaka then sought Chinese help in mediating with Naypyitaw, asked Seoul to urge Daewoo to desist from entering 'Bangladeshi waters,' and warned that it would do 'whatever was necessary' to defend its sovereign rights. To back up this threat, two other frigates were placed on alert. It was then that the Burmese 'suspended' their seismic work, claiming they had completed their survey, and withdrew from the disputed waters.[65]

Negotiations resumed in mid-November and though neither side conceded, they agreed to continue discussions and avoid repeating similar confrontations. The fact that despite a 'strategic partnership' Dhaka had forged with Beijing, China merely urged the two neighbours to amicably resolve the dispute while launching two new pipeline projects linking its Yunnan province to southern Myanmar, and a similar dispute over maritime boundary had festered with India for three decades suggested Bangladesh's search for energy security and the defence of its exclusive economic zone (EEZ) posed major challenges. Confirmation arrived on Christmas day in 2008 when two Indian naval vessels escorting an Australian survey ship were detected conducting surveys some 140 nautical miles south-west of Mongla port, within Bangladesh's EEZ. Dhaka promptly deployed a frigate to the area, dispatching a second combat platform from Chittagong.[66]

Despite warnings issued by the latter, however, the Indian vessels initially refused to leave.[67] Bangladeshi protests elicited an Indian suggestion that Dhaka send a delegation for negotiating with Delhi.[68] With deadlines for countries to file their maritime claims under the UN Convention on the Law of the Seas (UNCLOS) fast approaching,[69] Bangladesh's claimed EEZ was contested by both its neighbours. The fact that the Myanmarese-South Korean team had operated for months, surveying waters claimed by Dhaka and assembling an off-shore drilling rig there without being detected or challenged, and Indian ships refused to heed warnings from Bangladeshi naval vessels, underscored the limits to Dhaka's ability to defend its interests. The answers to these quandaries were not readily apparent during the election campaign or later, but these paled beside what might be considered existential threats to the country and its people.

6

A LAND OF ANGER—RIGHT, LEFT, CENTRE, AND THE OTHER

Abstract: Bangladesh's national narrative focuses on the dynamic among leaders of the Awami League, the BNP and the military as the key protagonists in the country's historiography. There is little acknowledgement of the roles played by other actors, and yet Bangladesh has been the stage of a much more diverse drama with a deeply divided cast of secondary players operating in the wings, or behind the scenes, occasionally bursting forth on the national consciousness by taking centre-stage. No national narrative would be complete without an account of their impact on shaping national politics.

Populist challengers to the status quo have arisen in many forms, and none more openly than the student community, especially young scholars seeking enlightenment at state-funded universities. The Dhaka University Central Students Union has played a central role in highlighting national issues, mobilising opinion, launching campaigns and pushing politicians to endorse and to join them since before the Partition. Its members played a key role in forging a national consensus against Pakistani efforts to impose Urdu as the country's sole state language, demanding an equal status for Bengali, organising an eventually successful campaign to that end, crystallising Bengali nationalist autonomist tendencies and precipitating the war of independence. In independent Bangladesh, they reflected and reinforced the fragmentation and polarisation dividing the polity, providing muscle—and often blood—to the perennial conflict among mainstream antagonists. Even under the state of emergency in 2007–8, they displayed their capacity to cause trouble.

But students have not been a monolithic corpus. Ideologically more active than the rest of the populace, they built and manned extremist fringes on the right and left. Islamist groups may have become a notorious subset in recent years, especially because of their links to substantial violence against the secular instruments of the state such as the police, the judiciary, and security forces, but a tradition of faith-based struggle against perceived oppression going back to early eighteenth century has been a part of Bengal's political history. The catharsis of internecine violence in 1970–71 deepened the divide; later events have engendered even more intensely passionate devout-vs.-secular conflict. Leftwing activism, beginning in the early twentieth century, has been an equally crucial part of Bengal's political dynamic. Idealism confronting repression precipitated equally violent responses. With the state denying legitimacy and space to such forces, they have withdrawn into the shadows but continue to operate from nooks and crannies and plague the populace wherever the state's writ proves weak and its reach attenuated. A continuing reliance of central authorities on these extremist fringes to counteract each other has afforded tacit legitimacy as successive rulers have used the marginals to their own ends.

Bangladesh grew from a reactive consciousness, first against the two-nation theory behind Pakistan's Islamist concept. Once freedom from that bond was attained, ruling elites fashioned a conceptual framework rationalising Bengal's continued partition, originally executed on a confessional basis but now the physical foundation of a secular republic. Bangladeshi nationalism, fabricated in contradistinction to the Indian other, lent purpose and meaning to a truncated land but has created elemental tensions with India.

Heroes and knaves in the wings

Bangladesh has been ruled by party-political professionals and military commanders, the latter usually taking on the guise of the former before being ejected from office with some violence, either by popular mobilisation, or by dissident fellow-officers. The four civilian governments elected in 1973, 1991, 1996 and 2001 themselves proved less than plural and 'democratic' in office. The first utterly dominated the parliament with an overwhelming majority, leaving no scope for a legitimate opposition to function within the representative system. The other three failed to keep the opposition in parliament. With the two main parties, the BNP and the Awami League, alternating in power, both demonstrated a similar lack of parliamentary faith when in opposition, boycotting the National Assembly on often flimsy pretexts. Opposition activists found violent agitation in the capital's streets more rewarding than acting within the constitutional framework.

All of these administrations were shown to have been corrupt, authoritarian and repressive—the first, as noted, turned Bangladesh into a single-party state; the remainder marginalised the opposition to the point of insignificance. Their competence in handling Bangladesh's myriad challenges varied but was never impressive. Neither of the major parties nor their leaders demonstrated a grasp of the complexity of their ward nor a capacity to address its many needs. Domestic and overseas critics repeatedly exposed their shortcomings and yet, the two main parties challenged reformers with insuperable odds while maintaining popular support. Charisma may explain some of this, but not all. A partial explanation of this intriguing phenomenon is provided by the interplay of a cast of subsidiary players who have never taken power themselves, but some of whom have played a crucial role in the initial success of those who did, while others have contributed to the fall of other mighty actors. Vigorous in their assertions and often violent in action, most are integral to the Bangladeshi experience; however, there is at least one such secondary actor which is essentially external but equally intrinsic to the narrative.

Dissonant and disparate in their role and influence, they have nonetheless helped to shape Bangladesh's political landscape since before its independence. No account of the country's recent history would be complete without an encounter, however brief, with four such categories—student activists, groups operating at the two extremes of the political spectrum, and the malleable concept of 'the other' defining the Bangladeshi 'self.' Among the four, activist students have stood out head and shoulders above the rest.

Scholars on the warpath

Student activism in Bengal began with the spread of 'modern' colonial education in the nineteenth century. The 'Young Bengal' movement, itself a product of the British imperial intermediary educational system, drew intellectual attention to the iniquities of the colonial dispensation. Its

271

members urged a revival of traditional Bengali–Indian values. However, the latter's specifics were ambiguous and the group's members' self-identification was a function of colonial values imbibed via imperial institutions. This meant the expression of their goals lay in non-conformist rejection of the present rather than any positive imagery of what they sought. In the last quarter of the nineteenth century, leading campaigners for the movement like Ananda Mohan Bose urged Bengali students to participate in politics which at the time was subtly but largely anti–colonial, but in the face of the restrictions on student politics imposed by British academic authorities, their efforts had only limited effect. Early in the twentieth century, with the consequences of the Great War roiling the imperial order, nationalist politics became a force among India's British-educated middle classes. There was much activism in the northern and western provinces.

In Bengal, it was not until 1928 that campaigners like Promode Kumar Ghoshal and Birendra Nath Dasgupta succeeded in establishing a formal body—the All Bengal Students Association (ABSA). Jawaharlal Nehru, the rising star of the Indian National Congress (INC), presided over the ABSA's inaugural function in Calcutta, while Subhas Chandra Bose, the fiery leader of the INC's activist wing, delivered the keynote address. Although the ABSA was not constitutionally linked to the INC, the two mirrored each other in organisational structure, and the ABSA was effectively the INC's student wing. The group was almost an exclusively Hindu organisation; Muslim middle classes sought at this time to keep their children away from what increasingly looked like another INC body.[1] However, some Muslim intellectuals in eastern Bengal may have been inspired by ABSA's successful launch. At a Muslim students' conference in Dhaka in July 1930, Muhammad Shahidullah of Dhaka University was asked to establish a Muslim students' organisation which emerged as the All Bengal Muslim Students' Association (ABMSA) in 1932. The vanguard of Bengali political activism thus mirrored the communal divisions polarising mainstream nationalist politics early on. The ABMSA soon attracted the attentions of Bengal's two Muslim parties, which pursued slightly different objectives. The Muslim League tended to represent Muslim landed and nascent industrial interests; the Krishak Praja Party, an exclusively Bengali organisation led by lawyers and other Muslim professionals, aimed at protecting the interests of peasants and farm-workers. ABMSA members promptly divided into supporters of the two parties, foreordaining the fragmentation of Bengali–Muslim student politics along class- and other lines.

The 1937 Indian legislative elections intensified student activism. Muslim League leader M.A. Jinnah set up an all-Indian Muslim Student Federation that year. Once the Muslim League established its authority across India as the principal representatives of Muslim political aspirations, with an electoral mandate post-1937, Muslim student activists were often drawn into the MSF fold. In Bengal, the industrial and trading house of the Ispahanis and the Nawab of Dhaka led the reorganisation of the Bengal chapter of the Muslim Students Association into the Muslim Students League (MSL), the Muslim League's student front. The MSL actively aided the Muslim League's campaign for the establishment of Pakistan. It was as a Muslim student activist that Sheikh Mujibur Rahman, then studying at the Islamia College in Calcutta, drew the attention of H.S. Suhrawardy, Bengal's Muslim League premier, as India approached dominion status. Suhrawardy's turbulent political career following the Direct Action Day which his acolytes executed on 16 August 1946 has been noted; Sheikh Mujib's reflected the tradition his generation established for East Bengal's students in subsequent decades.

After Partition, Mujib left for Dhaka where he registered as a university student, but his support for a junior member of staff who was facing disciplinary proceedings, and his role in organising protests on his behalf led to university authorities expelling Mujib before he could graduate. The future leader of the Bangladesh campaign had made his mark as student leader but his academic achievements were curtailed by his 'political' preoccupations. For those East Pakistani and, later, Bangladeshi, students who emulated this role–model, agitational activism would often take precedence over academic labours—even when many years later Mujib himself was the focus of 'student politics.'

In East Pakistan, political activism among students took off in 1948 when Jinnah, Pakistan's Governor-General, told a gathering of Dhaka's elite that Urdu alone was going to be the country's national language. With a chorus of 'no, no!' his audience, Dhaka University students prominent among them, told Jinnah how difficult the consolidation of Pakistan's unity was going to be. Student activists were led, among others, by Mohammad Toaha and Abdul Matin, future leaders in nationalist and leftist politics. Toaha wrote many of the articles, posters and leaflets for the movement.[2] Before Jinnah's visit, he and his comrades in the *Rash-*

trabhasha Shangram Committee (state language action committee) tried to submit a memorandum to Khawaza Nazimuddin, head of the provincial administration, on the language question, and he was arrested. Later, when Jinnah arrived, Toaha submitted a memorandum to him demanding national status for Bengali. He campaigned against the government's attempt to introduce the Arabic script for writing Bengali. After the police action on 21 February 1952, when four people were killed and others injured, Toaha was arrested again. Released two years later, he stood in provincial elections as a candidate of the United Front coalition challenging the Muslim League, and was elected as a member of the East Bengal provincial legislature.

Toaha's colleague Abdul Matin's passionate involvement in the 'language campaign' led to his being called '*Rashtrabhasha* (state language) Matin.' He gained fame on 24 March 1948 when Jinnah presided over the Dhaka University convocation, awarding graduation certificates. When Jinnah reiterated his position on the national language, Matin, waiting to receive his diploma, stood up at shouted 'No, it can not be!'[3] Other students then took up the refrain. Matin was a leader among students who formed the *Purbo* Pakistan *Jubo* League (East Pakistan youth league) in Dhaka in March 1951, and then, the *Chhatra* (student) League, both Awami League fronts and instruments of the incipient nationalist movement.[4] The following January, Matin attended a key session of the *Sharbodolio Rashtrabhasha Karmaparishad* (all-party national language action-committee) and went on to convene the Dhaka University Language Action Committee, organisations which drew support from East Pakistan's student and intellectual communities and the wider middle-classes for the recognition of *Bangla* as a state language, mobilising endorsement of the view that Bengalis were a distinct segment of the Pakistani polity which merited acknowledgement and respect from the Karachi–based state. However, Matin objected to the Chhatra League's selection of Sheikh Mujibur Rahman as its chairman, and was promptly fired.[5]

Dhaka's Nawab family, sponsors of the All Bengal Muslim Students League, supported Jinnah's state consolidation objectives which included Urdu's pre-eminence in national life and the resultant decline of Bengali in the Pakistani order. The MSL developed a strong faction which rejected this development. Shortly after Jinnah's 1948 speech, this more Bengali nationalist group broke away to form the East Pakistan Muslim Students

League (EPMSL). This band spearheaded what grew into East Bengal's 'language movement' which, as we have seen, generated the nationalist-autonomist movement that eventually led to Bangladesh's secessionist war of independence. The EPMSL's leadership of the 1952 'language martyrs' campaign and the subsequent elevation of Bengali to one of Pakistan's two national languages alongside Urdu did not go unnoticed by East Pakistan's mainstream politicians. Just as East Bengali political parties fissioned into factions, their efforts to attract student activists frag-mented student organisations into ideologically-grouped party-political fronts and wings.[6] Over the next few years, several major student organi-sations emerged in Dhaka and other cities and towns across East Paki-stan. The East Pakistan Students Union (EPSU), formed in 1952, was the student wing of the leftist parties fronted by the National Awami Party (NAP); Students' Force and National Student Federation (NSF) emerged to support factions of the Muslim League. The imposition of martial law in 1958 forced these and other groups and their party-polit-ical mentors into the political wilderness for eight years.

In 1966, Mujib launched his 'Six–point programme' demanding pro-vincial autonomy, catalysing a moribund movement into a dynamic force which threatened the Pakistani state's unity. His arrest and implication in the 'Agartala conspiracy case' mobilised East Pakistan as never before. Students were at the forefront of the protests which coalesced into a cam-paign embracing much of the politically active populace. To wrest Mujib from prison, students formed the *Sarbadaliya Chhatra Sangram Parishad* (all-party students' campaign council—SCSP) in January 1969, placing an eleven-point charter of demands incorporating both autonomist-na-tionalist objectives and socialist ideals.[7] The SCSP's initial success forced Ayub Khan to release Mujib and invite him to talks. Mujib acknowledged the students' contribution by ceremonially accepting from their leaders the title *Bangabandhu* (friend of Bengal). This recognition reflected a symbiotic relationship between Mujib and the SCSP's radical leadership. The latter initially supported the Awami League's six–point programme but faced with increasing violence and then Yahya Khan's martial law regime succeeding Ayub Khan's 'basic democracy,' it evolved into a sepa-ratist organ. The group's leadership developed the concept of a secular Bengali nation-state, named it 'Bangladesh,' and generated most of the associated symbolism, rhetoric and literature with which the indepen-dence campaign would be mounted.[8]

The SCSP and its subordinate organisations campaigned for Awami League candidates before the December 1970 elections, giving them a popular boost they could not have gained otherwise. The students could claim much of the credit for the Awami League's overwhelming victory in the polls. When Yahya Khan postponed the session of Pakistan's new-ly-elected National Assembly on 1 March 1971, the SCSP began implementing its planned separatist campaign, mobilising support. The following day, the group unfurled the newly-designed Bangladeshi flag, following it up on 3 March with a public rally in Dhaka where they proclaimed independence and declared Mujib the 'Father of the Nation.' A.S.M. Abdur Rab, Vice President of the Dhaka University Students Union (DUCSU), the core of student activism, formally hoisted the Bangladeshi flag at the university square called 'Bat-tala.'[9] They also announced that *Aamar sonar Bangla*, a song composed by Rabindranath Tagore eulogising an imagined 'golden Bengal,' would be the national anthem. Their nationalist aspirations, if not their separatist goals, found expression in Mujib's own address at the Paltan Maidan on 7 March.[10]

While forcing Mujib's hand to pin his standard to their separatist mast, the SCSP launched a non-cooperation campaign against Pakistani authorities across East Pakistan, demanding that all officials of the provincial administration and the general population only obey Mujib, who had earned an overwhelming popular mandate from the polls. Support for the Awami League's autonomist campaign and the SCSP's separatist programme was so intertwined that Bangladeshi historians would later surmise that 'if six–point failed, Joy Bangla nationalism must prevail.'[11] The Pakistani military's 'Operation Searchlight' on 25 March 1971 and Mujib's proxy proclamation of independence which followed 'gave an instant and automatic validation to the declaration of independence made by students on 3 March 1971.'[12] The students had been ahead of the politicians, a fact acknowledged by Tajuddin Ahmed's government-in-exile when it adopted the rhetoric introduced to the nationalist lexicon by the students in 1969–71.

Acting individually and in their organised groups, students played important roles in the war against Pakistani forces and their local supporters. They joined elements of the *Gonomukti Fouz* and the *Mukti Bahini* in large numbers, fighting valiantly, and many losing lives or limbs in the process. As has been noted, not all FFs, many of whom had interrupted their studies to fight Pakistani soldiers, were happy with the conduct of the war or its aftermath. The most visible expression of this difference came on 31 October 1972 when a large group of student-freedom fighters, opposing the Mujib government's reliance on 'the same old colonial bureaucratic administrative set up and the backward exploit-ative economic system,' formed the *Jatiya Samajtantrik Dal* (National Socialist Party—JSD), declaring its aim 'to establish socialism through social revolution.'[13] In its own view, 'within two years of its emergence JSD became the most powerful and effective opposition political organi-sation. The then Awami League government was very much afraid of JSD.'[14] In the early years of independent Bangladesh, Mujib and his party towered over all else, virtually unchallenged in their apparent patrimony over the country and its people. Against that backdrop, the emergence of a group of students—many of them armed and battle-hardened—as a dynamic opposition to the leader they themselves had lifted onto a plinth of nationalist struggle and national honour, was both ironic and a defining feature of the political landscape they were trying to fashion.

The turbulence which reshaped elite politics in 1975–76 fragmented and marginalised militant students, if temporarily. Mujib had banned right-wing activism; General Ziaur Rahman restrained other forms of campus militancy with equal vigour. However, once he assumed a party-political role, he too saw the advantages of having student wings of his new party at the major universities, most importantly, on the Dhaka University campus. With groups affiliated to the Awami League and the National Awami Party—the Chhatra League and the Students Union respectively—already ensconced and influential, his efforts to attract prominent student leaders to his camp met modest success. However, incumbency allowed him to attract both mainstream politicians and their campus acolytes and an initially unimpressive band of students did even-tually coalesce around the BNP. This, the *Jatiayatabadi Chhatra Dal* (nationalist students party—JCD), was chased out by well-armed Ban-gladesh *Chhatra* League (BCL) activists. To protect his own student-wing, Zia appointed an army officer to the Ministry of Home Affairs as Deputy Secretary with responsibility for maintaining peace on campuses. This official implemented a policy mirroring the former Awami League government's practice of arming its own young supporters with automatic and semi–automatic weapons.[15] The BCL's near-monopoly on firearms on university campuses was broken, and eventually, the JCD was able to chase out its rivals, taking control over most campuses. However, this success was achieved at the cost of frequent exchanges of fire between bands of armed 'students' across the country, some bloodshed, and the establishment of armed violence as an accepted instrument of control over academic blocks and halls of residence.

General Ershad followed Zia's footsteps, setting up student- and youth wings of his new party soon after deciding to embark on a party-political career. Now, with both the BCL and JCD arrayed against his authority, this proved a particularly difficult exercise.[16] Only when his aides managed to attract Ziauddin Bablu, leader of the DUCSU, to the Chief Martial Law Administrator's vision of Bangladesh, did the efforts begin to bear fruit. Nonetheless, the Jatiya Party's student wing, mirroring the factional weaknesses of the JP itself, never gained the cohesion or the influence of either the BCL or the JCD. In fact, when the latter joined hands under the banner of the All-Party Students Unity (APSU) in an anti–Ershad campaign, instead of countering this gathering threat against their leader, the JP's student wing scattered like straw in the wind. This failure to command mastery over the campuses weakened Ershad's authority in a key and highly-visible segment of national politics, contributing to the opposition campaign gaining courage and building momentum. The APSU's greater success, of course, lay in its ability to get Sheikh Hasina and Khaleda Zia to leave aside their differences and unite against Ershad in a unified challenge to his government. This united platform mobilised opinion and support across Bangladesh, which the army then refused to fight, persuading General Ershad to resign.

Following the 1991 democratic restoration, the JCD and the BCL alternated in power on campuses depending on whose party-political patrons were in office. In 1991–2006, the main opposition party rarely attended parliamentary sessions, electing, instead, to take its politics to the capital's streets. This is where their respective 'student wings' came into their own, engaging their opponents in violent confrontations, often using prohibited but freely flaunted firearms, spreading fear and shedding blood. In all instances after their parties won general elections, the student wings immediately raided university campuses, 'capturing' halls of residences, and forcing the previous incumbents to flee, while the police—barred by regulations from entering campuses unless invited by the university authorities—watched from the sidelines. Not surprisingly, university campuses became battlegrounds just before and after parliamentary polls, and elections to student bodies. The victors claimed the spoils—the power to distribute patronage ranging from the 'right' to extort contractors bidding for construction or supply contracts with the particular institutions, through obtaining benefits from the ruling party, to 'giving' out the right to highly subsidised and extremely prized food-and-board facilities at halls of residence.[17]

The fact that many of the 'students' rarely attended lessons or sat for exams did not appear to trouble either the academic authorities or the government of the day into taking corrective action. The involvement of non-student armed activists in campus violence and agitational politics which, in turn, led to closures of various universities, delaying exams and causing 'session jams,' did build up public sentiment 'against student politics altogether.'[18] But in the absence of support from the main parties, such sentiments remained just that. The growing number of teachers having graduated as student-activists before joining the faculty themselves getting involved in campus politics raised other concerns. 'Getting a first class, the ultimate in a student's life, also increasingly depended on which party the student was affiliated to.' A recent 'scandal' involving the award of first classes to more than fifty graduates in political science, an unprecedented largesse, raised eyebrows but no promised investigation or other administrative action followed.[19] If, however, there were any misapprehensions that students had shifted their focus on acquiring degrees and moved away from idealistic activism, violent disturbances challenging the military's authority in the summer of 2007 swiftly put paid to those.[20]

Embers beneath the ashes

Most of the campaigns in which student activists worked in the vanguard of mainstream politics, were centrist or a combination of centre-left activism. Conservative Islamists have often not featured in these struggles. However, in recent years, the *Islami Chhatra Shibir* (Islamist student camp—ICS), the student wing of the Jamaat-e-Islami, has drawn much national and international attention. The US-led 'global war on terrorism' (GWOT) which followed the al-Qaeda attacks in Washington and New York on 11 September 2001, and growing right-wing militancy across the subcontinent, including Bangladesh, have focused attention on Islamist activism, and the ICS has been under special scrutiny.[21] Although the ICS was formed after Jamaat-e-Islami was allowed back into the national political mainstream in the late 1970s, Islamist activism goes back a long way.

The Bengal chapter of the Jamaat was formed a year after the Muslim League passed the 'Pakistan resolution' in Lahore in 1940. Like the Indian National Congress, the Jamaat rejected the Muslim League's two-nation theory or the Partition which followed. Its early years in Pakistan were not especially happy. The Muslim League's moderate leaders found the Jamaat's assertions that divine law as revealed in the Koran took precedence over human jurisprudence a serious challenge. The Pakistani government's military crackdown on the Jamaat and allied religious groups in the 1950s ensured the Islamists were marginalised in the 'Muslim homeland,' but they were not extirpated. In East Pakistan, mirroring the *Chhatra* Union, the NSF and *Chhatra* League, the Jamaat built up the *Islami Chhatra Shangha* (Islamist student association) but this group only gained influence in 1969–70 when Bengali nationalist tendencies given expression by secular student bodies led to state intelligence organs supporting the Islamists. As the secular groups, working in close collaboration with the Awami League and other nationalist parties built up an autonomist movement which eventually turned separatist, Islamists and their student wing, and other pro-Pakistan elements, joined hands with the efforts of Pakistan's military-intelligence establishment to counteract the nationalist campaign.

In that zero-sum confrontation there was much violence and atrocities were committed by all sides.[22] The nationalists' victory, secured with 'secular' Indian military intervention, forced the Islamists' marginalisation. Thousands were detained and some were killed as 'pro-Pakistani traitors.'[23] They were prohibited from organising any activities and often socially ostracised. Seen by many as villains in a milieu charged with nationalist sentiments and 'anti–Pakistani' fervour, Islamists virtually disappeared from the national consciousness, sulking on the margins of society. There they subsisted, unsure of their future. Even after Sheikh Mujibur Rahman granted an amnesty, freeing around 33,000 'pro-Pakistan' Islamists in late 1973, they did not lose their stigma and were not fully rehabilitated. Only in the late 1970s, when Ziaur Rahman's non-secular 'Bangladeshi nationalism' built on the recognition of Islam's role in defining the Bangladeshi 'half-nation' as distinct from its non-Bangladeshi 'other' swept to power did the Islamists, and their student acolytes, now the ICS, return to the political centre-stage.[24] The process was eased by the arrival of Saudi and other Gulf Arab aid to Muslim seminaries and charities, the encouragement these provided to madrassa-trained *taleban* (students) to join the

CIA-sponsored *Mujahideen* guerrillas fighting Soviet and local communist forces in Afghanistan, a growing flow of workers to the Gulf from where many returned imbued with an austere version of Sunni Islam, and the establishment's supportive stance to religious revival. Still, the Islamist restoration did not prove to be easy; in fact, their return to eminence contributed to the alienation of the secularists, building momentum for the movement which, simmering even within the military, eventually devoured Zia.

In consonance with the Jamaat's quest for the establishment of an Islamist order, the ICS rejects the secular-rationalist *status quo* in favour of 'a struggle for changing the existing system of education on the basis of Islamic values, to inspire students to acquire Islamic knowledge and to prepare them to take part in the struggle for establishing (an) Islamic way of life.' ICS encourages the student community 'with the aim and determination to mould their character with morality and ideology enriched with modern scientific spheres of knowledge. The final programme of the organisation is to strive to build an ideal society for freeing humanity from all forms economic exploitation, political oppression and cultural servitude.'[25] The remarkable similarity in the final sentence of this polemic to Marxist-Leninist rhetoric underscores the irony in the tradition of violent confrontation between the ICS and its left-wing counterparts across Bangladesh since the 1970s.

The use of the same diction by both the rationalist-secularists on the Left and the devout believers on the Right to describe their goals while pursuing contradictory objectives underscores the volatility of the ideological struggle in which students often find themselves. The competition's zero-sum nature raises stakes, helping to institutionalise violence as an instrument of political pursuits. This conflictual hot-house of political activism prepares Bangladeshi students as they graduate to the similarly adversarial crucible of mainstream party-political life. One such experience was the rioting around the national mosque in Dhaka after Khaleda Zia stepped down in October 2006. During the post-BNP interregnum, clashes between pro- and anti–BNP activists grew violent. In one such confrontation mobs from the secularist camps grabbed hold of at least one young activist from the religious group, beating him to death in front of TV crews filming live. If the depth of polarisation dividing Bangladesh's political heart needed evidence, nothing could have demonstrated it any better. It was then that the sequence which led to the military forcing President Iajuddin Ahmad to step down as his own Chief Adviser and accept a new, army-backed CTG, unfolded.

When the president conceded and proclaimed a state of emergency, and a new CTG took office on 11 January 2007, student activists, along with their less academically inclined colleagues, withdrew from the streets. Rigorous enforcement of emergency strictures, the arrest of senior political and business figures, and threats of severe punitive measures may have succeeded in keeping the lid on student militancy for seven months. But then, in August 2007, Dhaka University exploded again. It began with an innocuous incident. To enforce emergency regulations, the army had established camps at various 'sensitive' locations including the Dhaka University campus. One of these was based at the Dhaka University gymnasium. As a result, one of the few non-academic outlets for the energies of the thousands of young students resident at the halls on the campus was taken out of action. Also, students here, the traditional home of student activism, were not used to seeing soldiers in their very midst. Many young scholars saw the soldiery as armed upstarts and usurpers of state power and resources, an adversary in their perpetual idealistic struggle to achieve perfection in national life.[26] On 20 August, latent volatility surfaced at a football match between the departments of Public Administration and Mass Communications and Journalism. Apparently, when a plain-clothes soldier berated in unseemly language a student for obstructing his view—perhaps inadvertently—scuffles broke out between groups of students and soldiers. When teachers intervened trying to restore calm, they too were roughly handled. The injured students needed medical help.

The Vice-Chancellor and the Proctor called on the camp commander responsible for the soldiers billeted on the campus and obtained assurances of 'appropriate action' against those responsible for unruly behaviour. However, the students, dissatisfied with military presence in their midst, and with rigorous enforcement of emergency regulations in a land which had experienced elected administrations spanning much of their conscious lives, wanted more. Processing across the campus shouting slogans, they gathered at the Vice-Chancellor's office and demanded a public apology from soldiers. This grew to a demand for the withdrawal of the camp from the campus. When a police contingent baton-charged the protesters injuring several, students lobbed bricks and other missiles at their tormentors, moving onto the streets. Protests began in Dhaka's other campuses. Students—and presumably less scholastically inclined activists—battled the police across the city that evening, causing injury to many and damage to property. Security personnel closed access to the university campus but violence had already escaped the dragnet.

A group calling itself 'Students against repression' met at the university cafeteria and set terms for peace: CAS, General Moeen Uddin Ahmed should apologise publicly for his troops' misconduct, all soldiers involved in the original and subsequent altercations with students should be punished, students injured in fracas with the military and the police should be compensated, and all those who had been arrested should be released immediately. Giving expression to the underlying tensions charging student militancy, the group also demanded that the army 'stop interfering in state affairs.'[27] If these demands were not met by 22 August, the group would call a strike at all of Bangladesh's schools, colleges and universities. Several teachers, including a well-known former left-wing activist, professor of biochemistry, M. Anwar Hossain, helped students to organise themselves in what soon became a country-wide campaign. Students' groups and faculty from major universities across Bangladesh supported their fellows in Dhaka and rioting spread. Late on 21 August, Chief Adviser Fakhruddin Ahmed went on national television apologising for the soldiers' conduct, promising to take disciplinary action and pledging to withdraw troops from the campus. But his assurances did not end the violence. On 22 August, the government imposed a curfew in six districts including Dhaka; universities were shut and students ordered to vacate halls of residence. Cellphone networks and internet access were suspended, student activists, a number of university teachers and journalists were arrested, and media control imposed. Curfew was relaxed six days later after control had been restored.

Many explanations were advanced of a minor incident triggering the sudden but intense outburst, the rapid spread of violence, and the involvement of teachers, amongst them: the CTG's economic failures—especially rising inflation, a drop in exports, and job-losses in the key textile sector; frustrations caused by devastating floods; the arrests of Khaleda Zia, Sheikh Hasina and many of their senior aides on corruption charges; uncertainties over restoration of representative governance, and an army-backed CTG 'overplaying its hand.'[28] Perhaps all of these factors combined to create a complex resentful context in which a small spark could ignite a major confrontation between the army-controlled state and the students who considered themselves the defenders of the nation's pluralist, democratic ideals. The iconic image to emerge from this episode was the photograph of a uniformed soldier trying to escape a flying kick administered by an evidently angry student. Swiftly circulated via the internet once access was restored, this photograph—more than that of a vehicle used by one of the army's handful of three-star generals turned on its side by students and set on fire—underscored the gulf between those who led the country and some of those on whose behalf they claimed to do so.

The army and the CTG restored calm and resumed control, emptying the streets of protesters by employing Draconian rigour—arresting many activists and threatening other potential challengers with severe punitive measures under emergency rules. But aware of the need to revive near-normalcy for major political parties to implement substantive reforms, the authorities soon offered an emollient face. The Generals and the cabinet promised to treat detained teachers sympathetically. They faced a challenge—university students were not a force to be treated with condescension, far less contempt. Although tensions were defused, the potential for trouble simmered and, occasionally, bubbled over on the slightest pretext. In August 2008, just months before scheduled parliamentary polls, the failure of the authorities to let Tareque Zia—held in special cells at the Bangabandhu Sheikh Mujib Medical University where he had reportedly fallen in the washroom and hurt his head—out for a CT scan led to rioting by students in Dhaka University, Bangladesh University of Engineering and Technology and the Dhaka College. A businessman, watching students torch a vehicle, was killed when gas canisters exploded in the fire. Members of the BNP's student wing—the JCD—already protesting against the government's failure to release Khaleda Zia although Sheikh Hasina had been bailed several months earlier, clashed with the police and blocked a major highway. Violence was also reported in Bogra, Ziaur Rahman's ancestral home and a BNP stronghold. The police restored calm, but the students' violent capabilities were obvious.

The rise of the 'righteous'

Established as a pointedly secular polity in violent rejection of its confessionally-defined Pakistani past, Bangladesh nonetheless gradually slid to the right. Part of this shift was party-political and confessionally sanctioned, but there was also a darker underbelly challenging the precepts on which the polity had been founded in 1971. By the late 1990s, militants identified as religious extremists had begun attacking symbols of Bangladesh's non-confessional political culture and 'moderate-Muslim' societal norms. Consider the progression:

Security concerns arose almost as soon as President Clinton arrived in South Asia on Sunday night, with the cancellation of his trip to a village in Bangladesh on Monday. Shortly before the start of Clinton's daylong visit to Bangladesh, White House spokesman Joe Lockhart announced the cancellation of a visit to the rural village (sic) of Joypura, 60 miles from the capital city of Dhaka, 'because of concerns raised by the Secret Service.[29] 20 March 2000.

Bangladeshi police arrested four suspected members of a militant Islamic group, Jamaat-ul-Mujahideen, in the village of Puiya. Officers also seized a football–size package with markings indicating it contained a crude form of uranium manufactured in Kazakhstan. Subsequent tests at the Bangladesh Atomic Energy Commission in Dhaka confirmed the 225–gram ball is uranium oxide, enough to make a weapon capable of dispersing radiation across a wide area if strapped to conventional explosives.[30] 30 May 2003.

A wave of grenade attacks on opposition chief Sheikh Hasina's rally on Bangabandhu Avenue yesterday left at least sixteen people killed and 200 including top Awami League leaders critically injured. Hasina, who was the apparent target of attacks carried out from buildings in front of the AL headquarters, escaped unscathed as activists formed a human shield to protect their leader.[31] 21 August 2004.

Former Finance Minister and a leading Awami League parliamentarian, Shah A.M.S. Kibria, was killed in a grenade attack at a rally in his Habiganj constituency in north-eastern Bangladesh on 27 January 2005, along with his nephew, Shah Manzur Huda, and three others.[32] 27 January 200.

Countrywide terrorist bomb attacks in August 2005, including the simultaneous detonation of over 500 bombs in multiple regions by Jamaatul Mujahideen Bangladesh demonstrated an ability to attack on a massive scale. It demonstrated that terrorists operating in this country are developing new methods of attack and improving the efficiency of existing ones, increasing the pressure on counterterrorist agencies.[33] 17 August 2005.

Six top militants including Jamaatul Mujahideen Bangladesh (JMB) supremo Abdur Rahman and his deputy, Bangla Bhai, were executed late Thursday night for killing two judges. They swung from the gallows between 11.45pm and midnight at four different jails amid tight security.[34] 29 March 2007.

The rise of Islamist radicalism and its violent expression in Bangladesh have attracted much national and international interest. But the current discourse often ignores the historical context in which extremism of the religious right subsists.[35] The cultural-secular driving forces behind the Bengali autonomist-nationalism which led to Bangladesh's war of independence created an atmosphere in which the movement's centre-left pre-bourgeois leadership could not but reject the role of religion—not Islam per se—in defining its anti–Pakistan politics. But the faith-vs.-culture identity crisis did not abate just because the new republic's ruling elite chose to ignore it. Bangladesh being constructed atop the ashes of East Bengal/Pakistan, partitioned from the rest of Bengal on the basis of a confessionally-defined intra-Bengal division, meant the existential reality of the religion's political role would return to haunt this newly refashioned state.[36] While the Bangladeshi state was superimposed over the residue of East Pakistan with relative ease, fashioning a Bangladeshi nation—to realise the imagined Bangladeshi nation-state—demanded more substantive changes than the simple renaming of places on administrative maps. And changes of that profundity could not be effected by a nine-month civil war which was ended by a third-party military intervention lasting a fortnight. The national elite do not appear to have grasped this fundamental challenge to developing a coherent national mythology.

One challenge comes from the history of Bengali Muslims—of indigenous, Bengali–speaking local leaders—who, emerging from the converted peasant stock looked down upon by not only the Hindu Bengali aristocracy, but also from the immigrant *Ashraf* Muslim elite, mobilised support and organised substantial, protracted and violent campaigns against powerful rulers. Devout Muslims imbued with Islam's egalitarian values, these leaders challenged what they saw as unacceptable oppression of their communities by Hindu Bengali, Muslim Afghan/Turkic, and Christian British overlords. Examples from nineteenth century Bengal attest to this powerful tradition of violent reaction to repression. Three episodes stand out, although there were many others across Bengal.

Early in the nineteenth century, Mir Nasir Ali, a local religio-political leader from the rural belt near the seat of the British East India Company's colonial power in Calcutta, began the process of resistance. A devout Muslim, he went to Mecca on pilgrimage. The experience may have deepened his sensitivities. On his return, he was appalled by the oppressive rule the Company-appointed Hindu landlord, Krishna Deva Raj, inflicted on the largely Muslim tenant farmers the fruits of whose labours he preyed on. Although the Company had secured the 'diwani' or governorate of Bengal, Bihar and Orissa from the Mughal Emperor and its power held up the landlord's revenue-collecting authority, Nasir Ali, popularly known as Mir Titu, decided to raise the standard of rebellion against these powerful adversaries. Using religious rhetoric to mobilise the local Muslim peasantry against repressive and hence illegitimate rulers, Mir Titu built an apparently imposing fortress at Narkelbaria village. Fashioned mainly with the local building material of choice, bamboo staves, his fortress was, however, a relatively frail edifice. With his 'capital' at this fort, Mir Titu established a 'government' which began collecting revenue from and administering the villages comprising much of Krishna Deva Raj's patrimony.

After months of sporadic clashes, the Company deployed a force of 100 English soldiers reinforcing 300 native Indian 'sepoys' with artillery to Narkelbaria. In a final engagement in 1831, this combined force besieged Mir Titu's fort and then pulverised it. Mir Titu, refusing to surrender, stood his ground and was killed alongside many members of his peasant militia. His 'Bengali Muslim' insurrection was bloodily ended, but the battle of his bamboo fortress entered the community's folk-lore, inspiring successive generations. Among those who followed, Haji Shariatullah was probably the best known. While Mir Titu was beginning his campaign, Shariatullah was in Saudi Arabia, where he had gone on pilgrimage to Mecca and Medina. A peripatetic religious scholar, he spent twenty years studying at various centres of Islamic scholarship in the Arab and Muslim world before returning to his eastern Bengali roots. Here, he was horrified to see the impact of British-Hindu exploitation of the Bengali–Muslim peasantry, made worse by the restrictions imposed on performing Muslim religious rites. Having acquired an appreciation of the austere orthodoxy of Sunni Islam's desert origins, Shariatullah gathered the most down-trodden of his fellows—descendants of Muslims converted from the lowest of Hindu castes and those even lower in the

Vedic hierarchy, the so-called 'untouchables.' He encouraged them to abandon pre-Islamic cultural traditions and rituals in favour of the 'essential obligations' demanded by Islam, or *faraiz*, in Arabic. His campaign thus gained popularity and notoriety as the '*faraizi* movement.' He forbade the practice of taking out colourful processions during the month of Muharram, when Shia Muslims commemorate the murder of Prophet Muhammad's grandson, Hussein, in ritualistic self-flagellation to symbolise their sorrow for having failed the family of Fatima and Ali, the prophet's only daughter and son-in-law. Shariatullah also prohibited all singing and dancing at weddings and other social festivals on the ground that such 'profane' activities were 'un-Islamic.'

As Hindu landlords and their Christian overlords had forbidden weekly 'Jumma' and annual 'Eid' congregations, Shariatullah declared the country as 'Dar-ul-Harb,' the realm of war, where such anti–Islamic strictures had to be fought and overturned. The *Faraizi* movement spread across southern East Bengal, challenging the Company's writ and the authority of the mainly Hindu landlords it superimposed on the Muslim peasantry. Forces deployed by local landlords against *Faraizi* zealots were unsuccessful in extirpating the threat to the colonial order. When Shariatullah died in 1840, the rulers hoped that the movement would die with him. They were mistaken. Shariutullah's efforts had struck a chord among Bengal's Muslim peasantry labouring under an unsympathetic and exploitative alien imposition whose legitimacy had not yet fully been established or acknowledged. Deepening religious devotion against a backdrop of socio-economic grievances that allowed no legal redress generated a self-sustaining momentum of orthodox belief and practice challenging the existing order.

Shariatullah's son, Muhammad Mohsin, popularly known as Dadhu Mian, took up his father's mantle and strengthened the *Faraizis'* grip over the districts of Bakerganj, Dhaka, Faridpur and Pabna. With Dadhu Mian's 'caliphs' administering the *Faraizi* enclave's subdivisions, a large chunk of eastern Bengal was 'liberated' from Hindu-British dominion. Only when the 'Sepoy Mutiny' initiated by the Company's Bengal Army rocked India, threatening British control in 1857, did British-Indian forces manage to arrest Dadhu Mian on charges of organising Muslim peasants in Faridpur into a rebel army against the British. He died in 1860 when the British succeeded in decimating the demoralised and divided *Faraizi* forces. As the British Crown took over the Indian Empire and administrative reforms addressed many local grievances, the movement died down. However, the experience of a Muslim-Bengali revolt against alien imposition, combining elements of Sunni Muslim orthodoxy and political-military organisation, left a deep impression on the community. While an areligious imperial superstructure erected a secular edifice, its veneer-like superficiality became apparent as the British moved towards a confessionally-defined polity in late-nineteenth and early twentieth centuries. The seeds of orthodox zealotry had been sown and the Subcontinent's political evolution nurtured its germination in modern Bengal.[37]

In Bangladesh, Mujib's 1973 amnesty to those who had collaborated with Pakistani forces in 1971, and his presence at the Organisation of Islamic Conference (OIC) summit in Lahore, Pakistan, the following year, the promulgation by the military-led administration in 1976 of the Political Parties Regulation enabling the outlawed Jamaat-e-Islami to resume political activities, Ziaur Rahman's insertion of Koranic quotes in the constitution's preamble in 1977, Ershad's proclamation a few years later that Islam was the state religion—and the general if unenthusiastic acceptance of these developments—pointed at Bangladesh's steady drift to the right. In the 1990s, with Jamaat aligned to the BNP administration, the legitimisation of Islamist politics was complete. Jamaat was not alone—'moderate' Islamist organisations like the Islami Oikya Jote, another BNP partner, and the Khilafat Movement, for some time an Awami League ally, pursued Islamist goals using peaceable rhetoric. Their increasing participation in the political mainstream, especially as partners to the ruling parties elected in 1991, 1996 and 2001, established them as 'normal' players. In that context their pursuit of a Shariah-based state, however unlikely, was seen as part of Bangladesh's political landscape. This built the backdrop against which the Islamist space expanded while the failings of the political-bureaucratic state to deliver essential services to a growing populace whose expectations had been heightened by politicians campaigning against military rulers, and then frustrated, increased support for 'moderate Islamists.'[38]

In the early years of the twenty-first century, Bangladesh was home to around two dozen Islamist groups, but just two these—*Harkat-ul-Jihad-al-Islami*-Bangladesh (campaign for Islamic holy war-Bangladesh, HUJI-B) and *Jamaat-ul-Mujahideen* Bangladesh (congregation of Bangladeshi holy warriors, JMB)—posed acute threats to the state.[39] Their ideological origins lay in the crucible of the US–Saudi–Pakistani covert campaign against the Soviet occupation of Afghanistan in the 1980s. Among the CIA-sponsored *Mujahideen* guerrillas were around 50,000 'foreign fighters', volunteers from Arab and other Muslim lands beyond Afghanistan and Pakistan, training with the largely Pashtun guerrilla groups fighting in eastern Afghanistan, and being radicalised in the process.[40] It appears some 2,800 of these fighters came from Bangladesh.[41] A group of the returnees from Afghanistan established HUJI-B in 1992.[42] Thought to have been initially led by Fazlur Rahman, one of the signatories of Osama bin Laden's 1998 *fatwa* against 'Crusaders and Jews,' HUJI-B has, in recent years, been led by several others. HUJI-B, the Bangladeshi chapter of HUJI based in Pakistan and active in Kashmir, was initially named *Harkat-ul-Ansar* (campaign of Islamist volunteers) but when, in 1995, its *al-Faran* band of operatives kidnapped and killed several Western tourists including Americans, in Indian-administered Kashmir, the US State Department placed the *Harkat-ul Ansar* on the list of international terrorist organisations. The Bangladeshi chapter of *Harkat-ul-Ansar* renamed itself HUJI-B, maintaining links with its Pakistani counterparts.[43]

With an estimated strength of 15,000 cadres,[44] HUJI-B is a looming if shadowy presence which is held responsible for a large number of attacks on officials, NGOs, girls' schools and, more prominently, eminent personalities. Mufti Abdul Hannan, initially the head of HUJI-B operations and more recently, the head of the organisation, was personally charged with plotting, leading and conducting many violent attacks on diverse targets. His alleged crimes included two prominent assaults[45]— one a bomb attack on the traditional Bengali New Year celebrations at the Ramna Gardens in Dhaka on 14 April 2001, killing ten people and wounding scores more; the other the grenade attack on Awami League leaders at Sheikh Hasina's rally in Dhaka on 21 August 2004 at which several party figures were killed or injured although Hasina herself escaped death. Following his detention in 2005, Hannan reportedly confessed to plotting or leading other attacks: an assault on the country's best-known living poet, Shamsur Rahman, on 18 January 1999; detonating bombs at the annual gathering of *Udichi*, one of Bangladesh's leading cultural organisations, in Jessore, in March 1999, killing 10 and wounding more than 100; planting a 76kg bomb at Kotalipara in Gopalganj just before the then Prime Minister Hasina was scheduled to arrive there for a visit in July 2000; a raid on a rally by supporters of Awami League leader Suranjit Sengupta in Sunamganj in July 2001; and a grenade attack on British High Commissioner Anwar Chowdhury at a Sufi shrine in Sylhet in May 2004.[46] Since 2005, RAB personnel have detained or killed many HUJI-B commanders and cadres; interrogation of the detainees has revealed a fascinating tale.

After HUJI-B's attempted bomb-attack on Sheikh Hasina in Kotalipara failed, the group reportedly tried again in Khulna, in May 2001. Hasina visited the south-eastern city to lay the foundation of a bridge across the Rupsha River on 30 May. Two days earlier, the police had detained fifteen men traveling on two boats in the vicinity of the spot where Hasina was to attend the ceremony. Police recovered military uniforms and jihadist literature from the suspects but did not find anything more incriminating. Later in the year, at Hasina's election rally in Sylhet, HUJI-B plotted another attack with bombs but these detonated prematurely, killing two activists instead. In October 1999, HUJI-B bombed a mosque of the Ahmadiya sect—which believes Mohammad was not the last prophet but one who was followed by others—in Khulna. Eight people were killed in the blasts but investigations soon ran into the sand. There is some indication that as Mufti Hannan's team launched into a series of violent attacks in the late 1990s, he and his acolytes were expelled from 'mainstream HUJI,'[47] although this has not been confirmed.

The other, equally active group, the Jamaat-ul-Mujahideen Bangladesh (JMB), has received focused attention from the authorities in recent years. The decapitation by execution of its leadership by Fakhruddin Ahmed's CTG shortly after taking office demonstrated its willingness to take tough action against Islamists convicted by the courts of breaking the country's laws. However, the JMB was not prepared to give up its violent struggle and was soon reportedly regrouping in remote areas where the state's writ reached only weakly.[48] Like other secretive extremist groups, the JMB has sought to conceal itself while carrying out attacks on its 'enemies'—institutions of the secular state, especially the judiciary. A series of dramatic attacks in 2005, growing domestic and external pressure and perhaps anxiety within the BNP-led ruling coalition to counter allegations of complicity, led to a crackdown against JMB leaders, six of whom were apprehended, some in theatrical fashion. Their trial uncovered some of the group's secrets, but public knowledge of its antecedents remains patchy.

The JMB was reportedly formed in rural Dhaka in 1998 with a view to replacing secular Bangladesh with a Shariah-ruled state by building 'a society based on the Islamic model laid out in the Holy Koran and Hadith.'[49] The organisation was led by a group comprising Sheikh Abdur Rahman, his deputy, Siddiqul Islam, a.k.a. *Bangla Bhai'* (brother of Bengal), Dr. Mohammad Asadullah al-Galib, and several others. Just as HUJI-B initially focused its activities in the south-west of Bangladesh, expanding its theatre of operations gradually, the JMB concentrated its early activities in the north-west. The group broke cover in May 2001 when eight of its members were arrested with twenty-five petrol bombs and documents describing its plans, in the railway town of Parbatipur in Dinajpur district.[50] In 2003, JMB members were believed to have been plotting to attack cultural functions commemorating the International Mother Language Day on 21 February, but their plans were foiled by accidental detonation of seven bombs at a hideout eight days earlier. In January 2005, four sets of bombs went off at cultural performances in Sherpur and Jamalpur in north-central Bangladesh and at Bogra and Natore in north-western Bangladesh, killing two people and injured nearly a hundred.[51] Having for years rejected claims by the opposition, civic bodies and the media that radical Islamists were behind most if not all the organised violence across Bangladesh, in February 2005, the Zia administration banned the JMB, having already banned its off-shoot, the *Jagrata Muslim Janata*, Bangladesh (awakened Muslim masses of Bangladesh, JMJB), a tightly-knit radical body localised in north-western Bangladesh. Both the groups worked under the same leadership. While the JMJB concentrated its attacks on left-wing radicals and occasionally other 'atheist' bodies and individuals, the JMB sought to transform Bangladesh into a Shariah-based state.

The JMB's most spectacular attack occurred, presumably in response to the government's decision to ban it, on 17 August 2005 when nearly 500 bomblets went off almost simultaneously at 300 locations in 50 cities and towns in 63 of the country's 64 administrative districts.[52] The breach of security at the Dhaka international airport, government buildings and major hotels caused anxiety.[53] A few bombs were located and defused before they could do any harm, but fifty people suffered injuries. There were only two fatalities—a child died in Savar near Dhaka, and a pedicab driver in Chapai–Nawabganj in the north-east. The precision, organisation, logistical resource-base, skilled manpower, and most of all, the terrorist imagination symbolised by the attacks demonstrated the JMB's potential capability to wreak havoc across the land.

Leaflets apparently left by the bombers at a number of the sites explained their goals:

We are the soldiers of Allah. We have taken up arms for the implementation of Allah's law the way the Prophet, *Sahabis* (the Prophet's companion-disciples) and heroic Mujahideen have implemented for centuries. If the government does not establish Islamic law in the country after this warning and, rather, it goes to arrest any Muslim on charge of seeking Allah's laws or it resorts to repression on *Alem-Ulema* (religious scholars), the Jamaatul Mujahideen will go for counteraction, *Insha Allah* (Allah willing).[54]

To prove it meant the substance of its message, one of its suicide-bombers killed two judges in the south-western town of Jhalakathi in mid-November, leaving leaflets repeating its juridical focus: 'We do not want *Taguti* (non-Islamic) law; let Quranic law be introduced. Law framed by humans cannot continue and only laws of Allah will prevail.'[55]

This particular sequence of attacks appeared to have forced the Zia government's hands. With suicide bombers killing judges, lawyers, policemen, court officials and bystanders at court houses, threatening the integrity and efficacy of the magistracy and judiciary, the government had to act. It ordered security services, particularly the RAB, to root out the extremists. Once the cabinet-level shift—made difficult by the presence of the Jamaat-e-Islami in it—had occurred and state machinery deployed to this new mission, with Indian agencies monitoring the border and granting no sanctuary to radicals of the religious right, conflict was inevitable.[56] Violent engagements followed, the media offering glimpses of dramatic encounters in which dozen of activists were captured or killed. The most significant was the apprehension of six top leaders including Abdur Rahman and Siddiqul Islam 'Bangla Bhai'. Interrogation of these men led to further arrests and their eventual trial. Seven top leaders of the JMB/JMJB front were tried by the Additional District and Sessions Judge in Jhalakati in 2006 for the murder of senior assistant judges Jagannath Pandey and Sohel Ahmed in a suicide bomb attack on 14 November 2005.[57] The court convicted them of plotting and masterminding the attack and sentenced them to death on 29 May 2006. The appeal process took several months. In early 2007, at the final stage of the process, President Iajuddin Ahmed rejected mercy petitions filed on behalf of the six convicted men in custody, leading to their execution in late March 2007.

As the JMB leaders also headed the JMJB, its activists also started falling into RAB's dragnet. Established in the late 1990s, the JMJB worked directly under Siddiqul Islam 'Bangla Bhai' although its leadership council comprised the JMB's top leaders. JMJB activists operated against militants of the radical left—the outlawed *Sarbahara* Party and the East Bengal Communist Party—in the north-western districts of Rajshahi, Naogaon and Natore. In this enterprise, they received the blessings of several members of the ruling coalition including ministers and MPs, local officials and police officers.[58] When the cabinet committee on law and order chaired by minister and BNP Secretary-General Abdul Mannan Bhuiyan ordered the arrest of Siddiqul Islam (*Bangla Bhai*) for taking what the minister described as the law in his own hands, junior ministers from the north-western Rajshahi areas, Aminul Huq, Fazlur Rahman, and Ruhul Quddus, opposed police action, insisting the JMJB was on 'a pro-people mission' liberating the region's populace from radical-left depredations. Despite this intra-governmental challenge facing early efforts to counter the group's activities, the police did assault a JMJB hideout at Khetlal in the north-western district of Jaipurhat in August 2003 when a gun-battle developed. Most of the JMJB activists fled but the police were able to arrest Abdur Rahman's brother Ataur Rahman and eighteen other militants, recovering documents which provided evidence of the JMJB's objectives and plans. However, on official orders the militants were released a few days later. Rahman later gave an interview to the press, blaming 'conspirators' for having misled the police into attacking a meeting of 'workers from Bogra, Jaipurhat, Rajshahi, Rangpur and other adjacent areas.'[59]

These confusing signals were cleared in late 2004 when police and RAB began chasing JMJB activists. By early 2007, battle was fully joined. Security forces had been given clear orders and were carrying these out. Key leaders of HUJI-B and JMB/JMJB were either dead or in custody awaiting trial. But the shadow of the 'righteous radicals' continued to loom large as Bangladesh approached the parliamentary polls scheduled for December 2008. Senior officials responsible for managing the operations against radical Islamists conceded the battle was far from won. Both HUJI-B and JMB were 'large organisations heavily influenced by the ideology and strategies of al-Qaeda and the Taliban.' While these groups did not have operational links with foreign terrorist organisations, they enjoyed the support of 'sections of political parties.' Also, the view that

Islamist extremists were mainly drawn from madrassa students was factually incorrect—militants arrested and being sought came from a wide variety of social and educational backgrounds, madrassa alumni making up only a modest percentage.[60] The arrest of former Deputy Minister Abdus Salam whose brother Tajuddin was thought to have masterminded the 21 August 2004 grenade attack on Sheikh Hasina's rally in Dhaka demonstrated the level of linkage between the radicals and mainstream politicians.

While the government's campaign had produced notable results, many challenges remained. The larger, more visible extremist groups had been pinned down and their leadership neutralised—but the campaign was being taken up by newer, smaller, and more shadowy bodies such as '*Allahr Dal*' (Allah's party), *Hizb-ul Tahrir* and *Hizb-ul Touhid*. These groups did not openly pursue totalitarian goals of taking power to build a shariah-ruled state—on the contrary, they focused on small projects like banning specific publications they considered 'unIslamic.' They were shifting ground in imaginative ways, finding cracks in the legal system which would allow them to pursue lesser, non-threatening objectives but which would keep them in the limelight and build support for their campaign. Perhaps one sign of their ability to keep a step ahead of a hostile legal system was to disband proscribed organisations, regroup and emerge as new entities under different names.[61] In September 2007—June 2008, a total of 245 militants of all stripes were arrested; of them, forty-five were members of *Hizb-ul Touhid*, thirty-five of the JMB, twenty-five from HUJI-B, and twenty-three members of '*Allahr Dal*.' The remainder came from other groups. In the same period, the courts sentenced seventeen militants—including seven JMB members—to death while eighty-six others had been given prison sentences of varying lengths.[62]

This offensive against the Islamists did not crush them; in fact, it may have encouraged the emergence of a new leadership as determined as its predecessors to pursue its radical goals. As Bangladesh prepared for polls in December 2008, the JMB emailed detailed explanations of its aims and aspirations, along with a link to its fairly sophisticated website, to a large number of Bangladeshis at home and abroad,[63] making clear its determination to maintain its base of operations. In the final days before the elections, security forces raided a number of Islamist hideouts, arrested several activists and recovered a large number of grenades, bombs and explosives for making more of these. Fears for the lives of the two main political leaders, Sheikh Hasina of the Awami League and Khaleda Zia of the BNP forced the government to take added precautions. Threats to members of the CTG, the RAB, army and police personnel[64] conveyed to RAB and police offices across the country suggested the Islamists were alive and that Bangladesh faced a long struggle with 'believers' seeking heaven on earth.[65]

The egalitarian threat

The challenge from the radical right was only a part of Bangladesh's background of insecurity. The tale of the radical left in Bangladesh is a narrative of austere ideological discourses turning into bloody campaigns against a hostile state, and occasionally, among fellow-travellers debating nuanced theoretical differences. The seriousness with which Fakhruddin Ahmed's CTG assessed the threat from the extreme left in the run up to the elections scheduled for December 2008 underscored the danger from the political spectrum's other end. The CTG, taking over a campaign against various 'Marxist-Leninist' groups from the BNP-led coalition,[66] reinvigorated the effort. As a result, in 2007–8, RAB personnel raided numerous hideouts, killed several leaders and activists and arrested many more.[67] Security services identified eighteen extreme leftist organisations which had fragmented from the handful of communist groups active in the early 1970s.

By late 2008, these factions were led by around forty key figures. They were especially active in thirteen north-western and southern districts where they attacked middle-peasants, police outposts, government offices and businesses from which they could extort money. Of the forty leaders, two were killed in 'crossfire' incidents in 2007–8; six had been detained by August 2008[68] when intelligence agencies urged the Ministry of Home Affairs to proscribe the bands so that these could be attacked more robustly and detained activists could not escape justice using legal loopholes.

The factions, described variously as Marxist-Leninist or Maoist, were[69]:

- Purbo Banglar Communist Party Marxist-Leninist (Lal Pataka) or East Bengal Communist Party M-L (red flag)—also known as PBCP M-L (red flag)

- PBCP M-L (Janajuddha) or East Bengal Communist Party M-L (people's war)—also called PBCP M-L (people's war)
- PBCP M-L (Rashed) or East Bengal Communist Party M-L (Rashed)
- Bangladesh Biplobi (revolutionary) Communist Party, or BBCP
- Bangladesh New Biplobi (revolutionary) Communist Party, or BNBCP
- BNBCP—Mrinal Group
- BNBCP—Sailen Group
- Sramajibi Mukti Andolon (workers' liberation campaign) or Gana Mukti Fouj (people's liberation army)
- Bangladesh Communist Oikkya Prokria (unity process)
- Banglar (Bengal's) Communist Party, or BCP
- Bangladesh Communist Juddha (war), or BCJ
- Sarbahara (proletarian) Group
- Sarbahara Sagar Group
- Sarbahara Party
- Sarbahara Zia Group
- Sarbahara Poresh Group
- Jashod Gono Bahini (national socialist party people's militia), and
- Regional Bahini

This fragmentation stressed the relative insignificance of ideological unity in contrast to the importance of personalities of leading cadres. These trends went back to the origins of radical nationalism and leftist activism in Bengal in the early decades of the twentieth century. Boosted by the 1905 partition of Bengal and largely a Bengali Hindu *bhadralok* phenomenon, radical nationalism took the form of 'terrorist' attacks against British officials and symbols of colonial rule with a view to forcing an end to the imperial order. Two secret revolutionary groups, *Anushilan Samity* (calisthenics association), established in 1902 and *Jugantar* (transition to a new era), formed a little later, became notorious among Bengal's British masters. Their members attacked British officials, police stations, trains and similar targets with high-visibility. Many activists were killed in encounters with the police while others were arrested, tried and executed. Many others were exiled to the remote penitentiary at Port Blair on the Andaman Islands in the Bay of Bengal.[70]

The other strand of the Bengali challenge to the imperial dispensation came from the Communist Party of India which was also established with a Bengali ideologue and activist at the forefront of the international communist movement. This was Manabendra Nath Roy, popularly remembered as M.N. Roy. His life reflected the rationalist rigour of dialectic materialism combined with a romantic belief in the individual's capacity to effect change and shape history. Roy, a polymath who chose an activist career, shaped the rise of radical leftist movements in South Asia. Born to a school teacher as Narendra Nath Bhattacharjee, he was thrown out of school in 1905 after attending a political rally in violation of school regulations. He then joined *Anushilan Samity*. While a student of chemistry and engineering, he experimented with bomb-making as an underground activist. In 1910, he worked with another famous Bengali revolutionary, Jatindra Nath Mukhopadhyay—*Bagha* (Tiger) Jatin, both leading members of *Jugantar*. The two of them were arrested that year and tried in the 'Howrah-Shibpur Conspiracy Case, 1910–11.' It was during their detention that they planned an India-wide insurrection. This abortive attempt was crushed in 1915 and Jatin was executed. Roy, traveling under one of his many pseudonyms, sailed to Batavia, and then to Shanghai, seeking German armed assistance against the British. This exercise failed. Over the next two years, he toured Japan, Korea, the Philippines, Mexico and the USA. Arriving in Palo Alto, California, in 1916, he took the name M.N. Roy to hide from British intelligence—the name stuck.

Roy married and moved to New York, living in the house of Lala Lajpat Rai, an Indian nationalist who, after the end of the Great War, would return to India, becoming a famous Congress leader. In New York, Roy studied Marxism at the public library. After the USA declared war on Germany in 1917, American police started arresting Indians on suspicion that they were German spies. Roy fled to Mexico where he learnt Spanish, French and German, and teamed up with left-wing American and Mexican intellectuals. He became popular with Mexico's ruling circles, and organised a Socialist Party Conference in Mexico City in August 1918. Lenin's envoy Michael Borodin was impressed with Roy's knowledge, skills and influence. Lenin invited Roy to attend the Second World Congress of the Communist International in Moscow in July-August 1920. The Congress debated the two theses presented by Lenin and Roy, accepting both. With the Congress over, Lenin asked Roy to head Comintern's Asian bureau based in Tashkent. Roy began an anti–British guerrilla campaign in Khorasan, chasing the British out of the province. His efforts led to the establishment of Communist Party of India in Tashkent in October 1920.

Roy was a member of the Comintern delegation sent to China to resolve the dispute between the Chinese Communist Party and the Kuomintang. On his return to Moscow, he fell ill and was taken to Berlin for treatment. He worked at the upper levels of Comintern until 1929 when he was expelled from it for writing articles critical of the organisation. Roy returned to India using the name of Dr. Mahmud and was arrested in Bombay in July 1931. Tried for sedition, he faced years of imprisonment. In 1932–36, he wrote a number of voluminous theoretical tomes in prison, the most famous being *The Philosophical Consequences of Modern Science*.[71] After being released in November 1936, Roy joined the Indian National Congress and organised the radical wing of the INC. This group supported Subhas Chandra Bose's effort to become the INC's president. However, Roy's differences with the Congress high command over a more combative approach to the British opposed by 'mainstream' leaders like Gandhi and Nehru forced Roy to leave Congress and set up the Radical Democratic Party with his supporters.

However, on the outbreak of the Second World War, considering declining imperialism a lesser evil than fascism, Roy lent support to the Allied war effort. In 1948, disenchanted with both Marxist thinking and bourgeois democracy, Roy disbanded the Radical Democratic Party. Analysing the unattractive aspects of his previous attachments in a book titled *Reason, Romanticism and Revolution*, Roy established the Radical Humanist Association as an alternative. He was a founder of the Renaissance Institute and in his final years, edited the quarterly journal *The Humanist Way*, formerly *The Marxian Way*.[72]

This transformation of the revolutionary activist and ideologue to a theoretician of the humanist movement both reflected and reinforced Bengal's intellectual ferment which gave rise to second-generation leftist groups, some of which pursued radical goals and evolved into organisms very different to their progenitors. Roy was a unique figure and not just among Bengal's modern radical leftist leaders, but he represented a tendency which gave rise to a plethora of practitioners who pursued egalitarian objectives with a cold detachment combined with a pragmatic style only true believers could rationalise. In spite of the loss of inspirational leaders like M. N. Roy and the atomisation of the communist organisational structure in the 1940s, leftist activists continued fomenting revolts among disadvantaged groups across Bengal.

In Eastern Bengal, they incited the 'Tebhaga movement' among peasants[73] from the northern districts in 1946–47 while much of South Asia was in the throes of pre-partition turbulence. Peasants and tenant farmers, rejecting the oppression of the share-cropping system, rose in revolt and many were killed or wounded in police action. Next, the Hajong tribe in the northern Netrokona area mounted an uprising; after it was crushed, sporadic peasant rebellions challenged the authority of the newly defined (East) Pakistan in Jessore, Sylhet and other districts. More than 3,000 communists were arrested and hundreds detained for years without trial.[74] It was in this context that the Pakistani government banned the Communist Party of Pakistan (CPP). Thereafter, the movement could only function as a series of clandestine cells and lay dormant until the late 1960s. Mirroring the fragmentation of post-imperial India, the Communist Party of East Pakistan grew out of the break up of the Communist Party of India and the establishment, in March 1948, of the CPP. The latter, banned in 1954, operated underground. In East Pakistan, its provincial leaders and activists worked under the cover of the Awami Muslim League (the Awami League's precursor) and the National Awami Party.[75] In 1966, following the schism between the Communist Party of the Soviet Union (CPSU) and the Chinese Communist Party (CCP) at the CPSU's 20th Congress, the CPP's East Pakistani wing fragmented.

The mainstream, pro-Moscow faction, led by Moni Singh, was willing to co-habit the political space with bourgeois-liberal democratic forces as it sought to build a more egalitarian society. The pro-Beijing faction, led by Mohammad Toaha, could not countenance such 'revisionism.' Under Moni Singh, the CPP's East Pakistan Provincial Committee, meeting clandestinely in 1968, formed a distinct party, naming itself the Communist Party of East Pakistan. The pro-Beijing faction held its first Congress in Sylhet in 1967, and named itself *Purbo Pakistaner* (East Pakistani) Communist Party Marxist-Leninist (initially, the PPCP M-L; later, EPCP M-L), with the goal of achieving an 'independent, people's democratic East Bengal.'[76] However, a substantial body within the EPCP (M-L), led by Mohammad Toaha and Abdul Haque, maintained that it was possible and necessary to achieve a 'democratic revolution' within the Pakistani state. In 1969, the secessionist faction, led by Deven Sikder, Abul Bashar, Abdul Matin, and Mohammad Alaudin, parted company with Toaha and Haque, forming what they named *Purbo Banglar* (East Bengal) Communist Party (PBCP).

In 1971, as the national campaign for autonomy turned into Bangladesh's war of independence, the EPCP (M-L) again fragmented. Toaha abandoned Haque, naming his faction the Communist Party of Bangladesh Marxist-Leninist (CPB M-L),[77] and deciding to engage in the anti–Pakistan war while not supporting the Indian forces or their *Mukti Bahini* allies. Haque's EPCP (M-L) found it difficult to support the transformation of the Pakistani bourgeoisie's eastern colony into a focus of the convergence of interest between the bourgeois Indian state and East Bengal's petite bourgeoisie. While the import of such theoretical nuances seen against the backdrop of East Bengal's civil war escaped many at home and abroad, for the participants in the debate these were defining issues. It consolidated a tradition of ideological schism and structural fragmentation characterising Bangladesh's leftist movement. In 1978, after Ziaur Rahman lifted most of the bans, encouraging radical leftists to give up violence and engage in 'bourgeois politics,' Abdul Haque's party would emerge as the Revolutionary CPB (M-L).[78] Given the wider regional context, especially the Marxist-Leninist-Maoist ferment threatening to tear apart eastern India in the late 1960s and early 1970s, this fragmentation was almost inevitable.

Naxalbari's insurrectionary legacy

While the CPP was splitting into pro-Moscow and pro-Beijing factions, in the neighbouring West Bengal state of India, the Naxalbari uprising was swelling into a substantial revolt. In 1964, following differences emerging within the CPI between its pro-Moscow and pro-Beijing factions over the 1962 Sino-Indian war, the latter formed the CPI (Marxist) which, nonetheless, was willing to collaborate with the Congress in pursuit of power within India's capitalist liberal-democratic system. In 1967, two Bengali communist leaders, Kanu Sanyal and Charu Majumder, left the CPI (M) and established the Organising Committee of the Communist Revolutionaries of India. Two years later on Lenin's birthday, 22 April 1969, Sanyal announced the establishment of the CPI (Marxist–Leninist) with Majumder as secretary. The two of them rejected the Congress-CPI (M) decision to set a land-ownership ceiling at twenty-five acres per head, demanding instead that peasants who tilled the soil be given possession. Rising against 'imperialists, feudal landlords and monopolistic capitalists',[79] CPI (M-L) mounted an insurrection against state power from its base in West Bengal's Naxalbari district. The *Naxalites* killed a number of landlords and the police struck back. The CPI (M-L) organised tenant-farmers, attacking members of the feudal class—often indiscriminately—but failed to take over their land and redistribute it among the peasants. This was later seen as a major failing.[80]

In June 1967, eleven people including women and children were killed in police firing[81] on a gathering of activists. The campaign now took on a momentum which local authorities failed to contain. Begun as a farmers' uprising against feudal repression, the *Naxal* campaign, using the slogan 'Land to the Tiller!' rapidly spread. It soon drew in urban students as violent flag-bearers, posing a challenge to the Indian state as represented by the Congress-led provincial government in Calcutta. The urban counterpart of the rural campaign, the *Naxalbari Sahayak Samity* (aid-Naxalbari association), was accused of bombing city-centre police stations and posts, and shooting members of the 'repressive state.' Despite the *Naxalites'* early successes, strong contradictions emerged between Majumder's rural insurrection and the urban insurgency mounted by Sanjay Mitra and his colleagues. The former saw feudalism and the state's support of it as the principal threat while the latter, with the Vietnam War in the background, viewed imperialism and its local associates as the key challenge. The two camps shared a belief in the importance of armed struggle in changing society's power relations, but while Majumder believed in the primacy of the annihilation of 'class enemies,' Mitra's comrades, convinced that they had to organise trades union and operate through the democratic process, established the National Liberation and Democratic Front, dedicated to aiding sub-national activists among Naga and Mizo montagnard nationalists, and marginal workers in agro-industry.[82]

Initially unaware of these internal contradictions between *Naxalite* factions, the Indian state imposed Draconian restrictions on radical activists, deployed substantial paramilitary and military forces to the state and launched a bloody counter-insurgency operation lasting several years, decimating *Naxalite* ranks and forcing the survivors to hide. In the meanwhile, in East Pakistan, the autonomist-nationalist movement rose through the anti–Ayub Khan movement in 1969, when diverse separatist tendencies coalesced around Mujib's Six–Point campaign on the one hand, and a radical leftist armed struggle theme on the other. In June 1969, two months after the formation of the PBCP, its leaders met in

Pabna and decided to follow the CPI (M-L)'s revolutionary line. This correspondence between radical leftists across the intra-Bengal boundary would influence the way the Bangladeshi campaign shaped up, the evolution of Delhi's support for it, and post-1971 political developments in independent Bangladesh. The pro-Moscow CPP supported the Awami League-led campaign. Moni Singh served as an adviser to Tajuddin Ahmed's government-in-exile while many CPP members fought Pakistani forces in the guerrilla war. The record of pro-Beijing factions was mixed: one group aligned to both the PCP and the PBCP saw the war as a conflict between the Pakistani bourgeoisie and an emergent Bengali bourgeoisie, and fought both Pakistani forces and Bangladeshi guerrillas; a group from the PPCP viewed the conflagration as an attempt by the Indian capitalist state aided by Soviet 'social imperialists' to capture East Pakistan, and fought alongside Pakistani forces against Bangladeshi guerrillas.[83] Delhi's insistence that the *Mukti Bahini* not recruit combatants from pro-Beijing communists ensured that the fragmentation within the East Bengali movement not only persisted, but was deepened during the war.

The one exception among pro-Beijing groups was the *Purbo Banglar Sarbohara Party* (East Bengali proletarian party—PBSP) which waged its own war against Pakistani forces in 1971. The PBSP emerged from the left-wing ferment in the wake of the CPSU-CCP split. In 1967, Siraj Sikder, a newly graduated engineer, established the Mao Tse-tung Thought Research Centre in Dhaka. It immediately attracted the wrath of *Jamaat-e-Islami* stalwarts who assaulted several members of the Centre.[84] In January 1968, Sikder and his comrades met at a jute mill worker's residence in Dhaka and established *Purbo Banglar Sramik Andolon* (East Bengal workers' movement). The group, unlike other pro-Beijing factions, viewed Pakistan as a colonial power and sought to liberate East Bengal and establish a 'democratic republic' there.[85] Sikder's opposition to 'US imperialism, Soviet social imperialism, Indian expansionism and feudalism'[86] combined with his view of China and its presumed ally Pakistan confounded many Bengalis. Mujib denounced his band as 'pro-Chinese provocateurs.'[87] This antagonism would persist into the 1970s.

The group began underground activities in mid-1968, first by 'capturing' a cyclostyle printer with which to publish its organ *Lal Jhanda* (red flag), expounding its theories. In January 1970, the group hoisted the immediately proscribed flag of East Bengal at various locations in Dhaka,

Munshiganj and Mymensingh. On 6 May 1970, Karl Marx's birthday, it bombed the Dhaka offices of the Pakistan Council, Islamabad's instrument of cultural integration among Pakistan's disparate provinces. In October, it expanded its target list, bombing several official buildings across East Pakistan, including the US Information Centre in Dhaka.[88] Soon after the Pakistani crackdown on 25 March 1971, Sikder decided to establish national resistance cells. On 30 April, he set up a militia— *Purbo Banglar Sashastra Deshpremik Bahini* (East Bengali patriotic armed force) which engaged Pakistani troops in combat; the PBSP, launched in June, served as the group's political platform.[89] Post-1971, the PBSP emerged as a major threat to the new order.

Sikder was elected PBSP president at the first party congress held in January 1972. He devoted much effort to building bridges with other like-minded groups and in April 1973, succeeded in forging a coalition of eleven left-radical organisations, *Purba Banglar Jatiya Mukti* (East Bengal national liberation) Front. He was elected its president. He then began an armed campaign against the petit bourgeois state with a view to establishing the rule of the Bangladeshi proletariat.[90] His comrades killed Awami League cadres, fought the police and were, in turn, persecuted by Mujib's loyal militia, the JRB. Partly to counter threats from the radical left with a political move, Mujib granted an amnesty to Islamists in November 1973, and released more than 30,000 of them from prison. The religious right and the radical left have since then engaged each other in mortal combat in a proxy engagement between mainstream proponents of two very different visions of Bangladesh. The course was thus set for believers from the extremities of the ideological spectrum to wage an elemental struggle for the soul of Bangladesh, tearing at its very fabric.

After Mujib promulgated a state of emergency in 1974, Sikder and his band went underground. His fighters received a boost when Colonel Mohammad Ziauddin, a renegade war-hero and former commander of the army's brigade in Dhaka, joined the PBSP, rising through the ranks to become Sikder's principal military adviser. In mid-1974, during the army's 'Operation Silver Lining' ordered by Mujib to arrest smugglers, owners of illegal fire-arms and assorted 'miscreants,' Sikder, Ziauddin and other PBSP leaders fled into the forested highlands of the Chittagong Hill Tracts, seeking to escape the dragnet laid by the JRB and intelligence agencies. When security services detected their move into the CHT, Mujib ordered the army to liquidate the PBSP. In December 1974, the army mounted 'Operation Dragon Drive,' its first major operational deployment since independence.[91]

Army battalions chasing the PBSP's leadership repeatedly came close to Sikder and Ziauddin but failed to apprehend either.[92] However, the threat was enough to force Sikder to abandon the CHT and seek refuge in Chittagong city where he was arrested by men of National Security Intelligence (NSI), the country's apex intelligence organ. He was brought to Dhaka where he refused to 'repent' before Mujib. According to widely disbelieved official reports, Sikder was being taken from Dhaka airport to the JRB camp in Savar north of the capital on 2 January 1975 when he tried to escape and was shot dead.[93] The military's operations across the CHT and elsewhere, death of the charismatic founder-leader, traumatic violence shaking Bangladesh in 1975–77 and the transformation of the country's political landscape fragmented the PBSP. As noted above, it broke up into a number of factions which themselves broke up. The faction often identified as the inheritor of the PBSP mantle is PBSP (Central Committee), an underground group which seeks armed revolution. In 2001, a faction split from PBSP (CC) to form the PBSP (Maoist Bolshevik Reorganisation Movement).[94] Like other extreme leftist groups, many PBSP factions too, by late 2008, were reduced to launching sporadic attacks on remote police posts, businesses and homes, robbing, kidnapping and extorting in campaigns seen more as a threat to domestic peace and tranquility than to Bangladesh's political order.

In the late 1970s, General Zia's efforts to bring the radical left out onto open politics largely succeeded; in the 1980s, General Ershad built on this legacy by co-opting many former 'underground' figures. The most visible transformation occurred in the ranks of the JSD which, following Colonel Taher's execution, changed its policy, accepting the legitimacy of operating within the liberal-democratic pluralist framework and abandoning violence. However, as large leftist organisations abandoned the path of armed struggle and revolutionary violence, fringe groups formed to occupy the space the former vacated. With the state's capacity to order collective behaviour relative to the left's disruptive abilities having steadily grown, it is difficult to see the disparate factions emerging as a credible threat to the state. However, in the early years of the twenty-first century, several bands from the PBCP stable caused such trouble in north-western Bangladesh that influential politicians were accused of aiding and abetting radical Islamists in launching a counter-attack on the left.[95] Factions of the PBCP were thus seen to pose a serious challenge to the state by directly threatening the status quo, and indirectly by subverting state power.

In its more recent resurgence, the PBCP hit the headlines in 1998 when the decapitated bodies of five of its members were found and identified in the western Kushtia district. Inquiries suggested they had been killed in a factional feud.[96] With violence mounting, the government launched an operation against radical groups active in south-western Bangladesh, including the PBCP, in April 1999. Six days later, PBCP cadres shot seven Awami League members dead in the western Chuadanga district. Over the next three years, the group killed policemen and members of the Awami League, BNP, and *Islami Chhatra Shibir*. Security personnel detained a large number of PBCP cadres while hundreds more surrendered. All were jailed, but shortly before handing power to the CTG in preparation for the October 2001 parliamentary elections, Prime Minister Hasina released hundreds of PBCP activists while others secured bail. The PBCP soon regrouped. In its efforts to disrupt state power and capture it through armed struggle, in January-March 2002, its cadres killed nearly one hundred individuals.[97] Polarisation between the extreme left and radical right mirroring the Awami League-BNP divide within 'mainstream politics' deepened the cleavage at the heart of political Bangladesh. As the major parties used the radicals at the respective extremities as instruments of competition, polarisation deepened beyond what would otherwise have been the case.

With an undeclared semi–civil war raging between the radical left on the one hand, and the Islamist right and security services on the other, RAB units hunted PBCP leaders and senior cadres in the western third of Bangladesh in 2004. PBCP (M-L) leader Mofakkhar Hossain managed to escape from his theatre of operations in late 2004, taking shelter in Dhaka's Mirpur district. Here he was identified and arrested by RAB personnel who, after questioning him on his activities in western Bangladesh, took him to Kushtia to hand him over to a RAB unit there. According to officials, the RAB convoy taking him from Dhaka was ambushed by his comrades. During a firefight between RAB staff and PBCP cadres, Mofakkhar Hossain jumped from the RAB vehicle he was in and tried to escape. Caught in the crossfire, he was killed.[98] His career had reflected the progress of the Bangladeshi radical leftist movement. He joined the Matin-Alauddin faction of PBCP (M-L) in the early 1970s, rising to the rank of party central committee secretary until 1999 when he was expelled. He and his supporters established another PBCP (M-L) which he led. In 2002, he and a comrade, Abdur Rashid Malitha, fell out, and 'expelled' each other. Mofakkhar's faction became PBCP (M-L) *janajud-dha* (people's war) while his rivals formed PBCP (M-L) *lal pataka* (red flag). At the time of his death, Mofakkhar's band was accused of having killed at least two hundred people over the past two decades.[99]

Since 2001, security forces have regularly engaged cadres of radical leftist groups which have gained notoriety for spreading fear with criminal violence. Although official data of encounters, arrests and casualties is not available, private media regularly report clashes and many journalists themselves have suffered at the hands of activists. Published reports of casualties suffered by radicals and security forces, while possibly incomplete, provide indications of the scale of the leftist challenge to Bangladesh: in 2005, security personnel killed 163 radical leftist cadres, lost three of their own, and eleven civilians were killed in cross-fire; in 2006, the figures were 139, five and twenty-eight respectively; 2007 saw a decline in clashes, with casualty figures dropping to seventy-two militants, and eight civilians; in the first eight months of 2007, security forces killed forty-one leftists, lost one of their own and one civilian was killed in the violence.[100] While the numbers of left-radicals killed fell under the army-backed CTG, the seniority of those eliminated appeared to have risen. Among those held or killed in raids and 'encounters' were regional, district or area commanders of various PBCP factions. In 2005, PBCP cadres killed members of mainstream parties, police officers and local figures opposed to or critical of their activities. Once the RAB and other security units were deployed in some numbers against them, the tide seemed to turn in 2006 when fifty-seven 'regional leaders,' 'area/district/divisional commanders' or 'top cadres' of the PBCP (M-L) 'red flag,' 'people's war' and other factions were reportedly killed in 'encounters.' Another twenty such ranking personnel were killed in 2007.[101]

This trend continued. In June 2008, RAB officials claimed 514 'extremists,' including senior figures, had died in 'crossfire' over the previous four years.[102] Their success was topped by the consecutive killing of Abdur Rashid Malitha alias 'Dada Tapan,' founder of the PBCP (M-L) 'people's war' faction, on 18 June, and Dr. Mizanur Rahman Tutul, leader of the PBCP (M-L) 'red flag' faction, on 30 June.[103] The demise of these two 'giants' of the extreme left, the arrest or death of hundreds of cadres, and the occasional surrender of others weakened the movement as Bangladesh approached an electoral end to the state of emergency in late 2008. However, the threat persisted. Security officials believed around 5,000 armed cadres loyal to nearly twenty extremist groups remained active.[104] In their fragmented and occasionally internecine campaigns they might not pose an existential challenge to Bangladesh's political order, but if experience is any guide, their very disunity and the ability to operate in unconnected cells rendered the challenge of managing them more complicated than it would otherwise have been.

The shadow of the looming 'other'

In 1971, Bangladeshis established their country in opposition to Pakistan's military-bureaucratic-political-oligarchic power-elite on the grounds that their electoral majority in the Pakistani dispensation had not only been denied its constitutional stature but had also been institutionally discriminated against since 1947. Pakistan's refusal to honour the pledge to transfer power to the majority party elected in December 1970, its military crackdown on Bengali nationalists, its widely-alleged 'genocidal' war on the Bengali 'nation,' its threat to execute Sheikh Mujib, the war-time support it received from the USA and China, its reluctant release of Mujib and tardy negotiations over the exchange of prisoners of war and other 'stranded' people, and its refusal to consider Dhaka's pleas to share pre-1971 assets and liabilities reinforced Bangladeshi outrage. Pakistan was the 'other' against which Bangladesh crystallised, fought, coalesced and emerged.

Bangladesh was everything Pakistan was not. Physical separation was reinforced by the rejection of the ideological-philosophical bases of earlier unity. Critique of the Pakistani past was a foundational factor in building the Bangladeshi present. In both the nature of the nation and the structure of the state, in domestic and foreign policy, in politics and economics, and in self-regard and attitudes towards the rest of the world, Bangladesh was the virtual opposite of the residual Pakistan. Without the Pakistani other to define itself against, Bangladesh would struggle to create its own identity. And yet, just over three and a half years later, domestic forces removed the ruling elite which had triggered the war of independence, defined its purpose and designed the contours of its outcome. The domestic dynamics which changed Bangladesh also changed the 'other' against which the country defined itself. The traumatic transition created a new ideational framework.

For most of the history of post-Mujib Bangladesh, in the eyes of a substantial segment of the ruling elite, India rather than Pakistan was the national 'other.' The widely-held view of the Awami League's proximity to Indian interests received a boost during Sheikh Hasina's premiership in 1996–2001 when the Ganges water-sharing accord and the CHT peace treaty stressed the advantages of cooperative policies. However, even Hasina had to bow to strong popular resistance to Indian demands for overland transit rights allowing movement of personnel and goods across Bangladesh, and exporting natural gas to India—despite pressures from Western energy firms with investments in the sector. This relatively static juxtaposition of India-Bangladesh interaction underwent visible change only after General Moeen Ahmed, CAS and the strongman behind Bangladesh's CTG in 2007–08, acknowledged Delhi's regional stature. He reviewed bilateral relations and the shift was formalised during his week-long visit to India in February 2008. However, whether this shift marked a fundamental and lasting change in relations remained unclear.

Bangladesh's many and variegated problems with India are rooted in consanguinity born of contiguity across contrived borders, structural differences, perceptual discontinuities, and their translation into policy contradictions—mutually reinforcing and confounding efforts to address their consequences. The philosophical-ideational differences between the two neighbours have been noted.[105] From the inception of relations during Bangladesh's war of independence when Delhi provided moral, material and legal support to the separatist movement represented by Tajuddin Ahmed's government-in-exile (GOE), India's approach had been unusual. Even when using formal instruments of diplomatic legality, Delhi maintained the charade that the GOE was based at 'Mujibnagar,' the border village where the GOE had taken its oath of office in April 1971, although in fact, it was located in central Calcutta.[106] Such deliberate reliance of the highest offices of both states on subterfuge laid a frail foundation on which to erect normal relations. The few Indian analysts who acknowledge the fact that many Bangladeshis see Delhi's role as divisive say this impression is a 'misunderstanding.'[107]

Delhi's support for the Awami League-led campaign rather than for the multitudinous resistance to Pakistani forces, and its formation of the

Mujib Bahini—distinct from the *Mukti Bahini* which formally took orders from the GOE, proved particularly contentious. Delhi established the former militia with Mujib-loyalists under the command of student leaders—Fazlul Haq, Sirajul Alam Khan, Abdur Razzaq and Tofael Ahmed—driven by fears that if Pakistan did not release Mujib and the *Mukti Bahini*'s popularity grew during the war, it could take over the nationalist campaign from the Awami League.[108] In 1972, the *Mujib Bahini* and its leaders split—Khan and A.S.M.A Rab reorganised their faction into the radical-left JSD, invited disillusioned war-heroes Colonel Abu Taher and Major Jalil into its ranks, and prepared to mount both political and insurrectionary challenges to Mujib. Haq—Mujib's nephew, with Tofael and Razzaq, led the Awami League's youth and student wings and assumed influential positions in the administration.

Indian assistance, critical to the war-effort, was seen as less than altruistic and driven by Delhi's calculations of its strategic interests: here was a rare opportunity to reduce India's regional rival to a rump state and gain a friend on the eastern flank; Pakistan's civil war, expected to push around fifteen million refugees into eastern India by early 1972, threatened its fragile politico-economic fabric; two Indian infantry divisions were fighting *Naxalite* radicals in West Bengal while two others were engaging Pakistan-aided Naga and Mizo separatists in north-eastern areas; Marxist-Leninist guerrillas were threatening to take over the East Bengali campaign—the danger of a pan-Bengali radical leftist group with operational linkages felt real. In that context, the need for a swift end to the ferment was quite obvious to Delhi.[109] This pragmatic *realpolitik*-driven motivation, while perfectly rational, appeared to rob India's substantial assistance to the Bangladeshi nationalist campaign of its moral authority. The 'looting' of Bangladeshi assets by victorious Indian troops swiftly eroded much of the affection with which they had been welcomed.[110]

Still, at the highest levels, cordiality was reflected in the intimacy expressed in the 1972 Treaty of Peace and Friendship incorporating security collaboration signed by the two prime ministers during Indira Gandhi's visit to Bangladesh in March 1972. Through this treaty, India and Bangladesh formally entered an alliance relationship. However, the purpose and content of the alliance became a source of much debate in Bangladesh as interpretations ranged from Delhi's offer of protection to Delhi's imposition of a protectorate.[111] Indian aid to the Bangladeshi separatist campaign was similarly assessed by Bangladeshi analysts as reflecting 'certain well-conceived and cogent calculations' of Delhi's 'strategic considerations.'[112] Wartime expectations having risen very high, post-war disappointment in one land was matched by frustration in the other.[113] This created a context in which subjective assessments of each other's performance generated emotionally charged responses not amenable to a rational pursuit of 'normal' diplomacy. Nonetheless, political proximity, physical contiguity and geographical reality encouraged the signature of several other agreements which, together, formed the practical bases of the alliance. Two of these dealt with what were, in Bangladeshi view, critical issues.

Water

The first, signed in November 1972, established a Joint Rivers Commission which would study problems and opportunities relating to shared watercourses 'in order to ensure the most effective joint efforts in maximising the benefits from Common River Systems' and utilise the region's water resources 'on an equitable basis for the mutual benefit of the peoples of the two countries.'[114] The early establishment of a framework for addressing a problem—mainly of equitably sharing water-flows in common rivers between the upper-riparian India and the lower-riparian Bangladesh—which had confounded Indo-Pakistani efforts, promised to finally resolve a critically important issue. And yet, India's decision to commission the Farakka Barrage in early 1975 and unilaterally withdraw Ganges water, reducing the water-flow into Bangladesh, and the failure of the two countries to reach a long-term agreement until 1996, underscored fundamental discord.[115] The depth of this dispute was reflected in the approaches the two sides took to addressing the issue and the divergent proposals they tabled.

Bangladesh urged regional and multilateral collaboration across river basins; India insisted on bilateral arrangements ignoring the geographical characteristics of watercourses draining river basins.[116] For more than two decades, Dhaka's stress on the opportunity costs of not adopting a regional approach was rejected; its proposal to augment lean-season Ganges water-flow by building reservoirs in Nepal received short-shrift from Delhi. India asked Bangladesh to build a canal linking the Brahmaputra River to the Padma instead, diverting 'surplus' water from this other major river flowing from India into Bangladesh, reducing arable land in a land-hungry country, with uncertain ecological consequences, and no means for Dhaka with which to control the water-flow into Bangladeshi territory.[117] Dhaka's reliance on Indian goodwill in ensuring drainage of the delta and its failure to secure Delhi's agreement on dividing the reserves of dozens of other rivers since 1972 have embittered relations and complicated the context; Bangladeshis think of India as having a stranglehold on a key element of their well-being.

The one agreement which was reached and then promoted as an example of the benefits of cooperation—the 1996 Ganges Water Sharing Treaty—received legal scrutiny after Bangladesh, instead of receiving the promised 67,516 cusecs, actually received only 55,556 cusecs in the first ten days of January 2008. Two Bangladeshi lawyers filed a public interest writ petition with the High Court claiming that the treaty did not protect Bangladesh's national interests and ought to be reviewed. The Government argued that the court had no jurisdiction over such an international treaty. On 19 June, the High Court ordered the government to explain why the treaty should not be reviewed 'according to the provisions of the Berlin Rules on Water Resources, 2004, and the provisions of the UN Convention on the Law of Non-Navigational Uses of International Watercourses, 1997.'[118] The thirty-year treaty posed a potential challenge to 'normal' bilateral relations.

Land and sea

In 1947–71, India and Pakistan had disagreed on the precise demarcation of their eastern land frontiers at several points where their troops had occasionally clashed. Both Indian and Bangladeshi governments hoped that on the strength of their alliance, they would resolve all the disputes. The priority given to this aspiration was manifest in a treaty signed by the two prime ministers during Sheikh Mujib's visit to Delhi in May 1974. The treaty specified the delineation of the Indo-Bangladeshi border in fourteen disputed stretches and set out the formulation for addressing the inherited issue of enclaves and exclaves.[119] There were dozens of these with thousands of people stranded in 'adverse possession' in a state of legal limbo. India and Pakistan had failed to resolve their fate; Gandhi and Mujib determined to end that dispute now. The treaty stated, 'The Indian enclaves in Bangladesh and the Bangladesh enclaves in India should be exchanged expeditiously, excepting the enclaves mentioned in paragraph 14 without claim to compensation for the additional area going to Bangladesh.'[120] The treaty would come into effect 'from the date of the exchange of the Instruments of Ratification' and would resolve a long-standing dispute. Bangladesh promptly ratified the treaty; India did not.

The enclaves had emerged from the complex evolution of relations among the region's successive rulers across dynamic frontiers—the Mughals, the *Nawabs* of Bengal, the royal family of Koch Bihar state and their various tributaries, the British East India Company, the kingdom of Bhutan with its shifting borders, and, eventually, the provinces of the British-Indian Empire. The complex nature of the problem meant that even at official levels, there often was disagreement over who owned which exclaves and where.[121] The most contentious issue to emerge from the 1974 accord dealt with the exchange of disputed territories and enclaves in and around north-western Bangladesh:

India will retain the southern half of South Berubari Union no. 12 and adjacent enclaves, measuring an area of 2.64 square miles approximately, and in exchange Bangladesh will retain the Dahagram and Angarpota enclaves. India will lease in perpetuity to Bangladesh an area of 178 metres x 85 metres *ijear 'Tin Bigha'* to connect Dahagram with Panbari Mouza (P.S. Patgram) of Bangladesh.[122]

It would take nearly two decades for the 'Tin Bigha corridor' to be handed to Dhaka. In the meantime, the several thousand people in the Dahagram and Angarpota enclaves, surrounded by not notably friendly Indian neighbours, subsisted in a legal limbo. Not citizens of the land in which they found themselves, they were boxed in their tiny islands within the Indian landmass; the country they were entitled to call their own was unable to extend the basic services even rural Bangladeshis might reasonably expect from their state. Their perennial plight, Delhi's apparent unwillingness to honour its commitments and Dhaka's inability to help its distraught citizens contributed to a wider malaise of mutual mistrust.[123] The Ershad administration's more friendly stance toward Delhi led, in October 1982, to Indian confirmation of the corridor's lease, allowing 'unfettered movement' of 'Bangladesh citizens including police, paramilitary and military personnel along with their arms, ammunition, equipment and supplies.' Bangladesh could administer the enclaves as it did other areas under national jurisdiction.[124] In short, Bangladeshi sovereignty over the enclaves would be effective. It was not to be.

Indian citizens from the neighbouring Kuchlibari, Dhaprahat and Mekhliganj townships organised the Kuchlibari *Sangram* (campaign) Committee and the Tin Bigha *Sangram* Committee. In March 1983, the committees filed three writ petitions in the Calcutta High Court challenging Delhi's decision to give Dhaka 'right of free passage' across Indian territory. These argued that the 1974 Land Boundary Agreement (LBA) was inconsistent with the 1958 agreement signed between Prime Ministers Jawaharlal Nehru and Feroze Khan Noon which acknowledged the borders between India and Pakistan as delineated by the Radcliffe Award of August 1947; a lease in perpetuity amounted to cession of Indian territory; and the 1974 and 1982 agreements diluted India's sovereignty over its own land.[125] Political and legal processes in West Bengal state and at the federal level in India then became entangled with the implementation of the 1974 and 1982 agreements.

On 1 September 1983, the Calcutta High Court disallowed the three petitions. The West Bengal state government then acquired the private plots of land making up the corridor. On 12 April 1984, the Kuchlibari *Sangram* Committee filed an appeal before a Division Bench of the Calcutta High Court. On 19 September 1986, the Division Bench upheld the High Court's previous judgment. The Bench also directed that the Indian constitution be amended to ensure that the once-disputed Berubari Union was not transferred, and the 1974 and 1982 agreements be noted in the constitution's relevant schedules to confirm that the corridor was transferred to Bangladesh and not Pakistan. On 18 December 1986, the Indian Government filed a 'special leave petition' in the Supreme Court against the directions issued by the Calcutta High Court on the grounds that these were extraneous to the petitioners' points of appeal. The Supreme Court accepted the petition in October 1987. In May 1990, the Supreme Court ordered that the lease be fully implemented. In November 1991, the Calcutta High Court dismissed another case challenging the Indian government's acquisition of land for the corridor. It was only then that, in March 1992, Delhi confirmed to Dhaka that the corridor would be operational by the end of June 1992.

This, however, only addressed a small part of the problem. As late as in December 2006, the enclave-exclave issue remained largely unresolved. At the time, India claimed 111 enclaves with a total area of 17,158.13 acres within Bangladesh while acknowledging the existence of fifty-one Bangladeshi enclaves with a total area of 7,110.02 acres lying within

India.[126] The 1974 LBA provided for an exchange of the enclaves; Delhi sought a joint survey/census of these to ascertain if their residents wished to transfer to the country within which they were going to be absorbed but Dhaka insisted such a survey/census was 'extraneous to the provisions of the LBA' and not a pre-condition to the exchange.[127]

Although in July 2006 Bangladesh agreed to participate in a 'joint visit' to the enclaves, none followed. For Bangladesh, at the receiving end, this protracted and unhappy process did little to endear its large neighbour. But this unhappiness paled beside the infelicity of being hemmed in and shut out behind an eight-foot-high, double fence of rolled barbed wire stretching between serried ranks of steel bars stretching along the length of the 2,545–mile India-Bangladesh border, apart from the riverine stretches. Following mass attacks on alleged Bengali immigrants by local vigilantes in many parts of north-eastern India in 1983, and the failure of complex legal procedures to identify and deport 'Bangladeshis,' Delhi began planning the erection of a fence along the Indo-Bangladeshi border in 1985. The objective was to 'check illegal infiltration, contain smuggling and to frustrate militants who were using the border route to cross over into India to commit subversive acts.'[128] India began constructing the fence along 'sensitive' sectors in the 1990s. Despite Dhaka's protests that no Indian militants enjoyed Bangladeshi sanctuary and that no Bangladeshis illegally migrated to India—both claims rejected by Delhi—Indian contractors and the Border Security Force (BSF) proceeded to build the fence.

The BSF and the Bangladesh Rifles (BDR) had occasionally engaged in firefights, especially when relations were fraught. Now, with India building a security fence close to, if not on, the border, tensions rose. Whenever Indians tried to erect a fence within 150 metres of the 'zero line,'—the border—BDR personnel opened fire on the grounds that a 1972 boundary agreement and guidelines agreed on in 1975 prohibited such constructions.[129] Delhi denied that the fence was a 'defensive structure' but, after repeated clashes in which both sides suffered many casualties, decided to erect the fence on Indian soil 150 metres away from the border. Bangladeshi protests faded, but a general feeling of hurt was not ameliorated. Indian farmers and landowners whose property fell on the wrong side of the fence began protesting, especially in Tripura and West Bengal states.[130]

Disputes over the maritime boundary mirrored those on land. In the late 1970s, as littoral states negotiated the UN Convention on the Law of the Sea (UNCLOS), and deposits of natural gas were discovered in the seabed off Bangladesh's shores, India-Bangladesh ties hit the buffers. A series of talks failed to resolve the issue. The two sides disagreed on which of the many channels of a border river dividing the *Sundarban* mangrove forest between western Bangladesh and India's West Bengal state was the main one. This meant they disputed the ownership of a tidal islet rising from silt deposits on the estuary. Giving it different names on their charts—Delhi called it *Purbasha* (eastern promise); Dhaka, South *Talpatty*—the two sides failed to resolve the dispute in talks held in 1980. The following year they came close to threatening violence. As Delhi deployed a naval survey ship with escort vessels to the area in early 1981, Dhaka sent in its missile boats to engage in a potentially escalatory cat-and-mouse game. The crisis ended only after President Ziaur Rahman was killed in an abortive coup and Bangladesh focused on domestic dissidence. However, the issue refused to die. In late 2008, with UN registration deadlines approaching and disputes over offshore hydrocarbon exploration once again in contention, the two sides met to resume discussions of disputed maritime borders after nearly twenty-eight years. As both sides presented documents supporting their contrary claims, the three-day meeting failed to produce an agreement on the precise location of the border river's 'mainstream.'[131]

In December 2008, weeks after a similar episode in the eastern Bay of Bengal with the Burmese Navy, Bangladesh faced another drama with the Indian Navy. A survey ship escorted by several Indian naval platforms entered waters disputed by Bangladesh and India just days before Dhaka was to hold parliamentary elections after two years of army-led emergency rule. Bangladesh also deployed its naval vessels and issued warnings to the alleged interlopers, while formally protesting to the Indian government. Delhi suggested negotiations but did not otherwise heed Dhaka's warnings. In the absence of agreed boundaries, Dhaka was reduced to complaining that India and Burma were collaborating in hydrocarbon exploration in parts of the Bay of Bengal which fell within Bangladeshi jurisdiction, but to little effect. Once again, no shots were fired in anger, but the fact that both navies had seen fit to deploy combat platforms to areas disputed by them pointed to the potential confrontation escalating to conflict with unpredictable consequences.

Insurgency

In the mid-1970s, as Bangladeshi nationalist forces emerged as the leading contenders for state power and Bengali nationalists, considered favourably disposed to India, were marginalised, relations chilled. Indian security forces offered sanctuary, arms and training to Bangladeshis opposed to the Ziaur Rahman regime in Dhaka. Guerrilla bands numbering several thousand Awami League loyalists, based at camps in India's Meghalaya state, attacked Bangladeshi border guards and towns for two years, inflicting many casualties and much damage.[132] At the same time, as the Chakma tribal *Shanti Bahini* guerrillas mounted their armed challenge to Bangladesh's writ in the Chittagong Hill Tracts (CHT), the Bangladeshi security forces struck back. Indian security services then set up camps for the guerrillas and for Chakma refugees fleeing from the CHT in the bordering Tripura state.[133] From their sanctuary here the insurgents would mount operations against Bangladeshi establishments with relative impunity.[134] It was only in the 1990s when peace talks between government officials and the guerrillas reached a degree of success that the camps began to be shut. However, until the CHT peace treaty was signed in 1997, all sides maintained the charade that the guerrillas were operating from within Bangladeshi territory although everyone knew otherwise. Between 1975 and 1977, India-based Bangladeshi militants had plotted and prepared for assassinating President Ziaur Rahman; only when Morarji Desai assumed the leadership in Delhi was the project shut down and the two states negotiated an end to the Meghalaya-based insurrection. Desai himself disclosed these dramatic developments.[135]

In recent years, India has accused Bangladesh of sheltering a large number of ethnic minority activists waging separatist wars in northeastern Indian states. At official- and cabinet level meetings, Indians have pressed demands that Bangladesh stop providing sanctuary and support to separatist militias from Assam and Tripura states, demolish all their alleged camps, detain their cadres and hand them over to Indian authorities.[136] Dhaka has denied extending sanctuary or other assistance to Indian guerrillas. However, the detention of Golap Barua a.k.a Anup Chetia, a senior commander of the United Liberation Front of Assam (ULFA)—Assam's most effective secessionist group—in the 1990s and his imprisonment on relatively minor charges suggested ULFA activists may have been using Bangladesh as a transit area if not a base. Dhaka's refusal to deport Chetia to Delhi despite strongly repeated requests has been seen extremely negatively in India's security circles.[137] Indian journalists, presumably working with the benefit of 'background briefing' by intelligence officials, have made serious allegations against the activities of ULFA and other Indian insurgent groups in Bangladesh.[138] In July 2008, a Delhi–based Indian journalist alleged that Anup Chetia, by lending one of the owners of a prominent Bangladeshi media group 'a few million dollars to reorganise his collapsed business' in the 1990s, had won ULFA a stake in the media house.[139] The Editor of the Daily Star, the flagship of the media group in question, wrote back refuting the allegations, protesting against 'the content of the piece, which is full of lies, distortions and inaccuracies.'[140]

The subtext of this exchange was an example of the deep mutual suspicions, misunderstanding and unhappiness colouring elite perceptions underpinning relations and policies. More recently, Indian security officials have accused Bangladeshi Islamist militants, especially those belonging to HUJI-B, of involvement in terrorist attacks in India.[141] Indian intelligence officers, briefing foreign journalists on the arrest of Islamists by Bangladeshi police near Indian-Bangladeshi borders, said, 'That brings in the global terror angle, and we're all too close to all this for comfort.'[142] Several thousand alleged Bangladeshi illegal immigrants in Jaipur, the capital of India's western state of Rajasthan, were incarcerated for long periods after a series of bomb blasts in the state in 2008. Senior Indian officials blamed HUJI for violent acts in Northeastern India–'HUJI has its presence in the northeast, and they have come from Bangladesh.'[143] Illegal immigration from Bangladesh, a major political issue in the 1990s, again gained prominence in 2008 when the Director-General of the BSF announced that between 1972 and 2005, the entry of over 1.2 million Bangladeshis had been cleared by immigration counters on the Bengal border, but 'there is no record that they have returned.'[144] In the same year, following a high-profile visit to India by Bangladesh's military leader, General Moeen Ahmed,[145] Bangladesh did hand over a number of detained guerrillas from north-eastern separatist groups to Indian authorities.[146] If the trend became policy, one bone of contention would have been buried.

Discordant vision and voices

The disputes are symptoms of the insecurity dynamics shaping Indo-Bangladeshi mutual perceptions. Ever since Bangladesh's transformation from a quiescent ally to a vocal critic of India's regional policy in the mid-1970s, contrasting views of the 'self' and 'the other' have coloured relations. Perhaps the most striking instance of this relativism in Bangladeshi thinking is the ego-perception of 'smallness.' Even with over 100 million people calling Bangladesh home, the elite there has consistently considered the country 'small.' Officially sponsored academic studies have theorised on the definition of 'small states' with a view to interpreting the framework sufficiently flexibly to include Bangladesh in the pantheon of such actors.[147] This could only be explained by relating Bangladesh's stature to India's, a giant on many counts. The geographical reality of being nearly surrounded by this looming presence sharing line-crossing similarities across contrived frontiers, combined with the need to establish nation-defining divergences which themselves generate dynamic tensions within the polity, ensures that Bangladeshis often see themselves juxtaposed to Indians. It is in this context that Bangladesh could be forgiven for perceiving threats to its territorial, political, economic and technological security and to its freedom of action.[148] Insecurity founded on the incompleteness and internal contradictions in the ideational bases of nation-statehood invariably pits India as both the mirror in which Bangladeshis see the reverse of who they are and the yardstick against which they must judge themselves. In short, Bangladesh can only define itself in opposition to India while assessing performance in comparison with India's. This combination of compulsions ties the two countries in an unhappy but symbiotic bond.

The complexity of this duality is not helped by elite-perceptions in India. Indian analysts note that while policy-pragmatism could be founded on rational assessments of shared economic interests between India and its neighbours, 'economic considerations are secondary to political-security factors' such as elite predispositions, priorities and preferences. The primacy of the political was evidenced by the severance of economic ties between India on the one hand and Pakistan and Bangladesh on the other early in their interactions, setting the tone for relations generally.[149] Others point out that while India's 'continual civilisational tradition and a sense of history' made nation-building relatively easy for

India's leaders, this was not the case for India's neighbours which had to fashion brand-new national narratives of distinct identities. Small states, unable to defend their own sovereignty and dependent on external aid, suffer from 'a pervading sense of insecurity.' Given some Indians' 'blatantly hypocritical' projection of India as a small or medium power, its neighbours become distrustful of Delhi. 'It is but natural for the smaller neighbours of India to entertain some misgivings about India's size and capability.' Insecurity is compounded by the divergence between India's secular democracy and the paths adopted by its neighbours. 'Extra-regional intervention' in the affairs of South Asian states where 'it is unrealistic to overlook that what happens to a population in one country is not totally without its impact on their kindred populations across the border' sets the context in which Delhi would not countenance 'foreign' meddling in the area, but could not itself ignore developments in neighbouring states.[150]

Other Indian analysts insist that small states see the world from peripheral perspectives, focused as they are on their own regional subsystem and concerned mainly with power-relations in their immediate environs. Just as large powers 'see little prospect of the small states remaining secure except in their protection, so do the small states tend to believe that they need the protection and patronage of large states to survive and develop.'[151] They point out that regional cooperation could offer an effective mechanism for securing the interests of the region's small states as long as extra-regional linkages were avoided—effectively ensuring the pre-eminence of the regional big-power. 'The important element of this aspect is that the regional approach should be oriented towards autonomous arrangements amongst the sovereign states of the region concerned rather than any great power patronage. Only such an approach can satisfy the requirements of national security.'[152] This legitimisation of India's role as the regional security manager is not widely welcomed in South Asia[153]; in Bangladesh, nationalist elites see it as a threat.

Dhaka's rejection of Delhi's supervisory pretensions became clear in 1998 when Sheikh Hasina's 'Delhi–friendly' administration took a diplomatic initiative to de-escalate a dramatic rise in regional insecurity after India and Pakistan tested nuclear weapons. Whether out of concern over potential risks to the region caused by this extraordinary development, and with conviction that Dhaka could and should seek to ameliorate its consequences, or out of naiveté, Hasina announced plans to consult both her Indian and Pakistani counterparts and offer her good offices in mediating between the two newly-declared nuclear neighbours. However, when she arrived in Delhi to meet the Indian leadership under Prime Minister A.B. Vajpayee, her hosts turned down her offer and demanded she 'pay attention to their views regarding insurgents and "infiltrators".' They also warned her against signing up a mooted status of forces agreement (SOFA) with the USA which would allow US forces to deploy to Bangladesh to assist with post-disaster relief and rehabilitation efforts.[154] This failed initiative was followed in mid-2000 by a series of exchanges of fire between the BDR and BSF leading to the deaths of several Indian border guards and Bangladeshi civilians.[155] The BSF started 'pushing in' many Bengali–speakers—alleged illegal Bangladeshi immigrants—across the border while the BDR pushed them right back out, insisting only those with proper identification documents verifying their citizenship would be accepted. Against this backdrop, relations would plunge unexpectedly as Hasina's Awami League government wound down.

Trade

Of the disputes deepening rancour, trade has been a key source of discord. The Ershad administration, hoping to open up the commercial sector and seeking improved relations with Delhi, encouraged trade relations. In FY 1987–88, imports from India stood at $143.70 million or 5.88 per cent of total imports. Exports to India hit $11.30 million, or 1.05 per cent of Bangladesh's total exports that year. By the last financial year of Ershad's rule, 1990–91, exports had reached $17.40 million while imports had more than doubled to $305.10 million. Dhaka's trade deficit rose from $132.40 million to $287.70 million.[156] As Table 6.1 shows, in the years since then, Bangladesh's trade with India, and indeed the world, has expanded substantially, as has Dhaka's trade deficit with Delhi, a source of much unhappiness, and the subject of considerable international discussion.[157]

This persistent, large and growing trade deficit with India, given an already uneasy relationship, was 'a great concern for Bangladesh.' Dhaka additionally bore the burden of 'the large volumes of informal imports from India across the land border which avoid Bangladesh import duties.'[159] If this trend continued, Bangladeshi economists feared trade diversion would be inevitable, creating efficiency loss, and reducing the

Table 6.1: Bangladesh-India trade development in 1987–2006, in $m[158]

F/Y	Exports to India	% of total	Imports from India	% of total	Trade deficit
1987–88	11.30	1.05	143.70	5.88	132.40
1988–89	8.90	0.69	179.70	6.57	170.80
1989–90	11.70	0.90	275.20	8.34	263.50
1990–91	17.40	1.04	305.10	9.36	287.70
1991–92	5.70	0.34	324.00	10.54	318.30
1992–93	7.70	0.37	355.30	10.59	347.60
1993–94	17.90	0.70	430.20	11.76	412.30
1994–95	38.20	1.30	644.70	14.82	606.50
1995–96	85.90	2.30	1049.10	17.32	963.20
1996–97	62.20	1.55	869.00	13.83	806.80
1997–98	50.80	1.05	786.50	12.01	735.70
1998–99	62.40	1.21	995.60	14.82	933.20
1999–00	78.20	1.43	636.30	8.44	558.10
2000–01	80.40	1.26	935.00	11.61	854.60
2001–02	59.10	0.97	1002.20	12.32	943.10
2002–03	62.10	1.02	1176.00	15.12	1113.90
2003–04	77.60	1.10	1740.70	18.34	1663.10
2004–05	143.66	1.76	2025.78	18.16	1882.12
2005–06	241.96	2.63	1868.00	15.20	1626.04

gains from trade. Another fear was that large-scale imports from India would 'displace domestic production,' and 'de-industrialise' Bangladesh.[160] Partly to counteract such dangers and also to spread commercial liabilities, Bangladesh has, since the 1990s, reduced tariff and non-tariff barriers and joined several regional trading blocs, most prominently, the South Asian Association for Regional Cooperation (SAARC)-sponsored South Asian Free Trade Area (SAFTA), and the Bay of Bengal Initiative for Multi–Sectoral Technical and Economic Cooperation (BIMSTEC) Free Trade Area. Additionally, Dhaka has played an active role in promoting the interests of the Least Developed Countries (LDC) bloc in the Doha Rounds of world trade talks. These initiative may in combination have boosted the country's collective commercial confidence, but structural dissonances within each of these 'arrangements'[161] and Bangladesh's own myriad weaknesses have conspired to rob these initiatives of the potential dramatically to improve the country's trade prospects.

Informal trade—or smuggling, followed the same pattern: large volumes of goods are smuggled from India to Bangladesh, but very little in the other direction. This suggested that in informal trade, too, India had a substantial surplus.[162] In 2002, a rough estimate of both 'bootleg' and 'technical' smuggled imports from India to Bangladesh amounted to around $500 million, or 42 per cent of recorded 'formal' imports. However, a study of the figures of both kinds of smuggling from India to Bangladesh suggested the actual value of goods smuggled from India into Bangladesh could be $900 million, about three quarters of Bangladesh's total recorded trade.[163] Dhaka insisted Delhi's protectionist policies obstructed the growth of Bangladesh's exports. Indian global imports grew at over 9 per cent annually in recent years, with many imports overcoming higher tariff than that applied to Bangladeshi goods—Dhaka enjoyed South Asian Preferential Trade Agreement (SAPTA) benefits. The slow growth of Bangladesh's exports to India was said to 'reflect fundamental comparative advantage factors, not discriminatory import policies.'[164] The appreciation of the Bangladeshi Taka/Indian Rupee exchange rate by about 50 per cent between the mid-1980s and 1999 would have contributed to the expansion of this virtually one-way trade.[165] Key factors were:

- Bangladesh's narrow export base
- Lack of complementarity in production
- Divergent productivity and management standards
- Structural and technological limitations
- Nominal and real appreciation of currency exchange rates
- Tariff and non-tariff barriers
- Inadequate banking facilities and underdeveloped capital markets
- Poor infrastructure and utilities facilities
- Political instability and weak governance, and
- Poor quality and lack of international competitiveness in products[166]

Bangladesh's unwillingness to acknowledge these internal factors and inability to address their consequences meaningfully in the absence of elite consensus on both relations with India and the roles of the executive and legislative branches of government have produced the pattern of pronounced imbalances. Passion born of a reliance on emotive subjectivity as opposed to the rigorous application of reasoned logic would ensure the persistence of this pattern. Absent fundamental shifts, no change could be expected.

Energy

This is not to say Dhaka alone was responsible for all the ill will. As the Indian economy took off in the 1990s and exploration by local and foreign agencies discovered substantial natural gas reserves in Bangladesh, pressure for exporting gas to India mounted. Foreign energy firms sought rapid recovery of exploration costs and repatriation of profit; multilateral lenders wished to speed up Bangladesh's economic growth; Indian commercial and bureaucratic interests worried that burgeoning development would require steady, secure and proximate supplies of energy; and sections of the Bangladeshi elite which could not see the logic of not exporting 'surplus' gas to India too urged Dhaka to export. Protracted and bitter debates followed. Those Bangladeshis who insisted the country's 'proven'—as opposed to 'estimated'—reserves were barely enough for meeting domestic demands and that the country would soon become a net importer, challenged the 'export camp.'[167] Even the allegedly 'pro-Indian' Awami League administration in 1996–2001 failed to turn popular opinion in favour of exporting gas. Once Dhaka's inability to export gas to India became clear, Delhi urged Bangladesh to build a pipeline linking Burmese gas fields to Indian industrial centres. This did not get very far either. Delhi's unhappiness was apparent as Indian analysts pointed to possible Bangladeshi attempts to use the 'China card' against India— 'Once Bangladesh becomes less inclined to allow a gas-pipeline to pass through its territory, China would succeed in delaying or seriously damaging India's attempts to secure overland access to Myanmar's gas fields. As for the Myanmarese junta, they would hardly mind selling their gas to China instead.'[168] In recent years, as industrial and domestic demand grew and the energy deficit rose in Bangladesh, some originally pro-export promoters have changed their minds.[169] But this has not helped trade relations, or indeed, relations generally.

Dhaka has, since the 1960s, pursued the establishment of a nuclear power-plant as a way out of serious energy shortages. Successive governments have failed, despite promises, to bridge the growing gap between energy supply and demand. Since the late 1980s, natural gas reserves have offered some hope. But with ageing power-plants generating only about 3,000 MWe while demand soared to 5,000 MWe, the economy and civic life have suffered. With proven reserves of 14 trillion cubic feet (tcf) of natural gas in twenty-three fields, more than 3 tcf already consumed by mid-2008 and production from fourteen operational fields providing only

1.6 billion cubic feet (bcf) daily, Bangladesh faced 'a total blackout by 2011.'[170] This urgency drove the CTG to seek the IAEA's help in installing a nuclear power-plant generating 600–1,000 MWe by 2015.[171] Parallel to that effort, in April 2005, Bangladesh signed an agreement with China on cooperation in the field of civil nuclear technology. The accord, confirmed during Fakhruddin Ahmed's discussions with Chinese leaders in Beijing in September 2008,[172] and designed to address Bangladesh's energy crisis, outraged key sections of the Indian establishment. Their anger underscored Delhi's emotional approach to its Bangladesh strategy.

One Indian analyst wrote: 'The most striking part about (sic) the China-Bangladesh nuclear deal is that it is more about politics than about economics. For Bangladesh, an alternative to the much-politicised international gas pipeline linking Myanmar and Bangladesh to India strengthens its negotiating hand. Furthermore, the deal allows Bangladesh to engage in that age-old trick of counterbalancing bigger powers, by playing the China card against India.'[173] Thirty months later, reflecting on Bangladesh's decision to seek Chinese help, following approval by the IAEA, in building a nuclear power-plant, a more openly official Indian commentary noted, 'China has been focusing on developing closer ties with Bangladesh in recent years in order to bring that country within its fold... Its (Dhaka's) eagerness to go in for this (nuclear) option while other sources of energy remain underutilised is indeed surprising. There are several other options available to improve the power situation in the country. Bangladesh has huge reserves of gas and coal, but strangely it does not seem to want to use these.[174] The author either was not aware or ignored the fact that a British energy firm's attempts to establish an open-cast coalmine in north-western Bangladesh had led to massive protests and multiple deaths, injuries and arrests, shutting the project down. As for 'huge reserves of gas,' at current rates of consumption, proven reserves were expected to be exhausted by 2011. Instead of building trust and cooperation, energy issues thus deepened Indo-Bangladeshi anxieties.

Transit

Khaleda Zia focused on commercial exchanges during her visit to India in early 2006. Although she had waited for the last year of her second term before going to Delhi, the trip did generate some positive responses, especially in trade affairs. Delhi pressed Dhaka to agree 'to make mutually

beneficial arrangements for the use of their waterways, railways and road-
ways for commerce between the two countries and for passage of goods
between two places in one country through the territory of the other.'
Back in Dhaka, Bangladesh's Foreign Secretary assured compatriots that
Zia had not granted India transit rights, only right to transport goods
across Bangladesh using its waterways,[175] in vogue since 1972. Transportation of Indian goods over land, and rail links, had been ended by Pakistani authorities on the outbreak of war in September 1965, and although
the two sides resumed a bus service and in 2008 a rail link, between
Dhaka and Calcutta, Dhaka would not grant India the right to transport
goods or personnel across Bangladesh over land. Notwithstanding Bangladeshi refusal to grant overland transit rights, India revived its proposals
in 2008. In mid-2008, Delhi presented fresh proposals covering both
road- and rail-links between north-eastern Indian states and the Indian
mainland across Bangladesh. Delhi proposed the revival of five railway
connections interrupted in 1965, and the construction of a sixth in eastern Bangladesh. Dhaka declined to sign an accord on the ground that an
elected government should take such a substantive decision.[176] The issue
of land-transit has become intertwined with both sovereignty and security
concerns in Bangladesh. Dhaka cannot countenance the transport of
military or security personnel and hardware across Bangladesh between
North-eastern Indian states and the Indian mainland; Delhi would not
let Bangladesh impose an intrusive verification and search regime on its
stores and personnel; Dhaka's long-standing request for transit rights
allowing Nepal to use Bangladeshi ports has perennially received a
brusque rebuff.

Investment

Bangladesh is concerned that its infrastructure would require significant
improvement to take the presumed load of added pressure from India's
transit movement, for which no financial support was forthcoming.[177]
There have also been problems with Indian investment programmes.
Once it became clear that Bangladesh was unable to sell natural gas to
India, several large investment proposals were made by Indian firms to
build manufacturing plants using Bangladeshi gas as either the feed-stock
or fuel. The most prominent of these offers came from Tata, one of India's
largest industrial houses.

The \$3 billion proposal, made half-way through Zia's second term, included the construction of a 1,000 megawatt gas-fired power plant, a 500 megawatt coal-fired power plant, a 1 million ton per year fertiliser plant and a steel mill capable of producing 2.4 million tons of hot rolled coil and other basic steel products. The 2004 proposal included a pledge by Dhaka to supply gas at \$1.10 per unit guaranteed for twenty years. Bangladesh rejected this proposed price as too low. In 2006, Tata made a fresh bid, offering to pay \$3.10 per unit of gas supplied to the proposed fertiliser plant, and \$2.60 per unit of gas to be supplied to the planned steel plant. The Zia administration found this unacceptable but did not give a decision[178] before leaving office. Fakhruddin Ahmed's CTG, after long deliberation, rejected the proposal. This dented the optimism generated by several similar proposals.[179]

Security-insecurity

In the end, it was the political dynamics between the two neighbours which determined if agreements were reached or broken, suspicion was deepened or replaced with trust, and a cooperative and benign framework functioned. Delhi accused Dhaka of ignoring or colluding with Islamist extremists who allegedly crossed the border to carry out terrorist attacks in India.[180] Indian security officials alleged that Afghan war veterans and more recent recruits from among madrassa alumni in the HUJI-B, numbering 15,000–20,000, have been allowed to collude with Pakistan's Inter-Service Intelligence Directorate (ISI) to mount attacks including some in India.[181] They were incensed when in the autumn of 2008 the Bangladeshi authorities allowed the group to float a political party—the Islamic Democratic Party (IDP)—to contest national elections.[182] Bangladesh's Election Commission refused to register the IDP as a political party, but Indian complaints did not cease. HUJI-B activists were accused of carrying 'lethal arms and explosives' into Assam in late September 2008 when seven of them were killed by Indian forces. In early October, the group was held responsible for a series of blasts in Agartala, capital of the Indian state of Tripura. Following these incidents, Delhi issued 'a high alert' and deployed a large number of troops along the Bangladesh-India border.[183] Senior Indian security officials have been fulminating against increased 'infiltration of Bangladeshis' into north-eastern Indian states, 'disturbing the demographic ratio of the country and also spreading the evil of separatism.'[184] They complained that this twin-threat had been aided by the proliferation of 'illegal madrassas' along the Bangladesh-India border, offering 'bases' to Bangladeshi 'terrorists' and 'infiltrators'. However, a Muslim student leader from India's Assam state promptly offered a large cash reward to the Deputy Inspector General of Police in Assam if he could prove these allegations were true![185]

The sharpest edge to India-Bangladesh relations was evident in perceptions of mutual insecurity. Despite the insubstantial offensive strength of Bangladesh's armed forces relative to that of India's,[186] any sign of Bangladesh adding to its defensive or deterrent capability caused anger and annoyance across the border. In May 2008, the Bangladesh Navy test-fired Chinese-made C-802 anti–ship cruise missiles from its Chinese-built frigate, *BNS Osman*, a 1500–ton *Jianghu* class platform built in 1989 and recently upgraded with Chinese assistance. The C-802 was thought to be capable of evading enemy defences and hit hostile vessels up to 120km away.[187] The range and accuracy of the missile in Bangladeshi inventory had 'Indian security agencies worried.'[188] Given the overwhelming superiority enjoyed by Indian forces across the spectrum of lethal capability, and the improbability of Bangladeshi operations other than purely defensive ones, that alleged anxiety hinted at likely frustrations felt in Delhi, boosting Bangladeshi fears that India expected to reign supreme as the regional hegemon, able to assert its will and impose its security interest on South Asian neighbours as it stepped out as a global actor. An increase in Bangladeshi deterrent capability could detract from the perception—if not the reality—of Indian invincibility in its own strategic backyard. The insertion of Chinese security interests, as instanced by the Bangladeshi frigate and cruise missile combination, may have deepened Delhi's unhappiness and tinged it with anxiety.

The C-802 was not the only source of Indian angst. 'Highly-placed intelligence' officials briefed Indian journalists on other aspects of Dhaka's missile-building ambitions. They noted that Bangladesh was negotiating with Turkish and German firms for the purchase of at least two types of surface-to-air-missiles (SAM) and related radars and other gear. The briefings were sufficiently detailed for the press to report that the Bangladesh Air Force was seeking to buy SHORAD (short-range-air-defence) missiles and radars from a Turkish vendor, and the 180km OTOMAT Mk-II SAM from the European MBDA company.[189] The Indian intelligence briefers neglected to stress that the SAMs were purely defensive weapons with the capability of deterring attacks by more powerful air forces, but lacked any offensive capability at all. Their unhappiness was explained by the complaint that 'Bangladesh has already set up a missile launch pad near the Chittagong Port with assistance from China. Breaking protocol, it did not bother to inform India about its missile tests.'[190] Again, Indian officials neglected to note that the tests were conducted near Kutubdia Island, a few miles from Chittagong, and broke no agreements.

Indian anxiety over Bangladesh's military modernisation, however modest in scale and scope, and Dhaka's lack of appreciation of Delhi's unease, were the obverse and reverse sides of the same security-insecurity dynamic. As each party sought to build up capacity for reasons which may not have any offensive content, the perceived balance which may have existed prior to the change was disturbed. The 'other' was troubled by the resulting 'disruption' and might feel forced to take steps to restore the status quo ante—which then led to further reaction. This dialectic of asymmetric responses ensured a lack of strategic stability in Indo-Bangladeshi security relations. Nothing exemplified the escalatory potential of such fluidity, and the elite anger which it reflected, better than the BDR-BSF clashes in April 2001, at a time when Sheikh Hasina's apparently 'Delhi-friendly' administration was in office in Dhaka. The fighting took place over a four-day period in the third week of the month around the disputed village of Padua[191] which lay on the border between the Indian state of Meghalaya and Bangladesh's north-eastern Sylhet district. The clashes were triggered by the attempts of the BSF, whose troops had occupied the village since 1971, to build a 'footpath' from an Indian camp in the village across a stretch of disputed territory some 300 metres wide to the state of Meghalaya.[192]

BDR officials later stated their local commanders asked the BSF to stop constructing the road in the disputed territory and when they refused, the BDR ordered them to withdraw. When BSF personnel refused to carry out this order, BDR soldiers opened fire and the BSF responded. Over the next few days, both sides used light, medium and heavy machine guns, small-calibre rockets and mortars. The intense exchanges of fire forced around 10,000 Bangladeshi and 1,000 Indian civilians to flee the area; sixteen Indian and three Bangladeshi troops were killed. The press played up nationalist sentiments—Indian media reporting that Bangladeshis had mutilated the bodies of Indian soldiers killed in action and that Indian authorities had refused to hand over the bodies to their families; Bangladeshi media reported Indian forces 'massing troops' along the border, declaring a 'red alert' and digging 'thousands of trenches.' Indian media, briefed by officials, reported that 3,000 BDR and Bangladesh army troops had besieged 'India's' Pyrdiwah outpost from where they took BSF soldiers hostage, killed them 'in cold blood' and mutilated their bodies before handing them back to Indian authorities.[193] Others claimed BDR troops had suddenly attacked the Indian outpost, captured three Indian troops and flown them on an army helicopter to Dhaka. This led to an Indian counterattack and the casualties which followed.[194] The Director-General of the BSF later said 'One of our patrols strayed and got caught by the BDR or Bangladeshi villagers on the other side of the border.'[195] Reports from Dhaka presented a picture heavily laden with hints of Indian heavy-handedness and the outrage felt by local civilians who lynched the BSF soldiers and mutilated their bodies before the BDR was able to retrieve and return these to India.

With parliamentary elections scheduled in a few months, Bangladeshi politicians exploited the conflict to suit their particular purposes. After ordering Bangladeshi troops to withdraw from Padua village to restore the status quo ante a month after the clashes, Sheikh Hasina rang her Indian counterpart, A.B. Vajpayee, to express 'regret' over the death of Indian soldiers. However, she also used the BDR's action to boost her nationalistic credentials by claiming her willingness to stand up to India. The clashes demonstrated the combination of mutual mistrust, resentment and anger simmering under the surface, ready to explode at the earliest opportunity. From the Indian perspective, its 'cautious approach' to the army-backed CTG, and Delhi's decision 'to do business' with General Moeen Uddin Ahmed, especially the very high-profile reception accorded to the Bangladeshi CAS,[196] were premised on the expectation that the General would 'clamp down on anti–India militants using Bangladesh as a safe haven,' and also respond to India's concern over 'illegal immigration.'[197] The generally positive response from Dhaka to these expectations—especially the extradition of a number of northeast Indian insurgents to Indian authorities by Dhaka—may have persuaded some Indian analysts that Dhaka and Delhi were ready for building a 'strategic partnership' to deepen the security collaboration initiated by General Ahmed.[198]

Whatever the success of General Ahmed's visit to India, organisations shaping the policy perspectives of his military power-base appeared to view Delhi in a more sinister light. An intelligence briefing conducted for service officers painted a gloomy picture of the activities of India's premier external intelligence organ, the Research and Analysis Wing (RAW), in Bangladesh. The briefer, turning Indian accusations against Bangladesh on their head, accused RAW of conducting grim 'black' operations in Bangladesh:

Creation of so-called Islamic Militant Outfit: Indian Agencies created so-called Islamic Militants in Bangladesh. They did it basically for two reasons. One, to make Bangladesh as a (sic) Islamic Fundamentalist State. Two, they wanted to counter the leftist ideology groups by creating so called "Islamic Fundamentalist" group.[199]

Create Condition Deteriorate the Law and Order Situation in Bangladesh (sic): Indian Agencies are making all out effort to create condition deteriorating law and order situation in Bangladesh. RAW is patronizing the extremist groups like JMB, HUJI etc.[200]

The fact that China had displaced India as Bangladesh's foremost business partner for the first time since 1989 troubled others who saw the 'military-backed CTG' as Delhi's 'perfect partner to deal with,' as it 'was and remains India's best bet in pushing for greater Indian presence on Bangladeshi soil.'[201] Indian analysts pointed out that over the first eighteen months of the CTG's tenure, India had gone out of its way to meet Bangladesh's expectations but Delhi's own expectations were far from being fulfilled by Dhaka. One MOD-sponsored analyst asked: 'the moot question is while the core Bangladeshi concerns are being met, albeit belatedly, what happens to India's core concerns? Notwithstanding the assurances from the Bangladeshi side, there is nothing to indicate that Indian security concerns, which have plagued bilateral ties for decades, are being addressed satisfactorily.'[202] Another analyst, following a similar argument to its logical conclusion, recommended: 'India has to approach Dhaka with much more aggressiveness and a greater sense of urgency. Maybe it is time for India to change its strategy. What India requires is a closer look at what other tools of international relations India can use to get Dhaka to the negotiating table. If the carrots do not work, is it time to look for a stick?'[203]

There was no evidence to suggest that such hegemonic discourse shaping Indian policy has been effective in establishing Bangladeshi perspectives congruent with Indian interests. Indeed, it is this that has encouraged the crystallisation in Bangladesh of the idea of India as the national 'other.' According to Dhaka's premier intelligence agency, Delhi has deployed its powerful external intelligence organ, RAW, to pursue objectives utterly subversive of Bangladesh's sovereignty, independence and integrity: 'In this regard the most important target of RAW is to render Bangladesh under Indian subjugation to make it dependent on Indian favour in every aspects (sic) beginning from the formation of the government and administration to politics, economics and defence policy making matters.'[204] The juxtaposition of these extreme views at the heart of the two establishments suggests it will take a lot of effort to redress mutual misperceptions. The fact that a complex political-security dynamic shaped and was in turn shaped by this malignant mix demonstrated the volatility of trans-frontier ties and the need for sophisticated diplomacy on both sides to manage the inevitable fluidity in relations. As Bangladesh approached another transition to a representative order after an authoritarian interregnum, there were indications of a recognition of India's importance to its future stability and prosperity, and hints of a shared anxiety to build on this recognition with policy alternatives on both sides of the border.[205]

EPILOGUE

A BLOOD-SOAKED RESTORATION

The Awami League's overwhelming victory in the parliamentary elections held on 29 December 2008, the scale of which surprised even some of Sheikh Hasina's senior aides,[1] and the reciprocal diminution of the BNP's legislative prowess, may have given the rulers a sense of invincibility. Although Awami League leaders repeatedly spoke about their intention to forge a national consensus on key issues by offering parliamentary posts to the BNP, the League's student wing mounted a traditional assault on university campuses, chasing out their counterparts from the BNP and its coalition partners. Not surprisingly, the BNP did not accept the Awami League's legislative sweeteners and, in fact, delayed the acceptance of election results and its MPs took their oaths of office several days after MPs from the Awami League-led coalition had done so. Although Khaleda Zia eventually led her colleagues to the assembly, she revived the practice of walking out of parliamentary sessions early on.[2]

The political parties had pledged, as part of the registration process for the December 2008 polls, to end all links to student wings and trades union affiliated with them. However, as soon as the Awami League's victory became clear, activists of the Chhatra League began raiding major state-funded university and college campuses, taking over halls of residence, evicting anyone unwilling to take orders, and dictating who could or could not enjoy the fruits of subsidised food and board. The campaign became so fraught that in Jahangirnagar, just outside the capital, factions of the Awami League's student wing engaged in internecine bloodshed, forcing the Awami League to declare at least one faction 'illegitimate.'

A more serious clash erupted at the campus of Rajshahi University in north-western Bangladesh. There, armed members of the Chhatra League engaged in combat similarly equipped activists of the Islami Chhatra Shibir, affiliated to the Jamaat-e-Islami, in mid-March 2009, killing the leader of the local chapter of the ICS, and only then forcing the authorities to shut the university down indefinitely. Representative restoration was now complete. The Awami League's decision to implement one of its campaign pledges—to bring to trial 'war criminals' accused of committing 'war crimes' during Bangladesh's war of independence—added fuel to right-wing ire, raising spectres of further disruptive divisions caused by ancient animus being dredged up from the country's troubled history.

But these incidents paled into insignificance when compared with the bloody mutiny by paramilitary soldiers of the Bangladesh Rifles (BDR) border guards in late February 2009. The BDR, a 67,000–man force organised into 'sectors' with specific areas of operational responsibility along the country's land borders, had, since 2002, been revamped, armed and trained into over forty light-infantry battalions. Although administratively the BDR came under the Home Ministry, it had historically been commanded by officers seconded from the army on tours lasting from three to four years. Since the reforms, BDR units received almost as many officers as were on the organisational table of the army's infantry battalions, and many of these officers were selected for deputation on the basis of professional merit. BDR soldiers themselves, trained at BDR schools of instruction, rose to the rank of Deputy Assistant Directors (DADs), comparable to Warrant Officers, but would not be given commissions.

Since the late 1970s, the BDR had celebrated 'BDR week,' its foundation anniversary, in the last week of February, with a series of events at its Peelkhana headquarters in Dhaka's city centre. Thousands of soldiers and hundreds of officers converged on Peelkhana during the festive week of parades, conferences, sports and professional competitions, award-giving ceremonies, cultural events, banquets, a spectacular nocturnal tattoo, and the Director-General's *Durbar*, at which rank-and-file soldiers raised their grievances directly with the commanding General in the presence of the force's senior officers at the spacious Durbar Hall. On 24 February 2009, Prime Minister Sheikh Hasina inaugurated the Week, delivering an address full of praise for the BDR's contributions to the nation in times of war and peace, and gave awards for gallantry to several soldiers in recognition of meritorious service. The following morning, as the Director General, Major General Shakil Ahmed, presided over the annual Durbar, a dispute broke out between troops and their commanders. As officers tried to subdue agitated soldiers, shots were fired and suddenly, the BDR was in mutiny.[3]

Judging by what some mutineers told the local and international media within the first few hours of killing their commanders, they had three sets of grievances: they wanted a raised pay-structure because they considered their compensation package iniquitous compared to that given to army counterparts—including the latter's opportunity to participate in lucrative UN peacekeeping missions from which they were excluded; they wanted army officers to be replaced with either their own or civilian officials because the officers allegedly did not treat them well; and they wanted 'justice' for many of their senior commanders who, allegedly, had embezzled large sums from 'Operation Dal Bhat,' an assignment in which the BDR had been ordered by the Caretaker Government in 2008 to set up a chain of retail stores and sell essential foodstuff at low prices. In short, corruption and injustice were their key grievances.[4]

Within hours, fifty-seven officers, ranging from the Director General and his Deputy, to all the sector commanders, senior staff officers and aides, were dead.[5] Mutineers took over the sprawling Peelkhana complex, broke open armouries and looted arms and ammunition, took members of the officers' families hostage, locking up women and children in the Quarter-Guard, ransacked officers' quarters, killed the Director General's wife and his guests—a retired officer and his wife—and others. There were reports of rape too.[6] Civilians travelling along busy thoroughfares just outside Peelkhana scattered as bursts of automatic fire rang out. Several were killed and others wounded. Soon, rebel soldiers brought out light- and medium machine-guns and mortars, deploying them at tactically commanding locations near the perimeter wall and the various gates which opened onto a by now agitated and anxious city. The Director General had called up Hasina as soon as mutineers had opened fire; other senior BDR officers similarly called their fellows in the army headquarters. The army ordered motorised units to move towards Peelkhana.

However, the Prime Minister determined that wider national interests demanded a 'political,' i.e. non-military, resolution of the problem. She ordered the military to remain beyond visual range of the rebels and invited their leaders to explain their demands personally. A fourteen-strong delegation led by a DAD visited the Prime Minister's official residence and laid out their demands. She announced a general amnesty for the rebels and was promised that they would surrender their arms and release all hostages. An official delegation led by the Home Minister visited Peelkhana, negotiating with the mutineers for several hours, receiving a few arms surrendered as a token of sincerity, and retrieving a number of officers, and their families early the following morning. When on the following day it became clear that the rebels would not surrender and pressure from the army grew, Hasina allowed the deployment of several tanks and assault units close to Peelkhana. She then issued a warning to the mutineers: either surrender and release surviving hostages, or face an army assault.

After nearly thirty-three hours had elapsed from the outbreak of violence, several hundred BDR troops still in Peelkhana surrendered to police and other law enforcement agencies. It was then that the army was allowed to go in to look for its officers and discovered that thousands of rebellious BDR men had escaped, leaving behind charred and putrefying bodies of dead officers in well-designed mass graves, in ponds within Peelkhana's sylvan precincts, and in sewers leading out of the headquarters. Many of the bodies had been mutilated and some had their eyes gouged out. It took several days before all the bodies had been found and identified. Once the attackers' brutality and the scale of their violence had become clear, the popular mood shifted. Until now, rebels speaking to TV stations and to the press had elicited public sympathy with allegations of the army officers' rough treatment of BDR personnel, unequal pay and allowances BDR rank-and-file received, and corruption among officers they sought to reveal. Media coverage initially sounded sympathetic to the mutineers. This now changed.

If the need for introspection was less than obvious, it became clear when Prime Minister Hasina held her own durbar with army officers in the Dhaka cantonment. With a number of survivors from the Peelkhana massacre present in their ranks, the officers were brutally frank with their political mistress. They demanded to know why she had not acted when the late Director General of the BDR had called her and informed her of the mutiny, why she had adopted a slow 'political' approach and negotiated with the rebels while they were killing serving army officers, why her fellow parliamentarians had repeatedly made vituperative comments about army officers in speeches in the assembly, and why she had allowed so many of the army's brightest officers to die so brutally without taking prompt action. One survivor asked why her government had allowed thousands of mutineers to flee the scene of their grisly crime unchallenged while just over a hundred army officers were not allowed to leave Peelkhana alive. For hours she patiently listened to the officers' anguished outbursts while taking note of their specific suggestions.[7] It was an unprecedented meeting in many ways.

Following this encounter, Hasina issued several orders, reversing earlier ones: the high-level official inquiry team headed by the Home Minister was dissolved; instead, a retired senior official would head a bureaucratic team manned by senior police, military, and administrative officials, including the newly-appointed Director General of the BDR. The amnesty she had announced on the first day of the mutiny would not apply to BDR personnel found guilty of murder, arson, rape and other crimes. Special tribunals would be established and appropriate laws enacted to try arrested mutineers. And the army would be deployed 'in aid of civil power' to mount 'Operation Rebel Hunt' in search of absconding rebels. The police filed cases against several named ring-leaders and a thousand anonymous mutineers. The Criminal Investigation Department (CID) mounted a forensic inquiry to collect evidence for the trial of suspected rebels while the army, too, began its own investigations under a senior General. The Chief of the Army Staff (CAS), who often met the Prime Minister in the mutiny's wake, reassured the press that the army remained 'subservient to the government.' This message was repeated by a senior military aide to Hasina in a TV broadcast. However, national and foreign analyses noted the rebellion's extremely disruptive effects on the administration.[8]

Conspiracy theories

Hasina noted threats to her own person as well as to her government and Bangladesh's democracy. Both she and her colleagues and political rivals spoke of conspiracies. Analyses and commentary, liberally laced with rumours and conjectures, raised questions about who the 'real conspirators' were. On this, as on most political issues, Bangladeshis were divided. The most elaborate conspiracy theory, presented as the gleanings from 'over a dozen of reliable sources,' claimed that 'a team of twenty-five trained foreign commandos entered Bangladesh illegally from India through various bordering areas on or within January 11, 2009. They were received and sheltered in Dhaka by individuals working under cover as diplomats.' These men, and apparently one woman, linked up with 'a small group of 10–12 BDR members' for the strike. The attack, originally scheduled for 24 February 2009, was delayed so as to avoid harming the Prime Minister and her entourage, who would be in Peelkhana on that day.

The 'final coordination and reconnaissance were done that day by some guests who attended the parade, masquerading as VIPs.' To finalise the plans, 'at about 10.30 pm, on February 24, a segment of the foreign killing squad and over twenty-five BDR soldiers—plus three young, leading politicians of the country—met in a briefing in one of suburban Dhaka residences. The precise timing of the operation and the responsibilities of each small group were decided in that meeting.'[9] This account provided other details of the exact sequence of the operation which unfolded at about 9.30am the following morning and ended with the flight of the plotters and rebels around thirty-three hours later. If this elaborate account hinted at India as the source of the trouble, Islamist politicians were more forthright. Indian media quoted a leader of Bangladesh Jamaat-e-Islami as saying that 'The killing mission was executed from Indian intelligence headquarters.' Proof was provided, according to this politician, by the fact that 'Indian media ran the news of the carnage citing Indian intelligence sources' before local Bangladeshi television channels did.[10] Khaleda Zia and her colleagues also criticised the government's handling of the crisis, claiming to have evidence of a deep-seated conspiracy, although not the one Prime Minister Hasina and her cabinet colleagues had referred to in their speeches.

The Indian media for their part struck in a totally different direction early on. The TV channel CNN-IBN and dailies like the *Times of India* and the *Indian Express* quoted official and intelligence sources citing detained BDR mutineers who had reportedly 'confessed' their crimes. According to these Indian outlets, these men told their interrogators that right-wing groups working with Pakistan's Inter Service Intelligence Directorate (ISI) and a senior BNP parliamentarian serving as an adviser to Khaleda Zia had instigated the mutiny and invested large sums of money in the enterprise.[11] This school claimed that during Khaleda Zia's second term in office in 2001–06, a large number of Islamists had joined state bureaucracies including paramilitary and armed services, and so 'There is every possibility that the BDR mutiny in Dhaka was backed by "pro-Islam" army officers.'[12] A somewhat more extreme and implausible Indian analysis inferred that 'The killings were carried out at the order of Riyadh, with adequate support from London, and put in place by a global terrorist network which includes a number of other players, such as the renegades in the Pakistani ISI, Wahhabi jihadis, and the foot soldiers of the British MI6–ISI–Saudi–protected international drug and gunrunner, Dawood Ibrahim.'[13]

Despite the passions aroused first by the mutineers' complaints of unredressed grievances and, then, by images of their savagery, many Bangladeshis—ever sensitive to possible slights to their sovereignty and independence—were deeply troubled by reports of Indian reaction to the mutiny. With the BDR's ability to maintain security on the Bangladeshi side of the border compromised by short-lived uprisings at several frontier towns as well as at the headquarters, Indian border security forces understandably took measures to prevent any infiltrations. However, the fact that the Indian Air Force had alerted its heavy and medium air transport units to prepare for probable operations in Bangladesh from Jorhat and Kalaikunda air bases close to the border caused anxiety in Dhaka. Over a thousand Indian paratroopers were flown from Agra to Kalaikunda 'to deal with any contingency which might arise due to the internal turmoil in Bangladesh,'[14] reminding the latter that India would act swiftly and violently to stabilise Bangladesh if Bangladeshis failed to do so themselves. The suggestion by a senior Indian Air Force officer that these preparations had been taken in hand for a 'humanitarian intervention inside Bangladesh' by the Indian armed forces did not allay nationalist fears among the putative beneficiaries of such stabilising operations.[15]

So, while Bangladeshis mourned their loss, buried their dead, grappled with the vexing flow of information emerging from the once-placid verdant island of bird-song in the centre of their frantically-paced capital city, and awaited the outcome of three separate inquiries into the bloodbath, questions hung in the air: why had grievances over pay and discrimination led to the sudden massacre of so many army officers—with mutilation and rape mixed in? How had the rebels managed to organise the initial attacks—well-timed and precisely located at the Durbar Hall where the BDR's top leadership could be decapitated within minutes just this once at an once-a-year-only event? What were Bangladesh's various security and counter-intelligence bodies doing while the attacks were being planned? Just who was behind this devastating assault on the state? How deeply into the system did their grasp reach? And, where could the next blow fall? A stream of gory media reports, a perplexing lack of clarity, popular mood swings and uncertainty raised the anxiety level in an otherwise anxious populace.

Although few answers were immediately forthcoming, several issues appeared to have become clearer than they had been before: national security, social civility, equity and a shared sense of justice were inextricably intertwined; and governance and service-delivery had suffered grievously while the political elite wrangled in internecine feuds, fragmenting the polity, deepening the divisive polarisation which rendered consensus on even fundamental issues improbable, fracturing any residual societal cohesion and increasing fragility. Now, a price had to be paid, mostly by those who had little control over their circumstances. Civil-military relations were not an esoteric category to be confined to academic and intellectual exercises—they were integral to intra-state dynamics and had to be managed well. Bangladeshis had become victims of the consequences of their own myriad follies—perhaps none more devastating than the elite's concentration on perennial and ritualistic power-politics as an instrument of acquisition by graft and a failure to grasp the acute urgency of elemental threats which challenged their long-term collective survival.

Damoclean swords

Climate change

The most urgently apparent of Bangladesh's long-term challenges stems from its geography in the context of changes to global climate. More than 40 per cent of Bangladesh's 'land area is within ten metres above sea level.'[16] In 2007, the UN body responsible for examining climate change issues, the Intergovernmental Panel on Climate Change (IPCC), reported Bangladesh's prominence among countries and regions most at risk from the danger of sea levels rising by 'tens of centimetres this century.'[17] The data for Bangladesh underscored the convergence of several troubling trends: in 1990–2000, the population living on land 0–10 metres above sea level grew at more than twice the national population growth rate; in

2007, the population in this zone stood at 62,524,000, or 46 per cent of the total.[18] Parallel to the threat from rising seas came news of Himalayan glaciers drying out. Since much of the Bengal Delta's water cycle relied on glacier melt-water charging the three major river systems with their hundreds of tributaries and distributaries carrying perennial flows with seasonal variations, the loss of such flows posed a severe threat to the delta's ecology.

The loss of fresh water flows from the north, compounded by upper-riparian withdrawals at Farakka in India, reduced the pressure at the estuaries of the Gangetic river system. This increased the northward intrusion of saline water from the Bay of Bengal, endangering the fresh-water biological cycles across western Bangladesh. Rising sea levels threatened to expand the scale of this southern threat even further. A consequent loss of agricultural productivity has been apparent for some-time. For instance, national and UN data suggest that salinity-affected land expanded from 1.5 million hectares in 1973 to 2.5 million hectares in 1997, with losses exceeding an estimated 3 million hectares by the end of 2007. Of the thirty-seven million people living in Bangladesh's twelve coastal districts, twenty million had already been affected by spreading saline intrusions.[19] The impact of rising salinity, however, was no longer restricted to coastal districts; about 200km north of the coast in Magura district, 72 per cent of all arable land showed signs of 'higher-than-acceptable' levels of soil salinity. Between 1948 and 2007, salinity in the rivers of the southern districts of Khulna, Bagerhat, Satkhira, Borguna, Pirojpur and Patuakhali had risen by 45 per cent.[20]

Changes to the water cycle, convergence of pressures from the north and south melding a reduction in fresh waterfowls and an increase in saline intrusions, damage done to cropland, vegetation and fisheries by the latter, and the risks facing subsurface aquifers added up to a grim challenge. Although the CTG, environmental NGOs and several donor countries acted to address some of these issues at a conference in London in 2008, there were no indications that any of the parties grasped the elemental nature of the threats facing Bangladesh or were prepared to take meaningful steps to meet these.[21] The Bangladeshi response to the threat appeared limited to *pro forma* enunciations of what had been done to address vulnerability to 'routine' natural disasters such as floods, storms, and storm surges from the Bay of Bengal. The government noted the investment of over $10 billion over thirty-five years 'to make the country less vulnerable to natural disasters.'[22] These involved building and repairing flood management schemes, coastal polders and river embankments, cyclone- and flood shelters, building major roads and highways on embankments higher than flood levels, and the establishment of a disaster warning system. Building on the National Adaptation Programme of Action issued in 2005, the CTG framed a six–point 'Climate Change Action Plan' in 2008 focusing on:

- Food security, social protection and health
- Comprehensive disaster management
- Infrastructure development and protection
- Research and knowledge management
- Mitigation and low-carbon development, and
- Capacity building and institutional strengthening[23]

The government noted that 'in the worst case scenario, unless existing coastal polders are strengthened and new ones built, sea level rise could result in the displacement of millions of people—'environmental refugees'—from coastal regions, and have huge adverse impacts on the livelihoods and long-term health of a large proportion of the population.'[24] The donor community, perhaps as sensitive to the scale of the impending crisis, noted that 'The impact of higher temperatures, more variable precipitation, more extreme weather events, and sea level rise are already felt in Bangladesh and will continue to intensify.'[25] Climate change would adversely affect Bangladesh in many areas—water resources, agriculture and food security, ecosystems and biodiversity, human health and coastal zones in particular. Predicted rainfall increases in the summer would worsen flooding; crop yields would fall by up to 30 per cent, creating 'a very high risk of hunger'; increased temperatures melting Himalayan glaciers would contribute to increased flooding, erosion, and mudslides during the wet season. Over the longer term, the disappearance of glaciers feeding the major river systems would threaten the delta's ecosystem in ways not fully understood. The impact on agriculture, which accounts for almost 20 per cent of the GDP and 65 per cent of the labour force, would be devastating for overall growth, the trade balance, and the levels of poverty and malnutrition.[26] The loss of coastal and low-lying land—which encompasses most agricultural areas—and the resulting destitution of tens of millions of already penurious people would trigger a 'boat people crisis' of such proportions which the world may not have witnessed.[27] And yet, judging by their action, neither Bangladesh's leaders nor their allies abroad appear to have woken up to the scope and scale of this impending crisis, and its consequences.

The poisoning of the wells

While climate change threatens Bangladesh's hydro-ecology on a macro level, millions of its people are already facing the affliction of arsenicosis caused by long-term arsenic poisoning in small doses, because of the quality of their drinking water. The result for many would be skin cancer, cancer of the bladder, kidney and lung, neurological effects, cardiovascular and pulmonary diseases, and diseases of blood vessels in the legs and feet. At best, victims can hope to get away with just hardening of patches on the palm and soles of feet, and changes in skin colour. Levels of arsenic in the water are so high across Bangladesh that the WHO has described it as 'the largest mass poisoning of a population in history.'[28] A 1997–8 study led by epidemiologist Allan Smith, a professor at the University of California, Berkeley, reported that between thirty-five million and seventy-seven million Bangladeshis faced exposure of arsenic in their drinking water. By late 2000, 'at least 100,000 cases of debilitating skin lesions' had already occurred.[29]

Ironically, this is the result of an otherwise successful effort to provide 'safe drinking water' to Bangladeshis. In the early 1960s, diarrhoea spread by contaminated water supplies killed over 100,000 children under five every year.[30] In the following three decades, nearly 7.5 million small tube-wells topped with metallic hand-pumps tapping into ground water at a depth of less than 200 metres were installed across the country by the Department of Public Health Engineering (DPHE). In 1970, only two percent of the population lived within 100 yards from a tube-well; by 1990, over 95 per cent did.[31] Standard water testing procedures did not include checking for arsenic contamination since that was not considered a problem in water supplies.[32] Arsenic in contaminated ground water leaching from rocks at the base of sub-surface aquifers was first confirmed in Bangladesh in 1993, a decade after over 200,000 cases of arsenic poisoning were recorded in neighbouring West Bengal.[33] In 1998, a British Geological Survey (BGS) study of tube-wells in sixty-one of the country's sixty-four districts found that 46 per cent carried arsenic above 0.010 milligrams per litre (mg/L) and 27 per cent, above 0.050 mg/L. This compared to the WHO's acceptable level of arsenic in drinking water for Bangladeshis at 0.05 mg/L and for Europeans and North Americans at 0.01 mg/L.[34] A second BGS survey in 2001 estimated that more than fifty million Bangladeshis drank arsenic-contaminated water; a local estimate in mid-2008 was closer to a hundred million.[35]

Despite much anxiety expressed by local and international scientific and public health communities since the late 1990s, national authorities appeared unable to acknowledge the consequences of what had for decades been state policy—providing 'safe' drinking water by installing tube-wells. In 2000–2008, more than 100,000 new, alternate, water points including shallow tube-wells, dug wells, rain water collectors and pond sand filters were installed, but only gradually.[36] Only in 2004 did the government issue a National Policy for Arsenic Mitigation which laid down procedures for identifying contaminated tube-wells, marking them with red paint and prohibiting their use. While this worked in so far as identification and marking went, providing alternate sources of safe drinking water proved less successful. The government's recommendation that people use 'clean' surface water for drinking was described by some scientists as 'risky.'[37] Also, by 2008, only half of the country's current stock of ten million tube-wells had been tested.[38] Fortunately, the cost of accurate detection of arsenic contamination had fallen and the Sono filter, invented in 2006, and capable of being locally manufactured at affordable costs, made it possible to decontaminate arsenic-tainted water at household level.[39] The DPHE, working with UNICEF, began pilot projects of delivering filtration kits in 2008, but without official policy changes and funding, this would be unlikely to deliver Bangladeshis safe drinking water on a national scale, and save them from mass poisoning.

By late 2008, it became clear that arsenic had infiltrated large elements of the animal- and human food chains across Bangladesh. Field surveys conducted by Japanese, British and local scientists showed that in the worst affected areas, arsenic appeared in water, soil, plants and 'all types of crops.'[40] In south-western districts, samples of the rain-fed *aman* and irrigated *boro* rice crops, ninety-four types of vegetables and fifty varieties of legumes and spices were found to be tainted with arsenic. Boro rice contamination was higher presumably because this variety relied on irrigation with arsenic-tainted ground-water. The districts of Faridpur, Satkhira, Chuadanga and Meherpur showed particularly high concentrations. The scientists noted that 'Daily consumption of rice with a total arsenic level of 0.08 microgrammes per gramme of rice would be equivalent to a drinking-water arsenic level of 10mg/L of water.'[41] Since rice constitutes about 70 per cent of the average calorie intake for Bangladeshis, the danger posed by food-chain contamination is substantial. Grappling with this scale of public-health crisis could challenge the government of any country.

Noah's capsizing arc

If there is one challenge which threatens Bangladesh in existential terms even if all its other demons are purged; that is, the phenomenon of an exploding population tied to a small deltaic flood-plain. In 1971, the population stood at 68 million; by 2000, it had nearly doubled to 131 million.[42] Six years later, it reached 144.3 million;[43] in 2008, it surpassed 153 million.[44] If the trend persists, in 2025, Bangladesh would be home to a population of between 182.2 million and 205.4 million.[45] If nothing was done to change direction, by 2035, Bangladesh's population would rise to at least 200 million and, by 2050, to 240 million.[46] With its population density of 1,007 persons per sq. km in 2005 already one of the highest in the world,[47] how well Bangladesh, one of the world's poorest countries, and 'softest' states,[48] would cope with the stresses generated by that level of demographic density, must be a key question to be addressed by its leaders and their allies abroad. Successive governments have included 'family planning,' a code for population control measures, in their policy programmes, but few leaders have taken any substantive steps to reduce Bangladesh's explosive demographic growth.

The one exception was General Ziaur Rahman, a military leader who took charge in late 1975 and kept control before being assassinated in May 1981. In 1976, Zia promulgated a comprehensive family planning programme to address what he considered 'the most pressing concern for the nation.'[49] He invited donors and NGOs to help implement the programme.[50] This collaboration laid a strong foundation for reducing the population growth rate. In the mid-1980s, approximately a decade after Zia launched his initiative, 25 per cent of women of child-bearing age, between fifteen and forty-nine, were using contraceptives. Efforts by donors, NGOs, and committed local field workers raised the use of contraceptives to 54 per cent by 2000.[51] Also, steady if slow development of public health facilities and general improvements contributed to an increase in life expectancy from 44.2 years in 1970 to 61.2 years in 2000.[52] At the same time, diverse pressures on the rural economy and a relative preponderance of investment in the main cities drove a process of urbanisation so that between 1970 and 2000, the share of the country's population living in urban areas grew from 11 to 23 per cent. The capital and the main port city saw dramatic increases; the population of Dhaka grew from 1.5 million to 10.2 million and Chittagong's, from 0.7 million to 3.3 million,[53] raising demands for basic services on municipal, regional and national administrations which they often could not meet.

A notable aspect of Bangladesh's demographic challenge is a so-called 'youth bulge,' offering an indication of the scale of socio-economic, and possibly political, pressures population issues will place on any government in Dhaka. Since independence, the ratio of people under fifteen to the total population has been decreasing, but because of the large base and steady growth of the absolute populace size, the under-fifteen cohort is likely to expand for some years yet. In 1970, this group stood at 45 per cent of the total population, falling to 39 per cent in 2000, and 37 per cent in 2005—compared to 28 per cent for Asia as a whole.[54] Despite the decrease in relative terms, the under-fifteen segment has continued to grow in numbers—from around thirty million in 1970 to fifty-six million in 2005; it is projected to grow to fifty-eight million in 2020.[55] With such a large body of fecund youths coming into the fertility cycle, Bangladesh's demographic problems are likely to haunt the country for decades to come.

So, a large population base, rapid growth, dependence on agriculture as a primary source of employment, and the steady shrinkage of arable land have combined to create enormous socio-economic pressures. In 1980–2005, per capita arable land declined from 0.12 hectares to 0.06 hectares; it is projected to decrease by another third in 2005–2030,[56] falling to possibly 0.04 hectares in 2025 when the population to land imbalance will become even more acute and possibly unsustainable.[57] To complicate matters, the availability of renewable water per capita has also fallen rapidly since the 1970s. In 1975, per capita renewable water supply stood at 16,543.80 cubic metres (cu.m); by 2000, it had been nearly halved to 8,778.44 cu.m; in 2005, it stood at 8,536.35 cu.m. If nothing changes, per capita renewable water supply could fall to just 5,893.81 cu.m,[58] around a third of the 1975 figure, in 2025. Over the longer term, Bangladesh's 'total fertility rate,' the number of children a woman would be expected to bear over her lifetime, is projected to fall to 1.85 in 2045–2050, but the high base rate and a slow progression mean that in 2050, Bangladesh's population could well rise to 254.59 million.[59]

Even ignoring the challenges posed by arsenic contamination or, indeed, the quality of governance, the combination of declining per capita arable land and renewable water supply on the one hand, and growing demands from a rapidly rising population on the other, could generate tensions which would threaten the fabric of social order. So, without being melodramatic it is possible to be pessimistic about Bangladesh's long-term prospects. If it were to overcome its apparently insuperable odds, there would be hope for South Asia and for the planet generally. If, however, it receives no help and succumbs to its myriad afflictions, it could presumably launch millions of people to deserting their sinking ship in a massive—and possibly even more horrendous—re-enactment of the flight of the refugees in 1971. However, given the fence along the border this time round, the desperation of the multitudes trying to escape the grim reality of their unbearable lives, this alternative conjures up possibilities which would not bear thinking about.

NOTES

PREFACE

1. S. Mahmud Ali, *Nation-building and the Nature of Conflict in South Asia*, unpublished Ph.D. dissertation, King's College, London, 1992, pp. 40–41.
2. Ali, *US-China Cold War Collaboration, 1971–1989*, New York: Routledge, 2005, ch. 3.
3. Ali, 1992, pp. 15–34.
4. Ali, *Cold War in the High Himalayas*, New York: St. Martin's Press, 1999.
5. Kissinger in *Memorandum of Conversation: New Delhi Advisers Meeting*, the White House, 31 July 1969; *ibid: Lahore Advisers Meeting*, the White House, 1 August 1969.
6. Directorate of Intelligence, *India/Pakistan*, TDCS-314/12990–71, Washington, CIA, 7 December 1971. For an exposition on Sino-US convergence against the Indo-Soviet alignment over Bangladesh, see Huang Hua, Kissinger, *Memorandum of Conversation*, New York City, the White House, 10 December 1971.

1. THE PAST AS PROLOGUE

1. Percival Spear, *the Oxford History of Modern India, 1740–1947*, Oxford: Oxford University Press (OUP), 1965, pp. 24–5; Ramakrishna Mukerjee, 'The Rise and Fall of the East India Company', *Monthly Review, 1974*, p. 267.
2. Literally gentlefolk, high-born nobility or gentry, usually with some foreign ancestry and owning property; a tiny but influential minority among Bengal's Muslims. *Atraf*, in contrast, comprised indigenous Bengali individuals who had no foreign ancestry and often belonged to the lower tiers of the Hindu caste hierarchy before being converted to Islam or having been descended from such converts. They comprised the bulk of eastern Bengal's tenant farmers and craftsmen. They were thought to lack what was considered social respectability. Tazeen Murshid, *The Sacred and the Secular: Bengal Muslim Discourses 1871–1977*, Calcutta: OUP, 1995, pp. 36–43.

349

3. The photographer Fritz Kapp captured many scenes of the visit; some of his photographs illustrated a number of contemporary publications reporting Curzon's progress.

4. Residual Bengal would have 42 million Hindus and 9 million Muslims; Eastern Bengal & Assam would be home to 18 million Muslims and 12 million Hindus.

5. S.A.T. Rowlatt et al., *Report of Committee Appointed to Investigate Revolutionary Conspiracies in India*, London: India Office, para.168; Political Department, *Memorandum on the History of Terrorism in Bengal, 1905–1933*, Calcutta: Government of Bengal, 1933, West Bengal State Archives.

6. Estimates of famine-related deaths vary but the lowest count stands at 1.5 million. Chris Williams, *The Things We Forgot to Remember: The Bengal Famine*, Milton Keynes: Open University, 7 January 2008.

7. K Hill, W Seltzer, J Leaning, SJ Malik, SS Russell, *The Demographic Impact of Partition: Bengal in 1947*, Cambridge: Harvard University Asia Centre, 2004, p. 3

8. Ibid. pp. 13–14.

9. Communal violence had bloodied Calcutta, the western districts of East Bengal with large Hindu communities, and the Noakhali district in the south-east, but in much of the rest of eastern Bengal, trouble had been limited.

10. Lawrence Ziring, *Bangladesh From Mujib to Ershad: An Interpretive Study*, Dhaka: University Press Limited (UPL), 1994, pp. 4–7.

11. Ali, 1992, pp. 40–1

12. Mijarul Quayes, *The Westphalian State in South Asia and Future Directions*, Dhaka: Bangladesh Institute of Peace and Security Studies, February 2008.

13. H.S. Suhrawardy to Liaquat Ali Khan, Calcutta, 11 June 1948, and 8 July 1948; Khan to Suhrawardy, Karachi, 13 July 1948.

14. On the nature and consequences of these changes, see Hamza Alavi, 'India and the Colonial Mode of Production' in John Saville and Ralph Miliband (eds.) *Socialist Register 1975*, London, 1975, pp. 160–97; Partha Chatterjee, 'The Colonial State and Peasant Resistance in Bengal, 1920–1947' in *Past and Present*, No. 110, February 1986, pp. 169–204; H. Bernstein, 'Production and Producers' in B. Crow and M. Thorpe (eds.), *Survival and Change in the Third World*, Oxford: Polity Press, 1988; C.H. Philpin and T.H. Ashton, Eds., *Agrarian Class Structure and the Economic Development of Pre-Industrial Societies*, Cambridge: Cambridge University Press, 1988. For an account of the rise of the *Jotedar* intermediary class and its mutation into the most influential rural *gushthi* (clan) group in rural East Bengal/Bangladesh, see Brigitta Boda, *In Pursuit of Power: Local Elites and Union-Level Governance in Rural*

Northwestern Bangladesh, Dhaka: Care Bangladesh, August 2002, especially pp. 4, 6–7, 9–13; Sirajul Islam, 'Social Stratification', *Banglapaedia*, Dhaka, 2006.

15. Ziring, op cit.
16. Keith Callard, *Pakistan: A Political Study*, London: Allen & Unwin, 1957, p. 24.
17. Ziring, p. 39.
18. Bhashani at a *Krishak Samity* (peasants' association) rally, 4 May 1958.
19. The criteria defining national security states are in Jack Nelson-Pallmeyer, *Brave New World Order*, New York: Orbis Books, 1992; and Michael Hogan, *A Cross of Iron: Harry S. Truman and the Origins of the National Security State*, New York: Cambridge University Press, 1998.
20. Hamza Alavi, 'Authoritarianism and Legitimation of State Power in Pakistan' in Subrata Mitra (ed.), *The Post-Colonial State in South Asia*, New York: Harvester Wheatsheaf, 1990; Richard Merritt, 'The Fragile Unity of Pakistan' in James Rosenau, Ed., *Linkage Politics: Essays on the Convergence of National and International Systems*, New York: the Free Press, 1969; Sumit Ganguly, *Conflict Unending: India-Pakistan Tensions since 1947*, London: Frank Cass, 2007, pp. 31–50; Ashok Kapur, *Pakistan in Crisis: The Ayub Khan Era, 1958–69*, New York: Routledge, 1991, pp. 68–72.
21. Lt. General Gul Hassan Khan, Chief of the General Staff during General Yahya Khan's rule, would later write, 'By 1969, the Sheikh (Mujibur Rahman) had become synonymous with all that the Six Points stood for. These were endorsed by his party enthusiastically, and no less heartily, though surreptitiously, by the Hindu minority in East Pakistan, with the tacit, yet warm, approval of India…The people of East Pakistan harboured many grievances against their fellow citizens in the West Wing…There was an element of truth in these accusations, but no one had apprised them that development in the West was not as considerable as they were led to believe. The local Hindus and the Indian propaganda had brainwashed the people of the East Wing effectively.' Khan, *Memoirs*, Karachi: OUP, p. 244.
22. 'A group of scholars in Vienna', 'Why Bangladesh', in Government of India (GOI), *Bangladesh Documents*, New Delhi: Ministry of External Affairs, 1971, pp. 15–22.
23. GOI, ibid. pp. 19–21.
24. Hasan Zaheer, *The Separation of East Pakistan*, Karachi: OUP, 1994, p. 189.
25. Hasan Gardezi and Jamil Rashid (eds.), *Pakistan: The Unstable State*, Lahore: Vanguard Books, 1983, pp. 178–9.
26. Sheikh Mujibur Rahman, *Amader Banchar Dabi: 6–dafa Karmashuchi* (Our Demand for Survival: 6–point Programme), Dhaka: Office of the President of the Awami League, 18 March 1966.

27. Ibid.

28. Ibid.

29. Shortly after President Richard Nixon arrived at the White House, his Assistant for National Security Affairs, Henry Kissinger, wrote that most people in East Pakistan 'have long felt the government has discriminated in favor of West Pakistan. Recent dissatisfaction has given new impetus to the separatist movement, and almost all opposition politicians advocate some degree of autonomy.' Kissinger to Nixon, *Ayub Khan's Situation*, the White House, 27 January 1969, p. 1.

30. Ibid. p. 2.

31. Ambassador Oehlert to Secretary of State, Rawalpindi, telegram-944, 29 January 1969.

32. Directorate of Intelligence (DOI), *The Situation in Pakistan*, Intelligence Memorandum, Washington: CIA, 6 February 1969.

33. Ambassador Oehlert to Secretary of State, Rawalpindi, telegram-1238, 5 February 1969.

34. Thomas L. Hughes, *Pakistan on the Brink*, Director of Intelligence and Research (INR) to Secretary of State, Washington: State Department, 20 February 1969.

35. Ibid.

36. Sheikh Mujibur Rahman, *Address to the Round Table Conference*, Rawalpindi, 13 March 1969.

37. Kissinger, *Ayub Khan Resignation*, Memorandum for the President, the White House, 25 March 1969. Kissinger feared that if East Pakistan reacted violently to these developments, 'the opportunities for foreign meddling, especially by the Communist Chinese, would be increased.' There was some speculation that the Army may have forced Ayub Khan out, but Yahya Khan's own account noted that Ayub had written to him on 24 March, asking him 'to fulfil my constitutional responsibilities to defend the country, not only against external aggression, but also to save it from internal disorder and chaos.' Yahya Khan to Richard Nixon, Rawalpindi, No. SS/17/5/69, 27 March 1969.

38. Yahya Khan, *Address to the Nation*, 26 March 1969.

39. Ibid. 28 November 1969.

40. Ibid.

41. Ibid. 28 March, 1970; *Legal Framework Order*, Gazette Extraordinary, Islamabad: the Government of Pakistan, 30 March 1970.

42. 'The Awami League Manifesto,' *Bangladesh Documents*, pp. 67–82.

43. Yahya Khan, *Address to the Nation*, 28 July 1970.

44. Casualty figures like these proved to be extremely sensitive but also difficult to ascertain. The most recent census was recorded in 1961 and the population

had grown significantly since. The worst-affected coastal districts included many low-lying sandbars and islands where vulnerable, poor and often landless families made destitute by river-erosion elsewhere sought refuge. The state machinery kept few records of such people and nobody could be certain of the precise toll. While East Pakistani press and politicians gave exaggerated accounts, West Pakistani counterparts downplayed losses. This difference reflected serious, perhaps irreconcilable, divergences. The sympathetic US Consul-General in Dhaka, Archer Blood, thought 'the death toll will not greatly exceed 300,000, if indeed it reaches that number. While brutal in its magnitude, it is nonetheless far short of a million and a half as had been predicted by one prominent newspaper.' Blood to Secretary of State, *East Pakistan Disaster Relief*, Dhaka, telegram-02417, 30 November 1970.

45. Sheikh Mujibur Rahman, *Press conference*, Dhaka, 26 November 1970. Others, too, noticed a lack of energy in Islamabad's response. See Kissinger, *Pakistan Relief-Situation*, Memorandum for the President, the White House, 20 November 1970; and *Pakistan Disaster Relief*, ibid. 27 November 1970.

46. Yahya Khan, *Press conference*, Dhaka, 27 November 1970. On Yahya Khan's role in building covert contacts between Washington and Beijing in 1970–71, see, Ali, 2005, pp. 9, 12, 14, 18–30.

47. Ray S. Cline, *Pakistan: Election Results Suggest Fresh Problems*, Director INR to Secretary of State, Washington: State Department, 8 December 1970.

48. ZA Bhutto, *Address Outside the Punjab Assembly Chambers*, Lahore, 20 December 1970.

49. Tajuddin Ahmed, *Statement by the General Secretary, East Pakistan Awami League*, Dhaka, 21 December 1970.

50. Yahya Khan, *Press Conference*, Dhaka, 14 January 1971.

51. Bhutto, *Press Conference*, Dhaka, 30 January 1971.

52. Lt. General Gul Hassan Khan, 1993, p. 258.

53. Bhutto, *Press Conference*, Peshawar, 15 February 1971.

54. Ibid.

55. Bhutto, *Address on constitutional issues*, Karachi, 28 February 1971.

56. Yahya Khan quoted in Ambassador Farland, *Possibility of East/West Pakistan Split—China's Role*, Islamabad: American Embassy, telegram-0944 to Secretary of State, 1 February 1971. Interestingly, Yahya Khan noted that 'a militarily insecure, independent, and geographically separated East Pakistan would represent a target of the highest priority' for China. Such an East Pakistan/Bengal would form a nucleus for Beijing to pull West Bengal and Assam into giving the 'damned Chinese precisely what they've wanted for years—a port on the Bay of Bengal and an outlet to the Indian Ocean.'

57. A judicial commission established by the Pakistani government later reported that the hijackers were Indian 'intelligence agents'. Hasan Zaheer, *The Separation of East Pakistan*, Karachi: OUP, 1994, ch. 9, fn.2.

58. See, for instance, Yahya Khan to Richard Nixon, Islamabad, 8 February 1971, and Nixon to Khan, the White House, 17 February 1971.

59. In Late February, Kissinger ordered an inter-agency study of US options vis-à-vis Pakistan's political crisis. He then advised Nixon that if Mujib's pursuit of autonomy was foiled, he was likely to declare East Pakistan's independence. Pointing out that Mujib was 'basically friendly toward the US,' Kissinger asked if Washington should adopt 'a more neutral stance toward' him. Nixon wrote, 'not yet—correct—but not any position which encourages secession.' Kissinger to Nixon, *Situation in Pakistan*, the White House, 22 February 1971, p. 2.

60. Farland to Secretary State, *My Feb.25 Session with Yahya*, Islamabad, telegram-1660, 25 February 1971.

61. The Pakistani military had, until then, a single infantry division deployed in East Pakistan. On 27 February, an airlift began bringing in two other divisions from the West. Lt. General Gul Hassan Khan, 1993, pp. 260–1.

62. Zaheer, 1994, pp. 147–9.

63. Blood to Secretary of State, *My Conversation With Sheikh Mujibur Rahman*, Dhaka, telegram-540, 28 February 1971.

64. Sheikh Mujibur Rahman, *Address at Paltan Maidan Rally*, Dhaka, 3 March 1971.

65. Lt. General Gul Hassan Khan, 1993, pp. 259, 262.

66. Justice Hamoodur Rahman, Justice S. Anwarul Haq, and Justice Tufail Ali Abdur Rahman, *Report of the Commission of Inquiry into the 1971 War*, Rawalpindi, May 1974, Part V, Chapter II, para 2. The report cites but does not corroborate an estimate by an independent investigator who claims that the number of 'helpless Biharis, West Pakistanis and patriotic Bengalis living in East Pakistan' killed during the conflict ranged from 100,000 to 500,000. Ibid. para 5.

67. Yahya Khan, *Address to the Nation*, 6 March 1971.

68. The Awami League secretariat issued statements incorporating these points on 7 March 1971.

69. The Yahya-Mujib-Bhutto exchanges are reported in Zaheer, 1994, pp. 149–159.

70. Z.A. Bhutto, *Press Conference*, Dhaka, 22 March 1971.

71. Major General Rao Farman Ali, quoted in Zaheer, 1994, p. 159.

72. Zaheer, 1994, p. 156.

2. WAR, INDEPENDENCE AND BLOOD-FEUDS

1. American Consul General to Secretary of State, Dhaka, telegram-978, 29 March 1971.

2. Major General K.M. Safiullah, *Bangladesh at War*, Dhaka: Academic Publishers, 1989, pp. 30–2.

3. Zaheer, pp. 166–7.

4. American Consul General to Secretary of State, telegram-986, Dhaka, 30 March 1971.

5. Ibid. telegram-959, 28 March 1972; telegram-978, 29 March 1971; telegram-986, 30 March 1971.

6. Ibid. telegram-959, 28 March.

7. Farland to Secretary of State, Islamabad, telegram-2954, 31 March 1971. However, Farland noted that this was an internal Pakistani problem. 'Since we are not only human beings but also government servants, righteous indignation is not of itself an adequate basis for our reaction to the events now occurring in East Pakistan.' US consulate staff in Dhaka virtually revolted against this point of view, Archer Blood representing their collective anger at official US reaction to Pakistani action in several strongly-worded signals—for instance, Blood to Secretary of State, Dhaka, telegram-1138, 6 April 1971; telegram-1249, 10 April 1971.

8. Lt. General Niazi quoted in Justice Hamoodur Rahman, Justice S. Anwarul Haq, and Justice Tufail Ali Abdur Rahman, *Report of the War Inquiry Commission*, Islamabad, 1974, Part V, Chapter II, para.10.

9. In 1986, Abdur Razzaq, a prominent student leader in 1971, told Syed Samadul Haq of the *Janamat*, a vernacular weekly published from Balham in south London, that Mujib had advised him—and presumably others—to cross the border should the military mount an attack, and seek help from particular Indian nationals. This help would include arms.

10. Zaheer, p. 167.

11. Yahya Khan, *Address to the nation*, Islamabad, 26 March 1971.

12. Major General K.M Safiullah, 1989, pp. 44–5.

13. Authoritative Pakistani authors claim Colonel M.A.G. Osmany, commander-in-chief of the Bangladesh Forces (BDF), had been plotting with Bengali officers for sometime before 25 March 1971. For instance, Lt. General Gul Hassan Khan (CGS of the Pakistani army in 1971), *Memoirs*, Karachi, OUP, 1993, pp. 270–1; Hassan Zaheer (senior Pakistani official in Dhaka in 1971), *The Separation of East Pakistan*, Karachi: OUP, 1994, pp. 164–5.

14. Safiullah, p. 56.

15. The other officers present at this conclave were Lt. Colonel Abdur Rab, Lt. Colonel Salehuddin Mohammad Reza, Major Kazi Nuruzzaman, Major Nurul Islam, Major Shaffaat Jamil, and Major Moinul Hossain Chowdhury. They would play key roles in the war and its aftermath. Ibid. pp. 78–9.

16. The proclamation was published in the Indian press on 18 April, a day after a government–in-exile under the premiership of Tajuddin Ahmed was sworn

in at a border village near Meherpur in Kushtia in eastern Bangladesh. The village was renamed *Mujib Nagar*, or Mujib's city.

17. Initially, the commanders were—Major Ziaur Rahman: Chittagong-CHT; Major Khaled Musharraf: Comilla-Noakhali; Major K.M. Safiullah: Sylhet-Brahmanbaria-Mymensingh; Captain Nawazish Ahmed and Captain Najmul Haque: Rangpur-Dinajpur; Major Abu Osman Choudhury: Kushtia-Jessore; Captain Jalil: Barisal- Patuakhali. Safiullah, 1989, p. 101. Over the following months, as the war ebbed and flowed, sector boundaries would be redrawn and commanders reappointed or changed. Eventually, there would be eleven sectors and three brigade-strength regular formations. For details of the sectors, see Emajuddin Ahmed, *Military Rule and the Myth of Democracy*, Dhaka: University Press Limited (UPL), 1988, pp. 43–5.

18. CIA, *Prospects for Pakistan*, SNIE 32–71, Langley, 12 April 1971, p. 3.

19. Ibid. p. 2.

20. Ibid. p. 3

21. Ibid. pp. 4–7.

22. Indira Gandhi, 'Resolution Moved in the Parliament,' *Loksabha Records*, New Delhi, 31 March 1971.

23. CIA, *Pakistan-American Relations: A Reassessment*, Langley, April 1971, pp. 2–23.

24. Theodore Eliot, Jr. to Henry Kissinger, *Contingency Study for Indo-Pakistan Hostilities*, Washington: State Department, 25 May 1971, p. 1.

25. Ibid. p. 2. Pakistani scepticism is reflected in Lt. General Gul Hassan Khan, 1993, p. 286.

26. Indian officials called the Bangladeshi regulars the *Mukti Fouj* (liberation army) and the irregulars, Freedom Fighters (FF). Indian partiality towards the latter was not explained to the regulars and caused some friction which carried on after Bangladesh had been 'liberated.' Safiullah, pp. 114–5.

27. *Contingency Study for India-Pakistan Hostilities*, p. 2.

28. Ibid. pp. 3–5.

29. Samuel Hoskinson to Henry Kissinger, *Indian Government Decisions on Pakistan Crisis*, the White House, NSC, 26 May 1971, pp. 1–2.

30. Ibid. p. 2.

31. Gandhi, *Statement in Lok Sabha on Situation in Bangladesh*, New Delhi, 24 May 1971.

32. Gul Hassan Khan, 1993, p. 290.

33. Ibid. p. 294.

34. Phrase used, for instance, in Lt. General Niazi's message from Eastern Command to CGS, GHQ, Dhaka, signal G-1265, 11 December 1971, as Bangladeshi and Indian forces advanced towards Dhaka: 'Our forces all sectors under extreme pressure (.) Isolated in fortresses and invested by enemy (.)

Enemy possess mastery of air (.) Local population and rebels out to destroy own troops (.) All communications cut off (.) Order issued 'last man last round' (.) But will be difficult to hold positions when weapons and ammunition exhausted in few days (.) Advice solicited (.)

35. For an account of this debilitating debate, see Khan, 1993, pp. 302–6.

36. S. Mahmud Ali, *US-China Cold War Collaboration, 1971–1989*, New York: Routledge, 2005, pp. 3–7.

37. For an account of Nixon's search for a secret approach to Mao Zedong and Zhou Enlai, see ibid, ch. 1; for a description of the role played by General Yahya Khan, see ch. 2.

38. Nixon and Kissinger discussed the Bangladesh crisis, and South Asian and great power relations generally on a number of occasions throughout 1971 and early 1972. Their views resonated with Pakistani and Chinese perspectives. See, for instance, the White House, *Memorandum of Conversation (memcon) between President Nixon and His Assistant for National Security Affairs (Kissinger)*, Washington, 4 June 1971, 9.42–9.51 am.

39. NSC, *Contingency Planning on South Asia*, NSSM-133, Washington, 12 July 1971, pp. 1–2.

40. Ibid. p. 2. US ambassador to India, Kenneth Keating, said Washington should not equate India and Pakistan and, instead, help India overcome the consequences of mostly Hindu refugees still crossing from Bangladesh at the rate of 100,000–150,000 every day. He said India sought a political settlement in East Bengal enabling the refugees to return home. This reflected the general view of the US Administration outside the White House. The White House, *Memcon between President Nixon, his Assistant for National Security Affairs Kissinger, and the Ambassador to India Kenneth Keating*, Washington, 15 June 1971, 5.13–5.40 pm.

41. In private conversation just before the Indian Foreign Minister Swaran Singh called on the US president, Kissinger told Nixon, 'I've told Yahya that he had a personal channel through me to you. I'm just trying to keep the Indians from attacking for three months…We have to keep them from attacking for our own reasons.' *Memcon among President Nixon, his Assistant for National Security Affairs, the Indian Foreign Minister, and the Assistant Secretary of State for Near Eastern and South Asian Affairs Joseph Sisco*, the White House, 16 June 1971.

42. Details of Pakistan's economic woes appear in Zaheer, 1994, pp. 185–236.

43. Contrasting great power interests and responses are described in *Contingency Planning on South Asia*, NSSM-133, op cit. pp. 7–9.

44. Nikolai Podgorny to Yahya Khan, the Kremlin, Moscow, 2 April 1971.

45. The White House, *Memcon among President Nixon, his Assistant for National Security Affairs, the Indian Foreign Minister, and the Assistant Secretary of State for Near Eastern and South Asian Affairs Joseph Sisco*, 16 June 1971.

46. Kissinger to Ram in New Delhi on 7 July 1971, cited in *memcon between Jagjivan Ram et al and Henry A. Kissinger et al*, the White House, New Delhi, 12 July 1971.

47. Ibid.

48. For details of this dramatic shift in great power relations, Yahya Khan's contribution to it and a resulting Sino-US sense of obligation to Pakistan, see Ali, 2005, pp. 27–40.

49. NSSM-133, op cit. p. 8.

50. Ibid.

51. The White House, *Memcon among President Nixon, the President's Assistant for National Security Affairs, and the Ambassador to Pakistan, James Farland*, Washington, 28 July 1971.

52. Ibid. State Department's 'pro-Indian bias' is reflected in State Department, *Scenario for Action in Indo-Pakistan Crisis*, Washington, 29 June 1971, especially pp. 3–8. An inter-agency analysis noted that 'If India attacked, our interests would be best served by a rapid Indian victory in East Pakistan followed by a swift withdrawal and installation of a Bangladesh government and a stale-mate on the Western front which left West Pakistan intact.' NSC, *Analytical summary of NSSM-133*, the White House, 12 July 1971. Nixon agreed with the second part of this recommendation but rejected the first and any linkage between the two.

53. Farland to Secretary of State, Islamabad, telegram-7164, 15 July 1971; Consul-General to Secretary of State, Dhaka, telegram-2814, 23 July 1971; American Embassy in Islamabad to State Department, Islamabad, telegram-6395, 25 June 1971, summarising report on East Pakistan's food situation by US Department of Agriculture official Joseph Ryan, filed at Islamabad's behest.

54. In an address to the nation on 28 June 1971, Yahya Khan promised to transfer power to civilian 'elected representatives' in East Pakistan within four months, after replacing MNAs and MPAs either killed or missing, or accused of committing 'heinous crimes', with fresh representatives chosen through by-elections.

55. Farland to State Department, Islamabad, telegram-7172, 15 July 1971.

56. The White House, *Memorandum for the Record: NSC Meeting on the Middle East and South Asia*, San Clemente, 16 July 1971.

57. The White House, *Memcon between the President's Adviser for National Security Affairs and the Soviet Ambassador, Anatoly Dobrynin*, Washington, 19 July 1971. Kissinger did not, however, root for Yahya Khan's leadership. He told colleagues, 'Yahya and his group would never win any prizes for high IQs or for the subtlety of their political comprehension. They are loyal, blunt soldiers, but I think they have a real intellectual problem in understanding why

East Pakistan should not be part of West Pakistan (sic). You will never get an acceptance of the Awami League from the present structure.'The White House, *Minutes of Senior Review Group Meeting*, Washington, 23 July 1971.

58. Rogers to Keating, Washington, State Department telegram-134596, 24 July 1971.
59. The White House, *Minutes of SRG Meeting*, Washington, 30 July 1971.
60. Ibid.
61. Zaheer, 1994, pp. 309–10.
62. Safiullah, 1989, p. 158.
63. Maurice Williams to the Secretary of State, *Mission to Pakistan to Review Relief, Refugee and Related Issues*, Washington, USAID, 3 September 1971, pp. 3, 10.
64. Ibid. pp. 5, 9.
65. Ibid. p. 7.
66. Ibid. p.p. 5–6.
67. Kissinger in *Minutes of Washington Special Action Group Meeting*, the White House, 29 November 1971. Assistant Secretary of State Joseph Sisco had led the secret exercise. Indian security services alerted Tajuddin Ahmed that 'Foreign Minister' Khandakar Moshtaque Ahmed's aides were secretly meeting US diplomats in India. The contacts immediately ended and Tajuddin Ahmed put Moshtaque on notice. He would lose his senior post shortly after victory against Pakistan. Kissinger to Alec Douglas-Home, the White House, *Memcon among President Nixon, the President's Assistant for National Security Affairs, the British Foreign Secretary, and the British Ambassador*, Washington, 30 September 1971; General Rao Farman Ali quoted in Zaheer, 1994, pp. 349–350; Clare Hollingworth reported in *the Daily Telegraph*, on 4 August 1971 that the Bangladesh government-in-exile would have held secret negotiations with Pakistani representatives 'were it not for the strong opposition of their military command under Col. Osmany who...has not unexpectedly gained ascendancy over the politicians.'
68. Office of National Estimates, *The Indo-Pakistani Crisis: Six Months Later*, Langley: CIA, 22 September 1971, p. 2.
69. Safiullah, 1989, p. 200.
70. Ibid. pp. 3–4.
71. Ibid. pp. 6–8.
72. Farland to Secretary of State, *Pakistan Internal Situation*, Islamabad, telegram-10043, 4 October 1971.
73. Secretary Rogers to Ambassador Farland, *US Leverage in Current Pakistan Crisis: US Policy*, Washington: State Department, 29 September 1971.
74. Nixon and Kissinger liberally used expletives to describe Mrs. Gandhi and

Indians in their private review of the meeting. The White House, *Memcon Among President Nixon, the President's Assistant for National Security Affairs, and the President's Chief of Staff*, Washington, 5 November 1971.

75. The White House, *Memorandum for the President's File*, Washington, 5 November 1971, 11.20 am in the Oval Office.

76. Harold Saunders, Samuel Hoskinson, *Memorandum for Dr. Kissinger: Gandhi Visit—Advisers' Meeting in Cabinet Room*, the White House, 4 November 1971.

77. Maurice Williams, *Memorandum for the Secretary*, Washington, USAID, 5 November 1971, p. 1.

78. Ibid. p. 2. The by-elections Yahya mentioned were being rigged by Pakistani Generals in the East. They chose the men who 'would be elected in the next provincial elections.'

79. Ibid. p. 4.

80. Ibid. p. 3.

81. NSC, *Analytical Summary: Contingency Paper- Indo-Pakistan Hostilities*, the White House, 11 November 1971.

82. Gul Hassan Khan, 1993, pp. 303–4.

83. The White House, *Memcon Among President Nixon, the President's assistant for National Security Affairs, and the Pakistani Foreign Secretary*, Washington, 15 November 1971.

84. The White House, *Memcon Among President Nixon, the President's Assistant for National Security, and Secretary of State Rogers*, Washington, 24 November 1971.

85. Zaheer, 1994, p. 354.

86. Gul Hassan Khan, 1993, pp. 321–2.

87. Safiullah, 1989, pp. 201–224.

88. The White House, *Memcon*, 24 November 1971. fn.83.

89. See, for instance, the White House, *TelCon between the President and his Assistant for National Security Affairs*, 26 November 1971, 10.42 am. Kissinger told Secretary John Connally, 'here we have Indian-Soviet collusion, raping a friend of ours. Secondly, we have a situation where one of the motives that the Chinese may have had in leaning towards us a little bit is the fear that something like this might happen to them. So that some demonstration of our willingness to stand for some principles is important for that policy. Thirdly, if the Soviets get away with this in the Subcontinent, we have seen the dress rehearsal for a Middle Eastern war.' The White House, *TelCon between Mr Kissinger and Secretary Connally*, 5 December 1971.

90. Nixon reminded Gandhi, 'In our conversations, I mentioned to you that President Yahya would be willing to take the first step in disengaging his forces on the frontier with West Pakistan provided India were willing to take

reciprocal action subsequently. I have not heard from you on that point, and I hope you would agree promptly to designate a representative who could discuss a limited disengagement with a representative named by President Yahya. On the frontiers of East Pakistan he has agreed to permit stationing of UN observers even if India does not reciprocate. Such steps would be in the interest of both India and Pakistan and of peace in the world. It is only in a defused situation that progress can be made in the direction of a political settlement for which we continue to work.' Nixon to Gandhi, the White House, 27 November 1971.

91. Nixon to Kosygin, the White House, 27 November 1971.

92. Lt. General Robert Cushman of the CIA, in the White House, *Minutes of Washington Special Action Group (WSAG) Meeting*, Washington, 29 November 1971.

93. Ibid. Maurice Williams

94. Ibid. Department of Defence official David Packard

95. Gandhi to Keating, New Delhi, 1 December 1971, quoted in Kissinger to Nixon, *Your Message to Mrs. Gandhi*, the White House, 1 December 1971.

96. Zaheer, 1994, pp. 360–1.

97. Lt. General Cushman, and Admiral Thomas Moorer, Chairman, JCS, in the White House, *Minutes of the WSAG Meeting*, Washington, 1 December 1971.

98. Kissinger to Nixon, *Information Items: India-Pakistan Situation*, the White House, 2 December 1971.

99. Reflecting deep anxiety, Yahya wrote: 'Gestures such as the stoppage of $2 million worth of arms supplies to India or delay in the signing of PL-480 and development loans are unlikely to change the Indian attitude at this stage. Therefore, I request for urgent consideration, Mr. President, the following measures: a) issuance of a personal statement by you, condemning India's aggression, aided and abetted by the Soviet Union, and calling for an immediate end to hostilities and withdrawal of opposing forces to safe distance behind their respective borders; b) issuance of a statement by you strongly advising Soviet Union to desist from militarily supporting India in its aggression against Pakistan; c) your agreement to my invoking Article 1 of the Pakistan-United States Bilateral Agreement of Co-operation signed on 5 March 1959 and meeting my request for military assistance in accordance with the provisions of the Agreement.' Yahya Khan to Richard Nixon, Islamabad, 2 December 1971. Nixon told Kissinger, 'We have a treaty and we have to keep it. That makes it imperative to cut off aid to India.' The White House, *TelCon between the President and His Assistant for National Security Affairs*, 2 December 1971. Library of Congress, Manuscript Division, *Kissinger Papers*, Box 370.

100. Lt. General Abdul Hamid Khan to Lt. General A.A.K. Niazi, Rawalpindi, GHQ, 3 December 1971, quoted in Zaheer, 1994, p. 362.

101. India-Pakistan Working Group, *Situation Report No. 18*, Washington, State Department, 3 December 1971. In a letter to Nixon, Mrs. Gandhi listed eight Indian airfields that she said had been bombed by Pakistani aircraft around 1730 Indian Standard Time on 3 December in 'premeditated and planned aggression'. She assured Nixon that 'the people and the Government of India are determined that this wanton and unprovoked aggression should be decisively and finally repelled once and for all.' Indira Gandhi to Richard Nixon, New Delhi, 5 December 1971.

102. *Situation Report No. 18*, ibid. As the Battalion Intelligence Officer and later, an anti–tank platoon commander, in the Divisional Reconnaissance and Support battalion deployed around Rahim Yar Khan at the time, the author was unaware of any such Indian offensive. Indeed, his battalion and Division were ordered to mount offensive operations across the border as part of 'Operation *Labba-ek*', which ran into the sands when the IAF responded on the morning of 5 December.

103. Title of one of the earliest authoritative accounts of the Indian operations in Bangladesh—Major General D.K. Palit, *The Lightning Campaign*, New Delhi, Thomson Press, 1972. General Aurora's command comprised Lt. General T.N. Raina's 11 Corps which mounted two divisional thrusts into western East Pakistan, Lt. General M. L. Thapan's 33 Corps which launched a Divisional thrust to neutralise the Pakistani 'fortress' in Hilli and capture north-Western East Pakistan; Lt. General Sagat Singh's 4 Corps which sent in its three modified mountain divisions to take control of eastern East Pakistan, and the 101 Communications Zone with division-sized forces reinforcing operations in north-eastern East Pakistan. Safiullah, 1989, pp. 205–11. With these Indian forces were the three *Mukti Bahini* brigades and sector troops numbering in their dozens of thousands.

104. Confirmed by Congressman Otto Passman, Chairman of Foreign Affairs Subcommittee of the House Appropriations Committee, in the White House, *TelCon between Mr. Kissinger and Congressman Passman*, Washington, 3 December 1971.

105. Admiral Moorer and DCI Helms in the White House, *Minutes of the WSAG Meeting*, Washington, 3 December 1971. Palit, 1972, p. 78, claimed not one IAF aircraft was destroyed.

106. The White House, *TelCon, Vorontsov–Kissinger*, Washington, 5 December 1971.

107. Following the March 1959 US-Pakistan Agreement of Cooperation, President Kennedy assured Ayub Khan, 'As a firm ally, Pakistan is entitled to the re-affirmation you have requested of the prior assurances given by the

United States to Pakistan on the subject of aggression against Pakistan. My Government certainly stands by these assurances.' Kennedy to Ayub Khan, the White House, 26 January 1962. The USA pledged similar aid including military assistance to India in case it suffered another round of 'aggression.' This agreement, signed by Prime Minister Jawaharlal Nehru and Ambassador J.K. Galbraith on 9 July 1963, was transmitted to State Department in US Embassy Delhi telegram-143 on the same day.

108. See, for instance, the White House, *TelCon between the President and his Assistant for National Security Adviser*, 6 December 1971, 12.02–12.06 pm.

109. India's Defence Secretary K.B. Lall noted on 4 December that Delhi had launched a 'no holds barred' offensive in the East. Directorate of Intelligence, *Intelligence Memorandum: India-Pakistan Situation*, Langley: CIA, 4 December 1971.

110. The White House, *Minutes of WSAG Meeting*, Washington, 4 December 1971.

111. The White House, *Memcon between President Nixon and His Assistant for National Security Affairs*, Washington, 6 December 1971, 6.14–6.38 pm. Kissinger had already told Nixon, 'if the Soviets and Indians get away with this, the Chinese and the United States will be standing there with eggs on our face. And they will have made us back down.' The White House, *TelCon between President Nixon and His Assistant for National Security Affairs*, Washington, 5 December 1971, 11 am. When Nixon agonised over dealing with India, a large democracy, Kissinger reminded him, 'They were the ones that made a treaty with the Russians. They are the ones that are now establishing the principle that force is the only method—the principal method for settling disputes...The Russians aren't going to give them $700 million in development aid.' The White House, *TelCon between President Nixon and his Assistant for National Security Affairs*, Washington, 4 December 1971.

112. Richard Nixon to Leonid Brezhnev, the White House, 6 December 1971.

113. The White House, *TelCon between President Nixon and His Assistant for National Security Affairs*, Washington, 4 December 1971, 12.15 pm.

114. Ibid.

115. The White House, *Memcon*, Washington, 6 December 1971, 6.14–6.38 pm.

116. The White House, *Minutes of WSAG Meeting*, Washington, 6 December 1971.

117. Joseph Sisco in ibid.

118. Yahya Khan to Richard Nixon, Islamabad, 7 December 1971.

119. Richard Nixon to Yahya Khan, the White House, 7 December 1971.

120. The White House, *Recording of a Conversation among President Nixon, Secretary of Commerce Maurice Stans, Assistant for National Security Affairs Henry Kissinger, Deputy Assistant for National Security Affairs Brigadier-General Alexander Haig, and President's Press Secretary Ron Ziegler*, 7 December 1971, 3.55–4.29 pm.

121. A.M. Malik to Yahya Khan, Dhaka, signal A-6905, 7 December 1971, 12.00 am.

122. Yahya Khan to A.M. Malik, Islamabad, signal A-4555, 7 December 1971, 7.25 p.m.

123. The White House, *Memcon among President Nixon, the President's Assistant for National Security Affairs, and Attorney General Mitchell*, Washington, 8 December 1971.

124. The White House, *TelCon between President Nixon and his Assistant for National Security Affairs*, Washington, 8 December 1971, 8.03–8.12 pm.

125. The White House, *Memcon between President Nixon and his Assistant for National Security Affairs*, Washington, 9 December 1971, 12.44–1.27 p.m.

126. A.M. Malik to Yahya Khan, Dhaka, signal A-4660, 9 December 1971, 6.00 pm.

127. Yahya Khan to A.M. Malik, Islamabad, signal G-0001, 9 December 1971.

128. A.M. Malik to Yahya Khan, Dhaka, signal A-7107, 10 December 1971.

129. Yahya Khan to A.M. Malik, Islamabad, signal G-0002, 10 December 1971.

130. The White House, *Memcon among President Nixon, the President's Assistant for National Security Affairs, and the President's Deputy Assistant for National Security Affairs*, Washington, 12 December 1971.

131. The White House, *Memcon between President Nixon and his Assistant for National Security Affairs*, Washington, 10 December 1971, 12.47–1.01 pm.

132. The White House, *Memcon among President Nixon, the President's Assistant for National Security Affairs, and the President's Deputy Assistant for National Security Affairs*, Washington, 12 December 1971.

133. Ibid.

134. Directorate for Plans, *Indian Prime Minister Indira Gandhi's Briefing on the Indo-Pakistan War*, Langley: CIA, 12 December 1971.

135. The White House, *Memcon between President Nixon and his assistant for National Security Affairs*, Washington, 12 December 1971, 11.04–11.14 am.

136. Theodore Eliot, Jr., to Henry Kissinger, *India-Pakistan: Refugee Problem*, Washington: State Department, 12 December 1971.

137. President of Pakistan to the Governor of East Pakistan, and Commander, Eastern Command, Islamabad, signal G-0013, 14 December 1971.

138. Henry Kissinger, *Memorandum for the President: Information Item*, the White House, 16 December 1971. Kissinger mentioned that the arrival of the USS Enterprise in the Bay of Bengal was 'generating considerable anti–American sentiment' in India.

139. Gul Hassan Khan, 1993, pp. 339–45.

140. Farland to Secretary of State, Islamabad, US Embassy, telegram-12804, 20 December 1971.

141. Ibid, telegram-12821, 20 December 1971.

142. Kissinger to Nixon, *Information Items*, the White House, 21 December 1971. While Bhutto picked up the pieces of Pakistan, Nixon and British Prime Minister Edward Heath met in Bermuda to restore a degree of normalcy to the region. They agreed that the situation needed response on three key issues: '(1) keeping West Pakistan afloat; (2) meeting the humanitarian requirements in the face of inevitable famine in Bangla Desh; and (3) finding a way of coming to terms with India as the most powerful country in the sub-continent.' The White House, *Memcon between Prime Minister Heath et al and the President et al*, Bermuda, 21 December 1971, 2.35 pm.

143. Spivack to Secretary of State, Dhaka: American Consulate, telegram-0010, 3 January 1972.

144. Mujib cited in Anthony Mascarenhas, *Bangladesh: A Legacy of Blood*, London, Hodder and Stoughton, 1986, p. 5; a London-based Bengali journalist who was present at Heathrow among the crowd on hand to receive Mujib told the author in 1992 that when informed by the senior Bangladeshi diplomat in London, Rezaul Karim, that he was now the president of Bangladesh, Mujib asked with surprise, 'haven't we just been granted autonomy?' He was soon corrected.

145. CIA, *National Intelligence Estimate-Bangladesh*, NIE32.1–72, Washington, 21 December 1972, p. 5.

146. As with several other aspects of Bangladesh's war of independence, the number of Bengalis, and non-Bengalis killed during the conflict remains a controversial and emotive issue. There is no agreement among the parties and observers and, without empirical evidence, widely varying estimates are all that historians have to hand. Major General K.M. Safiullah, a decorated war hero who was appointed the first Chief of Army Staff in independent Bangladesh, says 'hundreds of thousands of people died.' An association of freedom fighters, the *Muktijuddha Chetana Bikash Kendra*, citing a December 1981 UN report, says 1.5 million were killed. An academic observer of South Asian politics, Prof. Lawrence Ziring, says, 'the Pakistani army is believed to have killed in excess of one million Bengalis.' A US Library of Congress study reports, 'By the end of summer (1971) as

many as 300,000 people were thought to have lost their lives.' The CIA, in its 1972 National Intelligence Estimate, noted, 'According to the Bengalee government, a half million people died in the huge less.' The judicial commission Z.A. Bhutto set up in December 1971 to ascertain the circumstances in which Pakistani forces laid down their arms in the East and accepted a ceasefire in the West concluded that Bangladeshi allegations of Pakistani army responsibility 'for killing three million Bengalis and raping 200,000 East Pakistani women…are obviously highly exaggerated.' The commission accepted the Pakistani General Headquarters figure of 'approximately 26,000 persons killed during the action by the Pakistan Army' as 'reasonably correct.' Major General K.M. Safiullah, *Bangladesh at War*, Dhaka, Academic Publishers, 1989, p.xiv; Ahmed Sharif, Quazi Nur Uz-Zaman, Serajul Islam Chowdhury, Shahriar Kabir, Eds., *Genocide '71*, Dhaka, Muktijuddha Chetana Bikash Kendra, 1988, p. 13; Lawrence Ziring, *Bangladesh From Mujib to Ershad: An Interpretive Study*, Karachi: Oxford University Press, 1992, p. 72; James Heitzman and Robert Worden, *Bangladesh: A Country Study*, Washington: Library of Congress, 1989, 'The War for Bangladeshi Independence, 1971'; CIA, *National Intelligence Estimate-Bangladesh*, NIE32.1–72, Washington, 21 December 1972, p. 6, Justices Hamoodur Rahman, S. Anwarul Haq, Tufail Ali Abdur Rahman, *Report of the War Inquiry Commission* (Hamoodur Rahman Commission Report), Islamabad, 1974, Part V, Chapter II, paragraphs 31–34. As for the widely quoted figure of 3 million killed by the Pakistani forces in 1971, a London-based Bengali journalist who attended Sheikh Mujibur Rahman during his brief stay in London in January 1972 told the author in 1992 that asked about casualty figures by journalists and briefed by his local aides that '*teen lakh*' (Bengali for 300,000) Bangladeshis had lost their lives, Mujib used the phrase 'three million' in answering the question. Since then, official Bangladeshi statements have included allegations of 3 million killed and 200,000 women raped by Pakistani soldiers. See the Hamoodur Rahman Commission, ibid. paragraph 34.

147. A small detachment of Indian military helicopters, pilots and ground crew stayed back in Chittagong to provide logistics support to Bangladeshi forces which were taking over from Indian units at such stations as Ruma, Bolipara, Thanchi, Mowdok, and Ali Kadam in the CHT where *Chakma* militiamen recruited by Pakistan's Inter-Services Intelligence Directorate (ISI) had guarded training bases and sanctuary given by the ISI to India's rebel Mizo National Front fighters under the Mizo rebel leader Laldenga. Indian and *Mukti Bahini* units, entering the CHT in December 1971, encountered the only real indigenous resistance from these tribal fighters. This would have implications for Bangladesh's future development.

148. The Treaty was focused on defending Bangladesh from a hostile external environment rather than from domestic disruptions. In fact, clause i stipulated that 'each side shall respect the independence, sovereignty and territorial integrity of the other and refrain from interfering in the internal affairs of the other side.' Clauses ix–xi laid down the framework of bilateral security cooperation and mutual assistance in the event of external aggression.

149. Nixon to Mujib, the White House, 4 April 1972.

150. Secretary of State to Spivack, Washington: State Department, telegram-060873, 8 April 1972.

151. CIA, NIE32.1–72, 21 December 1972, p. 14.

152. Mascarenhas, 1986, p. 8.

153. CIA, 21 December 1971, p. 14.

154. Ibid.

155. CIA, 21 December 1972, p. 9.

156. Government of Bangladesh, *Annual Plan: Fiscal Year 1973*, Dhaka, 1972.

157. CIA, 21 December 1972, p. 8.

158. The origins of these commitments revealed the relative interest donors showed in stabilising the new republic: US—$335 million, India—$270 million, Soviet Union—$70 million, Canada—$65 million, Britain—$50 million, Japan and Western Europe less Britain—$113 million. CIA, ibid.

159. CIA, ibid. p. 11.

160. Ibid.

161. Ibid. p. 13.

162. Moudud Ahmed, *Democracy and the Challenge of Development*, Dhaka, University Press Limited, 1995, p. 4. The range of the estimate demonstrated the difficulty of obtaining credible data even for leaders from the country's top echelon. Ahmed served in several cabinets and, under General H.M. Ershad, rose to be his Vice President. Of this number, Bangladesh Forces (BDF) regulars added up to 25,000 men; 84,000 irregulars were registered with the *Mukti Bahini*. The remainder came from the various militias armed by India but operating under their own commanders, the best known being 'Tiger' Kader Siddiky's *Kader Bahini* active in Tangail. *Keesing's Contemporary Archives* (Keesing's), February 1972, p. 25109A; Muyeedul Hasan, *Muldhara Ekattar*, Dhaka, 1986, p. 240.

163. These clashes became so worrying, and the Tajuddin government's loss of influence so total that Tajuddin despatched his personal aide, Muyeedul Hasan, to seek Mrs. Gandhi's help. She sent Hasan to R.N. Kao, Director of the Research and Analysis Wing (RAW), India's external intelligence agency. Kao patiently listened to Hasan but then left without making any comment. In the late 1990s, Golok Majumder, who as Inspector General

of India's Border Security Force in 1971 was responsible for aiding the Bangladeshi war effort, told the BBC's Bengali Service that Delhi had set up the *Mujib Bahini* because it could not 'put all its eggs in the *Mukti Bahini* basket.'

164. *Keesing's*, p. 25109A.

165. Ibid.

166. Hasan, p. 240.

167. *Keesings*, p. 26693B.

168. Ibid. p. 25114B.

169. S. Mahmud Ali, *Civil-Military Relations in the Soft State: The Case of Bangladesh*, Bath: European Commission/European Network of Bangladesh Studies, 1994, p. 17.

170. Having spent over eleven years imprisoned by Pakistan's military rulers, Mujib told the CAS that he needed no army, that Mrs. Gandhi would come to his aid whenever he asked. General K.M. Safiullah to author in interview, 1991.

171. Arms Control and Disarmament Agency, *World Military Expenditure and Arms Transfers 1971–1980*, Washington, 1983, p. 40.

172. Senior Bangladeshis, such as CNS and Deputy Chief Martial Law Administrator, Rear Admiral M.H. Khan, would later complain that 'We have nothing. After liberation fifteen ships sailed to India with military equipment.' State Department, *Memcon: Secretary's Meeting with Bangladesh Naval Chief Khan*, Washington, 2 July 1976.

173. The JSD alleged a tiny Awami League elite representing only 8 per cent of Bangladesh's population but controlling 85 per cent of the national wealth had captured power in 1971 with help from India's 'land-based *bourgeoisie*' and Soviet 'Social-imperialist power'. The JSD's manifesto would proclaim its plans to overthrow a structure dominated by these 'exploiting classes.' See JSD, *Ghoshana Patra* (proclamation document), Dhaka, July 1973, pp. 7–11.

174. Colonel M. Ziauddin, 'The Hidden Prize', *The Holiday*, Dhaka, 12 August 1972.

175. Bureau of Intelligence and Research, *Bangladesh: The Euphoria Fades*, Intelligence Note, Washington: State Department, 8 June 1972.

176. Kissinger to Nixon, *Relief Assistance Totals for Bangladesh*, the White House, 15 July 1972.

177. Connally to Secretary of State, Islamabad, American Embassy telegram-5842, 6 July 1972.

178. Connally to Secretary of State, Tehran, American Embassy telegram-4084, 8 July 1972.

179. Ibid.

180. Ibid.
181. Moudud Ahmed, 1995, pp. 12–13.
182. Bangladesh Awami League at http://www.albd.org/autoalbd/content/view/111/44 accessed on 8 May 2008.
183. Ziring, 1994, p. 76.
184. Rogers to Sheikh Mujibur Rahman, Washington: State Department, 5 January 1972.
185. Harold Saunders and Samuel Hoskinson to Henry Kissinger, *Aid for Bangladesh*, the White House, 5 February 1973.
186. For an account of the process established by D.P. Dhar and Aziz Ahmed, representatives of Indira Gandhi and Z.A. Bhutto respectively, which led to the Simla Agreement, bypassing Bangladesh, see Kuldip Nayar, 'The roadmap which led to Simla accord,' *Gulf News*, 31 May 2003.
187. See, for instance, *Memcon: Bangladesh Ambassador's Call on Sisco*, Washington: State Department, 8 May 1973.
188. Rounaq Jahan, 'Bangladesh in 1973', in M.M. Khan and H.M. Zafarullah, *Politics and Bureaucracy in a New Nation—Bangladesh*, Dhaka: Centre for Administrative Studies, 1980, pp. 63, 70.
189. Bangladesh Election Commission, *Results of the Jatiya Sangsad Elections*, Dhaka, March 1973.
190. Theodore Eliot, Jr. to Henry Kissinger, *U.S. Wheat for Bangladesh*, Washington: State Department, 20 June 1973.
191. Daniel Newberry to Peter Constable, Dhaka, US Embassy, 27 August 1973.
192. Henry Kissinger in *Memcon—Meeting of the SRG*, the White House, 14 February 1974.
193. *The New York Times*, 20 October 1973.
194. *The Bangladesh Observer*, 4 September 1973. This phrase would interchangeably be used with 'miscreants' to describe perpetrators of violent acts against personnel or property belonging to the state or the ruling elite.
195. *Daily Ittefaq*, Dhaka, 30 November 1973.
196. 'The Political Significance of the Emergency Provisions,' *The Holiday*, Dhaka, 23 September 1973.
197. Ahmed, 1995, pp. 9–10; Ali, 1994, p. 17.
198. FF officers had received rapid promotions during and after the war so that Majors who had fought as Force- or Sector Commanders, had become Major-Generals and Brigadiers by the end of 1973; their contemporaries returning from Pakistan received promotion by one rank at best on repatriation. Consequently, at the command level, senior repatriates were subordinated to FF officers several years their junior in service. This was not unique to Bangladesh, but the across the board two-years ante-dated se-

niority granted to all FF personnel institutionalising FF seniority to repatriate personnel was. It also created a sense of victim hood and grievance among the latter, detracting from an already complicated integration process. Although Mujib had been anxious to get the soldiers back from Pakistan, his treatment of the returnees prevented the building of a cohesive professional military. A lack of professionalisation and widening cleavages among the ranks threatened cohesion. Mujib was not to know this. FF officers and men would kill him before the FF-repatriate fissures in the army made it vulnerable to internecine violence.

199. *The Bangladesh Observer*, Dhaka, 30 November 1973.
200. Kissinger in *Memcon—Meeting of the SRG*, the White House, 14 February 1974.
201. These were NAP (B), Bangla Jatiya League, Bangladesh Jatiya League, Bangladesh Gono Mukti Union, Bangladesh Communist Party (Leninist), and Krishak-Sramik Samajbadi Dal.
202. Emajuddin Ahmed in Khan and Zafarullah, 1980, pp. 160–1.
203. *Keesing's*, p. 25821B.
204. Anthony Mascarenhas, *Bangladesh: A Legacy of Blood*, London, Hodder and Stoughton, 1986, pp. 47–8. Lawrence Lifschultz, *Bangladesh: The Unfinished Revolution*, London, Zed Books, 1979, p. 103. This author, then a junior officer in the infantry, witnessed one instance where a young man, threateningly sporting an automatic weapon in public, was detained by soldiers and interrogated. He presented an official-looking document claiming the Secretary of the Home Ministry had issued him the weapon and ammunition for 'self-defence.' The officers detaining the young man, identified as an Awami League activist, were ordered by their superiors—who had received their instructions from the Prime Minister's Political Secretary—to hand over the youth to the local police. The latter, after treating the bearer of the weapon and his companions as honoured guests, released them to the JRB who escorted them out of the area.
205. Nurul Islam, 'What was it about the 1974 Famine?', *Scholars Journal*, 15 October 2005.
206. Habibul Haque Khondker, 'The Famine of 1974,' in M. M. Khan, J. P. Thorp, Editors, *Bangladesh: Society, Politics and Bureaucracy*, Dhaka: Centre for Administrative Studies, 1984, pp. 43–74, especially Tables 1 and 2.
207. The Deputy CAS, Major General Ziaur Rahman, responsible for supervising the army's Operation Silver Lining, told the Deputy Chairman of the Planning Commission that the Prime Minister had not been correctly briefed on the scale of smuggling which, he estimated, cost Bangladesh 500,000–1 million tons of grains annually. Deputy Chairman Nurul Islam considered this unlikely since 'head-load' smuggling could not account for

such massive shipments which would have required organised shipping using trucks and barges—this would be impossible to hide from the military.
Zia said even if soldiers had observed such large-scale movement, because
local Awami League leaders were involved in the smuggling operations,
there was little they could do. Awami League leaders, for their part, claimed
the army was targeting party cadres. Islam agreed smuggling had become
a regular feature since 1971, but did not believe its scale was big enough to
affect the local price of rice. Islam, 15 October 2005.

208. Nurul Islam, 15 October 2005.

209. Ibid.

210. Kissinger in State Department, *Memcon: Secretary Kissinger Calls on Bangladesh Prime Minister, Sheikh Mujibur Rahman*, Washington, 30 September
1974.

211. Nurul Islam, 15 October 2005.

212. Ibid.

213. State Department, *Memcon: Secretary Kissinger Calls on Bangladesh Prime
Minister, Sheikh Mujibur Rahman*, Washington, 30 September 1974.

214. Amartya Sen, 'Ingredients of Famine Analysis: Availability and Entitlement', *Quarterly Journal of Economics*, Vol. 96, No. 3, 1981, p. 451; *The Bangladesh Observer*, Dhaka, 23 October, and 2 November, 1974. For a detailed
analysis of the famine, see Sen, *Poverty and Famine: An Essay on Entitlement
and Deprivation*, Oxford: Scholarship Online Monographs, 1983, pp. 131–
154.

215. Habibul Haque Khondker, 1984, p. 23.

216. W. Haque, N. Mehta, A. Rahman, and P. Wignaraja, *Towards a Theory of
Rural Development*, Bangkok: UN Asian Development Institute, 1975,
p. 43.

217. D. McHenry and K. Bird, 'Food Bungle in Bangladesh,' *Foreign Policy*, Volume 27, No. 78, 1977, p. 78; Khondker, 1984, p. 23.

218. In late 1974, Mujib himself complained that four thousand party workers
including five MPs had been killed. Mascarenhas, 1986, p. 45; Lifschultz,
1979, p. 124.

219. The Amendment specified that 'when the National Party is formed a person
shall:
   a. In case he is a Member of Parliament on the date the National Party is
   formed, cease to be such member, and his seat in Parliament shall become vacant if he does not become a member of the National Party
   within the time fixed by the President.
   b. Not be qualified for election as President or as a Member of Parliament
   if he is not nominated as a candidate for such election by the National
   Party.

c. Have no right to form, or to be a member or otherwise take part in the activities of any political party other than the National Party.

The Fourth Amendment to the Constitution, cited in Mascarenhas, p. 57; Ahmed, 1995, p. 13.

220. Questions were later on raised about whether some troops had pursued Col. Ziauddin as vigorously as had the others, and whether he was, in fact, allowed to escape. The author took part in the operation and had a proximate view of events.

221. Mascarenhas, 1986, p. 46.

222. Lifschultz, 1979, pp. 98–149. Lifschultz, on the authority of unnamed US diplomats, makes the case that the CIA station chief in Dhaka, Philip Cherry, maintained covert contact with the plotters even after Ambassador David Eugene Boster ordered that all contacts be cut off. Lifschultz accuses the CIA of involvement in Mujib's assassination.

223. Mascarenhas, 1986, p. 54.

224. State Department, *The Secretary's 8.00 am. Staff Meeting*, Washington, 15 August 1975, p. 13.

225. Leaders of major professional and press organisations would swiftly join up; several senior bureaucrats and military officers, too, would apply for membership. Mascarenhas, p. 59.

226. Ibid. p. 44.

227. Bangladesh *Betar* (radio), *Bangabandhu's address at the Independence Day Rally*, Dhaka, 26 March 1975.

228. For details of and slightly differing perspectives on the coup, see Lifschultz, 1979, pp. 98–143; Mascarenhas, 1986, pp. 1–78; Emajuddin Ahamed, *Military Rule and the Myth of Democracy*, Dhaka: UPL, 1988, pp. 56–70; Lawrence Ziring, *Bangladesh from Mujib to Ershad: An Interpretive Study*, Karachi: OUP, 1992, pp. 96–108.

3. IN THE VALKYRIES' SHADOW

1. Mascarenhas, 1986, p. 63.

2. Ahamed, 1988, pp. 65–6; Lifschultz, 1979, pp. 119–43; Ahmed, 1995, pp. 12–16; Ziring, 1992, pp. 106–8.

3. Several authors noted Major Sharful Haq Dalim's radio announcement of Mujib's death and the imposition of martial law on the morning of 15 August, concluding that he was the coup leader. Others pointed to grievances harboured by Dalim and two colleagues, Majors M. Shahriyar and S.J. Noor, all three having been removed from service by Mujib on grounds considered unfair and saw this as the drive motivating the coup. Some described a key participant, Major Bazlul Huda, as another officer who had been cashiered by Mujib although Huda was in fact serving as a General-Staff Officer in the

Military Intelligence Directorate at the AHQ at the time of the coup. Yet others misconstrued the organisational structure, status and strength of the two battalion-strength units, 1st Bengal Lancers under the command of Major Farook (formally the unit's 2nd-in-Command), and the 2nd Field Regiment Artillery, under Major Rashid's command. Such inaccuracies challenge the credibility of the information and analyses published in several accounts. See, for instance, Habiba Zaman, 'The Military in Bangladesh Politics,' in M.M. Khan and J.P. Thorp, 1984, p. 89; Ahamed, 1988, p. 70, fns. 57, 58; Ahmed, 1995, pp. 13–15.

4. S. Mahmud Ali, 1994, pp. 10–12.

5. Prominent among them were Colonels Abu Taher and Mohammad Ziauddin, and Major M.A. Jalil, FF commanders who led the resistance on behalf of Tajuddin Ahmed's government-in-exile. They not only imbibed socialist theories, but in independent Bangladesh, began practising egalitarian values and challenging Bangladesh's *petit bourgeois* order before being eased out of service. They then joined two radical left-wing groups—Jalil and Taher the JSD, and Ziauddin, the PBSP all three rising to top positions in these organisations.

6. Ali, 1994, p. 12.

7. Ibid.

8. See Chapter 2; Ali, 1994, pp. 13–14.

9. One Sector Commander, Major M.A. Jalil, sought to prevent Indian looting of military hardware and non-military material from the Khulna area. He was dismissed and jailed for his troubles. Another, Colonel (later Lt. General and president of Bangladesh) Ziaur Rahman, commander of 'Z Force,' Bangladesh army's first regular infantry brigade, ordered his battalion commanders to secure tactically important ground surrendered by Pakistani troops before these could be taken over by 'green forces,' indicating Indian troops in their olive-green combat fatigues. The author, as an infantry regimental officer in 1974, was ordered to review the security classification of this and similar instructions issued by the Z Force commander during the war.

10. After the fall of the Mujib government, the Chief of Naval Staff, Rear Admiral M.H. Khan, visiting Henry Kissinger as a Bangladeshi DCMLA, told him 'We have nothing. After liberation fifteen ships sailed to India with military equipment.' Department of State, *Secretary's Meeting with Bangladesh Naval Chief Khan*, Washington, 2 July 1976.

11. Major General Safiullah to the author in an interview recorded in 1991.

12. Colonel M. Ziauddin, 'The Hidden Prize,' *The Holiday*, 12 August 1972; 'The Agony of Independence,' *The Far Eastern Economic Review*, Hong Kong, 16 August 1974.

13. Ali, 1994, pp. 12–13.

14. Ahamed, 1988, p. 70.

15. *Zindabad*, a Persian/Urdu word meaning 'long live' was widely used in Pakistan and among Muslim political groups across South Asia. *Joy Bangla*, (roughly translated to *vive le Bengal*), a Bengali call that became the nationalist war cry in 1970–71 and among the FFs during the war.

16. Ahmed, 1995, p. 16.

17. For the number of political prisoners held by the Mujib government, see Ahamed, 1988, p. 73. For the number of those released by Mushtaq, see Boster to Secretary of State, *Human Rights in Bangladesh*, Dhaka, American Embassy telegram-1532, 29 March 1976. Ahamed, ibid. says Mushtaq released none.

18. Boster, *Human Rights in Bangladesh*, ibid.

19. Ziring, 1992, p. 115, says Mosharraf acted 'possibly with Awami League collusion'; Ahamed, 1988, pp. 78–79, refutes this and claims that Mosharraf engineered the coup 'as a pre-emptive bid to prevent the radical forces from taking over control of the armed forces.' He cites no evidence. Most authors do report the exuberance with which Indian press and official media reported Zia's arrest, Mushtaq's eventual ouster and Mosharraf's assumption of the post of CAS.

20. Mascarenhas, 1986, pp. 98–99.

21. *The Frontier*, (Calcutta), 8 November 1975; Lifschultz, 1979, p. 8; Mascarenhas, 1986, p. 105.

22. Lifschultz, ibid.

23. Directorate of Plans, *Mukti Bahini Operations in the Rangpur-Mymensingh-Tangail Sector*, Langley: CIA, 3 December 1971.

24. Lifschultz, 1979, p. 50.

25. *Colonel Abu Taher*, Colonel Abu Taher Sangsad (Council), Dhaka, 2003.

26. According to the Colonel Abu Taher Sangsad, 'The army is still directed along its colonial lines. The ruling class has kept colonial service rules and structures of the Army intact and kept it away from the development process of the country. The Army is used with foreign collusion to settle power sharing among different factions of the ruling class. Consequently, there have been many examples of seizure of state power by the Army with the assistance of a section of the civil bureaucracy. The members of the armed forces have often protested against being used to repress the toiling people.' Ibid; also see, Lifschultz, 1979, p. 9.

27. Mascarenhas, 1986, p. 105; Lifschultz, 1979, p. 9; Ahamed, 1988, p. 79. Ahamed refutes the veracity of this widely believed allegation.

28. The Charter was presented to Zia by Colonel Taher, his rescuer-in-chief, at a gathering of radical soldiers who had rescued him from house arrest and

brought him to the 2nd Field Regiment Artillery barracks on 7 November 1975, Appendix I.

29. *Larai* (combat), Issue 6, Dhaka, JSD, November 1975; 'The Twelve Demands,', *The Far Eastern Economic Review*, 5 December 1975—cited in Lifschultz, 1979, pp. 9–10.

30. 'Political and Organisational Report: 7 November and Subsequent Events,' *Samyabad* (socialism), Issue 4, Dhaka, JSD, 23 February 1976, pp. 13–14.

31. Mascarenhas, 1986, p. 109.

32. Taher's acolytes would later explain this intriguing decision thus: 'On the 7 November, 1975, majority of the 'sepoys' and patriotic officers led by the valiant freedom fighter, retired Lt. Colonel Abu Taher, *Bir Uttam*, initiated an uprising against the conspiracies of a handful of senior officers. The aim of this historic soldiers'-people's uprising was to pave the way for the formation of a democratic national government and to shape the army as a production oriented, disciplined, powerful trained force suitable to safeguard the independence and sovereignty of the country. But this gallant effort was foiled and the senior officer in collusion with the vested quarters succeeded in restoring the old order.' Colonel Abu Taher Sangsad, op cit.

33. 'Political and Organisational Report: 7 November and Subsequent Events,' p. 14.

34. M.H. Chowdhury, M.A Hakim, Habib Zafarullah, 'Politics and Government: The Search for Legitimacy,' in Habib Zafarullah, Ed., *The Zia Episode in Bangladesh Politics*, New Delhi: South Asian Publishers, 1996, p. 24.

35. The author witnessed one such day-long episode late in February 1976 from close proximity in the Chittagong garrison.

36. H.A.K. Rono, 'Ekti oitihashik obhyuthhan: taar joy o pawrajoy' (an historic mutiny: its success and failure), in *7 November Revisited and Relevant Thoughts*, Dhaka, Colonel Taher Sangsad, 1982, pp. 45–7; Ahamed, 1988, p. 101.

37. For details of Taher's trial and execution, see Lifschultz, 1979, pp. 60–63.

38. Later, when he had become a party-political figure, Zia was asked by a senior legal adviser why he had enforced Taher's execution. He replied, 'I had no other alternative, the pressure from the army was too heavy.' After the tribunal had passed its sentence, Zia summoned forty-six senior-most military commanders to seek their views; 'all were in favour of this ultimate and final form of punishment.' See Ahmed, 1995, pp. 29–30, 34, fn. 58, 59.

39. Henry Kissinger told his rather cautious and reluctant inter-agency aides immediately after an apparently pro-American regime came to power following Mujib's assassination that Washington must check whether America was giving Bangladesh all the aid it could or Bangladesh could absorb—he did not think that was the case. 'I know we can't do a huge increase in aid.

But I think if people who think they are pro-US come to us and then get a technical lecture that unfortunately we can't do any more—there must be some manoeuvring we can do on food aid and some token increase in aid.' Kissinger insisted he wanted any Bangladeshi approach 'ought to get a friendly reception.' State Department, *The Secretary's 8.00 am. Meeting*, Washington, 15 August 1975.

40. On the process of militarisation of politics and economics in developing countries, see Robin Luckham, 'Militarism: Arms and the Internationalisation of Capital,' *IDS Bulletin*, vol. 8, no. 3, March 1977, pp. 38–40.

41. B.K. Jahangir, *Nationalism, Fundamentalism and Democracy in Bangladesh*, Dhaka: International Centre for Bengal Studies, 2002, pp. 52–3.

42. As a regimental and General-Staff officer serving at various units and headquarters in this period, the author experienced the bitterness and suspicions dividing the officers' corps.

43. Arms Control and Disarmament Agency (ACDA), *World Military Expenditures and Arms Transfers 1971–1980*, Washington: Defense Program and Analysis Division, 1983, p. 40. All figures in constant 1979 US dollars.

44. Ibid. pp. 40, 82. All figures in constant 1979 dollars.

45. Boster to Secretary of State, Dhaka: American Embassy telegram-0325, 19 January 1976.

46. Secretary of State to American Embassy Dhaka, Washington, telegram-170354, 10 July 1976.

47. For details of this conflict, see S. Mahmud Ali, *The Fearful State: Power, People and Internal War in South Asia*, London: Zed Books, 1993, pp. 162–203.

48. Ibid. p. 165.

49. Estimates of the Chakma population ranged from 350,000 to 400,000 out of a total non-Bengali population of 600,000. Ibid. p. 166, Table–1.

50. S. M. Ali, *Civil-Military Relations in the 'Soft State': The Case of Bangladesh*, Bath: European Commission, 1994, pp. 20–2.

51. As a General Staff Officer at 65 Brigade Headquarters and then at the 24th Light Infantry Division Headquarters in 1975–76, the author was briefed by senior commanders on the nature of the threat on several occasions. These two formations were successively responsible for managing the counterinsurgency operations in the CHT.

52. In 1978, the author was asked to discuss with J.B. Larma—while he was under treatment at the Dhaka Medical College hospital—the JSS/SB's demands. Larma sought extensive autonomy.

53. 'Hill Tracts Bleeds,' *The Holiday*, Dhaka, 30 May 1986.

54. *The Bangladesh Times*, Dhaka, 30 November 1976.

55. Ziaur Rahman, *Broadcast to the Nation*, Radio Bangladesh, Dhaka, 30 April 1977, Appendix II

56. T. Maniruzzaman, *Bangladesh Revolution and Its Aftermath*, Dhaka: Bangladesh Books International, 1980, pp. 217–8.

57. M.M. Khan and H.M. Zafarullah, 'The 1979 Parliamentary Elections in Bangladesh,' *Asian Survey*, Vol. 19, no. 10, 1979, p. 1023.

58. Chowdhury, Hakim and Zafarullah, op cit., p. 29.

59. Maniruzaman, 1980, p. 212.

60. Ibid.

61. Government of Bangladesh, *Economic Survey of Bangladesh, 1977–78*, Dhaka: Ministry of Planning, 1978, p. 105.

62. Akhtar Hossain, 'The Economy: Towards Stabilisation,' in Zafarullah, Ed., 1996, p. 72.

63. Ibid.

64. Ahmed, 1995, pp. 36–9, 43, 73–4.

65. Ibid. pp. 57–8, especially fn.5 and 6.

66. Ibid. p. 67.

67. Ibid.

68. Mascarenhas, 1986, pp. 145–6.

69. Ibid. Ahmed, 1995, pp. 67–8.

70. Ahmed, 1995, p. 68.

71. Ziaur Rahman, *Address to the Nation*, Dhaka, Radio Bangladesh, 2 October 1977.

72. Ahmed, 1995, p. 69.

73. Ibid. These were estimates; actual figures remained a secret. The findings of a two-member judicial commission of inquiry into the disturbances in Bogra in late September and in Dhaka in early October 1977 instituted by Zia were never published.

74. S. Mahmud Ali, 'The Demise of Zia: From Bloody Mutinies to Abortive Coups,' in Zafarullah, Ed., 1996, pp. 147–8.

75. Ahmed, 1995, p. 71.

76. Ahmed, 1995, p. 51.

77. Government of Bangladesh, *Results of the 1978 Presidential Elections*, Dhaka, Bangladesh Election Commission, 6 June 1978.

78. Chowdhury, Hakim and Zafarullah in Zafarullah, 1996, pp. 28–9.

79. Ibid. p. 33.

80. Government of Bangladesh, *The Bangladesh Gazette*, Notification no. 7/8/D-I/25/270, Part III, Dhaka: Ministry of Defence, 19 April 1979.

81. A.S. Haque, 'Bangladesh in 1980: Strains and Stresses—Opposition in the Doldrums,' *Asian Survey*, no. 21, 1981, p. 192; Ahmed, 1995, p. 140.

82. Ahmed, 1995, p. 141.

83. M.A. Halim, K.U. Ahmed, 'Foreign Affairs: Safeguarding National Interest,' in Zafarullah ed., 1996, pp. 130–6.

84. Ibid. p. 134.

85. Government of Bangladesh, *Flow of External Resources into Bangladesh*, Dhaka: Economic Relations Division, 1993, p. 47.

86. M.S. Huq, *Bangladesh in International Politics: The Dilemmas of the Weak States*, Dhaka: UPL, 1993, p. 259.

87. Akhtar Hossain, 'The Economy: Towards Stabilisation,' in Zafarullah, Ed., 1996, pp. 78–9.

88. Mascarenhas, 1986, pp. 150–1.

89. *The Holiday*, Dhaka, 19 April 1981.

90. This theory is elaborated, with much conjecture and modest evidence, in Jyoti Sen Gupta, *Bangladesh: In Blood and Tears*, New Delhi: Naya Prakash Publishers, 1981.

91. This theory was publicised by a US-based Bangladeshi academic. See, Zillur Rahman Khan, *Martial law to Martial Law*, Dhaka: UPL, 1984; also, Ahmed, 1995,pp. 148–50.

92. One of Bangladesh's best-known political scientists, Talukder Maniruzzaman, propounded this view in his *Group Interests and Political Changes*, New Delhi: South Asian Publishers, 1982.

93. See, for instance, Ahamed, 1988, pp. 123–8.

94. Ahmed, 1995, p. 153.

95. Ibid.

96. As a General-Staff Officer serving at the Army Headquarters at the time, the author was aware of these breaches of military protocol and the tensions they caused.

97. Ahmed, 1995, p. 154.

98. Ali in Zafarullah, ed., 1996, p. 154.

99. Ibid.

100. Mascarenhas, 1988, pp. 157–9.

101. A government guest house at the city centre dating back from the colonial era.

102. The government instituted a civilian commission of inquiry, a military court of inquiry and a court martial to try the officers accused of plotting and executing Zia's assassination. They also published a White Paper documenting the findings. The latter was published in August 1981.

103. Details of the 'operation' and its immediate aftermath appear in Ali in Zafarullah, ed., 1996, pp. 154–64; Ahmed, 1995, pp. 148–76; Ahamed, 1988, pp. 114–28; Mascarenhas, 1986, pp. 156–83.

104. Ahamed, 1988, p. 115.

105. Ahmed, 1995, p. 158.

106. Lt. Colonel A.Z. Tufail Ahmed, *Post Mortem Report: Major General M. A. Manzoor*, Chittagong: Combined Military Hospital, 2 June 1981.

107. On the legal controversies over the trial, see Ahmed, 1995, pp. 159–76.

108. Ibid. p. 173.

109. Ibid. p. 191.

110. Ibid. p. 192.

111. Bangladesh Election Commission, *Results of the Presidential Election*, Dhaka, 17 November 1981.

112. As the lead researcher monitoring the civilian bureaucracy's implementation of instructions issued by General Ershad as the country's CMLA, from the 'Research Cell' at the CMLA's Secretariat—effectively the cabinet office—in August-October 1983, the author heard this refrain from a number of senior officers engaged in administering the martial law regime under General H. M. Ershad.

113. Lt. General H. M. Ershad, 'Role of the Military in Underdeveloped Countries,' *Bangladesh Army Journal*, Dhaka: Army Education Directorate, January 1981, p. 12.

114. See, for instance, Ershad's comments in *The Guardian*, London, 7 October 1981; *The New York Times*, 14 October 1981; *The Bangladesh Observer*, Dhaka, 29 November 1981; and *The Holiday*, Dhaka, 6 December 1981.

115. B.M.M. Kabir, 'Bangladesh Politics in 1981–84: Military Rule and the Process of Civilianization,' *Chittagong University Studies*, Vol. 8, no. 1, June 1985, pp. 179–80.

116. Ali, 1994, p. 42.

117. Ahmed, 1995, pp. 232–5.

118. Ibid. p. 240.

119. Ali, 1994, pp. 42–3.

120. President Abdus Sattar in an interview with *the BBC World Service*, 21 January 1981.

121. Ahmed, 1995, p. 243.

122. Government of Bangladesh, 'Proclamation of Martial Law,' *Bangladesh Gazette Extraordinary*, Dhaka, 24 March 1982. Accounts of the putsch appear in Ahamed, 1988, pp. 131–6; Ziring, 1992, pp. 151–3; Ahmed, 1995, pp. 246, 249–52.

123. M. Ataur Rahman, 'Bangladesh in 1982: Beginning of the Second Decade,' *Asian Survey*, Vol. 23, no. 2, February 1983, p. 152.

124. Ali, 1994, p. 43, fn.32.

125. In 1986, the author was told by a General officer who had played a key role in the putsch that such action could not have been taken without planning and preparations spanning one, possibly two, years. This would be in consonance with the timing of Ershad's 1980 writing published in the *Bangladesh Army Journal* in January 1981. See fn. 113 above.

126. Ali, 1994, pp. 43–4.

127. Ibid. p. 44.

128. Ershad commanded 7 EBR, one of three Bengali–manned battalions of the EBR stationed in West Pakistan in 1971. His unit, deployed to the Sindh-Rajasthan sector as part of the Pakistani 18th Infantry Division, was ordered to disarm itself at the early stages of the war in the West. Ershad refused to surrender his battalion's arms and ammunition. As a result, his unit was redeployed several miles behind the frontline and surrounded with troops from neighbouring infantry battalions. This reduced the strength of the Division's manpower available for operations. The author, serving in a neighbouring unit, observed these events until his own arrest.

129. See, for instance, comments of Lt. Colonel Kazi Nuruzzaman (retd.), Chairman of the *Mukti Joddha Sangsad* (FF association), *The Bangladesh Observer*, Dhaka, 3 December 1981; and of General M.A.G. Osmany, *ibid*, 2 January 1982.

130. Ziring, 1992, p. 153.

131. Lt. General H.M. Ershad, *The CMLA's Address to the Nation*, Dhaka, Radio Bangladesh, 24 March 1982.

132. Ziring, 1992, p. 153.

133. President H.M. Ershad, *Address to the Nation*, Dhaka, Radio Bangladesh, 1 March 1985.

134. Government of Bangladesh, *Referendum ballot*, Dhaka: Election Commission, 21 March 1985.

135. Ahmed, 1995, p. 313.

136. The three fronts were all prefixed with *Natun Bangla* (new Bengali), and were the student, youth and labour wings of what became, in 1984, the short-lived *Janadal*, the people's party.

137. Ahmed, 1995, p. 316.

138. President H.M. Ershad, *Broadcast to the Nation*, Dhaka, Radio Bangladesh, 2 March 1986.

139. Ibid. 21 March 1986.

140. Among the other victors, *Jamaat-e-Islami* won ten seats, NAP and the Communist Party each took five, Muslim League and JSD (Rab) bagged four seats each, the rump BKSAL, JSD (Shahjahan Siraj) and the Workers Party won three each, NAP (Muzaffar) won two seats while independents took thirty-two. Government of Bangladesh, *Results of the National Assembly Elections of 7 May 1986*, Dhaka: Bangladesh Election Commission, May 1986.

141. This description of the Ershad administration, popularised by the BNP leader in her media interviews in this period, would be taken up by other opposition parties, including the Awami League, in later years as the anti–Ershad campaign gathered steam.

142. State Department, *Background Note: Bangladesh*, Washington: Bureau of South and Central Asian Affairs, March 2008.
143. Ahmed, 1995, pp. 324–5.
144. Ibid. pp. 256–7.
145. As the *ex–officio* chairman of the Dhaka Cantonment Golf Club's management committee, and an avid golfer, Ershad frequently hosted large groups of these entrepreneurs at the club where discussions ranged beyond sporting issues. Many of these men, suddenly developing a burning passion for the 18–hole course at weekends, flowered into wealthy entrepreneurs.
146. Ahmed, 1995, pp. 260–1.
147. Government of Bangladesh, *Preliminary Report of the Population Census*, Dhaka, 1991, cited in Ahmed, 1995, p. 282.
148. See chapter 1.
149. James Heitzman and Robert Worden, 'The Ershad Period: Achieving Stability, 1982–1983,' *Bangladesh: A Country Study*, Washington: Federal Research Division, Library of Congress, 1989.
150. In 1998, the author visited several 'Rural Health Centres' just an hour out of the capital's municipal limits. All had at least one building with a large notice-board; few had anything else. In one such shuttered building along the Dhaka-Maowa highway, overgrown with grass and weeds, cows and goats had broken in and were grazing contentedly. Not a medical orderly was in sight.
151. Government of Bangladesh, *The Drugs (Control) Ordinance 1982*, Dhaka, 12 June 1982.
152. The Right to Livelihood Foundation, *Report and Citation of Award*, Stockholm, 1992.
153. As opposed to police posts manned by a squad of constables and junior officers each; several such posts were managed and supervised by each *Thana*, and ensured law and order in their respective areas of responsibility.
154. Subsequent BNP administrations would change the name from *Upazila* to *Thana;* the chief executive officer would be called the *Thana Nirbahi* (executive) officer—TNO. Although different governments would adjust the brief and title of various officials, the TNO acronym would stick.
155. Ahmed, 1995, p. 303, fn7.
156. Despite efforts under successive administrations, this aspect of the criminal justice system did not improve. In April 2003, a High Court bench directed the government to withdraw all cases against children under twelve, and to immediately transfer all child-prisoners from jails to juvenile correction centres. See, for instance, 'HC order goes unheeded: 350 children continue to languish in jails,' *The Daily Star*, Dhaka, 28 June 2008.
157. Government of Bangladesh, *Martial Law Proclamation (2nd Amendment) Order 1982*, Dhaka: CMLA's Secretariat, 8 May 1982.

158. For arguments *pro* and *contra* on this issue, see Ahmed, 1995, pp. 268–79.

159. *The Military Balance 1984–1985*, London: International Institute for Strategic Studies (IISS), London, 1984, p. 97. The GDP grew by 1 per cent in 1982–83, and by 4.5 per cent in 1983–84; inflation was at 10 per cent in 1982–83, and 8 per cent in 1983–84. Ibid and *Military Balance 1985–1986*, London: IISS, 1985, p. 120.

160. Ibid. 1984, p. 141; ibid. 1985, p. 172. Figures are in current US dollars.

161. Ershad boosted Bangladesh-China relations, paying five official or state visits to Beijing during his rule—in November 1982, July 1985, July 1987, November 1988 and June 1990. His efforts, and Chinese reciprocation, led to considerable economic, diplomatic and military support flowing to Dhaka. China provided scientific-technical assistance, helped to build factories and bridges in Bangladesh, trained soldiers, sailors and airmen, and provided military hardware at 'friendship prices.' See *Sino-Bangladesh Relations*, Beijing: Ministry of Foreign Affairs, 22 October 2004.

162. B.M.N. Kabir, 'Bangladesh Politics in 1981–84: Military Rule and the Process of Civilianization,' *Chittagong University Studies*, Vol. 8, no. 1, June 1985, p. 182.

163. Arms Control and Disarmament Agency, *World Military Expenditures and Arms Transfers 1995*, Washington, 1996, pp. 63, 113. Financial figures are in current US dollars. GNP figures are estimates. Figures have been rounded off in source document.

164. Ali, 1993, p. 193.

165. Ibid.

166. Ibid. p. 195.

167. The Government of Bangladesh, 'Rangamati…Khagrachhari…Bandarban Hill Tracts District Local Government Council Act 1989,' *Bangladesh Gazette*, Dhaka, 6 March 1989.

168. The Government of Bangladesh, 'Hill Tracts (repeal of law, application and special provisions) Act 1989,' *Bangladesh Gazette*, Dhaka, 2 March 1989.

169. Ali, 1994, p. 53.

170. Ahmed, 1995, p. 327.

171. Ibid. p. 345, blames the BBC for this erroneous reporting. The author worked for the BBC World Service in London at this time and does not recall any deliberate attempt by his colleagues to obfuscate the truth.

172. The officer concerned later retired as a Brigadier-General. He narrated the day's events to the author in November 2006.

4. THE PLIGHT OF PARLIAMENTARY POLITICS

1. Ali, 1994, p. 55.

2. Sometime after retiring from service, General Nooruddin Khan would join the Awami League, be elected an MP and, later, serve as a minister in the 1996–2001 Sheikh Hasina cabinet.

3. Among them Major General Majidul Haq, Brigadier Hannan Shah, Colonel Mustafizur Rahman, Lt. Colonel Oli Ahmed and Major Mannan would later take up ministerial portfolios.

4. Except for Major Mannan, all had been associates of the late President Ziaur Rahman.

5. Government of Bangladesh, *Results of the Election to the Fifth National Assembly*, Dhaka: Bangladesh Election Commission, March 1991.

6. The 1972 constitution provided for fifteen such nominated seats reserved for women for the first thirty years of the country's independence. In 1978, Ziaur Rahman doubled the number by issuing Proclamation Order No. IV. Subsequent constitutional amendments legitimised that act.

7. Human Rights Watch (HRW), *Bangladesh: Political Violence on All Sides*, Vol. 8, no. 6, New York, June 1996, p. 6; Rehman Sobhan, 'Mediating political conflict in a confrontational environment,' in Syed Saad Andaleeb, Ed., *Political Culture in Bangladesh: Perspectives and Analyses*, Dhaka: UPL, 2007, p. 187.

8. Some authors have described the leadership of the two women at the helm of Bangladesh's two main parties as 'more indicative of a progressive political climate than a reflection of the country's dynastic, patronage-oriented political culture.' See K.A. Kronstadt, *Bangladesh: Background and U.S. Relations*, Washington: Congressional Research Service (CRS), 2003, p. 2.

9. A. Bilski and S.A. Belal, 'Waves of Destruction: Bangladesh Copes with Disaster,' *MaClean's*, 20 May 1991, p. 42; Major General H.C. Stackpole, 'Angels from the Sea,' *Proceedings/Naval Review*, Vol. 118/5/1,071, May 1992, p. 110.

10. Lt. Commander Frederick Gerheiser, USN, to Commanding General, Joint Task Force Sea Angel, *Bangladesh Cyclone Engineer Damage Assessment Report*, JTFJ4, 23 May 1991, para 3.

11. Major Paul McCarthy, *Operation Sea Angel: A Case Study*, Santa Monica: RAND, 1994, pp. 2–4.

12. Information provided to the author by armed forces officers during a field trip in 1992.

13. The operation was originally titled 'Productive Effort,' but after a Bangladeshi survivor saw the Marines arrive from the sea with help and allegedly called them 'angels from the sea,' it was changed to Operation Sea Angel. McCarthy, 1994, p. 6. fn.1. Apart from US forces from the Gulf and from Okinawa and Hawaii, fifteen military engineering personnel already in Bangladesh building schools in the northern Mymensingh district as part of

Exercise Baker Carriage II, were redeployed to the coast but because of a lack of heavy gear, their skills went unused. 84th Engineer Battalion (Combat) (Heavy), *84th Engineer Battalion's Participation in CJTF "Sea Angel,"* Schofield Barracks, Hawaii, 5 June 1991, para 4.

14. Major Mark Haselton, Commander Army Special Operations Forces team in Bangladesh, to Major Paul McCarthy, Hawaii, 16 March 1993.

15. US Air Force aircraft flew 194 missions delivering 2,430 tons of cargo; US Army helicopters flew 805 sorties distributing 891.5 tons of relief supplies; US Navy/Marine aircraft flew 969 sorties distributing 700 tons of relief supplies; US military teams supplied 266,000 gallons of drinking water and treated 15,000 patients in the affected areas. McCarthy, 1994, p. 31.

16. Stackpole, 1992, p. 112.

17. McCarthy, 1994, p. 1.

18. Stackpole, 1992, p. 114.

19. Information provided to author by armed forces officers during a field trip in 1992.

20. S. Aminul Islam, *The Predicament of Democratic Consolidation in Bangladesh*, Dhaka: Department of Sociology, University of Dhaka, not dated, p. 11.

21. Ibid.

22. During discussions in the parliament, Information Minister Nazmul Huda impugned the Islamic credentials of the Awami League and its leaders seated across the aisle. The latter immediately protested but Huda neither retracted nor was he disciplined. This, and the Speaker's refusal to table for discussion the opposition's allegation of corruption against several ministers triggered a walk-out by MPs from the Awami League, Jatiaya Party, Jamaat-e-Islami and several smaller parties on 1 March 1994. The BNP candidate's contested victory in the Magura-2 by-election on 20 March ensured the opposition would not return to the parliament. HRW, June 1996, p. 6.

23. Rehman Sobhan, in Syed Saad Andaleeb, 2007, p. 186.

24. The G5 comprised former Chief Justice Kamaluddin Hossain, former Attorney General Syed Ishtiaq Ahmed, former Foreign Secretary Fakhruddin Ahmed, senior journalist Faiz Ahmed, and Executive Chairman of the Centre for Policy Dialogue, a think-tank, which provided logistical support, Professor Rehman Sobhan. The G5 asked senior journalist Ataus Samad to act as their public face and contact for the media.

25. Sobhan, op cit, pp. 189–99.

26. Ibid, p. 199.

27. HRW, 1996, p. 7.

28. Ibid.

29. Compiled from *The New Age, The Daily Star*, and *Naya Diganta*, all daily newspapers published in Dhaka on 28 October 2006.

30. Charlotte Duncan, Cecilie Brokner, Dilara Choudhury, Lisa Hiller, Kathryn Uphaus, *Beyond Hartals: Towards Democratic Dialogue in Bangladesh*, Dhaka: UNDP, March 2005, pp. 32–3.

31. Most studies by national and foreign assessors take individual consumption of food containing 2112 kilo calories (kcal) daily as the baseline for calculating poverty. The Bangladesh Bureau of Statistics (BSS) uses the marginally higher baseline of 2122 kcal. On this basis, a very large proportion of Bangladesh's population fell below the poverty line. Although every administration, party and leader, barring neutral caretaker ones, have pledged to alleviate, even 'eliminate' poverty during election campaigns, progress has been modest.

32. UNDP, *Fighting Human Poverty: Bangladesh Human Development Report 2000*, Dhaka, January 2001, p. 21, especially fn.1 and 3; Government of Bangladesh, *Bangladesh Economic Review*, Dhaka: Ministry of Finance, 1999.

33. UNDP, January 2001, p. 23.

34. Z.R. Khan, 'Aspirations and Realities: Parliaments and the Democratic Culture,' in S. S. Andaleeb, 2007, p. 173.

35. UNDP, March 2005, pp. 32–3.

36. Z.R. Khan, 'Aspirations and Realities: Parliaments and the Democratic Culture,' p. 173.

37. Briefing given to the author by senior army officers during a field trip in 1997.

38. This line of analysis was widely noted in editorials and op-ed columns published in a number of Bangladeshi newspapers—e.g., *Dainik* (daily) *Ittefaq*, *Sangbad*, *The Bangladesh Observer*, and *The Holiday*, between 21 May 1996, the day after Biswas sacked Nasim, and 25 May 1996, after Nasim had quietly surrendered and left the AHQ.

39. Briefing given to the author by senior army officers during a field trip in 1997.

40. Ibid.

41. Ali, 1994, p. 57.

42. Ibid.

43. Compiled from *The Military Balance*, London: IISS, 1992, pp. 130–1; 1993, p. 137; 1994, pp. 152–3; 1995, pp. 156–7; 1996, pp. 158–9; 1997, pp. 152–3; 1998, pp. 154–5; ACDA, *World Military Expenditures and Arms Transfers 1997*, Washington, February 1999, p. 19. Figures are in current million US dollars except for GDP which is in billion US dollars. Separate account of actual defence expenditure as distinct from budget allocations in 1991 is not available in these sources.

44. ACDA, *World Military Expenditure and Arms Transfers 1997*, Washington, 1998, Table III, South Asia.

45. Wahiduddin Mahmud, 'National budgets and Public spending patterns in Bangladesh: A political-economic perspective,' in Andaleeb, 2007, p. 207.

46. Roger Robinson, *Bangladesh: Progress Through Partnership*, Washington: World Bank, 1999, p. 16.

47. Bangladesh's annual budget has two components. The current or revenue budget meets regular and recurrent expenditure on public administration, national defence, social sectors such as health and education, and payments of interest on foreign concessional loans. These costs are matched against revenue income. Any surplus left over from the collected revenue goes into project-wise allocations for developmental spending across the economy and especially in social sectors. The Annual Development Plan (ADP) budget funds major new infrastructural projects, but costs of maintaining existing stock come out of the revenue budget. ADP expenditure above and beyond the revenue surplus is met with foreign aid net of amortisation outlays. Ibid, pp. 208–9.

48. World Education Forum, *EFA 2000 Assessment: Country Reports—Bangladesh*, Dhaka: UNESCO, 2001, Tables 7A-7B. All figures in million Takas.

49. Ibid, Table 7C. All figures in million Takas.

50. Ibid. p. 4.

51. Ibid, pp. 5–6.

52. HRW, 1996, p. 7.

53. For specific examples of gross violations of human rights and other abuses, see ibid, pp. 8–21; attribution of blame to militants belonging to both ruling- and opposition parties is on pp. 21–2.

54. Islam, *The Predicament of Democratic Consolidation in Bangladesh*, op. cit., pp. 17–8.

55. Ibid. p. 18.

56. Ibid, tables 2 and 3, pp. 21–2.

57. Government of Bangladesh, *Elections to the Sixth National Assembly*, Dhaka: Election Commission, June 2006.

58. Ibid.

59. Z.R. Khan in Andaleeb, 2007, pp. 174–5. It would, however, have to wait until another CTG implemented these provisions in 2007–8. See chapter 6.

60. Government of Bangladesh, *Adverse impacts on Bangladesh due to withdrawal of dry season Ganges flow at Farakka and upstream*, Dhaka: Ministry of Water Resources, 1996.

61. B. Crow, A. Lindquist, and D. Wilson, *Sharing the Ganges: the Politics and Technology of River Development*, Dhaka: UPL, 1995, ch.1.

62. A concise account of Pakistani and Bangladeshi efforts to first pre-empt and then negotiate a dilution of the negative impact of the barrage's operations on Bangladesh up to 1983 appears in B.M. Abbas, *The Ganges Water Dispute*,

Dhaka, UPL, 1984. Abbas participated in or led many of the delegations which negotiated with Indian counterparts on this issue.

63. M.M. Rahaman, *The Ganges water sharing: A comparative analysis of 1977 Agreement and 1996 Treaty*, Espoo: Water Resources Laboratory, Helsinki University of Technology, 2006, Table II.

64. In October 1993, Zia expressed concern over the continuing withdrawal of water in the dry season at the Commonwealth Heads of Government Meeting (CHOGM) in Cyprus. Two years later, her government raised the issue of 'the misery of the people of Bangladesh' inflicted by the Farakka Barrage, at the 50th UNGA in New York. There was little positive reaction from India.

65. For an indication of the hospitality extended to her, see I.K. Gujral, *Suo moto Statement by the External Affairs Minister on the visit of Prime Minister of the People's Republic of Bangladesh to India and the signing of a Treaty on the sharing of Ganga Waters at Farakka*, Delhi: Ministry of External Affairs, 12 December 1996.

66. Rahaman, 2006, Table IV.

67. Ibid, Table III.

68. In early 1999, more than a year after a peace treaty had been signed between the government and the PCJSS, an army General told the author that while the military had suffered in the CHT operations and had been rewarded for its contributions, this essentially political problem needed a political solution and that the army was happy with the outcome of the agreement.

69. Amnesty International, *Bangladesh: Human Rights in the CHT*, London, February 2000, p. 10.

70. Bangladesh National Assembly, *Bangladesh Gazette Extraordinary: CHT Regional Council Act, 1998*, Dhaka, 24 May 1998, pp. 2–3. The gazette notification provides the details of the power, duties and functions of the chairman and members.

71. Amnesty International, February 2000, p. 6.

72. Government of Bangladesh, *The Agreement between the National Committee on Chittagong Hill Tracts constituted by the Government and the Parbattya Chattagram Jana Samhati Samiti* [CHT Peace Accord], Dhaka, 2 December 1997, Article D.2.

73. Ibid, Article D.4.

74. *Jumma* is derived from *jum*, which indicates the slash-and-burn technique of periodic cultivation used by montagnard farmers on the CHT's hill slopes. The tribal population collectively describes itself as 'the *Jumma* people' or the people who use the *jum* method of farming.

75. PGP, PCP and HWF, *Why we oppose Government-PCJSS agreement on Chittagong Hill Tracts*, Rangamati, 4 May 1998.

76. Amnesty International, February 2000, pp. 8–9.

77. Ben Sheppard, ed., *Jane's Sentinel Security Assessment: South Asia*, Coulsdon: Jane's, 1999, p. 63.

78. Amnesty International, February 2000, p. 9.

79. Carlo del Ninno, Paul Dorosh, Lisa Smith, Dilip Roy, *The 1998 Floods in Bangladesh*, Washington: International Food Policy Research Institute, Research Report 122, 2001, p. 2.

80. Before mid-1998, major floods triggered by simultaneous peaking had hit Bangladesh in 1954, 1974, 1987 and 1988, causing serious agricultural and nutritional problems and extensive infrastructural damage and economic losses, as well as losses of lives and livelihood.

81. The comparable average for 1988 had been thirty-four days. Bangladesh Water Development Board, 1998, cited in Ninno, Dorosh, Smith, Roy, 2001, p. 4.

82. Grameen Trust flood website: http://www.bangladeshonline.com/gob/flood98/foreign_1.html accessed in 1999 and cited in ibid, p. 5.

83. Ninno, Dorosh, Smith, Roy, 2001, p.*xvi*.

84. Ibid, p.*xvii*.

85. Ibid, p. 3.

86. The World Bank, *Bangladesh Poverty Assessment Report*, Dhaka, April 1998, ch.1.

87. Tercan Baysan, Syed Nizamuddin, Zahid Hussain, Zaidi Sattar, *Bangladesh: Annual Economic Update*, Dhaka: The World Bank, October 1997, p. 25.

88. Ibid.

89. Ibid.

90. Ibid, Table–4.1, p. 43.

91. The World Bank, *Bangladesh: An Agenda for Action*, Dhaka, 1996.

92. The World Bank, *An Agenda for Action: Status Report 1997*, Dhaka, January 1998, pp. 1–3.

93. K. Kapur, Z. Hussain, Z. Sattar, S. Nizamuddin, Min Tang, R. Khan, N. Rao, Y. Uehara, D. Ponzi, S. Ahmed, *Bangladesh: Economic Trends and the Policy Agenda*, Dhaka: The World Bank and The Asian Development Bank, May 1998, p. 1.

94. Transparency International Bangladesh, *Evidence to be submitted to the United Kingdom House of Commons International Development Committee Hearing on Corruption and Development*, Dhaka/London, 14 November 2000, p. 4.

95. Transparency International, *Nationwide Household Corruption Survey*, Dhaka, TI Bangladesh Chapter, 1997, pp. 1–2.

96. Ibid. p. 2.

97. TI Bangladesh, 14 November 2000, p. 4.

98. In Bangladesh, financial years begin on 1 July and end on 30 June the following year. FY 1998–99 ran from 1 July 1998 to 30 June 1999.

99. TI Bangladesh, 14 November 2000, p. 5.

100. Ibid. This report provides information on graft in banking, roads & highways, revenue collection, police, courts, local government and other sectors of public life.

101. Amin Sarkar, 'Political Economy of Sustainable Development in Bangladesh,' in S. S. Andaleeb, ed., 2007, p. 259.

102. Ibid.

103. Ibid.

104. Muzaffer Ahmad, *Governance, Structural Adjustment & the State of Corruption in Bangladesh*, Dhaka: Transparency International Bangladesh, 2000, pp. 1–2. Percentages have been rounded off.

105. Ibid, p. 3.

106. Ibid.

107. Ibid, p. 5.

108. *The Daily Star*, Dhaka, 24 April 2000.

109. Aqil Shah, 'Regional Reports: South Asia,' in *Global Corruption Report 2001*, Berlin, Transparency International, 2001, p. 47.

110. Ibid, pp. 43–4.

111. UNCTAD, *World Investment Report 2001*, New York: UN Publications, 2000, cited in ibid, p. 45.

112. American Chamber of Commerce, *Chittagong Port: Concerns and Solutions*, Dhaka: AmCham press release, 31 January 2001.

113. *The Independent*, Dhaka, 2 October 2000.

114. TI-Bangladesh, 'The costs of corruption in Bangladesh,' in Shah, 2001, p. 45.

115. Ben Sheppard, Ed., 1999, pp. 64–5.

116. Ibid, p. 62.

117. Paul Burton, Ed., *Jane's Sentinel Security Assessment: South Asia*, Coulsdon: 2000, p. 72.

118. Ibid, p. 74.

119. Hasina quoted in ibid, pp. 72.

120. Compiled from *The New Age*, *The Daily Star*, and *Naya Diganta*, all dailies published in Dhaka on 28 October 2006.

121. These were some of the points made by the donors at the meeting of the Bangladesh Development Forum coordinated by the World Bank in Paris in mid-2000. A World Bank official involved in the discussions unofficially briefed the author in Dhaka in December 2000.

122. UNDP, *Beyond Hartals: Towards Democratic Dialogue in Bangladesh*, Dhaka, March 2005, p. 32. The GDP is calculated in constant market prices. Figures are in million Takas (Tk.m).

123. Ibid, Table 4.1.

124. On separate field trips in 2000, the author was invited to two such 'round tables' where eminent scholars, newspaper columnists and retired bureaucrats with party-political affiliations exchanged views on how to 'save' the country. One was organised by the editor of a prominent daily; the other, by an NGO. The recommendations which emerged sounded rational and self-evident. However, there was little intermediation between these scholarly exercises and the street battles which raged between the supporters of the government and its violently vocal critics.

125. An official inquiry into Brigadier-General Shabab Ashfaq's death concluded he had shot himself although the reasons for his taking such drastic action were not apparent. Brigadier-General Kalam Shahed, the commander who refused to lend his name to institutionalised financial impropriety, and one of the very few serving officers with a doctoral degree, is currently employed by a Western government.

126. Ben Sheppard, Ed., *Jane's Sentinel Security Assessment: South Asia*, Coulsdon: Jane's, 1999, p. 74; Paul Burton, ed., ibid, Coulsdon, 2001, p. 81.

127. In 2004, during a visit to Bangladesh, the author was told by the then Chief of Air Staff that the MiG-29s were unsuitable for the designated purpose for which they had been procured. In 2000, the Bangladeshi Defence Attache in Delhi told the author that he had been warned about this particular aircraft by senior Indian Air Force officers operating the same model on the ground that its rapid climb-rate, useful in the air-defence role, meant its engines burnt out rapidly and had to be frequently changed, at great expense. Cheaper alternatives existed. As for the Daewoo-built frigate, the *BNS Bangabandhu*, named after Hasina's father, it was taken out of service for several years by the successor BNP government, docked for an extensive and expensive refit, renamed, and then commissioned anew.

128. For defence budget allocations and actual expenditure in 1996–2001, see *The Military Balance*, London: IISS, 1997, pp. 152–3; ibid, 1998, pp. 154–5; ibid, 1999, pp. 160–1; ibid, 2000, pp. 167–8; ibid, 2001, pp. 161–2.

129. Ibid. Also see Ben Sheppard, 1999, pp. 70–71; Sheppard, 2000, pp. 80–81; Paul Burton, 2000, pp. 82–83. Military manpower figures vary. Later editions of *The Military Balance*, London: IISS, 2001, pp. 161–2, and 2002, p. 128, put the total at 125,500.

130. Allocations are made as part of the revenue budget and the largely foreign aided ADP. All figures are in million Tk. World Education Forum, *The EFA 2000 Assessment Country Reports: Bangladesh*, Dhaka: UNESCO, 2001, Tables 7A and 7B.

131. Ibid, Table–7C.

132. Ibid, pp. 3–4.

133. Ibid, pp. 5–6.

134. IBRD and the World Bank, *To the MDGs and Beyond: Accountability and Institutional Innovation in Bangladesh*, Dhaka, January 2007, pp. 11–12.

135. Ibid, p. 13.

136. Ibid, pp. 13–15.

137. Each of the cases listed here was covered at length by the main vernacular dailies like *Ittefaq* and English-language ones like *The Daily Star* as the facts became known over several days . For concise accounts, see Amnesty International, *Bangladesh: Torture and Impunity*, London, November 2000, especially pp. 5–6.

138. For details of widespread violation of citizens' rights and abuses by a wide range of state functionaries and organisations under Sheikh Hasina's premiership, see UNDP, *Human Security in Bangladesh: In Search of Justice and Dignity*, Dhaka, September 2002.

139. UNDP, *Human Development Report 2001*, New York: UN Publications, 10 July 2001.

140. For details of resource allocations to the health sector and their outcome, see Tulshi Saha, *Bangladesh Service Provision Assessment Survey 1999–2000*, Calverton, Maryland, National Institute of Population Research and Training (NIPORT), 2002; and NIPORT, ORC Macro, Johns Hopkins University and Centre for Health and Population Research, *Bangladesh Maternal Health Services and Maternal Mortality Survey 2001*, Calverton, Baltimore and Dhaka, December 2003.

141. United Nations, *United Nations Records Bangladesh's Achievements*, Information Department press release, New York, 9 July 2001.

142. International Parliamentary Union, *Bangladesh: Last Elections*, Geneva, report at IPU website at http://www.ipu.org/parline-e/reports/2023_E.htm accessed on 4 August 2008.

143. Paul Burton, Ed., *Jane's Sentinel Security Assessment: South Asia*, Coulsdon: Jane's, 2002, p. 109.

144. S.A. Islam, 'Book Review', in *Bangladesh e-Journal of Sociology*, Vol. 4, no. 1, January 2007.

145. Government of Bangladesh, *Results of Parliamentary Elections 2001*, Dhaka: Election Commission, October 2001.

146. Ibid; Burton, 2002, p. 113.

147. This phrase was widely used by Awami League spokesmen in the election's aftermath. In late-2002, a leading member of the party's cultural wing in Dhaka insisted to the author these allegations were true, although he did not present any evidence.

148. Waresul Karim, *Election Under a Caretaker Government: Empirical Analysis of the October 2001 Parliamentary Election in Bangladesh*, 2nd edition, Dhaka: UPL, 2007, p. 254.

149. Islam, January 2007.

150. Steven Dunaway and Shigeo Kashiwagi, Eds., *Staff Report for the 2001 Article IV Consultation*, Dhaka: International Monetary Fund (IMF), 8 April 2002, p. 1.

151. *IMF Concludes 2001 Article IV Consultation with Bangladesh*, Public Information Notice (PIN) no. 02/54, Washington: IMF, 15 May 2002.

152. Dunaway and Kashiwagi, Eds., April 2002, p. 4.

153. IMF, 15 May 2002.

154. Dunaway and Kashiwagi, Eds., 2002, p. 6.

155. IMF, 15 May 2002.

156. Saifur Rahman, Bangladeshi Finance Minister, to Horst Kohler, Managing Director, IMF, *Memorandum of Economic and Financial Policies*, Dhaka: Ministry of Finance, 4 June 2003, p. 1.

157. Ibid, p. 2.

158. Ibid, p. 8.

159. Ibid, p. 5.

160. Saifur Rahman to Rodrigo de Rato, Managing Director, IMF, *Memorandum of Economic and Financial Policies*, Dhaka: Ministry of Finance, 8 July 2004, pp. 2–3.

161. Ibid, p. 3.

162. Ibid, p. 4.

163. Saifur Rahman to Rodrigo de Rato, *Memorandum of Economic and Financial Policies*, Dhaka: Ministry of Finance, 26 May 2005, pp. 1, 4.

164. Ibid, p. 1.

165. Ibid, p. 2.

166. Ibid, pp. 7–10.

167. Jonathan Dunn, 'Growth in Bangladesh,' in *Country Report no. 05/242*, Washington: IMF, July 2005, p. 5.

168. Ibid, pp. 6–10.

169. Saifur Rahman to Rodrigo de Rato, *Letter of Intent*, Dhaka: Ministry of Finance and Ministry of Planning, Government of Bangladesh, 9 January 2006, p. 1.

170. Saifur Rahman to Rodrigo de Rato, *Memorandum of Economic and Financial Policies for 2006*, Dhaka: Ministry of Finance, 9 January 2006, pp. 1–2.

171. Ibid, p. 3.

172. Ibid, p. 4.

173. Steven Dunaway, Anthony Boote, Eds., *Fifth Review Under the Three-Year Arrangement Under the Poverty Reduction and Growth Facility, and Request for Waiver of Performance Criteria, extension of the Arrangement, and Rephasing*, Washington: IMF, 6 October 2006, p. 4.

174. Bangladesh Bureau of Statistics, *National Accounts Statistics*, Dhaka, Government of Bangladesh, June 2007; Rezaul Khan, 'Bangladesh,' in *Asian Development Outlook*, Manila: ADB, 2008, table 3.15.1, p. 157.

175. See, for instance, the assessment by Rezaul Khan, ibid, especially pp. 157–9.
176. Compiled from *The New Age*, *The Daily Star*, and *Naya Diganta*, all dailies published in Dhaka, on 28 October 2006.
177. Ibid.
178. Compiled from *Parliament Watch: 2001–2006*, Dhaka: Transparency International-Bangladesh, February 2007.
179. The 2001 and 2006 Corruption Perception Indices are accessible at http://www.transparency.org/policy_research/survey.s_indices/cpi
180. See Haroon Habib, 'The sacking of a president,' *Frontline*, Madras, 06–09 July 2002.
181. Informal exchanges with the author in Dhaka in January 2008.
182. Compiled from Colonel Christopher Langton, Ed., *The Military Balance*, London: IISS, 2003, p. 288; ibid, 2004, p. 313; ibid, 2005, p. 234; ibid, 2006, p. 229; ibid, 2007, p. 313; FY2006 GDP growth figure taken from *IMF Executive Board Concludes 2007 Article IV Consultation with Bangladesh*, PIN no. 07/75, Washington: IMF, 29 June 2007, p. 1.
183. *Key Indicators of Developing Asian and Pacific Countries: Bangladesh*, Manila: ADB, 2007, p. 178. This conservative estimate is challenged by UNICEF in it's *State of the World's Children 2008*, Geneva, 5 August 2008, p. 114, recording a population of 155.99 million in 2006. If true, this latter figure would cast most indicators in a more worrying light. Another donor agency report records the population at 144.30 million in 2006. See Aloysius Milon Khan, *Country Fact Sheet: Bangladesh*, Dhaka: DFID, May 2008, p. 1, citing Bangladesh Bureau of Statistics, World Bank and UNDP sources.
184. *Key Indicators of Developing Asian and Pacific Countries: Bangladesh*, Manila: ADB, 2007, p. 178.
185. UNICEF, 5 August 2008, p. 114.
186. Ibid, p. 134.
187. Ibid, p. 130.
188. IMF, PIN no.07/75, 29 June 2007, p. 2.
189. UNICEF, 5 August 2008, p. 138.
190. Compiled from Paul Burton, Ed., 2001, pp. 79, 92; Colonel Christopher Langton, Ed., *The Military Balance*, London: IISS, 2003, pp. 135, 336; ibid, 2004, p. 354; ibid, 2005, p. 234; ibid, 2006, p. 229; ibid, 2007, p. 313; ibid, 2008, p. 339. (Figure for FY2007 is budgetary allocation rather than actual expenditure.)
191. Informal briefing to author by Dhaka-based army officers in December 2000.
192. Informal briefing to author by Dhaka-based army officers in June-July 2003.

193. 'Dhaka Lynchings Spread Alarm,' *BBC News Online: South Asia*, 10 December 2001.

194. Human Rights Watch (HRW), *Judge, Jury and Executioner: Torture and Extrajudicial Killings by Bangladesh's Elite Security Force*, New York, December 2006, p. 16.

195. 'Troops Resume Dhaka Crime Fight,' *BBC News Online: South Asia*, 18 February 2003.

196. HRW, December 2006, p. 18.

197. Ibid.

198. Ibid, p. 3; also see Suhas Chakma, Editor, *SAARC Human Rights Report 2006*, Delhi: Asian Centre for Human Rights, 2006, pp. 4–6 for a detailed critique of RAB action.

199. 'K.M. Hasan steps aside for the sake of people,' *The Daily Star*, Dhaka, 29 October 2006.

200. One of them, former CAS, General Hasan Mashhud Chowdhury, said, 'From the very start it was clear that the president was a party-man...He was not detached from his party in the least...and had totally failed in his job as a neutral administrator.' General Chowdhury quoted in ICG, *Restoring Democracy in Bangladesh*, Brussels, 28 April 2008, p. 6.

201. National Democratic Institute, *Survey on the Integrity of the Voter's List*, Washington and Dhaka, 10 December 2006.

202. ICG, 2008, p. 7.

203. The swift posting and retirement of several Generals after President Iajuddin Ahmed was forced to step down as Chief Adviser and accept an army-imposed CTG on 11 January 2007 reinforced this belief.

204. The Club comprised the envoys of Australia, Canada, the EU, Japan, the UK and the USA who represented Bangladesh's largest donors. In late January 2008, the author met several of the envoys at a social gathering hosted by the German Ambassador in Dhaka.

205. European Commission, *European Commission suspends its Election Observation Mission to Bangladesh,'* Brussels, 11 January 2007.

206. Department of Public Information, *United Nations Says Bangladesh Political Crisis Jeopardises Electoral Legitimacy*, New York: UN Secretariat, 10 January 2007.

207. Renata Dessallien made a press statement in Dhaka to this effect on 11 January 2007. It was reported by virtually the entire national press on the following day.

5. A 'REFORMIST' INTERREGNUM

1. Shafiq Alam, 'Sheikh Hasina sworn in as Bangladesh PM, democracy restored,' *Agence France Press (AFP)*, Dhaka, 6 January 2009; Anis Ahmed,

'Hasina takes oath as new Bangladesh prime minister,' *Reuters*, Dhaka, 6 January 2009; 'Hasina sworn in as Bangladesh's prime minister,' *Associated Press (AP)*, Dhaka, 6 January 2009.

2. 'Bangladesh: The nice side of democracy, shame about the democrats,' *The Economist*, 8–14 November 2008 (UK edition), p. 72.

3. Briefings received by the author from officials and analysts during visits to Dhaka in January 2008 and January 2009.

4. Informal discussions with donor community officials in Dhaka, 22 January 2009.

5. Khaleda Zia alleged such 'conspiracies' to establish 'a puppet government' in her campaign speeches just days before the election. See 'Khaleda doubts EC neutrality, fair polls.' *The Daily Star*, Dhaka, 19 December 2008.

6. In past elections, party leaders such as H.M. Ershad, Sheikh Hasina and Khaleda Zia had often contested the maximum number of seats allowed and, having won all or most of them, relinquished all but one. The vacated seats then usually went to their own party colleagues in by-elections which followed. The leader's popularity was thus leveraged to maximise the party's gain.

7. International Crisis Group, *Bangladesh: Elections and Beyond*, Brussels, 11 December 2008, p. 3.

8. Ibid, p. 4.

9. 'EC warns BNP for violating electoral code of conduct,' *The Daily Star*, Dhaka, 10 November 2008.

10. 'EC warns AL,' *The Daily Star*, Dhaka, 11 November 2008.

11. 'RPO, party constitution overlooked,' *The Daily Star*, Dhaka, 18 November 2008.

12. 'BNP constitution, RPO choked,' *The Daily Star*, Dhaka, 28 November 2008.

13. On 14 December, the CTG approved the Emergency Powers (Repeal) Ordinance 2008; it was then signed by President Iajuddin Ahmed. The following day, the government issued a gazette announcing that the Emergency Powers Ordinance 2007 and Emergency Powers Rules 2007 on the basis of which the CTG had administered the country since 11 January 2007, would be repealed on 17 December.

14. 'Emergency revoked,' *The New Age*, Dhaka, 17 December 2008.

15. Government of Bangladesh, *Gazette notification: Emergency Powers (Repeal) Ordinance 2008*, Dhaka, 15 December 2008. Theoretically, members of the parliament elected on 29 December could, in future, gather a sufficiently large majority to overturn these caveats, but by challenging elements of the legal framework within which representative governance was restored, they would potentially be putting their own election to question.

16. In mid-2008, General Masud Chowdhury, who had played a leading role in his capacity as the General Officer Commanding, 9 Infantry Division stationed in and around Dhaka, in the army's assumption of effective control on 11 January 2007, was placed under the Ministry of Foreign Affairs. In late 2008, he took up a diplomatic assignment as the country's envoy to Australia.

17. By the time Sheikh Hasina assumed office as prime minister in January 2009, many of these had expired, but 96 remained active and needed to be either ratified or disposed of by the newly elected legislature. BBC Bengali Service, *Probaha*, broadcast on 7 January 2009 at 1330 GMT.

18. 'Emergency revoked,' *The New Age*, Dhaka, 17 December 2008.

19. Shakhawat Liton, 'No easy going yet for court-clearing aspirants; disqualification on the cards even if elected; EC decides to launch legal battle,' *The Daily Star*, Dhaka, 21 December 2008.

20. In the First Information Report (FIR) recorded by the police, complainant Azam Chowdhury alleged that Sheikh Hasina's cousin, Sheikh Fazlul Karim Selim, had taken Tk 30 million from him in exchange for awarding the contract to build key elements of Siddhirganj Power Plant near Narayanganj outside Dhaka. In July 2007, the police submitted a charge-sheet before the court indicting Sheikh Hasina, her sister Sheikh Rehana, and cousin Selim. See 'Azam Chowdhury applies to withdraw case against Hasina.' *The New Nation*, Dhaka, 15 December 2008.

21. 'Tk 1 crore extortion: Plaintiff wants to drop case against Tareque,' *The Daily Star*, Dhaka, 18 December 2008. Both Tareque Rahman and Arafat Rahman were released in the summer of 2008 and allowed to travel abroad for medical treatment as part of an informal agreement with Khaleda Zia who herself was later released under bail to lead her party's election campaign. Cases against Sheikh Hasina, too, were suspended as she led the Awami League's campaign.

22. J.A. Manik and Emran Hossain, 'Anti–graft drive stumbles on TAC; HC order against TAC catches government off guard; over 80 percent corruption cases stuck into HC stay,' *The Daily Star*, Dhaka, 15 November 2008.

23. 'It's legally verified, affirms ACC chief,' *The Daily Star*, Dhaka, 23 December 2008.

24. Sheikh Hasina, *Address to the Federation of Bangladesh Chambers of Commerce and Industry (FBCCI)*, Dhaka, 23 December 2008, reported in the BBC Bengali Service radio programme *Probaha*, broadcast at 1330 GMT on 23 December 2008.

25. As guests invited to the military's Armed Services Day reception in late November, the 'two Begums' exchanged pleasantries during a brief, 'managed encounter.' There were no substantive talks between the country's two most influential politicians.

26. Owen Lippert, *Proposal Summary: Poll-Level Electoral Return Map*, Washington: National Democratic Institute, at http://www.ndibd.org/election_analysis.php accessed on 8 December 2008.

27. Bangladesh Election Commission, *Number of Candidates (Party-wise)*, Commission's website at http://www.ecs.gov.bd/English/QLTemplate1.php? Parameter_QLSCat_ID=55 accessed on 29 December 2008. However, on another page of the Commission's website, the list of 'Political Parties Registered with the Election Commission' only named thirty-two parties, at http://www.ecs.gov.bd/Bangla/MenuTemplate1.php?Parameter_MenuID=53 also accessed on Election Day, i.e., 29 December 2008. The explanation is provided by the separate representation of several factions of a few parties in the former list but not in the latter.

28. *The Economist*, 8–12 November 2008, Op cit.

29. The Election Commission's website, http://www.ecs.gov.bd cited by the IGC, *Bangladesh: Elections and Beyond*, op cit, p. 2, fn. 3. However, the number of registered voters fell—probably owing to the death of some—to 81,058,698 on the day before polling. Of them, women voters made up 41.23 million and men, 39.82 million. Election Commission website, http://www.ecs.gov.bd/NewsFilesEng/32.pdf accessed on 28 December 2008.

30. *The Economist*, 8–12 November 2008.

31. Asif Zakaria, 'HuJI "Plans to kill" Hasina: CNN-IBN,' Dhaka, *bdnews24.com*, Dhaka, 20 December 2008; 'Huji suicide squad ready: Target Hasina; We are taking it seriously: SSF Chief,' *Shamokal*, Dhaka, 21 December 2008.

32. Shariful Islam and Aminul Islam, 'Hasina ready to sacrifice life for country,' *The Daily Star*, Dhaka, 22 December 2008.

33. Qadir Kollol's report from Dhaka, broadcast by the BBC Bengali Service, *Probaha*, 24 December 2008, at 1330 GMT. Sheikh Hasina challenged the BNP's contention by alleging that the latter was seeking to either not take part in the polls or prevent voting from going ahead, especially since 'it was the past BNP-led administration which had aided the Islamists.' Sumon Mahbub's report from Dinajpur broadcast in the BBC Bengali Service's *Probaha* programme, ibid.

34. Rokhsana Amin, 'Banned militant group chief held with explosives,' Dhaka, *Channel I TV*, 17 November 2008.

35. Bangladesh's continuing struggle with the rivalry between its secular-rational framework and the apparent determination of the violently devout fringes is charted in Anupam Ray, *Islamic Radical Ideologies and South Asian Security*, Washington: Centre for Strategic and International Studies, 27 October 2008.

36. ATM Shamsul Huda, in an interview with the BBC Bengali Service, broadcast in *Probaha* transmitted on 1 January 2009 at 1330 GMT.

37. Bangladesh Election Commission, *Number of Candidates (Party-wise)*, Commission's website at http://www.ecs.gov.bd/English/QLTemplate1.php? Parameter_QLSCat_ID=55 accessed on 29 December 2008.

38. Election Commissioner Sakhawat Hossain, in an interview with the BBC Bengali Service's *Pratyusha* programme, broadcast on 28 December 2008, at 0130 GMT. The CTG deployed 50,000 soldiers, 70,000 policemen, 6,500 members of the RAB and 466,000 members of part-time *Ansar* auxiliaries. Shafiq Alam, 'Bangladesh votes under heavy security,' Dhaka, *AFP*, 29 December 2008; 'Polls to witness record security,' *The Daily Star*, Dhaka, 29 December 2008.

39. These early results were 'unofficially' published by the Election Commission which would not announce 'official' results until all complaints and questions had been resolved. A party-wise distribution of the seats won was summarised by the BBC Bengali Service at its website at http://www.bbc.co.uk/ bengali/accessed on 30 December 2008.

40. *Bangladesh Elections 2008*, BBC Bengali Service website at http://www.bbc. co.uk/bengali/indepth/cluster/2008/12/081218_bdelection_2008.shtml accessed on 6 January 2009.

41. For a reasonable explanation of the elections' dramatic outcome, see Mahmud ur Rahman Choudhury, 'Why the AL won and the BNP lost the election-2008,' *The Bangladesh Today*, Dhaka, editorial, 31 December 2008. An optimistic assessment appears in 'Bangladesh's elections: The tenacity of hope,' *The Economist*, UK edition, 3–9 January 2009, pp. 39–40.

42. 'Bangladesh ex–PM Zia alleges "unprecedented" poll rigging,' *bdnews24.com*, Dhaka, 31 December 2008.

43. 'Two dead, dozens injured in Bangladesh post-election violence,' *bdnews24. com*, Dhaka, 31 December 2008.

44. BNP Secretary-General Khandker Delwar Hossain's interview with the BBC Bengali Service, broadcast in *Probaha*, transmitted on 2 January 2009 at 1330 GMT.

45. The BBC Bengali Service interviewed the Awami League's middle-ranking leaders and activists on the new line-up in its *Probaha* programme broadcast at 1330 GMT on 7 January 2009.

46. 183 posts of *Upazila* Chairmen went to Awami League-backed candidates, 59 to BNP-supported ones, Jamaat-e-Islami members secured 18, Jatiya Party members, 10, CPB and the Workers Party took one each, other parties won 13 while independents took 10 chairs. 'AL-backed candidates win "marred" upazila polls,' *The Financial Express*, Dhaka, 24 January 2009.

47. See, for instance, 'Violence, rigging mark upazila polls,' and 'CEC blames ministers, MPs for influencing upazila polls,' *The New Age*, Dhaka, 23 January 2009.

48. Informal discussions with non-partisan observers from the press and commercial classes in Dhaka in January 2009.

49. Oxfam, *Cyclone Sidr: One year on, more than a million still struggling in Bangladesh*, Dhaka and Oxford, 12 November 2008.

50. IMF Directors pointed to these challenges in their consultations with Bangladesh's leaders in late June 2007. Kalpana Kochar and Anthony Boote, Editors, *Staff Report for the 2008 Article IV Consultations*, Washington: IMF, 27 August 2008, p. 1

51. In a land awash in rumours helped by the rigours of Emergency regulations, reports of money changing hands between contractors supplying victuals to the 'fair price' shops and those linked to officials managing the latter spread rapidly but were never brought to court. Briefings received by the author from Bangladeshi political analysts during a visit to Dhaka in January 2009.

52. Kalpana Kochar and Anthony Boote, Editors, 27 August 2008, p. 3.

53. Ibid.

54. 'Bangladesh's election: The tenacity of hope,' *The Economist*, UK edition, 3 January 2009, pp. 39–40.

55. Vinaya Swaroop, *Global financial crisis and its likely impact on Bangladesh*, Dhaka: World Bank, 26 November 2008.

56. Ibid.

57. Asian Development Bank, *Bangladesh: Political and Economic Update*, Manila: January 2009, para.7.

58. Ibid, para 11.

59. Ibid, para 12.

60. Ibid, para 14.

61. Prominent among them were Agriculture Minister, Motia Chowdhury, who had served in the same capacity in Hasina's previous cabinet, and Finance Minister, A.M.A. Muhith, who had taken the same portfolio under General Ershad in the 1980s.

62. Ashutosh Sarkar, '1972 constitution to be restored, says Barrister Shafique,' *The Daily Star*, Dhaka, 8 January 2009; 'Government to form expert body to review constitution,' ibid, 12 January 2009.

63. Sahara Khatun, quoted in Mahfuz Anam, 'Commentary—Sheikh Hasina's cabinet: Gutsy but risky,' *The Daily Star*, Dhaka, 10 January 2009.

64. Alexander Nicoll, Editor, *South Asia's disputed waters*, Strategic Comments, London: IISS, December 2008.

65. For accounts of developments, see 'Bangladesh asks China for help in Myanmar sea row,' *Reuters*, Dhaka, 5 November 2008; 'Myanmar stops disputed gas exploration—Bangladesh,' *Reuters*, Dhaka, 6 November 2008; 'Burma rejects Bangladeshi demand to stop gas drilling,' *Xinhua*, Yangon, 6 Novem-

ber 2008; 'Myanmar pulls warships from disputed waters—Bangladesh,' *AFP*, Chittagong, 6 November 2006; 'Burma rejects 'mistakenly' made demand over water territory by Bangladesh,' *MRTV-3*, Nay Pyi Taw, 6 November 2008; 'Myanmar refuses to withdraw in dispute with Bangladesh,' *Kyodo*, Yangon, 7 November 2008.

66. 'Indian ships enter Bangladesh waters,' *bdnews24.com*, Dhaka, 26 December 2008.

67. Reported in BBC Bengali Service programme *Pratyusha*, broadcast at 0130GMT on 27 December 2008.

68. 'Delhi's reaction lacks diplomatic demeanour,' *The New Age*, Dhaka, 28 December 2009; 'Indian ships leave Bangladeshi "territorial waters",' *Press Trust of India*, New Delhi, 28 December 2008, 0921 GMT.

69. Myanmar must formally table its claim by 21 May 2009, India by 29 June 2009 and, Bangladesh, by 27 July 2011. Alexander Nicoll, December 2008.

6. A LAND OF ANGER—RIGHT, LEFT, CENTRE, AND THE OTHER

1. The INC was constitutionally a secular nationalist organisation, but its success led, as we have seen, in 1906, to the establishment in Dhaka of the All India Muslim League, an avowedly Muslim political party. In the early inter-War years, the Bengali nationalist *Swadesi* campaign and the Non-cooperation movement against British colonial authorities were led and manned almost entirely by Hindu activists. While the INC and its acolytes pursued 'all-Indian secular nationalist' goals, their frequent use of Hindu religious iconography and rhetoric—*Bharat Mata* (mother India) and *Bande Mataram* (hail, mother!) being notable instances—dissuaded many Muslims from joining in and, indeed, in many cases, drove many Muslims to the confessionally-based Muslim political groupings. Student activism too reflected these general tendencies. This further polarised the colony's nationalist politics, with outcomes which would bloodily reverberate far into the future.

2. Bashir al-Helal, *Bhasha Andoloner Itihas*, Dhaka: Agami Prokashani, 2003, ch. 2.

3. *Ekusher Smriticharan '80*, Dhaka: Bangla Academy, 1980, p. 113.

4. al-Helal, 2003, p. 58.

5. *Banglabazar Patrika*, Dhaka, 30 *Magh* 1399.

6. Mohammad Hannan, 'Student politics,' in *Banglapedia*, Dhaka: Asiatic Society of Bangladesh, at http://www.banglapedia.org/httpdocs/HT/S_0568.HTM accessed on 18 August 2008.

7. See chapter 1.

8. Perhaps the most evocative slogan of the campaign, *Joy Bangla!* (Victory to Bengal!), which emotionally united much of Bangladesh's population between

1971 and 1975, emerged from the process initiated and led by the SCSP. This slogan countermanded the symbolism behind *Pakistan Zindabad* (long live Pakistan!), the Pakistani equivalent which had been used as the national 'mantra' for the Pakistani state and society.

9. Literally, 'underneath the banyan boughs', this square acquired a semi–mythical status as the rendezvous for student activists gathering at the campus to form processions and rallies. See, http://www.geocities.com/athens/ithaca/3873/prelibhist.htm?200822 accessed on 22 August 2008.

10. See chapter 1.

11. *Banglapedia*, op cit.

12. Ibid.

13. Colonel Abu Taher Sangsad, *J.S.D: The Political Party Colonel Taher Belonged* (sic), Dhaka, 2003.

14. Ibid, 'Foreword.'

15. As a junior army officer, the author apprehended and disarmed several such youths in 1974; as a General Staff Officer in the late 1970s, he was aware of the implementation of this policy by the same Home Ministry, now under different management.

16. As a temporary member of the Implementation Monitoring Cell at General Ershad's Chief Martial Law Administrator's Secretariat in 1983, the author was able to observe the proceedings from a proximate position.

17. Mahbub Kamal, 'When good turns to bad,' *The Daily Star*, Dhaka, 25 May 2008.

18. Mohammad Hannan, 'Student Politics,' *Banglapedia*, op cit. On the continuing challenge of 'session jam,' see President Iajuddin Ahmad's comments in 'Session jam key reason behind high cost of education,' BangladeshNews24.com.bd, Dhaka, 8 April 2008.

19. Mahbub Kamal, 'When good turns to bad.'

20. See chapter 6, pp.282–4.

21. Indian intelligence officials accuse the ICS of 'working to support Islamist subversive action and agenda in many regions of India, particularly in areas bordering Bangladesh,' in collusion with the ISI (Inter-Services Intelligence Directorate- Pakistan). They say the ICS recruits and indoctrinates 'fanatic youth. A significant number of them were reportedly sent to Pakistan and Afghanistan during the reign of the Taliban regime where a large number of fanatic youth come (sic) under the direct command of Osama bin Laden.' They provide no evidence substantiating this and many other accusatory assertions against the ICS. See *Islami Chhatra Shibir (ICS)*, at the 'South Asia Terrorism Portal' at http://satp.org/satporgtp/countries/bangladesh/terroristoutfits/ICS.htm accessed on 20 December 2007; another Indian analyst says many leaders and cadres of Muslim militant groups such as the Jamaat-

ul-Mujaheedin Bangladesh (JMB), Jagrata Muslim Janata Bangladesh (JMJB) and Harkat-ul-Jihad-al-Islami Bangladesh (HUJI-B), which have been identified by Bangladeshi authorities to have been behind a series of attacks on secular institutions and personalities in the first decade of the twenty-first century, are former ICS members. See, R. Upadhyay, *Islami Chhatra Shibir of Bangladesh—A Threat to Democracy*, Noida: South Asia Analysis Group, Paper no. 2275, 27 June 2006.

22. A rare account of this appears in Ishrat Firdousi, *The Year That Was*, Dhaka: Bastu Prakashan, 1996.

23. Late on 16 December 1971, after the Pakistani garrison had surrendered to its Indian captors in Dhaka, 'Tiger' Kader Siddiky, commander of one of Bangladesh's best known 'non-official' guerrilla forces—the 'Kader Bahini'— bayoneted several such 'traitors' to death before a cheering crowd as foreign photographers took pictures which were then flashed around the world.

24. Some of the first clashes, reflecting tensions between secular and devout political forces occurred on the campuses of the Chittagong University and the Chittagong Medical College in the late 1970s. Later, conflict spread to other major campuses, most significantly at Rajshahi University, at the northwestern end of the country. As a staff officer at the Zonal Martial Law Administrator's Headquarters in Chittagong in the mid-1970s, the author monitored some of the early clashes in the south-east of Bangladesh.

25. ICS recruitment documentation quoted in 'Bangladesh Islami Chhatra Shibir: Objective,' in *Wikipedia*, accessed on 17 December 2007.

26. The All-Party Students Unity coalition which forged a front not only among themselves but also among the major political parties against General Ershad's rule in 1990, encouraged the use of non-partisan and more 'universal' polemics in mobilising support against the military. The practice declined as the Awami League-BNP divide resumed during the 1991–2006 democratic restoration, but in August 2007 that universalistic rhetoric returned as student activists took to the streets.

27. Compiled from Emily Wax, 'Bangladesh's Epicenter of Political Tumult: Students and Teachers at Dhaka University Fulfill a Tradition of Protest, and Pay the Price,' *The Washington Post*, 23 September 2007; Randeep Ramesh, 'Bangladesh imposes curfew after three days of student riots,' *The Guardian*, London, 22 August 2007; Adam Pal, 'Bangladesh: Students defy the brutality of the military dictatorship,' *In Defence of Marxism*, 17 September 2007.

28. Ibid.

29. *Security concerns stop Clinton visit to Bangladesh town*, New Delhi, CNN, 20 March 2000. The White House did not announce the change of plans— cancelling Clinton's overnight stay in Dhaka, and all programmes outside the security perimeter of the US embassy there—until just before he left

Delhi for Dhaka. A senior Bangladeshi intelligence officer informally told the author later in the year that Indian security officials urged the President's Secret Service detail to cancel his Dhaka programmes outside the embassy on security grounds after the presidential entourage arrived in Delhi. The Bangladeshi hosts were not consulted, merely informed of the changes.

30. Alex Perry, 'A Very Dirty Plot,' *Time*, 9 June 2003.

31. 'Assassination attempt on Hasina,' *The Daily Star*, Dhaka, 22 August 2004. The Awami League blamed the BNP-Jamaat coalition government for the attack in which the leader of the party's women's wing, Ivy Rahman, was killed. An Awami League activist, who was present at the rally at the time and was wounded in the grenade blasts, later filed a case against twenty-eight named individuals including Prime Minister Khaleda Zia, her son and BNP official Tareque Rahman, Jamaat chief Matiur Rahman Nizami, a number of senior BNP and Jamaat officials, and activists. 'Victim sues Khaleda for Aug 21 grenade attacks,' *The Daily Star*, Dhaka, 6 June 2007.

32. Even after three years, Kibria's widow and son were not satisfied that 'a proper investigation' had been conducted into his death. 'After a carefully limited investigation some local BNP leaders were identified as the culprits… If these people were involved, they could only have acted on the instructions of much more powerful individuals who could realistically have had a motive to kill someone of the stature of my husband.' Asma Kibria, 'Is it not yet time for justice?' *The Daily Star*, Dhaka, 24 October 2007. Also see, Iqbal Siddiquee, 'No headway yet in Kibria killing case,' *The Daily Star*, Dhaka, 26 January 2008.

33. Farooq Sobhan, M. Shafiullah, Shahab Khan, *Countering Terrorism in Bangladesh: A Strategy Paper*, Dhaka, Bangladesh Enterprise Institute, July 2007, p. 1. Accounts vary as to the number of bomblets which went off in dozens of cities and towns almost simultaneously in sixty-three of the country's sixty-four districts. Two people were killed and dozens injured in the explosions, but it clearly was a symbolic show of potential force, indicating the capacity for wreaking countrywide havoc if the perpetrators so wished. See, Bruce Vaughn, *Islamist Extremism in Bangladesh*, Washington: CRS, 31 January 2007, p. 2. In India, the blasts raised fears the bombers had demonstrated the sophistication, organisation and precision necessary for 'taking the government and opposition and parliament.' Vipin Agnihotri, 'Bangladesh Serial Blasts,' *Counter Currents*, 23 August 2005.

34. Julfikar Ali Manik and Shariful Islam, 'Six JMB militants hanged,' *The Daily Star*, Dhaka, 31 March 2007.

35. Farooq Sobhan et al, 2007, Bruce Vaughn, 2007, and Maneeza Hossain, *Broken Pendulum: Bangladesh's Swing to Radicalism*, Washington: Hudson Institute, 2007, are examples of such contemporary discussion of religious

radicalism in Bangladesh. None of them explores pre-1947 Islamist tendencies or radical politics utilising Islamist motifs among Muslim Bengalis. Their otherwise reasonable studies treat the rise of Islamist extremism as though this has emerged *de novo* triggered by the 1979 Islamist Revolution in Iran, and the US-led proxy war against the Soviet invasion of Afghanistan, mounted on Christmas Eve that year. By ignoring the deeper roots of the phenomenon, they reduce the subject of their attention to a purely reactive category with little local relevance, and consequently, lower the substantive value of their labours.

36. Some authors have acknowledged this crisis of identity while still insisting it is a manageable challenge amenable to administrative and party-political measures. Hossain, 2007, pp. 4–7, 53–7.

37. For more on the Faraizi Movement, see Tazeen Murshid, *The Sacred and the Secular: Bengal Muslim Discourses, 1871–1977*, Calcutta: Oxford University Press, 1995, pp. 50, 59, 88, 98, 122, 194, 292, 328.

38. Hossain, 2007, pp. 16–8.

39. Rohan Gunaratna, *Trends in Asian Terrorism*, paper presented at the Bangladesh Institute of Peace and Security Studies (BPSS), Dhaka, 30 December 2007.

40. S. Mahmud Ali, *US-China Cold War Collaboration, 1979–1981*, New York: Routledge, 2005, p. 181.

41. Ali Riaz, citing official documents, in 'Islamist Militancy in Bangladesh: What's to be done?' *The Progressive Bangladesh*, Dhaka, 20 March 2008. This was not surprising—a number of Bangladeshis had drifted into Lebanon in the 1970s, joining Palestinian bands in their campaign against Israeli forces during the Lebanese civil war. But the impact of the Afghan operations appears to have been much deeper.

42. P.G. Rajamohan, 'Harkat-ul-Jihad-al-Islami Bangladesh (HUJI-BD)', in *South Asia Terrorist Portal*, Delhi, not dated, accessed on 20 December 2007; Ali Riaz, 'Islamist Militancy in Bangladesh: What's to be done?' op cit.

43. Rajamohan, op cit.

44. Estimates vary. Ali Riaz, 2007, cites government documents which claim HUJI-B's ranks range around 10,000–15,000; Rajamohan, op cit, thinks HUJI-B might have 15,000–20,000 cadres; Paul Burton, Editor, *Jane's Sentinel Security Assessment: South Asia*, Issue 11, Coulsden, 2003, p. 112, asserts HUJI-B has 15,000 members.

45. '21 August, Ramna blasts: another suspect held; Mufti Hannan remanded,' *The Daily Star*, Dhaka, 29 November 2007.

46. Ibid; Bibhas Saha, 'Two Harkatul operatives held: police suspect their involvement in Ramna Batamul bomb attack,' *The New Age*, Dhaka, 28 November 2007; 'HUJI cadres attacked poet Shamsur Rahman, Mufti Hannan

tells interrogators,' *The Daily Star*, Dhaka, 30 November 2007; 'Grenade attack on Anwar Chowdhury: Charges framed against HUJI man Zandal,' *The Daily Star*, Dhaka, 1 July 2008.

47. 'HUJI's subversive designs started from Khulna Division.' *Prothom Alo*, Dhaka, 4 May 2008. HUJI-B's activities allegedly included identifying and killing 'apostates.' See, for instance, 'HUJI-B killed homeopathic physician Azizur Rahman after declaring him apostate,' *Prothom Alo*, Dhaka, 3 May 2008.

48. 'JMB cadres regrouping in remote northern areas; most of the cases remain stalled owing to legal loopholes,' *The New Age*, Dhaka, 18 August 2008.

49. Julfikar Ali Manik, 'Bangla Bhai active for six years,' *The Daily Star*, Dhaka, 13 April 2004; 'Terrorism: A Tragic Tale of Continued Denials,' *the New Age*, 27 September 2005.

50. 'Jamaatul Mujahideen Bangladesh (JMB),' *South Asia Terrorism Portal*, http://www.satp.org/satporgtp/countries/bangladesh/terroristoutfits/JMB.htm accessed on 18 December 2007.

51. '35 Hurt in Jamalpur and Sherpur blasts,' *The New Age*, Dhaka, 13 January 2005; '2 killed, 60 hurt in bomb attacks on Jatra shows,' *The Daily Star*, Dhaka, 16 January 2005.

52. Maneeza Hossain, 'The Rising Tide of Islamism in Bangladesh,' *Current Trends in Islamist Ideology*, Washington: Hudson Institute, 16 February 2006.

53. *The Columbia World Dictionary of Islamism*, New York: Columbia University Press, 2007, pp. 69–70.

54. 'Leaflets ridicule democracy,' *The Daily Star*, Dhaka, 18 August 2005.

55. 'JMB suicide bomber kills 2 judges,' *The Daily Star*, Dhaka, 15 November 2005.

56. There is some indication that opinion inside the BNP-Jamaat coalition in power in Dhaka was divided over what to do with the two groups. Following a series of vicious attacks mounted by the JMJB, it was proscribed in 2004, but its sister-body, the JMB, was only banned in February 2005.

57. Of them, six men were in custody: Abdur Rahman, Siddiqul Islam, JMB Majlish-e-Shura (highest decision-making body) member and Rahman's son-in-law Abdul Awal, JMB's military commander and Rahman's youngest brother Ataur Rahman, another Shura member Khaled Saifullah, and the bomber who killed the two judges but himself was detained severely injured, treated to recovery and then tried—Iftekhar Hasan Mamun. The seventh suspect absconded and was tried *in absentia*.

58. Julfikar Ali Manik and Shariful Islam, 'Six JMB militants hanged,' *The Daily Star*, Dhaka, 31 March 2007.

59. See, for instance, Abdur Rahman's interview in *The Daily Star*, Dhaka, 17 May 2004.

60. Bangladesh Home Secretary Abdul Karim's address as the chief guest at a conference titled 'Trend of Militancy in Bangladesh and Possible Responses' at the Bangladesh Enterprise Institute, Dhaka, 28 February 2008; *The Daily Star*, Dhaka, 29 February 2008.

61. Zohra Akhter, *Trend of Militancy in Bangladesh: August 2007–2008*, Dhaka, Bangladesh Enterprise Institute, 28 February 2008.

62. Bangladesh Enterprise Institute, *2007–2008 Trends in Militancy in Bangladesh*, Dhaka, 11 June 2008; 'Militants regrouping for attacks,' *The Daily Star*, Dhaka, 12 June 2008.

63. The author was among the recipients.

64. 'Banned Islamic Militant JMB Threatens Bomb Attacks on Advisers,' *The Daily Star*, Dhaka, 8 September 2008.

65. See 'JMB reorganising afresh under leadership of Abu Kayed Talim: Regional commander Mohammad reveals in Chittagong court,' *Dainik Ittefaq*, Dhaka, 19 June 2008; 'JMB cadres regrouping in remote northern areas,' *The New Age*, Dhaka, 18 August 2008.

66. See, for instance, Ahmed Hussain, 'News Flash: Purbo Banglar Communist Party founder Mofakkhar killed in RAB action,' *Asian Tribune*, 19 December 2004.

67. 'Leader of Purbo Banglar Communist Party (PBCP Marxist-Leninist) executed,' *People's March*, 31 July 2008, at http://ajadhind.blogspot.com/2008/07/leader-of-purbo-banglar-communist-party.html accessed on 27 August 2008.

68. 'Govt to ban 18 armed groups,' *The Daily Star*, Dhaka, 8 September 2008.

69. Ibid.

70. The Indian Government turned the Port Blair prison complex into a national memorial and museum, highlighting the often cruel fate of the several thousand inmates transported from the mainland, many never to return alive. The memorial is an obligatory destination for India's leaders, especially its President and Prime Minister. The author visited the complex in September 2007. The relatively small number of Muslim revolutionaries imprisoned or executed there were from other parts of the Indian empire, mainly what is now Andhra Pradesh. Bengali prisoners almost to a man came from the upper strata of Hindu middle- and professional classes.

71. A prolific author, Roy published many other books. In 1937–45, he published *Materialism, The Historical Role of Islam, Science and Superstition, Man and Nature, From Savagery to Civilization, The Philosophy of Fascism, The Ideal of Indian Womanhood, Letters from Jail*, and *India's Message*, among others. Later, in 1940–46, he wrote several other books including *India and War, Alphabet of Fascism, The Constitution of Free India, People's Freedom, Poverty or Plenty, The Problems of Freedom*, and *Jawaharlal Nehru: The Last Battle for*

Freedom. In 1947, he appraised post-revolution Soviet Union. The following year, he revised Marxism in two volumes titled *Beyond Marxism* and *New Humanism.*

72. T. Hossain, 'Roy, Manabendra Nath,' *Banglapedia,* Dhaka, Asiatic Society of Bangladesh, at http://www.banglapedia.org/httpdocs/HT/R_0243.HTM accessed on 9 February 2010.

73. 'Te bhaga' literally meant three portions and came from the share-cropping system in which the land's produce—irrespective of the sharecropper's investment in seeds, fertiliser, labour, time and other costs—was divided into three equal portions. The tenant got one and the landlord took the remaining two. Communist activists incited tenants and share-croppers to revolt against this system.

74. Mohiuddin Ahmed, 'Radical Politics,' *Banglapedia,* ibid. at http://www.banglapedia.org/httpdocs/HT/R_0007.HTM accessed on 9 February 2010.

75. Muazzam Hussain Khan, 'Communist Party of Bangladesh,' *Banglapedia,* ibid. at http://www.banglapedia.org/httpdocs/HT/C_0318.HTM accessed on 9 February 2010.

76. Md. Nurul Amin, 'Maoism in Bangladesh: The Case of the East Bengal Sarbohara Party,' *Asian Survey,* vol. 26, no. 7, July 1986, pp. 759–73.

77. M. Rashiduzzaman, 'Bangladesh 1978: Search for a Political Party,' *Asian Survey,* vol. 19, no. 2, Part II, February 1979, pp. 191–7.

78. 'Abdul Haque,' *Banglapedia,* op cit, at http://www.banglapedia.org/httpdocs/HT/H_0049.HTM accessed on 9 February 2010.

79. Kanu Sanyal quoted in 'Echoes of Naxalbari', *Himal Magazine,* Kathmandu, December 2007, cover feature.

80. Ibid.

81. Sanjoy Mitra, another former *Naxalite* leader, quoted in ibid.

82. Ibid. On India's Naga and Mizo separatist campaigns, see S. Mahmud Ali, *The Fearful State: Power, People and Internal War in South Asia,* London, Zed Books, 1993, pp. 22–68.

83. Mohiuddin Ahmed, 'Radical Politics,' *Banglapedia,* op cit.

84. Md. Nurul Amin, July 1986.

85. Ibid.

86. Ibid.

87. N. Adil, 'Storm over Timor Sea,' *The Financial Express,* Dhaka, 8 April 2006.

88. Amin, July 1986.

89. Muazzam Hussain Khan, 'Sikder, Siraj,' *Banglapedia,* at http://www.banglapedia.org/httpdocs/HT/S_0382.HTM accessed on 9 February 2010.

90. Ibid.

91. See S. M. Ali, *Civil-Military Relations in the 'Soft State': The Case of Bangladesh,* Bath, European Commission/University of Bath, 1994, pp. 19–22.

92. There were some suggestions that, reluctant to capture one of their own highly regarded and decorated war-heroes, some army units avoided detaining Ziauddin. The disappearance of one battalion from the 'radio net' for a number of days during which the operational 'hammer' would have closed in on the 'anvil' and shut the trap on the PBSP leaders was not, to the author's knowledge, adequately explained. The author served as a staff officer and then as the commander of an operational group in one of these battalions during the operation.

93. Muazzam Hussain Khan, op cit; the most popularly-held accounts, unsupported by evidence, claimed Sikder was killed by his guards in a staged 'escape' effort. As a member of the military security service in 1978–9, the author frequently came across left-wing assertions to this effect.

94. M.J. Alam, 'Ten outlawed parties active in half of Bangladesh,' *Dainik Ittefaq*, Dhaka, 30 May 2004.

95. In 2007–8, the army-backed CTG arrested several BNP politicians on suspicions of aiding and abetting the JMB and JMJB as instruments of coercion against left-extremists in north-western Bangladesh. They included former MPs and state ministers.

96. Compiled from Bangladeshi press reports, published by the South Asia Terrorism Portal at http://www.satp.org/satpgrtp/countries/bangladesh/terroristoutfits/PBCP.htm accessed on 15 September 2008.

97. According to the same accounts, from 1998 to April 2002, PBCP cadres killed eighteen comrades from rival factions, allegedly over turf issues. South Asia Terrorism Portal, ibid.

98. Ahmed Hussain in *Asian Tribune*, 19 December 2004.

99. Ibid.

100. Compiled from Bangladeshi press reports, published by the South Asia Terrorism Portal at http://satp.org/satporgtp/countries/bangladesh/database//lwekilled2008.htm accessed on 11 September 2008.

101. South Asia Terrorism Portal at http://www.satp.org/satporgtp/countries/bangladesh/terroristoutfits/PBCP.htm accessed on 15 September 2008.

102. RAB Additional Director General Colonel Gulzar Uddin Ahmed quoted in 'Twenty top leaders of seven extremist organisations are still operative,' *Prothom Alo*, Dhaka, 22 June 2008; also see Amanur Arman, 'Forty Bangladesh outlawed group chiefs "at large"', *The Daily Star*, Dhaka, 20 June 2008.

103. 'Janajuddha founder killed in shootout; his woman accomplice also killed,' *The Daily Star*, Dhaka, 19 June 2008; 'Twenty top leaders of seven extremist organisations are still operative,' *Prothom Alo*, Dhaka, 22 June 2008; 'Leader of Purbo Banglar Communist Party (PBCP Marxist-Leninist) executed,' *Peoplesmarch*, 31 July 2008, at http://ajadhind.blogspot.

com/2008/07/leader-of-purbo-banglar-communist-party.html accessed on 27 August 2008.

104. Amanur Arman, 20 June 2008.

105. Ibid.

106. Indira Gandhi to Tajuddin Ahmed, conveying India's diplomatic recognition of Bangladesh, New Delhi, Prime Minister's Office, 6 December 1971; the letter was addressed to 'His Excellency Mr. Tajuddin Ahmed, Prime Minister of the People's Republic of Bangladesh, Mujib Nagar.' It is difficult to imagine that the prime minister of India was unaware of the seat of the Bangladeshi GOE being located in Calcutta.

107. Smruti Pattanaik, 'Internal Political Dynamics and Bangladesh's Foreign Policy Towards India,' *Strategic Analysis*, Delhi, Institute of Defence Studies and Analysis (IDSA), vol. 29, no. 3, July-September 2005, p. 396.

108. Talukdar Maniruzzaman, *Radical Left and the Emergence of Bangladesh*, Dhaka, Mowla Brothers, 2003, p. 100.

109. Major General D.K. Palit, *The Lightning Campaign*, Salisbury, Compton Press, 1972, pp. 38, 63.

110. The confiscation of Pakistani military equipment surrendered in Bangladesh especially rankled with Bangladeshis. C.H. Bateman, 'National Security and Nationalism in Bangladesh,' *Asian Survey*, vol. 19, no. 8, 1979, p. 751. Indian analysts claim Delhi confiscated this ordnance to prevent it from falling into the hands of 'Left-wing guerrillas.' They also claim India eventually returned all such captured stores. J.N. Dixit, *Liberation and Beyond: India-Bangladesh Relations*, Delhi, Picus Books, 2003, pp. 147–8; Pattanaik, 'Internal Political Dynamics and Bangladesh's Foreign Policy Towards India,' p. 402. Bangladeshis deny they received all Pakistani *materiel*.

111. Shahiduzzaman, *Alliance Reliability in the Post-Cold War Context and Bangladesh's Military Strategy*, paper presented at 'International Conference on Bangladesh and SAARC: Issues, Perspectives and Outlook,' Dhaka, Bangladesh Institute of International and Strategic Studies (BIISS), 23–24 August 1992, p. 5; A.K.M. Abdus Sabur, *Bangladesh-India Relations: Retrospect and Prospects*, ibid., p. 4.

112. M.G. Kabir and Shaukat Hassan, *Issues and Challenges Facing Bangladesh Foreign Policy*, Dhaka, Bangladesh Society of International Studies, 1989, p. 34.

113. In 1990, the author, on a brief visit to the National Defence College in New Delhi, was told by a member of the faculty that after the war in 1971, 'we thought you'd join us.' Although the speaker would not elaborate, the author assumed he meant Delhi's expectations, perhaps unstated and limited to military circles engaged in planning and executing India's 'lightning campaign,' were that post-Pakistan East Bengal would join hands with

India in some form. Against that backdrop Dhaka's post-1975 stance towards Delhi must have deeply hurt Indian sensibilities.

114. Subimal Dutt, High Commissioner of India in Bangladesh, and Shafiqul Huq, Secretary, Ministry of Flood Control and Water Resources, Government of Bangladesh, *Agreement on the Establishment of a Joint Rivers Commission*, Dhaka, 24 November 1972, Article-4.

115. See chapter 4.

116. B.M. Abbas, 'Regional cooperation for river basin development,' M.A. Hafiz and Iftekharuzzaman, Eds., *South Asian Regional Cooperation: A Socio-Economic Approach to Peace and Stability*, Dhaka, BIISS, 1985, pp. 112–122.

117. Bangladesh's objections to the Indian proposal appear in ibid, pp. 118–21.

118. 'Bangladesh court may tell Government to review India water treaty,' *The New Age*, Dhaka, 20 June 2008.

119. The disputed stretches were 'Mizoram-Bangladesh sector, Tripura-Sylhet sector, Bhagalpur railway line, Sibpur-Gaurangala sector, Muhuri River (Belonia) sector, remaining portion of the Tripura-Noakhali/Comilla sector, Fenny River, rest of' Tripura-Chittagong Hill Tracts sector, Beanibazar-Karimganj sector, Hakar Khal, Baikari Khal, Hilli, Berubari, and Lathitil-la-Dumabari.' Indira Gandhi and Sheikh Mujibur Rahman, *Agreement between the Government of the Republic of India and Government of the People's Republic of Bangladesh concerning the demarcation of the land boundary between India and Bangladesh and related matters*, New Delhi, Ministry of External Affairs (MEA), 16 May 1974.

120. The two governments agreed that enclaves demarcated in areas for which maps had been prepared should be exchanged 'within six months' of these 'strip maps' being signed by official envoys. The maps were to be signed 'as early as possible and in any case not later than the 31 December 1974.' Maps of other areas already demarcated were to be printed by 31 May 1975 and signed by envoys soon afterwards so that territories in adverse possessions in those areas were exchanged by 31 December 1975. In areas still to be demarcated, enclaves were to be exchanged within six months of their strip maps being prepared and signed by envoys. Ibid.

121. Authoritative Indian and Bangladeshi accounts offer differing claims. For instance, Prof. K. Moudood Elahi, writing in the semi–official *Banglapedia* compilation, states Bangladesh claims 119 exclaves located in Indian territory while India claims 73 exclaves located in Bangladesh. See Elahi in 'Enclaves,' *Banglapedia*, Dhaka, at http://www.banglapedia.org/httpdocs/HT/E_0054.HTM accessed on 9 February 2010. An Indian account of comparable reliability states there are 111 Indian exclaves in Bangladeshi territory and 51 Bangladeshi exclaves in India. See Alok Kumar Gupta and Saswati Chanda, 'India and Bangladesh: Enclaves Dispute,' *South Asia Ar-*

ticles, New Delhi, Institute of Peace and Conflict Studies, article no. 493, 6 May 2001. Accounts of the physical size and populations of these exclaves/enclaves similarly vary widely.

122. *Agreement between the Government of the Republic of India and Government of the People's Republic of Bangladesh concerning the demarcation of the land boundary between India and Bangladesh and related matters*, New Delhi, MEA, 16 May 1974, paragraph 14.

123. In early 1984, as the executive editor of *Bangladesh Today*, a news magazine published in Dhaka, the author commissioned a study of the conditions in which the residents of the two enclaves lived. The findings were published in the magazine. Other Bangladeshi publications too reported the lack of basic health, education, criminal justice and administrative services.

124. P.V. Narshimha Rao to A.R. Shams-Ud-Doha, *Terms of Lease in perpetuity of Tin Bigha Area*, New Delhi, MEA, 7 October 1982, paragraph 4.

125. MEA, *Tin Bigha—a Proper Perspective*, New Delhi, March 1992.

126. Pranab Mukherjee, Minister of External Affairs, answer to question by Dr. Murli Manohar Joshi, MP, question no. 1691, *Rajya Sabha Q&A*, New Delhi, MEA, 7 December 2006; ibid, answer to 'unstarred question no. 811 by Shri Prabodh Panda, Yogi Aditya Nath, Shri Nikhil Kumar,' *Lok Sabha Q&A*, New Delhi, MEA, 22 October 2008. The most exhaustive academic study on the subject, however, offers different figures. Brendan Whyte, *Waiting for the Esquimo: An historical and documentary study of the Cooch Behar enclaves of India and Bangladesh*, Melbourne, School of Anthropology, Geography and Environmental Studies, University of Melbourne, 2004, says India claims it has 106 exclaves within Bangladesh while Bangladesh lays claim to 92 exclaves located in India (p. 21). Whyte admits that the India-Bangladesh Boundary Commission had identified 111 Indian and 51 Bangladeshi 'exchangeable enclaves' (p. 445). The wide range of varied claims published by various Indian and Bangladeshi authors is also recorded (pp. 444–5). Estimates of land areas and populations of these enclaves are noted (pp. 434–5). For the purpose of the present work, official claims made by the Indian Minister for External Affairs—which elicited no rejoinders from Dhaka—are accepted as such.

127. Pranab Mukherjee, ibid, 7 December 2006.

128. Syed Sajjad Ali, 'Fencing the Porous Bangladesh Border,' *WorldPress*, datelined Agartala, India, 14 December 2006.

129. Pushpita Das, 'India-Bangladesh Border: "A Problem Area for Tomorrow",' *Strategic Comments*, New Delhi, IDSA, 8 December 2006.

130. Ibid. Also, Subir Bhaumik, 'Livelihoods on line at Indian border,' *BBC News*, at http://news.bbc.co.uk/go/pr/fr/-/2/hi/south_asia/4622317.stm accessed on 11 January 2008. A photograph of BSF troops patrolling along

the fence appears in 'A special report on migration,' *The Economist*, UK edition, 5 January 2008, p. 9.

131. Press Trust of India (PTI), *India-Bangladesh maritime border talks begin*, Dhaka, 15 September 2008; Raheed Ejaz, 'Indo-Bangladesh maritime talks end inconclusive,' *The New Age*, Dhaka, 18 September 2008.

132. See, for instance, Christopher Sweeny, 'Small engagement at Jamalpur,' *The Guardian Weekly*, London, 19 September 1976. As a General-Staff Officer at the headquarters of the BDR in this period, the author regularly visited troubled border areas, and attended funerals of BDR personnel killed in these encounters.

133. The Chittagong Hill Tracts Commission, *Life is not Ours*, London, 1991, p. 16; Syed Anwar Husain, 'Ethnicity and security of small states,' in M.A. Hafiz, A.R. Khan, Eds., *Security of Small States*, Dhaka, BIISS, 1987, p. 48.

134. Indian involvement in the Chittagong Hill Tracts insurgency is recorded in Syed Kamaluddin, 'A tangled web of insurgency,' *Far Eastern Economic Review*, Hong Kong, 23 May 1980; 'The Indian Hand,' and 'The Civil War in Chittagong,' *The Sunday*, Calcutta, 6–12 July 1986, pp. 35–6; John Laffin, *War Annual 1*, London, Brassey's, 1986, p. 23.

135. Leo Rose, 'The US and South Asian Regional Issues,' in M. A. Hafiz and Iftekharuzzaman, Eds., 1985, p. 216. As a member of the Bangladeshi delegation which negotiated an end to the 'northern insurgency' with the Indian government in May 1977, the author was aware of the complex nature of the negotiations preceding their eventual success.

136. Paul Burton, Ed., *Jane's Sentinel Security Assessment: South Asia*, Coulsdon, 2002, p. 117.

137. In early October 2008, Indian media reported that Bangladesh had 'now become a more dangerous neighbour for India than Pakistan,' with Dhaka allegedly 'providing facilities for training to northeast extremist organisations. There are 110 terrorist training camps in Bangladesh.' Kunal, 'Bangladesh is the new terror training ground,' *Rashtriya Sahara*, Delhi, 7 October 2008. The Director-General of BSF, Assam, Ashish K. Mitra, briefed Indian journalists on 1 September 2008 that after Dhaka tried to deport the ULFA leader, Anup Chetia, and eight of his comrades to India, Chetia sought legal protection against deportation. Mitra confirmed that in a reversal of past practice, Dhaka had already handed over eight Indian insurgents and India had returned seven Bangladeshi wanted criminals. Some changes were apparent. See, 'ULFA leader appeals against deportation,' *The Asian Age*, Calcutta, 2 September 2008.

138. See, for instance, a detailed report by a 'special correspondent' titled 'Indian Intelligence campaign starts against Bangladesh media,' *Naya Diganta*, Dhaka, 24 August 2008.

139. Kalyan Barooah, 'ULFA has stakes in Bangla media,' *The Assam Tribune*, Guwahati, 29 July 2008.

140. 'Bangla Editor Denies ULFA Nexus Report,' *The Assam Tribune*, Guwahati, 29 August 2008.

141. Pushpita Das, 8 December 2006.

142. Alex Perry, 'A Very Dirty Plot,' *Time*, 9 June 2003.

143. Inspector-General of the BSF for Assam-Meghalaya-Manipur, I.K. Mishra, quoted in 'BSF admits HUJI presence in northeast,' *The Sentinel*, Guwahati, 7 October 2008.

144. A.K. Mitra quoted in Nishit Dholabari, 'Missing: A million Bangla visitors,' *The Telegraph*, Calcutta, 26 August 2008.

145. For an Indian assessment of the visit's import, and that of the reciprocal visit to Bangladesh by his Indian counterpart, see Subhash Kapila, *Bangladesh: Visit of Indian Army Chief Significant*, Noida, South Asia Analysis Group, Paper no. 2778, 23 July 2008. Dr Kapila's paper, however, is inaccurate in claiming that General Moeen Uddin Ahmed 'trained in the Pakistan Military Academy and served in the Pakistan Army.' Such factual errors raise possibilities of misplaced inferences being drawn on the bases of which inappropriate recommendations are then made.

146. Rezwan Biswas, 'BDR hands over 18 "All-Tripura Tiger Force" cadres,' *Amader Shomoy*, Dhaka, 15 September 2008.

147. A.R. Khan, M.H. Kabir, 'The security of small states: A framework of analysis,' in M.A. Hafiz, A.R. Khan, Eds., 1987, pp. 3–19; A.I. Akram, 'The security of small states in the South Asian context,' ibid, p. 132, notes that Bangladesh's large 'population burden' makes it a small state.

148. R.P. Barston, 'Diplomacy and security: dilemmas for small states,' ibid, pp. 230–45.

149. Mohammed Ayoob, 'The primacy of the political: SAARC in comparative perspective,' in M.A. Hafiz, A.R. Khan, Eds., 1987, especially pp. 67–8.

150. K. Subrahmanyam, 'Problems in nation-state-building: perceptions and realities,' in ibid, pp. 187–211.

151. Bhabani Sen Gupta, 'Regional organisations and the security of small states,' in M.A. Hafiz and A.R. Khan, Eds., *Security of Small States*, Dhaka, BIISS, 1987, pp. 263, 273, 275.

152. Jasjit Singh, 'Insecurity of developing nations, especially small states,' in ibid, p. 30.

153. Zillur Rahman Khan, 'Multiculturalism and neutrality: the applicability of the Swiss model to the security of small states,' in ibid, p. 315.

154. Paul Burton, Ed., 2002, p. 117.

155. Ibid, p. 118.

156. Mamta Chowdhury, 'Growth in India and its impact on Bangladesh economy,' *Peace and Security Review*, vol. 1, no. 1, Dhaka, Bangladesh Institute of Peace and Security Studies (BIPSS), 2008, p. 72.

157. See, for instance, Shafiq Ahmed and Shantayanan Devarajan, Eds., *India-Bangladesh Bilateral Trade and Potential Free Trade Agreement*, Dhaka, The World Bank, 2006.

158. Mamta Chowdhury, op cit.

159. Shafiq Ahmed and Shantayanan Devarajan, 2006, p.*xiii*.

160. M.M. Rahman, *Bangladesh-India Bilateral Trade: Causes of Imbalance and Measures for Improvement*, Sydney, University of Sydney, June 2005, cited in Mamta Chowdhury, p. 69.

161. Sharif M. Hossain, 'Bangladesh and Free Trade Area: Regional and Bilateral Routes,' A.R. Khan, Ed., *BIISS Journal*, vol. 26, no. 3, Dhaka, BIISS, 2005, especially pp. 392–3.

162. Shafiq Ahmed and Shantayanan Devarajan, 2006, p.*xiv*.

163. Ibid, p.*xxiv*.

164. Ibid, pp.xiv–xv.

165. Ibid. p.*xiv*.

166. Mamta Chowdhury, op cit, p. 70.

167. This is the argument explained in considerable detail to the author by Shahidur Rahman, then a senior engineer with the Bangladeshi state hydrocarbon agency during an informal briefing session in October 1999 in Dhaka.

168. 'China to help Bangladesh produce nuclear power,' *The Acorn*, Delhi, The Indian National Interest, 15 April 2005.

169. Informal discussions with British energy industry and diplomatic figures with interests in Bangladesh at the Royal Institute of International Affairs (Chatham House), London, 17 July 2008.

170. 'IAEA approves Bangladeshi nuclear power plant,' Dhaka, *Reuters*, 24 June 2007.

171. *Bangladesh aims to set up a nuclear power plant by 2015*, Dhaka, PTI, 24 September 2007.

172. 'China to help Bangladesh to set up Rooppur nuclear power plant,' *The New Age*, Dhaka, 25 September 2008.

173. 'China to help Bangladesh produce nuclear power,' *The Indian National Interest*, Delhi, 15 April 2005.

174. Anand Kumar, 'Bangladesh's quest for nuclear energy,' *Strategic Comments*, Delhi, IDSA, 17 October 2007. The fact that the IDSA is a strategic research organ of the Indian Ministry of Defence indicated the authoritative nature of this perspective.

175. Smruti Pattanaik, *India-Bangladesh Relations After Khaleda's Visit*, Article no. 1983, New Delhi, Institute of Peace and Conflict Studies, 7 April 2006.

176. Masumur Rahman Khalil, 'India wants road transit facilities from Bangladesh by 18 July 2008,' *Naya Diganta*, Dhaka, 9 July 2008.

177. Discussions with Bangladeshi analysts in Dhaka in January-February 2008.

178. Smruti Pattanaik, 'Bangladesh and the TATA Investment: Playing Politics with Economics,' *Strategic Comments*, Delhi, IDSA, 11 May 2006.

179. For an angry Indian reaction to the collapse of the Tata deal, see Sandeep Bhardwaj, 'India-Bangladesh Relations: Are the Carrots Working?' *South Asia Articles*, Delhi, Institute of Peace & Conflict Studies, 12 August 2008.

180. See, for instance, B. Raman, 'Unending Terrorism', *The Times of India*, Delhi, 29 July 2008; 'Harkat "Lesson" Letter,' *The Telegraph*, Calcutta, 28 September 2008; Rakesh Singh, 'More terror looms over Delhi,' *The Pioneer*, Delhi, 29 September 2008.

181. 'Stop HUJI in its tracks,' editorial, *The Pioneer*, Delhi, 1 October 2008. Rakesh Singh, 'More terror looms over Delhi,' *The Pioneer*, Delhi, 29 September 2008, says 'Intelligence inputs indicate that the Pakistan-based Inter-Services Intelligence (ISI) organised a meeting in Dhaka on August 17 with representatives of the Lashkar-e-Tayyeba (LeT), Harkat-ul-Jehad-al-Islami and ULFA (United Liberation Front of Assam) leader Paresh Baruah to carry out pan-India terror attacks.'

182. Julfikar Ali Manik, 'Huji leaders float party with govt nod,' *The Daily Star*, Dhaka, 29 September 2008; 'Stop HUJI in its tracks,' editorial, *The Pioneer*, Delhi, 1 October 2008.

183. Raju Das, 'Massive troops (sic) deployment along Indo-Bangla border,' *The Assam Tribune*, Guwahati, 3 October 2008.

184. Sandeep Kumar Das, 'Illegal madrassas along northeast's international border refuge of terrorists,' *Panchjanya* (Hindi weekly), Delhi, 5 October 2008; 'AASU, ABSU slam Dispur,' *The Telegraph*, Calcutta, 7 October 2008.

185. Ibid. Also see Nishit Dholabhai, 'Missing: A million Bangla Visitors,' *The Telegraph*, Calcutta, 26 August 2008.

186. For recent estimates of the two countries' military expenditure, orders of battle, tables of organisations and equipment and strategic orientations, see James Hackett, Ed, *The Military Balance*, London, IISS, February 2008, pp. 329–31, 341–46 (India), and pp. 339–41 (Bangladesh).

187. 'Bangladesh Navy successfully test fires long range missile,' *The Daily Star*, Dhaka, 13 May 2008.

188. 'Bangladesh building missile arsenal,' *The Times of India*, Delhi, 12 September 2008.

189. Ibid.

190. Ibid.

191. Known as Pyrdiwah in India.

192. Nishanthi Priyangika, 'India-Bangladesh border still tense after worst clash in 30 years,' *World Socialist Web Site*, 21 May 2001, at http://www.wsws.org/articles/2001/may2001/bang-m21_prn.shtml accessed on 27 February 2008.

193. Kalyan Choudhuri, 'Disturbed border,' *Frontline*, vol. 18, issue 9, Chennai, 11 May 2001.

194. Ibid.

195. Ibid.

196. In Delhi, General Moeen Uddin Ahmed was atypically received by the Indian President, Prime Minister, Defence Minister as well as his Indian counterpart, General Deepak Kapoor.

197. Anand Kumar, 'Could India and Bangladesh be friends?' *Asia Sentinel*, Hong Kong, 12 March 2008.

198. Subhash Kapila, *Bangladesh-India Strategic Partnership: The Imperatives*, Noida, South Asia Analysis Group, paper no. 2765, 11 July 2008.

199. Directorate General of Forces Intelligence, *RAW—Its Role and Activities; special emphasis on Bangladesh*, Dhaka, December 2008, Phase-2: Details of Activities of RAW in Bangladesh, Para 'k'.

200. Ibid, Para 'n'.

201. Sandeep Bhardwaj, 'Indo-Bangladesh Relations: A Golden Opportunity Missed?' *South Asia Articles*, Delhi, Institute of Peace & Conflict Studies, 6 August 2008.

202. Sreeradha Datta, 'Will Bangladesh Address India's Security Concerns?' *Strategic Comments*, Delhi, IDSA, 24 July 2008.

203. Sandeep Bhardwaj, 'Indo-Bangladesh Relations: Are the Carrots Working?' *South Asia Articles*, Delhi, Institute of Peace & Conflict Studies, 12 August 2008.

204. Directorate General of Forces Intelligence, December 2008, op cit, 'Conclusion.'

205. 'Pranab Mukherjee set for mid-January visit: Iftekhar,' *bdnews24.com*, Dhaka, 4 January 2009.

7. A BLOOD-SOAKED RESTORATION

1. See, for instance, interviews with Awami League leaders by the BBC Bengali Service on its *Probaha, Parikrama, Prabhati* and *Pratyusha* programmes broadcast at 0030GMT, 0130GMT, 1330GMT and 1630GMT on 30 December 2008 and 31 December 2008.

2. One contentious issue was the Awami League's decision, given its overwhelming majority, to slash the number of front-bench seats allocated to BNP MPs. The BNP challenged this decision and boycotted the parliament's opening sessions, returning only after the Awami League agreed to increase the BNP's allocations marginally.

3. Accounts of exactly what triggered the mutiny and how an alleged grievance over pay and allowances led to massive bloodshed with the virtual decapitation of the BDR's leadership in the hands of its troops within a few hours remained sketchy. Surviving officers who escaped, later gave accounts of what had happened. Perhaps the most detailed accounts emerged from Lt. Colonel Syed Kamruzzaman, and Major Syed Manirul Alam. Their recollections appeared in Ahmede Hussain, 'The Bloody Durbar,' *The Star Weekend Magazine*, Dhaka, 6 March 2009, and Kazi Hafiz, 'The tale of a surviving army officer,' *Amar Desh*, Dhaka, 1 March 2009.

4. A number of mutineers were interviewed on local TV channels on the first day of the mutiny. The BBC Bengali Service too carried such interviews in its programmes on the day. Also see, Fidel V. Ramos, 'Killings in the Philippines and Bangladesh,' *NewsBreak*, Manila, 11 March 2009.

5. The precise number of officers killed remained uncertain for many days. Initially, it was assumed that most of the 150–odd officers, the combined total of officers stationed at the headquarters and others who had arrived from outstation units to attend the annual reunion, had been killed. As details emerged of survivors, the number of serving officers killed by the mutineers came down to fifty-seven. This did not include the members of their families, civilians killed inside Peelkhana and outside, or BDR troops who may have resisted the rebels. See Lt. Colonel Mahmudur Rahman Choudhury (retd.), *Institutional Capacity and the State*, presentation at a conference organised by the Bangladesh Institute of Peace and Security Studies, Dhaka, 21 March 2009; Khaled Iqbal Chowdhury, 'BDR Mutiny: Security implications for Bangladesh and the region,' *BIPSS Special Report, Dhaka, BIPSS*, 5 March 2009; '200 BDR rebels arrested, 130 officers still missing,' *The Indian Express*, Delhi, 27 February 2009; 'More graves found at BDR HQ; toll climbs to 77,' ibid., 28 February 2009; Haroon Habib, '42 more bodies recovered from BDR headquarters,' *The Hindu*, Chennai, 28 February 2009.

6. Major-General Razzaqul Haider, a retired former Director-General of the BDR, in interview with Farhana Haider, *Analysis*, radio documentary broadcast by the BBC World Service, London, on 9 March 2009.

7. Audio clips of the exchange, held behind closed doors, were published on YouTube a few days after the event when the government ordered that this and other sites playing these clips be blocked across Bangladesh. See, for instance:
http://www.youtube.com/watch?v=Wpmr4gKFHww,
http://www.youtube.com/watch?v=eWI3Ybe2hfs&feature=related,
http://www.youtube.com/watch?v=a6wt4wt2HNE&feature=related,
http://www.youtube.com/watch?v=zYNtSyryIhs&feature=related,
http://www.youtube.com/watch?v=C8f2FG6rjns&feature=related, and

http://www.youtube.com/watch?v=uvNft-ppJwQ&feature=related, all accessed on 16 March 2009.

8. See, for instance, Somini Sengupta, 'Bangladeshi Premier Faces a Grim Crucible,' *The New York Times*, 14 March 2009, Abhijit Bhattacharya, 'Dangerous Complications,' *The Telegraph*, Kolkata, 10 March 2009; 'Editorial: A Critical Test,' *The Hindu*, Chennai, 28 February 2009.

9. M. Shahidul Islam, 'Foreign Military Intervention Likely? Intelligence failure caused BDR disaster,' *The Holiday*, Dhaka, 6 March 2009.

10. 'Islamists blame India for Bangladesh mutiny, as FBI agents arrive,' *The Hindustan Times*, Delhi, 9 March 2009.

11. 'Indian media points fingers at SQ Chowdhury,' *Bdnews24.com*, 1 March 2009.

12. Sreeram Chaulia, 'Power play behind Bangladesh's mutiny,' *Asia Times*, 3 March 2009.

13. Ramtanu Maitra, 'Mumbai Two in Bangladesh: Saudi Attempt To Assassinate Hasina Fails; Threat Remains,' *Executive Intelligence Review*, Washington, Vol. 36, No. 10, March 2009.

14. Ibid.

15. M. Shahidul Islam, 'Foreign Military Intervention Likely? Intelligence failure caused BDR disaster,' op cit.

16. Gordon McGranahan, quoted in 'Climate Changes: Study Maps Those At Greatest Risk From Cyclones And Rising Seas,' *ScienceDaily*, International Institute for Environment and Development, 28 March 2007.

17. Two others were the Maldives, an archipelago of coral reefs in the Indian Ocean, and the Mekong Delta in southern Vietnam. Bangladesh, sitting atop the Bengal Delta, led the pack.

18. *ScienceDaily*, 28 March 2007.

19. IRIN, *Bangladesh: Battling the effects of climate change*, UN Office for the Coordination of Humanitarian Affairs, Geneva, 16 December 2008; ibid, *Bangladesh: Rising sea levels threaten agriculture*, 1 November 2007.

20. Ibid.

21. Foreign media have been pointing to these challenges with urgency in recent years. See, for instance, Emily Wax, 'In Flood-Prone Bangladesh, a Future That Floats,' *The Washington Post*, 27 September 2007; Jeremy Page, 'Climate of Fear in Sinking Country,' *The Times*, London, 2 February 2007; Leonard Doyle, 'Bangladesh in dread of rising sea levels,' *The Independent*, London, 15 March 2001.

22. Ministry of Environment and Forests, *Bangladesh climate change strategy and action plan 2008*, Dhaka: Government of Bangladesh, September 2008, pp. xv–xvi.

23. Ibid.

24. Ibid, p. 1. The document goes on to say, 'It is essential that Bangladesh prepares now to face the challenge ahead and safeguard her future economic well-being and the livelihoods of her people.' The Action Plan itself, however, appears to be based on the assumption that routine reinforcement of current levels of adaptation and mitigation activities would be sufficient for addressing the challenges so eloquently described.

25. The World Bank, *Climate Change: Bangladesh Facing the Challenge*, London, 8 September 2008, p. 1.

26. Ibid, p. 2.

27. Major General Muniruzzaman, President, Bangladesh Institute of Peace and Security Studies, *Briefing on Bangladesh*, London: Portcullis House, 2 December 2008.

28. Prof. Allan Smith of the University of California, Berkeley, quoted in the *Bulletin of the World Health Organization (WHO)*, Geneva, September 2000; also see, WHO, 'Researchers warn of impending disaster from mass arsenic poisoning,' *Press Release no. 55*, Geneva, 8 September 2000.

29. Ibid. For a case study focusing on the Matlab *Upazila* in eastern Bangladesh providing a framework for analysing the challenge and outlining ways of mitigating some of its consequences, see Md. Jakariya, *Arsenic in tubewell water of Bangladesh and approaches for sustainable mitigation*, doctoral dissertation, Stockholm: Department of Land and Water Resources Engineering, Royal Institute of Technology, May 2007.

30. IRIN, *Bangladesh local filter to combat arsenic tainted water*, UN Office for the Coordination of Humanitarian Affairs, Geneva, 10 January 2008.

31. Ibid.

32. WHO, *Press Release no. 55*, op.cit.

33. Ibid.

34. IRIN, *Bangladesh local filter to combat arsenic tainted water*.

35. IRIN, *Bangladesh: Arsenic detector saving lives*, 9 July 2008.

36. Ibid.

37. Mustak Hossain, 'Scientists urge Bangladesh arsenic strategy change,' *Science and Development Network*, 14 December 2006.

38. IRIN, *Bangladesh: Arsenic detector saving lives*.

39. IRIN, *Bangladesh local filter to combat arsenic tainted water*.

40. IRIN, *Arsenic in food chain raises health concerns*, 19 September 2008.

41. Ibid.

42. The World Bank, *World Development Indicators, 2002*, Washington, 2002, cited in C. Christine Fair, Clifford Grammich, Julie DaVanzo, and Brian Nichiporuk, 'Demographics and Security: The Contrasting Cases of Pakistan and Bangladesh,' *Journal of South Asian and Middle Eastern Studies*, Vol. XXVII, No. 4, Summer 2005, p. 56.

43. Aloysius Milon Khan, *Country Fact Sheet: Bangladesh*, Dhaka, Department of International Development, May 2008.

44. CIA, *The World Fact Book—Bangladesh*, Washington, 2008, at http://www.cia.gov/library/publications/the-world-factbook/print/bg.html accessed on 17 December 2008.

45. Population Action International, *People in the Balance: Interactive Database*, Washington, at http://216.146.209.72/Publications/Reports/People_in_the-Balance/Interactive/peopleinthebalance/pages/?c=12 accessed on 26 December 2008.

46. Aloysius Milon Khan, May 2008.

47. Fair, Grammich, DaVanzo and Nichiporuk, 2005, p. 57.

48. For an explanation of political 'softness' of states, see Syed Mahmud Ali, *Civil-Military Relations in the 'Soft State': The Case of Bangladesh*, Bath: University of Bath/European Commission, 1994.

49. Fair *et al*, 2005, pp. 56–7.

50. John Caldwell, Barket-e-Khuda, Bruce Caldwell, Indrani Peiris, and Pat Caldwell, 'The Bangladesh Fertility Decline: An Interpretation,' *Population and Development Review*, Vol. 25, No. 1, March 1999, pp. 67–84.

51. Fair, *et al*, 2005, p. 57.

52. World Bank, *World Development Indicators, 2002*, Washington, 2002, cited in Fair et al, p. 57.

53. Fair, et al, p. 58.

54. Ibid.

55. United Nations Population Division, *World Population Prospects: The 2002 Revision*, New York, 2003, cited in Fair, et al, ibid, fn.10.

56. Ibid, p. 58; for additional details, see Robert Engelman, Richard Cincotta, Bonnie Dye, Tom Gardner-Outlaw and Jennifer Wisniewski, *People in the Balance: Population and Natural Resources at the Turn of the Millennium*, Washington: Population Action International, 2000.

57. Population Action International, *People in the Balance: Interactive Database*, op cit.

58. Ibid.

59. UN Population Division, *Long-Range Population Projections*, New York, 30 June 2003, p. 18.

APPENDICES

Appendix I
The 12–Point Charter of Demands of the Sepoys

1. Changing the structure of the armed forces: Our revolution is not for changing only the leadership; this revolution is in the interest of the poor classes. We have accepted you as our leader in this revolution. For that reason, you are to express very clearly that you are the leader of the poor classes, and change the structure of the armed services. For many years, we have served as soldiers of the rich classes. They have used us as tools of their own interests; the 15 August incidents are an instance. This time round, we have rebelled not for the rich or on their behalf; this time round, we have revolted along with the masses. From now on, the armed services will build themselves up as defenders of the interests of the masses.

2. Release of all political prisoners: We demand the immediate release of all political prisoners.

3. Confiscation of properties of corrupt officials and individuals: Properties owned by corrupt officials and individuals should be immediately confiscated; their money held in foreign banks should be brought back to the country and invested in the interest of society.

4. Ending discriminations between armed services officers and other ranks: We demand an end to all discrimination between officers and other ranks and the payment of salaries to each according his work and capability.

5. Ending recruitment of officers from privileged classes: We demand that officers be recruited from among capable other ranks and not from special schools such as cadet colleges and public schools.

6. Changing existing colonial practices: We demand the termination of the many colonial practices still current in the armed services, and immediate changes to the dehumanising patterns of conduct in force in garrisons.

7. Enhancing salaries of other ranks: We demand increased salaries for the other ranks and the immediate abolition of the system of providing accommodation to their families on payment of rent.

8. Abolition of the 'batman' system: We demand the immediate abolition of the batman system under which soldiers are required to work as personal servants of officers in their family quarters.

9. Establishment of the Revolutionary Soldiers' Organisation: We call for the establishment of a revolutionary army organisation for the entire Dhaka garrison.

10. Role of the Revolutionary Soldiers' Organisation: The Revolutionary Soldiers' Organisation would function as the central policy-making body for the armed services. General Ziaur Rahman would take any decision regarding the armed services only after consulting this organisation.

11. Co-ordinating role of this central organ: This central policy-making group would co-ordinate the policies and activities of other such organisations in the other garrisons, and enlist the support of revolutionary students, farmers, workers and common citizens of the country.

12. Future role of the armed services: The revolutionary army, in association with progressive and revolutionary students, peasants and workers would play its role in bringing about a revolution in society.\

Appendix II

General Ziaur Rahman's 19–Point Programme

1. To preserve the country's independence, integrity and sovereignty at all costs
2. To reflect the four fundamental principles of the constitution in all spheres of national life
3. To make the nation self-reliant in every possible way
4. To ensure the participation of the people at every level of the administration, in development programmes and in the maintenance of order
5. To strengthen the economy by according top priority to agricultural development
6. To ensure that no one went hungry, by making the country self-sufficient in food
7. To ensure clothing for everybody, by increasing production of textiles
8. To take all measures to ensure that no one remained homeless
9. To rid the country of illiteracy
10. To ensure a minimum level of medical care
11. To give women their rightful place in society and to organise and inspire the young for building the nation
12. To give necessary incentives to the private sector for the economic development of the country
13. To improve workers' conditions and to develop healthy labour-management relations in the interests of increased production
14. To encourage the spirit of public service and nation-building among government employees and to improve their financial situation
15. To check the population explosion
16. To establish friendship with all countries on a basis of equality and especially to strengthen relations with Muslim countries
17. To decentralise the system of administration and develop and strengthen local government
18. To establish a social order based on justice and free from corruption, and
19. To safeguard the rights of all citizens irrespective of religion, colour and sect and to consolidate national unity and solidarity.

GLOSSARY

Allahr Dal	God's party.
Andolon	movement/campaign.
Anushilan Samity	calisthenics association; an early Bengali youth organization.
Ashraf	of noble birth, aristocrat.
Atraf	common.
Awami	people's, popular.
Bagha	tiger-like, courageous; title given to an anti-imperial Bengali freedom fighter.
Bangabandhu	friend of Bengal; title given to Sheikh Mujibur Rahman.
Bangabhaban	Bengal's mansion; Bangladesh's presidential palace.
Bangla	Bengali language; geographic Bengal.
Bangladesh Awami League	party established by H.S. Suhrawardy; later, led by Sheikh Mujibur Rahman and then by his daughter.
Bangladesh Jatiyatabadi Dal	party established by General Ziaur Rahman; later led by his widow.
Bangladesh Krishak Sramik Awami League	framework of one-party rule established by Sheikh Mujibur Rahman in 1975; politically marginalised since his assassination.
Bhadralok	gentle-folk; Westernised intermediary middle classes precipitated by Bengal's exposure to British administrative, commercial and educational enterprises.

Bihari	generic term describing non-Bengali-speaking north-Indian immigrants to East Pakistan.
Bikalpa Dhara	literally, an alternative stream; political grouping set up by BNP co-founder and former President of Bangladesh, Badruddoza Chowdhury, after his ouster.
Biplobi Gonobahini	revolutionary people's militia; radical leftist organization.
Biplobi Shainik Sangstha	revolutionary soldiers' association; radical leftist cells secretly established within the armed forces, covertly linked to the *Biplobi Gonobahini*.
Chhatra	student.
Dal	party.
Deobandi	generic description of orthodox Sunni Muslims adhering to the literal teachings of the *Dar-ul-Uloom* seminary at Deoband in northern India.
Faraizi	an early religio-political movement among Bengali Muslims, fashioned around the obligatory religious duties dictated by Islam.
Ganatantrik	democratic.
Ganatantri Dal	democratic party.
Ganatantrik Oikkya Jote	democratic unity front; a coalition of Islamist organizations.
Gram Sarkar	village government.
Gonobahini	people's militia.
Harkat-ul-Jihad-al-Islami	movement for Islamic holy war; radical Islamist organization.
Islami Chhatra Shibir	Islamist students' camp—student wing of the Jamaat-e-Islami party.
Jagrata Muslim Janata	awakened Muslim masses; radical Islamist group allied to the JMB.
Jamaat-e-Islami	Islamic congregation; main Islamist party in Bangladesh.
Jamaat-ul-Mujahideen	congregation of holy warriors; radical Islamist group.

Janadal	people's party; a short-lived political organization.
Janajuddha	people's war; a radical leftist faction.
Jatiya Party	national party; party established by General H M Ershad.
Jatiya Rakkhi Bahini	national security force; militia established by Bangladesh's first administration with Mujib-loyalists trained by Indian officers, for internal security operations.
Jatiyatabadi Ganatantrik Dal	nationalist democratic party; a centre-right grouping.
Jatiya Samajtantrik Dal	national socialist party; radical leftist group formed by breakaway factions of the Awami League's student wing and freedom fighters.
Jotedar	rich peasants and intermediate landowners.
Juba	youth.
Juddha	war.
Jugantar	transition to a new era; early Bengali anti-imperialist organization.
Jumma	slash-and-burn method of hill farming; Montagnards practising this method.
Kader Bahini	militia led by Kader Siddiky.
Karbari	traditional Montagnard leader administering a Union of several hill villages.
Karmachari	employees.
Khas land	literally, the best/special land; land owned by the state.
Khilafat	caliphate.
Krishak Praja Party	peasants and tenant farmers' party.
Lal Jhanda/Pataka	red flag; faction of radical left-wing political activists.
Lok Sabha	lower house of the Indian parliament.
Mughal	Mongol-Turkic imperial dynasty established by Zahiruddin Muhammad Babur who captured Delhi in 1526; the Empire ended with the British Crown's assump-

tion of power following the Indian Mutiny in 1857.

Muhajir	immigrant, refugee.
Mujahideen	holy warriors.
Mujib Bahini	militia established in 1971 by Indian authorities from among Awami League loyalists; maintained outside the control of the Bangladeshi government-in-exile.
Mukti Bahini	Liberation army; generic description of freedom fighters combating Pakistani forces and their local allies during Bangladesh's war of independence in 1971.
Nawab	Muslim prince; local ruler reigning under Mughal suzerainty across India.
Naxalbari Sahayak Samity	Aid-Naxalbari association; group formed to support the radical leftist insurrection against feudal figures and their state sponsors in northern reaches of India's West Bengal state—around Naxalbari village—in the late 1960s.
Naxalite	Generic term describing radical leftist activists engaging in violence against feudal landed families and their supporters within the state machinery.
Niyamita Bahini	regular force; Bangladeshi resistance forces comprising rebel units from Pakistani military formations, and subsequently raised units built around that core.
Noor-i-Khuda	divine light; *Sufi* mystical concept of all creations being suffused with the creator's grace and thus meriting respect.
Pahari Chhatra Parishad	Hill Students' Council; organization in the Chittagong Hill Tracts.
Pahari Gano Parishad	Hill People's Council; popular organsation in the Chittagong Hill Tracts.
Paltan Maidan	originally a military parade ground, this large open space in Dhaka has tradition-

	ally been used by politicians for holding rallies.
Parbattya Chattagram Janasanghati Samity	Chittagong Hill Tracts people's solidarity association; Montagnard autonomist grouping established by Chakma leader M. N Larma; established an armed wing called *Shanti Bahini* to fight for autonomy.
Praja	subject; tenant-farmers.
Purbasha	literally, eastern promise; name given by India to coastal islet whose ownership was disputed with Bangladesh.
Purbo Banglar Communist Party	East Bengal's Communist Party.
Purbo Banglar Sarbahara Party	East Bengal's Proletarian Party; radical leftist party established by Siraj Sikder and reinforced by the entry of a prominent cashiered military commander; fragmented into factions after Sikder's murder.
Purbo Banglar Shashastra Deshpremik Bahini	East Bengal's armed patriotic force; an underground militia seeking to take over the state.
Purbo Banglar Sramik Andolon	East Bengal's workers' campaign.
Purbo Pakistan Communist Party	East Pakistan Communist Party.
Rashtrabhasha Sangram Committee	State-language campaign committee.
Ryot	tenant-farmer.
Sangram Parishad	struggle/campaign council.
Sarbadaliya Chhatra Sangram Parishad	All-party students' campaign council.
Sepoy	trooper; rank-and-file soldier.
Sepoy Biplab	soldiers' revolution.
Shamyabadi Dal	egalitarian party; socialist party.
Shanti Bahini	peace force; armed wing of the Chittagong Hill Tracts people's solidarity association.

Sramik Karmachari Oikkya Parishad	workers' and employees' unity council.
Sufi	mystical sect of Islam whose savants played a key role in converting the lowest strata of Bengal's Hindu populace to Islam between the tenth and thirteenth centuries.
Sundarban	mangrove forests along Bangladesh's south-western coasts.
Swadeshi Andolon	literally, campaign for indigenous products; a nationalist campaign across much of Britain's South Asian empire in the early twentieth century.
Swadhin Bangla Betar Kendra	independent Bengal radio station; radio station operated by Bangladesh's Government-in-Exile from Calcutta.
Swanirbhar Andolon	self-sufficiency campaign.
Taleban	literally, students; generic term signifying Islamists emerging from seminaries and campaigning, often violently, to impose their orthodox views on society.
Thana	police station; administrative area around such stations.
Upazilla	sub-district; subordinate administrative area under districts.
Wahabi	Sunni Muslims adhering to the teachings of reformist Muhammad ibn Abd-al Wahab (1703–1792); seen to demand a literal and austere interpretation of Islam's tenets.
Zamindar	landlord; Indians given ownership of land by the British East India Company on condition that they regularly collected revenue from their tenants and handed over a proportion to the Company while keeping the remainder for themselves.

ABBREVIATIONS

ABSA	All-Bengal Students Association.
ABMSA	All-Bengal Muslim Students Association.
ADB	Asian Development Bank.
AFD	Armed Forces Division.
AHQ	Army Headquarters.
AID	Agency for International Development.
AL	Awami League.
APSU	All-Party Students Unity.
ASEAN	Association of South East Asian Nations.
BAF	Bangladesh Air Force.
BAL	Bangladesh Awami League.
BBCP	Bangladesh *Biplobi* (revolutionary) Communist Party.
BNBCP	Bangladesh *Nutan Biplobi* (new revolutionary) Communist Party.
BCL	Bangladesh *Chhatro* (students) League.
BD	Basic Democrat.
BDF	Bangladesh Forces.
BDR	Bangladesh Rifles.
BIMSTEC	Bay of Bengal Initiative for Multi-Sectoral Technical and Economic Cooperation.
BKSAL	Bangladesh Krishak Sramik Awami League.
BLF	Bangladesh Liberation Force.
BMA	Bangladesh Medical Association.
BNP	Bangladesh Nationalist Party.
BSF	Border Security Force.
BOP	Border Outpost.
CAS	Chief of the Army Staff.

CCP	Chinese Communist Party.
CENTO	Central Treaty Organisation.
CGS	Chief of the General Staff.
CHT	Chittagong Hill Tracts.
CIA	Central Intelligence Agency.
C-in-C	Commander-in-Chief.
CMLA	Chief Martial Law Administrator.
CNS	Chief of the Naval Staff.
CO	Commanding Officer.
COAS	Chief of the Air Staff.
COS	Chief of Staff.
CPB	Communist Party of Bangladesh.
CPI	Communist party of India.
CPI-M	Communist Party of India—Marxist.
CPI-ML	Communist Party of India—Marxist-Leninist.
CPP	Communist Party of Pakistan.
CPSU	Communist Party of the Soviet Union.
CSP	Civil Service of Pakistan.
CTG	Caretaker Government.
DAC	Democratic Action Committee.
DCAS	Deputy Chief of the Army Staff.
DCI	Director of Central Intelligence.
DCMLA	Deputy Chief Martial Law Administrator.
DESA	Dhaka Electricity Supply Authority.
DFID	Department for International Development.
DGFI	Directorate General of Forces Intelligence.
DOD	Department of Defence.
DSCSC	Defence Services Command and Staff College.
DUCSU	Dhaka University Central Students Union.
EBR	East Bengal Regiment.
EBRC	East Bengal Regimental Centre.
EEC	European Economic Community.
EPCP	East Pakistan Communist Party.
EPMSL	East Pakistan Muslim Students League.
EPR	East Pakistan Rifles; Emergency Powers Regulations.
EPSU	East Pakistan Students Union.
FDI	Foreign direct investment.
FF	Freedom fighter.

FFE	Food for education.
GHQ	General Headquarters.
GOB	Government of Bangladesh.
GOC	General Officer Commanding.
GOI	Government of India.
GOP	Government of Pakistan.
HDC	Hill District Council.
HuJI-B	*Harkat-ul-Jihad-al-Islami* (movement for Islamic holy war)—Bangladesh.
HWF	Hill Women's Federation.
IAEA	International Atomic Energy Agency.
IAF	Indian Air Force.
ICS	*Islami Chhatra Shibir* (Islamic students camp).
IDP	Islamic Democratic Party.
IMF	International Monetary Fund.
INA	Indian National Army.
INC	Indian National Congress.
ISI	Inter-Services Intelligence Directorate.
JAL	Japan Airlines.
JCD	*Jatiyatabadi Chhatra Dal* (nationalist student party).
JCO	Junior Commissioned Officer.
JI	*Jamaat-e-Islami* (Islamic congregation).
JMB	*Jamaat-ul-Mujahideen* (congregation of holy warriors) Bangladesh.
JMJB	*Jagrata* Muslim *Janata* (awakened Muslim masses) Bangladesh.
JRB	*Jatiya Rakkhi Bahini* (national security militia).
JRC	Joint Rivers Commission.
JSD	*Jatiya Samajtantrik Dal* (national socialist party).
KSP	*Krishak Sramik* (peasants, workers) Party.
LFO	Legal Framework Order.
MDG	Millennium Development Goals.
MFA	Multi-fibre Arrangement.
MNA	Member of National Assembly.
MPA	Member of Provincial assembly.
MSF	Muslim Student Federation.
MSL	Muslim Student League.
NAM	Non-aligned Movement.

NAP	National *Awami* (people's) Party.
NCB	Nationalised commercial bank.
NCO	Non-commissioned Officer.
NDC	National Disaster Committee.
NGO	Non-governmental Organisation.
NSF	National Student Federation.
NSI	National Security Intelligence.
NWFP	North West Frontier Province.
OIC	Organisaion of Islamic Conference.
PAF	Pakistan Air Force.
PBSP	*Purbo Banglar Sarbohara* (East Bengal's proletarian) Party.
PBCP	*Purbo Banglar* (East Bengal's) Communist Party.
PBCP-ML	*Purbo Banglar* (East Bengal's) Communist Party—Marxist-Leninist.
PCJSS	*Parbattya Chattagram Janasanghati Samity* (Chittagong Hill Tracts people's solidarity association).
PDB	Power Development Board.
PGR	President's Guard Regiment.
PIA	Pakistan International Airlines.
PLA	People's Liberation Army.
POW	Prisoner-of-war.
PPCP	*Purbo Pakistaner* (East Pakistan's) Communist Party.
PPP	Pakistan People's Party.
PSO	Principal Staff Officer.
RAB	Rapid Action Battalion.
RAT	Rapid Action Team.
RAW	Research and Analysis Wing.
REB	Rural Electrification Board.
RMG	Ready-made garments.
SAARC	South Asian Association for Regional Cooperation.
SAFTA	South Asian Free Trade Area.
SAM	Surface-to-Air Missile.
SAPTA	South Asian Preferential Trade Agreement.
SB	*Shanti Bahin;*, Special Branch.
SCSP	*Sarbodoliyo Chhatro Sangram Parishad* (all-party students campaign council).
SEC	Securities and Exchange Commission.

SHORAD	Short-range Air Defence.
SKOP	*Sramik Karmachari Oikkya Parishad* (workers', employees' unity council).
SOE	State-owned enterprises.
SPA	Special Powers Act.
SRG	Senior Review Group.
UNCLOS	United Nations Convention on the Law of the Seas.
UNGA	United Nations General Assembly.
UNSC	United Nations Security Council.
ULFA	United Liberation Front of Assam.
USSR	Union of Soviet Socialist Republics.
WB	World Bank.
WSAG	Washington Special Action Group.
VAT	Value-added Tax.
VDP	Village Defence Party.
VGF	Vulnerable Group Feeding.
ZMLA	Zonal Martial Law Administrator.

INDEX